Megacities and Global Change
Megastädte und globaler Wandel

Herausgegeben von
FRAUKE KRAAS, MARTIN COY, PETER HERRLE und VOLKER KREIBICH

Band 27

Christian Obermayr

HOUSING THE POOR

The Right to the City and Policy Arrangements in Urban Indonesia

Franz Steiner Verlag

Published with the support of Austrian Science Fund (FWF): PUB 899-G. The research reported in this publication was jointly supported by the ASEAN-European Academic University Network (ASEA-UNINET), the Austrian Federal Ministry of Education, Science and Research (BMBWF), the OeAD – Austria's Agency for Education and Internationalisation, and University of Innsbruck.

FWF Der Wissenschaftsfonds.

This publication was subject to an anonymous, international peer review process.

Cover illustration: The image shows informal shacks along one of the narrow alleys in the old town of Surabaya. The photo was taken by the author during the field work in 2015.

Bibliografische Information der Deutschen Nationalbibliothek:
Die Deutsche Nationalbibliothek verzeichnet diese Publikation in der Deutschen Nationalbibliografie; detaillierte bibliografische Daten sind im Internet über dnb.d-nb.de abrufbar.

Franz Steiner Verlag, Stuttgart.
www.steiner-verlag.de

Layout und Herstellung durch den Verlag
Satz: DTP + TEXT Eva Burri, Stuttgart
Druck: Beltz Grafische Betriebe, Bad Langensalza
Gedruckt auf säurefreiem, alterungsbeständigem Papier.
Printed in Germany.
ISBN 978-3-515-13348-7 (Print)
ISBN 978-3-515-13349-4 (E-Book)
https://doi.org/10.25162/9783515133494

Acknowledgements

The topic of housing and informal settlements drew my interest for the first time in the now long-distant year 2008, when I had the opportunity to visit one of the favelas in São Paulo as a student of Martin Coy. Since that experience I wanted to study these strange and fascinating settlements. I could not foresee that this would develop into a year-long research journey. During this journey, I met many people who influenced me in one way or another and helped me to realise this work. To all of them I owe thanks, but it is impossible to name everyone.

Martur nuwun or *terimah kasih* goes to all Indonesian colleagues and friends who welcomed me warmly in their country and supported me in scholarly, organisational, and cultural ways. In particular, I would like to thank Nurhadi, Wawan, Widiyanto, Winny, Ita, and Happy. Your support was invaluable. I owe gratitude to all interview partners for their openness and the patience with which they endured my endless questions. The fieldwork, however, would have failed without the help of four people. Maida, Diana, Dwikki, and Charisma, thank you for your support, the many intensive discussions, and your friendship.

I would also like to express my thanks to all colleagues in Innsbruck. This applies in particular to the members of the Working Group Development Studies and Sustainability Science. They advised me not only on scholarly issues, but supplied me above all with mate, coffee, and chocolate. I am indebted to Martin Coy who motivated me to do this work and supported me in all matters.

Thanks also go to my parents who made these studies possible in the first place. Most importantly, my deep thanks goes to my wife Marina. She lived with me through the ups and downs of this research journey, endured my long absences, proofread the whole book, and was always ready to prevent me from giving up. Without you this journey would not have come to a successful end.

Thank you!

Table of Contents

List of Figures

List of Tables

List of Boxes

List of Boxes

Abstract

The world is in the middle of a global housing crisis. The number of people living in slums is rising every year and the goal of achieving adequate housing for all, as articulated in the Sustainable Development Goals (SDG 11), remains a distant dream. Proper means to counteract this system-inherent crisis through sound housing policies have not yet been found. The results are sprawling informal settlements that fit into the mosaic of an increasingly fragmented urban landscape as places of marginality and exclusion. Some countries, however, show a contrary trend, as for example Indonesia. In this country, the housing situation has improved for many residents over the last decades and innovative urban policies have emerged in several cities. Searching for the reasons for this success, the aspect of local governance has increasingly moved into focus in recent years. Often, it is assumed that specific modes of governance can be linked to success or failure of applied housing policies.

Against this background, this book aims to gain a better understanding of the relationship between modes of urban governance and emerging housing policies in order to achieve adequate housing for all. This goal is approached from different perspectives and by means of two case studies, the Indonesian cities of Surabaya and Surakarta, which have become known for their progressive policies. A first perspective puts the case studies into context and analyses previous housing strategies and associated paradigms at the international and national level. A second, theoretical perspective conceptualises the policy arrangement approach as an analytical framework for urban governance and develops a normative compass for 'adequate housing' and 'sound housing policies' based on Henri Lefebvre's right to the city. The third perspective is empirical and examines housing policies and modes of governance in the two cities, applying the policy arrangement approach and related qualitative methods (Interviews, surveys, Net-Map method). In the fourth comparative perspective, the two case studies are compared and evaluated with the help of the normative compass developed.

The four different perspectives each confirm in their own way the importance of urban governance for the possible emergence of sound housing policies. From a theoretical perspective, it is argued that both governance and housing policies should be oriented toward a normative goal, namely the right to the city. By applying this normative basis, it becomes possible to create the necessary foundation of governance that allows and promotes a societal transformation. The empirical research revealed that less hierarchical modes of governance with multiple actors involved in governance processes, shared power relations, and inclusive discourses are more likely to produce housing policies that are people-centred, participative, and actually benefit marginalised groups. However, the analysis also shows that the two cities studied still have a long way to go to ensure that all residents have equal access to urban resources, as the right to the city demands.

Keywords: Housing policy, adequate housing, governance, right to the city, policy arrangements, modes of governance, Indonesia, Surabaya, Surakarta

Zusammenfassung

Die Welt befindet sich in inmitten einer globalen Wohnungskrise. Die Zahl der Menschen in Marginalsiedlungen steigt kontinuierlich an und das Ziel angemessenen Wohnraum für alle zu erreichen, wie es in den Nachhaltigkeitszielen (SDG 11) artikuliert wird, ist nur eine ferne Illusion. Mittel und Wege dieser systemimmanenten Krise durch geeignete Wohnungspolitik zu begegnen sind bisher nicht oder nur in Ansätzen gefunden worden. Das Resultat ist eine weitere Ausbreitung von informellen Siedlungen, die sich als Orte der Marginalität und Exklusion in das Mosaik einer immer deutlicher fragmentierten Stadtlandschaft einfügen. In einigen Ländern lässt sich aber auch eine gegenläufige Tendenz beobachten, so zum Beispiel in Indonesien. Dort ist es gelungen die Wohnsituation für Viele zu verbessern und in mehreren Städten zeigen sich innovative Ansätze im Wohnbereich. Auf der Suche nach den Gründen für diese Erfolge rückte in den letzten Jahren immer mehr der Aspekt der lokalen Regierungsführung in den Fokus. Vielfach wird vermutet, dass bestimmte Formen von Governance eng mit dem Erfolg oder Misserfolg von angewandter Wohnungspolitik verbunden sind.

Vor diesen Hintergründen ist es das Ziel der vorliegenden Arbeit ein besseres Verständnis des Zusammenhangs zwischen Formen städtischer Governance und daraus hervorgehenden Wohnungspolitiken zu erlangen, um angemessenen Wohnraum für alle zu verwirklichen. Eine Annäherung an dieses Ziel erfolgt anhand von zwei Fallbeispielen, den indonesischen Städten Surabaya und Surakarta, die für ihre progressive Politik bekannt geworden sind, und aus verschiedenen Perspektiven. Eine erste Perspektive setzt die Fallbeispiele in den Kontext und analysiert bisherige Wohnbaustrategien und damit assoziierte Paradigmen auf internationaler und indonesischer Ebene. Eine zweite Perspektive ist theoretisch, adaptiert das Konzept der Policy Arrangements als Analysekonzept für städtische Governance und entwickelt basierend auf Henri Lefebvre's Recht auf Stadt einen normativen Kompass für „angemessenes Wohnen" und eine „inklusive Wohnungspolitik". Die dritte Perspektive ist empirisch und operationalisiert das Analysekonzept zur Untersuchung von Wohnungspolitik und Formen der Governance in den beiden Fallstudien durch einen Mix aus vornehmlich qualitativen Methoden (Interviews, Befragungen, Net-Map Methode). In der vierten vergleichenden Perspektive werden die beiden Fallstudien gegenübergestellt und mithilfe des entwickelten normativen Kompasses bewertet.

Die vier verschiedenen Perspektiven bestätigen jede auf ihre Weise die Wichtigkeit von städtischer Governance für das mögliche Entstehen einer inklusiven Wohnungspolitik. Aus theoretischer Perspektive wird argumentiert, dass sowohl Governance als auch Wohnungspolitiken auf ein normatives Ziel ausgerichtet werden sollten, nämlich auf das Recht auf Stadt. Erst diese normative Basis ermöglicht es die nötige Grundlage einer Governance zu schaffen, die eine gesellschaftliche Transformation zulässt und befördert. Die vergleichende empirische Forschung ergab, dass weniger hierarchische Formen der Regierungsführung mit vielen am Regierungsprozess beteiligten Akteuren, geteilten Machtverhältnissen und inkludierenden Diskursen eher zu einer Wohnungspolitik führen, die alle Bewohner der Stadt miteinbezieht, partizipativ ist und tatsächlich einen Nutzen für marginalisierte Bevölkerungsgruppen hat. Die Analyse machte allerdings auch deutlich, dass die beiden untersuchten Städte noch einen weiten Weg zu gehen haben, um allen StadtbewohnerInnen gleichermaßen den Zugang zu städtischen Ressourcen zu ermöglichen, wie es das Recht auf Stadt einfordert.

Keywords: Wohnpolitik, Angemessenes Wohnen, Governance, Recht auf Stadt, Policy Arrangement, Modes of Governance, Indonesien, Surabaya, Surakart

1 Introduction

What is so interesting about housing policies? I have been asked this question many times over the last years, ever since I became interested in the topic of housing. I used to respond in a simple way, disregarding the complexity of the topic: 'We cannot allow the existence of one billion people living in slums!', 'We live in the 21st century; there must be a way to improve the living conditions of the poorest', or 'We need a right to adequate and affordable housing for all!'. Such were my direct answers and they satisfied most people. Usually, they agreed, and recognised the importance of studying this topic. At the same time, however, they did not understand slogans such as 'the right to the city' or immediately judged them to be ideologically charged, and regarded the whole issue of housing the poor to be something from the past, an issue already overcome in advanced societies.

It was not until the financial crisis in 2008, when discussions on housing reappeared in the so-called 'developed countries'[1] that slowly, people began to become aware of the fact that housing is not a given right in a capitalist world. In the precise moment when the employees of Lehman Brothers were leaving their offices carrying boxes with their belongings, the importance of housing markets as part of the circuits of capital accumulation with its inherent tendency to produce recurring crises (Harvey 1978) became evident. Loan defaults in the housing sector had induced a severe crisis in the financial sector, resulting not only in the near bankruptcy of whole countries but more concretely in the expulsion of thousands of families in North America and many countries of the European Union (Crump et al. 2008; Alexandri & Janoschka 2017). The crisis had shown quite plainly that a right to adequate housing does not exist, at least not everywhere and for everyone.

In most countries of the Global South the housing question has never left the table. While some industrialised countries only recently and only intermittently experienced serious housing backlogs, the housing challenge faced by developing countries is much

1 In this work, the terms 'industrialised countries', 'Global North' and 'developed countries' are used synonymously just the same as 'Global South' and 'developing countries'.

more serious. Here, rapid urbanisation processes, never before seen in their severity, result in fast-growing urban agglomerations and extensive urban landscapes. Usually, these urbanisation processes take place uncontrolled and produce an increasing housing shortage. Despite considerable economic growth, a significant part of society – the underprivileged – remain excluded and, due to the inherent logic of capitalism, formal markets have proven unable to provide sufficient amounts of adequate housing for the poor. Consequently, informal settlements in various stages of consolidation are sprawling in the cities of the Global South and informality as a way of life has long since become one of their characteristics (Roy & AlSayyad 2004).

The housing question is closely linked to two other debates: the discussions on the urban age and planetary urbanisation. The idea of the so-called *urban age* was born in 2007, when the United Nations, based on their demographic records, proclaimed that for the first time in human history more people lived in urban than in rural areas (UN-DESA 2014). In this perspective, cities are seen as the home to the majority of the population, as the places where the future of humanity will be decided.

Urbanisation is seen as a serious threat to the goal of sustainability, because urban fabrics produced today will shape our cities for decades to come (WBGU 2016a). Due to path dependency, structures cannot be changed easily in the short or medium term, having serious impacts on all dimensions of sustainability. Economically, cities are major drivers of globalisation processes, producing fragmented landscapes at all spatial scales, resulting in increased inequality and the exclusion of 'the useless' or 'the underprivileged' – those not needed in the global economy. Ecologically, these hubs of the global economy consume most of the produced energy and contribute with their emissions most significantly to climate change, ie 70 % of global CO_2 emissions are produced in cities (WBGU 2016b). Socially, cities have become the melting pot of a world characterised by increased inequality and social fragmentation. By denying equal opportunities for all, including such a basic right as 'the right to adequate and affordable housing', social cohesion in urban areas is threatened with serious challenges for political stability.

The debate on urbanisation can be linked further to a second discussion about *planetary urbanisation*. Perceiving urbanisation not only as a demographic process, some scholars argue that an 'extended urbanisation' is affecting every spot on our planet, no matter how peripheral (Brenner 2013; Brenner 2014a). Global cities – homes to transnational enterprises – push forward the commodification of their hinterland and expand and intensify their land grab to every spot on earth (Leon 2015). There, the logics of capital accumulation destroy and transform the 'old' landscapes, expelling original residents. Those dispossessed are then pushed to the gates of the cities, contributing significantly to the uncontrolled dynamics of spatial and demographic urban growth. Adopting this perspective, urbanisation becomes more than a process describing the growth of urban areas or the proliferation of lifestyles, but a process affecting and transforming all places on earth, incorporating them into the circuits of capital accumulation and producing fragmented landscapes characterised by poverty and inequality.

The highest dynamic of urbanisation can be witnessed in developing countries. On the African and Asian continents alone, 1.4 million people are added to the ranks of the world's citizens every week (UN-DESA 2018a). Of course, the demographics these statistics are based on as well as the perspective on 'the urban' and 'urbanisation' must be questioned critically (Brenner & Schmid 2015). It can be agreed that it is the Global South which will have to cope with an estimated 95 % of global urban growth by 2050 (Davis 2006). Whole urban areas, including housing units and services, must be planned, financed, and constructed in a sustainable way for an estimated number of 2.5 to 3 billion new urban residents by 2050 (UN-DESA 2018a). Identified as a second wave of urbanisation after industrialisation, the consequences of urbanisation have clearly become one of the most serious challenges in the 21st century (OECD 2015: 27–28).

1.1 The housing question and the challenge of slums

Increased urgency characterises the debate on urbanisation and its most serious consequence: the lack of affordable and adequate housing. Different actors are responsible for housing production: private developers, individuals, and the government. These groups have generally distinct and sometimes opposing interests: in the case of private individuals it is mostly to satisfy their housing need; developers seek the highest possible returns on their investments; and governments might act to make profits or for the public good. Developers and the government usually work in the formal housing sector while individuals produce housing for both the formal and informal markets. Due to the priority of the logics of profit-seeking over the logics of satisfying housing needs – in other words, the dominance of exchange value over use value (cf. box 2), most housing stock is produced only for medium- or high-income households. This leaves a lack of adequate housing for the poor (an affordability crisis) who must rely on informal housing markets to satisfy their housing need.

Strong urbanisation processes reinforce this lack of adequate housing, causing a skyrocketing demand in many cities of the Global South. In 2014 an estimated one billion people, or one third of the world's urban population, lived in slums (UN-Habitat 2016: 203), a term used to describe various kinds of marginal settlements (cf. box 1). Even if relative numbers are decreasing in most parts of the world, forecasts predict the world's slum population to grow by up to two billion by 2050 (UN-DESA 2013: 10). Consequently, some scholars draw an apocalyptic picture for our future world, picturing a 'planet of slums' (Davis 2006).

This proliferation of slums raises some important questions: Why are the numbers of slum dwellers still increasing? Is this tendency deeply rooted in our capitalist mode of production? Is the international community unable or unwilling to address this challenge? What strategies, measures, and initiatives have been introduced?

Box 1: Slums

Several diffuse terms have been used to describe deteriorated and run-down urban areas with inadequate housing conditions (eg favela, marginal settlements, squatter, shanty towns, *kampung kumuh, colonias populares,* etc), but the term 'slum' has become a catch-all word for various kinds of marginal settlements in different temporal, social, legal, and spatial manifestations (UN-Habitat 2003a; Bronger 2007).

Slums are often perceived as overcrowded and dirty places, associated with poverty and criminality. However, past geographical research has shown that they are by no means homogeneous places (Mertins 1984; Bähr & Mertins 2000; Wehrhahn 2014). What they have in common are some or all of the following: deteriorated or provisional housing conditions, high population densities, insecure tenure, inadequate infrastructure, insufficient provision of public services, and a lack of economic opportunities. These characteristics limit the dwellers' ability to satisfy even their basic needs, resulting in poverty and exclusion from society (Deffner 2006; Perlman 2010: 316–326; Rothfuß 2014).

The 'challenge of slums' (UN-Habitat 2003a) has been accepted as a fundamental development concern by the international community since the 1970s. During the first two conferences on human settlements (Habitat I in 1976 and Habitat II in 1996) governments acknowledged a fundamental right derived from the Universal Declaration of Human Rights: the right to adequate housing for all (Art. 48; UN 1948). Commonly, slums are perceived as a problem, and informal and marginal areas have become frequently subject to interventions by state authorities. Views on the extent and nature of these interventions, however, differ widely among practitioners and scholars. They have developed over time, following paradigmatic changes in the international debate. Since the mid-20th century several paradigm changes on 'adequate' strategies for slum areas have occurred: In the decades before the United Nations called for the first conference on human settlements in 1976 (Habitat I) slum areas were widely neglected in most developing countries and, if any, conventional housing strategies such as state-financed social housing were preferred. Subsidised flats in multi-storey buildings were constructed to accommodate low-income residents, but soon this model was abandoned as too cost-intensive (Bähr & Mertins 2000; Mertins 1984).

Facing the worsening housing conditions and growth of slum areas in many cities, the social housing approach was abandoned after the Habitat I conference. Based on the pioneering work of the architect John Turner (1968a) who emphasised the self-help ability of slum dwellers, a new paradigm emerged: aided self-help. Substantially influenced by the World Bank, different project-based approaches were tried in the following two decades: core housing, sites and services schemes, and slum upgrading programmes. At the end of the 1980s the enthusiasm for these programmes slowly vanished, as the desired impact on the housing crisis was not achieved (Werlin 1999; Pugh 2001).

In the wake of the second Habitat Conference (Habitat II) in 1996, the view gained ground that the self-help approach must be lifted from project-based interventions to comprehensive strategies which are multidimensional, combining physical improvements with other socio-economic measures (Helmsing 2002; Chiodelli 2016; Nuissl & Heinrichs 2013). Governments were now identified as having a key role in creating an appropriate environment enabling all stakeholders to act in concert. This 'enabling approach' stresses the need for supporting the private sector as the main provider of low-cost housing units, for involving the community in planning and managing issues, and for empowering local governments by local capacity building (Burgess 1996; Keivani & Werna 2001b).

The call for 'better government' (Werlin 1999: 1531) has become noticeably hegemonic, emphasising the need for better government institutions. Generally, it is accepted that comprehensive housing policies embedded in a better governance framework, often termed as 'good governance' (Grindle 2007), are needed. How such a framework should look, which principles it should follow, and which actors should shape it is much disputed and ideologically charged. Often the term is connoted with neoliberal ideas of dominant international actors, such as the World Bank.

Three main points can be derived from this brief history of housing policies: first, there is a general acknowledgement that market forces are unable to solve the challenge of slums and that some kind of state intervention is needed. Second, local governance is seen as decisive for the success of housing policies. Third, two opposing views on how the housing challenge should be addressed characterise the debate on policies and interventions: on the one hand, the dominant position is that slums can be improved by trusting the self-help abilities of slum dwellers and facilitating their efforts by creating an appropriate environment. Promoting inexpensive enabling policies by means of market integration of slum dwellers, land titling programmes (Soto 2002), and making the residents 'bankable' are seen as an important part of the solution (Jones 2012; Roy 2014). This neoliberal view is dominant and propagated by most development agencies. On the other hand, it is argued that slums are a phenomenon caused by the structural conditions of capitalist economies which can only be properly addressed by massive and cost-intensive state intervention such as social housing (Marx et al. 2013; Nuissl & Heinrichs 2013). Critical scholars take this alternative view, challenging the hegemonic position of neoliberal approaches on housing policies. Considering the failure of formal housing markets over the last decades – estimations suggest that up to 85 % of the new housing stock is created informally every year (Aguilera & Smart 2016) – and the ongoing proliferation of informal settlements, they argue that alternative approaches, such as 'the right to the city', must be considered and translated into pro-poor housing policies.

All three points are included in the Quito Declaration, the final declaration resulting from the Habitat III summit in 2016. This declaration, which is called the 'New Urban Agenda' (NUA), provides principles, visions, and implementation guidelines for sustainable urban development. Although not made explicit in the paper, alternative approaches considering the right to the city are recognised as being in line with the vision outlined in the NUA.

> We share a vision of cities for all, referring to the equal use and enjoyment of cities and human settlements, seeking to promote inclusivity and ensure that all inhabitants, of present and future generations, without discrimination of any kind, are able to inhabit and produce just, safe, healthy, accessible, affordable, resilient and sustainable cities and human settlements to foster prosperity and quality of life for all. We note the efforts of some national and local governments to enshrine this vision, referred to as 'right to the city', in their legislation, political declarations and charters.
> (UN 2017: par. 11 of NUA)

The leading role of national and subnational governments is highlighted as being decisive for reaching this vision by adopting people-centred approaches that translate into effective urban policies at all levels. A strong urban governance that empowers all relevant stakeholders is seen as crucial (UN 2017: 8).

Cities are increasingly discussed not as a problem, but as the solution for the grand challenges faced by humanity. This is already mirrored in the Sustainable Development Goals (SDGs) adopted in 2015, where for the first time a stand-alone urban goal was included, stating the aim to make cities safe, inclusive, resilient, and sustainable (SDG 11). Cities are highlighted as crucial for achieving sustainability (Parnell 2016; Caprotti et al. 2017) and in the first among several targets of SDG 11 the commitment to address the housing question is expressed:

> By 2030, ensure access for all to adequate, safe and affordable housing and basic services and upgrade slums.
> (SDG 11, Target 1;UN 2015a)

Both documents, the SDG 11 and the New Urban Agenda, are important reference documents, but despite such strong commitments it remains highly questionable whether the outlined goals will be reached. The challenge to find adequate urban policies in the housing sector remains unsolved. Despite some impressive success stories, eg the Kampung Improvement Programme (KIP) in Indonesia or the Million Houses Programme in Sri Lanka (Joshi & Sohail Khan 2010; Yap 2015), scaling-up pilot programmes and transferring good practices to other cities and regions frequently failed. Against ever-increasing numbers of slum dwellers the strategies from the past must be rated as insufficient. Some authors even see signs of an unfolding housing crisis being global in scale (Wetzstein 2017; Misselwitz 2018). Thus, I argue for the importance of considering alternative perspectives on urbanisation and normative directions that could possibly point out other more suitable solutions for housing policies promoting the shared vision of 'cities for all' (UN 2017: par. 11 of NUA).

1.2 Capitalist urbanisation, neoliberalism, and the right to the city

> What [...] are we to make of the immense concentrations of wealth, privilege, and consumerism in almost all the cities of the world in the midst of what even the United Nations depicts as an exploding 'planet of slums'?
> (Harvey 2012: 4)

The continuing lack of housing for the poor can be linked to urbanisation processes (causing increasing demand), to government failure (local and national governments overstrained), and to market failure (formal markets unable or unwilling to provide enough housing). All three aspects are related to logics inherent in the capitalist mode of production. Most scholars in critical urban theory nowadays agree that urbanisation and capitalism must be seen as connected, as a nexus (Rossi 2017). David Harvey contributed significantly to this understanding, outlined first in *Social Justice and the City* (Harvey 1979) and deepened in *Limits to Capital* (Harvey 2006). In his conceptions, he identified a close relationship between the urban and capitalism via the tendency of capital to mitigate its crisis tendencies of overaccumulation (Marx 1867 [1965]) by switching capital from the productive circuit (the first circuit of capital) to a second circuit, the built environment (ie all physical structures such as houses, transport systems, office buildings, etc). By huge investments in infrastructure projects and large-scale office or housing developments, accumulation can be maintained, at least for a certain period. This temporal fix averts the crisis caused by overaccumulation in the first circuit of capital. The process of switching is mediated by the state and large financial organisations which require appropriate communication networks and management infrastructure. These structures are provided in cities functioning as hubs of the global economy. Depending on their involvement in the primary or secondary circuits of capital, cities obtain different roles (origin or destination of capital flows) and become linked in a global spatial division of labour (Krätke 2014). In the light of this theory, the current wave of urbanisation, in particular the expansion of the real estate sector, can be explained as a necessary and inevitable process caused by the logic of accumulation in capitalist economies.

Since its beginning in the 1970s, this general tendency of capitalist urban development has been reinforced and rescaled by the ascendency of neoliberalism and globalisation. After the crises of the Keynesian system in those years, logics of deregulation, flexibilisation, entrepreneurialisation, privatisation, and individualisation have become prominent means to maintain the current accumulation regime (Leitner et al. 2007b). The principles of neoliberalism have become the dominant mode of regulation and due to intensifying globalisation these logics spread everywhere, helping to commodify all corners of the world (Belina et al. 2013; Harvey 2007).

For cities, neoliberalism meant first and foremost the shift to another management system (Müller & Sträter 2011: 147–152). Steering the city in an entrepreneurial way is nowadays seen as 'best practice' and the term 'urban governance' emerged, emphasising the incorporation of other stakeholders in the management of urban areas as neoliberal policy experiments (Brenner & Theodore 2003). Austerity policies, privatisation of urban services, self-responsibility of the residents, but astonishingly also participatory and liberal approaches are since that time the global dogma of good urban policies. Cloaked as an efficiency increase, the proliferation of neoliberalism has one deeply inscribed goal: the financialisation of urban policies and possibly all aspects of urban life (Rossi 2017). Achieving this would allow a smooth capital switch from the first circuit to other circuits of capital accumulation (on the circuits of capital cf. Harvey 1978; Belina 2011; on neoliberalism cf. Brenner & Theodore 2002; Leitner et al. 2007a).

Box 2: Use value and exchange value

Use value and exchange value are central terms conceptualised by Karl Marx in his theory of commodities (Marx 1867 [1965]: 49–98). Use value is the practical utility of an object determined by its physical properties (Abrahamson 2014: 99). All goods possess a use value when they are socially recognised as useful. Exchange value, in contrast, is the worth of a commodity in relation to others, the monetary price a commodity can achieve in a market (Castree et al. 2013: 545).

Both terms are central in Marxist thinking, where they are interpreted as contradicting elements of commodities. A flat has use value for its tenant, which is socially recognised depending on size, location, and equipment. The same flat has exchange value for its owner, expressed in the profit it generates by rent relative to the profit other investments would yield (Abrahamson 2014: 99).

What do these considerations mean for housing production and how can they explain the global housing crisis? One could expect that a redirection of investments to the second circuit (ie to urban fabrics) would produce enough housing units for all, but this is not the case. Of course, as already noted by Friedrich Engels (1892 [1970]: 194), the logic of capital accumulation dictates to be reluctant when investing in working-class housing since the resulting structures are unlikely to yield proper returns on investments. Moreover, in the housing sector the capital is switching to high-rise office buildings and luxury real estate assets because these types of urban fabric promise a better amortisation. Housing is only produced for those who are part of the 'formal' society, for the middle and upper class, and for those who are creditworthy. The increasing demand for such investments raises the land prices in all cities over the world, making it even more difficult if not impossible for individuals to satisfy their housing needs at an affordable price. From this perspective it becomes clear why the challenge of slums still exists and why markets are unable to provide adequate and affordable housing for all.

The lack of housing expresses itself spatially in the proliferation of informal areas and run-down quarters in our cities. This expression is only one of the stones in the mosaic of space produced by our society. Clearly, under the current capitalist mode of production in its latest configuration (following neoliberal principles and reinforced by globalisation processes) we have produced fragmented landscapes characterised by rising inequalities and segregation on all geographical scales (Scholz 2002, 2003; Coy 2004). One among many fragments, though most visible and disturbing, are sprawling slum areas (Coy & Kraas 2003). Is there no way to redirect capitalist urbanisation to achieve a more inclusive development? A development which ensures, to use UN terminology, that no one will be left behind (UNGA 2015)?

Both scholars and activists of various social movements have considered and theorised alternative development paths. One concept in particular distinguishes itself and has become increasingly prominent over the last decades: the concept of *the right to the city*. The French philosopher Henri Lefebvre coined this term in the 1960s (Lefebvre 1968 [2016]) as a 'cry and demand' for a radically different urban experience. In his work, Lefebvre drafted a 'possibility', a different urban world where use value has triumphed over exchange value (cf. box 2). In this utopia, citizens are in charge of the production of urban space. The right to the city then is a demand and also a cry for help of those who are marginalised in today's cities, whose right to access and use urban space and to participate in urban development is denied. It is a demand for a different production of space (Ronneberger & Vogelpohl 2014: 263–265).

Considering the housing domain, the local level, or – more precisely urban governance, is identified as decisive for the appearance of specific housing policies. Here, the interplay between the two opposing perspectives can be witnessed. Depending on the dominant perspective among stakeholders, distinct modes of governance form and with them housing policies that differ in terms of their style and outcome. For residents of informal settlements this can mean several scenarios: they might get financial support from local governments to improve their homes; they might get formalised, receiving an official land title; or be made 'bankable' using the mortgage system and be included in the capitalist world. Local governments might also perform forced evictions to redevelop urban areas for business districts or medium-income housing complexes. Another possibility is to resettle them with a participatory approach to social housing units, giving incentives for their individual economic development. It can also mean many other measures in between. What is clear is that it is the mode of governance and its inscribed perspective on housing that is decisive for the design of housing policies and in turn for the impact on the lives of informal dwellers.

1.3 Conceptual background and research questions

The discussion so far on the housing challenge and its causes leads us to the following conclusions: There is a dramatic lack of affordable and adequate housing worldwide, so the number of slum dwellers continues to rise. The problem has been recognised internationally and there have been a variety of projects, programs, and strategies to address the challenge. However, most strategies failed or were insufficient. Increasingly it is acknowledged that better local governance is needed to create and implement sound housing policies. From a superior perspective, it has become clear that rising inequality, segregation, and fragmentation in urban areas are system-inherent and will remain so within the dominant societal formation and its mode of regulation. Based on the theories of Henri Lefebvre, it should therefore be considered to imagine a world within another social formation, the 'urban society'[2], in order to derive better strategies to address the housing challenge.

These fields form the conceptual background of this work. The central point is the juxtaposition of the elements of two successive formations ('space-time configurations') in order to derive possible recommendations for an alternative production of space. In figure 1 the current formation, which Lefebvre calls an 'industrial society', and a possible future formation – the possible-impossible world of an 'urban society' – are juxtaposed. Both formations have specific levels ('space-time levels'): Below a general abstract level (the global order), consisting of abstract regulatory entities (eg state, market, laws), there is a mediating level of governance, characterised by specific policy arrangements. Depending on the characteristics of these arrangements specific policies are created that steer 'spatial practices'.

Our current formation – the 'industrial society' – is characterised by the hegemony of neoliberalism as a regulatory force and its rationale in substantially shaping modes

2 The term 'urban society' is used in this work in the sense of Henri Lefebvre, who refers to a new societal formation that follows the industrial society, ie the current societal formation. He developed this theory through his historical preoccupation with the process of urbanisation, in which he concludes that there is a succession of 'continents' or societal formations, which make a possible future formation appear on the horizon: the 'urban society'. For a more detailed explanation, see chapter 5.

of urban governance and urban policies around the globe. The switching of capital from the first to the second circuit inherent in the current formation demands repeated investments in the built environment. Together, both factors are the logics behind the production of today's urban space. The results are fragmented landscapes, rising inequality, and sprawling slum areas. In contrast to this, there is a future formation, 'the becoming' or the 'urban society', which can be conceived in a theoretical and normative way. The mode of regulation of such a formation would no longer be completely subject to the logic of capitalism, but use value would have triumphed over exchange value and the right to the city for all would have been realised. The 'spatial practice' would be characterised by adequate housing for all and inclusive cities which guarantee access to urban resources for all.

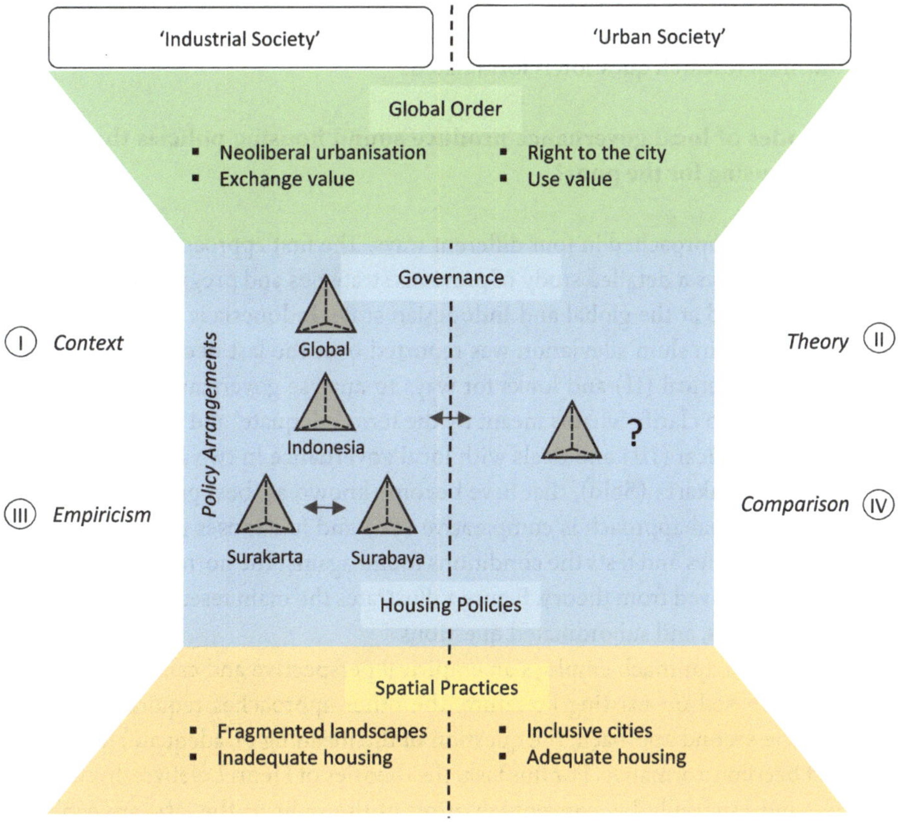

Fig. 1 Conceptual background
Source: Illustration by author

This concept, however, remains vague at a critical mediating level: that of governance, which is decisive for steering spatial practices. The crucial question is therefore how the governance level of such an 'urban society' could be characterised in order to achieve the normative goal of an inclusive city that provides housing for all. The governance level has also become more and more important in housing studies. It is increasingly recognised that neither specific types of housing programmes, nor specific actors, nor the legal, cultural, or socio-economic framework conditions of specific countries, nor global housing paradigms are decisive for sound housing policies. Rather, the policy outcomes seem to be the result of an interplay of all these factors (Bredenoord et al. 2014; Nuissl & Heinrichs 2013).

Following these reflections, it becomes apparent that an approach is needed which focuses on the formation conditions of sound housing policies. Based on the assumptions that governance conditions are correlated with the (non-)formation of adequate housing policies and that specific local governance conditions do promote the emergence of sound housing policies, the main objective of this study is to explore and compare the circumstances under which such policies evolve. Out of these considerations, the main research question is formulated:

Which modes of local governance produce sound housing policies that realise adequate housing for the poor?

This question is approached in four different ways. The first approach is contextualising (I) and employs a detailed study of previous strategies and programmes that have been implemented at the global and Indonesian scale. Indonesia is chosen since tremendous success in slum alleviation was reported over the last decades. The second approach is theoretical (II) and looks for ways to analyse governance and for a normative direction to clarify what is meant by the term 'adequate' and 'sound'. The third approach is empirical (III) and deals with local governance in two Indonesian cities, Surabaya and Surakarta (Solo), that have become known as 'best practice' examples. The fourth and final approach is comparative (IV) and juxtaposes modes of governance in the two cities and tests the conditions found against the normative foundation of governance derived from theory. Figure 2 illustrates the main research question, the four research fields, and subordinated questions.

While the first approach employs an empirical perspective and can be realised relatively easily based on existing literature, the other approaches require conceptual work. For the second approach, the question of the meaning of 'adequate', the discussion must become normative. For this task, the theories of Henri Lefebvre, his writings on cities, and especially his conceptualisation of the right to the city, are explored. This theoretical contribution provides a normative compass to imagine appropriate governance configurations and housing policies. For the empirical approach, an analytical concept is needed to analyse local governance. Such a concept is available from the governance literature: policy arrangements (Arts et al. 2006). Its holistic nature makes it possible to analyse practices and structure conditions in the housing sector such as the actors' decisions and power relations, but also formal and informal institutions (rules) and discourses, altogether forming specific arrangements. It can also be

Main research question and research fields

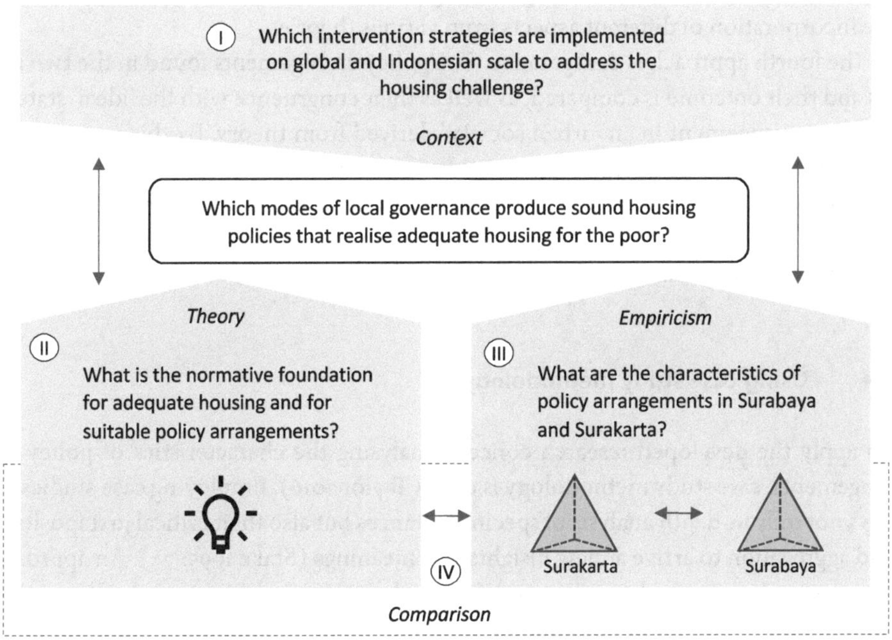

Subordinated questions

I. *Context*
- What is the housing situation globally and in Indonesia?
- What paradigms shape(d) the global discourse on housing the poor?
- What are rules of the game and central actors in Indonesia's housing domain?
- Which measures, strategies, and programmes were applied and to what effect?

II. *Theory*
- What does Lefebvre's 'right to the city' and his 'urban society' mean?
- Is the concept of policy arrangements suitable to analyse local governance?
- What do Lefebvre's theories offer to conceive of adequate housing and appropriate policy arrangements?

III. *Empiricism*
- What intervention strategies and programmes are realised for the poor and what do they achieve?
- Which actors are relevant in the housing domain and what influence do they hold?
- What strands shape the local discourse on housing the poor?
- What are the formal and informal rules of the game?

IV. *Comparison*
- What are similarities and differences of the identified policy arrangement in Surabaya and Solo (content and organisation)?
- To what extent are global and national recommendations implemented at the local level?
- Do identified housing policy arrangements respect the right to the city and adequate housing?

Fig. 2 Main research question, research fields, and subordinated questions
Source: Illustration by author

applied in different urban environments and at different scales, allowing a comparative approach. In addition, it has multiple linkages to other theoretical strands, promoting the incorporation of different aspects from various theories.

The fourth approach is comparative. The policy arrangements found in the two cities and their outcome is compared, as well as their congruence with the 'ideal' state of a policy arrangement in an 'urban society' derived from theory. By this comparison, the results of the first three research fields can be related to each other. This makes it possible to achieve crucial insights on policy arrangements that promote adequate housing for the poor. All four approaches with their subordinate questions contribute to answering the main research question from different angles.

1.4 Using case study methodology

To apply the developed research concept analysing the characteristics of policy arrangements, case study methodology is used (Taylor 2016). Employing case studies allows not only in-depth analysis of specific instances but also their critical juxtaposition and aggregation to arrive at new insights and meanings (Stake 1995: 74). An approach that compares case studies is instrumental in drawing conclusions on the theoretical assumptions about the governance environment under which inclusive and adequate housing policies are possible and furthered.

As the item of analysis, the governance environment of urban entities is chosen: the administrative unit of cities. There is much discussion in the literature on the importance of the local scale for the result of policies (Helmsing 2002; Kersting et al. 2009; Ghosh & Kamath 2012), but local governance environments and their entangled policies are increasingly recognised as a crucial factor determining the success of realised measures (Cohen 2006: 78). It is at the city level where national policies are realised and it is their governance structure, the way strategies are turned into action, which determines success or failure (Devas 2004). Thus, the local policies on the city level are chosen as the object to be analysed in this study. By using cities as cases, it becomes possible to analyse their governance environments and the comparison allows the identification and categorisation of applied housing strategies, implemented measures (good practices), characteristics of local policy arrangements, as well as obstacles and challenges for the common goal of inclusive housing policies.

A sufficient analysis demands at least two cases that cover a broad range of applied strategies in the housing sector but are still comparable. Two Indonesian cities, Surabaya and Surakarta (Solo), are selected for this study. Since both cities are located in the same national context, the laws and rules are similar and national programmes do apply in both cities. Thus, the institutional and political variables can be controlled (Pierre 2005: 455). However, the observed policy outcome in the housing sector does differ significantly in both cases, raising the question of which other variables might be relevant. Here, my conceptual approach comes in, focusing on these other factors and arguing that the interrelated dimensions of specific policy arrangements are responsible for differing policy outcomes.

Of course, the distinct historic trajectories of both cities must be taken into account. It might be argued that cities are different due to their historic pathways, which have produced different socio-economic, demographic, and structural realities and thus result in a distinct character. Referring to specific hidden knowledge bases inherent and unique in all cities, Löw (2008: 78–80) argues that this pattern, what she calls '*Eigenlogik*', is deeply inscribed in the actors' routines and practices, structuring the logics of their actions (Berking & Löw 2008; Löw 2008). From this point of view, differing policy outcomes in distinct cities are not surprising.

Löw's notion has an important consequence for the comparative part of this study. Case study methodology used here aims to produce both intrinsic knowledge, focusing on knowledge about particular cases, and instrumental knowledge, using insights of the cases to illuminate a wider issue (Stake 1995: 3–4). While the applied concept gives a deep insight into the governance environment of the housing domain of each city taken for itself, the subsequent comparison relies on generalisation of patterns and categories. This generalisation might have produced problematic results, as it remains to be discussed if, or to what degree, the analysis concept developed here is able to capture the *Eigenlogik*, the specific character, of the selected cases properly. Thus, it is necessary to discuss the findings of this comparative approach carefully and to consider appropriate reinterpretations against the contextual background of the two cities.

1.5 Two Indonesian cities as cases

Two cities located in Indonesia are selected as cases for this study. This has two reasons: First, the country is reported as very successful in mitigating its housing problems. Despite strong and enduring urbanisation processes, Indonesia managed to improve the living conditions of 21.2 million slum dwellers between 2000 and 2010 (UN-Habitat 2008c: 39–40). This achievement is *a priori* impressive, since the country had to cope with the devastating consequences of the Asian Crisis, a large-scale economic crisis in the late 1990s, which had severe socio-economic consequences. The second reason is that Indonesia introduced far-reaching reforms in the beginning of the 2000s (decentralisation and democratisation) that meant a radical political change for the country, leaving cities with increased power to steer their own development. The centralist regime, under which the government in Jakarta controlled all policies, gradually changed (Kersting et al. 2009: 171–175; May 2015). Power and responsibility were devolved to lower-level government bodies, giving them a greater say in their own affairs (Firman 2010; Hudalah et al. 2013a). Due to this process, Indonesian cities today have more power to influence national policies, implement them on their own terms, and even create and design their own local policies, at least to a certain degree. This new freedom enabled local governments to decide more freely on the design and implementation of local measures. For this reason, cities have begun to develop innovative approaches and programs to cope with their housing challenges (Bunnell et al. 2013). Two of these cities that are internationally recognised as models for 'good practices', owing their success to a new generation of local leaders (UN-Habitat 2015a: 166), are chosen for this study: Surabaya and Surakarta (Solo) (cf. figure 3).

Fig. 3 Major cities and urban areas in Central and East Java
Source: Illustration by author

Surabaya, the capital of East Java Province, is the second largest city in Indonesia with more than three million inhabitants (UN-Habitat 2013: 160). The agglomeration covers more than six million people (World Bank 2015a: 150–151) and the city with its work opportunities draws migrants from all over Indonesia. Due to strong urban growth – an average annual change of 3.3 % is reported for the urban area (World Bank 2015a: 150–151) – housing problems such as a lack of housing for the poor and vast informal areas are well-known in this city. In response, numerous intervention strategies have been developed, the origins already dating back to the colonial rule of the Dutch (Bawole 2007: 38–41). Since that time, several measures have been realised, ranging from social housing to community-based slum upgrading. The latter has become renowned in Indonesia since the 1970s as the Kampung Improvement Programme (KIP). Since 1976 it has been adapted nationwide, received support from the World Bank, and is considered to be very successful (Silas 1992). In Indonesia and among international experts, Surabaya is known for innovative urban policies and many practitioners look at this city as a model for urban development. KIP has meanwhile evolved from an upgrading programme, focusing explicitly on physical-structural issues, to a more comprehensive programme, taking into account also economic and social issues (Asnawi 2005: 69–72). Several urban policies have been awarded as 'best practice' by UN-Habitat, the United Nations Human Settlement Programme (UN-Habitat 2002b, 2008a). Recently, under the progressive mayor Tri Rismaharini (since 2010), the city has introduced a number of advanced initiatives to improve the city's *kampungs*[3] in many respects.

The other case city, Surakarta, more commonly known as Solo by its inhabitants[4], is a medium-sized city with approximately 500,000 inhabitants in Central Java Province. Home to Javanese culture and an important centre for national politics, the city has become famous for its innovative urban policies in the last decades. The success of these policies can be measured not only by the reports of a number of scholars (Phelps et al. 2014; Taylor 2015; Obermayr 2017), but also by the successful career of its main driver, Joko Widodo (known as 'Jokowi'). He substantially shaped the city's policies as mayor between 2005 and 2012, became governor of Jakarta in 2012, and was elected president of the republic in 2014. During his time as mayor, he introduced people-centred policies, considering the demands of relevant stakeholders and the citizens, and focusing particularly on the informal sector and informal settlements. He introduced a new political style in the city, the political will to listen to marginalised groups, and a commitment to solve their problems (Obermayr 2017: 170). Several policies of Solo have gained attention, most of all the participatory relocation of Solo's street vendors, awarded as 'best practice' by UN-Habitat (UN-Habitat 2008d), and the participatory resettlement of informal squatter settlements (Bunnell et al. 2013; Obermayr & Sandholz 2017).

1.6 Outline and scope

Nine different parts structure this study, illuminating the main research question from different scales and perspectives (cf. figure 4). After the introduction (Part I), the conceptual foundation is presented, consisting of two conceptual-theoretical fields (Part II). The first field explores Henri Lefebvre's theories of the production of space and the right to the city, deriving the normative direction for this study. The second

---

3 The *kampung* is an Indonesian settlement type (cf. chapter 18.2 for details). For better readability the Indonesian word *kampung* is appended in the plural with an [s] to '*kampungs*' in this work, even though this is grammatically incorrect.

4 The city's official name is Surakarta and this name is found often in government documents and maps. However, since the residents call their city 'Solo' this denomination is also preferred in this study.

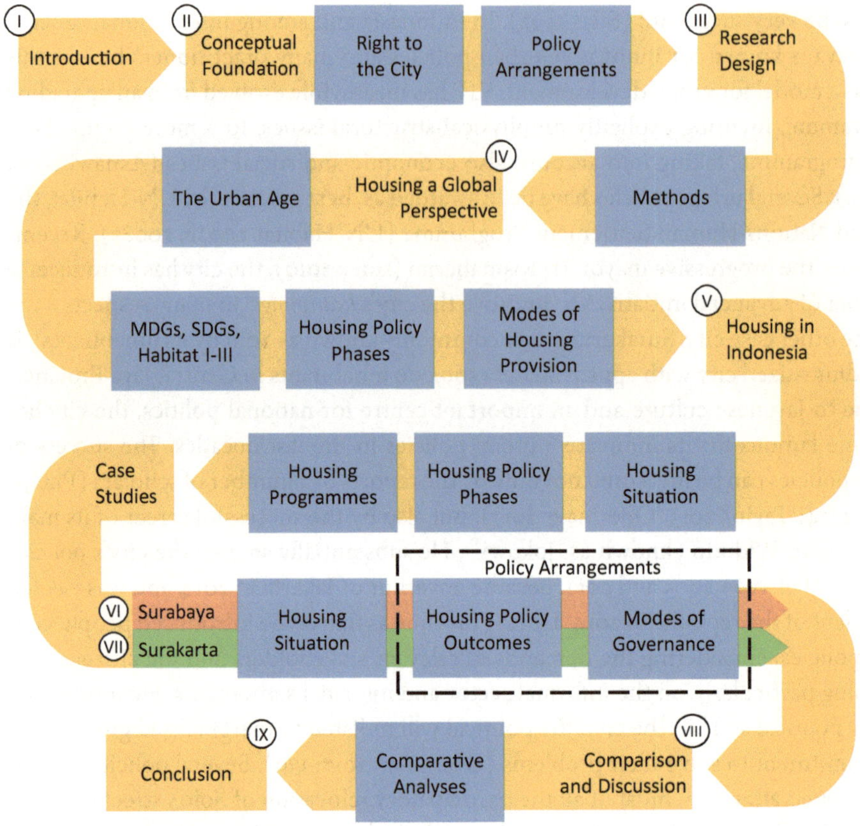

Fig. 4 Research outline
Source: Illustration by author

field conceptualises and adapts the framework of policy arrangements for analysing local governance. The corresponding research design, including methods of data collection and analysis, are presented thereinafter (Part III). After these theoretical and methodological parts follows the main section of the study. Parts IV and V deal with housing policies on the global and national level in order to contextualise the two case studies. From a global perspective, Part IV analyses the state of housing and associated housing policy recommendations and discourses. Latest trends in urbanisation are illustrated, followed by an examination of milestones and global conferences on human settlements. From this analysis dominant discourse strands, changing paradigms, distinct housing policy phases, and intervention strategies are identified and related to modes of housing provision in developing countries. The next part deals with housing issues in Indonesia (Part V). The country's cities and settlements, recent urban developments, and its housing situation are comprehensively explored. Indonesia's housing policies are examined thereinafter, identifying distinct phases, actors involved, and outcomes for the poor. Parts VI and VII present the two case studies: the cities of Surabaya and Surakarta (Solo). Both cities are comprehensively studied in terms of their housing situation, the content of their housing policies, and specific policy arrangements in place. The four dimensions of policy arrangements are analysed in detail, detecting specific and distinct configurations of governance in the housing domain for both cities.

In Part VIII, a comparative analysis is carried out (between cities, between scales, and against theory). Differences and similarities between both cities are identified as well as constraints and obstacles for achieving the common goal of adequate housing for all. The comparison between different scales (global to local) reveals the degree of congruence in housing policies between the global, national, and local scale. The comparison against theoretical findings makes it possible to evaluate content and outcome of policy arrangements considering the normative foundation. Based on these comparative analyses, Part IX summarises the results and provides an outlook for further research.

I. CONCEPTUAL FOUNDATION

Two conceptual-theoretical fields form the conceptual foundation of this work. The first field explores critical urban theory, seeking for a normative foundation for adequate housing and local governance. The theories of Henri Lefebvre are explored in detail, including in particular his perspectives on the production of space, the right to the city, and the 'urban society'. The second field deals with conceptual questions about how to analyse local governance. As an analytical framework, the approach of policy arrangements is conceptualised to be employed later on for the empirical analysis. The study of these theories leads to a normative understanding of what adequate housing and appropriate policy arrangements should look like in order to achieve a social transformation towards a possible alternative urban reality (the 'urban society'). The following questions guide this chapter:

What is the normative foundation for adequate housing and for suitable policy arrangements?

- What do Lefebvre's 'right to the city' and his 'urban society' mean?
- Is the concept of policy arrangements suitable for analysing local governance?
- What do Lefebvre's theories offer to conceive adequate housing and appropriate policy arrangements?

The first conceptual field deals with the search for normative directions, for alternative ways to produce space. Henri Lefebvre's conception of the production of space (Lefebvre 1974 [1991]), and his right to the city (Lefebvre 1968 [1996]) are examined to explore the 'urban society', a radically different possible-impossible space-time configuration of society (Lefebvre 1970 [2003]). The second conceptual field is concerned with theories of medium reach, which are necessary for the concrete analysis of policy arrangements or modes of governance producing specific housing policies. In this section, theoretical complexes of theories of urban political economy, ie regime theory (Moosenberger & Stocker 2001) as well as governance theory (Kooiman 2003) and institutional theory (North 1990), are briefly assessed in order to culminate in the approach of policy arrangements (Arts et al. 2000). This approach is employed later on for the analysis of housing policies for the poor in the two case study cities.

In international reference documents on cities, such as the New Urban Agenda (2016), the call for 'adequate housing' is articulated. Usually, the term 'adequate' is not clearly defined, but referred to as the normative goal. It is stated that policies should be implemented that enable all urban dwellers to participate equally in the resources and possibilities provided by the city (UN 2017). This normative discussion needs backing from a theoretical point of view and for this task, the writings on cities of the French philosopher Henri Lefebvre (1974 [1991], 1968 [1996], 1970 [2003], 1968 [2016]) are of particular use.

In his work, Lefebvre conceived an urban 'possibility', a vision of how the urban experience could be in contrast to what we experience today as reality in our cities. This thinking about 'the possible' is of particular use when reflecting on urban policies, since it opens the eyes to a new perspective, shedding light on new directions and alternative development paths. For a clear understanding of Lefebvre's abstract notions on 'the urban' as a possibility, however, it is necessary to discuss the foundations of his conceptions.

2 Conceptions of Space

To begin with, it is necessary to explore common conceptions of space and to be explicit about the concept of space used by scholars of critical urban theory: that of socially produced space, the site, medium, and outcomes of historically specific societal relations (Brenner 2012). Thus, abstractions from the actual world are necessary to identify possibilities for '[...] another, more democratic, socially just and sustainable form of urbanisation even if such possibilities are currently being suppressed through dominant institutional arrangements, practices, and ideologies' (Brenner 2012: 11). It is this specific space concept which distinguishes critical urban theory from neoclassical urban analyses, allowing the development of specific frameworks for understanding the production of space in capitalism and conceptions of radical alternatives. In this chapter, common theories of space are discussed, arriving at Lefebvre's notion of 'the production of space' (Lefebvre 1974 [1991]) which is the foundation of his conception of 'the urban' (Lefebvre 1970 [2003]) as a radically different vision of an 'urban society'.

2.1 Space in geography

Unlike other social sciences, which discovered the importance of space only recently[1], geography as a discipline has a long and controversial tradition of discussing the significance and meaning of space. As a spatial science, the interest of geography has always been to comprehend, analyse, and explain things in space. What is located where? What natural and human-induced processes happen in space? Such were the principle questions being asked by geographers in the past and remain important questions today. Over the course of the 20th century, however, other questions became more influential (Wardenga 2002): can space be conceptualised as an element of human action? If so, how can we do that? Which kind of human action produces what spaces?

---

1 At the end of the 1980s, space was rediscovered as an important factor and perspective across various disciplines. This paradigmatic shift is also described as a 'spatial turn'.

Clearly, something had happened: the new questions imply underlying changes in the understanding and conception of space. In all these questions, a very specific comprehension of space is inscribed, informed by distinct interpretations and imaginations of space having emerged in the discipline. Often, conceptions are mixed in the research process, confusing the reader about the central interest of a particular study and making discussions on space difficult. Therefore, the next paragraphs briefly summarise the different conceptions of space in geography.

The Austrian geographer Peter Weichhart gives a comprehensive overview of numerous categorisations of space used by scholars of various disciplines (Weichhart 2018: 79–97). Instead of asking 'what is space?' which only leads to controversial and endless discussions of definitions, he asks 'how is space conceptualised in research?' which results in the categorisation of seven different spaces and their interrelations. This classification includes: the use of space as a vague but actually existing part of earth including all its elements (*Raum*$_1$ as in *Gebirgsraum* or 'mountain area'); space perceived subjectively, an interpreted image of reality labelled with stereotypes (*Raum*$_{1e}$ as in the 'Ruhr area'); the conception of space as a container, a three-dimensional space filled with all kinds of physical-material things having a specific position (*Raum*$_2$); space understood as a logic structure formed by immaterial relations between elements (*Raum*$_3$ as in *Farbraum* or 'colour space'); space understood as 'spatiality', as an attribute or characteristic of physical-material 'things' which is only formed by their relation (*Raum*$_4$, eg a nuclear chain reaction forms only when different critical 'things' are brought together in one place); space as a epistemological concept, as an *a priori* way to perceive things (*Raum*$_5$) and the understanding of space as socially constructed by human action (*Raum*$_{6s}$).

Depending on the research questions asked, scholars have shown interest in all of the mentioned concepts of space, but for geographical research four of these concepts are most prominent (Wardenga 2002; Freytag et al. 2016: 4): The oldest one is the conception of *space as a container* (Weichhart's *Raum*$_1$ and *Raum*$_2$). This is probably the best known conception of space, used commonly in everyday life. Space is seen as a three-dimensional entity, which is filled with all kinds of physical-material things (eg settlements, mountains, soils, transport systems, etc). When removing all objects in this container, only space remains. As human beings, however, we cannot perceive space as such, which is why we focus on physical-material objects located in an imagined space in relation to other objects. Thus, space becomes the way we perceive physical objects. When we try to comprehend space, we tend to do so by creating (abstract) demarcations. We demarcate space using specific categories and create territories – containers – in our minds. These territories might be the borders of a city or a country; and we fill these containers with content, with specific social, cultural, and economic characteristics. According to this view, the whole territorial organisation of our society is based on the concept of space as a container (Freytag 2014: 14–15).

For geography this conception of space was – and still is – very important, most of all for regional and cultural studies. In this perspective, spaces are seen as entities, assuming their existence in reality are the result of natural and anthropogenic factors which have formed a specific and unique landscape (Wardenga 2002). Problems with this space concept are that borders might be interpreted as naturally given (even though they are man-made in all cases), cross-border relations might be concealed, and there is a danger of tying certain characteristics to an assumed homogeneous population of a respective territory (Freytag 2014: 14–15).

During the 1960s and 1970s, with the upcoming quantitative methods of the 'spatial approach', this older perspective of space was increasingly extended by another conception of space, that of *space as a system of relations* (Weichart's $Raum_{3}$). Such a conception sees space as constituted, based on the interrelationships and linkages between physical-material objects exceeding the borders, of *a priori* imagined areas of the container space, ie relations between places of production and consumption or the spatial dimension of social networks. Based on statistical regionalisation new spaces were demarcated as a logical and organising system (eg commuter areas of cities), assuming that a completely positivist regionalisation of earth could be achieved. Even though this spatial approach meant an extensive working field for geographers, it also became obvious that the areas produced are only a cognitive and abstract creation of scholars, an invented organisation of things (Wardenga 2002; Weichhart 2018: 83).

Taking up this notion and anticipating upcoming cognitive approaches from behavioural geography during the 1970s, another conception of space emerged: that of *space as the sensory perception* of individuals or organisations (Weichhart's $Raum_{1e}$). In this understanding, the experienced spaces of individuals, their perception of spaces with its subjective meaning and symbology is the centre of focus. If one asks how individuals, groups, or organisations comprehend and value existing container spaces, the answers are very heterogenic. With this approach it becomes obvious that 'real spaces' are valued and demarcated very differently, challenging notions of an 'universal reality' and 'real existing spaces'. This perspective opens one's eyes to the fact that spaces are always dependent on the perception of individuals, which are continuously creating individual mental maps of the world (Freytag et al. 2016: 4).

2.2 Constructed space

Based on the understanding of space as a result of sensory perception, the latest conception of space became prominent in geography: that of *constructed space* (Weichhart's $Raum_{6s}$). In this perspective, regions are seen as constituted through spatial structures, which are produced and constantly reproduced by collective actions of society. According to Benno Werlen (1999, 2008), individuals are shaped by the world, but also shape the world with their everyday actions. This process, what he called *'alltägliches Geographie machen'* organises and forms the physical-material and symbolic appearance and configuration of the world. This produced configuration of space is in itself a resource or a constraint for further actions of individuals; it limits and promotes possibilities of action. In contrast to all previous conceptions, in this perspective spaces are conceived not as the spatial reflection of socio-cultural conditions, but as the product of social actions (Weichhart 2018: 323–326).

As we have seen in this short history of space, concepts in human geography, the ontological framework of space underlying concrete research questions shifted from container space to constructed space. This does not mean that the older space concepts are abandoned. Quite to the contrary, they are continuously applied implicitly or explicitly in human geography and other disciplines. What has happened, however, is a paradigmatic shift. Research questions are not confined asking only 'What do we see in space?', 'Where is it located?' and 'How are things related?' but extended to questions such as 'Who produces spaces out of what interest?' and 'Which spaces are produced by what kind of human action?' (Wardenga 2002).

Scholars adopting the perspective of constructed space are less interested in space itself, but in the linkages between societal phenomena and spatial aspects mediated by individual or collective actions. From this perspective, it is the actions of individuals who together as a collective produce and reproduce both spatial patterns and structures – ie physical material configurations formed by socio-economic actions – and immaterial perceptions of space – ie linguistically constituted cognitive constructions (Freytag 2014: 12). All three aspects – actions of individuals, the physical-material configurations, and cognitive constructions – are interlinked in various ways, restricting and/or reinforcing each other. Research adopting this perspective focuses on these linkages, but weights the three aspects in a different way.

This now prominent conception of space has informed critical theory and was the starting point for the development of critical-material research on space. Such research is particularly interested in the analyses of societal practice and processes of the production of space trying to identify and abstract universally valid interrelations. Doing this, the goal is to arrive at rules and laws of physical-material configurations and patterns in socially constructed space (Belina & Michel 2007: 8).

These considerations need further theoretical backing, which has been first and foremost provided by the French philosopher Henri Lefebvre (Lefebvre 1974 [1991]). Lefebvre was concerned with the task of understanding societal relations, individual actions, and possibilities for change. For this endeavour, he theorised space as both socially produced and fundamental for all human actions. He argued that space and society are linked in a profound way, space being simultaneously the expression and the prerequisite, the context for social relations and the development of society. At the end of the 20th century, the work of Henri Lefebvre was rediscovered as a source of inspiration for a revived discussion on space in the social sciences (Soja 1989).

3 Thinking with Lefebvre

The French scholar Henri Lefebvre developed a comprehensive theory of space, seeing space not as a physical-material object and not as a pure idea or imagination, but as a complex result of societal production processes. His goal was to develop a new science of space, which is not concerned with objects in space but comprehends space as a production process. His understanding developed over time and is implicitly already inscribed in his publications *The Urban Revolution* (1970 [2003]) and *The Survival of Capitalism* (1973[1976]). In his work *The Production of Space* (1974 [1991]) he presented it in a more elaborated form (Schmid 2005: 192). In order to understand his work, it is necessary to take a short trip into his epistemological thinking.

Lefebvre's epistemology

There are four constants in Lefebvre's writings: a specific understanding of the term 'praxis', a radical criticism of philosophy and scientific practice, a specific approach to Marxism, and a very specific dialectic. Especially the latter – his dialectic of the 'simultaneous' – needs clarifications, since it is the epistemological basis of his work, a creative contribution, especially for his theory of 'the production of space'.

Henri Lefebvre (1901–1991) studied philosophy in Paris in the early 1920s, after which he became a philosophy teacher and then, in the 1960s, professor for sociology in Strasbourg and later on at Paris Nanterre University. Already during his studies, he became deeply disappointed with his subject, which turned into intense criticism, as he found philosophers of his time producing theories out of touch with the real world. Lacking practical relevance, philosophy did not address the pressing questions of his time in his view. As professor in Strasbourg and Paris he came in contact with social movements, particularly during the 1968 student revolts. These experiences informed his way of thinking, and he regarded theory production never as an end to itself, but reasoned that theory must always be bound to social practice and social movements (Schmid 2005: 73–75).

Due to this critique of philosophy, he also turned early to historical materialism and joined the French communist party in 1928 from which he was expelled in 1958. His relation to communism was always ambivalent. On the one hand, Marxist writings were the cornerstone of his own theoretical conceptions, on the other hand he criticised the most influential work of Karl Marx, *Das Kapital* (Marx 1867 [1965]), as being too reductive and homogenising rationality. For him other writings of Marx were more important, in particular *The Economic and Philosophic Manuscripts of 1844* (Marx & Engels 1844 [1988]). From this starting point, he developed many of his conceptualisations: his understandings of praxis and production as well as his dialectic developed further from the 'German dialectic' of the 19th century.

Praxis and production

For Lefebvre, the term praxis came to be of utmost importance as he engaged with the writings of Marx, Engels, Hegel, and Feuerbach. He adopted Marx's idea of the self-production of the human being: humans – as part of nature, as natural beings – produce and reproduce themselves, creating the world and shaping it (Marx 1844 [1968]: 544–546). 'By acting man modifies Nature [sic!], both around and within him. He creates his own nature by acting on Nature. He transcends himself in Nature and transcends Nature in himself' (Lefebvre 1940 [2009]: 106).

For Marx it is human labor which produces everything, but for Lefebvre it is more than that. For him the fundamental category of being is human 'action'[2] subsuming all productive activities of humans including labor under this term. He emphasises the creative character of human actions, seeing them as the foundation stone of society: 'Practice [the sum of all actions] is seen as both a beginning and an end, as the origin of all thought and the source of every solution, as a fundamental relation of the living man to Nature [sic!] and to his own nature' (Lefebvre 1940 [2009]: 89). Praxis then is more than only practices, it is moreover the '[…] total activity of mankind, action and thought, physical labour and knowledge' (Lefebvre 1940 [2009]: 100). In this understanding the term praxis unites 'action' and 'thought' bringing together the practical and the theoretical dimension which has been customary separated in sciences, in everyday life, and even in languages.

Directly connected to praxis is the term 'production'. By acting, humans as social beings produce themselves and all material-physical and mental-abstract things. Products of social practice are not only their own life, history and consciousness, societal relations, the whole world (including time and space), but also abstract timeless things: knowledge, artworks even feelings are included (Schmid 2005: 85).

---

2 Lefebvre intentionally used the French term *action*, which covers a wider semantic content than only practice or activity, more than the German terms *Handlung* or *Tätigkeit*. The term *action* includes activity and practice, action, resistance, and with it more liberating moments, it means all expressions of human beings in their totality (Schmid 2005:81).

In contrast to Marx, for Lefebvre production and praxis are more than only economic practices. For him the classical Marxist analysis of labor, value of labor, and capital perspective was too narrow, reducing human actions to that of labor, concealing in that way other social practices. For Lefebvre this dominance of economic actions over other social practices became only a historical category, a principle of the dominant regime, that of capitalism (Schmid 2005: 87).

Dialectical thinking

Throughout his life, Lefebvre occupied himself with the development of his own very specific dialectic. It was always a work in progress and, depending on the writings one is reading, new questions are addressed, new aspects are included, modifying his dialectic further. Therefore, a stringent and universally valid presentation of his dialectic is not possible. Nevertheless, the roots are clear: the dialectic of Hegel and Marx, which he tried to develop further and to apply in his own research (Schmid 2005: 88).

Lefebvre accepted Hegel's view that all thinking is rooted in contradictions and exemplified it by referring to the practice of establishing a word or term (Lefebvre 1940 [2009]: 19). He argues that by establishing a term, the determination – the identity – of this term can only be comprehended in relation to its own negation – a second term. 'The "other", the second term, is equally as real as the first, it is on the same plane, at the same level or degree of reality and in the same "sphere" of thought. It negates, makes manifest and completes the first term, by expressing its one-sidedness' (Lefebvre 1940 [2009]: 21).

By putting a term, thus, also its opposite meaning, its antonym, is established. By negating this antonym, it is not the first term that reappears, but a third term, which negates the antonym but transcends the first term in something new. 'Within the Third Term [sic!] the first term is found again, only richer and more determinate, together with the second term, whose determination has been added to the first determination. The Third Term [sic!] turns back to the first term by negating the second one, by negating therefore the negation and limitation of the first term. It releases the content of the first term, by removing from it that whereby it was incomplete, limited and destined to be negated […]' (Lefebvre 1940 [2009]: 22). This means, the first term receives its determination from this dialectical movement. The first term is transcended; Lefebvre uses the German word *aufheben*, which means both overcoming and preserving. 'The Third Term unites and transcends the contradictories [of the first and second term] and preserves what was determinate in them' (Lefebvre 1940 [2009]: 22).

By the dialectical movement of *affirmation – negation – negation of the negation* or *thesis – antithesis – synthesis* a term's determination is created, it is *aufgehoben* – the first term is simultaneously overcome and preserved, it is transcended into a third term – *the Becoming* (Schmid 2005: 90). 'In thought as in reality they [the first and the second term] pass into one another all the time, and are thus set in motion and enter into the Becoming [the third term] [...]' (Lefebvre 1940 [2009]: 20).

In contrast to Hegel, Lefebvre's third term does not symbolise a synthesis, a solution, or a compromise, but it is 'the Becoming', which has transcended the contradictions of the first two terms. In this term, for Lefebvre, the indefiniteness can be found – 'the possible' – to be realised by action (by social practices) and involving the possibilities of both failure and success (Schmid 2005: 92–93).

Lefebvre's three-dimensional dialectic

Lefebvre combined the material thinking of Marx with the dialectic of Hegel and developed his own tri-dimensional image of reality. For him the three dimensions are social practice, abstract thinking, and the third, the transcendent sphere. He argues that the contradictive character of the first two dimensions is transcended through dialectical movement into a third sphere.

Social practices are for Lefebvre the starting point of everything, of life and all contradictions. The opposite of practice, the dialectical contradiction, the antonym, is for him the second dimension: abstract thinking, produced knowledge, expressed in writings, representations, and models of reality. The third dimension is a form of transcendence, which can be put neither solely in the sphere of thinking nor in the sphere of practice. It negates and preserves both spheres by transcending them, by lifting them to another stage, 'the Becoming'. For Lefebvre, all things that cannot be reduced to models, behavioural patterns, or attitudes by the means of abstraction characterise 'the Becoming'. The third is to be found in praxis, in the daily life, in human practice (Schmid 2005: 108–110).

This dialectical movement between the three dimensions is Lefebvre's epistemological framework. It can be traced in all of his writings. By applying this framework, it becomes possible to discover or determine new horizons of 'the Becoming', new possibilities and chances (Schmid 2005: 112). Clearly, this dialectical movement can be observed in the development of his most famous theory: *the production of space.*

4 Lefebvre's Production of Space

Lefebvre goal was to discover or develop an *unitary theory* (Lefebvre 1974 [1991]: 11) of space bringing together the three fields of mental, social, and physical space and overcoming their separation, which he saw as a product of western philosophy. This aim demands a theoretical occupation with all three fields, as he admitted himself '[...] we are concerned with logico-epistemological space, the space of social practice, the space occupied by sensory phenomena [...]' (Lefebvre 1974 [1991]: 11–12).

Lefebvre grounded his theory on a long-term occupation with philosophical questions on space and on intense criticism of common conceptions developed in philosophy and spatial sciences. Conceptions of space as container and space as a system of relations are for Lefebvre only philosophical abstractions, thus *representations of space*, one of his moments in the *production of space* (ie one of the dimensions in his theory of space). He argued that common scientific concepts of space always try to conceptualise space in an abstract way, giving primacy to the mental world, thereby consolidating this primacy and neglecting social practice (Schmid 2005: 198–200).

He argued further that space can be understood neither solely from a physical-material perspective nor solely from a mental-conceptual perspective. Both aspects alone, he stressed, are not enough to comprehend space. Space cannot be created immediately from the mind by means of conceptualisation, space is not only a mental construction, but also based on materiality. Materiality alone is equally not suited to comprehend space. Space is more than only material objects with specific localities. It is neither subject nor an object. Moreover, space is societal reality and this reality, so he argued, can only be understood as a societal production process (Schmid 2005: 205).

So who produces space? In Lefebvre's understanding these are neither abstract ideas, nor material things but a third aspect, the social sphere, individuals, and collectives (Schmid 2005: 203). Based on these considerations, Lefebvre arrived at his basic hypothesis: '(Social) space is a (social) product' (Lefebvre 1974 [1991]: 26).

With the incorporation of the third field, the social field, Lefebvre succeeded in overcoming the duality between the mental and the physical field, between subject and object. In his theory of the production of space he shaped a double triad of terms, which he called dimensions, formants, or moments, where he differentiated between three types (Lefebvre 1974 [1991]: 38–39; Schmid 2005: 192):

1. **perceived space** (*espace perçu*) – **spatial practice**
2. **conceptualised space** (*espace conçu*) – **representations of space**
3. **lived space** (*espace vécu*) – **representational space**

He argued that the production of space is constituted from three dialectically linked production processes, which are mutually dependent: First, a material production process connected to *spatial practices*, the perceivable aspects of space. Second, a process of knowledge production creating *representations of space*, ie conceptualised space, and third, the production of meaning which is connected to *representational spaces*, the lived space (Guelf 2010: 146).

These three formants or moments happen simultaneously; space is simultaneously conceptualised (mental), perceived (material), and lived (social). All three aspects are closely related; they imply each other, and are a prerequisite for each other. Together, they constitute the production of space (Schmid 2005: 207–208). Based on history, the three moments have different weight for the production of space. Each societal formation produces its own specific space. The relations are not stable; they are conflictual, but sometimes also congruent (Schmid 2005: 227).

4.1 Spatial practice (*espace perçu*) – perceived space

> The spatial practice of a society secretes that society's space; it propounds and presupposes it, in a dialectical interaction; it produces it slowly and surely as it master and appropriates it. From the analytic standpoint, the spatial practice of a society is revealed.
> (Lefebvre 1974 [1991]: 38)

For Lefebvre, social practice produces *perceived space* (*espace perçu*), ie '[...] relatively objective and concrete space that a person reacts to in her daily environment' (Purcell 2003: 577). Everything that human beings perceive with their senses constitutes this perceived space; it is the space where actions of collective actors are inscribed in material objects. *Spatial practice* is thus the material aspect of collective social practice; it projects social practice to the terrain (Schmid 2005: 211). It is a production and reproduction process, creating specific places and spatial ensembles with particular configurations, which are characteristic for different variations of social formations.

Examples of such places are squares, street corners, market places, or shopping malls. These places are simultaneously material-perceived and abstract-conceived places. Everyone seems to know the meaning of these places; the terms describe not only specific localities but also their usage. They express specific social practices (Schmid 2005:

211). Based on these considerations, social practice can be observed empirically: in architecture, in planning, in daily life and in spatial reality. All societal relations produce 'their' social space. These emerging spaces cannot be clearly defined and demarcated; they overlap and penetrate each other. Together, as networks and configurations, they are articulated as spatial reality. Networks and connections modify and transform this perceived space: streets and railroad networks, flight connections, business networks, urban networks, for example. Also goods and their markets are part of the social existence and therefore part of social practices. The whole economy can be explained as a system of connections, of flows of energy, capital, goods, and labour, controlled and secured by organisations. Social practice creates these circuits and networks (Schmid 2005: 215).

4.2 Representation of space (*espace conçu*) – conceptualised space

> Conceptualised space, the space of scientists, planners, urbanists, technocratic subdividers and social engineers, as of a certain type of artist with a scientific bent – all of whom identify what is lived and what is perceived with what is conceived. (Arcane speculation about Numbers [sic!], with its talk of the golden number, moduli and 'canons', tends to perpetuate this view of matters.) This is the dominant space in any society (or mode of production). Conceptions of space tend, with certain exceptions to which I shall return, towards a system of verbal (and therefore intellectually worked out) signs.
> (Lefebvre 1974 [1991]: 38–39)

Lefebvre's *representations of space* are constructed by discourses, maps, plans, language, signs. Here, abstract spaces are conceived: '[…] ideas about space, creative mental constructions […]' (Purcell 2003: 577). All attempts of so-called experts (scholars, planners, etc) to conceptualise space fall in this category; they do not produce space itself, but they create abstract representations of space. These representations have great influence on social practices – concepts of space are inscribed as precondition of all social practices – and are thus decisive for the production of space reflecting dominant modes of production (Schmid 2005: 217; Guelf 2010: 133).

According to Lefebvre, representations of space produce knowledge, which is simultaneously objective and revisable. Generally, he distinguishes between knowledge and cognition, seeing knowledge on the one hand as shaped by ideology and power, as an instrument to control reality, as something that can reach truth but is not real. Cognition on the other hand, has the task of reveaing this two-faced characteristic of knowledge, destroying 'old truths' and opening the way to another knowledge, to the 'possible' (Schmid 2005: 101).

Examples for representations of space are manifold. One would be urban planning. Experts conceptualise space in spatial plans; they give order to patches of space for example by creating zoning rules. In this way, specific spatial practices are allowed, fostered, or restricted in certain areas, and spatial practices in those patches are greatly defined. While conceptualising space, however, the same experts are not free from their own conception of space underlying their work. In their minds, space is conceived as empty; as space that they can design and shape according to their will (Schmid 2005: 218).

Lefebvre chose the second concept, representations of space, to be similar to his third moment, that of representional space, also to show that conceptualised and lived space cannot be comprehended independently. He argues that all social reality is shaped by the dialectic between conceptualised and lived, experienced space. That means that every spatial practice is always lived before it is conceptualised. The lived and the abstract space are therefore the basis and the expression of spatial practice. He argues further that conceptualised space tends to dominate lived space, tending to suppress it and with it social practice (Schmid 2005: 220).

4.3 Representational space (*espace vécu*) – lived space

> Space as directly lived through its associated images and symbols, and hence the space of 'inhabitants' and 'users', but also of some artists and perhaps of those, such as a few writers and philosophers, who describe and aspire to do no more than describe. This is the dominated – and hence passively experienced – space, which the imagination seeks to change and appropriate. It overlays physical space, making symbolic use of its objects. Thus representational spaces may be said, though again with certain exceptions, to tend towards more or less coherent systems of nonverbal symbols and signs.
> (Lefebvre 1974 [1991]: 39)

Representational spaces are difficult to define; they contain the totality of all spatial associations and experiences (Vogelpohl 2011: 238). They are produced by experiences loaded with meaning, with symbology; these spaces are lived, not conceptualised. They are qualitative, dynamic, and rational and they are characterised by difference. They include the imaginary world and symbology, and have their origin in lived space, in daily life, and thus also in individual and collective history. These spaces represent social relations: societal values, traditions, dreams, and collective experiences. Often they are in conflict with different representations of space (Schmid 2005: 223).

It is very difficult – if not impossible – to grasp these spaces of social meanings theoretically as well as empirically. Experiences, or lived space, cannot be seen or observed; it is not the object of discourses. For Lefebvre, lived space can only be comprehended if space is connected to social practices, which are both a spatial practice and representations of space. In other words, lived space, and with it the social meanings inscribed in it, cannot be separated from its flip sides, the material and mental side of social practice.

4.4 The three dimensions of the production of space

Lefebvre's comprehension of space is that of a production process happening in three dialectical intertwined dimensions or moments (cf. figure 5). Lefebvre labels each of these three dimensions with two terms, which he intentionally left without a precise definition. As is usual in Lefebvre's dialectic, the starting point for comprehending space is the perceivable aspect of social practices: the first dimension, the conceptual pair 'spatial practice – perceived space'. From this starting point, the second dimension, 'conceptualised space – representations of space', is already included as the antonym, since space cannot be perceived without conceptualising it.

This conceptualisation, however, is always connected with a specific goal and therefore it is connected to ideology and power. An analysis of these two dimensions alone would fail to explain societal reality. Thus, Lefebvre introduced the third of his dimensions, the transcending dimension: 'representational space – lived space'. He argued that beside the material aspect of social practice and its conception this practice is also lived and experienced, with symbology and meaning attached to it. It is this symbology which constitutes the third dimension, 'lived space – representational spaces'. On the one hand, they overlap material aspects produced by social practices by giving meaning to them or their configuration, on the other they are entangled with conceptualised spaces, which already contain symbolism but tend to dominate lived space (Schmid 2005: 226–227).

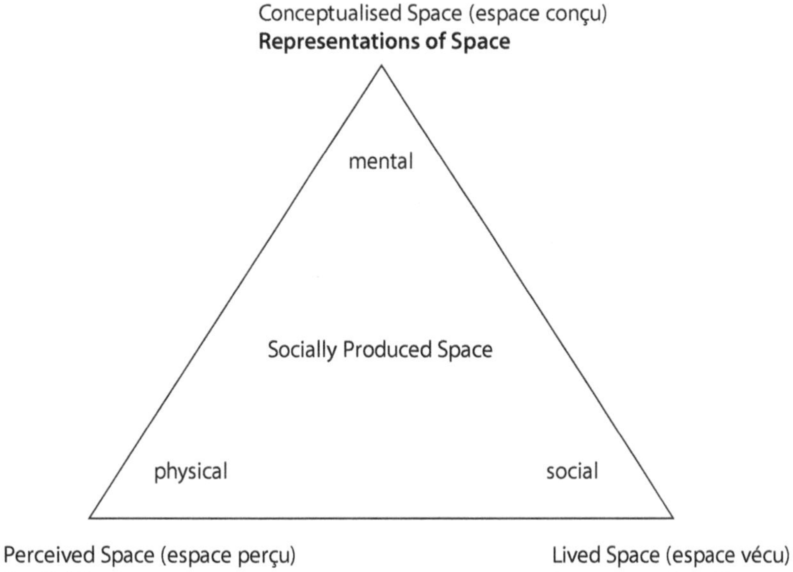

Fig. 5 The three dimensions (moments) of the production of (social) space
Source: Illustration by author

Lefebvre intentionally used a pair of terms to describe each of his dimensions, contributing to the dialectic between the individual and the collective. The first individualistic set of terms means the perceived, the lived, and the conceptualised sphere of a subject (an individual), which manifests itself in social practice. The second set of his terms – spatial practice, representations of space, and representational space – refer to the societal (collective) production process of space (Schmid 2005: 230). Lefebvre refers to both situations. All six terms create a conflictual field reflecting the contradictions between the individual and societal perspective. His double triad of terms, therefore, includes both perspectives and describes the reality of a space that cannot be comprehended but can be perceived, conceived, or experienced collectively or individually (Schmid 2005: 244–245).

An example of a Lefebvrian-inspired understanding of the production of space can be provided when imagining the process of establishing a freshly built urban quarter within a city. Architects and urban planners conceive this new quarter, the streets are laid out in a specific fashion, the land is divided into plots, and the usage of every plot is determined by zoning rules; everything is planned following specific principles and urban models. This is a representation of space, the space collectively conceptualised by individuals. When people move into this quarter, which is let's say situated at the outskirts of the city, they will have to adapt their spatial practices to this new space, ie how they use this space. Depending on their home within the quarter and established physical-material locations of shops, schools, and stations for public transport, they will have very individual perceptions of these spaces resulting in very individual perceived space. As their place of work may still be located in the city centre, they will use the local public transport station to reach their destination on a daily basis. Depending on their preferences or available time, they might choose different routes to reach this local station, creating different perceived space every day. If there is no such station, they might have to rely on individual transport to reach their place of work. If traffic gets too dense by collective spatial practices, the urban planners might think it necessary to extend the public transport system to this area. The mental and the material dimensions are connected. Finally, people moving into this new quarter live in the new quarter and assign meaning to each physical-material object they can find and also to the quarter as a whole. The school will have a different meaning for someone with children compared to someone without. The existence of restaurants, sport facilities, public parks, or pubs may have (very different) meanings to some, none to others. These meanings, which are derived from living in that area, are inscribed to the material world also collectively, as representational spaces.

The connection between socially produced space and time can be iilustrated by another example – that of a street. A street may be conceptualised by urban planners to be a public, accessible, and safe place with the purpose of connecting different places. During the day, the street may become a place of encounter and communication when for instance a number of street-hawkers have chosen to occupy this street for their business. At night, however, the street may become an unsafe place, a place of criminality. Some Individuals may thus perceive the same street as unsafe during the night, but as safe and friendly during the day. They will inscribe different meanings to the street depending on time and will adopt their spatial practices accordingly. These meanings then, representational spaces, and connected spatial practices may be contrary to the way the street was originally conceptualised. Urban planners might react to these circumstances, trying to adjust the usage by the introduction of new regulations or sanctions, which in turn again change spatial practices and representational spaces. What should have become clear is that it is an ongoing threefold production process happening simultaneously that produces social space.

4.5 The particular of Lefebvre's dialectic

We have seen that Lefebvre is using the 'German dialectic' of Marx, Hegel, and Nietzsche to arrive at his theory of the production of space. There is something very particular about Lefebvre's dialectic which distinguishes it from the classical dialectic and is, according to Schmid (2005: 306–308), his most novel contribution. Schmid argues further that this particularity is frequently misunderstood or misinterpreted.

Lefebvre's starting point was the classical dialectic of Hegel with its 'thesis – antithesis – synthesis', where by using a term, at the same time its antonym, its negation, is established as a second term. By negating this antonym, the first term is transcended (*aufgehoben*) into a third term, a synthesis (cf. chapter 3). In contrast to this, Lefebvre is using three terms and every term can be understood as a starting point, as a thesis and simultaneously as the synthesis of the other two terms. They are dialectically related on one another. Every term is the result of the dialectical movement of the other two terms, emerging from the process of transcendence or *aufheben*. As such, every term thus contains the contradictions of the other two terms which have been transcended into it (Schmid 2005: 312). By conceiving this concept, Lefebvre has created a *triadic dialectic*, which does not result in a synthesis but connects the three terms that continuously interact in manifold ways (from conflicts to alliances).

This triad of dimensions is not necessarily a spatial one, for Lefebvre it is a general principle. As such he applies it to many fields in his research (Schmid 2005: 313; Vogelpohl 2011: 234). When applied to the production of space, however, it can be concluded that social space is comprised of three things: materiality, cognitive conceptions, and experienced things. These three fields cannot be separated and together they form social space. The three dimensions of the production of space are of equal value, none is privileged: space is simultaneously perceived, conceived, and experienced. There is no starting point, no thesis; space is always incomplete and continuously produced by these three production processes (Schmid 2005: 313).

4.6 Consequences of Lefebvre's production of space

Lefebvre's theory has radical consequences for the epistemology of research: Adopting his theory and accepting that there is not space *a priori* to social practice, research is not concerned anymore with modelling space or categorising space, but with the patterns of societal space production. Artefacts in space and material things, but also discourses or symbols, the visible results of these production processes are not the object of analysis, but the collective production activities and with it the inscribed societal relations move to the centre of interest (Schmid 2005: 204).

Lefebvre understands space as a social product, produced not naturally but by the interests and demands of specific actors of society. Second, he comprehended space as historically specific, arguing that the characteristics of space reflect the social system, the form of society in a particular point in time. Third, he regarded space not as a fixed thing, but as an entity that is always changing, always in motion, space as a process. That means that space cannot in fact be steered in a certain direction, but is the mirror of the respective social relations in a society which are always conflictual and highly contested (Ronneberger & Vogelpohl 2014: 254–259).

As an illustrative example for the determination through history, Ronneberger & Vogelpohl (ibd.) refer to the space produced in capitalist economies, the space we live in. The capitalist mode of production expresses itself in specific peculiarities of space; it cannot exist without such expressions: infrastructure, the whole built environment (communication systems, transport systems, etc), investment opportunities (hotels, housing units, office blocks, etc), planning documents (eg spatial development plans), and specific perceptions of available options for action and decision-making. All these aspects are deeply shaped by dominant configurations of our society and economy – a societal configuration valid during a period in time. Depending on the era, the three dimensions of the production of space, the three moments – spatial practice, the representations of space, and representational spaces – are different in terms of their characteristics and their weight for the production of space. Space reflects the condition and context of its production.

The three dimensions cannot be separated; they imply and contain each other. Social space consists of three spheres: concrete materialities, a mental construct, and social sensations. From a societal perspective, the material world has no existence without mentally conceptualising it and without living and experiencing it. The mental world alone equally does not exist; it needs as a basis the material and lived sphere. In addition, the lived sphere also has no existence without materialities and without the conceptualisation that structures it. Space is simultaneously perceived, conceptualised, and lived. Each of the dimensions is transcended in the two others (Schmid 2005: 313).

None of the dimensions can stand alone, but their relation is conflictual and they compete for dominance. In the current societal formation, Lefebvre understands representations of space – knowledge production – as dominating, shaped by those who hold power and control the productive forces (Belina & Michel 2007: 17–19). This societal production process rules over the others, exerting its homogenising logic, but cannot succeed, since it is part of the dialectical movement, of Lefebvre's triadic dialectic, where each dimension transcends the other two dimensions in itself. Even if one dimension dominates the production process, it is the interplay of all three dimensions that produce social space (Guelf 2010: 135).

The analytical distinction in Lefebvre's three dimensions not only enables space to be understood as a process, but also moves the focus to an exploration of the possibilities for far-reaching changes for societal transformations. Space is the historical expression and prerequisite of societal relations and development; it is produced by social practices informed by social needs and interests; it is the end result of production and sets simultaneously its conditions, providing in itself the seeds for change (Gottdiener et al. 2016: 127). Not only can single dimensions change, but also their relations. This implies that radical changes, eg a societal transformation, can only happen with wide-ranging changes of all three production processes. A changing representation of space for instance, as the introduction of a new urban model – 'sustainable development' – would imply, cannot succeed without changes in the other dimensions of the production process; also spatial practices and lived space must change. Equally, changing power relations or changing institutions might induce change in one of the dimensions, but these shifts do not necessarily imply a possible transformation (Ronneberger & Vogelpohl 2014: 254–259).

Lefebvre exemplified the value of his theoretical approach in his theory of the 'urban'. By switching the perspective away from the analysis of things in space towards the patterns of societal space production he arrives at new cognitions. In this theory, the object of analysis is not the 'city', but the process of urbanisation, understood as the societal production of 'urban' space. For that reason and for a full understanding of his theoretical thinking, his 'production of the urban' must be examined.

5 Lefebvre's Theory of the 'Urban'

Lefebvre contributed significantly to the development of critical urban theory. In an effort to explain intensifying urbanisation processes after World War II, he developed several approaches and ideas that resulted in a comprehensive theory of the 'urban'. This theory can also be seen as the foundation of his later theory development of the production of space. His notion of an upcoming 'urban society' is an important cornerstone for this study, since it provides a normative direction. For that reason, this chapter examines Lefebvre's theory of urbanisation from its beginnings, arriving at his demand of a right to the city. Considering today's urbanisation processes, Lefebvre's theory and his demand is more meaningful than ever before.

5.1 Observing urbanisation

After World War II, Lefebvre witnessed the proliferation of modern lifestyles and the expansion of urban areas in France. These two aspects of urbanisation seemed to happen simultaneously in both urban and rural areas, bringing about deep transformations of society. He approached this phenomenon by a specific phenomenological approach, which was uncommon at the time: focusing on changing practices of daily life, which he saw as the constituting characteristic of the emerging modern society (Ronneberger & Vogelpohl 2014: 251–252).

As many other western countries, France underwent deep societal change in the 1960s, which was referred to as 'modernisation'. This era was characterised by the upcoming fordistic mode of production, by mass consumption and mass production (Grell 2014). Lifestyles and working processes seemed to be increasingly programmed and homogenised, a development that also shaped the production of space. Old city centres were judged as incompatible with modern ways of life. Oriented at the paradigmatic guideline of a 'functional city' (cf. box 3) attempts were made to redevelop inner-city areas to be car-friendly and in the cities' peripheries, large-scale housing blocks as well as space-consuming areas with single-family homes were developed (Schmid 2011: 26).

Interestingly, Lefebvre's decisive encounter with urbanisation processes happened not in urban areas but in the countryside: in Mourenx, a new town established around an industrial complex in a deeply traditional and rural area. There, Lefebvre analysed the arrival of modern life as it changed practices of daily life in a profound way. He identified the proliferation of functionalism, monotone working processes, and the bureaucratic city in the countryside (Ronneberger & Vogelpohl 2014: 252). Only after this did he begin to focus also on structural changes within cities. During these studies he coined the term 'bureaucratic society of controlled consumption', describing the emerging societal reality as programmed and steered by the state within a framework of mass consumption and mass production (Schmid 2005: 118–119). Later on, this socio-economic configuration became known as 'fordism' in regulation theory (Kipfer et al. 2013: 126).

For Lefebvre, this analysis of societal reality became the starting point for approaching the process of urbanisation (Schmid 2005: 121). His work resulted in his publications *The Right to the City* (Lefebvre 1968 [2016]) and *The Urban Revolution* (Lefebvre 1970 [2003]), which are today seen as the roots of critical urban theory. After years of studying societal transformations caused by urbanisation, he introduced his work *The Urban Revolution* with a – for 1970 – ground-breaking hypothesis: 'society has been completely urbanised' (Lefebvre 1970 [2003]: 1).

Box 3: The functional city and the Athens Charter

The Athens Charter is a list of 95 theses and demands concerning urban development, framed during the fourth International Congresses of Modern Architecture (Congrès Internationaux d'Architecture Moderne, CIAM). The congress took place in Athens, Greece, in 1933 and the architect Le Corbusier published the charter in 1941. Concerned by living conditions in European cities at the time, architects and urban planners assessed European cities as chaotic, overcrowded, polluted, and unhealthy. The consequences of industrialisation and the dominance of private over public interests were seen as factors disturbing the balance between economy, administrative control, and social cooperation (§ 71–73 of the Athens Charter, Mumford 2002; Hilpert 2000).

To re-establish this balance and as a solution, the key proposal of the charter was the functional separation of urban space according to its function for satisfying the residents' basic needs: housing, working, recreation, and mobility. This meant a systematic classification of urban space into clearly separated functional areas according to their dominant use (residential, industrial, etc) and connected by traffic axes. The intention was to create a modern, less dense, healthy, and orderly city (Heineberg 2017: 137).

For European urban development, the charter became of great significance after World War II. The logic of functional separation was implemented in urban planning and new, large-scale housing projects and satellite cities as well as industrial complexes and shopping areas emerged in urban peripheries, upholding the idea of car-friendly towns. Unintended consequences were social tensions in the peripheral high-rise apartment blocks and an intensifying and collapsing traffic system. By the late 1970s, it was acknowledged that the charter had failed, but the functional separation is still maintained in the building codes of many countries (Leggewie 2015; Mumford 2002).

5.1.1 Marx & Engels explaining urbanisation?

Based on his empirical findings of studying daily life in the 1960s, Lefebvre searched for theoretical explanations for urbanisation processes and the consequences he was witnessing. Since classical urban theory of the Chicago School (eg Park et al. 1925), which were mainstream at that time, could not provide satisfying answers, he turned to Marxist writings in his search to understand the ongoing transformations of urban and rural areas (Schmid 2005: 123). Marx and Engels had not explicitly theorised urbanisation, since they had only witnessed the beginning of this all-encompassing process during their lifetimes. Nevertheless, they had provided two important fragments, linking cities and industrial capitalism.

The first fragment can be found in Friedrich Engels work, *Condition of the Working Class in England* (1845 [1969]), in which he analysed the industrialisation process and its consequences in 19th century England. Engels identified the connection between industrialisation and urbanisation, the tendency of industrial capitalism to centralise both population and capital in one place, creating rapidly growing villages and cities:

> Population becomes centralised just as capital does; [...] A manufacturing establishment requires many workers employed together in a single building, living near each other and forming a village of themselves in the case of a good-sized factory. They have needs for satisfying which other people are necessary; handicraftsmen, shoemakers, tailors, bakers, carpenters, stonemasons, settle at hand. The inhabitants of the village, especially the younger generation, accustom themselves to factory work, grow skilful in it, and when the first mill can no longer employ them all, wages fall, and the immigration of fresh manufacturers is the consequence. So the village grows into a small town, and the small town into a large one. The greater the town, the greater its advantages. It offers roads, railroads, canals; the choice of skilled labour increases constantly, new establishments can be built

> more cheaply, because of the competition among builders and machinists who are at hand, than in remote country districts, whither timber, machinery, builders, and operatives must be brought; it offers a market to which buyers crowd, and direct communication with the markets supplying raw material or demanding finished goods. Hence the marvellously rapid growth of the great manufacturing towns.
> (Engels 1845 [1969]: 42–43)

According to Schmid (2005: 124), Lefebvre found a second fragment on the role of the city in Marxist writings: in Karl Marx's *Grundrisse* (1858 [1983]). In this work, Marx discussed from a historic perspective the dialectical contradiction between city and country and its role in the formation of capitalism. He stated that the relationship between city and country had changed over time: while the country ruled over the city in ancient and medieval times, in modern times this relationship has been reversed, resulting in a rule of the city over the country. He found that the city opened the possibility for an existence not based on land ownership and identified this as the decisive condition for the development of capital. A new form of property had emerged, based solely on work and exchange. In that way, Marx concluded, the contradiction between city and country had been decisive for the historic development of capitalism (Schmid 2005: 123).

Two important aspects on urbanisation can be derived from Marx and Engels. First, the finding that industrialisation and urbanisation are related processes, whereby industrialisation reinforces urbanisation, and second, that the city-country dichotomy had been decisive for the formation of capitalism. Both aspects represent important components for Lefebvre's urban theory, but could not provide answers for the urban experience at his time: the crisis of the city in the 1960s.

5.1.2 The crisis of the city and Lefebvre's strategic hypothesis

In the 1950s and 1960s, Lefebvre joined contemporary criticism of functional urban development and planning. Based on Marx and Engels, he added his own reflections to the process of urbanisation: he regarded it as a dual process taking place simultaneously in the city and in the countryside, and transforming both (Schmid 2005: 126).

In rural areas, he noticed, urbanisation was ruining agrarian society by bringing industrialisation and destroying those elements constituting rural life. A web of urban fabric – termed *tissue urbain* by Lefebvre[1] – was sprawling, rapidly encompassing everything in a more or less dense sheet (Schmid 2005: 126–127). 'As a result, the tra-

---

1 With 'tissue urbain' Lefebvre meant "[…] all manifestations of the dominance of the city over the country. In this sense, a vacation home, a highway, a supermarket are all part of the urban fabric" (Lefebvre 1970 [2003]: 4). Later, this term was taken up by David Harvey as the term 'built environment' (Harvey 1978).

ditional unit typically of peasant life, namely the village, has been transformed. Absorbed or obliterated by larger units, it has become an integral part of industrial production and consumption' (Lefebvre 1970 [2003]: 3). The *tissue urbain* does spread everywhere, but does not result in homogenised space, it leaves moreover some places untouched, those that are '[...] stagnant and dying, those that are given over to nature' (ibid.: 4). This process goes along with the proliferation of urban values (urban clothes, urban amenities, the urban lifestyle) and urban rationality (Schmid 2005: 127).

In the cities, Lefebvre also identified major transformations. In keeping with the guiding principle of functional urban development (cf. box 3), inner-city areas as well as the cities' outskirts were converted to make them suitable for modern life. Large-scale housing projects with high-rise apartment blocks were developed as well as massive, space-consuming areas of single-family homes (Schmid 2011: 26). The cities exploded, Lefebvre noted, breaking up and dissolving themselves into fragments: into industrial complexes, suburbs, residential areas, and satellite towns (Lefebvre 1970 [2003]: 10).

For Lefebvre, this development meant a crisis of the city, apparent in the modernisation of life entailing a homogenisation of lifestyles. Monotony became prominent, not only at the place of work, but also in the housing environment – as functionalist machines of living, whether standardised single-family homes or equally standardised multi-storey apartment blocks. From the perspective of the city, he argued, urbanisation meant the expansion of urban areas, urban networks, trade, the formation of new urban peripheries and centralities (Schmid 2005: 128). He concluded with a radical thesis: the traditional city, so he argued, was imploding, it was in danger of disappearance.

From these two perspectives Lefebvre grasped the process of urbanisation as *implosion – explosion* (Lefebvre 1970 [2003]: 14), a dual crisis engulfing both the city and the country: an explosion of urban fabrics, urban values, and lifestyles and a simultaneous implosion, a destruction of the traditional city (Schmid 2005: 136). He saw this process happening on a global scale, no matter what political regime, and as a process slowly approaching a point where the duality between city and country is disappearing, transcending – '*aufgehoben*' – into something new, a mesh of elements forming a landscape which is entirely urban. Based on these reflections, Lefebvre put forward his strategic hypothesis: 'society has been completely urbanised' (Lefebvre 1970 [2003]: 1).

This hypothesis means on the one hand a state of society, an urban world, where all places on earth and every aspect of society has been urbanised. On the other, it includes an object, it implies a definition: 'An urban society is a society that results from a process of complete urbanisation' (Lefebvre 1970 [2003]: 1). With the term *urban society* he defined a virtual object, a possible, a potential future in order to analyse the pathway towards it: 'We can assume the existence of a virtual object, urban society; that is a possible object, whose growth and development can be analysed [...]' (Lefebvre 1970 [2003]: 3). He introduced this term as a mean to develop a new urban theory. 'The expression urban society meets a theoretical need [...] it is an elaboration, a search, a conceptual formulation [...] to build theory from a theoretical hypothesis' (Lefebvre 1970 [2003]: 5).

5.2 Three approaches towards urbanisation

5.2.1 Space-time axis of urbanisation

Based on his strategic hypothesis that 'society has been completely urbanised' (Lefebvre 1970 [2003]: 1) Lefebvre approached the phenomenon of urbanisation in three ways. In a first step, he took a historical perspective and developed a space-time axis of the western city, in which he differentiated and described several types of cities (*political city, mercantile city, industrial city*). On this axis (cf. figure 6), the origin represents pure nature and the end point marks a 100 % urbanised society (Schmid 2005: 132–133). All types of cities described are comprehended as specific urban formations, which run through a historic sequence of ascension, zenith, and decline. Every new formation rises from the ruins of the old (Lefebvre 1970 [2003]: 7–22). Lefebvre connected each of these city types, and thus urban development, with one dominant production process, adopting the classical periodisation of history already developed by Marx and Engels: ancient, feudal, and capitalist modes of production. Each of these modes of production, Lefebvre argued, has produced a specific type of city – and a specific type of space.

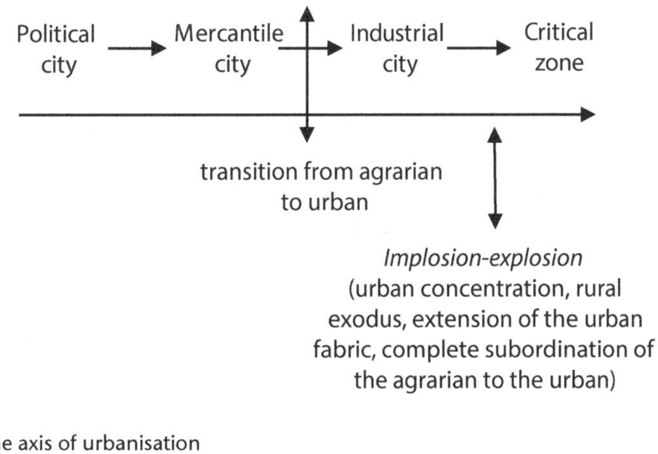

Fig. 6 Lefebvre's space-time axis of urbanisation
Source: Reprinted from Lefebvre (1970 [2003]: 15)

The periods of transition from one city type to another are characterised by critical phases. According to Lefebvre, one of these critical phases appeared during the transition from the mercantile city to the industrial city: in that phase, society became increasingly based on capital instead of land ownership and an increasing number of people made a living outside the agricultural sector. Industrial production soon outpaced agricultural production in terms of productivity and the city began to dominate the country in economic, social, and political terms: 'From this moment on, the city would no longer appear as an urban island in a rural ocean' (Lefebvre 1970 [2003]: 11).

The era of industrialisation produced and reinforced urbanisation processes. The emerging industries were initially not urban at all; quite to the contrary, they were established outside the historic cities. Early industries favoured places close to raw materials, energy, and good transport linkages. They appeared more as an emerging 'non-city' (Lefebvre 1970 [2003]: 13), a counter-thesis of the city. Over time, however, industrialisation slowly encroached on the traditional cities since they offered access to cheap labour, capital, and markets. The city allowed the concentration of the forces of production. The results were the foundation of new industrial towns and the gradual transformation of existing cities into industrial cities (Schmid 2005: 135–136). The urban reality had changed radically: all characteristics of historic cities had disappeared. Markets and capital have destroyed all obstacles, have broken the city into tiles, and have created the industrial city, '[...] a shapeless town, a barely urban agglomeration, a conglomerate, or conurbation like the Ruhr valley' (Lefebvre 1970 [2003]: 14).

Lefebvre concluded that the industrial revolution produced or at least reinforced urbanisation, a process gradually destroying the country and dissolving the city and resulting in another critical phase. He called this process 'implosion-explosion', manifesting itself in 'the tremendous concentration (of people, activities, wealth, goods, objects, instruments, means, and thought) of urban reality and the immense explosion, the projection of numerous, discjunct fragments (peripheries, suburbs, vacation homes, satellite towns)' *(Lefebvre 1970 [2003]: 14)*. What remains is an urbanised landscape and a totally urbanised society.

At first glance, Lefebvre's space-time axis seems to be a trivial description of the historic development of the western city. It is more than that. Lefebvre succeeded in understanding the city as a historic configuration, shifting his analytical focus from the city to the process of urbanisation. He found that urbanisation has encompassed everything – the city, the country, and society as a whole – slowly approaching a critical zone where the rural-urban divide is vanishing, approaching its dialectical transcendence. Lefebvre's space-time axis of urbanisation has revealed a movement from nature over the urban-rural dichotomy towards its transcendence into an 'urban society'. From this result, Lefebvre concluded that urbanisation as a phenomenon has stretched out over all of society which is why also the analysis of this phenomenon must be attempted from a macrosocial perspective (Schmid 2005: 140).

5.2.2 Space-time continents and the 'urban society'

In a second step, Lefebvre analysed urbanisation from a macrosocial perspective. He created space-time fields of society, which he termed 'continents': the *rural*, the *industrial*, and the *urban* continent. He defined them as ways of thinking, living, or practice, as societal formations forming often, but not necessarily, a historical sequence. All three continents overlap each other, are mutually intertwined, and in some societies, they exist simultaneously. As an example for such cases, Lefebvre revers to developing countries, which undergo all three continents simultaneously (Lefebvre 1970 [2003]: 32).

As the rural continent, Lefebvre identified a societal formation dominated by traditional, rural life and agricultural activities. The satisfaction of human needs dominates in this societal formation. He connects all three continents also to a specific city type: The city of the rural continent is the political city, where a coherent division of labour between mental and material work, between agricultural and mercantile production, between city and country, prevails (Lefebvre 1970 [2003]: 32–34). The city in this continent is not yet permeated by economic rationality, by the production of commodities; squares and streets were still places of communication and encounter, use value dominates (Vogelpohl 2011: 235).

As the industrial continent, Lefebvre identified a societal formation where rationality, productivism, and exchange value dominate. Labour is the most important factor in this formation. In the name of rationality and efficiency, laws, technology, and the state are organised in a way to establish and enforce a general order that follows the logic of commodities (Lefebvre 1970 [2003]: 35). The city in this continent – the industrial city – is the place where this logic becomes evident: it is the place where surplus value is accumulated, realised, and distributed. Production processes tend to reach out on a global scale and in the name of rationality and highest possible efficiency, everything is acquired: knowledge, labour, life, and space. All aspects are organised, planned, and measured in terms of productive performance and homogeneity (Schmid 2005: 143).

From a future perspective – that of the urban continent succeeding the industrial continent – the industrial continent appears in another light: 'from its own perspective, it [the industrial continent] was productive and creative, in control of nature, substituting the freedom of production for the determinism of matter. In fact – in truth – it was radically contradictory and conflictual. Rather than dominating nature, industry ravaged it, destroyed it completely. Claiming to substitute a consistent rationality for the chaos of spontaneity, it separated and dissociated everything it touched, it destroyed connections by instituting a reign of homogenous order. For industry, the means became an end and the end a means: production became strategy, productivism a philosophy, the state a divinity' (Lefebvre 1970 [2003]: 176).

Inherent to the industrial continent is the urban continent, a societal formation slowly emerging from industrialisation: the 'urban society'. According to Lefebvre, industrialisation and urbanisation represent a conflictual and complex double process, where industrialisation produces urbanisation. One could say urbanisation is the antonym of industrialisation and both processes form a dialectical unity heading to their transcendence – their *Aufhebung* – into something new: the 'urban society'. In this new societal formation, both processes are simultaneously overcome and preserved.

From this perspective, Lefebvre predicts nothing more than the end of the 'industrial continent' superseded by the arrival of an 'urban continent'. He argues that over the course of two centuries, industrialisation has produced a world dominated by economy and labour, and economic logics have been inscribed into all aspects of human life. Industrial revolution becomes, from this perspective, a period in time-space containing or producing another revolution: the urban revolution.

Society has run through an era of economic growth characterised by a turmoil of the economic production forces and this revolution is followed by a societal revolution – the urban revolution, resulting in the 'urban society'. Lefebvre describes this 'urban society' (often referred to as 'the urban') as a virtuality, which puts an end to the dominance of economic logics, creating a new draft of the human being, freeing the desire, and giving rise to the dominance of use value over exchange value (cf. box 2). It is the desire which is the most important aspect of the urban continent (Schmid 2005: 145, 2018).

This 'urban society' is not reality yet, it is an outlook, it is 'the possible'. It is slowly emerging as '[...] a mental and social form, that of simultaneity, of gathering, of convergence, of encounter (or rather encounters). It is a quality born from quantities (spaces, objects, products). It is a difference, or rather, an ensemble of differences' (Lefebvre 1968 [1996]: 131). Simultaneity, encounter and difference; these are the characteristics of an 'urban society'. In the 'urban' different elements of society encounter each other, articulate their differences, and negotiate their conflicts. It gives meaning to industrial production. A physical space and a specific point in time (simultaneity) is needed to allow encounters between social groups and individuals. Only in such a way, from social practices arising from encounters, can change and innovations happen. Development thus becomes nothing more than transcended differences and the urban revolution must be understood as a successful overcoming of the industrial continent, where homogenisation, fragmentation, and a hierarchical production of space dominated (Vogelpohl 2011: 236–237).

This future development remains uncertain. Lefebvre terms it as the 'possible-impossible', a virtuality which gives meaning, a goal for action (Schmid 2005: 147). This prediction of the future, an upcoming era of 'the desire', shows some surprising similarities to the de-growth and the sustainability debates of our times (eg. Martínez-Alier et al. 2010; Redclift 2005), but Lefebvre's 'urban society' is more than that. It is an utopian world where labour and productivism has become meaningless, a world ruled by the desire, playfulness, and pleasure (Schmid 2005: 148). Lefebvre's notions of the emergence of an 'urban society' builds on the implosion of the city, the disappearance of the traditional city. This comes with a contradiction: If the city is disappearing due to urbanisation processes, how can the prevalence of the city as built form, as image, as ideology, and as social reality be explained? For this task, Lefebvre used a third lens to shed light on the phenomenon of urbanisation.

5.2.3 Space-time levels

Lefebvre's third step of analysing urbanisation was concerned with the search for a new definition of the city congruent with the urban theory developed in his first two analytical steps. He approached this task by searching and conceptualising the linkages between the historic development of the city and macrosocial developments, a question untouched by his first two analytic steps. For that reason, he established three space-time levels (*niveaux*) of societal reality: the private level, P, the global level, G, and a mediating level, M (Kipfer et al. 2013: 124; Schmid 2018).

Lefebvre defined the private level, P, as the practical, sensual reality, the *close order*; as relations between individuals or groups which constitute society; the level of daily life. In opposition to this close order, he placed the global level, G, as the *distant order*, the highest level of societal reality. This level is an abstract, transcendental domain dominated by the actions of powerful organisations, such as the state or the church, which significantly shape societal reality by establishing rules and order. It is at this level where those in power execute their strategies and promote their 'representations of space'. Abstract macro processes, such as industrialisation and urbanisation, happen at this level. It is the level of capital markets and commodity exchange dominated by powerful actors, who impose rules and order by means of planning, and extend this configuration globally. As the third level, he defines a level, M, mediating between level P and G. This is the level of the city, where the 'urban' evolves. The central task of this level is to mediate between the two other levels (Schmid 2014: 70).

All three levels are historically specific, intertwined, and have mutual and complex relations. The global level is above the mediating level, but the latter contains also parts of this distant order. In the city, the distant order can be perceived and vice versa, the mediating level is part of the distant order. The distant order consolidates itself on the mediating level and employs rules and regulations to steer the private level. The city embraces the private level; it is the form for private life; it allows the exchange of information, the submission of commands from the distant order directed to the private level. In this conception, it is the task of the city (the level M) to translate and mediate between 'close' (level P) and 'distant' (level M) order (Schmid 2005: 165).

In this conceptualisation, the city becomes a projection of society on the terrain and the three levels inscribe themselves in it with specific materialities. The distant order is projected on the terrain through the organisation of the built environment: highways, ministries, cathedrals; the level M is represented by streets, squares, public buildings, public space; and the level P is represented by private buildings, residential blocks, slums, and villas. A clear classification remains impossible; all aspects are interwoven (Schmid 2005: 166–167).

5.2.4 The centrality of the city

From this third analytical step, the characteristics of the city become more evident: the city has a societal function; it is a mediator between the private and the general level, and it unites the different elements of society. The city is a centre; its essential characteristic is its centrality. The city has always been the centre of capital accumulation, but this is only one aspect of its centrality. The city concentrates not only capital, but also people, products, symbols, knowledge, wealth, and technics. It is the place where all things come together; it creates a situation, where everything converges, a condition where exchange, assemblies, and encounters become possible (Schmid 2005: 175–178). 'The urban is, therefore, pure form: a place of encounter, assembly, simultaneity. This form has no specific content, but is a centre of attraction and life' (Lefebvre 1970 [2003]: 118). Centrality is the form of the city; it can be filled with anything: an empty square can be used for a festival, a demonstration, or it can be a terrifying place of power. The meaning of the city, therefore, depends on its content and this content is defined by historic formations of society and is subject to an ongoing transformation (Schmid 2005: 178). Depending on the historic situation, the city assembles different elements of society, which encounter each other, react, and create possibly something new, a surprising outcome, an innovation. For this reason the form of the city, its centrality, must be understood as a productive process. It is the form of centrality which allows *different* elements of society to *encounter* each other in *simultaneity* (Schmid 2005: 186–187). Summarising, three characteristics of the city can be derived (Schmid 2014: 72):

1) The city is a **specific level of social realty**, the level of mediation
2) The city is a **social form.** Its characteristic is centrality
3) The city is a **specific place**, a place of difference, encounter, and simultaneity

Arriving at this cognition, a specific quality of the city becomes evident. The city becomes productive since its centrality allows the assembly of various parts of society. The place of encounter of opposing elements of society, of contrasting opinions and lifestyles, creates a milieu where innovations and new ideas prosper and is the best place to cultivate 'the urban' (Purcell 2013a: 150). Therefore, the city's centrality is an essential societal resource, which allows the possible to happen, and is thus crucial for societal transformations. This resource is contested. Centrality allows for the encounters of differences, crucial for future developments, but also creates conflicts. The access to centralities might be controlled by certain groups and might be denied to others. The homogenising rationality from the global level with its rationale of functionalism might attack the ability of the city to create places and moments of encounter (Vogelpohl 2011: 237).

5.3 Consequences of Lefebvre's theory of the 'urban'

Lefebvre's analysis of urbanisation has radical consequences for urban studies. He criticised the existing concepts of the city in his time – eg (Park et al. 1925; Wirth 1938; Christaller 1933 [2006]) – for representing only historic and theoretical categories of the city, dependent on respective societal situations and particular theoretical perspectives, which are directed by specific research interests (Schmid 2005: 27). These concepts would be nothing more than representations of space based on imaginations, facts derived from produced knowledge and ideology (Schmid 2005: 161).

With Lefebvre's notion of an 'explosion of the city', the classical and dominating understanding of the city (eg of the Chicago school) as an object of analysis, as a clearly definable, city-like socio-spatial unit has become obsolete (Brenner 2014b: 14–19). Simultaneously, also the definition of the city as a counterpart to the country – the area beyond – becomes invalid since the urban-rural divide is disappearing. Instead, Lefebvre developed an understanding of the city as a historical category of urbanisation that is slowly disappearing. With this cognition, he performed a change of perspectives implying an analytical shift towards the process of transformation and its inherent potential, the formation of a completely urbanised society. For knowledge production, this notion implies that a science of the city has become obsolete and should be replaced by a science of urbanisation (Schmid 2005: 159–161).

A number of scholars have added their conceptual thoughts to Lefebvre's notion of an 'implosion and explosion' of the city in the late 20th century. The emerging urban configurations, which have nothing to do with the city in its classical sense, are described for instance by Sieverts (1997), who coined the term *Zwischenstadt* – the in-between city – for the expansion of urban fabrics and lifestyles in formerly rural areas. Also Garreau's edge cities (Garreau 1992) or McGee's *desakota* (McGee 1991) try to theorise the appearance of new urban configurations. In various publications, Brenner and Schmidt have taken up Lefebvre's theory, refining it to their concept of planetary urbanisation (Brenner, 2014a; Brenner & Schmid, 2015; Schmid, 2018). This move is a claim to abandon the 'city' as an object of analysis and to reconceptualise an urban theory without an outside, where cities become only one of the expressions of capitalist urbanisation. Keeping up Lefebvre's spirit, the worldwide expansion of capitalism is understood as a broad process producing socio-spatial and socioecological transformations appearing as manifold terrains of urbanised conditions including all areas operationalised for capitalist accumulation (Brenner 2014b: 14–19).

Lefebvre succeeded in developing a new theory of urbanisation based on contemporary critics of the urban development in the 1950s and 1960s and on theoretical fragments excavated from Marxist writings. He conceptualised urbanisation as a process of 'implosion': dissolving and transforming the traditional city and 'explosion': expanding the *tissue urbain* over the country. From this point of departure – the dual crisis of city and country – he derived a strategic hypothesis: that of the complete urbanisation of society. From this perspective, it becomes possible to comprehend urbanisation as a macrosocial and a historical phenomenon. Consequently, Lefebvre's analyses of the urbanisation process follows these two perspectives at first in two analytical steps: that of a historic analysis of the city (the space-time axis of urbanisation) and that of a macrosocial perspective of the process of urbanisation (creating space-time continents) (Schmid 2005: 149–151).

In a first step, he approached the city from a historic perspective (the space-time axis), where he identified the process of urbanisation as linked to industrialisation and as responsible for the destruction of the city. With this analysis, the city becomes a historic configuration of urbanisation, characterised by rise, zenith, and destruction, and the urban crisis of the 1960s a critical phase of transition. In a second step, he creates societal fields or formations (space-time continents) and analyses the city as part of the macrosocial development process. He draws a sequence of these continents (the rural, the industrial, and the urban), where industrialisation produces urbanisation (Schmid 2005: 154). These analyses reveal a virtual object on the horizon – the 'urban society' – an upcoming societal formation where economic rationality, the dominance of exchange value, is replaced by another world, where productivism has become meaningless and use value is prioritised (cf. chapter 5.2.2).

During Lefebvre's first two analytical steps, however, the city as an object of analysis becomes obsolete. For that reason, Lefebvre performs a third analytical step (space-time levels), where he searched for the linkages between the historic development of the city and the macrosocial development process towards an 'urban society'. He created three interconnected space-time levels of societal reality (private level, P, global level, G, and a mediating level, M), where the city is the mediating level, M.

Lefebvre arrives at a definition of the city as a mediator, a social and mental form characterised by its centrality, and the place of difference, encounter, and simultaneity. This form can be filled with anything. Its content is historically specific; it is contested and it is the result of societal confrontations. The centrality of the city thus becomes essential since it allows the encounter of differences. These encounters create conflicts but are also crucial for new developments. They are the ground to cultivate the 'urban society'. Powerful groups might control access to this centrality, or it might be attacked by the global order, which is why the emerging 'urban society' remains uncertain; it is 'the possible'. Lefebvre sees the centrality of the city as decisive for the development of an 'urban society'. It is such an understanding of the city that is central to the demand for the right to the city.

6 The Right to the City

The concept of the 'right to the city' has witnessed political and scholarly renaissance over the last decades. Against the background of an unfolding crisis of today's cities and triggered by the first translation of Lefebvre's work into English in the 1990s (Lefebvre 1968 [1996]), vivid discussions have emerged among social activists, scholars, and in political circles. Charters have been developed and adopted based on the right to the city, such as the Montréal Charter of Rights and Responsibilities (2006), the Mexico City Charter for the Right to the City (2010) or the World Charter for the Right to the City (2005), to name a few (Purcell 2013a: 141; WBGU 2016a: 155; Brown & Kristiansen 2009: 22–26). Most remarkable is the development of the *Estatuto da Cidade* – the *City Statute* in Brazil, which became national law in 2001 (cf. Fernandes 2007; Mengay & Pricelius 2011). Referring to the right to the city, it has established a new concept of land ownership, emphasising the social value of urban land and a requirement for democratic participation in urban planning (Brown & Kristiansen 2009: 7). At the international level, the United Nations Educational, Scientific and Cultural Organisation (UNESCO) and UN-Habitat have taken up the idea and have initiated a public debate since 2005, trying to conceptualise the right to the city as a vehicle to realise the broader agenda of human rights (Purcell 2013a). Despite remaining controversial, for the first time the concept found entry in an internationally negotiated document: The New Urban Agenda (2016) (Scruggs 2016; UN 2017). Nor has the scholarly debate come short of discussion, having produced a wide array of interpretations and controversies (cf. Attoh 2011; Duff 2017; Harvey 2008; Holm & Gebhardt 2011; Kipfer et al. 2013; Kuymulu 2013; Marcuse 2010; Purcell 2002, 2013a, 2013b; Schmid 2011).

6.1 Interpretations of the right to the city

When looking at the extensive field of interpretations and attempts at operationalisation of the concept, a number of strands can be identified referring to discussions on the right to the city. Grassroots movements and social organisations have used the idea mainly as a slogan for unifying the goals of different initiatives (Mayer 2011) and international organisations have pushed forward the concept as an inspiration to achieve their wider goals of poverty reduction, full realisation of human rights, and initiatives for good governance. The attempts of local governments to adopt declarations and charters based on the right to the city can be associated in this context. All attempts have in common that they demand a better life in the city, a more just city, more inclusion, more participation, less segregation, and access to urban resources for all, particularly for marginalised groups. They try to implement the right to the city as a collection of claims and individual rights, rarely challenging the existing space-time configuration of capitalist accumulation. Doing this, they dilute the meaning of Lefebvre, as his theories are understood here, who imagined another possibility, the vision of another space-time configuration, that of an 'urban society'.

The academic debate on the right to the city intensified in the 1990s with the English translation of Lefebvre's work and the spatial turn in social sciences. From the 2000s onwards, this discussion was further leveraged as a response to the mushrooming of social movements, which took this term as their buzzword against the increasing commodification of urban space, demanding more just and more democratic cities (Grell 2014; Kipfer et al. 2013; Holm 2013). The debate circles around central questions: is the right to the city a suitable concept, only a slogan or a utopia worth considering? Except for South America, the debate remains a discussion in the Global North (Holm & Gebhardt 2011: 9–10).

Excavating Lefebvre's original text, scholars have found several dimensions of the right to the city. Two meanings of city are distinguished (cf. Holm & Gebhardt 2011; Grell 2014): city meant as physical form (access to it) and city meant in its form as a result of production processes (access to this production processes and to all the dimensions of the production of space) (Holm & Gebhardt 2011: 7). The following rights are commonly associated with the right to the city (WBGU 2016a: 155; Grell 2014; Holm & Gebhardt 2011; Purcell 2002):

1. **The right to participation:** the right of the inhabitants of cities to have a say in any decision with consequences on the production of urban space, whether they hold citizenship or not. Inhabitants are to play a central and direct role in all decisions that produce urban space in their cities (Purcell 2002).
2. **The right to difference:** the right of the inhabitants of cities to be different, to live different lifestyles,and to have urban space that allows difference, to places in the city where encounters and confrontations between social groups and cultures are possible. Only if such places of difference exist might the city become a possible place for societal innovations.
3. **The right to appropriation:** the right of all inhabitants of cities to collectively (re) appropriate the city, to use urban space for their need and desire, to utilise the advantages and resources of the city in an equal and just way. It is the right of the people to be physically present in the city, and to physically access, occupy, and use urban space (Mitchell 2012).

4. **The right to centrality:** the right of all inhabitants of cities to access places of societal wealth, urban infrastructure, and urban knowledge. This includes physical access as well as access to debates about future development paths. Lefebvre identified centrality as a crucial characteristic of the urban. Centrality is the form of the city; its content is always contested. The right to the city is synonymous with its right to centrality, the right to the city demands therefore reoccupation of centrality by the people (Schmid 2005: 184).

Most scholars refer to the right of participation – access to decisions made on urban space – and the right to appropriation – access to urban resources, the right to access, occupy, and use urban space – as the main two meanings of the right to the city (WBGU 2016a: 156). In many ways, attempts are made to institutionalise or operationalise the right to the city. Empirical studies as well as translations for practitioners, however, remain rare.

6.2 Institutionalisation and operationalisation of the right to the city

The wide array of interpretations of the right to the city can be seen as a 'black box' or 'fuzzy concept' (Attoh 2011: 678), blurring the meaning and purpose of the concept, but its capaciousness can also be interpreted as its strength, as it allows solidarity across political struggles (Mitchell & Heynen 2009). Most obvious, this strength is unfolded as a uniting element – a rallying cry – for social mobilisation. Social movements interpret Lefebvre's right to the city and the associated right to difference as a tolerating element of different views on urban development and use it as a source of legitimation and orientation providing a uniting element for initiatives founded for quite different topics on urban policies (Holm & Gebhardt 2011: 19–21; Holm 2013: 8). The best example for such an organisation is The Right to The City Alliance in the United States (cf. box 4).

The right to the city inspires not only movements in the Global North, eg anti-gentrification movements in the United States or squatter milieus in Germany, but also organisations in some regions of the Global South (eg slum dweller and housing activists in Brazil). In developing countries, the central demands are comparatively far more pressing: human dignity, affordable housing, urban services, and adequate livelihoods are the central topics (Mayer 2011: 70–74). Lefebvre's notions, such as the right to centrality, the right to difference, the right to appropriation, or the right to participation, are extracted and translated into respective regional and thematic contexts. All protest movements have in common one central demand, the demand of non-exclusion from access to material and immaterial resources of the city (Schmid 2011: 25–34). This might be the demand not to be gentrified, to have a say in urban policies, to have access to urban space, or not to be evicted from one's present home.

Box 4: The Right to the City Alliance

The Right to the City Alliance was founded in 2007 as an umbrella organisation of community-based organisations in the United States. In the beginning, its demands focused on countering tendencies of gentrification and displacement of low income people (Right to the City Alliance n. d.). By now (2019), the organisation has grown to a union of 45 initiatives demanding justice and democracy in topics ranging from environmental justice to human rights and democracy. The Alliance recognises that the issues they are fighting for (eg housing, homelessness, LGBT-rights to space and rights to culture) are interrelated and need a common platform to exert power towards change. They found this common ground in the concept of the right to the city, understood as '[...] the right for all people to produce the living conditions that meet their needs' (Perera 2007). The organisation adopts a human rights perspective with the goal to '[...] urbanise human rights, [...] to ground them in real lives and struggles [...]' (ibid.). Direct action on the ground to take control of their own neighbourhoods is equally emphasised as struggles for better inclusion (eg participatory budgeting) by advocating for new national law on urban development (Purcell 2013a: 144).

In the last two decades, movements for a right to the city have gradually gained momentum, culminating in urban protests – eg associated with the Arab spring or the occupy movement. This development has put Harvey to reflect admirably: 'It [the right to the city] primarily rises up from the streets, out from the neighbourhoods, as a cry for help and sustenance by oppressed peoples in desperate times' (Harvey 2012: xiii).

Urban protests activists have increasingly begun to connect globally, coming together at the Social Forum of the Americas or at the World Social Forum (cf. Fernandes 2007; Kipfer et al. 2013: 127–129). The results were the foundation of international non-governmental organisation (NGO) alliances (eg the Habitat International Coalition) and the development and endorsement of a number of charters in many parts of the world (eg the World Charta for the Right to the City (2004), Montréal Charter of Rights and Responsibilities (2006), the Mexico City Charter for the Right to the City (2010)). These charters are not legally binding, rather are used for orientation and for expressing the willingness to move in a certain direction.

The exception is the City Statute of Brazil. This document became national law in 2001 and with this achievement, Brazil has moved to the forefront in institutionalising the right to the city. Since that date, in all decisions about urban development, the social value of space (not only its exchange value) is to be considered and appropriate measures for citizen participation in urban planning are to be implemented (Fernandes 2007). The instruments for implementation are the tools of urban planning, eg the obligation for municipalities to develop local master plans determining the social use of all properties (including possibilities to impose sanctions) and the possibility to demarcate zones of social interest (Mengay & Pricelius 2011: 251–252). In addition, a process to formalise squatter settlements[2] is postulated. Property rights are not removed, but beside exchange value, now also the social needs of the inhabitants are to be considered (Purcell 2013a: 142).

Nearly two decades after its implementation, however, a lack of success of the City Statute is reported (Rolnik 2013c; Caldeira & Holston 2015). While the significance of its jurisdictional institutionalisation is acknowledged, a gap between *de jure* and *de facto* implementation can be witnessed (Friendly 2013). Caldeira and Holston (2015) conclude that the executive and legislative branches of government are not sufficiently obliged to ensure implementation, allowing many municipalities to ignore determinations written in respective master plans. Nevertheless, the City Statute remains a milestone in the institutional acknowledgement of the right to the city.

Since 2005, the United Nations have also reviewed comprehensions of the right to the city and a public debate on urban policy was initiated. The concept was put on the agenda of the fifth World Urban Forum in 2010 and in their flagship report, *State of the World Cities 2010/11: Bridging the Urban Divide* (UN-Habitat 2008c), the concept has become a central element (cf. box 5). In line with adopted charters, UN-Habitat and UNESCO pursue the goal of anchoring the right to the city in the jurisdictional sphere. Operationalisation is then to be carried out by creating adequate principles and translating them into law and regulations to be implemented on the local level. The goals are to use it as a vehicle for the full realisation of human rights and to initiate governance reforms oriented at the principles of 'good governance'.

For practitioners working in the sphere of urban planning, the right to the city has remained an abstract concept with few examples of application. Some architects have tried shrinking it to a right that can be operationalised by introducing measures of morphological diversity and social mixture in their urban strategies (Kipfer et al. 2013: 128). Beside these attempts, however, it remains unclear how the right to the city can be utilised on the local level.

---

2 Article 183 of the city statute regulates the formalisation of housing without land titles (informal settlements). It is stated that an individual who has occupied a land plot for living purposes not larger than 250 m^2 and for more than five years can become the legal owner and apply for a land certificate (Mengay & Pricelius 2011: 249).

Box 5: UN-Habitat's interpretation of the right to the city

One major UN body, UN-Habitat, outlined an interpretation of the right to the city in one of their flagship reports, *State of the World's Cities 2010/2011. Bridging the Urban Divide* (UN-Habitat 2008c). In that report, the right to the city is interpreted as 'a vision for an alternative, adequate and ideal city [...] a city where mutual respect, tolerance, democracy and social justice prevails'. Such a city is to be achieved by a holistic, balanced, and multicultural type of urban development focusing at the gradual realisation of the universally recognised human rights. 'The "right to the city" must not be viewed as a new legal instrument, but instead subsumes a wide range of universally recognised human rights into a single claim for enforcement in urban areas' (UN-Habitat 2008c: 122).

Local authorities are to realise this agenda. The right to the city is seen as a platform for implementing initiatives and policies at the municipal levels in all policy arenas (land use, planning, etc) with the goal of achieving inclusiveness. It is reasoned that such approaches are hampered by obstacles related to governance (eg disjuncture between policy aims and processes, lack of capacities and technical skill, weak organisations, unclear coordination between agencies, etc), with the argument that better governance would be the requirement for realising the right to the city (UN-Habitat 2008c: 122–134).

Anne Mikoleit (2014) states that some examples of a direct or indirect operationalisation of the right to the city do exist: Alternative forms of the production of space, where urban pioneers, research groups, cultural and artist communities, and others try to create open, non-capitalistic spaces where interaction, exchange, and communication is centred. Examples of such spaces would be temporal appropriation of space, intermediate use of barren areas, urban gardening, regional and local embedded economies, or cooperating housing associations, to name a few. These initiatives have in common that they try alternative concepts of coexistence in the realms of housing, economy, and the use of urban resources. As labs of urban and social innovation they challenge the existing paradigm of neoliberal urban development and might point us in the direction of alternative urban development in the sense of Lefebvre's 'urban society', where use value dominates (Mikoleit 2014: 115–124).

Mikoleit also identifies some characteristics of urban policies which promote the emergence of such alternatives. These characteristics can be related to the concept of policy arrangements: He argues that pioneer projects or labs of social innovation should be formally included in urban development practices by establishing adequate rules. Urban actors, especially the authorities, should be characterised by openness with regard to such projects, patience, and the readiness to negotiate alternative ideas. A respective urban discourse would be shaped by openness without prejudice with regard to the named practices (Mikoleit 2014: 115–124).

6.3 Only a collection of rights?

Efforts to institutionalise the right to the city aim at a wide variety of goals. Beside sectoral demands, these are often related to governance reform striving to reach 'good governance' and the full realisation of human rights. These attempts are not necessarily in line with Lefebvre's thinking. They do not desire to change the existing system or to imagine and conceptualise Lefebvre's 'urban society'. Rather, they strive to establish the right to the city as a codified synthesis of rights to be guaranteed by the liberal-democratic state (Purcell 2013a: 143–144; Wachsmuth 2018). The World Charta for the Right to the City(2005), for instance, lists a number of existing human, citizen, and social rights and recommends that local governments work on their realisation by implementing suitable legal frameworks and instruments[3]. Brazil's City Statute, as another example, indeed strives for an implementation of the right to the city, but does so only as a more participative form of liberal and representative democracy. Even the most progressive implementation in Brazil's municipalities leaves the power to shape urban space in the hands of administration and landowners (Mengay & Pricelius 2011: 263–264). In a similar way, the United Nations understand the right to the city as a principle, a collection of rights that might be a good vehicle for realising human rights. The goal proposed is 'inclusion', focusing on marginalised groups and the notion of integrating them into the existing system (Purcell 2013a: 143).

Such approaches counteract Lefebvre's meaning of the right to the city. Formalisation of the informal sector and informal settlements with the goal of inclusion, as proposed by UN-Habitat for instance, would stabilise the current system by advancing the commodification of possibly all aspects of human activities in the circles of capital accumulation. Notwithstanding the goals of such approaches, from a critical perspective, this strategy can be interpreted as a seizure of the right to the city by capitalist accumulation. In such a way the right to the city is in danger of being depoliticised, not striving for transformation to another 'urban', but achieving change by governance

---

3 In the World Charter for the Right to the City the right to the city is defined '[...] as the equitable usufruct of cities within the principles of sustainability, democracy, equity and social justice. It is the collective right of the inhabitants of the city [...]' it is '[...] interdependent of all internationally recognized and integrally conceived human rights, and therefore includes all the civil, political, economic, social, cultural and environmental rights which are already regulated in international human rights treaties' (World Charter for the Right to the City 2005: Art. I.2).

reform promoting greater participation within the existing system (Mayer 2011: 62–69). This approach, therefore, is not in congruence with Lefebvre's meaning, who forecasted a shift of the current space-time configuration and saw it as the obligation of urban scholars and experts to help such a far-reaching change towards an 'urban society' to evolve.

Other issues related to the operationalisation of the right to the city are rarely considered in the public realm and in policy circles. Attoh (2011) and Harvey (2012) point out that the right to the city is more a collective rather than an individual right. Therefore, attempts at institutionalisation would trigger many tensions and contradictions with existing human rights, liberty rights, or socio-economic rights. An introduction of the right to the city would post costs and trade-offs against other individual rights (Attoh 2011).

Purcell (2002) supports this critical view, by raising attention to geographical scale and emerging issues with democratic decision-making, should the right to the city be translated into law. Considering concrete decisions on urban space, eg the construction of a new coal power plant, he asks who is to be entitled to have a say in this decision? Every inhabitant of the city? All people affected by the predicted pollution, or everyone obtaining electricity from the new plant? In other words, are the rights of inhabitants of a neighbourhood put first or the rights of all residents of a city (Purcell 2006)? Purcell argues that the geographical scale of a political community holding the right to the city would have to be defined in every case anew (Purcell 2002).

Mayer (2011) adds, that 'hip' urban spaces, created by alternative groups of creative people and artists, where urban life is prospering and use value dominates, regularly become the focus of commodification tendencies. Activists, formally fighting for the rights of marginalised groups or for their right to live alternative lifestyles, are in constant danger of trading their convictions for personal advantages. In such a way neoliberal tendencies are frequently hijacking those spaces, created initially as an alternative to the existing space-time configuration (Mayer 2011: 66).

Summarising, it can be said that the right to the city is in danger of being reduced to a right fixed and limited to a state-centred perspective. Some try to operationalise it as a concrete legal right, such as access to urban space, to participate in decision-making, or to sectoral rights such as the 'right to housing'; others translate it for their purposes of governance reform. These reductions may be useful to translate demands into tangible reforms, but they miss Lefebvre's broad transformational perspective (Kipfer et al. 2013: 127–129).

6.4 Lefebvre's meaning of the right to the city

> Streets are meant to be a place of encounter, but the streets of Los Angeles are empty.
> (Friedmann 1995)

All interpretations, attempts at institutionalisation, and operationalisation of the right to the city point us to the question of what Lefebvre really meant by his demand for the right to the city. To find an answer it is useful to consider both the context in which his publication emerged and Lefebvre's whole intellectual legacy.

Lefebvre's essay, *The Right to the City*, was published prior to his other publications, *The Urban Revolution* and *The Production of Space* and also prior to the irruption of protests in May 1968. His work therefore must be read in that context. He was sensitive to an atmosphere of unrest, to a situation where forthcoming riots seemed to be inevitable (Harvey 2012). For Lefebvre, the transformation of urban and rural landscapes he was studying meant a crisis of the city as he understood it, a crisis of the fordistic city (cf. chapter 5.1.2). It was this development which drew Lefebvre's criticism, and against this transformation he put the right to the city as a cry – a response to the existential pain of the crisis of everyday life – and a demand for an alternative urban life (Harvey 2012).

Lefebvre's concept was born in a city witnessing an essential crisis. Urban development in Paris of 1968 had made clear once again that the possibilities to create, shape, and design cities are unevenly distributed. 'Only few, the hegemonic economic class, hold that power and make the cities to their desires and at public expenses' (Etzold 2011: 189–190). The powerless, the underprivileged were increasingly excluded and segregation tendencies were proliferating. Against the loss of urban qualities, the eviction of many from inner-city areas, and the functionalist modernisation, Lefebvre postulated the right to the city, meaning the right to urban life, to centrality, to places of encounter and interaction (Holm & Gebhardt 2011: 7).

In his following publications, Lefebvre specified the meaning of his right to the city within his wider urban theory. In his work *The Urban Revolution*, Lefebvre sketched another world, an emerging new societal formation, which he called an 'urban society' (cf. chapter 5.2.2). He also postulated the disappearance of the countryside and the traditional city, but the re-emergence of the latter as a place of centrality (cf. chapter 5.2.4). With this cognition, he revealed the crucial characteristics of the city: it is a form characterised by centrality. This form can be filled with anything, its content is always disputed and depends on negotiations and struggle between social groups or individuals. It is this access to the qualities of the city, the access to its centrality, which constitutes the basis for Lefebvre's demand for a right to the city (Schmid 2018).

> The right to the city cannot be conceived of as a simple visiting right or as a return to traditional cities. It can only be formulated as a transformed and renewed right to urban life. It does not matter whether the urban fabric encloses the countryside and what survives of

> peasant life, as long as the 'urban', place of encounter, priority of use value, inscription in space of a time promoted to the rank of a supreme resource among all resources, finds its morphological base and its practico- material realization.
> (Lefebvre 1968 [1996]: 158)

In Lefebvre's thinking, it is another societal formation – the 'urban society' – which is to be achieved. This 'urban society' is a virtuality, a utopian world, another societal configuration where use value has triumphed (cf. chapter 5.2.2). The right to the city than means two things: 1) the right to a transformed and renewed urban life – this would be the 'urban society'; and 2) the right to concrete places, the morphological base, which allow the cultivation of this new societal formation – this would be a place of centrality, the city. Common interpretations usually refer only to the second aspect mentioned here, reducing the transformational perspective of the right to the city to more tangible rights (right to appropriation, right to participation). Unlike common interpretations, with the right to appropriation, Lefebvre means not only the right to occupy already existing urban space, but also the right to produce urban space in such a way that it meets the needs of all inhabitants. Space must be produced in such a way that a full and complete usage of the advantages of the city, of centrality, becomes possible (Lefebvre, 1996, p. 179). That means access to wealth, urban infrastructure, and knowledge but most of all access to places where encounter with other societal groups and individuals is possible.

Use value for the inhabitants, thus, must be the prime consideration in decisions that produce urban space. The conception of urban space as private property, as a commodity to be monetised (or used to monetise other commodities) by the capitalist production process, is specifically what the right to appropriation stands against. The right to the city, therefore, is an anti-hegemonic demand for a transformation of society based on specific rights and the acknowledgements of these rights (Mayer 2011: 62–69).

Following Lefebvre's transformational perspective, the city with its characteristic of centrality is to be understood as a resource of society, a place where social practices are allowed that might bring about change and innovation. In such a milieu, Lefebvre argues, the possible-impossible, a utopian world, can be cultivated and might slowly emerge. The right to the city, thus, is much more than an intention to highlight the legal right to a particular physical space or the demand for more participation, it is meant to emphasise the importance of 'the urban', a '[...] form of spatial and social centrality produced in a convergence of radical or revolutionary politics' (Kipfer et al. 2013: 129). What does the city in an 'urban society' look like? Here Lefebvre provides us with some answers: it is a place of encounter, assembly, and simultaneity of different elements of society. A place where diverse groups of people (re)produce the city by their social interactions (Abrahamson 2014: 249–250). With these characteristics, the city becomes the decisive place for innovation and change, for the production of another alternative societal formation – the 'urban society'.

Lefebvre did not envisage the implementation of a few small changes and demands, but rather had a vision of a fundamental shift in societal power constellations controlling the production of the city. He intended not limited solutions in urban planning, but a redistribution of power over the urban process, a redistribution of urban resources to be equally used by the city's inhabitants (Holm & Gebhardt 2011). Consequently, many authors (eg Grell 2014; Harvey 2012) interpret Lefebvre's right to the city, the demand for 'a transformed and renewed right to urban life' (Lefebvre 1968 [1996]: 158) not only as a socio-spatial struggle against undesired urban developments (eg segregation), but also as a revolutionary demand against the primacy of economic logics of exchange value (Kipfer et al. 2013: 127–129). It is, thus, more than only the right to the resources a city embodies, it is not a property-based individualistic right, but a collective right to (re)appropriate and design the city, a challenge against hegemonic liberal and neoliberal market logics.

> The right to the city is, therefore, far more than a right of individual or group access to the resources that the city embodies: it is a right to change and reinvent the city more after our hearts' desire. It is, moreover, a collective rather than an individual right, since reinventing the city inevitably depends upon the exercise of a collective power over the processes of urbanisation. The freedom to make and remake ourselves and our cities is, I want to argue, one of the most precious yet most neglected of our human rights.
> (Harvey 2012: 4)

What to do with this cognition intellectually? When interpreting Lefebvre, Harvey (2012) suggests, it is our task as scientists to imagine an alternative world, which stands in contrast to our world characterised by overaccumulating capital with all its political, environmental, and social consequences. We should imagine a new city, not trying to reawaken the traditional cities, but to reconstitute a very different kind of city. This city is already there, it lives within the multiple alternative practices and projects where alternatives are tested. Our task is then to study these alternatives, identifying obstacles that hinder them from breaking through.

The right to the city means a right to urban life (not the traditional city), a right to renewed centralities, a right to places of encounter and exchange, a right to associated rhythms of life and a right to use these places and moments as one wants. This urban life needs a morphological base to be cultivated – the new city we need to imagine (Schmid 2005: 184–185).

6.5 The right to adequate housing

The right to adequate housing is derived from the Universal Declaration of Human Rights, where it is seen as one of the components of the right to an adequate standard of living (UN-Habitat 1996 § 8; UN-Habitat 2009b; UNHRC 2007, 2014). It has been recognised in a number of conventions, declarations and UN resolutions (UN-Habitat 2002b) and is also referred to as the 'right to live in security, peace and dignity' (UN-Habitat 2009b: 3). The basis for the right to adequate housing is § 28 of the Universal Declaration of Human Rights:

> Everyone has the right to a standard of living adequate for the health and well-being of himself and of his family, including food, clothing, housing and medical care and necessary social services, and the right to security in the event of unemployment, sickness, disability, widowhood, old age or other lack of livelihood in circumstances beyond his control. (UN 1948 art. 25)

The right to adequate housing contains freedoms and entitlements. Freedoms include protection against arbitrary interferences in one's home, including forced evictions as well as the freedom to choose a place to live. Entitlements are security of tenure, equal access to adequate housing, and participation in housing-related decision-making at national and community levels (UN-Habitat 2009b: 3). The minimum conditions that shelter should fulfil to be considered as adequate housing are presented in table 1.

Table 1 Minimum conditions for shelter to be considered as 'adequate housing'

Condition	Specification
Security of tenure	– Legal protection against evictions
Availability of services	– Safe drinking water, adequate sanitation, energy for cooking, heating, lightning, etc
Affordability	– Housing costs must not threaten other human rights
Habitability	– Sufficient living space – Permanent structures – Physical safety – Protection against natural hazards
Accessibility	– Access to the amenities of the city (services, etc) – Respect special needs of disadvantaged groups
Location	– Not located on hazardous sites
Cultural adequacy	– Respects cultural identity

Source: Table by author. Based on UNHRC (2007), Kothari (2007), and UN-Habitat (2009b: 3–4)

A common misinterpretation is that the right to adequate housing includes an obligation of the state to provide housing for all or a right to land ownership. For that reason, some governments (eg the US delegation) opposed an adoption of this right during Habitat II. The United Nations clearly state that this is not the case. Governments are not obliged to supply the housing stock for their entire population; rather they have to work on appropriate legislative, organisational, and political environments and to implement measures to protect the right to adequate housing against third parties and to guarantee its gradual fulfilment. This includes basic supply and availability of housing stock as well as measures that prevent homelessness, foster the inclusion of marginalised and disadvantaged groups, and guarantee security of tenure. At a minimum, governments must show that they are making every possible effort with the resources available to better protect and promote this right (UN-Habitat 2009b: 33; UNHRC 2014). Equally, land ownership is not a right to be given by the state. It is moreover the task of governments to guarantee the right to land, as legal recognition is critical for protecting the right to adequate housing (UNHRC 2007: 10)

In connection to the right to adequate housing as declared by the United Nations, the right to the city is frequently mentioned. The United Nations interpreted the right to the city as a vision for an alternative, ideal city, as a vehicle for the gradual realisation of the universally recognised human rights. It is also seen as a concept to counter the exclusion of marginalised groups. Governments have to give special attention to those groups, which the right to adequate housing is denied. Among others, these are dwellers of sub-standard and informal settlements. Governments have the obligation to recognise and protect their right to settle on urban land by implementing policies that sanction forced evictions and regularise informal settlements with the active participation of their residents (UNDP 2005: 38–42). National housing policies and housing plans must be implemented that progressively realise the right to adequate housing for all. Therefore, housing policies that realise the right to adequate housing must be first of all inclusive and pro-poor housing policies.

The right to the city is certainly in line with this argumentation, but as we have seen in chapter 6.4, Lefebvre's understanding goes beyond this interpretation. In post-war Europe, in many respects the right to adequate housing as presented here was satisfied by functionalist mass-housing (Holm 2015: 4). This massive housing construction helped to satisfy the demand, but the price was high: other qualities of the city were lost in the resulting planned settlements, which are permeated by rationalist logics (Lefebvre 1974 [1991]: 108). These quarters are far from being a space where cultural exchange, communication, and encounter of different social groups is possible, even though in some cases they might be appropriated by their inhabitants (Holm & Gebhardt 2011: 8). The city as an open space of communication and exchange was not to be found in functional tenements. In developing countries, this functional urban development is largely reproduced today. Oriented at western models, the functionalist city is still an important and prevailing paradigm of urban development. Functional separation and mass housing projects are often seen as adequate means to cope with rapid urbanisation processes in the Global South.

From this perspective, the right to adequate housing as defined by the United Nations is an important framework for housing development, but considering the insights from Lefebvre's right to the city, the definition of adequate housing should be extended. The conditions of adequate housing – outlined in table 1 – must be regarded as the *minimum* basis for sound housing policies. Adequate in terms of Lefebvre's right to the city would mean more; it would also encompass a right to places of encounter and exchange, a right to associated rhythms of life, and a right to use these places and moments to ones' desire. The right to participation, difference, appropriation, and to centrality, in other words, to all resources that are offered by cities, should be incorporated. In this sense, adequate housing policies for the poor would not just be designed with the goal of providing housing supply at the best technical and available standards, but would also consider the creation of urban life as an equally important factor for the realisation of the right to adequate housing. The second aspect cannot be easily conceptualised or designed by urban planners, since it is created by residents in their day-to-day spatial practices. It would moreover be the task of planners to allow and promote these processes. This might be achieved by reducing planning and steering efforts, by encouraging residents' participation in decision-making and urban planning, by creating and allowing places of encounter and communication, and by promoting the appropriation of urban space.

7 The Analysis Concept: Policy Arrangements

With the cognitions gained from Lefebvre's theories, the question emerges of how his comprehensive theoretical framework can be translated for an empirical study on housing policies. Adopting Lefebvre's perspective that another space-time configuration of society does exist and is already emerging, it is the task of scholars to find indications for such an evolution, wherever and whatever the level, the scale, and the dimensions might be. Due to its centrality, the city as a form is predestined to find such indications, even though they do not necessarily emerge there (Vogelpohl 2011: 241). For this reason, the city level is chosen as the scale of analysis.

Considering the production of housing, it must be asked how an 'urban' mode of housing production would be different to the 'current' mode of housing production. Similarly, it is to be asked how 'urban' housing policies would differ from 'current' housing policies. Thus, it is the task of this study to explore and analyse housing policies that are oriented at – or even might already be – in congruence with Lefebvre's 'urban society'. For achieving this task, it is necessary to imagine and search for housing policies that would be characteristic for the 'urban society'. Using case study methodology, cities where supposedly alternative housing policies have already evolved must be selected as cases. These housing policies then must be comprehensively analysed, testing them against their congruence with Lefebvre's 'urban society'. In such a way, the goal is to reveal obstacles and fractures that allow an alternative production of urban space in the housing domain.

As we have seen, the production of space is a production process happening in three dialectical intertwined dimensions (moments): space is conceptualised, experienced, and lived by individuals and these individuals collectively produce representations of space, spatial practice, and representational space. Housing policies are designed by experts, urban planners, architects, urbanists, among others, and they – together – produce knowledge about space, their conceptions or representations of space, that are valid during specific societal formations. Therefore, this study focuses on the representations of space produced by experts and their translation into spatial practices in the two case study cities, seeking to test them against the normative frame of an emerging 'urban society'. Doing this is already a contribution to the realisation of the 'urban society'. Lefebvre proposed an intellectual approach which he called *transduction,* to be employed alongside induction and deduction (Lefebvre 1970 [2003]: 5). Appling this approach would mean, for example, to compare continuously current conditions of an investigated phenomenon against the possible conditions of an 'urban society'. By describing and interpreting, having in mind a possible alternative and revealing obstacles to achieve them, a contribution is already made to help 'the possible' to emerge (Vogelpohl 2011: 241).

Representations of space, which structure and constrain spatial practices as well as representational spaces, are the outcome of processes of policy-making. Specific housing policies are produced predominantly by housing experts, urban planners, urbanists, and others at the local, the national, and the international scales. Housing policies are designed at all three scales by the interactions of actors in the housing domain. These actions are structured by institutions as well as formal and informal rules – set up by macro-societal developments and knowledge systems and through interactions between actors in day-to-day policy-making – that allow and determine individual conduct.

For analysing this policy process at the city level, a suitable concept is needed. It should be comprehensive, covering both organisation and content of policy-making, and it should be replicable, allowing for policies in different contexts to be compared. In political science and public administration multifarious concepts for public policy analysis exist, which can be borrowed. The literature body on urban governance is an important starting point for such concepts.

7.1 Urban governance

In common understanding, policy-making refers to the actions taken by governments, the decisions made to govern a spatial area. From the 1990s onwards, it was observed and acknowledged that the process of governing is increasingly not only based on state actors, but has become a coordinating process also involving actors from the public sector and civil society. This process was called 'governance', a term that describes the substantial changes observed in the way societies are organised (Pierre 2006; Benz et al. 2007; Kooiman & Jentoft 2009). Although there is no single definition, governance generally relates to '[…] the process of goal-oriented coordination and management involving governmental and non-governmental actors' (Castree et al. 2013: 195). Together, manifold actors co-determine the outcomes of policy-making. Often, this process of change is referred to as a 'turn' or 'paradigmatic shift' 'from government to governance' (Arts & Tatenhove 2006: 33). In academic literature, 'governance' is used and applied in different ways. It became a buzzword for describing a theoretical framework to study governance processes, it is also used as a normative concept in itself when referring to 'good governance' and is also applied as an empirical object of study, analysing and comparing different governance modes and their evolvement (Pierre 2005; Kersting et al. 2009: 14–16).

The development observed, termed as a shift 'from government to governance', was explained as a reaction to the changing relationship between state, civil society, and markets caused by macro trends, such as globalisation, individualisation, democratisation and decentralisation. The old paradigm of governing (government) encompassed an organisational mode led by the state, characterised by command-and-control mechanisms and top-down policy-making. In contrast, the new way of governing (governance) is characterised by new instruments and steering mechanisms and a multitude of actors participating in policy-making. Network-like arrangements of public and private actors and public-private partnerships were seen as characteristics of this. Some authors also refer to this development as multi-actor governance, network governance, multi-level governance, or informal governance (Kearns & Paddison 2000; Arts & Tatenhove 2006: 33).

Explanations for this development vary. Some attribute these changes to new requirements caused by macro-societal changes; others criticise the retreat of the state as a neoliberal project of submitting all possible aspects of life to the logic of capital accumulation (Belina et al. 2013: 126). The first perspective sees the old mode of governance as insufficient to cope with arising challenges, requiring optimisation through a shift to a new mode of governance (Kearns & Paddison 2000). Beginning in the 1980s, the hierarchical top-down management of state affairs was judged as ineffective, inefficient, and illegitimate to cope with day-to-day challenges. Governments and their bureaucracies were perceived as underperforming in terms of efficiency and unable to address the needs of all societal groups (Rakodi 2003: 525). Traditional urban planning approaches were regarded as inefficient and the prevailing top-down hierarchy would not allow any participation of the public in decision-making processes. The second perspective takes a critical stand, seeing deregulation and privatisation of government affairs and the subsequent transfer of multiple functions of city governments to private actors as highly problematic (Purcell 2002: 101).

Whatever explanation is highlighted, the observable result is the same: the emergence of new forms of governance, where governing processes are based on multiple actors, blurring the boundaries between public and private, formal and informal, and resulting in a fragmented governance landscape (Rakodi 2003: 542). Even though responsibilities were privatised or transferred to communities or individuals, most authors argue that the state retains most of its power, since decisions on policy processes are in the end still controlled by state actors (Matthews 2012; Taylor 2007).

This development became most visible at the local level. It were the lowest tiers of government that most significantly felt global socio-economic changes. Urbanisation, economic globalisation, decentralisation, and demands for participation caused raising obligations for city administrations. Rapid urbanisation has been causing an ever-increasing demand for infrastructure, housing, and services. Economic globalisation has made cities more vulnerable to the ups and downs of the economy and has intensified inter-city competition for business investments (DiGaetano & Strom 2003:

367–368). Decentralisation reforms and the devolution of power has left city administrations with increased control to design their own policies, but also with increased obligations (Helmsing 2002; Brenner 1999). Simultaneously, the public demands more influence on decision-making. All these developments led to an overload of tasks for administrations. In many cases, they proved unable to meet them due to insufficient financial and human capacities (Kearns & Paddison 2000; Suri & Taube 2014).

The introduction of new forms of governance combined with neoliberal reforms (privatisation and deregulation) at the local level were seen as the solution to these challenges (Cohen 2006). To optimise the outcome of policies and increase efficiency, it was proposed to reduce the role of governments in implementing measures and leaving this task to others, namely civil society and the private sector. The role of government should be only to create an enabling environment, guiding policies by incentives and rules wherever possible (Helmsing 2002). In such a way, it was thought to enable initiatives and the private sector to operate and carry out government programmes and measures. The goal of this shift in governance was to improve service provision to meet the needs for more participation, to reduce costs, and to improve policy outcomes. From the 1990s onwards, international aid organisations, the World Bank, and the United Nations highlighted this other mode of governance as desirable, as a precondition for successful policies, as 'good governance' (World Bank 1992; Doornbos 2001; UN-Habitat 2003b, 2009a).

Also the scientific interest in the governance of cities increased since the 1990s, as did research fields identified as local or urban governance (Holtkamp 2007; Bogumil & Seuberlich 2014). Numerous studies on local (or urban) governance reforms appeared (Kersting et al. 2009; Holtkamp 2007). Many of them conceptualise modes of governance and related principles (Lin et al. 2015; Kooiman & Jentoft 2009) and try to measure the performance of governance and governance arrangements on different levels (Fukuyama 2013; Rakodi 2003). Also, in publications related to housing interventions, governance has been used as an important reference (Minnery et al. 2013; Suhartini & Jones 2019). Frequently, concepts and tools were searched for in order to analyse and compare modes of governance between cities and to connect them with performance indicators (DiGaetano 2009; DiGaetano & Strom 2003).

7.2 Approaches to analyse public policy

Different approaches try to analyse public policy in the urban realm. Depending on their focus, they can be roughly categorised along the continuum between structure and agency, a dualism intensively discussed in the social sciences (Giddens 1984; Werlen 2008; Veronika Deffner & Christoph Haferburg 2012; Weichhart 2018). Following rational choice theories that see actors as rational and well-informed individuals, some of the approaches rather emphasise the actors' conduct and capacities to act. From this perspective, the observed governance constellations and policy output is predominantly the result of aggregated actions of individuals. The approaches of regime theory (Stone 1993) and growth machine theory (Logan & Molotch 1987) can be assigned to this category. The other category of approaches puts more emphasis on structure, or the system, as being decisive for determining actors' interactions. From this perspective, observed conditions of policy outcomes and governance modes result from structural conditions that are inscribed via rules and regulations into the organisation and content of policies. These rules pre-structure scripts of interactions for actors, leaving little choice for agency. Regulation theory (Heeg 2014) and all variants from institutional theory (cf. box 6) can be subsumed in this structural perspective (Leroy & Arts 2006: 8).

Two approaches have become most prominent in urban political economy: regime theory (Stone 1989) and the growth-machine theory (Logan & Molotch 1987). Both approaches are rooted in the United States, emphasising the importance of coalitions between governmental and non-governmental actors, especially the privileged role of economic elites, in shaping urban policies. This can be attributed to the political system of the United States, where local governments depend much more on local economies (local governments can go bankrupt and local taxes are very important for city budgets) and economic actors play historically a pivotal role (Harding & Blokland-Potters 2014: 101).

Regime theory is based on the cognition that there is a set of arrangements or regimes '[...] by which public bodies and private interests function together in order to be able to make and carry out governing decisions' (Stone 1989: 6). Power is seen as fragmented and regimes as sets of collaborative arrangements are the means through which actors assemble the capacity to govern (Moosenberger & Stocker 2001: 812). The regime perspective therefore focuses on such arrangements, their evolution, their consolidation, and their change (Kern 2016: 126). Private business elites or rentiers (in the case of the growth machine thesis) are identified as holding the prime position among actors in the urban realm, outweighing the interests of other urban players. In the growth machine thesis (Logan & Molotch 1987), which focuses on property values and the rent seeking-activities of entrepreneurial elites, it is even stated that the development of a city is run by these elites, who use a rhetoric of urban renewal and enhancing overall economic development of a city, but in reality seek to maximise their profits by the expansion of exchange value. Logan and Molotch (1987) showed that the consequences are the destruction of the use values of neighbourhoods and communities, as property and housing values go up and residents are displaced. Consequences are heightened inequalities and fragmentation in cities.

Urban political economy approaches have established a perspective which is similar to the governance perspective. It is recognised that urban authorities are only one among several actors governing a city and that the process of governing is a policy-making process of negotiation between different interests, based on formal and informal communication and interactions (Bogumil & Seuberlich 2014: 45). Coalitions of interest groups do exist, formed between actors depending on interactions and power relations. Together these actor coalitions form arrangements or regimes that are stable for specific periods and dominate urban development. These arrangements can be interpreted as one of several models of urban governance (Pierre, 2005: 452).

What structural and agency-oriented approaches agree upon is that decisions on policies in cities are shaped on the one hand by institutions (formal and informal rules and regulations) and on the other by interactions of the actors involved. The different approaches usually recognise both aspects, but vary by emphasising one aspect or the other. Institutions guide and define, constrain and allow possible actions of actors by assigning them not only possibilities for action but also the means, resources, and power, to do so. Actors on the other hand are those who willingly shape their actions following their interests or the interests they represent (in the case of political actors). Actors are those who choose to mobilise their power, who decide actively to form coalitions in order to pool their resources and who (re)shape, consciously and unconsciously, intuitions through their interactions (Bogumil & Seuberlich 2014).

From this short review it has become clear that both structure and agency are important to direct urban development. Moreover, both aspects must be seen as a dialectical relation, since both aspects constitute each other, structures are contained in actions and vice versa. Only few approaches try to overcome this duality in public policy analysis. One of them, the policy arrangements approach, which enables the analysis of specific policy domains within a city, incorporates also a discursive dimension and links arrangements formed on the ground with political and societal macro-processes (Arts & Tatenhove 2000; Leroy & Tatenhove 2000; Arts et al. 2000; Arnouts et al. 2012). For that reason, the approach is presented in more detail in the next section.

Box 6: Institutional theory

There is a wide discussion in political, economic, and social sciences on institutional theory which has intensified in the last decades (Affolderbach & Mössner 2014). Institutional theory was initially developed as a criticism of neoclassical approaches and their abstract models that assumed the existence of rational actors and neglected social context. Institutional approaches emphasise the importance of institutions – often referred to as informal and formal rules and regulations – for influencing or structuring human conduct. In the last few decades institutional approaches have gained ground and an 'institutional turn' has been observed in the 2000s (Jessop 2001).

At the end of the 19th century, institutional economy had emerged as a non-marxist alternative to neoclassic approaches, recognising institutions as important for political and economic questions. Further developments in the

1930s resulted in the approaches of the 'new institutional economy' which regarded institutions in a narrow sense as constraints and demarcations of human action (Affolderbach & Mössner 2014: 179). After a decrease of interest on the topic due to the quantitative revolution in social sciences, the 1970s and 1980s saw a revival of institutional approaches, now under the term 'neo-institutionalism' (Scott 2014: 30–54). In these approaches, social practices are regarded as embedded in political and social institutions and a myriad of strands emerged in the disciplines (most of all in sociology, economics, and political science). Examples are 'normative institutionalism' (seeing social practice as embedded in rules of appropriateness), 'rational-choice institutionalism' (social practice as a function of rational perceived rules), and 'historical institutionalism' (investigating the path dependency of decisions) to name a few. Decisive for neo-institutional approaches was the cognition that the decisions of organisations are much more shaped by socio-cultural, cognitive, and institutional factors and less by rational choice than previously assumed (Affolderbach & Mössner 2014: 181).

Today, the institutional perspective is used in sociology, political, economic sciences, sociology, and also geography (Coy 2001; Bork et al. 2011; Etzold 2011). Even though there is an increased comprehension of institutions, an increased recognition of their importance for individual actions, the difficulties in observing and analysing them empirically are not solved. Institutions are both cause and consequence of (economic) development, but relations are complex and vary over time and space (Affolderbach & Mössner 2014: 188).

Nevertheless, institutional theory has been adopted most of all in public-policy analyses and governance analyses to explain changing institutions and mechanisms of coordination and steering among actors and their networks (Kooiman 2003). What remains is a widely acknowledged perspective that helps to reveal societal routines, scripts, and informal actions and coordination. In spatial planning and policy-making, the perspective is also a means of questioning simplistic policy transfers of 'best practices' to other contexts and of explaining their frequent failure (Amin 1999).

7.3 The institutionalisation of policy arrangements

Institutional dynamics in environmental policies in Europe of the 1970s and 1980s was the focus of a research programme carried out at the Department of Political Sciences at Nijmegen University, the Netherlands, by Jan van Tatenhove, Bas Arts, and Pieter Leroy (Tatenhove et al. 2000b; Arts & Leroy 2006). The goal was to develop and conceptualise a research framework that could explain institutional dynamics shaping changes in policy content, strategy, rules, and organisation that were observed in empirical studies. These observations were discursive shifts in the naming and framing of environmental policies and desired modes of governance, as well as the occurrence of new forms of practices in day-to-day policy-making (multi-actor, multi-rule, and trans-boundary character). As a result, three integrated concepts were developed, which attempt to explain institutional dynamics by the concepts of *institutionalisation* and *policy arrangements* and link them to broader societal and political developments with the concept of *political modernisation* (cf. box 7) (Leroy & Arts 2006).

The authors identified that many scholars described changes in European environmental policies from an evolutionary perspective and connected them to new forms of governance. They argued that major changes in the political field, regarding interrelations between state, market, and civil society, a process which they called political modernisation (cf. box 7), is followed by the emergence of specific policy arrangements. These policy arrangements form from the interactions of actors, but are structured by the wider political context. If the context is changing, eg the famously referred to change 'from government to governance' as the prime and dominant mode of organisation of a society, they argue that also the policy arrangements in specific policy domains are adapting to these conditions. However, they state also that these arrangements originate from interactions of actors who are not free in their decisions, as the institutions in which they manoeuvre are shaped by political-societal macro-processes, but still have the freedom to make their own decisions. That means policy arrangements are the result of the institutionalisation of macro-processes on the one hand, but are simultaneously produced by actors through their interactions. Structure and agency are both relevant.

Box 7: Political modernisation

Political modernisation was one of the concepts developed by Jan van Tatenhove, Bas Arts, and Peter Leroy (Tatenhove et al. 2000a). The concept refers to a macro political-societal development process defined as the '[...] the shifting relations between state, markets and civil society in political domains of societies […]' (Arts & Tatenhove 2006: 29). In other words, the concept describes the shifting modes of governing observed over the last decades and conceptualised in governance theory.

Several phases of political modernisation are distinguished. Each phase is characterised by specific discourses on governance and interrelations between state, civil society, and markets. These phases are seen as the context for the institutionalisation process producing policy arrangements in the different policy domains (Tatenhove et al. 2000a). The concept thus makes it possible to link observed (re)configurations of policy arrangements back towards shifting relations of governance at a superior scale. From a Lefebvrian point of view (cf. chapter 6.5) the described changes must not be seen as changes of the space-time configuration of society, but can be described as changes in the 'space-time levels' of society (the global level G).

The central concept developed to explain institutional dynamics was the concept of institutionalisation. Institution theory was the main inspiration, particularly the evolving debate on neo-institutionalism from the 1980s onwards (cf. box 6). Institutionalisation is understood as a twofold process, as '[…] the phenomenon whereby over time day to day actors behaviour solidifies into patterns and structures, whereas these patterns in turn structure day to day actors' behaviour' (Leroy & Arts 2006: 7) and as '[…] the gradual sedimentation of meanings into rules of behaviour and organisational structures, that in turn reproduce and recreate these meanings' (ibid.).

This means that both the interactions of actors *and* changes on a superior scale influence the process. On the one hand, it is acknowledged that day-to-day activities, the interactions of actors, solidify into routines of action (ie informal institutions) and specific constellations of governance on the ground. This means for instance that the way a problem is addressed and which actors are involved is subject to informal rules. On the other hand, institutionalisation is also a process influenced by developments on the macro scale, meaning socio-economic and political changes. These changes influence institutions on the ground in manifold ways (political modernisation). The organisation of local governments, certain divisions of tasks and power, and the existence of a government branch for a certain sector are shaped by these structural conditions.

Since institutionalisation is a twofold process, it is regarded as having high potential to integrate the structure-agency duality as well as the substance-organisation duality (Giddens 1984; Hay & Wincott 1998). Therefore, it became the crucial basis for theory development.

> Institutionalization refers to the phenomenon whereby patterns arise in people's actions, fluid behaviour gradually solidifies into structures, and those structures in their turn structure behaviour. When applied to policy processes, institutionalization refers to the fact that relatively stable definitions of problems and approaches to solutions gradually arise in and around policy, more or less fixed patterns of divisions of tasks and interaction develop between actors, policy processes develop in accordance with more or less fixed rules and so on. (Arts et al. 2006: 96)

The aspects of political modernisation and actors' interactions both have influence on the institutionalisation process. A gradual stabilisation occurs during this process in its normative, regulative, interactive, and cognitive dimensions. In each of these dimensions, patterns gradually solidify. More or less fixed patterns of rules of the game (formal and informal) emerge, shared perceptions of problems and their solutions as well as suitable strategies become dominant, and a specific division of tasks among actors as well as allowed and banned actions become stable and well-known by all actors (Leroy & Arts 2006: 10). In other words, institutionalisation results in a stable pattern within a policy domain, in the production and reproduction of policy arrangements (Tatenhove & Leroy 2000: 17).

7.4 Policy arrangements

From the concepts of institutionalisation and political modernisation, the third concept emerged: the policy arrangement approach. Policy arrangements are defined as '[...] the temporary stabilisation of the content and organisation of a policy domain' (Arts et al. 2006: 96), whereby policy domain refers to all policy practices regarding one thematic issue (eg environment, housing). Drawing on the structuration theory of Giddens (1984) and anticipating a neo-institutional perspective (cf. box 6), it is argued that the process of institutionalisation results in the emergence of stable patterns, in specific arrangements, specific content, and organisation within a policy domain. In other words, a temporal stabilisation emerges regarding how problems are perceived and defined, what the desired solutions are, how these solutions might be reached, what rules of interactions and formal procedures should be used, just to name a few examples.

For the empirical analysis, four dimensions (*discourse, power, actors,* and *rules of the game*) of the content and organisation of a policy domain are identified (Arts & Tatenhove 2000; Arts et al. 2006): Discourses refer to the content or substance of a policy arrangement, meaning the objectives, ideas, and principles followed in a policy domain. The organisation of a policy arrangement is understood as a social system where the actions of actors are structured by rules and resources (cf. Giddens 1984). Individual agents form policy coalitions with other actors to reach their common goals; their resources (influence and power relations) determine their success and the rules of the game set the scene, as they define, through formal and informal conventions (institutions), how agents interact within a policy domain (Arts & Tatenhove 2000). These four dimensions of a policy arrangement are interconnected, and together the four dimensions form the tetrahedron illustrated in figure 7 and figure 8.

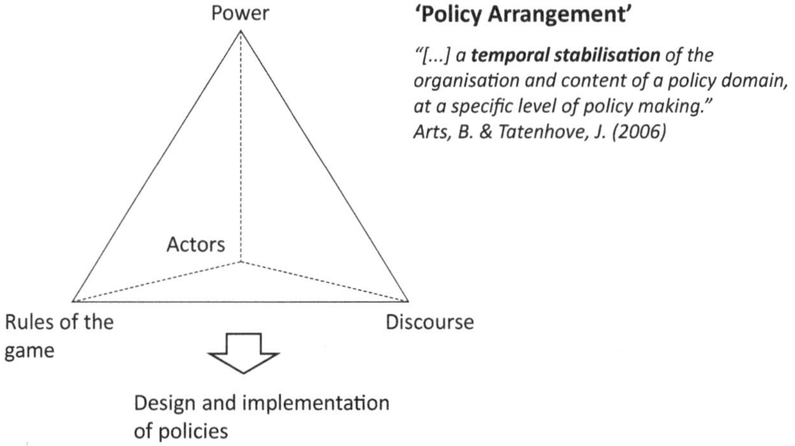

Fig. 7 The four dimensions of a policy arrangement and their outcome
Source: Adapted from Arts et al. (2006: 99)

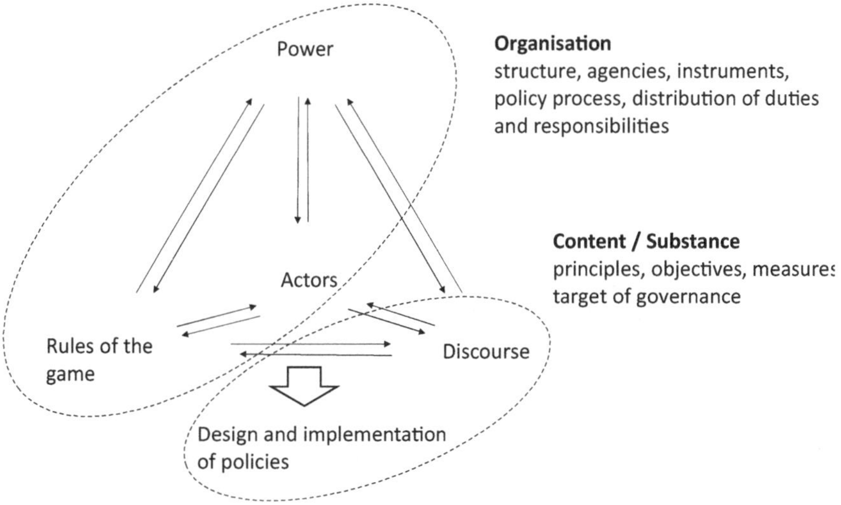

Fig. 8 Organisation, content, and related dimensions of a policy arrangement
Source: Illustration by author. Based on Arts et al. (2006: 99)

Policy arrangements are the result of institutionalisation processes reflecting day-to-day interactions as well as societal and political trends on the macro level. Therefore, they are under constant pressure of change. Any change to one of the dimensions of the tetrahedron might induce change to one of the other dimensions. The appearance of new actors, for instance, may be followed by an introduction of new elements to the prevalent discourse or may lead to another distribution of resources. Similarly, new ideas or concepts (eg sustainable development) might find their entrance towards the arrangement via the dimension discourse. Gaining more importance, such a concept might create legitimacy for specific actors, increasing their influence, or might be the nucleus for new coalitions (Lifferink 2006: 48).

Change is always related to one of the dimensions, but the cause might lie within or outside the arrangement. External causes refer to the influence of socio-economic or political shifts on a superior level (political modernisation), internal change is based on the interactions of actors. Both factors continuously structure the properties of policy arrangements, while actors' behaviour is simultaneously constrained by these structural properties. Both aspects, however, might induce change to one of the dimensions, causing the whole arrangement to be reconfigured (Arnouts 2010: 27).

Policy arrangements are also not to be found only at the city scale. It is imaginable, for instance, that depending on the policy domain arrangements might form at all levels of government or at the international scale. Simultaneously, actors involved in a domain might be members of different policy arrangements at the same time or on multiple scales. Therefore, a variety of policy arrangements coexist in the same spatial unit, their ways of governing might differ greatly (hierarchical top-down vs. participative bottom-up), and they can border and also overlap each other (Arts et al. 2000: 53 ff.).

7.4.1 Actors

Actors is one of the dimensions of policy arrangements. In theories of practice considered in social geography, actors are understood as individuals. Benno Werlen states that only individuals are capable of acting, not organisations, collective actors, or other groups (Werlen 2008: 283), but mentions also that '[...] there are no actions that are solely individual' (Werlen 2008: 290, translated by author). Even though only individuals perform actions, he refers here to the notion that these actions are also an expression of the respective socio-cultural context. This is one of the reasons, why some scholars also allow for more complex actors, such as groups or organisations (Weichhart 2018: 255). Of course, individuals remain the basic units of these quasi-actors. Institutions can constitute such social entities where individuals share collective beliefs or goals and act according to common norms, values, or codified rules. Such entities can be considered according to their capacity to act; they have become quasi-actors (Mayntz & Scharpf 1995: 49).

Quasi-actors or complex actors can be differentiated into *collective* and *corporative* actors (Blum & Schubert 2011: 54–55). Collective actors are associations of individuals who cooperate and share the same action orientation, but without a high degree of organisation and without sharing their resources (eg social movements). Individual members of a corporative actor, in contrast, pool their capacities to act. Their resources are centralised and their action orientation is determined hierarchically (in the case of government agencies or companies) or by majority (in the case of political parties). Corporative actors thus can be interpreted as an actor with goals, an action orientation, and resources, with the capacity to act (Mayntz & Scharpf 1995: 49).

In the policy arrangement approach, a wide understanding of actors is used, incorporating individual as well as corporative actors. According to Lifferink (2006), each of the dimensions of a given policy arrangement can be used as a point of departure for empirical analysis depending on the research questions. In the case of this study, it seems appropriate to start with the actor dimension, to identify all actors involved in the arrangement of a policy domain.

In this work, actors are understood as both corporative actors and individual actors, but the former are in the centre of attention. This is in consequence of the research level – the city – and the research object – housing policies – which is a domain close to the government and usually hierarchically organised. Nevertheless, from case to case, individual actors are considered. In congruence with the policy arrangement approach, in accordance with governance theory, and comprehending a wide term of institutions (cf. chapter 7.4.2), the analysis is not limited to political agencies or actors but includes all actors relevant for the housing domain. This also includes actors from non-governmental spheres, such as academics and civil society organisations. The goal is to reveal actor networks and their relations, power constellations, and relevant institutions.

The empirical data collection reflects these definitions. Since information is derived mainly from expert interviews, the researcher receives a mixture of clues on institutions and action orientations that might represent those of the interviewee's organisation or his or her own. Both are considered, with an attempt to differentiate from case to case. Individual actors are assumed as having internalised the institutions and action orientations of the organisation with which they are affiliated (ie their government agency or their organisation) and are thus regarded as suitable representatives for their organisation. This approach is a necessary and pragmatic reduction, neglecting the micro-scale, but considered as necessary to reduce complexity. When considered necessary – eg in cases where the actions of individuals are decisive for decision-making or in opposition to their organisation –individual action orientations and institutions are also incorporated.

Inspired by regime theory, the policy arrangement approach identifies actor networks and policy coalitions within a policy arrangement (Arts et al. 2000: 57–59). It is argued that each coalition consists of a number of agents who share the same action orientation and cooperate to reach their goals. They might be bound by a common interpretation of a policy discourse, by power relations, sharing the same resources, or by the institutional setting (Arts & Tatenhove 2004: 4). Arnauts (2010: 29) describes that there might be only one coalition of actors operating together within an arrangement, or more than one coalition with opposing goals struggling against each other. A policy arrangement might also be characterised without any coalitions.

For operationalisation in this study, focus is placed on actor networks and actor coalitions (cf. table 2). Using social network analysis examining data collected from different empirical methods, actors involved in the housing policy network are identified for each city as well as their relations and position within the network. By interpreting these findings and considering relevant institutions, power relations, and applied policies, conclusions on existing actor coalitions can be drawn.

Table 2 The actors dimension: criteria analysed and related questions

Dimension	Criteria	Related questions
Actors	Actor network	– Which actors are (not) involved? – What are the actors' relations?
	Actor coalitions	– What actor coalitions exist?

7.4.2 Rules of the game

Rules are another dimension of the policy arrangement approach. 'Rules of the game' set the scene for the interactions of agents in a social system; they delineate a policy domain and the possibilities and constraints of individual actors within the domain. Formal and informal rules can be distinguished, which are referred to as institutions[4] in scholarly literature (Mayntz & Scharpf 1995: 40). In the organisational sphere, formal institutions determine for instance which rules are legitimate, which procedures are used, what tasks are allocated to which agency, and how the competences are divided. Informal institutions are part of (political) culture determining actions of individuals often also unconsciously. In the policy-making process, for instance, informal institutions determine how interests are articulated, who is involved in the process and who is not, and how decisions are made and measures are implemented (Arts & Tatenhove 2004).

Rules and regulations in societies have become the subject of research in many disciplines, a research field known as institutional theory. In this field, various strands can be distinguished, which are characterised by different definitions of institutions

4 Commonly, the term institutions is simultaneously used for social entities (organisations) and for rules that structure behavioural patterns (Mayntz & Scharpf 1995: 40). Throughout this work social entities are denoted as 'organisation(s)', to prevent misunderstandings.

and their power over actors' conduct. Originating from the cognition that actions of individuals are not only decisions of their free will, it was attempted to conceptualise possibly all (hidden) rules limiting or allowing human actions. Some approaches try to explain actions with rational-choice approaches, seeing the actions of individuals as based on logical considerations of available options, while other approaches place more emphasis on structure, trying to incorporate social, cultural, and political factors and seeing them as more significant for individual action (the structure-agency debate).

From the wide body of literature on institutions, no clear definition of institutions emerges, reflecting the differing understandings with respect to research perspective, discipline, and tradition. Most scholars refer to North (1990), who defined institutions as '[...] the rules of the game in a society or, [...] the human devised constraints that shape human interaction' (North 1990: 3). Senge (2011: 91–96) proposed that a rule is only an institution if it is socially binding (ie it has the power to enable or constrain human actions), permanent (ie observable on a regular basis), and decisive (ie relevant for individuals and/or society). Rules can become institutionalised, which is a process and also a status: a process when social interactions and relations are not questioned anymore and have become routines; a status when a rule forms societal reality by defining what is important and what the scope of actions is (Affolderbach & Mössner 2014: 181).

Commonly, formal and informal institutions are discussed (North 1990: 36–53). Formal institutions would be '[...] codified and written rules, directives and contracts that are outlined in constitutions, laws, company directives or contracts. In contrast, informal institutions subsume cultural norms, customs and routines' (Etzold et al. 2012: 188). All in all, institutions appear to be an amalgam of societal rules, standards, laws, informal agreements, routines, cognitive representations and cultural traditions, expectations, and accepted decision-making processes (Affolderbach & Mössner 2014: 180–181).

For understanding institutions as causal for social practices, Scott (2014) developed three pillars of institutions according to their functions (Etzold et al. 2012: 186; Senge 2011: 85). In a narrow sense, he defined *regulative institutions*, which are more or less codified rules and regulations that allow or confine human conduct (eg formal law, regulations, and contracts). Actors decide rationally to follow these rules, since they fear sanctions if they do not. Such rules are largely defined by the state or other hierarchical systems of domination and recognised by others as legal or illegal practices (Etzold 2013: 25). *Normative institutions*, as Scott's second pillar, are based on values: '[...] conceptions of the preferred or the desirable [...]' (Scott 2014: 64); and norms: '[...] specify how things should be done [...]' (ibid.). Together, norms and values define moral obligations and social expectations. They structure social practices, as actors sometimes have internalised them, or actors might rationally judge their conduct against them in order to decide if their actions are appropriate. If not appropriate or illegitimate, actors must fear social exclusion. As the third pillar, Scott refers to *cultural-cognitive institutions,* the influence of shared conceptions, understandings, and logics of action on social practices. Every actor interprets – perceives and conceptualises – the world differently, resulting in symbolic representations of the world. Cognitive frames determine in such a way for example '[...] what information receives attention, [...] how it will be interpreted, thus affecting evaluations, judgements [...]' (Scott 2014: 67) and in the end social practice. It is this multifaceted understanding of institutions that has extended narrow conceptualisations of institutions as rules of actions (Senge 2011) towards wider conception seeing institutions as habitualised social practices (Etzold et al. 2012: 186).

Neo-institutionalism is characterised by the acknowledgement that institutions shape social practices significantly, but also recognise that actors have some individual power over their actions, to choose from given institutional scripts and shape the institutional context with their decisions (Schulze 1997). One specific variant of neo-institutionalism highlights this dualism of structure and agency more clearly, an approach known as *actor-oriented institutionalism* (cf. Mayntz & Scharpf 1995; Etzold et al. 2012). Advocates of this approach recognise the duality of institutions and social practices, trying to integrate them, or even refer to it as a dialectic relation: 'Institutions are a medium and outcome of social practices, while social practices are a medium and outcome of institutions' (Etzold et al. 2012: 187). In their view, neither social practices nor institutions are dominant: social practices of actors structure institutions and social practices as routines and strategies are also structured by institutions. Actor-oriented institutionalism is based on neo-institutionalism as it was formed in political sciences. Institutions are used in a narrow way, focusing on regulative institutions, but institutions can be created or reconfigured by actors. Therefore, institutions are not seen as a determining aspect of practices but are an enabling and simultaneously restricting factor. The epistemic interest is to study the interactions between corporative actors (cf. chapter 7.4.1), which is to be seen as easier with a narrowly defined institutional term. This narrow understanding of institutions in actor-oriented institutionalism is similar to the comprehension of institutions in the policy arrangement approach.

For operationalisation in this study, focus is placed on Scott's regulative institutions (codified rules and regulations) (cf. table 3), neglecting normative (values and norms) and cultural-cognitive institutions (shared conceptions and understandings) to reduce complexity. All three types of institutions are deeply entangled and reflected in discourses, and verbal acknowledgement of problems, in the housing policy network and finally in actors' practices. They are addressed using thick description of housing policies within the case studies. Regulative institutions encountered during the fieldwork are examined on the national and city scales, revealing the formal and informal laws and regulations that structure actors' competences and responsibilities in the housing domain.

Table 3 The dimension rules of the game: criteria analysed and related questions

Dimension	Criteria	Related questions
Rules of the game	Regulative institutions	– How are tasks, competences, and resources allocated? – What institutions are relevant for decision-making and policy implementation?

7.4.3 Power

As one of the components of policy arrangements, power is assumed as a prerequisite element of policy-making (Arts & Tatenhove 2004). Actors have power depending on their ability to utilise resources in relation to other actors, while institutions and discourses co-determine the kind and amount of resources each actor holds. Power is regarded as the capacity of actors to achieve outcomes by 'determining political decisions, [...] dominating public debates, defining policy issues, setting agendas, or even changing the rules of the game' (Arts & Tatenhove 2004: 5). The nature and amount of actors' resources is defined by structural and dispositional accounts.

Three pillars of power are distinguished by Arts and van Tatenhove (2004: 13–16): *relational power, dispositional power,* and *structural power.* Relational power is the capacity of actors to achieve outcomes in interaction (power as capacity). Dispositional power shapes this capacity by defining the position of an actor within an organisation and within a policy network (Clegg 1989: 83–84). Institutions mediate this process since they determine the division of allocative and authoritative resources[5] and with it the actors' relative autonomy or dependency. Structural power refers to the capacity of macro-societal structures to influence the nature and conduct of actors via (legitimising) discourses and institutions (Giddens 1984: 256–258). Considering this power concept, power is *structural,* manifesting itself in the uneven distribution of resources, it is *dispositional,* to be revealed in the actors' relations of autonomy or dependency, and it is *relational,* depending on the capacity of agents to mobilise resources to achieve certain goals (Arts & Tatenhove 2004: 5).

This power concept used for the policy arrangement approach is similar to the general debate on power in social sciences (cf. Allen 2003). Structural approaches consider power to be situated in institutions determining individual actions. Action-oriented approaches, in contrast, locate power with individuals and their capacity to act. This

5 The terms allocative and authoritative resources were shaped by Anthony Giddens in his work *The Constitution of Society* (Giddens 1984: 258). Under allocative resources, he subsumes property, land, technology, the material features of the environment, the means of material production, and produced goods. By authoritative resources he refers to the organisation of social time space, to the authority or control over the ways in which social life is organised and distributed over space (Allen 2003: 44).

capacity is seen as shaped by both societal structures and institutions as well as through individual resources and potentials. In post-structuralist discourse theory, it is argued that power originates less from individuals or social structures, but is determined by discourses, by superior knowledge systems which guide and determine individual actions (Mattissek & Prossek 2014: 200).

In this work, all three aspects are considered as interconnected factors, but relational power is the aspect of focus. Since the point of departure in the empirical study is the actor corner in the policy arrangement tetrahedron, the main interest is to study relational power or the capacity of actors to act. The allocation and division of resources, the authoritative and allocative resources resulting from individual, dispositional, and structural accounts, predominantly determines this capacity. Since the policy domain investigated (the housing domain) is largely dominated by government agencies, allocative resources (material features) can be neglected, though not excluded, assuming that authoritative resources play a larger role. These resources, the power of domination, are largely derived from the position of actors within the policy network (dispositional power).

Power is determined by the actors' capacity to act, but actors might be regarded as *influential* without acting in certain situations. Government actors might choose to use their capacities or might choose not to do so. This is reflected in another concept closely related to power, an approach focusing on influence. Willer et. al. (1997) state that actors exert influence in a policy domain when they choose to mobilise their capacities to act. Even if an actor decides not to use his or her capacities in certain situations, the actor might nevertheless be regarded as influential if prior actions are remembered. That means that actors in a policy domain have a reputation; they are regarded as influential by other actors based on expectations and past experiences.

From this theoretical account, two criteria are chosen for empirical operationalisation: resources and influence (cf. table 4). The first criterion measures potential power of actors, based among other things on the position of actors within the policy network and within their organisation (dispositional power), which implies an uneven distribution of resources. Such resources are predominantly authoritative resources, among others expert knowledge, funds and personal, legal means, and instruments. In addition, power received from legitimising discourses, actor coalitions, and institutions[6] might be employed as a resource. This potential power is assessed by a social network analysis focusing on dispositional centrality. The second criterion is influence, measuring the power reputation of actors assessed by other actors, indicating the actual use of power. This criterion is operationalised using the Net-Map method, by

6 Rules and regulations can be interpreted as resources of government actors; they enforce them only if the interest to apply them outbalances the interest to make an evasion (Zimmer & Sakdapolrak 2013; Bourdieu & Wacquant 2013).

surveying the reputation of actors based on the appraisal by other actors in the same network (cf. chapters 12.4 and 12.5 for details).

Table 4 The dimension power: criteria analysed and related questions

Dimension	Criteria	Related questions
Power	Resources (relational power)	– What is the position of actors within the housing policy network? – What dispositional power does each actor hold?
	Influence	– What is the perceived influence assessed by other actors in the network?

7.4.4 Discourse

The fourth of the dimensions of policy arrangements is the discourse dimension. In the policy arrangement approach, the term is narrowly understood as 'policy discourse', referring to the content or substance of policy-making (as opposed to organisation). Policy discourses are considered as 'dominant interpretative schemes ranging from formal concepts to popular story lines, by which meaning is given to a policy domain' (Arts et al. 2000: 63). This middle-range understanding of the term subsumes the narratives and principles of actors involved, their definition of policy problems, targets, and solutions (Wiering & Immink 2006; Contesse et al. 2018; Dang et al. 2019). They are created in the interactions of actors and signify common understandings and perceptions of procedures (how things should be done) and the (non-) importance of issues. Policy discourses are in this understanding considered as the outcome of policy- and decision-making processes, but do in turn also shape these processes significantly.

This understanding of the discourse dimension is a simplified version with necessary reductions compared to the comprehensions of the wide body of literature on discourse theory. Since the 1990s, discourse theory has gained popularity in human geography, strongly influenced by the writings of Michel Foucault, Ernesto Laclau, Chantal Mouffe and others (Mattissek & Glasze 2015: 41–42). From these roots several conceptual and theoretical approaches as well as methodological operationalisations have evolved (Keller 2011). Two of them are *critical discourse analysis* developed by Siegfried Jäger (1993) and *problem-oriented discourse field analysis* introduced by Thomas Jahn and Alexandra Lux (2009). Based on Foucault and Link (1990), Jäger's critical discourse analysis provides a useful comprehension of discourses as the verbal account of social praxis, as an institutionalised manner of speaking tied to practices and thus exerting power (Jäger 1993: 152). For Jäger, a discourse consists of several *discourse strands* that are entangled and it is the task of discourse analysis to disentangle and explain these strands. This comprehension is taken up by Jahn and Lux (2009), who consider these discourse stands to together form a *discourse field*, a thematic context where negotiation processes about common views on problems and solutions take place (Jahn & Lux 2009: 11). Some of the discourse strands might appear more important than others: they are *hegemonic*, representing presumably assured knowledge and having achieved dominance over other strands during a specific period of time. Other discourse strands are *counter-hegemonic* (they are not widely acknowledged and question the dominant strand) or *marginal* (they do exist, but are at the moment of minor importance). These strands continuously struggle for dominance in a discourse field and significantly influence actors' relations and practices as well as institutions in place. By identifying distinctive strands within a discourse field and the actors' positions and their assessment of knowledge (shared beliefs), problem-oriented discourse field analysis makes it possible to reconstruct and understand the reason for social practices and thus the origin of applied policies (Jahn & Lux 2009: 13).

In Liefferink's understanding (2006: 58–59), a distinction must be made between two levels of discourse fields that influence policy arrangements: the first level refers to a *superior* discourse field, where general societal relations (ie general ideas, values, and norms about the organisation of a society) and the preferred mode of governance are negotiated. The second level refers to a more *subordinated* discourse field that defines ideas and concepts about a specific policy problem at stake. At this level, different discourse strands exist that represent ideas about causes of the policy problem and approaches to possible solutions.

For operationalisation in this study, the discourses inherent to the housing policy arrangement of the respective city are investigated, omitting the analysis of superior discourses. Two criteria are examined (cf. table 5): 1) the current housing policy discourse in the discourse field of 'housing policies', focusing on various discourse strands in urban policies, and in dealing with the low-income population in the housing domain; and 2) shared beliefs within actor coalitions, meaning the way problems are defined and what approaches to solutions are considered as appropriate. Both criteria are analysed, employing thematic analysis of content and language practices collected from expert interviews (cf. chapter 12.2). By coding the verbal transcripts and searching for patterns and recurring themes, dominant discourse strands are revealed and presented for each case study.

Table 5 The dimension discourses: criteria analysed and related questions

Dimension	Criteria	Related questions
Discourses	Policy discourse strands	– What discourse strands exist in urban policies? – What are actors' views and narratives for dealing with low-income population in the housing domain?
	Shared beliefs within actor coalitions	– How are problems defined and what approaches to solutions are dominant?

8 Conceptualising Policy Arrangements in an 'Urban Society'

Lefebvre's theories can be brought together in one framework incorporating also the analytical concept of policy arrangements. Based on Schmid (2005: 316–330), three elements of societal space-time reality are identified and arranged in one matrix (cf. figure 9). These are space-time configurations – the continents of societal reality, or historically specific societal formations; space-time levels – the levels of societal reality; and space-time dimensions – the three production processes of the production of space. Even though Lefebvre did not explicitly conceive such a schematic illustration, it is included here to allow a better comprehension.

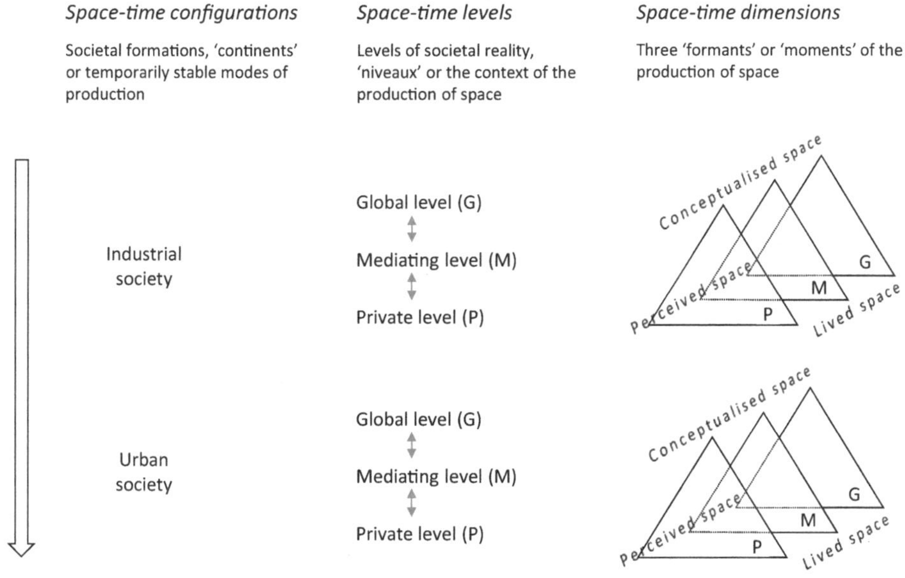

Fig. 9 Matrix of Lefebvre's theories: space-time configurations, space-time levels, and space-time dimensions
Source: Illustration by author

Space-time configurations: In his occupation with the phenomenon of urbanisation, Lefebvre conceived space-time configurations of society. These configurations are ways of thinking, living, or practice that form historically specific 'continents', or societal formations. According to Lefebvre the world is in a transition from an 'industrial' to an 'urban society', which he describes as a virtuality, a future utopian world where economic logics have become meaningless, and use value dominates exchange value (cf. chapter 5.2.2). Depending on the space-time configuration of society, the three dimensions of the production of space differ in their value. In the industrial continent, the 'spaces of representation – conceptualised space dimension' tends to dominate the other two dimensions, while in the upcoming urban continent, the 'representational space – lived space dimension' becomes more important.

Space-time levels: For each of these space-time configurations, Lefebvre categorised three space-time levels (cf. chapter 5.2.3): the global level, G – a general abstract level; a mediating level, M; and a private level, P – the level of daily life. The level of the 'distant' order, the global level, G, consists of abstract and regulatory entities: state, market, laws, regulations, religion. At the mediating level, M, Lefebvre places the city, as a social form characterised by centrality, as a place that allows difference, encounter, and simultaneity. The private level, P, is constituted from everyday practices. All three levels are interlinked and each level has its own dimensions of the production of space. The relations between the three levels differ, depending on the space-time configuration of society. In the industrial society for instance, the level G and P dominate level M (ie the urban level), while during a societal formation of the urban continent the mediating level, M, becomes more prominent. Likewise, the conceptualised space of an 'urban society' on the level M differs widely from the conceptualised space of the level M in an 'industrialised society'. A practical example would be the functionalist conceptualisation of space with its separations of residential, industrial, and commercial zones in an industrialised society as compared to an alternative conceptualisation of space, which allows the aggregation of these three zones in one place with fewer rules. Similar to that, 'perceived space' of an industrial society on the level M is that of an urban fabric characterised by fragmentation and inequality, while that of an 'urban society' would be that of an inclusive urban fabric recognising demands for the right of the city, allowing places of encounter and difference.

Space-time dimensions: At each of these space-time levels of societal realty, a separate but interlinked production process of space is happening. In his theory of the production of space Lefebvre conceptualised three dialectical interlinked space-time dimensions that produce societal reality: 'perceived space – spatial practice'; 'conceptualised space – representations of space'; and 'lived space – representational space' (cf. chapter 4). From an individual perspective, space and its material aspects are perceived by human senses, but cannot be perceived without conceptualising them and they are lived and experienced in people's daily lives. From a societal perspective, the simultaneous practices of individuals produce networks of communication and interaction, resulting in a pattern, in specific 'spatial practices'. Spatial practices are linked to collective 'representations of space', where knowledge and ideology are merged. Inherent in these two dimensions are 'representational spaces', where meaning and symbology is inscribed. It is a threefold production process of space: material production, knowledge production, and production of meaning (Schmid 2005: 318–319). Through their spatial practices human beings produce material realities, the perceivable aspects of space. By conceptualising space, they produce knowledge and within their daily lives, they produce meaning, a symbolic order – in other words, representational spaces that are imposed on material objects. Depending on societal conventions, space is defined and demarcated; a representation of space is created and communicated in discourses, illustrations, and pictures. These representations are contested and constantly negotiated anew.

The scheme presented here remains necessarily vague. However, it can be operationalised by envisioning the levels and dimensions of an 'urban society'. In a subsequent step, these notions can be traced empirically by searching for alternative production processes of space, by evaluating their congruence with Lefebvre's 'urban society', by finding obstacles for the evolution of this new formation.

How is space characterised in the 'urban society'? Anne Vogelpohl (2011: 238) proposed some of the characteristics of space in an 'urban society'. Spatial practice would be constituted from spaces of encounter, build orders would not be ruled by functionalism, and all citizens would collectively use and appropriate urban space. Representations of space would not be dominated by planned social life. Space would be conceptualised in such a way that there is not one single dominant conceptualisation of space. Such a representation would not be *a priori* designed at rationality and efficiency, designed to generate economic surplus value, but would be dominated by use value for the inhabitants of a city. Powerful actors of urban planning would set the framework conditions to allow manifold representational spaces happening simultaneously. In other words, they would allow manifold lifestyles to happen simultaneously in a city. A city in such a society would be a city of tolerance and inclusion, a city that allows the conflictual negotiation of space among diverse groups and sees this not as a problem, but as its decisive resource. In such a city, adequate housing for all would be a matter of course. In an 'urban society', conceptualised space would not dominate anymore; it would provide the framework that acknowledges the needs and desires of people to be transferred to individual and collective spatial practices.

Since the 'urban society' is 'the becoming' – the utopia to be achieved – such a characterisation is, of course, incomplete and depends on subjective knowledge and preferences. This incompleteness is reflected in table 6, where the three space-time dimensions for each of the two space-time configurations 'urban society' and 'industrial society' are juxtaposed.

Table 6 Characteristics of the production of space in the 'industrial society' and the 'urban society'

'Industrial society'	'Urban society'
General characteristics	
– Homogenisation and fragmentation – Representations of space dominate, everything is planned and organised – Exchange value penetrates all aspects of space	– All dimensions are of equal weight and aim to maximise difference – Use value overrules exchange value
Conceptualised space – representation of space | knowledge production	
– Strict build order, ruled by functionalism – Physical space and social life is planned – One representation of space dominates, orientated at efficiency and rationality – Experts produce factual knowledge – Exchange value dominates	– Build orders not ruled by functionalism – Social life is not planned – Multiple conceptualisations of space exist simultaneously – Openness of urban planners/architects to alternative knowledge – Representations of space oriented at people's needs and desires; individual representations are allowed
Perceived space – spatial practice | material production	
– Access to public space is limited and closed for some groups – Homogenised (exchange value) and fragmented space (divided in parcels) – Inclusion and exclusion	– Public space can be designed and used by all citizens – Spaces of encounter, assembly, exchange and simultaneity exist – Urban space is not functionally separated but its usage is self-determined by inhabitants
Lived space – representational space | production of meaning	
– Representations of space dominate representational spaces (do not consider or respect meaning of space)	– Multiple representational spaces coexist not ruled by representations of space – Conceptualised space respects representational spaces (meaning)

Source: Table by author

The mediating level, M, is focused on in this work, as this level will be of greater importance in the future formation compared to the 'industrial society'. It is the level of the city where all things are concentrated, where innovations flourish and where first indications of an emerging 'urban society' might be found. By imagining how the city as a mediating level, M, should look in the new societal formation, we approach the question of its characteristics in a theoretical way. This work focuses on one of the three moments of the production of space at city level: the representation of space. This conceptualised space is understood as the result of a political process that is decisively shaped by prevailing policy arrangements. Actors with different degrees of power, influenced by discourses and in their actions limited by formal and informal rules, determine policies and conceptualised space. Against this background this work seeks to explore how policy arrangements that would produce the desired representations of space in an 'urban society' might look. Therefore, the characteristics of a possible policy arrangement in an 'urban society' are conceived based on interpretations of Lefebvre's theories. These characteristics are of course incomplete, subjective, and normative, but are seen as a necessary step to develop target knowledge for a societal transformation (cf. table 7).

Table 7 Characteristics of policy arrangements producing representations of space in an 'urban society'

Rules
– Rules (eg build orders, land-use plans) are not static, not strictly oriented on functionalism
– Development plans take up and include pioneer projects, social innovations
– Allowing the co-existence of different approaches for land use
Actors
– Manifold actors from different sectors and professions
– Networks of actors determine policies
– Openness towards innovative, alternative projects and approaches
– Patience and readiness in coping with social groups proposing alternatives
Power
– Sharing decision-making and power among stakeholders
– Equal power relations (no dominance of business elites)
– Possibilities of participation
Discourses
– Policies are oriented at use value
– No prejudices against alternative concepts, practices, and lifestyles
– Promotion of alternative lifestyles and 'difference'

Source: Table by author

The municipal policies in an 'urban society' would aim to create as many places with urban life as possible. This means places where life pulsates, places of encounter, where the most diverse elements of society come together, exchange ideas, and resolve their conflicts. These places would be equally accessible for everyone, could be used according to individual needs, and would not be subject to the logics of capitalist exploitation. The inhabitants of the city would have a say in all matters of the production of space. Diversity, and a variety of lifestyles and social groups would be commonly recognised as a central resource of the city.

Translated into housing policies, this means that in an 'urban society' the city administration would develop mixed-use districts in which functions were no longer separated. The old dormitory cities of the suburbs would be a relic of the past and new districts would no longer be developed top-down, but in collaboration with and by the residents. Planning as a discipline will not have not vanished in such a new society, but will have changed dramatically. Plans would now be developed more flexibly and include only as much as necessary and as little as possible. Planning would be conducted in such a way that the other dimensions of space production were not hindered as is the case in past planning procedures of the 'industrial society'. This is achieved by applying fewer and more flexible rules that allow residents to appropriate space. Only they are capable of producing 'representational space' and it is this moment of space production that must be allowed to create a liveable city. Places of encounter are an important element of these new cities, and must be extensively promoted. The city government needs to find a balanced approach that navigates between planning and non-planning with the goal of achieving a renewed form of urban life.

With regard to appropriate housing policies for the poor, policies should respect the right to participation and appropriation. This means designing policies in such a way that residents are given as much say as possible and above all are given far-reaching opportunities to realise their individual production of space. The administration should set the framework conditions and allow people to design their homes and neighbourhoods mostly in self-help. However, this must not be steered by ideology. Regulating urban space is by no means a God-given law. On the contrary, the informal city also has a right to exist and should be seen as an enrichment. The ideology of formalisation is nothing else but a homogenising tendency of the 'industrial society', which tries to subject everything to the capitalist logic. A housing policy based on use value would try to take as much housing as possible away from the market by socialisation. Other forms of organisation would be promoted (eg housing cooperatives). These organisations would be public, so that market logics were no longer the central driver of urban development. By these means expropriations might be stopped, creating an inclusive city and achieving adequate housing for all. In this sense, 'adequate' would not only mean housing affordability and housing quality at technical standards of the time, but would also include the right to a vibrant urban life, the right to have a say in decisions on urban space, the right to live one's life to one's desire: the right to the city.

Based on these considerations, it is now a matter of devising and conceiving the characteristics of policy arrangements which appear to be suitable for producing the desired housing policies outlined here. Considering the actors dimension, such a policy arrangement would certainly be characterised by an actor network, not of single powerful actors determining policies. Only in such a way could a high degree of diversity be guaranteed, and actors would represent all strata and sectors of society, rather than being composed only of government officials. Power in such an arrangement would also be more evenly distributed among actors, since more people would have a say in decisions on the production of space in their city. The key actors in a policy arrangement organised in this way would also have certain skills and common goals. They would be open to new ideas from citizens, actively promote them, and be trained to interact with civil society actors and to accept and take up their ideas. Diversity in terms of land use, social groups, and lifestyles would be commonly seen as a central resource of the city and it would be the task of a city administration to actively promote it by allowing and protecting different lifestyles. The rules in such an arrangement would be characterised by flexibility and exceptions. Planning would not try to pre-design any aspect of physical space, but rather promote flexible spatial design that is allowed to change. Informal spaces would also be conceived as a central feature of the city that have a right to exist and are an enriching feature.

In addition to this theoretical approach, this study also tries to find an answer to the question of suitable policy arrangements in an 'urban society' by means of an empirical approach. For this purpose, the policy arrangements of the cities Surabaya and Solo are examined as case studies, since these cities have become known in the past for the progressive character of their urban policies. In a subsequent comparison, it is investigated whether and to what extent the policy arrangements analysed empirically correspond to the characteristics of the normatively desirable policy arrangement described here or not. It is hoped that this theoretical, empirical, and comparative approach will provide some clues as to which aspects of governance constellations need to be adopted in order to produce better housing policies and to achieve the goal of adequate housing for all.

9 Summary: Seeking a Normative Foundation from Theory

This chapter has examined two conceptual-theoretical fields. Approaching the central research question from a theoretical angle, the normative foundation for adequate housing and suitable policy arrangements has been laid, drawing on theories of Henri Lefebvre. For analysing local governance, the concept of policy arrangements has been operationalised to be employed for the empirical and contextual approach in the next chapters. The following questions guided this chapter:

<u>What is the normative foundation for adequate housing and for suitable policy arrangements?</u>
- What do Lefebvre's 'right to the city' and his 'urban society' mean?
- Is the concept of policy arrangements suitable to analyse local governance?
- What do Lefebvre's theories offer to conceive adequate housing and appropriate policy arrangements?

The theoretical framework of Henri Lefebvre is the meta-theoretical background of this work and provides its normative foundation. His theory of the production of space and his approach towards urbanisation open up a new perspective for urban studies in general. His theories lead to the realisation that the current 'industrial society' and its social production of space on its three levels of societal reality is only one episode in a historical sequence of societal formations. This recognition makes it possible to imagine a future formation, or space-time configuration, that of an 'urban society'. As in today's debate on post-growth, Lefebvre imagines a new societal formation in which economic logic no longer stands above everything and in which use value has triumphed over exchange value.

Lefebvre also conceives of different levels of societal reality, which he calls space-time levels (global, mediating, and private levels). These levels make the characteristics of the future formation easier to analyse, and from Lefebvre's writings, we can derive various clues as to how these levels might look, and how the production of space would then function. Lefebvre also formulates the right to the city in order to help the new formation to break through. By this right, he means two things in particular: the right to a changed urban world (a reformed and renewed urban life shaped by difference, encounters, and simultaneity) and the right to the place that is to bring about this change (the city). He understands the city as a mediating form that connects the different elements of society and concentrates them in one place. In it, exchange, assembly, and encounter are made possible, creating a milieu in which innovation and new ideas can flourish. In this way, the city becomes a central resource for societal transformations. Possible change will begin here. The right to the city is a 'cry and demand' for such places from which the transformation towards an 'urban society' might succeed.

From these considerations, the central question of this thesis has developed, which seeks ways to facilitate the spatial practice (inclusive cities and adequate housing) of an 'urban society' through appropriate governance conditions. The study focuses on the mediating level of the city and looks for the conditions for the emergence of housing policies that decisively shape housing production. Such policies can be understood as the outcome of one of the three moments of the production of space, the representations of space, conceived by politicians, planners, and architects, and whose expression is manifested in spatial practice. Representations of space at city level are the result of a process of policy-making. Therefore, it was necessary to find a suitable analytical concept to examine this process. This was achieved by drawing on theories of urban governance and employing the policy arrangement approach. The four dimensions of this approach were operationalised as actor networks, regulatory institutions, resources and influence as well as policy discourse strands. Together, they form specific arrangements that shape the design and outcome of housing policies. These criteria can be applied in case studies and thus make it possible to compare individual aspects as well as entire arrangements. In addition, this analysis grid also makes it possible to test the existing arrangements against a desirable arrangement, conceived as a possible policy arrangement in an 'urban society'.

The recognition of an emerging 'urban society' and the demand for a right to the city are helpful for establishing a normative compass for *suitable* policy arrangements, *sound* housing policies and *adequate* housing. With regard to the meaning of adequate housing, the United Nations have already defined minimum standards: security of tenure, availability of services, affordability, habitability, accessibility, safety, and cultural adequacy. Considering insights from the right to the city, this definition should be extended. To define adequate housing, the right to participation, appropriation, difference – all resources offered by the city – should be incorporated. Equally important for adequate housing are not only housing conditions at best technical standards, with access to urban services and so on, but also access to a renewed urban life. Only those housing policies are to be regarded as 'sound' which take into account not only the minimum requirements for adequate housing, but also try to create conditions to allow such a renewed urban life to unfold. The latter, however, cannot be devised by planners or architects, but can only be created by the residents themselves in their everyday social practices.

Therefore, a planning culture is needed that is willing to allow and actively promote such practices. This can be achieved, for example, through flexible planning that considers participatory processes and the appropriation of space from the very beginning, and does not prevent these processes through a rigid set of rules. Based on these insights into what adequate housing should mean and what sound housing policies would look like, the question of the nature of policy arrangements that are capable of producing such housing policies arises. The network of actors in an optimal arrangement would not be hierarchical, but would be characterised by a multitude of actors from different sectors who are actually involved in the decision-making processes. Rules would be flexible and not oriented to strict guidelines, but would leave room for experimentation. Government actors would be capable of actively engaging with new ideas from civil society and would not negate alternative concepts and lifestyles on a discursive level from the onset. On the contrary, the diversity of social groups and actors would be understood as a central resource of the city, a resource that can generate innovation, and would therefore be actively promoted. In such a way, theory tells us, the 'urban society' would be furthered and with it the goal of inclusive cities and adequate housing for all.

II. METHODOLOGY

10 Research Design

In order to achieve the exploratory goal of this study – identifying the characteristics of policy arrangements setting the scene for the production of housing in two Indonesian cities – a primary qualitative research design is employed, using case study methodology and several qualitative and quantitative methods of data collection and analysis. In contrast to a quantitative research design that strives to be representative by using large samples and tends to generalise the results in the search for general rules and laws, a qualitative research design is characterised by an in-depth investigation of a smaller number of cases, putting emphasis on detailed descriptions and interpretations (Mattissek et al. 2013: 34–38). Since this research is basic and exploratory, aiming at expanding scientific knowledge on the research object as well as on the analytical concept, a qualitative approach is considered most suitable. Qualitative methods make it possible to explore and capture perceptions and complex interpretation patterns of a not-yet-covered phenomenon best (Hollstein 2006: 20). This is the case for the concept of policy arrangements, since to my knowledge it has never been applied in the housing domain.

One of the methods in a qualitative research design is case study methodology (Taylor 2016; Flick 2019: 107–109). Employing case studies enables not only the performance of in-depth analysis of specific instances but also their critical juxtaposition and aggregation to arrive at new insights and meanings (Stake 1995: 74). Cases are seen as concrete entities bounded within space and time: '[…] a specific, a complex, functioning thing' (ibid: 2). A case might be for instance a person over a week or an organisation over three months. There are single cases (one individual, group, town, or country) and multiple cases (several individuals, groups, towns, or countries) (Taylor 2016: 584). This study uses an approach that compares multiple cases – two cities – to draw conclusions on the characteristics of their policy arrangements in the housing domain.

The analytical concept of policy arrangements requires specific types of data – primary and secondary data – and analytic lenses – institutional, actor-oriented, and discourse-analytical – for each of its dimensions at different scales. Therefore, a mixed-method approach is employed (Kelle 2014). Since the conceptual approach is

Table 8 Methods of data collection and data analysis

Data collection	Data analysis
– Problem-centred expert interviews (n = 50) – Standardised expert survey (n = 23) – Influence network mapping (n = 22) – Unsystematic observation – Literature survey – Collection of secondary data (*in situ*) – Informal discussions – Photo documentation	– Thematic analysis – Social network analysis – Systematic and critical literature review

exploratory, as is the research object, it was decided to triangulate data, perspectives, and methods. In such a way shortcomings from the usage of single methods, perspectives, or data sources can be eliminated, creating deeper insights into the research object (Flick 2011; Kelle 2014: 157).

Several methods of data collection and analysis are used (cf. table 8). The main empirical methods for the collection of primary data were problem-centred expert interviews, influence network mapping, and a standardised expert survey. In addition, data and information were gathered during three field visits by unsystematic observation, participation in local conferences, informal discussions, photo documentation, and the *in situ* collection of secondary data. The subsequent analysis was conducted using systematic and critical literature review (Huff 2008: 147–178), thematic analysis (Braun & Clarke 2006), and social network analysis (Jansen 2006; Fuhse 2018). Besides a large body of literature (academic literature, policy papers, and planning documents collected *in situ*), which were systematically reviewed, statistical data on the two cities were also explored and analysed.

These methods were applied to gather knowledge and information on the dimensions of *local* policy arrangements, but also the global and national scales must be considered. Policy arrangements can form in different domains often associated with sectoral policies (eg housing, economy, health) and at different scales (global, national, regional, local) (cf. chapter 7.4). The dimensions at these scales are entangled (ie actors or discourses can be located in more than one arrangement and at different scales simultaneously) and influence each other (eg the global discourse can have impact on very local arrangements). Therefore, while focusing on the policy arrangements in place at the local level, the influence of other scales must be included.

For operationalisation, all three scales are subject to analysis, although with different intensity and empirical methods. Figure 10 presents the research design, including research questions related to scales, the policy arrangement dimensions analysed, methods of data collection, received data and information as well as analysis methods. On each of the three scales – global, national, local – only specific policy arrangement dimensions are analysed. At the global scale, the analysis is limited to the 'discourses' dimension, while at the national scale the 'actors', 'rules of the game', and 'applied policies'

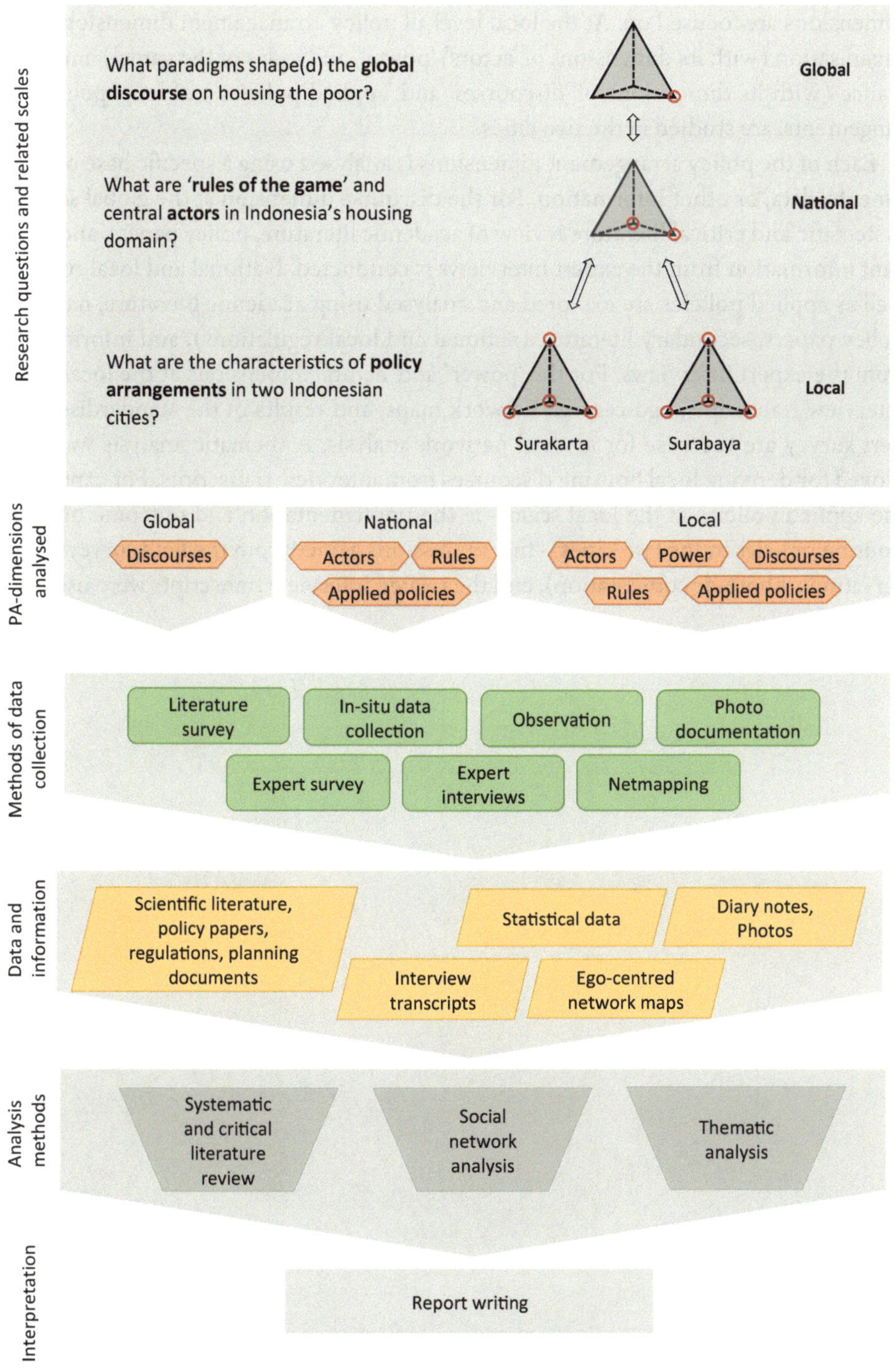

Fig. 10 Research design
Source: Illustration by author

dimensions are focused on. At the local level all policy arranagement dimensions, the organisation (with its dimensions of 'actors', 'power', and 'rules of the game') and substance (with its dimensions of 'discourses' and 'applied policies') of local policy arrangements, are studied in the two cities.

Each of the policy arrangement dimensions is analysed using a specific base of documents, data, or other information. For the discourse dimension at the global scale, a systematic and critical literature review of academic literature, policy papers, and relevant information from the expert interviews is conducted. National and local rules as well as applied policies are explored and analysed using academic literature, national policy papers, secondary literature (national and local regulations), and information from the expert interviews. For the 'power' and 'actors' dimensions at the local scale interview transcripts, ego-centred network maps, and results of the standardised expert survey are the base for a social network analysis. A thematic analysis was employed for deriving local housing discourses from interview transcripts. For capturing the applied policies at the local scale – ie the implementation and outcome of local housing policies in the two cities – the impressions gained from the field surveys (observations, photo documentation), and the related interview transcripts were used.

11 Fieldwork

Empirical data were collected during several fieldwork phases in the years 2014 and 2015. Covering an overall period of eight months, the research stay was divided into three periods (cf. figure 11). An initial phase of two months had an explorative character, aiming at the establishment of relations with important stakeholders in the two

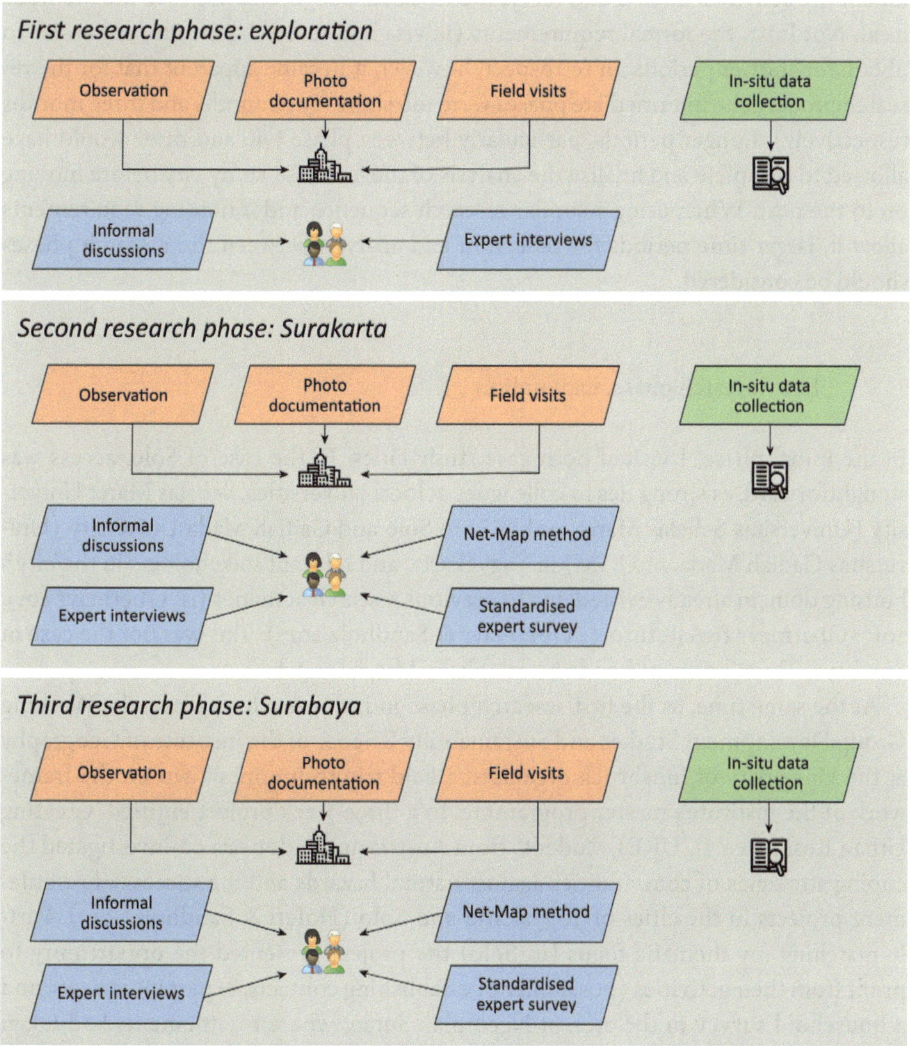

Fig. 11 Research phases and applied methods
Source: Illustration by author

cities and the preparation of the other phases. During the second and third research stay, the main part of the empirical work in the two case study cities of Surabaya and Surakarta (Solo) took place. Three months were spent in each city with the goal of collecting data and information about respective hosing policies and relevant stakeholders. In this chapter, the activities and methods used during the three research phases are described.

Such a fragmentation of the research activities into more than one phase has advantages. The phases in-between were helpful for reflection, and made it possible to document the activities carried out, revise the research design, and improve the methods used. Not least, the formal requirements (ie visa and research permits) are easier to obtain for shorter periods. In retrospect, however, it became apparent that for the research process, the intermediate phases were too short (two months and three months respectively). Longer periods, particularly between phase two and three would have allowed to complete and finalise the analysis of the first case-study city before moving on to the next. When using a similar research sequence and if funding requirements allow it, larger time periods for reflection and analysis between the research phases should be considered.

First research phase: exploration

In the initial phase, I visited both case study cities. In the case of Solo, access was straightforward, as strong ties to colleagues at local universities, Sebalas Maret University (Universitas Sebelas Maret, or UNS) in Solo and Gadjah Mada University (Universitas Gadjah Mada, or UGM) in Yogyakarta, and relevant stakeholders in the city's housing domain already existed due to previous research activities (cf. Obermayr 2013, 2017; Obermayr & Astuti 2016; Obermayr & Sandholz 2017). This was not the case in Surabaya. There, contacts had to be established from scratch.

At the same time, as the first research phase in Indonesia took place, the Working Group Development Studies and Sustainability Science of the Institute of Geography at the University of Innsbruck organised a field trip to Indonesia within the framework of the institute's master programme. In a three-week project entitled 'Creating Urban Resilience' (CURE), students from Austria and Indonesia co-investigated the coping strategies of communities against natural hazards and the success of resettlement projects in the cities of Yogyakarta and Solo (Höferl & Sandholz 2017). Partly matching my thematic focus (in Solo) the project presented the opportunity to profit from their activities (possibility of establishing contacts, expert interviews, and a household survey in the area of Ngemplak Sutan, where resettlements had taken place). By co-organising and joining the fieldwork during the group's week-long stay in Solo, I was able to obtain connections with new contacts and benefit from their data collection.

After completing the CURE project in Solo, snowball sampling was used to establish contacts to relevant stakeholders of Surabaya's housing sector. Once again, local universities in the city were my entry point. Due to the strong support of scholars from the State University of Surabaya (Universitas Negeri Surabaya, or UNESA) and the Sepuluh Nopember Institut of Technology (Institut Teknologi Sepuluh Nopember, or ITS), contacts to an increasing number of stakeholders in the housing sector outside the academic field (especially to municipal authorities, community-based organisations, or CBOs, and NGOs) were established. Many informal talks and discussions on my research plan provided me with first-hand information and advice that allowed me to adapt research activities to the local context.

In this initial phase of the fieldwork, I gained valuable insights and information. The activities within the CURE project, the informal discussions, observations during the field surveys, the collection of secondary data, and valuable advice from Indonesian scholars and professionals formed the basis for the subsequent research phases. In that way, it was possible to gain a first overview of the characteristics and spatial extent of marginal settlements within both cities, ongoing research activities on the topic as well as existing strategies and implemented measures of the urban authorities in the housing sector.

Second research phase: Solo

The second empirical research phase focused on the case of Solo. The goal was to gain a comprehensive overview on strategies in the housing sector, applied measures, and the characteristics of Solo's policy arrangement. Several methods were carried out: problem-centred expert interviews, influence network mapping, and a standardised expert survey. Altogether, 25 interviews were conducted with relevant actors in the housing domain, namely the involved municipal government agencies (12), the local university, UNS (4), one national government agency (1), a local NGO (1), and community representatives (5). Beside content-related questions, the Net-Map method (13) and a standardised expert survey (11) characterised the interviews. Those two methods aimed at the detection of ties and power relations among the actors.

Beside these methods, also observations, field surveys, and photo documentations were carried out in several areas of Solo. Together with local experts, and accompanied by UNS students helping with translations, different areas were visited, to get impressions about the implemented measures of the city authorities in the housing sector (ie social housing units, areas where 'slum-upgrading' initiatives were carried out, and areas where people where resettled from squatter settlements). Especial focus was placed on those areas where the municipal authorities had carried out resettlements. During these visits, the opportunity for informal talks and interviews with key people from the communities were used to gather information and data on the outcome of this type of housing intervention. The second research stay was also used to collect secondary literature. Spatial and development plans related to housing as well as relevant data on housing, slums, resettlement, and other information could be obtained from the interviewees and from the local university library.

Third research phase: Surabaya

The third empirical research phase focused on the city of Surabaya. All methods used in Solo were replicated in Surabaya in order to collect data and information on Surabaya's housing policies and its policy arrangement in a similar way. Altogether, 25 interviews were conducted in Surabaya, with officials of municipal (12) and provincial (2) agencies, academic scholars (2), community representatives (4), local NGOs (1), and residents in social housing units (4). In order to get information on ties and power relations in the housing domain during the interviews also the Net-Map method (9) and the standardised expert survey (11) was carried out wherever possible.

The collaboration with UNESA and ITS proved of particular value in Surabaya. Together with scholars and students from these two research institutions different areas of the city were visited. In one way or another, these areas were targeted by the city's housing policies or socio-economic improvement programmes (ie target areas of the Green and Clean Programme, the Economic Empowerment Programme, KIP, social housing units and slum and squatter areas along the coast line, river channels, and railroad tracks). Unsystematic observation, photo-documentation, and research diary notes documented the impressions from these field surveys.

For the assessment of the impacts of the city's housing policies, I decided to choose the city's social housing programme and relocation measures for a deeper analysis. In the case of the social housing programme, an area was chosen where three generations of social housing blocks had been realised: Penjaringan Sari I, II and III. This area was selected, as it best covers the evolution of the social housing programme over the last decades. In the case of the relocation measures, the riverbank communities at Kali Jagir were chosen for a deeper investigation. In that area previous research already existed and recent evictions testified to the urgency of the problem. In both areas, several interviews were conducted with residents.

12 Methods of Data Collection and Analysis

This chapter explains the main methods of data collection and analysis used in more detail. These are literature survey and systematic review, problem-centred expert interviews and thematic analysis, influence network mapping and social network analysis as well as a standardised expert survey. The procedure of data collection and analysis as well as limitations are outlined.

12.1 Literature survey and systematic review

A large amount of material was collected during the whole research project by an ongoing literature survey: academic literature, conference proceedings, reports produced by NGOs and international organisations, and newspaper reports. These materials contextualise the case studies; they provide the historical, socio-economic, and geographical background. In addition, during the field trips other materials were collected *in situ*: government-internal documents, such as unpublished reports on housing issues, spatial and development plans, programme-specific documents, regulations, maps and also quantitative data on demographics, the socio-economic situation and housing conditions in the two cities. All these information are secondary data, ie data collected by someone else and available for the researcher in textual, visual, or numerical form (Tyrrell 2016; Castree et al. 2013: 455).

Various civil servants generously provided much of the secondary data collected *in situ*. In this regard, the openness and helpfulness of Indonesian officials was remarkable. Another important source for secondary data were the libraries of the local universities (UGM, UNS, and ITS). Particularly, the library of the housing and settlement lab (Lab Perumahan dan Permukiman) at the faculty of architecture at ITS in Surabaya proved valuable. The collection there includes a treasure of research reports and official documents (regulations, spatial and development plans, etc) related to housing in Surabaya and Indonesia.

To analyse this material, several types of literature review were employed. Anne Sigismund Huff (2008: 147–178) distinguishes between *literature survey, critical review, systematic review*, and *supportive search*. While a formal literature survey is the starting point of research projects, delimitating the research domain, the critical review is a much more focused literature review of selected articles and books concerned with concepts and existing arguments. Systematic review of previous works addresses existing scholarly work as well as all kinds of documents from other sources (eg policy papers or government-internal reports). Supportive search is carried out at a later stage of the project when specific problems occur. All four types of literature review were conducted in this study, depending on the sources and the stage of the project. The results are a detailed description of the context of the two cases, achieving explanatory value by discovering the nature – the *Eigenlogik* (Berking & Löw 2008) – of the two cities.

12.2 Problem-centred expert interviews and thematic analysis

The main empirical data-collection method used in this study was the method of problem-centred expert interviews (Mattissek et al. 2013: 175–178; Flick 2016: 214–225). This method was chosen since experts have knowledge about the kind of housing policies and the procedures of implementing them as well as their own interpretations and perceptions of the housing challenge. Both are in the interest of this study. The latter is of particular relevance, since these interpretations and perceptions might structure the conditions of action for other actors. The method makes it possible to identify relevant governance procedures and to reconstruct experts' knowledge on housing issues. The findings are used to develop typologies and new theory (Flick 2016: 216). The interviews conducted were semi-structured. In contrast to structured interviews, where detailed scripts with questions are used, semi-structured interviews rely on a guide rather than a script. This type of interview leaves enough space for the interviewee to focus on issues he or she regards as particularly relevant (Longhurst 2016).

In the fieldwork phases, altogether 50 interviews were conducted, of which 25 took place in Solo and 25 in Surabaya. The interviewees were mostly government officials, working in different departments and at various administrative levels (national, province, city, *Kelurahan*, RT, and RW) of the respective city having a stake in the housing sector. Other interviewees were from civil society, namely from research institutions, NGOs, or residents from the community. The latter consisted of local leaders in regions affected by government intervention in the housing sector, individuals working for CBOs, or other persons involved in the city's housing policy.

The interviews were conducted in close cooperation with the local universities, UNS in Solo and UNESA and ITS in Surabaya. Scholars of these universities, in particular the departments of geography, architecture, and sociology, were the ideal starting point. They were not only prepared to share their knowledge on the housing situation in the respective cities, but assisted me also with the selection of suitable individuals to be interviewed. Another source to select relevant actors or agencies was the knowledge gained from the literature review. From that source important actors, especially non-governmental, could be identified and selected for an interview. Not least, by using a snowball system and asking for further suitable individuals or agencies during the interviews more and more contacts became available.

Each interview took at least one and up to three hours. Usually it took place at the interviewee's office, in the case of government officials, or sometimes also at the participant's home. All interviews were semi-structured and open, steered by a rough guideline of questions ordered by thematic fields, which had been prepared in advance. At the beginning of the research process, the interview guideline was more explorative and open, allowing also narrative passages. Later, with more accumulated knowledge on respective housing policies and involved agencies, the interview guide was adapted and became more focussed and problem-centred.

The interviews were conducted in English when possible, otherwise in Bahasa Indonesia. Since my language skills in Bahasa Indonesia reached only an intermediate level during my research stays – enough for daily interactions and simple conversations, but not sufficient for complex conversations – at least one translator was present during all interview appointments. In Solo, two students from the faculty of engineering at UNS and in Surabaya two students from the geography department of UNESA helped as translators. These four students were selected based on their study progress (post-graduate), their English skills, and existing experience with empirical social research. To ensure the best results, they were briefed ahead of each interview, during which the semi-structured interview guide was discussed. As experienced during previous research (Obermayr 2017) and the CURE project (cf. chapter 11), the translators' background in social sciences and experiences in empirical research proved to be of more importance for the successful application of problem-centred interviews than language skills. This experience was considered when selecting suitable translators.

During the research stay, the four students slowly became more than translators; they became research assistants. Since they accompanied me not only during the interview appointments, but also frequently during the field visits, they became quite involved in the research activities. Prior to and after the interviews, they were also ready for intensive discussions. Sharing impressions, comparing perceptions and gained knowledge as well as clarifying misunderstandings improved the results significantly. All interviews were documented using a smartphone for voice recording and taking notes in a research diary. In addition, the discussions afterwards were captured, noting content, structural settings (room, time, and individuals present) and additional information on each interviewee (affiliation, name) and subjective impressions. This postscript became later useful for analysis and interpretation (Flick 2016: 213).

Two other methods accompanied the problem-centred expert interviews: the influence network mapping and a short standardised questionnaire. Usually, each appointment started with the problem-centred interview; after approximately an hour, we proceeded to the Net-Map method, producing an ego-centred network map. Afterwards a short standardised questionnaire concluded each appointment. Both methods are explained in the following chapters (cf. chapter 12.3 and 12.5).

Applying those three methods during one appointment was time-intensive and experiences were mixed. Some interviewees disagreed with applying influence network mapping and/or the standardised survey due to limited time availability or for other reasons. Nevertheless, roughly 50 % of the participants endured all three methods, providing me sufficient information. Table 10 and table 9 list all interview partners including their function or occupation. All interviewed actors were categorised in several groups, assigned to one of three sectors – civil, private, or government – and to respective levels (international, national, province, city, or neighbourhood).

Table 9 Interviewed stakeholders and experts in Surabaya

No.	Date	Function or occupation	Group	Sector	Level
26	17.10.2014	lecturer at ITS	research Institution	civil	city
27	26.08.2015	employee of BAPPEKO	government agency	government	city
28	03.09.2015	employee of DCKTR	government agency	government	city
29	03.09.2015	employee of DCKTR	government agency	government	city
30	04.09.2015	employee of DPBT	government agency	government	city
31	07.09.2015	employee of DinSos	government agency	government	city
32	08.09.2015	employee of BAPERMAS	government agency	government	city
33	08.09.2015	employee of DPU	government agency	government	city
34	09.09.2015	employee of DinSos	government agency	government	city
35	01.10.2015	employee of DPU	government agency	government	province
36	05.10.2015	lecturer at ITS	research Institution	civil	city
37	07.10.2015	employee of DPU	government agency	government	province
38	08.10.2015	lecturer at ITS	research Institution	civil	city
39	09.10.2015	employee of BAPPEKO	government agency	government	city
40	10.10.2015	member of PWS	NGO	civil	neighbourhood
41	10.10.2015	resident of *kampung* Baru	individual	civil	neighbourhood
42	10.10.2015	resident *rusun* Penjaringan Sari II	individual	civil	neighbourhood
43	12.10.2015	employee of BAPPEKO	government agency	government	city
44	13.10.2015	RT in *kampung* Brateng	individual	civil	neighbourhood
45	13.10.2015	rusun Management Gunung Sari	professional	private	neighbourhood
46	05.01.2016	lecturer at DWCU	research Institution	civil	city
47	16.10.2015	Employee of BAPPEKO	government agency	government	city
48	20.10.2015	resident *rusun* Penjaringan Sari III	individual	civil	neighbourhood
49	20.10.2015	resident *rusun* Penjaringan Sari II	Individual	civil	neighbourhood
50	20.10.2015	resident *rusun* Penjaringan Sari II	Individual	civil	neighbourhood

Table 10 Interviewed stakeholders and experts in Solo

No.	Date	Function or occupation	Group	Sector	Level
1	24.09.2014	lecturer at UGM	research Institution	civil	city
2	28.09.2014	local RT, *Kel. Pucang Sawit*	individual	civil	neighbourhood
3	28.09.2014	local RT, *Kel. Sewu*	individual	civil	neighbourhood
4	28.09.2014	local RT, *Kel. Pucang Sawit*	individual	civil	neighbourhood
5	28.09.2014	local RT, *Kel. Pucang Sawit*	individual	civil	neighbourhood
6	29.09.2014	employee of BAPERMAS	government agency	government	city
7	29.09.2014	employee of BPN	government agency	government	national
8	29.09.2014	member of *Pokja Kel. Pucang Sawit*	CBO	civil	neighbourhood
9	30.09.2014	head of *Kel. Mojosongo*	government agency	government	neighbourhood
10	30.09.2014	head of *Kel. Pucang Sawit*	government agency	government	neighbourhood
11	01.10.2014	lecturer at UNS	research institution	civil	city
12	10.10.2014	lecturer at UNS	research institution	civil	city
13	02.04.2015	employee of DTRK	government agency	government	city
14	02.04.2015	employee of DTRK	government agency	government	city
15	05.04.2015	employee of BAPERMAS	government agency	government	city
16	07.04.2015	employee of BLUD	government agency	government	city
17	08.04.2015	employee of BAPPEDA	government agency	government	city
18	09.04.2015	employee of BPN	government agency	government	national
19	10.04.2015	employee of BAPPEDA	government agency	government	city
20	13.04.2015	consultant for PNPM	professional	private	city
21	15.04.2015	employee of DPU	government agency	government	city
22	15.04.2015	employee of DPU	government agency	government	city
23	15.04.2015	member of YKK	NGO	civil	city
24	17.04.2015	housing developer	developer	private	city
25	22.04.2015	lecturer at UNS	research institution	civil	city

The information gathered from the interviews included recorded audio files and notes taken in a field diary including the postscript. Notes were transferred to digital documents and subsequently tagged, categorised, and saved to a database for later usage. The recorded audio files were transcribed word-for-word utilising the software 'Listen N Write Free' in the language used during the interviews (Bahasa Indonesia or English). Then the transcripts were translated into English creating a text corpus of documents for further analysis.

In a next step, a thematic analysis was conducted as an approach to analyse discourses (Braun & Clarke 2006; Flick 2019: 474–482). Similar to qualitative content analysis (Mayring 2000, 2015), this method employs coding techniques (Cope & Kurtz 2016: 650) to search for themes and patterns in textual data, but was considered as more appropriate, since it allows greater detail and is more straightforward. The thematic analysis followed roughly the six steps outlined by Braun & Clarke (2006): 1) becoming familiar with the data, 2) creating initial codes, 3) combining codes to overreaching themes, 4) reviewing themes, 5) defining themes, 6) producing the report. In this study, the policy arrangement approach already provides initial codes for data classification (actors, rules, discourses, power, and applied policies). Therefore, in a first iteration, the data was classified according to these codes. In a second iteration, sub-codes were developed for each of these categories inductively from the data. This was applied for all categories, but found to be particularly useful for the category of discourses. In that case, codes were assigned to all explicit statements of interviewees ('semantic approach') on urban policies as well as the subtext, ie underlying assumptions of the interviewees ('latent approach') (Flick 2019: 475).

This second iteration resulted in a larger number of codes, which were in a third iteration generalised to overreaching themes within the category of discourses. This generalisation process was based on several patterns found in the transcripts (similarity of perceptions among actors and their frequency). The three iterations resulted in coding guidelines (cf. figure 12). Depending on the policy arrangement category, the findings of this thematic analysis were included in the social network analysis, in the description of rules of the game and applied policies (content), or directly presented and interpreted in the two chapters on discourses for each city (cf. chapter 25.2 for Surabaya and chapter 29.2 for Solo).

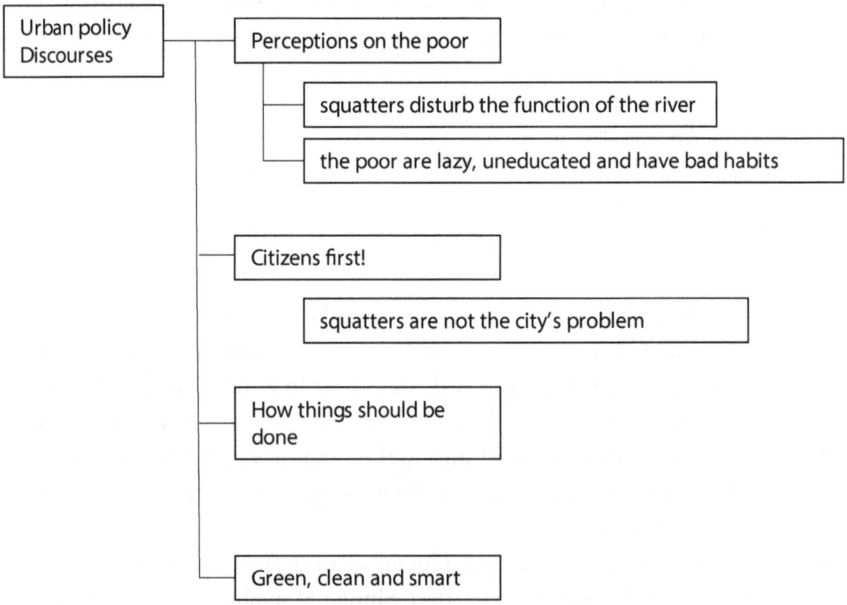

Fig. 12 Excerpt from the coding guide of expert interviews in Surabaya (category of discourses)
Source: Illustration by author

This method of data collection and the analysis method has some limitations. The first limitation is related to translations. During the expert interviews, undertone and context was sometimes lost in the translation. Although there were the word-for-word transcripts, there is an inevitable loss when translating them into English. In the case of interviews conducted in English, there were also some setbacks, since for the interviewees it was naturally more difficult to express themselves in a foreign language. The second limitation is related to the analysis method. Associating codes with phrases and paragraphs is always subjective and based on the habit and experiences of the researcher. To minimise these limitations intense informal discussions with research assistants and colleagues from the partner universities were carried out to clarify possible misunderstandings.

12.3 Influence network mapping: Net-Map

In order to analyse the policy arrangement dimensions of 'actors' and 'power' during the expert interviews, the Net-Map method developed by Eva Schiffer (2007; 2010) for influence network mapping was employed. This method produces ego-centred network maps, including perceived influence of actors that were subsequently analysed using a social network analysis. Besides data generation for social network analysis, the Net-Map method makes it possible to visualise and understand networks of actors that include power relations. Based on the literature review (Jansen 2006; Herz et al. 2015; Steinbrink 2013) the described approaches of network analysis and influence network mapping were customised, developing a unique procedure for the empirical application. The goal was to derive an overall influence network for the housing domains in both cities. The developed method identifies relevant actors, their linkages, and their influence in the housing domain during three steps:

1. Step (actors): the interviewee writes down names of all actors in a specific network;
2. Step (linkages): the interviewee draws lines between him- or herself (= *ego*) and these actors (= *alteri*), describing their relations;
3. Step (influence): the interviewee places 'power stones' on each actor to describe their influence.

For each Net-Map-interview an A3-sheet, coloured post-its, and power stones (in my case small Eiffel Towers) were prepared in advance. Three circles were already drawn on the A3-sheet around the centre, where the ego was to be placed. Each of the circles represents a category of interaction between the *ego* and *alteri* to be placed in one of the circles. Frequencies of interaction decrease with increasing distance from the centre (cf. figure 13).

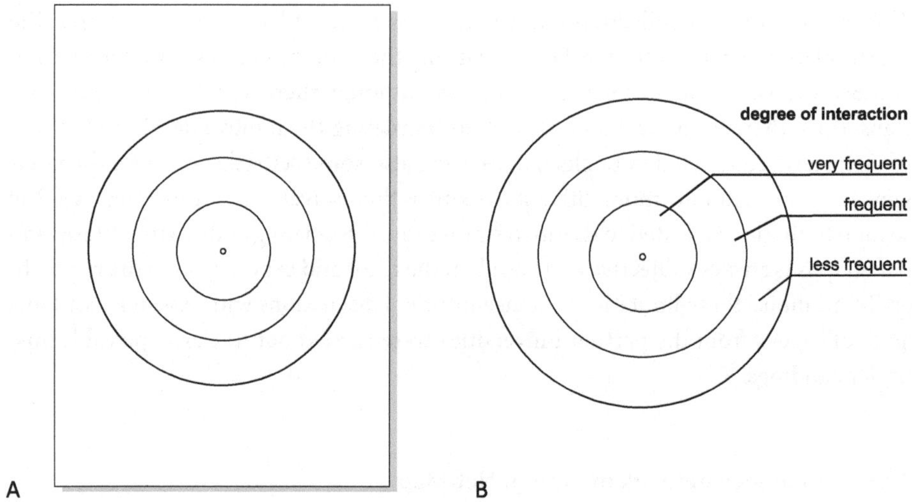

Fig. 13 The prepared 'map' used for the Net-Map method (A) and explanation of the circles (B)
Source: Illustration by author

After holding a pre-test of this Net-Map method with a lecturer at UNS in Solo, the method was slightly modified to mitigate some limitations. The method was included as a subsequent phase in each of the expert interviews. In the beginning, I showed the prepared materials to the interviewees and explained the method. None of the interviewees was familiar with the method and the explanation took some time. Overall, 22 ego-centred networks were created, thirteen in Solo and nine in Surabaya. Of the thirteen participants in Solo, nine were from various government agencies, two from the private and civil sector respectively. In Surabaya, in turn, eight of the nine Net-Map interviews were conducted with government officials and only one with a scientist from a local university. Table 11 and table 12 show the participating interviewees.

The Net-Map method started with the application of a name generator: The interviewees (= *ego*) were asked to write down the names of individuals, government agencies, and civil or private organisations (= *alteri*) which they consider as relevant for housing policies in the respective city (The exact question was 'What organisations, individuals or institutions do you consider as important for the city's housing policies?'). These names were written on post-its, and the interviewees were asked to stick them on the A3-sheet around the ego in the middle. It was explained that they should consider their organisation or themselves in the centre of the sheet and the three circles would represent three degrees of interaction with other actors. The inner circle would mean 'very frequent interaction', the second circle would mean 'frequent interaction', and the third circle would mean 'less frequent interaction'. Each post-it had to be placed in one of the corresponding circles. During this procedure often additional actors came to mind and were subsequently written down and placed on the network map.

When all post-its were assigned and no further names popped up, the participants were asked to describe the relations of their organisation with all *alteri*. The task was to specify the nature and direction of relation between actors. Three categories were provided to be drawn on the sheet by different colours: 'cooperation', 'information', and 'command'. An arrow indicated the direction, if possible. When all relations were drawn accordingly, interviewees had to perform the last step: the positioning of power stones. Ten power stones were provided for each network map and the rule was declared that one actor could hold a maximum number of three stones. This rule forced the interviewees to weight their choice carefully and to distribute their power stones more widely.

Table 11 Net-Map participants in Surabaya

No.	Date	Function/Occupation	Group	Category	Level
27	26.08.2015	employee of BAPPEKO	government agency	government	city
28	03.09.2015	employee of DCKTR	government agency	government	city
29	03.09.2015	employee of DCKTR	government agency	government	city
30	04.09.2015	employee of DPBT	government agency	government	city
33	08.09.2015	employee of DPU	government agency	government	city
34	09.09.2015	employee of DinSos	government agency	government	city
35	01.10.2015	employee of DPU	government agency	government	province
37	07.10.2015	employee of DPU	government agency	government	province
38	08.10.2015	lecturer at ITS	research Institution	civil	city

Table 12 Net-Map participants in Solo

No.	Date	Function or occupation	Group	Category	Level
13	02.04.2015	employee of DTRK	government agency	government	city
14	02.04.2015	employee of DTRK	government agency	government	city
15	05.04.2015	employee of BAPERMAS	government agency	government	city
16	07.04.2015	employee of BLUD-GLH	government agency	government	city
17	08.04.2015	employee of BAPPEDA	government agency	government	city
18	09.04.2015	employee of BPN	government agency	government	national
19	10.04.2015	employee of BAPPEDA	government agency	government	city
20	13.04.2015	consultant for PNPM	professional	private	city
21	15.04.2015	employee of DPU	government agency	government	city
22	15.04.2015	employee of DPU	government agency	government	city
23	15.04.2015	member of YKK	NGO	civil	city
24	17.04.2015	developer	developer	private	city
25	22.04.2015	lecturer at UNS	research institution	civil	city

The Net-Map method worked well with most participants, relaxing the atmosphere of the interview situation in many cases. The results provided a good basis to become an overview of actor constellations and their power relations in each city. Besides the generated data, the method was also useful to find other actors for the next interviews. The ego-centred network maps were documented by taking photos (cf. figure 14). The method also has some limitations. Much depends on the interviewee – whether he or she is willing and open-minded to proceed with such an uncommon method. Some interviewees rejected right away, stating that they do not have sufficient knowledge about the housing sector or judging the method as pointless. With others, it became clear during the first phase of the interview that the interviewee would not be suitable for the Net-Map method (lacking knowledge or dismissive attitude). In such cases, I decided to skip the method and proceed to the standardised expert survey immediately (cf. chapter 12.5).

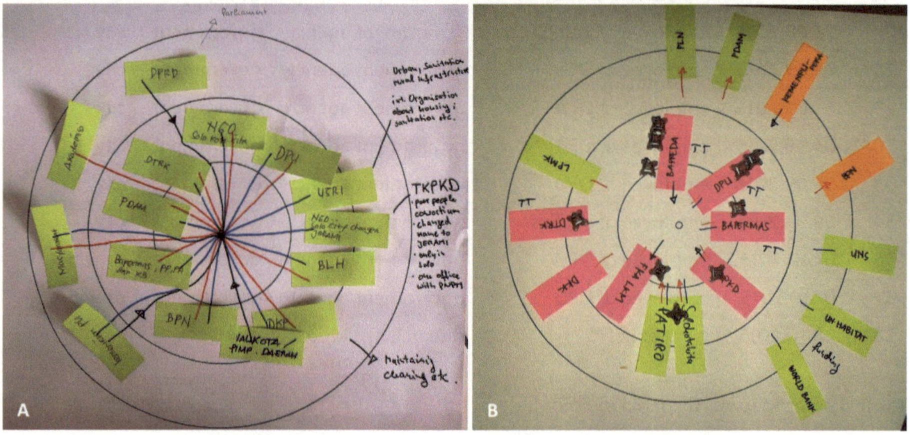

Fig. 14 Resulting ego-centred network maps: *ego*, *alteri*, and relations (A), with power stones (B)
Photos: Christian Obermayr, 2015

Naturally, the resulting network maps are more or less comprehensive and detailed. It depends largely on the interviewees' time schedule, their understanding of the method, and their willingness to participate. No pattern related to status, level of education, or affiliation could be identified – even though there was a slight tendency considering the person's position (individuals holding higher positions showed less willingness to spend much time with this method). The coloured post-its were not as useful as expected. It was intended to use the colours for a categorisation of the named *alteri* right away (ie colour x for NGOs; colour y for government agency etc). In practice, most participants did not use the colours for various reasons (for some it was too confusing; for others the categorisation of some institutions was not clear etc).

Another issue was the correct understanding of several terms used. It was necessary to discuss these terms in nearly all interviews to reach a common understanding. Instead of 'power' the term 'influence' was used, seen as less negatively connoted.

Nevertheless, 'influence' was also often misinterpreted as 'command power' and not as the ability to shape (applied) housing policies. Similar to that, the predefined actor relation categories 'funding', 'cooperation', 'information' and 'command' were also subject to various misunderstandings. While the problem with 'influence' could be solved by clarifying the definition of the term, the actor relation categories were in most interviews subject to discussion and did not work very well. In some cases, they were abandoned in favour of a more open discussion on exchange relations and their directions, which proved more valuable. In other cases, they worked well and gave additional qualitative information.

12.4 Social network analysis

In order to analyse the policy arrangement dimensions of 'actors' and 'power', a social network analysis is employed investigating common influence networks of the housing domain in each city. Developed as a stand-alone theoretical and methodological perspective during the 1960s (Jansen 2006: 37; Serdült 2002: 128), social network analysis is today increasingly used for the analysis of social networks in different disciplines, also in geography (Kratzer & Ammering 2019; Steinbrink 2013). Social networks can be defined as a set of actors (individuals and organisations) that are linked by different relationships (eg command, funding, information exchange, collaboration, friendship) (Newman 2010). Since actors are embedded in such a structure, it is the social network which determines significantly their capacity to act (eg their ability to influence political processes) (Jansen 2006: 17–18). Thus, it is of interest to develop common influence networks stacking together ego-centred network maps and use social network analysis for analysis (Schiffer & Hauck 2010: 239).

Social network analysis is a quantitative method for the analysis of relational data of an overall network (Steinbrink 2013: 15), which consists of social actors (*nodes*) and their relations (*edges*) within a predefined boundary (Serdült 2002: 128). The method is based on graph theory and allows the calculation and visualisation of statistics of the network. Thereby the overall structure of the network as well as relational attributes of embedded actors (eg their position) can be analysed.

In this study, several metrics calculated by social network analysis are of particular interest. Some consider the overall network structure, eg the number of actors involved or density of the network. Others are related to power and influence of actors. For the latter, the analysis offers a number of centrality indicators that allow drawing conclusions on actors' *dispositional power*, as one of the resources defining the capacity of actors to act (on the power concept underlying this analysis cf. chapter 7.4.3). Commonly the indicators *degree centrality*, *closeness centrality*, and *betweenness centrality*, developed by Freeman (1978), are used to determine the importance of actors in social networks (Steinbrink 2013: 45). *Degree centrality* measures the number of relations an actor has to other actors. Actors with a high degree centrality function as a hub in the network, indicating high communication *activity* and importance for the diffusion of information. Betweenness centrality measures the extent to which a specific actor must be passed to reach other parts of the network. Actors with high betweenness centrality function as gatekeepers since they can *control* communication (they can decide whether information can pass or not). Closeness centrality considers the distance of an actor to all other actors in a social network. This is an indicator for *efficiency* or independence from other actors (Jansen 2006: 132–137).

For the analysis several steps were performed:

- Delimitation of the network
- Data preparation and actor categorisation
- Calculation of statistics
- Analysis of overall network structure actors' attributes
- Interpretation and illustration

In a network analysis, the first step is to specify the boundary of the social network under investigation. Who is part of the network and who is not? This delimitation was done according to the snowball system used for the empirical methods of data collection. All actors were included that resulted from the Net-Map method or were mentioned during the expert interviews and the informal discussions. In addition, actors predefined by document analysis for the standardised expert interviews (cf. chapter 12.5) as well as actors mentioned additionally during this method were included.

The second step is data preparation and actor categorisation. The ego-centred networks received from the Net-Map method were translated into MS Excel tables to be imported in the network analysis software Gephi. The actors and relations of all 22 network maps were imported, resulting in tables with 137 nodes (72 in Solo and 65 in Surabaya) and 345 edges (193 in Solo and 152 in Surabaya). For every node (actor), the following six indicators were included: (1) a unique ID, (2) level, (3) actor type, (4) the sum of denomination, (5) the sum of power stones assigned and (6) the indicator 'influence'. Influence was calculated by summing up the overall number of denominations and power stones assigned for each individual actor. Values for the administrative level were generated considering the level where most activities of a respective actor are carried out. The following values were assigned: international, national, province, city, and neighbourhood. The category 'neighbourhood' was assigned to all actors below the city level, including for instance individuals, *kelurahan* authorities as well as CBOs that are not explicitly active on the city scale.

Actor categorisation by type proved to be more difficult than expected, but since it was required for the network analysis, it was decided to develop a generalised categorisation in four classes: government, civil, private and international organisation. Each of these classes consists of several sub-classes (cf. figure 15). Government agencies (eg Kementerian, Dinas, Kelurahan), state-owned companies (eg Perumnas, PLN) and government institutions (ie all representative bodies of the people: LPMK, Mayor, DPRD, APEKSI, etc) as well as mentioned government programmes[1] were subsumed in the category of 'government'. Under the category of 'international organisations' multilateral organisations (eg World Bank, UN, ADB) and development cooperation organisations (GIZ, USAID, etc) were subsumed. The category of 'private' consists of private companies (eg construction companies), banks, developers (investors), associations (eg advocacy groups), and professionals (eg consultants, notaries, programme facilitators). In the fourth category, 'civil society', research institutions (universities and other research institutions), NGOs (eg UPC, ACHR), CBOs (eg BKM, Pokja), individuals, and the community[2] were included.

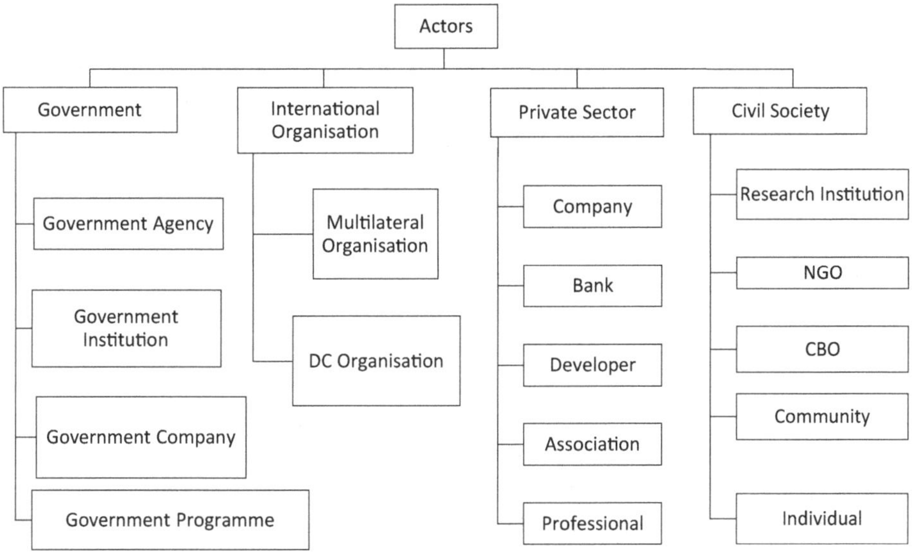

Fig. 15 Actor categorisation used for the social network analysis
Source: Illustration by author

A similar procedure was used for the tables containing the relations (edges) between the actors (nodes). This table consists of four columns with the indicators 'source', 'target', 'ID' and 'intensity'. Source and target define two nodes that are connected by an individual edge, ID is a unique ID assigned to each edge and intensity is the frequency of interaction, as assed by the interviewees (values min. 1 to max. 3). In cases when there were different assessments of the same actor relation by two different interviewees, the mean was assigned (integer number) or the higher value was chosen. This procedure of data preparation resulted in four tables: edges and nodes for each city

1 Sometimes government programmes were mentioned as actors. Usually the interviewees meant the working group established around a specific programme.
2 The 'community' was frequently mentioned as an actor by the interviewees.

(cf. table 13 and table 14). Since the network was perceived as rather small, information collected from the other methods (actors and linkages) were also included into the tables. For all nodes and edges added from these additional sources, the indicators 'influence' for nodes and 'intensity' for edges were set to 1 (the lowest value).

After successful data preparation and software import, the actual analysis was performed. The data was explored and statistics for the overall network and the centrality indicators were calculated (betweenness centrality, closeness centrality, and degree centrality). The analyses showed that both perceived influence indicators gained directly from the interviewees as well as centrality indicators calculated from the network graph reveal interesting aspects of the networks. In fact, the two types of indicators complement each other very well. By triangulating those indicators, new insights into the influence networks of the housing domain in the two cities could be gained. The networks were subsequently illustrated and interpreted by stressing different characteristics of the network and attributes of actors. The results are presented in the respective chapter for each city (cf. chapters 25.1 for Surabaya and 29.1 for Solo).

The employed analysis method has some limitations. The data collection method for social network analysis is decisive for the quality and size of the resulting networks. The Net-Map method produced several ego-centred maps, but due to a limited number of participants, the number of actors and relations collected was considered too low. Furthermore, these maps included already a bias resulting on the one hand from the selection of participants (most participants were government officials) and on the other from the design of the method (the ego in ego-centred maps inevitably has a high degree centrality). Due to these limitations, it was deliberately decided to include actors and relations from other sources (expert interviews and the expert survey) to increase the size of the network. The question must be raised as to whether this approach manipulates the collected data and in turn the results of the quantitative analysis too much or if it is a necessary step to make the results of social network analysis meaningful at all. For further studies using the data collection method of Net-Map or similar methods producing ego-centred network maps, it should be considered to ask the interviewee to draw relations between all actors in the network as well, instead of only between *ego* and *alteri*.

Table 13 Excerpt from the nodes table of Surabaya

ID	Name	Type	Level	Sum denomination	Sum power	Influence
11	BAPPEKO	government	city	7	16	23
22	KPUPR	government	national	3	9	12
2	DPU-CK	government	city	4	7	11
				(...)		

Note: Each node has seven indicators. 'Sum of denomination' indicates the number of times an actor was named in all Net-Map interviews. 'Sum power' indicates the summed value of all power stones assigned to this actor. 'Influence' is the sum of denominations and power.

Table 14 Excerpt from the edges table of Surabaya

ID	Source	Target	Intensity
1	11	5	3
2	11	6	2
3	11	7	2
	(...)		

Note: Each of the edges has four indicators. Source and target values are the IDs of nodes that are connected by the respective edge. Intensity is a value for frequency of interaction (min = 1, max = 3).

12.5 Standardised expert survey

A standardised expert survey was carried out as a backup for the Net-Map method and as a means of eliminating some of the limitations by methodological triangulation. It was not clear whether the Net-Map method developed would work well, due to its experimental and time-consuming characteristics. Furthermore, it was of particular interest how the interviewees would rate the influence of actors identified from literature review. For that reason, it was decided to develop a network questionnaire to supplement in an ideal case the ego-centred network analysis performed previously. The questionnaire contained only one question – 'In your opinion, how big is the influence of the following organisations on Solo's (Surabaya's) housing policy?' – and represented simultaneously the end of all interviews carried out. The question aimed at a simple assessment (on a scale between 1 = lowest influence to 4 = highest influence; 5 = unknown) of predefined government agencies and other organisations of global, national, or local scale. An option to add additional organisations was provided. The questionnaire was pretested during the first interviews in both cities and minimal adjustments were made (some actors were eliminated since they did not exist anymore or were considered as not relevant).

Not all of the 50 interviewed persons agreed to fill in the questionnaire, mainly due to the already long-lasting interview duration. However, there were 23 respondents, 12 for Solo and 11 for Surabaya. While the interviewees were filling out the questionnaire, which took only five to ten minutes, the researcher was present to answer any questions, without trying to influence the results. Table 15 and table 16 list all respondents, their occupancy, and affiliation.

The data collected were subsequently analysed using MS Excel. For each city, a table was developed listing all predefined actors from the questionnaire and those actors added by the interviewees (rows) as well as the numeric answers in separate columns. Three additional columns were added: level, sector1, and sector2, assigning values from the actor categorisation (cf. chapter 12.4). Two values were calculated for each actor: mean influence (I) and sum of denominations (D). Both values, the interviewees' assessment of influence, but also recognition of specific actors, were seen as important indicators for the actors' 'actual influence' (AI). Therefore, both values were combined by multiplying the mean influence and the proportional count of mentions (ie proportional count of mentions excluding those organisations not known by the interviewee). In that way the values for actual influence were calculated for each actor.

D = sum of denominations   N = number of respondents (= maximum of denominations)

I = mean influence   AI = actual influence

$$AI = \mathrm{I} \times \frac{D\,(\times 3)}{N}$$

In cases where additional items (additional organisations) were mentioned by the interviewees, the sum of denominations (D) was multiplied by the factor 3 (bold in formula). This was done since an explicit mentioning of an additional actor was regarded as of significance and to be weighted appropriately. An actor mentioned only by one interviewee, for instance, became a denomination value of three instead of one. The result is a table ranking actors in Surabaya and Solo according to their influence in the housing sector. This table was a useful supplement to verify and compare with the results from social network analysis. Related rankings are presented in table 32 for Surabaya and table 38 for Solo. The method of course has its limitations. The number of interviewees is too low, limiting data reliability. Most of the actors were predefined, and the interviewees added few additional actors (Surabaya: eight additional actors, Solo: 13 additional actors). These additional actors were included in the social network analysis. Overall, the standardised expert survey was valuable for crosschecking and broadening the results achieved from the Net-Map method.

Table 15 Survey respondents in Surabaya

No.	Date	Function or occupation	Group	Sector	Level
27	26.08.2015	employee of BAPPEKO	government agency	government	city
28	03.09.2015	employee of DCKTR	government agency	government	city
29	03.09.2015	employee of DCKTR	government agency	government	city
30	04.09.2015	employee of DPBT	government agency	government	city
32	08.09.2015	employee of BAPERMAS	government agency	government	city
33	08.09.2015	employee of DPU	government agency	government	city
34	09.09.2015	employee of DinSos	government agency	government	city
35	01.10.2015	employee of DPU	government agency	government	province
37	07.10.2015	employee of DPU	government agency	government	province
38	08.10.2015	lecturer at ITS	research Institution	civil	city
43	12.10.2015	employee of BAPPEKO	government agency	government	city

Table 16 Survey respondents in Solo

No.	Date	Function or occupation	Group	Sector	Level
13	02.04.2015	employee of DTRK	government agency	government	city
14	02.04.2015	employee of DTRK	government agency	government	city
15	05.04.2015	employee of BAPERMAS	government agency	government	city
16	07.04.2015	employee of BLUD	government agency	government	city
17	08.04.2015	employee of BAPPEDA	government agency	government	city
18	09.04.2015	employee of BPN	government agency	government	national
19	10.04.2015	employee of BAPPEDA	government agency	government	city
20	13.04.2015	consultant for PNPM	professional	private	city
22	15.04.2015	employee of DPU	government agency	government	city
23	15.04.2015	member of YKK	NGO	civil	city
24	17.04.2015	developer	developer	private	city
25	22.04.2015	lecturer at UNS	research institution	civil	city

III. HOUSING – A GLOBAL PERSPECTIVE

Housing issues are a globally discussed topic and the agenda setting of international organisations significantly shape the global housing discourse. The ever-changing hegemonic strands of this global discourse take effect on national and even at local scales. National housing programmes orient at this international debate and influence in turn the cities' housing policies as well as concrete measures taken on the ground. In other words, if and how a certain strategy of housing the poor (eg social housing) is applied, and at what scale, is determined not least by the international discourse. For that reason, it is essential to explore global housing policies and intervention strategies for the poor to identify changing phases and guiding principles.

This chapter thus takes a global perspective on the state of housing in our cities and associated housing policies. After identifying the latest trends in urban development and slum settlements, the global conferences and milestones on human settlements are analysed, extracting dominant strands and paradigms shaping the international discussion on housing. Based on this review the historic development of intervention strategies – their success and failure – is assessed revealing their impact on specific modes of housing provision in the Global South. The chapter concludes that sound housing policies must take on multiple forms, contextualised to local circumstances and adopting a variety of approaches to have positive effects for the goal of achieving adequate and affordable housing for all. The following questions guide this chapter:

Which intervention strategies are globally discussed to address the housing challenge?
- What is the housing situation on a global level?
- What paradigms shape(d) the discourse on housing the poor?
- Which strategies were applied to what effect?

13 The Urban Age – an Urban Crisis?

Urbanisation is the dominant process of the 21st century. Vast parts of the world are transforming in demographic, spatial, and socio-economic terms. Urban landscapes, new urban corridors, and metropolitan regions cover increasingly the Earth's surface. As Lefebvre predicted (1970 [2003]), the *tissue urbain* is spreading across all continents, encompassing the physical-material world and gradually eliminating the urban-rural dichotomy (Bähr 2005; Fassmann 2004: 49–50). In social terms, the urban way of life has become hegemonic, also intruding in areas where urban fabrics are still rare. This development is driven by population growth, migration patterns, and socio-economic transformations. Cities have become the preferred space to live for the majority of humanity, their attractiveness rooted in their centrality: the availability of socio-cultural infrastructures (education and healthcare facilities) and economic opportunities. In the Global South, people move to the cities pulled by the dream to find a better life, but also pushed by diminishing livelihood conditions in the peripheries, caused by the penetration of globalisation and modernisation into the rural realm (eg mechanisation of agricultural activities). In these regions, urbanisation is happening often without a simultaneous extension of urban economies, resulting in sprawling informal settlements, characterised by inadequate housing conditions and poverty. Some authors refer to this process also as the urbanisation of poverty (Davis 2006: 208–215).

Acknowledging this development, the United Nations have proclaimed the entrance of humanity into a so-called *urban age*. Since 2008, more than half of the world's population is living in cities and this trend is likely to continue for the next decades. In 2018, the UN estimated that 4.2 billion people lived in urban areas and only 3.4 billion in rural areas, reaching a global urbanisation degree of 55.3 % (UN-DESA 2018b). Average annual growth rates of urban population are slowly declining (1.9 % in the period 2015–2020), but in absolute numbers, urban population growth continues, expanding from 4.38 billion in 2020 to 5.94 billion in 2040. These figures imply the necessity to accommodate in our cities approximately 1.6 billion people over the next two decades (ibid.). Urbanisation degrees are distributed unevenly, countries in the Global North usually showing a higher proportion of their residents living in cities compared to countries of the Global South (Bähr 2005: 35–38). It is the latter, however, where most of the actual urban growth is taking place. Figure 16 illustrates absolute numbers of population growth and shares of urban and rural areas at the global level for several periods since 1990s.

Two observations are of high significance: first, total population growth seems to approach its zenith sometime during the period 2015–2020 with an annual increase of approximately 80 million people. Second, nearly all of this growth is happening in urban areas. Shortly after 2020, rural population will reach its maximum and is even expected to decline from then on. Population increase in urban areas is expected to stagnate, though at high levels, and more than 90 % of urban growth will be happening in cities of the Global South. This current wave of urbanisation is unprecedented in human history, even outpacing urbanisation during industrialisation in European cities (Bähr 2005: 40–43). Although the population data have to be interpreted with care[1], they show that urbanisation is an ongoing process for the next decades, having massive consequences for cities, predominantly the urban centres located in Africa and Asia.

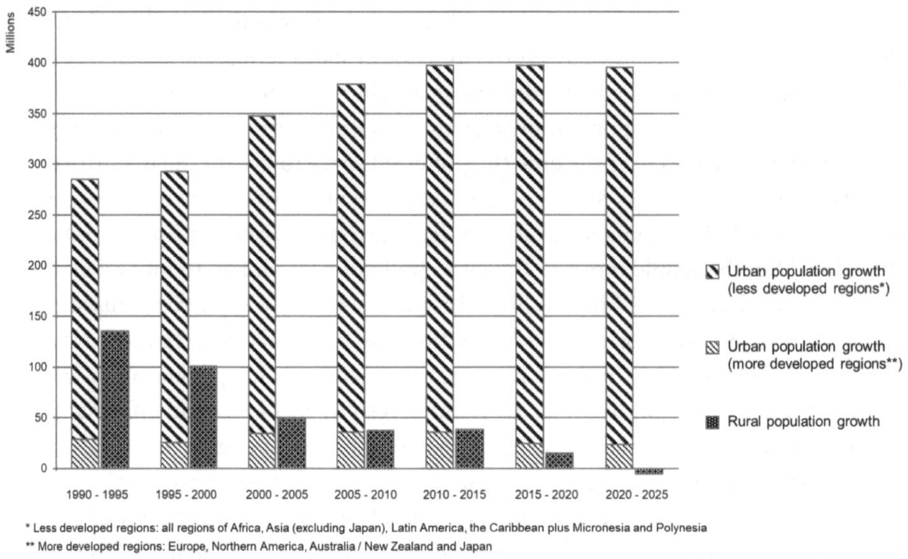

Fig. 16 The world's population growth in rural and urban areas 1990 to 2025
Source: Illustration by author. Data adopted from UN-DESA (2018b)

Coping with this development is one of the most severe challenges for cities in developing countries. Pressure is put on all dimensions of urban development: Adequate

1 Definitions of urban and rural regions vary across regions and countries and the increased blurring of urban boundaries makes it difficult to differentiate. For statistical purposes, abstractions and reductions are made, which are reflected in the resulting data presented here. These factors must be kept in mind when interpreting population data at all scales (Scholz 2006: 38).

infrastructure for the provision of public services, such as water, electricity, and sanitation, is needed as well as adequate transport systems, housing, and employment. Public administrations often lack the capacity and are in most cases overstrained. In the search for shelter and without support, migrants move to slum and squatter settlements to construct their own houses incrementally. These settlements are densifying and new informal settlements are sprawling rapidly, encompassing all available land in the cities or in their peripheries, no matter whether they are located in hazardous areas, and without paying attention to existing property rights. It is estimated that approximately half of the total urban population in developing countries is living in marginal settlements (a catch-all term for settlements with inadequate housing conditions), where inadequate housing standards and insufficient or lacking services are the standard condition.

As a visible expression of poverty, these marginal settlements have become the most striking characteristic of many contemporary cities. It was not until the adoption of the Millennium Development Goals (MDGs) in 2000 that the United Nations attempted to count the world's slum dwellers for the first time. In a first assessment for the year 2001, it was estimated that 921 million people lived in slums (UN-Habitat 2003a). In the follow-up flagship reports on the state of world cities this number was reduced to 700 to 800 million for the same year (UN-Habitat 2008c, 2013, 2016). This variety in data exemplifies the difficulties of finding clear definitions of 'slums' and consistent methods of calculation. It also raises doubts on the value of global slum targets, as for instance the target articulated in the MDGs 'to achieve, by 2020, a significant improvement in the lives of at least 100 million slum dwellers' (MDG target 7.D). In 2015, the United Nations reported that this target has been easily achieved, having raised more than 300 million out of inadequate housing conditions (UN 2015b: 60). It is not only these numbers that have to be questioned, but also their interpretation. Most improvements are reported for India, China, Indonesia, Turkey, and Vietnam (ibid.), but it remains unclear whether this achievement can be attributed to the implementation of appropriate policies, strategies, and measures on the ground or more simply to rapid economic growth. In addition, the logics behind such statements must be taken into account, since UN-Habitat and all national governments reporting on slum conditions in their countries have a clear interest in justifying their own existence by proving their success.

The latest numbers of those living in inadequate housing conditions is presented in figure 17 for the MDG regions[2]. In the year 2014, this figure shows that most of the global slum dwellers live in Eastern Asia (253 million), Sub-Saharan Africa (201 million), and Southern Asia (191 million). For all MDG regions, except Northern Africa,

---

2 Millennium Development Goals Regions (MDG-regions) are a country classification developed by the UN statistic division.

the data presented here show a stagnating or increasing tendency considering the period of 1990 until 2014. The challenge of slums is most serious in Sub-Saharan Africa, where the number of slum dwellers doubled from 1990 to 2014. These data raise the question of whether we are in the middle of a global housing crisis, considering that roughly 900 million people (2014) are living in conditions that are considered uninhabitable. Of course, the data might be interpreted differently when looking at proportions of slum dwellers as compared to the growing urban population. UN-Habitat and reporting countries follow this interpretation, highlighting their success. From that perspective, the proportions of urban population living in slums has come down from 46.2 % in 1990 to 29.7 % in 2014, a trend presented for all regions.

What remains from these statistical data are two stories that can be told. One would acknowledge the success of measures to improve slum conditions in the world's cities and would report widespread success in slum alleviation. The other story explains that absolute numbers of slum dwellers are on the rise, pointing at increasing poverty and inequality. A serious urban crisis is unfolding on a world scale that needs urgent attention.

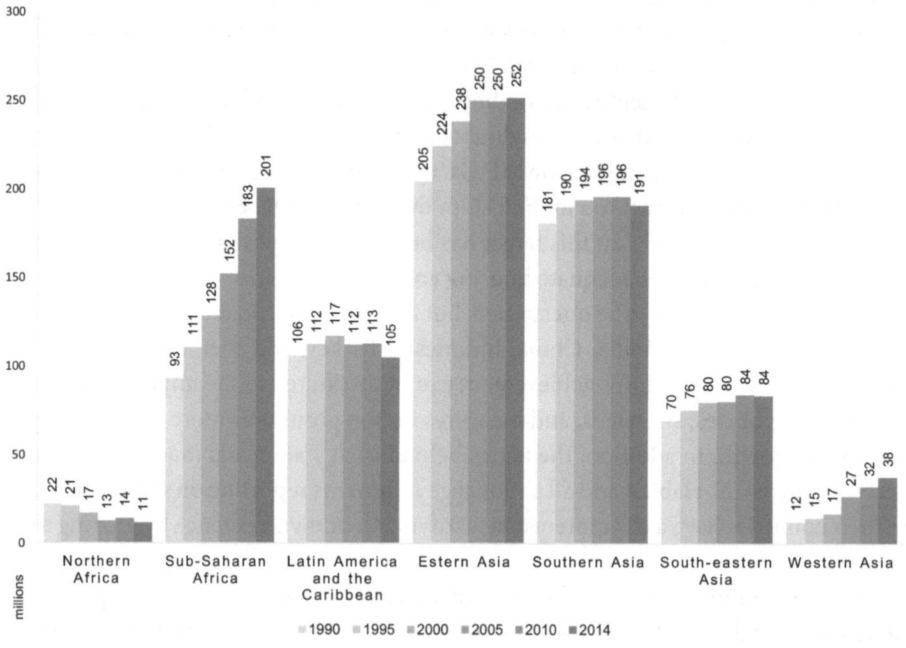

Fig. 17 Urban slum population by region
Source: Illustration by author. Data adopted from UN-Habitat (2016: 203)

14 Conferences and Milestones

During the 20th century, the consequences of rapid urbanisation were recognised as one of the most important challenges for human development. After a phase of neglecting or ignoring the challenge after World War II, the housing question became an internationally discussed topic in the 1960s. Major milestones since that time are illustrated in figure 18. The World Bank began to set up programmes in the late 1960s and the United Nations convened the first global conference on human settlements in 1976 (Habitat I). Since that time, the so-called Habitat conferences are held in 20-year intervals (Habitat II and Habitat III) in order to discuss the latest urbanisation trends, exchange experiences, formulate recommendations, and adopt declarations to steer this development. The two major organisations involved in global housing advocacy – the World Bank and the Human Settlement Programme (UN-Habitat) – have worked on several flagship reports where they lay out their recommendations. Two of these reports are worth mentioning: the World Bank's 1993 report entitled *Enabling Markets to Work*, which introduced a new era for dealing with slums and housing issues, and UN-Habitat's 2003 report *The Challenge of Slums*, which represents the first global assessment of the complex challenge of marginal settlements. The goal to create cities

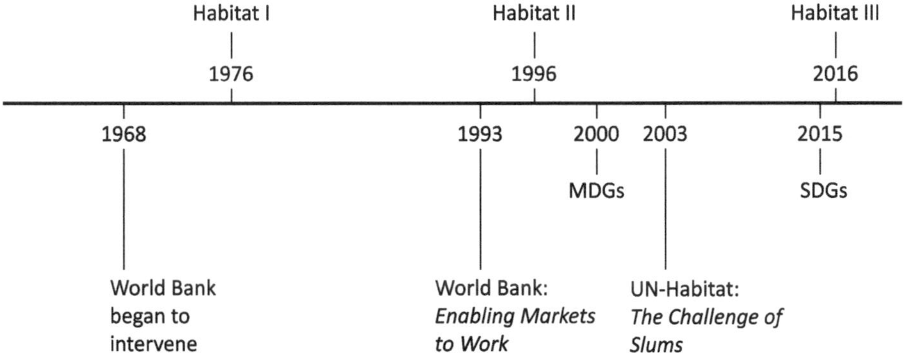

Fig. 18 Conferences and milestones in the global housing discourse
Source: Illustration by author

without slums and a more sustainable urban development found entry in the MDGs and the SDGs, where cities have become increasingly recognised as important places where the future of humanity will be decided.

This chapter addresses these conferences and milestones and illustrates central results with a specific focus on the housing question and the challenge of slums (cf. chapters 14.1–14.3). Two subsequent analytic sections address the changing actor constellations that have shaped the global discussion and outcome documents of the Habitat conferences (cf. chapter 14.4). By juxtaposing the results, several fields of discussion and changing priorities in advocacy on housing policies are revealed (cf. chapter 14.5).

14.1 Conferences on human settlements – Habitat I and Habitat II

Facing the unacceptable qualities of life in urban settlements, the United Nations called for a global conference on human settlements in 1976, known as Habitat I. For the first time in a UN conference, preparatory meetings were held with the aim of also including the perspectives of non-governmental groups and housing experts (Oestereich 1996: 57). Outcomes of the conference were a raised awareness among governments of the need to address insufficient settlement conditions globally. Commitments were made to establish ministries and agencies responsible for urban development and spatial planning (Cohen 2015: 3) and to recognise that qualities of life in cities need to be improved, focusing on the satisfaction of basic needs (UN-Habitat 1976: 4). It was agreed upon to establish civil society organisations focusing on urban issues (Cohen 2015: 3) and to form new UN bodies such as the United Nations Centre for Human Settlements (UNCHS) and the United Nations Commission on Human Settlements. Later, in 2002, these two bodies merged into the United Nations Human Settlement Programme, known as UN-Habitat[3] (Cohen 2015; WBGU 2016a: 117).

In the central outcome document, the so-called Vancouver Declaration, the international community committed itself to improving the quality of life in human settlements as their central goal (UN-Habitat 1976). Different strategies and principles to reach this goal were outlined: International cooperation, better national and international funding, more efficient spatial planning tailored to local circumstances, non-discrimination of disadvantaged groups, and broad participation of residents in

3 The United Nations Centre for Human Settlements and the United Nations Commission on Human Settlements were merged after the Habitat II conference and the adoption of the Millennium Development Goals in 2002. The two UN bodies were strengthened into a fully-fledged UN programme, the United Nations Human Settlement Programme, or UN-Habitat (UNGA 2002). The duties of UN Habitat are the design of settlement policies and technical assistance. Originally founded to address all aspects of human settlements, the agency is today mostly concerned with the creation of policies for sustainable urban development (WBGU 2016a: 117).

the planning and construction process. Even though inherent to the document, no explicit focus on slums or slum upgrading as strategy were made (Jehle 2017: 42).

In the two decades after the Habitat I conference, the challenge of housing had not disappeared, but had reached crisis proportions. Intensifying urbanisation processes and increased economic globalisation had resulted in increased marginalisation and exclusion tendencies in urban areas. In 1996, the second United Nations Conference on Human Settlements took place in Istanbul, known as Habitat II. This conference was more ambitious than Habitat I, since framework conditions had changed[4]. The topics of sustainability, a universal right to adequate housing (cf. chapter 6.5), and the principle of subsidiarity had been increasingly discussed on the international level. NGOs had become more important, having appeared as a symptom of the failure of many political systems to deliver basic services (Oestereich 1996: 59–60). A two-year-long preparation process, giving room for networking activities and sharing of experiences, preluded the conference. Its open design allowed the participation of a wide array of actors (Burgess 1996). Not only national representatives from 171 governments joined the event, but also participants from local governments, NGOs, and community groups (Bähr & Mertins 2000). The central foci were a reaffirmation of the goal of *adequate shelter for all* and the new goal of *sustainable human settlement development.*

The key outcome of Habitat II was a comprehensive document, known as the Habitat Agenda. This global action plan contains over 100 commitments and 600 recommendations for national and local governments. Key commitments were to improve cooperation and participation of all actors in planning and decision-making processes, including local governments and community representatives, to foster international cooperation in sharing knowledge and experiences, to allocate adequate financial means, and to implement a system for monitoring progress towards the two goals of the Habitat Agenda (UN-Habitat 1996). Governments were seen as key to achieving the goals by implementing national action plans and adopting the principles of 'good governance', setting up capacities to create an environment that enables all relevant actors to play an effective role for the development of housing and sustainable cities.

Termed as a 'turning point' in settlement policies by UN-Habitat, the increasing belief is expressed that solutions are reachable. In retrospect, however, scholars from dif-

---

4 The focus on 'sustainable human settlement development' can be attributed to the context in which Habitat II took place. In the early 1990s, a series of other global conferences were held (eg the United Nations Conference on Environment and Development, 1992), addressing global threats to the environment (loss of biodiversity, climate change). Facing these challenges, sustainable development was agreed upon as the key priority for human development in the 21st century. Another contextual point for Habitat II was the end of the cold war confrontation in 1989. The west had triumphed and state-led economies had failed. The 1990s were thus characterised by a belief in multilateral solutions for global challenges and a reduced role of the state for efficient policies. These beliefs were in large part influenced by the Washington Consensus and are reflected in the global conferences of the 1990s and the guiding principles of less state involvement and enabling policies were seen as decisive for the solution of the housing question (Cohen 2015: 5).

ferent disciplines looked at the outcomes of Habitat II more critically. Cohen (2015), for instance, states that while different stakeholders from various disciplines had participated, cross-disciplinary debates had been rare during Habitat II, leaving the discussions on housing policies a topic for experts only. Sustainable human settlements were adopted as a goal, but the increasing interdependence of cities in a global system and the rising issue of climate change had not found the attention needed (ibid.). Finally, no real changes were made to the content of the urban policies and no real ideas were put forward. Following the general discourse of the 1990s on better governance, the steering role of governments as an enabler for other actors in the housing domain was highlighted. Less state involvement and enabling of markets, politics, and communities were seen as the adequate means to promote self-help of the communities and achieve increased efficiency in housing production. What had been reached, however, was a clear acknowledgement of the need to address the challenge of slums, the surprising anchoring of the right to adequate housing in the final declaration, and commitments to the principles of participation, an increased role of local governments, and policies of slum upgrading (Neudert 2001: 64–66; Parnell 2016: 532). In order to measure success, it became the obligation of national governments to report their progress to UN-Habitat, strengthening the role of this UN body, but no monitoring or control instruments were established.

14.2 MDGs and SDGs

The problem of a lack of monitoring mechanisms for measuring development was addressed shortly after the Habitat II conference, at the UN General Assembly in 2000, known as the Millennium Summit. Based on the key outcomes of the UN conferences of the 1990s, measurable goals for humanity in the 21st century were adopted – the MDGs. Summarised in the Millennium Declaration, the eight goals contain commitments and targets in the fields of poverty, education, health, sustainability, gender equality, democracy, human rights, and environmental protection. In the context of housing, goal 7, to 'ensure environmental sustainability' with its sub-targets 'by 2020, to have achieved a significant improvement in the lives of at least 100 million slum-dwellers' (target 7D) and 'to halve, by 2015, the proportion of the population without access to safe drinking water and basic sanitation' (target 7C) are of importance (UN 2001). The distinguishing element contrasting all prior declarations was that quantitative and time-bound targets had been formulated for each goal. By the establishment of statistical databases relying on agreed-upon indicators, it was intended to create a monitoring and reporting system measuring progress towards the MDGs. In such a way, the hope was to commit governments more seriously to address the development challenges in their countries.

The obligation of monitoring target 7D fell to UN-Habitat (UNDP 2005: 109–116). Criticism on the target was articulated as being set too low (Bazoglu 2005; Bunting 2005; UN 2010: 63), the time frame being too long (UN-Habitat 2008c: 46–47), the language used for defining slums being insufficient (Gilbert 2007), and diversity of slums across geographies not being taken into account (Soederberg 2017). In the following years, UN-Habitat struggled to develop consistent indicators or a database on slum dwellers, resulting in a first estimation of people living in slums, a number roughly set to 921 million (UN-Habitat 2003a; Obermayr 2017: 44–45; Moreno 2005). What is of importance here is less the actual numbers of people living in slums, and more the obligation and efforts taken to create databases on slums. This effort consequently strengthened the topic on a world scale (Bazoglu 2005). The explicit entrance of an *urban* issue in key United Nations declarations and not least the further strengthening of UN-Habitat as the major agency for housing issues were further positive results (Auclair 2005: 9). In the Millennium Development Goals report of 2015, the outcomes of all targets were evaluated (UN 2015b). The report showed ambivalence, with some targets reached, others remaining a challenge. It was announced that the slum target (goal 7D) had not only been reached, but had even been surpassed threefold by lifting more than 320 million people out of slum conditions (United Nations 2015: 7, 2015: 60). The UN had to acknowledge, however, that due to urbanisation, slum improvements failed to hold pace with the growing absolute number of slum dwellers (UN 2010: 62).

In 2015, the next round of establishing goals for human development took place and resulted in the adoption of the SDGs. Based on the MDGs, but broader in scope, 17 goals with an associated 169 targets to be achieved by 2030 were established, '[...] seeking to complete what [the MDGs] did not achieve' (UNGA 2015). Integrating issues of poverty eradication, health, education, food security, and nutrition with a wide range of economic, social, and environmental objectives was seen as essential to contributing to the general goal of sustainability (UN 2015a; UNGA 2015). In contrast to the MDGs, which were largely relevant for the Global South, the SDGs are universal, including countries of the Global North as well, and give greater weight to absolute ecological limits (Parnell 2016: 529). All of these goals are interconnected in a nexus, and many have a connection to the urban realm (UN 2018: 10). It is highly remarkable that a stand-alone goal on cities was also included in the SDGs: Goal 11 'Make cities inclusive safe, resilient and sustainable'. Compared to the housing goal of the MDGs (target 7D), with its commitment to improving housing conditions of 100 million slum dwellers, the target was significantly scaled up: 'by 2030, ensure access for all to adequate, safe and affordable housing and basic services and upgrade slums' (SDG 11, Target 1;UN 2015a).

Arguments for this increased interest in cities were the recognition that humanity had entered into an urban age in demographic and socio-economic terms. The management of urbanisation was identified as crucial for achieving the SDGs, increasingly seen not as problematic, but as an opportunity to overcome existing global challenges

(Kraas & Mertins 2014; UN 2018). Cities were now perceived as hubs of economic activity, as places of innovation and change, as key agents where the transformation towards sustainability could take place (UN-Habitat 2014a). This emphasis on the urban realm also highlights the importance of sub-national governments – and thus the necessity of devolution – in implementing the SDGs (Parnell 2016).

Even more than the MDGs, the SDGs give emphasis to data collection, monitoring activities, and associated indicator development. For every target, indicators are discussed in an attempt to measure urbanisation and sustainability. Without measurement there are no data, without such data, there are no targets, and without targets, no programmes can be implemented (Caprotti et al. 2017: 7). 'What gets measured, gets done' (World Bank 2016a: 107). These are the common arguments, but critical voices question their feasibility. It is argued that standardised indicators across countries and cultures might reduce the meaning of sustainability, decontextualising development in its social and local meanings (Caprotti et al. 2017).

The difficulties and the logic behind the focus on indicator development can be exemplified with SDG 11 and its associated 15 indicators. Methodological difficulties start with the problem of defining cities, the necessity to invent new methods of data collection and integration, and the need of capacity development for governments to adopt a 'smart and sustainable city agenda' (UN 2018: 23–35). Only reliable data, it is argued, enable governments to implement 'evidence-based policy-making' (UN 2018: 30). Thus, '[...] there is a significant amount of time and resources that must be invested in [...] national statistical systems and other partners' (ibid.). The increasing belief that everything needs to be benchmarked using big-data approaches and new technologies raises the question of whose interests might be behind the implementation of such a 'smart city' agenda. Notwithstanding possible positive outcomes of such initiatives for governance structure and policy procedures (Fromhold-Eisebith & Eisebith 2019), they can also be seen as a means of opening up governance for business interests (Caprotti et al. 2017: 3–4).

At first glance, the MDGs and the SDGs are an advancement for housing issues, since they define clearly measurable goals and targets for approaching the housing challenge. Upon closer inspection, it becomes apparent that they remain silent or vague on how, by whom, and with what support the goals should be achieved (Satterthwaite 2016: iii). The benchmarking processes, so strongly advocated for, should be questioned (Soederberg 2017). The development of standardised indicators can be seen as a political way of inscribing a particular world-view – that of a neoliberal world of competitive states and entrepreneurial individuals. Such a view threatens to reduce the meaning of ambitious goals, limiting them to measurable entities (Death & Gabay 2015: 608). Not least, benchmarking practices are in the hands of the United Nations and national governments, serving their interests to easily claim success and to evade clearly binding commitments (Soederberg 2017).

14.3 Habitat III – The New Urban Agenda

The adoption of the SDGs in 2015 fell amidst the preparation activities for the third conference on human settlements – the United Nations Conference on Housing and Sustainable Urban Development, or Habitat III. For that reason, it is not surprising that the outcome document signed in Quito in 2016, the New Urban Agenda (NUA), includes much of the debates around the SDGs. The agenda sets out standards and principles for '[...] the planning, construction, development, management and improvement of urban areas' (UN 2017: iv). Well-managed urbanisation is seen – similar to the SDGs – as a 'powerful tool for sustainable development' (ibid.). Similar to the preluding Habitat conferences, the preparation processes for Habitat III took several years trying to involve as many stakeholders and voices as possible. The conference was seen as a unique opportunity to review global goals and strategies for more sustainable cities and deem a paradigm change necessary (WBGU 2016b). The conference was expected to result in a '[...] concise, focused, forward-looking and action-oriented outcome document' (Evans et al. 2016: 86).

The resulting document of Habitat III, the NUA, consists of two parts: the Quito Declaration on Sustainable Cities and Human Settlements for All and the Quito Implementation Plan for the New Urban Agenda. The declaration entails 22 paragraphs presenting the shared vision on sustainable urban development, principles, and commitments and a call for action. The implementation plan is much larger and covers a further 153 paragraphs arranged in three sections. The first section outlines transformative commitments for sustainable urban development considering the three dimensions of sustainability (§ 24–80). The second section covers considerations of effective implementation (§ 81–180), giving advice for governance structure (§ 85–92), urban and territorial planning (§ 93–125), and the means of implementation (§ 126–160). A last section (§ 161–175) is concerned with the follow-up and review process (UN 2017; Garschagen & Porter 2018: 117).

Some points stand out (Garschagen & Porter 2018: 118): First, the NUA is an agenda for all urban areas. Similar to SDG 11, it does not focus only on developing countries, but is to be applicable also in the Global North, recognizing that all cities and urban settlements urgently need to work toward a sustainable urban future. Second, the NUA calls for *inclusive* urbanisation and *inclusive* economies, expressing an increased recognition that the current model of urbanisation and economic growth has not resulted in a balanced world with socio-economic benefits for all, but is causing increased inequality and fragmentation. The fundamentals of our economic model, however, are not questioned. Third, the NUA stresses the role of subnational governance as being key for driving action towards urban sustainability, urging decentralisation and financial empowerment of local authorities. This move is remarkable, even though local authorities are quite often only mentioned in relation to national governments (Satterthwaite 2018: 122). Fourth, it is argued that sustainability cannot be achieved by governments alone, but needs backing from other parts of society, explicitly from the private and civil sectors. Fifth, the NUA calls for improvements of governance and spatial planning. This is not a new call, but a recognition that current structures are inadequate to cope with the challenges of climate change, inequality, and fragmentation (Garschagen & Porter 2018).

The foci of the NUA (UN 2017) become more clear when taking a closer look at the implementation section (§ 81–180). This section starts with the general way seen as appropriate to implement the commitments to sustainable urban development (cf. § 81, § 126). Enabling policy frameworks at all tiers of government are regarded as crucial, complemented by international cooperation, the mobilisation of financial resources, capacity development, and the sharing of best practices. Recommendations are given for urban governance (to be more decentralised, § 85–92) and for planning and managing spatial urban development (territorial planning, housing, mobility, services, and culture, § 93–125). Two issues are seen as the most important means for implementing the NUA: better financial frameworks (activating the private sector, better debt management, inclusion of multilateral funds and financial institutions, etc, § 130–146) and capacity building (better use of information and communication technologies, ie creating capacities for e-governance, monitoring, and data generation § 147–160).

Housing as a topic is not perceived as standing alone, but as an issue to be integrated into the three dimensions of sustainability (cf. § 31–34, § 46). As in the Vancouver Declaration, the right to adequate housing is recognised and the commitment to '[…] promote national, subnational and local housing policies that support the progressive realization of the right to adequate housing for all as a component of the right to adequate standard of living […]' *(UN 2017: § 31)* is reaffirmed. In the implementation section (§ 81–180), paragraphs concerned with housing policies are only one among many issues covering § 105–112. Here, ideas to realise the right to adequate housing are outlined: Participatory planning, the principle of subsidiarity (§ 105), social inclusion (§ 106), and integrated housing approaches (§ 108) are seen as the basis for affordable and sustainable housing options. The options to be developed and promoted are diverse and include rental housing, co-housing schemes and collective tenure, incremental and self-build schemes, and giving special attention to upgrade slums and informal settlements (§ 107). Strategies for upgrading are recommended to go beyond the improvement of physical conditions alone (§ 109) and to be backed by adequate rules and regulations (§ 111) as well as an efficient monitoring system (§ 110). It is acknowledged that financial and human resources must be allocated for this task (§ 109). Well-placed and well-distributed housing schemes, with 'the people's need at the centre' are to be given priority over 'peripheral and isolated mass housing developments' (UN 2017: § 112).

The content and length of the NUA has raised criticism: Satterthwaite (2018) argues that the NUA reaffirms only commitments and goals, which had already been provided by previous declarations, but remains vague and silent on the questions of how and by whom these commitments should be fulfilled. He concludes that the NUA is 'not new and not really an agenda' (Satterthwaite 2018: 122). Considering how little impact Habitat I and Habitat II declarations had on policy formulations and actions on the ground, most scholars are pessimistic as to whether the NUA can be different (ibid.). Matthias Garschagen and Libby Porter (2018) summarise that the NUA is too fuzzy in its formulations, '[...] it calls for too much at the same time' (ibid.: 119), does not set any priorities and gives '[...] little insight into the concrete implementation policies and measures' (ibid.: 119). Other scholars go even further and argue that the NUA reaffirms a techno-managerial approach, advocating – as the SDGs do – for the need to measure sustainability by indicators, trusting in science and technology and the idea of 'smart cities' for achieving sustainable urban development (Caprotti et al. 2017; Kaika 2017).

The NUA includes also 'the right to the city', but does not question the hegemonic development model of modernisation and economic growth. The ongoing process of real-estate financialisation are not addressed, the latest global mortgage crisis of 2007–2008 is not reflected, and state interventions in housing markets are further discredited (Unger 2016; Schechla 2016). Instead, efforts are put forward to cure the symptoms of a failing political economy (Kaika 2017). Housing for all is to be achieved by market mechanisms, prominently through 'partnerships' with the private sector. The right to the city has been included in the NUA – a historic achievement – but has not moved to the centre as desired by lobbying activities from NGOs and CBOs (Bertuzzo & Nest 2016; Scruggs 2016). Articulated demands for more state intervention, redistributions of land, legalisation of informal settlements, or the ban of market-driven land development in the housing sector were disregarded (Bertuzzo & Nest 2016). From this point of view, the NUA is not a paradigmatic shift, as proclaimed by itself. Known strategies are reaffirmed and the current model of political economy is not questioned.

An important shift in the Habitat discourse is the urban-centric focus of the NUA. This is already apparent in the framing of the declaration. While In Habitat I and II a 'balanced urban-rural development' was called for, it is now an '*urban* agenda' (Schechla 2016). Surely understandable considering the discursive turn towards 'urbanity', the reasons for urbanisation (eg rural-urban migration) are left aside. Although there are many reasons why people move from rural to urban areas, an important one is the penetration of capitalism into rural areas. Small-scale farming activities are vanishing, farming is increasingly becoming a corporate business, a development associated with land grabs and land dispossessions (Edelman et al. 2013). These processes have contributed significantly to the growth of cities, but were ignored in Habitat III (Soederberg 2017).

Overall, the NUA is a global agreement on challenges and adequate responses with regard to urbanisation, suggesting a holistic and crosscutting approach towards sustainable urban development (Hague 2018). It gives recommendations for desired spatial development and all connected issues, but does not provide concrete advice on how to implement these recommendations. Two things are highlighted as means of implementation: capacity building (strengthening of monitoring capacities etc) and the development of better financial frameworks. Cities and local governments have moved to the centre, obliged with the task to create enabling environments and partnerships. Financial resources for this endeavour are to come from national governments, international development aid, the private sector, and multilateral financial institutions (funds and banks). Considering the vagueness of the document, the missing guidelines for local implementation and the weak follow-up mechanisms, the NUA cannot be considered as a path-breaking milestone in urban development at all. It represents moreover a comprehensive catch-all of what needs to be done for more sustainable cities, but neither gives concrete advice nor inspires urgent action (Citiscope 2016). Nevertheless, the NUA plays a decisive role for guiding national housing policies, since it serves as an important reference for national governments.

14.4 Changing actors' influence on Habitat conferences

Different actors have shaped the outcomes of global Habitat conferences. Since Habitat I, an increasing number of actors have become involved, influencing in significant ways the outcome documents. Actors range from national, regional, and local governments, to development organisations, to multilateral lending organisations to NGOs, CBOs, and individual experts in academia and planning. Over the time period covered here (1976–2016), their influence on the conferences and on their results is assessed based on a review of original documents and secondary literature. This qualitative assessment results in a shifting weight of actor groups at the three major Habitat conferences (cf. figure 19).

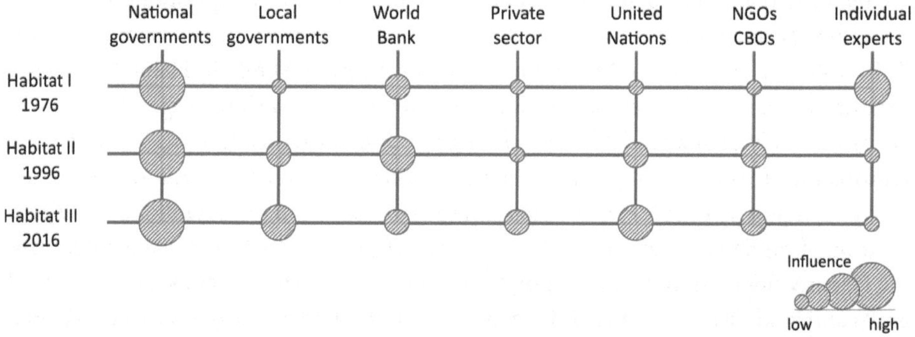

Fig. 19 Assessment of selected actors' influence on the outcome documents of each Habitat conference
Source: Illustration by author

National governments clearly were the most influential actors shaping the outcome documents of Habitat I–III. Since the conferences are in the end multilateral negotiations between states, national governments are the actors holding most negotiation and decision-making power. The influence of local governments has increased over the years. Though not equipped with equal decision-making power, they have slowly appeared as important actors together with an increased recognition of the principle of subsidiarity since Habitat II (Evans et al. 2016). They have organised in international platforms, such as the United Cities and Local Governments (UCLG), and in Habitat III they are recognised as crucial factors implementing policies on the ground.

Two international organisations have decisively shaped the housing discourse: the World Bank and the United Nations. While the World Bank's priorities traditionally favour market-based solutions combined with an ideology of home ownership (UN-Habitat 2016: 53), UN-Habitat's position is more diverse, putting more emphasis on social and environmental issues (Pugh 1997). The World Bank was already involved in housing programmes around the globe in the early 1970s, and has continued ever since to propose policies and intervention strategies. During the 1980s and 1990s, the organisation significantly dominated the debate, advocating for neoliberal reforms. The World Bank's power is based on its hegemonic role in the general development discourse, its accumulated knowledge on housing issues over the last decades, and, most importantly, its lending power (Waeyenberge 2017: 3–4). After the financial crisis of 2007–2008 and due to the rise of a multipolar world order, the World Bank's influence diminished somewhat. Likewise, the bodies of the United Nations – UNESCO, the United Nations Development Programme (UNDP), and most importantly, UN-Habitat (formally UNHCS) – have slowly evolved as an important actor addressing housing issues. This is visible in the constant development of UN-Habitat to a more important programme, today obligated to guide and monitor urban development on a world scale. Meanwhile, UN-Habitat has become the most influential actor for housing issues within the UN system, but UNESCO and UNDP are also working on topics related to urbanisation (Gomes da Silva 2018: 294–297).

In the years after Habitat I, non-governmental organisations formed, lobbying for their perspective on solving the housing challenge and functioning as a platform uniting the interest of many NGOs around the globe. Especially since the 1990s, NGOs and CBOs have been on the rise, increasingly organised in global networks, such as Habitat International Coalition (HIC) and Shack Dwellers International (SDI), demanding that their voices be heard. In contrast to that, the influence of individual experts diminished. In Habitat I, they played a decisive role (eg J. Turner) and had much influence on the Vancouver Declaration. With an increased number of parties involved over time, however, the influence of individuals on outcome documents is unavoidably reduced. In addition, the private sector has become more important in the housing discourse. Supported by the World Bank, the view has gained ground that only private investments can produce housing at scale. Representatives of the private sector, mostly from the real estate sector, increasingly demand to be involved, lobbying for their interests. Beside housing production, consultancy and smart technologies have also become emerging business fields. This influence can be traced in the debate on communication and information technologies and the adoption of a 'smart city' agenda in the Quito Declaration.

From this review of actors in the housing debate, the conflictual negotiation processes during the Habitat conferences can be imagined. During Habitat II, for instance, the Bretton Woods institutions (World Bank and IMF) advocated for market-based solutions in an era where state interventions were disregarded. The United Nations instead tried to oppose this view, advocating for rights-based approaches, searching for alliances among NGOs (Massiah 2016). In Habitat III, the different interests of all actors involved were negotiated again. The results are compromises, which explain the vague and catch-all formulations of the New Urban Agenda.

14.5 Changing priorities of the Habitat conferences

The debates on housing behind the Habitat conferences and the adoption of the MDGs and SDGs show changing priorities over the years 1976 to 2016. By juxtaposing the goals, outcomes, commitments, advised housing programmes, and changing approaches, several fields of the discussions can be traced (cf. table 17). These are:
- Sustainability/sustainable urban development
- Cities/subsidiarity/local governments
- Information technologies/monitoring/smart city
- Commitments/strategies
- Rights-based approach
- Discourse/basic needs/enabling/governance
- Housing policies/self-help/slum upgrading/comprehensive habitat approach

Sustainability has found entrance in the debate on housing since Habitat I with the adoption of the goal 'sustainable human settlements'. The perspective has become dominant that sustainable urban development is crucial for reaching overall sustainability (SDGs and Habitat III). Connected to this is the changing conceptualisation of the city considering the 'urban turn' of humanity. While in Habitat I and II, human settlements where the focal point, this has changed towards a perception of the city as opportunity and pathway towards sustainability (SDGs and Habitat III). With cities becoming the focal point, local governments and the principle of subsidiarity also gained influence. Already mentioned as important in Habitat I, strong local governments equipped with resources and acting as enablers are seen as crucial in Habitat III for implementing sound measures and strategies on the ground.

The commitments and strategies for urban development have remained largely the same over the years. They were simply broadened: Already in Habitat I better international cooperation, better financial frameworks, improved spatial planning practice,s and more participation opportunities were endorsed. This range of strategies

Table 17 Central goals, outcomes, commitments, strategies, and discourses of Habitat I–III, the MDGs and SDGs related to housing

Milestones	Goals related to housing	Outcomes	Commitments	Strategies for urban development	Housing programmes and practices	Conceptualisation of the city	Changing Discourse
Habitat I 1976	– Improve the **quality of life** in human settlements	– Awareness raising	– International cooperation – International and national funding – Participation – Spatial planning	– Focus on territorial planning and housing (excluding the environment) – Establishment of ministries, agencies, NGOs, and UN bodies focusing on urban issues	– Failure of conventional housing policies is acknowledged – Turner's ideas of **self-help** moves to the forefront	– Human settlements as places that need to be improved	– Satisfaction of **basic needs**
Habitat II 1996	– Adequate shelter for all – Sustainable human settlements	– **Right to adequate housing** is adopted – Acknowledgement that the challenge of slums needs to be addressed	– International cooperation – International and national funding – Participation – Monitoring – Sustainable urban development	– National action plans – **Capacity building:** enabling of all actors – Knowledge transfer of **best practices** – Public-private partnerships – Strengthening of local authorities	– **Self-help** remains the dominant paradigm; now involving NGOs and CBOs – Slum upgrading – **Deregulation** of housing markets – Comprehensive habitat approach	– Human settlements as places where sustainable development action is taking place, including the environment	– **Enabling approaches** (market, political, and community enablement) becomes dominant – **Good urban governance** – Subsidiarity
MDGs 2000	– Human development – Cities without slums	– **Time-bound quantifiable targets** – Raising urban issues to the international agenda for the first time	– **Creation** of a monitoring and benchmarking system – Establishment of **databases** on slums, sanitation, drinking water	– Focusing on **indicators,** data, and benchmarking	– No explicit reference to programmes or practices	– No explicit focus on cities or human settlements	– Focus on **monitoring** and benchmarking

Milestones	Goals related to housing	Outcomes	Commitments	Strategies for urban development	Housing programmes and practices	Conceptualisation of the city	Changing Discourse
SDGs 2015	– Sustainable development – Access for all to adequate, safe and affordable housing and basic services	– Time-bound quantifiable targets – **Stand-alone goal on cities** – More comprehensive than MDGs	– Improvement of the monitoring and benchmarking system – Strengthening of the local level of governments (acceptance of **devolution**)	– Focusing on indicators, **data, and benchmarking** – Global urban agenda on sustainable development	– Slum upgrading	– Cities as drivers of global environmental change – **Cities as pathways** towards sustainable development	– Focus on **monitoring** and benchmarking
Habitat III 2016	– Sustainable urban development	– Recognition of sustainable urban development as crucial for sustainable development – **Urban turn** of humanity is recognised – Right to adequate housing is reaffirmed – **Right to the city** is mentioned	– International cooperation – Better international and national funding – Better governance frameworks (stronger state) – Address **inequality** and create inclusive cities	– **Local governments** are crucial (enablers) – Capacity building (enablement of all actors) – Knowledge transfer (best practices) – Better involvement of private sector and civil society – Better use of **information technologies** – Improve spatial planning	– **Comprehensive habitat approach** as part of sustainable urban development – Development of diverse housing options (rental, self-help, co-housing, slum upgrading, etc) – **Smart city** initiatives	– **Cities as opportunity** – Cities as innovative spaces – Cities as development agents – Cities as leaders of action	– **Enabling approach** dominates – Smart City – Subsidiarity

Source: Table by author

was extended with capacity development, best practice transfers, and public-private partnerships (Habitat II), leading to a call for greater involvement of the private sector and civil society and a better use of communication and information technologies (MDGs, SDGs, and Habitat III). What has been new since the MDGs is the commitment to improve the monitoring and benchmarking systems. Indicator development and 'smart city' initiatives have thus also become a central field of debate in Habitat III. Underlying the discussion, but recognised, is the 'right to adequate housing'. A rights-based approach was adopted in Habitat II and reaffirmed in Habitat III, where also the right to the city has found entrance in the debate.

The background discourse changed from a focus on the quality of life and basic needs (Habitat I) towards the enabling approach and good urban governance (Habitat II). Implicit in this change are recommendations for housing policies: conventional housing programmes were disregarded (Habitat I), changing to self-help approaches and slum upgrading (Habitat II) and finally the perspective that comprehensive habitat approaches as part of sustainable urban development are preferable, allowing a diverse variety of concrete housing options (Habitat III). The general focus of the discussions changed from improving the quality of life in human settlements solely within developing countries towards the need for sustainable urban development in all cities, whether in the Global South or the Global North. The goals to provide adequate shelter for all, and to reach cities without slums, are still applicable, but goals became more comprehensive over the last decades, seen in a broader context, with the aim of achieving overall sustainability.

15 Global Discussions on Housing

The global discussion on housing is characterised by contrary opinions and changing paradigms. It is agreed that strategies and interventions are needed to overcome the global housing crisis (cf. chapter 13) and to achieve affordable and adequate housing for all (Gilbert 2009). Views on the extent and nature of intervention, however, differ widely among practitioners and scholars. Recommendations and principles agreed upon at the Habitat conferences have a significant impact on national and local actors (cf. chapter 14.4). For national housing ministries, local governments, and place-based NGOs and CBOs the outcome documents serve as guiding principles for translating them into national housing policies and concrete actions on the ground.

In the following sections, the discussion on adequate housing policies is traced from a historic perspective, identifying main paradigms and associated intervention strategies over the course of the 20th century. Subsequent formal and informal modes of housing provision are analysed, relating them to intervention strategies and assessing their respective contribution to the global housing provision.

15.1 Housing policy paradigms – phases of international policy advice

In the past, numerous strategies of intervention in the housing sector have been carried out. Already in the European and US cities of the 19th century, the housing question was a central concern (Gould 1900; Dyos 1967; Engels 1892 [1970]). Approaches have been developed, ranging from public housing, direct subsidies, private-sector incentives, rent controls, resettlements, sites and services approaches, or slum-upgrading strategies, to clearances and wider governance reforms (Kumar 2008; Bredenoord et al. 2014; Gilbert 2004a, 2004b).

From a historic perspective, three phases of the housing policy advocacy of international organisations can be identified. In a first phase after World War II public housing was the favoured strategy, followed by a phase where aided self-help was seen as the solution, and the latest phase where the enabling approach is preferred (cf. figure 20). These three general phases include a number of intervention strategies that are

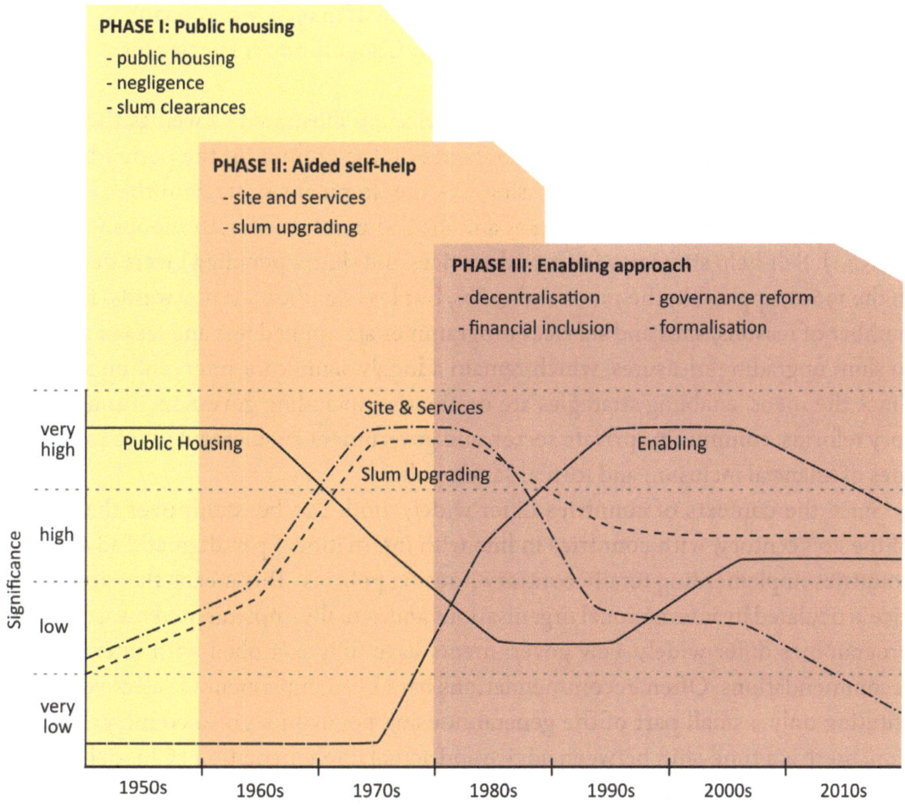

Fig. 20 Three phases of international policy advice for housing interventions and significance of specific interventions between the 1950s and 2010s
Source: Illustration by author

favoured during each period (UN-Habitat 2003a: 129; Obermayr 2017: 56–57). They do not represent a coherent and chronological policy evolution towards better solutions, but are overlapping phases of policy advice, which materialise differently on the ground, dependent on contextual circumstances and path dependencies in each country. Newer strategies replace older approaches, adjusted to changing realities or trying to overcome encountered shortcomings. However, older approaches also prevail or are revived after a period of absence.

The three phases represent periods in time when a specific perspective on solving the housing question dominates. At the beginning of each phase, the (new) idea rises slowly, is tested in pilot projects until it breaks through, at which point it is acknowledged as a working and sound new strategy. This happens ultimately with the adoption of declarations negotiated at international conferences. At least two such paradigmatic changes have occurred since the 1950s. The first change occurred roughly around the Habitat I conference in 1976 when 'public housing' was eventually replaced by 'self-help' and the second change happened after Habitat II in 1996, when 'enabling' became the advised recommendation (Pugh 1997, 2001; Choguill 2007; Harris 2015; Chiodelli 2016; Bredenoord et al. 2014).

In figure 20 the three phases of policy advice are illustrated as well as the significance of some selected intervention strategies on the ground for the period between the 1950s and the 2010s. Public housing was the dominant strategy in the 1950s and 1960s, became abandoned in the 1980s and 1990s, but returned in the 2000s (cf. chapter 15.1.1). Self-help strategies (sites and services and slum upgrading) were developed in the 1960s, applied in the 1970s and 1980s, but lost significance afterwards. Due to a number of reasons, sites and services programmes are applied less and less in contrast to slum upgrading measures, which remain a highly significant intervention strategy. Since the 1980s, enabling strategies are on the rise, including governance and regulatory reforms, community, private sector, and government enablement as well as measures of financial inclusion and formalisation policies.

Since the contexts of countries differ widely, both can be found over the course of the 20th century, with countries in line with international paradigmatic advice and countries implementing totally contrary housing policies. This means that policy advice articulated by international organisations and actually implemented measures and programmes differ widely. Few governments have fully complied with international recommendations. Often, recommendations have been implemented selectively, constituting only a small part of the general housing policy in a given country. In addition, there is a time-shift between advice and actual implementation (Chiodelli 2016). These factors are one explanation for the wide variety of applied housing policies and the prevalence of detrimental and ostracised measures, such as slum clearances and forced evictions (UNCHR 1993).

15.1.1 Negligence, public housing, and slum clearances – 1950s to 1970s

In a first phase after World War II, when urbanisation trends became more massive and informal settlements started to sprawl in countries of the Global South, international agencies and public authorities remained astonishingly silent. The international community was not committed to housing policies for the poor yet and government turned a blind eye to the problem. The growth of informal settlements was widely seen as a temporary condition that would disappear with increased economic development. Policy-makers assumed that the market would handle the problem of absorbing informal dwellers gradually into the formal city (Milbert 2006: 302; Chiodelli 2016). Urban authorities in most developing countries simply neglected the increasing housing problems. Physical urban planning was a center of focus, but areas with inadequate housing conditions were not addressed in planning documents and only few countries developed specific strategies for the housing sector (UN-Habitat 2003a: 130).

If any, conventional housing strategies such as state-financed public housing were preferred during the 1950s, 1960s, and 1970s. Trying to imitate European models (Flagge 1999; UN-Habitat 2003a: 123–124), mass housing programmes were initiated, with multi-storey buildings constructed to accommodate low-income dwellers. Some of the flats were sold to the residents (pay-off in long-term installments) or rents were subsidised (Mertins 1984). The underlying assumption behind this policy was that public housing would replace informal settlements and eventually erase unhealthy living conditions and perceived disorder (Andavarapu & Edelman 2013: 185–186). The objectives were not only to accommodate the poor population, but for the public houses to fulfill other goals as well: they were visible symbols of a government's commitment to the welfare of its people and in addition to that, housing could be provided for civil servants and supporters of political elites, consolidating political patronage systems in many countries (Tibaijuka 2009: 169–170). Another goal was city beautification. In an effort to 'tidy up' the city, demolishing informal settlements became common and an accepted strategy. Public housing served as a useful justification for these actions. The story told was that people affected by slum clearances would be better off when resettled in public housing units (cf. box 8).

The public housing programmes were confronted with many problems. To meet the promise of affordability, construction was bound to be done as cheaply as possible. For this reason, industrial building techniques were used, with the hope that costs could be lowered by the rationale of standardised mass production, but shortages of skilled labour and materials led to higher costs than initially expected (Wekesa et al. 2011: 241). Another means of reducing costs was to construct the blocks on cheap land, which was only available in urban peripheries. This entailed a number of consequences for the new residents, such as a lack of infrastructure for basic needs (eg schools), high mobility costs (large commuting distances), and stigmatisation. Standardised design did not consider the actual needs of the low-income groups regarding size, architecture, and physical characteristics (Keivani & Werna 2001a: 84). As a result, most of the flats were very small, inadequate for larger families, equipped with communal kitchens and toilets, and of overall poor quality. With no common space for home-based business activities, vital for most informal workers (Evers & Korff 2000), and confronted with rules and regulations alien to their culture, the new residents faced difficulties in adapting (Tibaijuka 2009: 169–170). For these reasons, most units constructed in public housing programmes were inadequate, of poor quality, expensive, overcrowded, and soon showed signs of deterioration due to insufficient maintenance.

Box 8: Slum clearances, evictions, and resettlements

Demolishing and clearing informal settlements and resettling the inhabitants in public houses was a common strategy from the 1950s to the 1970s. Nowadays, evictions are carried out for a variety of reasons, among them: to provide space for infrastructure projects, urban redevelopment, city beautification, or prestigious international events (Plessis 2005; UN 2014). Officially, slum clearances were frequently justified to be crime prevention and a means of eradicating an 'eyesore' of the city. In reality, informal areas are often seen as a threat, since they elude governmental control, and there is a strong interest in commodifying the high-value land occupied by low-income groups (Davis 2006: 103–127; Chaudhry 2014; Follmann & Trumpp 2013). Often, evictions are carried out with the use of force and the United Nations have declared such procedures as a gross violation of human rights (UNCHR 1993). Despite this strong commitment against forced evictions, UN-Habitat estimates that two million people are forcibly evicted every year (UN-Habitat 2009b: 21). Unlike eviction, resettlements can be done in agreement and in cooperation with the affected people. Resettlements are allowed only in the most exceptional cases: they must be authorised by law, be solely for the purpose of general welfare, follow international human rights law, and ensure adequate and fair compensation (UN-Habitat 2009b: 5; Kothari 2007).

Resettlements from informal settlements to public housing units were investigated by Janice Perlman (1976, 2010) in the case of favelas in Rio de Janeiro. She identified benefits and shortcomings in her study on informal dwellers, who were relocated to public tenements in a more peripheral location. She reports a significant loss of income due to longer commuting distances and additional expenses for paying rent, services, or mortgage loans. Since people were moved to different locations, the social network of neighbourly help collapsed. Urban amenities (movies, beach etc), the whole urban experience, was lost to the resettled people and they felt excluded from the city. The physical aspects, such as water, sanitation, or electricity, however, improved in their new home (Andavarapu & Edelman 2013: 186).

In the end, most programmes did not reach the urban poor. The units were simply too expensive. Low-income groups in developing countries work usually in the informal sector and receive only irregular and low salaries. In most cases, they are unable to pay regular rent, even at low rates and heavily subsidised (Obermayr 2017: 58; Mertins 1984; Neudert 2001: 55–56). If directly allocated to low-income people, units became subject to *'raiding'* by the middle class, as housing rights, even tenancy, is usually sold on. Affordability for low-income groups was not reached and the vast majority of public houses became occupied by members of the middle class (Choguill 2007: 146; Davis 2006: 66–74; Pugh 1997: 1561–1562).

By the end of the 1960s, the failure of public housing became obvious. The scale of intervention was, with some notable exceptions – Singapore, Hong Kong and South Korea (Zhu 2007; UN-Habitat 2003a; Chen et al. 2013) – very small, contributing to only 10 % of all housing produced (World Bank 1993). The programmes were too costly, houses were inadequately designed, poorly constructed, located in urban peripheries, had maintenance problems, and were subject to 'raiding' by the middle class (Bähr & Mertins 2000). These factors put public housing beyond the reach of the urban poor. The results were that most countries cut back their public housing programmes in the 1970s, even though in some countries public housing remains well established as a key instrument of housing policy (Tibaijuka 2009: 169–170). Advantages and disadvantages of public housing are summarised in table 18.

Table 18 Pros and cons of public housing

	Pros	Cons
Public Housing	– Action is highly visible – Market logics do not apply – Improved physical living conditions	– Resource intensive (high costs) – Maintenance problems – Low quality of materials used – Poor and inadequate design – Involves resettlement – Location in urban peripheries – Not for the poorest segment of low-income groups – Problem of tenant selection (reward for own supporters? ethnicity?)

Source: Table by author. Based on Harris (2015: 127–128), Tibaijuka (2009), and Wekesa et al. (2011)

15.1.2 Aided self-help: slum upgrading and sites and services – 1960s to 1980s

In the early 1970s, cities and governments began to worry about the worsening housing conditions and the continuous growth of informal areas in many cities. Considering the very limited financial means in most developing countries, the high costs of public housing schemes, and the fact that most of the housing stock is produced informally, strategies were considered to assist these self-build activities. Public housing, as a policy transfer from the Global North, had widely failed in the Global South and trickle-down effects of economic growth did not deliver. It became clear that intervention strategies were needed that were more tailored to the particularities of the urban situation in developing countries. The findings of most scholars in the 1960s (Abrams

1964; Mangin 1967; Turner 1968a) backed the view that strategies and approaches were needed for supporting the self-help abilities of the cities' inhabitants. At the forefront of these discussions was the work of the architect John Turner.

In his work on informal settlements in Peru, John Turner (1968a; 1977, 1968b) found that the sprawling informal settlements in the Global South were not 'slums of despair', but were mainly neighbourhoods of optimism and progress (Bromley 2003). These settlements were not stagnant; they consolidated over time due to the capacity and knowledge of residents to build and improve their homes. Based on these observations, Turner argued for a change of perspective, and offered a counter-narrative: Informal urban settlements should not be seen as a problem to be ignored or demolished, but as a solution for the housing crisis to be supported. Large quantities of housing at affordable prices and easily adaptable to changing circumstances were already produced informally (Bower 2016: 85–86), providing the lion's share of housing supply – 50 to 80 % – in the Global South (Bredenoord & Lindert 2010: 281). For these reasons, Turner concluded, not a centralistic, hierarchic state system with inadequate and costly public housing, but a more autonomous system of dweller control over the housing process with the 'freedom to build' was the solution to the housing crisis (Asnawi 2005: 52–57; Turner & Fichter 1972).

The central idea of the self-help approach was to recognise and support this informal mode of housing production. Adequate solutions would comprise assisted self-help for households, supporting their incremental building activities. This support might include building materials, technical advice, land to build on, access to credit, micro-finance, regulation of tenure, and gradual provision of community services. Nevertheless, people had to build themselves, relying on their own capabilities and resources, not necessarily their own labour, though their own land and financial means. In this approach governments were seen to have a supporting role, leaving the build process to the people, who could manage it according to their needs (Bredenoord & Lindert 2010; Gottdiener et al. 2016). 'Helping the poor to help themselves' became a common catch phrase in the 1970s and for housing policies a new paradigmatic approach was born: aided self-help. (Chiodelli 2016: 4; Gottdiener et al. 2016: 126; Andavarapu & Edelman 2013).

In 1973, the World Bank began to work in the housing sector rushing to this new strategy (Pugh 1994, 1997, 2001). The new approach fitted into its neo-liberalist attitude, as it promised to be pragmatic, viable, cost-effective, and eliminate the high subsidies of public housing schemes (Pugh 1997). Turner's original idea of dweller control in the building process was co-opted by neoliberal principles, stripped of its main intention of supporting the people to produce their own space as a community, and reduced to the principles of economic efficiency (Bower 2016: 90–91). Loans for the first generation of aided self-help programmes were introduced under the premise of affordability, full cost-recovery from beneficiaries, and replicability[5]. As project-based intervention strategies, *sites and services schemes* and *slum upgrading programmes* were designed and implemented. These two approaches were seen as complementary, the former providing new housing stock, the latter improving conditions in existing slums and squatters. The World Bank hoped that cost recovery would demonstrate the profitability of such approaches to private developers, encouraging them to become more engaged in this segment of housing production (Chiodelli 2016; Waeyenberge 2017; World Bank 1993). Soon, the projects mushroomed in the larger cities around the globe and by 1976, at the Habitat I conference, aided self-help had become the hegemonic strategy for coping with marginal settlements.

Sites and services projects work by the provision of developable building lots already connected to basic services (access to roads, electricity, drinking water, and sewer systems). In a second step, these lots are assigned to eligible households who are provided with basic materials and loans on favourable terms to actually build the houses. Sometimes also core housing units, a basic one-room shelter or a sanitary room, were provided (Mertins 1984; Bähr & Mertins 2000; Obermayr 2017: 60). The main rationale was to imitate the incremental house building activities from the informal sector: houses built incrementally according to the dwellers' needs (Keivani & Werna 2001a: 86). Additionally, formal land titles would allow households to improve and become eligible for mortgage loans. Although the specifics of the projects varied, they were often located at urban fringe areas, where land could be acquired at low cost. The drawback of such peripheral locations were high costs for infrastructure connection and additional expenses for mobility for the new inhabitants (Bredenoord & Lindert 2010).

Slum upgrading projects aim to improve the existing housing stock, infrastructures, and living conditions of slum settlements. World Bank-supported programmes usually had three principles: basic infrastructure (water supply, sewer systems, electricity, sidewalks etc), secure land tenure (to protect against eviction) and access to credit. In reality most programmes focused on infrastructure (Chiodelli 2016: 2; Wekesa et al. 2011: 242). Key elements of such projects were formalisation – ie regularisation and recognition of tenure, meant as an incentive for residents to improve their homes, as well as resident or community participation by contributing their manpower to the upgrading process (Bähr & Mertins 2000). Participation was in most cases easy to achieve since mutual support structures and strong social networks already existed in most informal settlements.

---

5 Full cost recovery was important for target countries since they did not have the means to subsidise such housing schemes and also for the World Bank since the bank's creditworthiness depends on the effectiveness and efficiency of its loan-assistance programmes. A good reputation is necessary for raising funds on international capital markets (Pugh 2001: 404–405; Choguill 2007: 146).

Self-help programmes proved their feasibility in the 1970s and 1980s and, compared to conventional strategies, they had significant advantages in terms of scale, costs, and community participation. Slum upgrading schemes had a larger impact than sites and services, since the latter faced higher costs and available land was scarce. Imitating informal housing processes largely failed, since the advantages of informality ie the ability to evade costs (building permits, regulations, taxes) cannot be copied in formal processes, resulting in higher costs (Jones & Ward 1994; Wekesa et al. 2011). The number of houses built or upgraded was not enough to improve the situation. Francesco Chiodelli (2016: 2) notes that between 1972 and 1980 only three million people benefited from sites and services projects and the housing of eight million people were improved in World Bank projects. Compared to annual urbanisation rates and housing demands this result was not much more than a drop in the bucket (Chiodelli 2016).

Self-help strategies did not work at scale since they faced many challenges. They were not easily replicable and cost recovery was not reached in most projects, especially with slum upgrading. Corruption, bad management, poor maintenance, the limited availability of cheap land, and incompatibility with other reforms were some of the problems (Bähr & Mertins 2000; Mukhija 2001). A poor governance system characterised by incapacity, conflicts of competences, patronage, and corruption contributed to the poor outcome of the programmes (Pugh 1997: 1563). In addition, the attitude towards informal settlements did not change easily among the authorities. The view of slums as a disgrace of the city to be demolished remained strong and with some exceptions (eg KIP in Indonesia, cf. chapter 20.1) the self-help programmes remained pilot projects of the international agencies but were not integrated into national housing policies (Chiodelli 2016: 4; Tibaijuka 2009: 171).

From the beginning, self-help strategies also came under attack from a neo-Marxist perspective. Rod Burgess (1978, 1982) and others (eg Davis 2006) criticised that self-help would be nothing more than a recognition of market mechanisms and a withdrawal of the state from its historic responsibility to deliver housing for the people. By fighting the housing crisis with the means of neoliberalism – privatisation, regularisation, and access to credit – the argument goes, self-help programmes help to include informal areas in the circuits of capital accumulation, expanding and consolidating the capitalist system. From this point of view, the intrusion of capitalism exacerbates the housing crisis since the root cause, the capitalist mode of production itself, is not questioned (Davis 2006; Asnawi 2005: 52–57).

One of the main critical points is that self-help strategies did not reach the poorest segment of society. This was particularly the case for sites and services schemes, but also to a lesser extent for *in situ* slum upgrading. Sites and services programmes were seen as a means to allow low-income groups to enter the formal home ownership market. In reality, however, the projects were still too expensive (high bureaucratic costs) and the requirements for eligibility (eg regular income) was not easy to fulfil for the urban poor (Pugh 2001). For an estimated 20 % of the urban population the programmes remained beyond their reach (Choguill 2007). *In situ* slum upgrading also had difficulties in reaching the poor. Consequences such as gentrification, exclusion, speculation, and middle-class raiding occurred (Desai & Loftus 2013). Improved housing conditions, infrastructures, and regularisation unavoidably bring about higher house prices (*filtering up*), higher housing expenses (formalisation entails municipal taxes and rates for communal services), and higher rents for tenants. Upgrading thus might be beneficial for homeowners, but might also drive out low-income renters. Higher expenses might also encourage owners to sell their upgraded homes to members of the middle class and move on to a new squatter site. Therefore, in many cases urban areas were upgraded, but the original dwellers were expelled (Keivani & Werna 2001a: 88). These unintended consequences further worsened the situation for the low-income population. Advantages and disadvantages of sites and services and slum upgrading approaches are summarised in table 19.

Facing these challenges and anticipating lessons learned in *the 1970s*, self-help approaches evolved in terms of procedures and aspects at the centre of focus. While the first generation of slum upgrading projects focused almost solely on infrastructure, from the 1980s onwards the projects shifted to include also socio-economic, environmental, and organisational aspects of improvement (cf. box 9). The projects also started to involve community members more directly by demanding their participation not only in construction work, but also in planning, management, and implementation. The main rationale behind increased community participation was cost reduction. Projects remained the same, but by assigning tasks to the community, costs could be further decreased. Slum upgrading projects were increasingly favoured since they were less costly and more easy to implement than sites and services schemes (Bähr & Mertins 2000: 22–24). In general, a shift from top-down projects towards bottom-up approaches, where projects were undertaken cooperatively by local governments and community groups and facilitated by NGOs, was observable (Wekesa et al. 2011: 242).

By the late 1980s the enthusiasm for self-help programmes slowly vanished since the desired impact on the housing crisis was not achieved. Turner's approach was recognised as an advancement from conventional housing strategies and the projects proved that inhabitants of informal settlements were capable of building their own housing, if allowed to and adequately supported. Scaling-up pilot programmes and transferring them to other cities and regions, however, frequently failed (Burgess 1978; Keivani & Werna 2001a). Poverty and inadequate institutional and socio-economic framework conditions were held responsible, preventing a resounding success. The recognition gained ground that approaches that are more comprehensive were needed to improve living conditions in slum areas. Focusing on infrastructure and services was not enough; governments would also have to address issues such as land tenure, cost recovery, institutional frameworks, and community responsibility (Werlin 1999; Pugh 2001).

Box 9: Lessons for successful slum upgrading

Slum upgrading has evolved since the 1970s and today it is recognised as an important means to improve living conditions and urban fabrics in slum areas. At first, upgrading projects had focused solely on physical improvements of infrastructure and improvement of buildings. After decades of application, it became clear that this was not enough to achieve long-lasting effects. It was recognised that a multi-sectoral and multi-stakeholder approach that includes '[…] the physical, social, economic, organisational and environmental improvements undertaken cooperatively and locally among citizens, community groups, businesses and local authorities' (Wekesa et al. 2011: 245) was needed (UN-Habitat 2009b). Key elements of successful upgrading strategies were identified:

Physical upgrading and availability of public resources: Key elements of slum upgrading are the provision of basic services (water, electricity, sewer systems), physical infrastructure (health centres, roads, schools, etc) and direct or indirect financial means (eg direct subsidies) for home improvements (Westendorff 2004: 211; Nuissl & Heinrichs 2013).

Security of tenure: Slum dwellers need a guarantee that their settlements are accepted by local authorities and are no longer threatened by removal. Formal land titles are not necessarily needed (titling strategies can even be counterproductive; cf. box 10); other forms of land rights may be sufficient. Only if inhabitants are convinced that their tenure is secure will they consider investing time, labour, and money to improve their homes (Bredenoord & Lindert 2010: 279; Wekesa et al. 2011; UN-Habitat 2016: 62).

Strong local governments: Local governments must be equipped with adequate competencies and means (capacities, staff, finance, materials, knowledge) to guide and supervise upgrading projects. Local governance arrangements are needed that embrace a positive and optimistic attitude towards slum dwellers (Werlin 1999: 1531).

Community participation und multiple stakeholders: The upgrading agenda should be set by the people, as should decision-making, planning, and implementation (Roy 2005). To achieve this, a strong representative and democratic community organisation is needed as a key element of upgrading committees. These committees should involve local authorities, community leaders, and NGOs with the responsibility of encouraging community participation, building capacity, and supervising the projects (Minnery et al. 2013; Wekesa et al. 2011) *"The broader, more participative and integrated the approach to slum upgrading, the more successful it is likely to be"* (UN-Habitat 2016: 58).

To address these issues, the international discussion moved slowly to a new approach in the 1980s considering whole housing sector development. Self-help approaches were not abandoned, but the need to integrate them into wider housing policies became pressing (Davis 2006: 79–81). A move towards city-wide and integrated habitat and governance approaches took place (Bredenoord & Lindert 2010: 280).

Table 19 Pros and cons of sites and services and slum upgrading approaches

	Pros	Cons
Sites and services	– low costs – houses according to dwellers' needs – security of tenure – house as financial asset	– low output – negotiations, agencies, staff, bureaucracy; resulting in higher costs – inadequate site locations – inadequate cost recovery – poor housing quality – availability of land
Slum upgrading	– avoid eviction (retain social networks, access to work) – regularisation of land (security of tenure) – house as financial asset – neighbourhood cooperation may foster community – smaller investments than sites and services	– increased housing costs by improved standards – gentrification, filtering up, middle-class raiding – inadequate cost recovery – high-densities remain – no new housing stock

Source: Table by author. Based on Tibaijuka (2009), Milbert (2006), Bredenoord & Lindert (2010), and Harris (2015)

15.1.3 The enabling approach and wider urban policy – 1980s until today

With the recognition in the 1980s that self-help strategies would not be the panacea for the housing crisis, the international community moved on to promote whole-sector approaches and settlement-wide action. Based on the experiences of the 1970s with self-help approaches and in an attempt to mitigate their limitations, progressive reforms took place on strategic policy development as well as the operational design and implementation of self-help programmes. Slum upgrading programmes were conceptualised more broadly (cf. box 9), and the focus moved from projects towards the development of whole-sector housing policies (Pugh 2001: 406–408).

The call for broader policies culminated in 1988 in the UN *Global Strategy for Shelter to the Year 2000* adopting the fundamental principle of '[…] an enabling approach, whereby the full potential and resources of all actors in the shelter production and improvement process are mobilized' *(UNCHS 1988: para. 14)*. Together with the flagship report of the World Bank (1993) *Housing: Enabling Markets to Work*, a new paradigmatic approach was born: the enabling approach.

The perspectives on enablement and their influence on applied housing policies varied between UNCHS and the World Bank. While the World Bank embraced a neoclassic perspective on enablement, UNCHS also adopted economic orthodoxies but elaborated more on organisational issues and citizen participation (Pugh 1997: 1563–1565). Both perspectives of enablement are recommendations, advice for governments, but the World Bank ideas became more influential, since it could enforce its perspective through loan programmes allocated under conditions (Pugh 2001).

In essence, the enabling approach seeks to create an environment where markets produce adequate and affordable housing for all – also for low-income groups – and governments are rescaled, restricted to handle only the legal and regulatory framework conditions. Self-help approaches remained positively connoted, but within the context of wider urban policy (Bredenoord & Lindert 2010). The goal to enable people to help themselves did not change; it was rather attempted to moderate structural deficits identified in the whole housing sector and governance frameworks. An enabling environment was to be achieved not by a coherent strategy but by a bundle of measures and reforms (Sengupta et al. 2018: 857). Direct interventions in governance systems were attempted, intending to induce far-reaching changes in the institutional, bureaucratic, and regulatory systems of countries. The underlying assumption was that the market would do its magic once the right business-friendly environment was created. Burgess (1996; 1997) distinguishes three types of enablement: Market, government, and community enablement.

Market enablement means to create an adequate environment for the formal and informal private sector to provide market solutions for urban services and housing production. From this neoliberal perspective, the state should withdraw from all direct activities in urban services and housing production, and instead focus on removing market obstacles and encouraging activities of the private sector. This can be done by enacting adequate rules and regulations for example on how land is used and how housing construction is regulated (building permits, building codes, materials allowed, organisational form etc). It was expected that market enablement would produce an increased supply of housing and services while simultaneously reducing prices to more affordable levels (Helmsing 2002; Mukhija 2001).

Government enablement means to empower local governments by decentralisation and to change their role in housing issues. It was argued that only strong local authorities, equipped with decision power, human competencies, and financial resources devolved and allocated by the central state would fulfil their new role as enabling governments. Enabling local governments seek to involve all actors in formulating and implementing government policies and programmes while providing adequate legal and financial frameworks. Local authorities are to guarantee the supply of land, housing security, credit, and basic services, but are not to implement direct interventions. (Helmsing 2002: 320–323; Pugh 2001: 406–408; Keivani & Werna 2001a).

Instead of direct interventions, local governments should promote community enablement as a strategy to coordinate and foster the efforts of communities to initiate, plan, implement, and manage urban self-help programmes. An environment of mutual acknowledgement and cooperation should be created, where individuals and communities, mediated by NGOs and CBOs, would be empowered to initiate their own actions under the principles of self-organisation, self-management, and broad participation (Helmsing 2002: 320–323; Neudert 2001: 62–63). In other words, governments' role should not be to do something directly, but to enable others to do something for themselves (Chiodelli 2016: 6–7).

The World Bank's adoption of the enabling approach must be seen in the context of a general revision of development economics following the debt crisis of the 1980s. Advocated housing policies became aligned with policy approaches recommended in other fields of development (Mukhija 2001). Structural adjustment programmes and the upcoming neoliberal ideology pushed forward principles such as deregulation and privatisation. These principles were also reflected in the World Bank's perspective on enablement outlined in their flagship report *Enabling Markets to Work* (World Bank 1993). In this report, it is argued that the housing sector should be handled as any other economic sector, recommending the privatisation of housing delivery (Mukhija 2001). Inadequate housing stock and conditions were seen as a symptom of market failure and governments should not deal with this symptom, but should address the causes: barriers that restrict markets from working properly. Removing these barriers would then create efficient housing markets doing their magic. The goal was to develop formal housing systems that were capable of providing housing for all strata of population (Helmsing 2002; Pugh 1997).

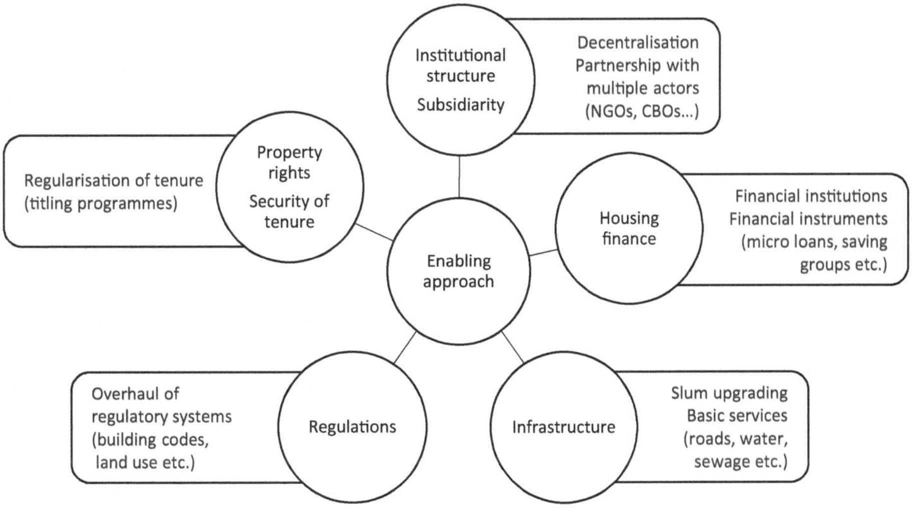

Fig. 21 Five pillars of action of the World Bank's enabling approach and associated measures
Source: Illustration by author

The World Bank established 5 pillars of action (World Bank 1993): (1) property rights, (2) basic infrastructure, (3) housing finance, (4) regulations and (5) vertical and horizontal subsidiarity (cf. figure 21). Steps to be taken are a regularisation of tenure in informal settlements, the provision of basic infrastructure (roads, services), the development of financial instruments and institutions (mortgage finance instruments, micro loans, credit associations), an overhaul of regulatory systems (building codes and land use), a revision of the organisational structure of the state, and the promotion of a multifactor approach (Helmsing 2002; Chiodelli 2016; Pugh 2001: 406–408).

The housing policies advocated by the World Bank shifted dramatically by adopting this approach in the early 1990s. The private sector and middle-income countries became the main recipient of World Bank loans instead of public institutions and low-income countries. Housing finance, formalisation policies, and institutional reform replaced individual self-help projects. In the 1990s, nearly half of the World Bank's shelter portfolio was dedicated to housing finance (Waeyenberge 2017: 3–4; UN-Habitat 2016: 52). Governments were advised to sell their public housing stock, abandon any tenant protections in place, and liberalise their mortgage markets (Rolnik 2013a). The overall goals were to reduce government subsidies to a minimum and to extend the reach of financial markets in the housing sector. Not least, including the poor and informal areas in financial circuits were seen as an important mean to contribute towards macro-economic development (Pugh 2001: 406–408).

At the Habitat II conference in 1996 national action plans were adopted based on the enabling approach. Enabling had become the new unchallenged paradigm. Self-help programmes were still regarded as relevant, but as a component of more holistic strategies. Good governance, partnership, participation, and multiple actors became the new buzzwords of the late 1990s (Neudert 2001: 64–66). Remarkably, it was recognised – also among World Bank economists – that deregulated markets alone would not deliver for low-income groups (Mukhija 2001; Harris 2015: 128–130). Not a reduced and passive state role, but an active and flexible role of local authorities embracing their new responsibilities and functions was acknowledged as being of importance (Harris 2015: 128–130; Pugh 2001: 416–417). In this regard also NGOs and CBOs were increasingly highlighted as essential vehicles for improving access of the poor to housing finance by initiating and implementing new lending methods, micro-credit, or community saving groups (Waeyenberge 20179–10).

The enabling approach was fundamentally criticised for its close ties to neoliberal principles. Focusing on market-based solutions for housing, demanding a retreat of the state, and promoting the expansion of housing finance would not reach those in need, but perpetuate an insufficient system. Indeed, the enabling approach appeared in an international environment of neoliberal supremacy (Smets et al. 2014: 2–3), endorsing the belief that the private sector would be more efficient in housing delivery than the state (Daniel & Hunt 2014: 204; Mukhija 2001). Cloaked by phrases such as empowerment, enabling, participation, and inclusion, the approach called in essence for a roll-

Box 10: Housing finance and formalisation

Two of the World Bank's pillars of action became particularly influential in the 1990s and 2000s: housing finance and security of tenure (Harris 2015: 128–130). The absence of formal housing finance markets in most countries of the Global South was identified as one of the main obstacles preventing private markets from working for low-income groups (Pugh 1997: 1563–1565). Without credit, so the argument goes, people had to borrow from informal sources to finance their housing projects at a much higher cost and private developers were more reluctant to work in such an insecure framework. Thus, the establishment of financial institutions, micro-credit schemes, saving groups, incentives for mortgage providers to move down the markets (guarantees), and others would be the proper means to replace public housing finance at full cost recovery and improve access to mortgage loans for low-income dwellers (Waeyenberge 20179–10; Ferguson & Smets 2010). Making them bankable would include them in the formal market system and allow them to construct their housing incrementally (Jones 2012).

The other aspect focused on was security of tenure to be achieved by formalisation. In the self-help programmes, lacking security of tenure had been the main obstacle in people's decisions of whether to invest in their homes. In line with a home ownership ideology, and in an attempt to regularise informal settlements, titling programmes were seen as the solution. The idea was that people could only use their property as collateral for getting mortgage loans if they held a formal title to their land. This view was supported by some academics, most famously by Hernando de Soto. In his work *The Mystery of Capital* (2002) he argued that a lot of 'dead capital' was buried in informal settlements, which could be 'freed' and used as a financial asset by providing proper land titles. In one stroke, informal dwellers would become homeowners, secured against evictions and enabled to take on mortgage loans. Having secured ownership and access to credit, they would be encouraged to invest in their property to improve their houses (Marx et al. 2013: 203–206). Numerous titling programmes carried out over the last decades, however, showed that the situation is more complex (Gilbert 2002; Campbell 2013; Galiani & Schargrodsky 2010; Geoffrey et al. 2009; Supriatna 2016). One of the drawbacks was that only *de facto* homeowners profited from formalisation, but not the poorest or tenants (Gilbert 2011: 86). Pretending to improve housing conditions, the measures were rather a welcome tool to restructure property relations for accumulation and control (Porter 2011: 118).

From this criticism it can be concluded that it is not necessarily the land title which guarantees security of tenure, but more so formal or informal rules (Handzic 2010; Nakamura 2016; Reerink & Gelder 2010). In fact, informal recognition can provide the same tenure security than freehold, but without unintended consequences of gentrification and expulsion of the poor (UN-Habitat 2016: 62).

back of the state from direct and indirect housing interventions, leaving the impression that governments should give up their attempts to improve the living conditions of the poor (Bredenoord & Lindert 2010). Ingredients of the enabling approach, such as the dominance of home ownership ideology, private property, extension of financial markets, and perception of the housing sector as an economic sector can be seen as a political strategy to perpetuate the dominance of neoliberalism. By creating and extending investments in housing markets and by facilitating capital switching between the circuits of capital accumulation the financialisation of housing can be seen as another fix for the crisis tendencies of the capitalist system (Sassen 2009; Soederberg 2014; Aalbers 2008, 2016; Rolnik 2013a). Presupposing that the responsibility for poverty is in the hands of the poor, enabling strategies can be justified (Roy 2005: 148).

For more than three decades, the World Bank and UN-Habitat have advocated the enabling strategy. In many countries this approach has delivered housing on scale, but outcomes regarding target groups are mixed and dependent on local circumstances. The ease of building regulations and liberalisation of housing finance markets led to incentives for the building industry, resulting in higher quantitative output (UN-Habitat 2016: 62). Better access to mortgage financing and general housing finance for a larger part of societies was achieved (Harris 2015). In addition, security of tenure has improved in many cases due to formalisation efforts (UN-Habitat 2016: 61; Ferguson & Smets 2010).

The main problem of the enabling strategy, however, is that most of the measures are beneficial for the middle class rather than the poor (Sengupta et al. 2018). For the latter, things can even get worse. Formalisation is beneficial for homeowners only, not for renters, and housing finance remains unreachable for those with an irregular and low income. Therefore, the high expectations to achieve a better financial inclusion of the poor are not justified (Mader 2018). By extending the formal housing stock and enabling more people to obtain mortgage finance, negative consequences are increased land prices followed by rising housing costs and rents. In many cases, this leads to intensified gentrification processes with negative consequences. Many slum dwellers are not eligible to benefit from this strategy; they have to rely on informal mechanisms to enhance their housing conditions incrementally (Ferguson & Smets 2010). This has not changed despite the efforts to extend housing finance down the income ladder. Even as homeowners with formalised titles, they usually work in the informal sector and cannot afford monthly payments or are not eligible. Community saving groups and micro-credit for housing might become an option (Ferguson & Smets 2010), but these initiatives are not widespread yet. Pursuing an enabling approach, governments have abandoned other housing programmes or measures, such as rent controls. Some governments also refrained from extending their efforts to construct public housing or have even sold off their existing social housing stock (UN-Habitat 2007). While channelling available resources to enabling policies, self-help programmes were neglected and, if applied, often focused only on physical upgrading instead of multi-sectoral and integrated approaches. These developments have made more tense the situation of housing markets for low-income groups (UN-Habitat 2016). The building industry was enabled to scale up its activities, but due to insignificant profit margins and higher risks, private developers remain reluctant to build at the lower end of the housing market (UN-Habitat 2002a: 53). Once again, the private sector has proven unable to provide adequate and affordable housing for the poor.

Even the United Nations in their latest city report of 2016 admit that the enabling strategy has failed or is about to fail:

> [...] the housing policies put in place over the last 20 years through the enabling approach have not succeeded in promoting adequate and affordable housing. Governments have backed away from direct supply without giving sufficient consideration to the markets and regulatory framework to enable other actors in the process to step forward and provide adequate and affordable housing. (UN-Habitat 2016: 65)

This statement acknowledges the shortcomings of the enabling approach, but sees the reasons for this not in the approach itself, but in an insufficient implementation. The UN admits that many efforts have been taken to formulate more comprehensive housing policies, but these strategy documents have rarely been effectively turned into action. Weak or lacking institutions, ineffective mechanisms, lack of legal frameworks and tools such as land registration systems, limited financial resources, and absent political will are still challenges not easy to overcome (UN-Habitat 2002a: 4–5).

At first glance, the enabling approach seemed to be more suitable to address the housing challenge due to its holistic nature. However, it also had shortcomings: it distracted attention from the housing question, it further fostered a retreat of the state from its social responsibilities, and implementation proved much more complicated than intended (Bredenoord et al. 2010). So far the government actors' lacking capacities to manage such an approach have been held responsible for its failure (Chiodelli 2016: 6–7; Tibaijuka 2009: 172–176; Smets et al. 2014: 4). The most important problem with the enabling approach, however, was that the private sector could not deliver for all segments of society. No matter what efforts were taken, for the poorest, for those working in the informal sector, home ownership and formal credits were no option at all. By relying solely on the private sector to deliver housing it was the middle class that benefitted; the poor faced adverse effects (Chiodelli 2016: 6–7). Despite these insights, the enabling approach is still the most propagated and recommended approach towards housing and in the New Urban Agenda 'enablement' is an important phrase, even though mentioned less prominently than before. Table 20 summarises advantages and disadvantages of the enabling approach.

Table 20 Pros and cons of two components of the enabling approach: housing finance and formalisation

	Pros	Cons
Housing finance	– Lower interest rates than in the informal sector – Better access to secure credit – Encourages private sector to construct housing for low-income groups – Reduced reliance on government aid (reduced costs for governments)	– Not for the poor, since income is irregular and too low – Higher housing costs for the poorest part of society – Private sector tends to focus on middle class – Fewer efforts for the urban poor
Formalisation	– Financial assets for low-income people – Reduced reliance on government aid (reduced costs for governments)	– Global finance takes over housing sector – Free circulation of capital in housing markets – Increased vulnerability for global financial crisis

Source: Table by author. Based on Rolnik (2013a) and UN-Habitat (2016)

15.1.4 Latest practices – public housing back on the table?

Despite the fact that enabling policies are still advocated on the international level, many countries have fallen back to older strategies, which is taking shape in the re-emergence of mass-scaled supply-driven housing programmes in some regions of the world (Buckley & Simet 2015; Croese et al. 2016; Waeyenberge 2017). The enabling approach did not deliver rapid results, did not reach the poor, and left the perception that governments would abandon the housing question. Against accelerating poverty, increasing inequality, and rising numbers of slum dwellers, many countries opted to change their housing policies again and reengaged in low-income housing delivery. Brazil and India, for instance, introduced enabling policies in the 1990s, but recently introduced state-administered large-scale housing programmes. These programmes are not public housing programmes, but materialise as subsidised housing solutions for the urban poor, to be delivered by commercial developers, as for instance the Minha Casa Minha Vida programme in Brazil (Sengupta et al. 2018: 866). Beside this, other strategies are also revived. Perlman (2017: 9–11) also reported an increase in slum eradication through clearances since the 2000s in Brazil. This continuing trend to relocate slum dwellers is also notable in Africa and Asia (cf. Smets et al. 2014; Croese et al. 2016; Saharan et al. 2018).

15.2 Modes of housing provision in developing countries

The discussion on housing circles around one central question: How should governments intervene in the housing sector? As we have seen in the three phases of policy advice, this question cannot be answered easily. We can only approach possible responses for different contextual backgrounds. For that endeavour, it is useful to recall the possibilities of intervention for governments: what options do governments have in the housing sector? Governments can aim at an improvement of quantitative numbers of housing and they can improve the housing quality in existing settlements. It is largely agreed upon that improving housing quality and living conditions in existing settlements is to be done by various forms of upgrading activities (cf. box 9). Much more disputed is the search for effective methods for improving the quantitative housing production. The literature indicates that intervention strategies are country- and group-specific, suggesting that one-size-fits-all approaches are unlikely to achieve sound results (Keivani & Werna 2001b; Rojas 2018).

For designing country-specific intervention strategies, it is necessary to understand what modes of housing provision compose the housing sector in a given country. Only then does it become possible to find an answer to the question of what interventions are most suitable. Ramin Keivani and Edmundo Werna (2001a, 2001b) have developed a useful conceptual model in this regard (cf. figure 22).

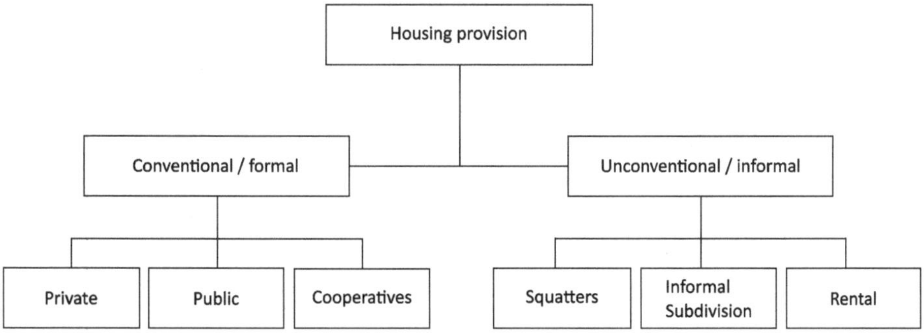

Fig. 22 Modes of housing provision in developing countries
Source: Illustration by author. Based on Keivani & Werna (2001a)

They found that different modes of housing provision do exist in developing countries, which can be roughly separated into conventional (formal) and unconventional (informal) housing production[6]. Formal actors in accordance with legal practices produce conventional housing, while housing constructed informally does not follow legislation, land use plans, or building standards. They subdivide these two major classes further into three subclasses each. Depending on the national context (eg macro-economic development, degree of financial integration in global markets, availability of mortgage finance, path dependencies of housing production, etc) each country's housing production relies more or less on these modes of housing provision. While in developed countries most of the housing stock is created conventionally, in the Global South the informal production is much more significant. Estimations range from 60 to 80 % of all produced housing (Hernández et al. 2010: 12; Bredenoord & Lindert 2010: 281).

15.2.1 Formal and informal modes of housing provision

In the formal sector, three general modes of housing provision exist: housing can be provided through the formal private sector (individual owner-occupiers or developers), the public, or by cooperatives. In the informal sector, housing is provided through squatting (illegal occupation of land for housing purposes), informal subdivisions, or rental housing. All six modes of housing production can be further subdivided, eg by types of squatter settlements, by history of formation, and others.

Formal private sector housing provision can take on many forms, from individual house-building by owner-occupiers to large-scale projects carried out by developers. Depending on the structure of the housing market in a given country, commercial housing developers are more present or not. In developing countries, this mode of housing provision is responsible for roughly 20 % of all units produced (Keivani & Werna 2001a: 90). If housing finance markets are 'underdeveloped', individual owner-occupiers tend to dominate formal private production. However, under specific conditions (ie incentives by the government, a large supply of mortgage finance, a situation of ongoing economic growth, etc) commercial developers might also contribute significant numbers. This happened in Thailand in the 1980s and 1990s, when the Thai government succeeded in a massive extension of private sector housing production. Already celebrated as a panacea for the housing question and as a successful market enablement (Dowall 1989), the implosion of the housing bubble in 1997 and the subsequent Asian financial crisis proved the opposite (Sheng & Kirinpanu 2000). The hous-

6 The distinction of housing production into conventional and unconventional modes is for conceptual reasons only. In reality, both sectors are connected in a complex continuum of interrelations. Informality does not imply poverty. Nor are informal subdivisions only created by the poor, or private individuals with owner-occupation always rich. What is important here is that metropolitan expansion is increasingly driven by informal urbanisation (Roy 2005: 149).

ing experiment had been beneficial for some, but made housing less accessible for the lowest income groups (Yap 2015).

In the formal public sector, direct and indirect interventions in housing provision can be distinguished as modes of housing production (Keivani & Werna 2001a: 84–86). Governments have introduced state-financed public housing programmes as a means for direct interventions in the housing sector, and the project-based self-help programmes of the 1960s and 1970s as indirect intervention strategies (sites and services and slum upgrading). Both intervention strategies had their shortcomings – public housing provision in general failed to reach scales for successfully addressing the housing question (cf. chapter 15.1.1).

Keivani and Werna (2001a) distinguish another mode of formal housing production, which was not mentioned yet and is often neglected in scholarly literature due to its supposed insignificance: cooperative housing. In many countries various housing cooperatives have appeared since the early 20th century, self-managed or state-supported, as providers of housing stock for their members (Bredenoord & Lindert 2010: 285–286; Ganapati 2010). Various forms of housing cooperatives exist, eg professional organisations, trade organisations, associations of teachers, taxi-drivers (Keivani & Werna 2001a: 88). These organisations work by pooling their resources in formal organisations to take measures (negotiations for land, mortgage loans, etc) to fulfil the housing needs of their members. Cooperative housing was not very significant in the Global South but has gained influence since the 1980s in some countries (eg India) due to the retreat of the state associated with neoliberal policies and the enabling approach (Ganapati 2014).

More significant than formal modes of housing production are the modes of informal housing production: squatting, informal subdivision, and informal rent agreements (Obermayr 2017: 33–40). During the acceleration of urbanisation in the 1950s and until the 1980s, squatting became the only option to gain access to housing for migrants and the poorest parts of the population (Davis 2006: 96). Squatting can be defined as an 'illegal occupation of land by households for their shelter purposes' (Keivani & Werna 2001a: 75), happening by processes of infiltration or invasion. Infiltration is a slow formation process, where in absence of state control residents slowly occupy land over several years. Invasion, in contrast, is an organised and planned process, where a number of households decide to take a free piece of land as their new home. Literally overnight, the land is occupied and simple shacks are erected (Hardoy & Satterthwaite 1989; Obermayr 2017: 38). In both types of squatter settlements, very simple structures are built in the initial stage, but over the years the inhabitants, dependent on their income and perceived security of tenure, improve these structures. Often, the residents organise in neighbourhood associations, CBOs and NGOs, which disseminate knowledge and technical assistance, guarantee loans, and have the important task of negotiating with authorities about connections to services (road network, power supply, water, etc). Consolidation activities happen incrementally and over several years, requiring flexible short-term loans that fit the insecure income conditions common for most dwellers in squatter settlements. Formal banks do not provide such unsecure loans, which is why the dwellers usually depend on their relatives and friends obtaining informal loans that fit their abilities of repayment. Depending on social cohesion, and the negotiation success of local leaders and NGOs, the consolidation process might be supported by governments' slum upgrading programmes (Keivani & Werna 2001a: 75–78).

The second mode of informal housing provision are informal subdivisions or 'semi-legal squatting' (Davis 2006: 44). In this process private developers and investors enter into a partnership with landowners to develop their land and sell it afterwards (UN-Habitat 2016: 54). The process is semi-legal, since on the one hand, *de facto* landowners have authorised the activities, but on the other hand, building rules, planning frameworks, and zoning regulations are usually violated. The settlements are characterised by a planned layout, a peripheral location, high security of tenure, non-conformity with urban development plans or construction standards, and a high degree of self-help housing (Baross & Linden 1990: 2–7; Obermayr 2017: 37). After completion, the units are sold – including sale documents – to middle-income or the upper segment of low-income groups. These new inhabitants consider themselves as owners, having obtained a *de facto* claim to their property. In contrast to squatter settlements, not community associations, but private developers take on the task of negotiating with governmental agencies to ensure this *de facto* security and service provision. In many cases, these developers also provide loans for the house purchase. Later on, when all plots are sold and developers withdraw from the area, CBOs and NGOs may form, similar to squatter settlements, to represent the interests of the community (Keivani & Werna 2001a: 78–80). Since the 1980s, this mode of production has clearly become the dominant one in the Global South, providing the vast majority of all housing units produced internationally (Roy 2005).

Another informal mode of housing provision is informal rental housing. First-time migrants to cities and some groups of low-income dwellers usually have no means to purchase informal subdivisions nor social connections to join squatter settlements as owner-occupiers. Therefore, their only option to find shelter is rental accommodation. Rental housing is also attractive for the poor, since it is often centrally located and offers varying types, sizes, and contractual arrangements suitable to different needs (Rojas 2018: 10; Yap 2015: 5). Whole areas are even specialised for this type of accommodation, eg villa 31, an informal settlement near the central railway station of Buenos Aires, which accommodates significant numbers of migrants (Benwell et al. 2013). Since formal rental options are often very low in scale, informal tenancy is the widespread option (Gilbert 2015). These rented housing options are characterised by bad living conditions, high rents, and, due to the exploitive landlord-tenant relation, are highly exploitive, offering only a minimum of security of tenure. Dwellers in such accommodations are thus highly vulnerable. With economic development of specific

Table 21 Modes of housing provision and associated target groups

Mode of housing provision			Target groups	Notes
Formal	Private	**Individual homeowners**	High-income groups	– Private market for high income groups
		Commercial developers	High- and middle-income groups; Upper segment of low-income groups	– Unsuitable for poorest households – Investment for middle class
	Public	**Social housing**	Low-income groups, government employees	– Dominant 1950s to 1970s – State-financed – Mismatch with residential needs – Poor quality, high costs, poor maintenance, peripheral location
		Slum-upgrading	Low-income groups, homeowners	– Security of tenure, basic services – May induce gentrification and expulsion
		Sites and services	Low-income groups, not the poorest, homeowners	– Imitation of informal subdivision – Self-help to reduce costs, many actors and bureaucracy – Peripheral location, inadequate technical assistance, low output
		Cooperative	Low- to middle-income groups	– Only in some countries – Low output
Informal		**Squatters**	Poorest and first-time migrants	– Dominant between 1950s and 1980s – Formation: Infiltration and Invasion – Incremental consolidation – Strong group cohesion and representation (NGOs, CBOs) – Informal housing finance
		Subdivisions	Low- and middle-income groups	– Dominant since the 1980s – Informal developers – Peripheral location, planned layout, sale documents, informal housing finance from developers
		Rental	First-time migrants and low-income groups	– Conditions vary due to available stock and government interventions – Mostly inadequate living conditions – High rents – Central locations

Source: Table by author. Based on Keivani & Werna (2001a, 2001b)

cities, this type of accommodation tends to fall in scale, but for some groups it remains the only or the preferred option to obtain shelter due to their life situation. Advantages are the central location and sometimes, dependent on available stock and recognition by local governments, also relatively low rents (UN-Habitat 2003a: 109–111; Keivani & Werna 2001a: 80–82).

The described modes of housing provision in developing countries are summarised in table 21. Every mode can be associated with specific target groups depending on available income and other factors. Formal modes of housing provision in general serve high- to middle-income groups and informal modes provide the housing stock for the poorer parts of society. This recognition is not new, but the analytical categorisation makes it possible to derive suggestions for policy interventions. If housing provision for low-income groups are to be improved, those modes of provision that are clearly beneficial for this target group should be the centre of focus. That means that if governments decide for instance to promote the private mode of housing provision by market enablement, this may be beneficial for upper-income groups and may also reach some of the poor, but first-time migrants or the poorest groups will not be reached. Therefore, beside these efforts, simultaneously also other measures must be introduced that promote other modes of housing provision and clearly target the lowest income groups.

15.2.2 Changing modes of housing provision and associated intervention strategies

Over the years, the proportions of these modes of housing provision for overall housing production have changed. Estimations on proportions are not available – only rough assessments for specific countries. These are illustrated in pie charts for the modes of formal and informal housing provision (cf. figure 23 and figure 24). When interpreting these charts, we must bear in mind that informal housing provision is much more important for the overall housing production in the Global South, accounting for 60 to 80 % of all new housing stock produced per year.

Formal modes of housing production did not change much between the 1960s and 2000s. Private production – promoted by market enablement – remains the dominant mode. Due to the international policy discourse public housing has become less significant, supplying less than 10 % of the overall conventional production of housing units (Smets et al. 2014: 2). In some countries, cooperative housing has been on the rise, contributing slowly increasing proportions. Also sites and services schemes, non-existent in the 1960s, are now adding small numbers to the available housing options.

More important changes have occurred in the informal modes of housing production. Back in the 1950s to the 1980s squatting was the main mode of housing production in the Global South. A lack of state control and the availability of undeveloped land were the main reasons why squatting had become the main option to satisfy housing needs. These circumstances, most importantly the availability of land, have noticeably changed over the last decades. Today, informal subdivision is the most significant mode of housing provision, contributing up to 70 % of all housing produced informally (Bähr & Mertins 2000: 20). Proportions of formal rental housing is insignificant in the

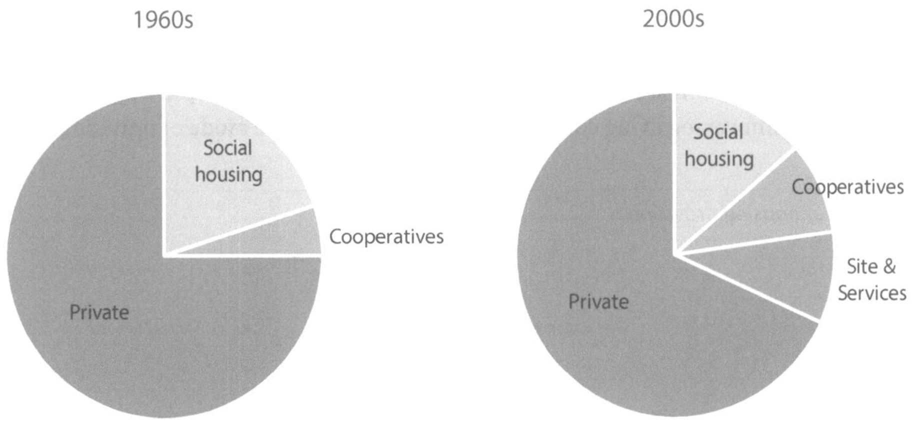

Fig. 23 Modes of formal housing production and their shares in developing countries, 1960s and 2000s
Source: Illustration by author. Proportions are rough estimations based on Keivani & Werna (2001a) and UN-Habitat (2003a)

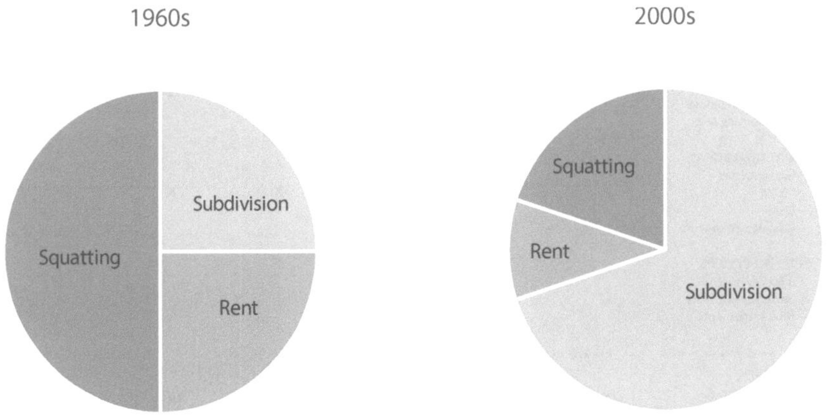

Fig. 24 Modes of informal housing production and their shares in developing countries, 1960s and 2000s
Source: Illustration by author. Proportions are rough estimations based on Keivani & Werna (2001a) and UN-Habitat (2003a)

Global South, since governments continue to promote home ownership, discouraging the extension of rental markets. With economic growth, proportions of informal rental housing tend also to decrease (Keivani & Werna 2001a: 81).

Housing intervention strategies applied during the three phases of housing policies can be analysed according to their effect on specific modes of housing provision (cf. figure 25). All interventions applied so far have targeted either private or public formal modes of production or the dominant informal modes of production, squatters and informal subdivisions. Clearly, the focus has always been on conventional housing provision, since it cannot be in the interest of the state to allow or promote informal activities within its jurisdiction. Therefore, all interventions targeting unconventional modes of housing provision aim at formalising these modes of provision in some way in the first place, not at improving living conditions without changing the mode of provision.

Modes of housing provision

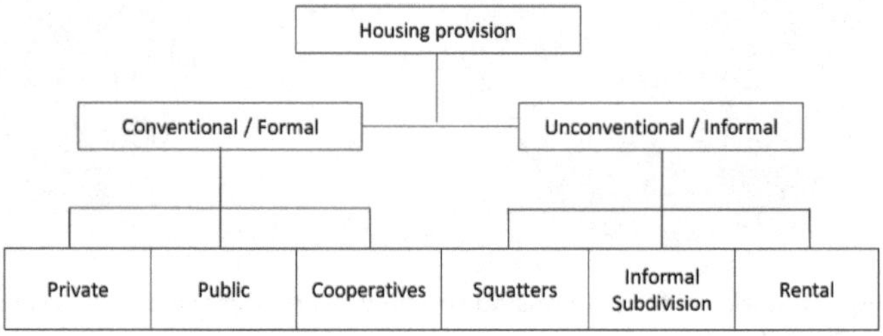

Housing intervention strategies

Phase	Strategy	Private	Public	Cooperatives	Squatters	Informal Subdivision	Rental
Phase I Public housing	Slum clearances	–	–	–	X	X	–
	Resettlement	–	–	–	X	X	–
	Social housing - Infrastructure - Industrial standard - New housing units	–	X	–	–	–	–
Phase II Aided self-help	Slum upgrading - Infrastructure - Titling - Credit - Existing settlements	–	X	–	X	X	–
	Site & services - Infrastructure - Basic housing units - New settlements	–	X	–	–	–	–
Phase III Enabling approach	Financing - Access to credit - Financial institutions and instruments	X	–	–	(X)	(X)	–
	Rules - Titling - Land-use and building regulations	X	–	–	X	X	–
	Institutional structure - Decentralisation - Subsidiarity - Participation	X	X	–	–	–	–

Impact of housing intervention strategies on specific modes of housing provision: **X** high **(X)** medium – none

Fig. 25 Modes of housing provision and associated housing intervention strategies during three phases of global housing policy advocacy
Source: Illustration by author

Three matters stand out (cf. figure 25): First, interventions targeting conventional provision have moved from the public mode of housing provision during the first and second phase of housing policies towards private modes of housing provision during the ongoing enabling phase. Second, interventions in the unconventional mode of housing provisions have moved from slum-upgrading, infrastructure provision, and home improvements towards the change of regulations, titling programmes, and the overhaul of building and land use regulations. Third, cooperative and rental housing provision has been astonishingly ignored in all three phases of recommended housing policies.

Government interventions in the housing sector, whether direct or indirect, always aim at one of these modes of housing provision. Since each mode targets the housing needs of specific groups (cf. table 21), associated interventions might be beneficial for some parts of society, but might also have harmful consequences for others. Interventions that promote formal private sector provision, for example, might be beneficial for middle-income groups and upper segments of low-income dwellers, but are simultaneously harmful for first-time migrant since these measures could have negative effects on informal rental markets, decreasing the available stock and increasing the rents for this part of society. Therefore, no single intervention focusing on one mode of provision can solve the housing question; a plurality of approaches to be applied simultaneously and adapted to national and local circumstances is needed to mitigate adverse effects of well-intended measures that might harm other segments of society.

16 Summary: Towards a Multiplicity of Approaches

This chapter has illustrated and analysed the global housing situation, conferences and milestones addressing the housing question, and changing housing policy paradigms as well as formal and informal modes of housing provision. The following questions guided the analysis:

Which intervention strategies are globally discussed to address the housing challenge?
- What is the housing situation on a global level?
- What paradigms shape(d) the discourse on housing the poor?
- Which strategies were applied to what effect?

The global housing situation shows alarming trends. Population growth has become entirely focused on urban areas and the lack of affordable and adequate housing is increasingly visible in rising absolute numbers of slum dwellers on a global scale. This urban crisis has been acknowledged in international conferences on human settlements and manifold strategies have been developed to address the challenge. The recommended approaches advocated by main actors – the World Bank and UN-Habitat – show changing paradigms for sound housing policies, evolving from social housing over project-based self-help strategies towards the enabling approach and comprehensive sector policies. The right to adequate housing and minimum conditions for housing have been outlined, to be achieved by inclusive pro-poor housing policies. On the ground, applied strategies are more blurred, partly following international advice, but also pursuing the manifold varieties of available options to intervene in the housing sector. The latest paradigm of enabling is increasingly questioned and many countries have revived older strategies of mass-scale public housing, slum clearances, and slum upgrading approaches. Against the increasing lack of adequate housing, the efforts are unsatisfying.

The changing housing discourse has not been immune to the general ascendancy of neoliberal principles visible in the declarations and resulting recommendations of Habitat I to Habitat III (Soederberg 2017). The broad set of principles, consisting of minimal state intervention, privatisation, commodification of housing, and individualisation is visible in many self-help initiatives and in the enabling approach. The promotion of such strategies is not a means to solve the housing question for all, since it promotes housing provision for middle- and high-income groups, and despite the successful extension of housing markets, the argument of 'filtering-down' cannot be sustained against empirical evidence (Keivani & Werna 2001b; Chiodelli 2016; UN-Habitat 2016; Sengupta et al. 2018).

The extension of private housing markets alone is not enough to solve housing issues for all parts of society and the private sector, whether formal or informal, does not work for the poorest, since its main driver is profit-seeking (Bredenoord & Lindert 2010; Yap 2015). The view of the housing sector as an economic sector and the extension of housing finance appears more as a means to avoid crisis tendencies of capitalist accumulation, allowing and maintaining an easy switching of capital between the circuits of capital accumulation and sustaining the currently dominant economic formation.

This development is reflected in applied housing policies, characterised by the tension between the perspective of housing as a good with use value and housing as a good with market value (Smets et al. 2014: 2). These two conflictual perspectives have produced opposing views associated with the role of the state in housing interventions: the older perspective argues that the housing challenges needs to be addressed by comprehensive and cost-intensive state interventions, a major push for quantitative housing production as a task of the state, and a focus on the need to provide more social housing. The newer perspective emphasises a more market-based view, seeing the role of governments as an enabler, obligated to give incentives for all actors to produce more housing stock: the private sector and the urban poor themselves. Depending on historic experiences and the countries' individual context, these two competing perspectives are inherent to specific housing interventions applied.

The second perspective has become hegemonic, favouring housing policies that highlight owner-occupation as the preferred form of tenure and focusing on improved housing markets to achieve high rates of ownership. This is not necessarily desirable, however, since there are rich countries with very low home ownership proportions (Gilbert 2011: 82–83). It is moreover necessary to abandon this logic of home ownership, financialisation, and commodification, which threatens the right to adequate housing, and focus instead the goal of solving the shelter problems in the Global South (Rolnik 2013b; Waeyenberge 2017).

A more nuanced view on actual housing provision is needed. Considering specific modes of housing provision for specific target groups is important as is the recognition that most housing is produced informally. Neither the formal sector nor well-intended interventions have produced the bulk of shelter for urban populations. The solution for the urban poor is rather found in informal self-build housing, using a range of user-defined and community-managed techniques. This informal housing is produced in an ongoing social process, recognising the value of space and everyday social practices. It is easily adaptable, reacting to changing conditions, as settlements consolidate over the years (Bower 2016: 85–86).

Past intervention strategies, however, have aimed mostly at the formal sector or were intended to regularise informal developments. These strategies should be reconsidered. If the goal is really to improve housing conditions and provide adequate and affordable housing at scale, it is hard to understand why the informal modes of housing production are ignored in such a profound way. Informal housing should be accepted instead as the main provider of housing and approaches must be developed to promote the informal modes of housing production. This means anticipateingand planning the extension of informal settlements, fostering upgrading activities, and considering other modes of housing provision as well (Gilbert 2011: 85).

It does not mean that governments should turn away from their applied housing policies. The enabling approach was an important achievement with its components of market, government and community enablement. In many cases, the approach has resulted in improved governance, more efficient land markets, provision of basic infrastructure and services, and improved housing finance (conventional mortgage loans, subsidised interest rates, micro-finance, or community shelter funds). Also slum upgrading activities should be continued, securing tenure by recognition not necessarily by formalisation, and with the strong involvement of communities in the implementation planning, and maintaining stages (Choguill 2007: 147–148). Public housing is also an important component of housing policies, which needs massive investments (Marx et al. 2013: 203–206).

Informal housing provision is also not a panacea (UN-Habitat 2016: 54), but informal ways of housing delivery should be incorporated in overall housing policies and other modes of provision should be considered. The rental sector, for instance, is extremely relevant in some cities for housing provision – 62 % and 49 % of citizens in Cairo and Lagos, respectively, live in rented housing (Tibaijuka 2009: 97) – but is widely neglected in studies and applied policies (Yap 2015: 5). In addition, cooperative housing might have potential not yet activated.

In summary, it can be concluded that there is no one-size-fits-all approach for sound strategies to address the housing question. Best practices do not work in every place. Instead, all modes of housing delivery should be taken into account (Rojas 2018). In the New Urban Agenda this is acknowledged by recommending diverse housing delivery options (§ 105–112) to be integrated in comprehensive housing policies within an enabling policy framework (UN 2017). Applied housing policies, thus, must be tailored to the context and deploy an interplay of approaches that addresses different modes of housing provision and specific income groups. Strategies solely based on market enablement, public housing, or self-help are likely to fail. Instead, massive state investments are needed, with a need to increase government spending in the housing sector above rates that are commonly below 2 % of countries' GDPs (Gilbert 2011: 81) and deploy these resources not only for measures 'setting the scene' for the private sector, but also towards direct and indirect housing production and improvements.

IV. HOUSING IN INDONESIA

This chapter contextualises the case studies, examines Indonesia's national housing situation and analyses its housing policies (organisation and content). To do this, a first section introduces the country and illustrates the latest social, economic and political trends. After that, Indonesia's cities and settlements, their distinctive elements, and the country's housing situation are examined. A third section explores the content of Indonesia's housing policies from a historic perspective, identifying housing policy phases, actors, and rules of the game. This analysis is deepened in the successive section by exploring different housing programmes and their evolution, including mechanisms, procedures, and outcomes. The final section critically assesses the impact of housing policies with a special focus on low-income groups. The following questions guide this chapter:

Which intervention strategies are implemented on the Indonesian scale to address the housing challenge?

- What is the housing situation in Indonesia?
- What are rules of the game and central actors in Indonesia's housing domain?
- Which measures, strategies, and programmes were applied to what effect?

17 Social, Economic, and Political Trends in Indonesia

In order to contextualise the study this first section introduces Indonesia and analyses latest development trends. Three aspects related to the housing question are illustrated and discussed in more detail: the population and urbanisation development, poverty rates, and data on slum developments. After the presentation of the latest political developments and their significance for national housing policies, a special feature of the Indonesian administrative system is outlined. This is important for an understanding of the mechanisms applied in various housing programmes.

17.1 Introducing a diverse country

The Republic of Indonesia is a tropical country in South East Asia, consisting of approximately 18,000 islands covering an area of 1,919 km^2 between the two continents of Asia to the north and Australia to the south. Approximately 6,800 of its islands are inhabited by 265 million people (2018), making Indonesia the 4th most populated country in the world (BPS 2019d, 2019b). The five largest islands are Java, Sumatra, Kalimantan (Borneo), Sulawesi, and the western part of Papua Island (cf. figure 26). Of these, Java Island (henceforth 'Java') has always been the political, cultural, and economic heart of the country. It was on Java where the historic Javanese kingdoms formed, and four of the five largest cities are located on this island (UN-Habitat 2015a; World Bank 2015a). Within the island, everything is concentrated to the west, namely towards the metropolitan region of Jakarta. Located at the island's north-western edge, the Indonesian capital has developed into a megacity-region with 22 million inhabitants producing 17 % of Indonesia's GDP (BPS 2019d).

Indonesia is an ethnically diverse country. Beside the two most dominant groups – Javanese and Sundanese, 40.6 % and 15 % of the total population, respectively – it is also home to countless other ethnic minorities with various cultures and languages. Estimations range from there being 300 to 800 different languages. Over the centuries, the Malay language in different variations has become the *lingua franca,* disseminated by sea traders to every corner of the archipelago. This formed the basis of today's of-

Fig. 26 Indonesian provinces and capital cities
Source: Reprinted from CartoGIS Services, College of Asia and the Pacific, The Australian National University (2013)

ficial language: Bahasa Indonesia. Seen as a unifying element for Indonesia's various ethnic groups, this language is strongly promoted by the state, and every Indonesian is required to gain proficiency, most commonly as his or her second language (Gamino 2012; Obermayr 2017: 75–77).

This diversity is also reflected in socio-economic terms, showing wide disparities. There are two patterns: one is a centrum-periphery disparity, the other one a west-east disparity. Java can be considered as the economic and political centre. With 140 million people, more than half of Indonesia's population is crammed on this island and nearly 60 % of the country's GDP is generated there (BPS 2019d: 87). The other regions are less populated and considered as periphery. The farther away from Java, the lesser 'developed' are these regions, as shown in indicators such as share of GDP per capita, the Gini index and Human Development Index (HDI) (BPS 2019c). These indicators also reveal a clear west-to-east gradient. Generally, the western islands show less poverty and a higher degree of human development.

Contrasting impressions from Indonesia's regions underpin this picture. In Papua, large areas are still covered by rainforest, infrastructure is poor, poverty rates high, and many tribes still follow traditional beliefs – not one of the five religions officially acknowledged by the state[1]. In contrast to this, there is the vibrant capital of Jakarta, where one after another skyscraper reaches out to the sky and where people live westernised, 'modern' lifestyles. Similar to that, the global inflow of tourists has deeply influenced the traditional way of life on the Hindu island of Bali, transforming it into an exotic holiday destination. At the northern edge of Sumatra, by contrast, in the province of Aceh, a strict interpretation of Islam has become the basis for the region's law. The two largest islands, Kalimantan and Sumatra, are increasingly targeted by processes of globalisation, visible in the spread of oil palm plantations and resource-extracting industries inevitably transforming vast areas and local livelihoods (Novira 2017).

Governing this culturally diverse, multi-ethnic state with its large socio-economic disparities is a difficult duty. Fears of state disintegration have always been a strong rationale behind government policies since independence (1949). The state motto of 'unity in diversity' (*Bhinneka Tunggal Ika*) and the state ideology of *Pancasila* form the base of the Indonesian state[2]. The motto is deeply rooted in Javanese culture, expressing a longing for harmony and stable societal relations. Diverging views and opposition are seen critically, perceived as undermining consensual decision-making (Frings 2012). The state philosophy acknowledges multiple cultures and languages in the country, but also emphasises unity, meaning that sovereignty of parts will not be tolerated. The latter has produced several clashes and struggles over the last 70 years, namely the Maluku conflict, the East-Timor occupation, and the smouldering conflicts for independence in Aceh and Papua. To prevent separatist tendencies and to promote unity, the national government has promoted several measures, eg the large scale transmigration programmes[3], a unifying language, and far-reaching decentralisation policies in more recent times (David 2012; May 2015).

In the last two decades, Indonesia has shown improvements in many fields, illustrated by social and economic indicators (cf. table 22). Economic growth was sustained at average rates of 5 % annual GDP increase over the last years and the international

1 Five religions, namely Islam, Christianity, Hinduism, Confucianism, and Buddhism, are acknowledged in Indonesia. The belonging to one of these five religions is obligatory and written on identity cards and passports. Most Indonesians consider it necessary to follow one of these religions and atheism is not accepted.

2 Five interconnected and interrelated principles were put in the preamble of the Indonesian constitution of 1945 as the central pillars of the nation. Known as *Pancasila*, they are to be followed by all Indonesians regardless of their ethnicity or their political beliefs. These principles are: 1) belief in God 2) humanitarianism and internationalism 3) national unity 4) democracy 5) social justice and prosperity (Dahm & Ptak 1999: 230–231; Obermayr 2017: 87).

3 Transmigration policies were already introduced during colonial times (from 1905) to ease the uneven distribution of population in the country and to strengthen control over more remote areas. Known as *Transmigrasi*, the efforts included a redistribution of population from Java Island to more peripheral regions, where new agrarian colonies were founded. The programmes continued and intensified under Suharto's regime and by 2001 over five million people had been resettled from Java island (Vorlaufer 2009: 74–77; Scholz 1992).

financial crisis of 2007–2008 barely affected the country (JICA 2018). This economic resilience was attributed to the strong and continued domestic demand. Indonesia is meanwhile classified as a middle-income country (OECD 2010). In addition, social indicators, such as the HDI, the Gini coefficient, or the poverty degree, show a positive trend. Population growth remains high and the country is continuously urbanising, causing an ever-increasing demand for infrastructure, housing, and urban services.

Table 22 Indonesia: selected social and economic indicators

Indicator	Source	Value
Population 2018 (million)	[a]	265
Annual population growth 2017 (%)	[c]	1.14
Urban population 2015 (million)	[d]	138
Urbanisation degree 2015 (%)	[d]	53
Average GDP growth 2014–2018 (%)	[f]	~5
GDP per capita 2018 (US$*)	[g]	4,284
Human Development Index 2018	[e]	0.71
Gini coefficient 2018 [2014]	[e], [f]	0.38 [0,41]
Poverty degree 2019 [2014] (%)	[a], [f]	9.42 [10.96]
Poverty line in Rp. per person per month 2019 (in €**)	[a]	442,000 (~ 29.50)
Average salary in Rp. per person per month 2019 (in €**)	[a]	2,800,000 (~ 187)
Share of urban population living in slums 2018 [2015] (%)	[e]	7.42 [9.21]
Households with access to improved drinking water 2018 [2014] (%)	[e]	73.7 [68.4]
Households with access to improved sanitation 2018 [2014] (%)	[e]	69.3 [61.1]

Sources: Table by author. Data compiled/calculated from **[a]** Badan Pusat Statistik Indonesia – BPS (2019b: 31), **[b]** BPS (2019d), **[c]** United Nations Department of Economic and Social Affairs, Population Division – UN-DESA (2019), **[d]** UN-DESA (2018b), **[e]** BPS (2019c), **[f]** Republic of Indonesia (2019), **[g]** World Bank (2019)
Notes: * Data are in constant 2010 U. S. dollars. ** Exchange rate: 1€ = Rp. 15,000 (09/2019, received from https://fxtop.com)

17.2 Improvements in poverty levels

Poverty levels remain high in Indonesia, but the poverty degree has gradually declined in both urban and rural areas. According to the central statistics agency (Badan Pusat Statistik, or BPS), 25 million people, or 9.42 % of the total population, lived in poverty in 2019 (cf. figure 27). Coming down from its peak after the Asian economic crisis in 1998, the degree has significantly dropped below the threshold of 10 % in 2019. Only in 2006 was a small increase recorded, caused by an oil price hike on international markets. Interestingly, the national poverty degree continued to drop afterwards, even during the international financial crisis of the years 2007 and 2008.

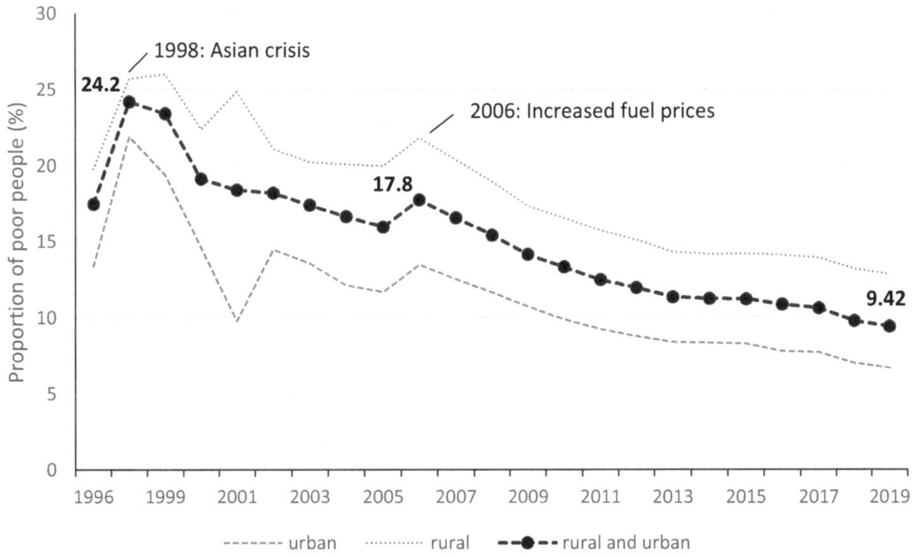

Fig. 27 Share of population below the Indonesian poverty line in rural and urban areas, 1996–2019
Source: Illustration by author. Data from Badan Pusat Statistik Indonesia – BPS (2019b: 51)

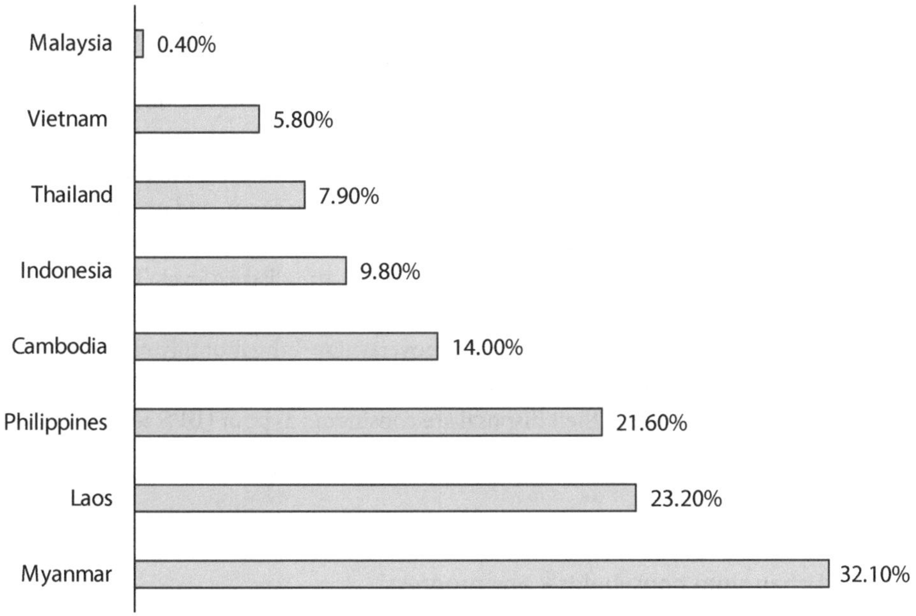

Fig. 28 Share of population below the national poverty line in 2017 for selected countries in South East Asia
Source: Illustration by author. Data from Asian Development Bank, ADB (2019)

The data on poverty reveal also a contrasting spatial distribution on the national and local level. Poverty is more severe in peripheral regions as compared to core regions. This statement is more valid for Java Island compared to the other islands and it is true for the west of the country compared to the east. In the eastern provinces of Papua or Maluku, for instance, poverty degrees of 27.53 % and 17.69 % respectively are recorded for the year 2019, while only 3.57 % of Jakarta's inhabitants are considered poor (BPS 2019b, 2019d: 20). Poverty is also more severe in rural than in urban areas. Cities generally offer better job opportunities and more possibilities of employment, which is why the poverty degree in rural areas is generally higher (cf. figure 27). This pattern is one of the reasons for the continuing rural-urban migration and the growth of urban agglomerations. Decreasing poverty rates can be attributed to continued economic growth and to the government's poverty alleviation efforts. Compared to other nations in South East Asia, Indonesia shows remarkable success (cf. figure 28). In 2019, 9.8 % of the population were recorded as living below the average Indonesian poverty line (cf. box 11).

Box 11: The Indonesian poverty line

The Indonesian poverty line is calculated separately for each city and district as well as for the national and provincial scale based on consumption expenditures. Since 1984, BPS has published data on poverty at the national and provincial level. For this task, a poverty line is calculated based on a consumption bundle consisting of food (to satisfy 2,100 calories per person per day) and non-food items. This bundle is revised from time to time and consisted for instance of 52 food and 47 non-food items in 2005 (ADB 2006: 19). The underlying data source is the National Socioeconomic Survey (Susenas), a survey conducted on a regular basis. Over the years, the methodological approach has changed several times and since 2002 poverty lines are also calculated at the district level. There are slightly different approaches across districts, choosing specificity over comparability (Priebe 2014). In 2019, the national poverty line – the monthly minimum consumption expenditures per capita – was set to Rp. 442,000 (~ 29.50€). All residents who have less at their disposal are considered as poor (BPS 2019b).

17.3 Urban slum households – any progress?

Similar to the poverty trends, the numbers of people living in inadequate housing also shows a positive trend. Estimating the number of people living in urban slums or in inadequate housing has always been a difficult if not impossible task. Since definitions of all terms differ widely (What is urban? What is a slum? What does adequate housing mean?), are not standardised and change over time on national scales, resulting databases are necessarily inconsistent, if not useless. This is also the case for Indonesia. Depending on the source, there are many contradicting datasets and opinions. While some authors state an expansion of slum areas and increasing slum population for Indonesia (Hartono 2009; Stalker 2007), the statistical divisions of the United Nations and Indonesia's central statistics agency, BPS, report resounding success. Both agencies use similar criteria to define slums[4], but report differing numbers. According to BPS the proportion of urban households in slums was 9.21 % in 2015 and has come down to 7.42 % in 2018 (BPS 2019c). When considering figures of the United Nations, the share of the urban population living in slums decreased dramatically from 50 % in 1990 to 22 % in 2014 (cf. figure 29). The differing numbers might be caused by different criteria used, but both datasets show a decreasing trend of slum dwellers. Absolute numbers are stable due to ongoing urban growth – with 29 million people living in

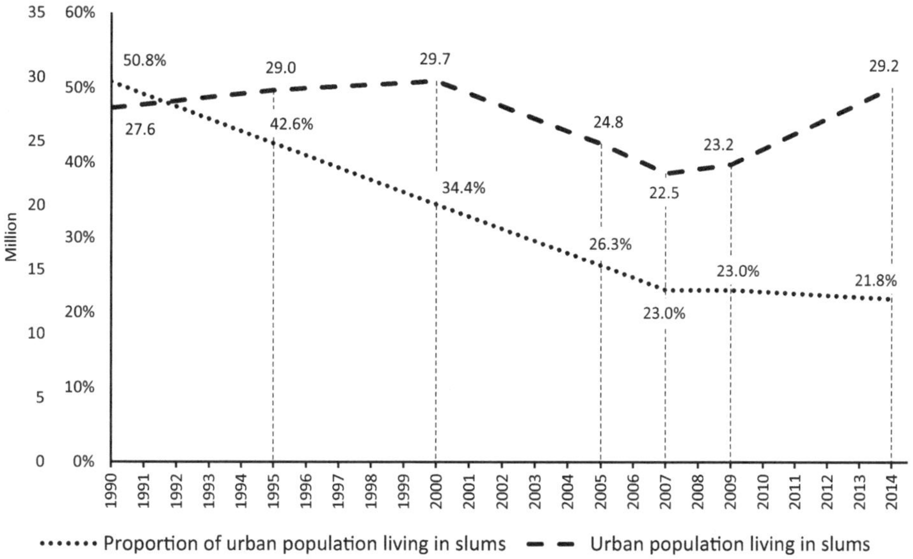

Fig. 29 Estimated number of slum dwellers in Indonesia, 1990–2014
Source: Illustration by author. Data from UN-Habitat (2015b)

4 UN-Habitat has defined a slum household as "[...] a group of individuals living under the same roof in an urban area, lacking one or more of the following amenities: access to basic services, durable structural quality of housing, sufficient living area, security of tenure" (UN-Habitat 2008c: 33). BPS uses four indicators to determine a slum household: 1) access to adequate drinking water 2) access to proper sanitation 3) quality of housing (roof, floor, and wall conditions) 4) sufficient living area above 7.2 m² per person (BPS 2019c). If one criterion applies, a given household is considered as slum.

inadequate housing in 2014 – but Indonesia can be considered as a good practice example in both poverty reduction and slum alleviation (UN-Habitat 2008c, 2010: 126, 2013: 149, 2015a: 75).

17.4 Recent developments since 1998: *Reformasi*

The year 1998 was fateful for Indonesia. After only two presidents (Sukarno, 1945–1967 and Suharto 1967–1998) had ruled the country for the last 50 years, a real opportunity to change the whole political system had emerged. General Suharto, who had ruled the country for over 30 years with his authoritarian system called 'New Order' (*Orde Baru*) lost his grip on power and stepped down. In that year, the country was hit hard by the Asian economic crisis of 1997/1998, shattering most achievements from the boom years of the 1980s and 1990s (Firman 1999; Furman et al. 1998). Within days, the Indonesian currency lost its value, industries went bankrupt, and the financial sector collapsed.

This monetary crisis (*Krisis Monetar*, or *Krismon*) was followed by mass unemployment and social unrest. Foreign debt (in US dollars) could no longer be serviced and it became increasingly clear that the economic boom of the 1980s and 1990s had been built on sand. With dwindling economic success, the regime lost its legitimacy and the pillars of the system – ie corruption, collusion and nepotism surrounding the Suharto clan and the ruling elites – were no longer accepted. Demonstrations and riots erupted in many cities and calls for reform became omnipresent. After violent clashes and ethnically motivated riots with more than 500 dead in Jakarta, Suharto lost his backing and had to resign in 1998 (Firman 1999; Schiel 2015; Obermayr 2017).

A new era had begun, soon to be known as *Reformasi*, where far-reaching changes towards democracy and decentralisation took place. During the *Krismon* many regions called for greater autonomy, increasing the pressure for more resource sharing and devolution. The centralistic government of Suharto had drained the country by allocating all resources and development efforts to Jakarta and Java, resulting in increased disparities. In this centralistic system everything related to administrative matters was regulated and planned by the central government (Usman et al. 2008: 6). Shortly after the first democratic election in 1999, the parliament thus enacted laws for fiscal and political decentralisation. Power and state functions were devolved to lower tiers of government. Mayors and district heads are now directly elected, no longer appointed by the central government (May 2015). The hierarchical relationship between these government levels was eliminated and for the first time also a direct election of the president was introduced (Obermayr 2017: 90; Vickers 2005: 197–209).

After years of reforms, much has been achieved. Indonesia has become a decentralised electoral democracy with general political and economic stability (JICA 2018; Wicakasono 2006: 156). Cities and regions now have a substantial development budget and have begun to take initiative, expanding their investments in urban public services and infrastructures that had previously been controlled by Jakarta (Suhartini & Jones 2019: 21–22). They are still obliged to implement national instructions, but have the freedom to adjust these instructions to local circumstances (Asnawi 2005: 27). In addition, they have limited freedom to steer their own development. The results are the emergence of many innovative policies at the local level. The process is, however, not complete and challenges of governance and missing capacities remain (Roberts 2014: 137–140). Initially, local authorities were overstrained with their new responsibilities and obligations and progress in capacity-building was slow (Atkinson 2004: 39–47). In many cases, the decentralisation of power also brought a decentralisation of corruption to the cities and districts (Schott 2015: 112–113). A challenge remains the 'new order thinking' persisting in the governance system, and the country's elites are still interspersed with persons close to the old regime. In a society and administrative apparatus with 50 years of obeying orders, it is not easy to establish a democratic culture (Hadiz 2008: 2–14).

The reform era has also paved the way for the emergence of a new generation of leaders (UN-Habitat 2015a: 166). The current president of Indonesia, Joko Widodo, better known as Jokowi, rised through the ranks from local politics without connections to the Indonesian elites and the Suharto clan, a career that would not have been possible in the New Order era (Kusno 2013). Elected mayor of Solo in 2005, he based his successful leadership on improvements in bureaucratic performance and the willpower to introduce comprehensive policies with a new political style (Obermayr 2017). Based on this success he soon became governor of Jakarta in 2012 and president of the republic in 2014 (Aspinall & Mietzner 2014: 351).

Jokowi's inauguration caused a major shift in Indonesia's development policies. The priorities outlined in the medium-term development plan (RPJM 2014–2018) are human resource development, key sector development, and a balanced regional development. Less emphasis is now placed on economic growth, but connectivity and regional development are more pronounced (JICA 2018). Local development outside Java, particularly in Indonesia's east, became a priority, as did better infrastructure development to increase general connectivity. To achieve this in the face of a limited national budget, private sector investment was encouraged by incentives and public-private partnerships were promoted.

By cutting fuel subsidies in 2014, more funds became available for this new focus of development policies (infrastructure and regional development). A political commitment to develop the regions was made and by endorsing a new Village Law in 2014 (UU 06/2014) even more autonomy and funds were given to the local level (Howes & Davies 2014: 171). Other achievements of the Jokowi administration are the introduction of an universal health care system, aiming to establish full health care coverage for all Indonesians by 2019 (JICA 2018: 78–79). Furthermore, Jokowi reintroduced the One Million Houses Programme (Program Satu Juta Rumah, or PSR) in 2014, a massive effort to increase the nation's housing production and reduce the housing backlog (cf. chapter 20.6).

17.5 Administrative levels and the significance of the local RT/RW system

Indonesia's administrative system has some particularities that are important in order to understand the introduction and operating mechanism of specific housing policies. There are five official administrative levels, but also two levels that are more informal (cf. figure 30). Both play a role and the lowest tiers of administration, the informal levels, have become of particular importance for the application of housing policies through community organisations and self-help.

Indonesia is divided in 34 provinces (*provinsi*), consisting of 416 rural regencies (*kabupaten*) and 98 urban areas (*kota*) with equal legal status. These administrative units are further subdivided into 7,240 sub-districts (*kecamatan*), composed of 83,931 urban and rural villages (*kelurahan* and *desa*), which are the smallest formal administrative units (Bawole 2007: 73). One *kelurahan* is a quarter within a city with 10,000 to 30,000 residents. At each administrative level, there are various sectoral agencies and offices that form Indonesia's public administration (BPS 2019d: 8). This bureaucratic body is often considered oversized and bloated, since it employs more than 4.2 million civil servants (2018) requiring one third (33.8 % in 2016) of the national state budget, the *Anggaran Pendapatan Belanja Negara*, or APBN[5] (BPS 2019d: 10; Rusliandy & Megawati 2016).

A distinctive characteristic of Indonesia's governance system is the existence of two more informal administrative levels: the administrative units *Rukun Warga* (RW) and *Rukun Tetangga* (RT). These levels are situated at the community and neighbourhood level, below the *kelurahan* level. Introduced during the Japanese occupation in World War II in the manner of Japan's neighbourhood associations, they have become an additional, more informal administrative system closer to the citizens (Peters 2013: 22; Sullivan 1992; Schott 2015: 79). The two units can be translated as community unit (RW) or neighbourhood unit (RT). A RW unit consists of three to five – sometimes up to ten – RT units, which in turn are responsible for 20 to 100 households. One person, the Ketua RT or Ketua RW, heads each of these units. Usually this person is also referred to as RT or RW, meaning the person, not the administrative unit. While the local RT is consensually elected during community meetings, the local RW is chosen by associated RTs as their contact person to the *kelurahan* administration. From a residents' perspective, the head of a RT unit is required to be a sincere and honest

5 The Indonesian government has the medium-term goal to shrink the public sector to 3.5 million civil servants and expenses to 28 % of the national budget (Rusliandy & Megawati 2016).

person and usually someone with high social or economic status is chosen. Since the assumption of this office is not connected to any remuneration and rather means a lot of voluntary work, the only reward for those taking on the job is respect and honour.

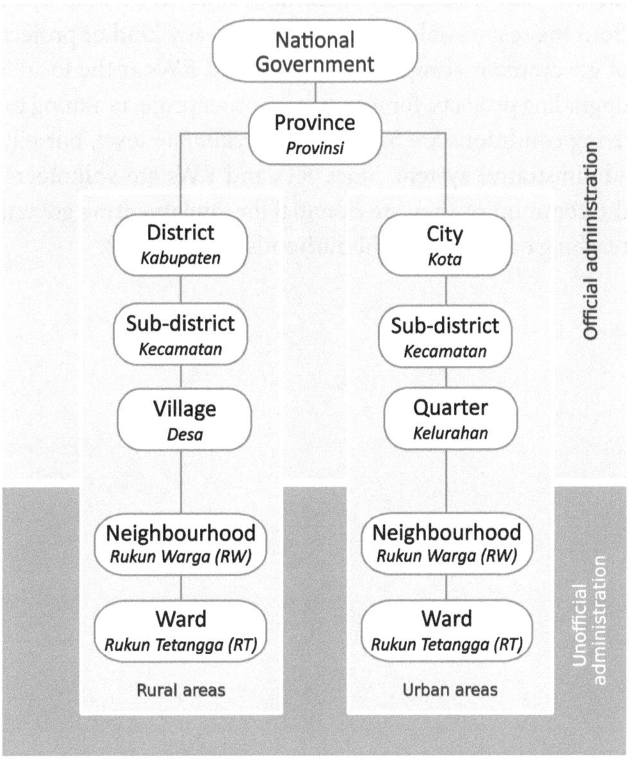

Fig. 30 Administrative levels in Indonesia
Source: Reprinted from Obermayr (2017: 78)

Since its introduction, the purpose of the system has changed. In the beginning, its main function was surveillance and control, and in the New Order era it additionally became a means for mobilising the community (King & Idawati 2010: 217–221). Whenever a new project was implemented in a top-down manner, the support of the community could be easily mobilised. After the reform era (from 1998 onwards), the functions of surveillance and mobilisation became less important in favour of the goal of improving community welfare. During monthly meetings the latest issues in each RT are discussed and individuals can propose their ideas concerning improvements for the community (eg infrastructure, health). If these proposals receive enough support among members in one RT, they are implemented on behalf of the community. This bottom-up process might be supported by government funds at a later stage.

In the last decades, this system has become the main vehicle for local governments to reach their citizens. As the interface between government and community, RTs and

RWs have the role of representing their area as local leaders and are required to handle and support all governmental day-to-day activities that involve 'their' neighbourhood or community. All bureaucratic transactions, for instance, eg business permits, identity cards, or land transactions, have to be accompanied by a permission letter from the responsible RT. Furthermore, any kind of project introduced at higher tiers of government always involves RTs and RWs at the local level. Most of the *kampung* upgrading projects, for instance, or other projects aiming to improve infrastructures or living conditions are happening at *kelurahan* level, but rely strongly on the unofficial administrative system. Since RTs and RWs are volunteers and trusted persons from the community, they are essential for implementing government programmes and for reaching out to the neighbourhoods (Jones 2017).

18 Indonesia's Cities and Settlements

This section explores the characteristics of Indonesian cities and settlements, traces their origin, and examines recent urban developments. One distinct element of the Indonesian city is highlighted in particular, since it is home to the majority of the population: The Indonesian *kampung*. The section arrives at an assessment of the country's housing situation, annual housing need, and production.

18.1 Origins and characteristics of the Indonesian city

Indonesian cities were founded in three different historic phases, tracing back their origin either to Hindu and Islamic kingdoms or to European foundations during colonial times (1602–1942) (Zahnd 2005). Upon the arrival of the Europeans from 1600 onwards, arguably only few towns – urban structures in a European sense – were encountered, mostly along the Strait of Malacca or in other coastal regions. Besides these towns, not many urban areas existed and most locals lived instead in a dense system of smaller villages (Rutz 1985: 47–67; Obermayr 2017: 92). It has been argued that no cultural concept of 'the city' existed before the arrival of the Dutch, even though this can be challenged as a Eurocentric perspective (Evers 2007; Zahnd 2005).

In their fight for domination, the arriving Europeans established trade and military posts on strategically favourable spots or incorporated existing villages along the coastlines of Java and Sumatra. Soon, the Dutch became the most important force, overcoming all competing powers and securing the archipelago as their colony. The presence of the Europeans and their exploitative activities entailed increasing trade and interchange among settlements, furthering in that way urban growth. Dutch influence was strongest in the cities located at Java's north coast, namely Batavia (today's Jakarta), Semarang, and Surabaya (Röll 1981: 68–79; Rutz 1985; Obermayr 2017: 93).

After Indonesia acquired independence, urban growth intensified, caused by increased rural-urban migration. Urban authorities did not react with adequate measures. New officials who lacked training and experiences had replaced the government officials of the colonial administration. Reinforced by political instability and economic downturns, the result was a chaotic urban development, characterised by the absence of the state. There were some exceptions. Indonesia's first president, Sukarno, proclaimed the goal to develop Jakarta from a colonial city into an international metropolis with monumental buildings and supra-regional flair. Beside these plans for the capital, however, urban development planning remained rare or non-existent. It took until the late 1960s when the first national development plans and first master plans for Javanese cities were made, for this to appear (Zahnd 2005: 46–47; Ford 1993).

In the decades that followed, development efforts were concentrated on the largest cities in Java. They were favoured in national development plans and benefited greatly from resource allocation. The results were widening regional disparities and for other cities this meant neglect and less priority (Ford 1993; Zahnd 2005: 49). These disparities were one of the factors producing social unrest and demands for greater regional autonomy leading to the far-reaching changes of the *Reformasi* era (Roberts 2014).

Today, various elements of this history are visible in the appearance of Indonesian cities. Hindu, Islamic, and European influences have mixed up, creating a unique urban landscape (Guillot 2005). Larry R. Ford (1993) distinguishes three city types: coastal cities, interior towns, and palace cities. Coastal cities such as Jakarta, Semarang, or Surabaya and interior towns such as Bogor and Bandung were strongly influenced by the Dutch, apparent in the existence of historic European architecture and planned city structures. Palace cities, in contrast, were founded by Islamic or Hindu rulers and show more distinctive layouts. What all three types have in common are a linear structure of the traditional centre oriented at the compass rose – a Javanese layout (Silas et al. 2012), remnants of an European quarter, usually a Chinese quarter nearby, and an irregular pattern of residential areas – known as *kampungs* – filling all patches in-between (Rutz 1985: 68–76). All these elements have been continuously reshaped and transformed over the decades, but are still visible upon closer inspection.

18.2 Kampungs

One important aspect distinguishes Indonesian cities and is greatly neglected in academic literature: The *kampung*. *Kampungs* are an indigenous Indonesian settlement type, a collection of houses forming a clustered neighbourhood with a strong sense of belonging and community. Originally the term described a village located outside of the city, shaped by rural traditions (Bawole 2007: 38; Sudarmo 1997: 236). Meanwhile many of these rural villages have been included in the cities and have become urban *kampungs* characterised by dense and compact patterns, irregular structures, and high population densities (Spreitzhofer 2007). They are self-constructed through incremental processes without a formal planning process and building codes, using local materials. Depending on location, urban *kampungs* are purely residential, mixed-use, or commercial areas. Most of them are residential quarters, essential for the provision of low-income housing, but they fulfil also other functions. They host small-scale businesses of all kinds, homebased industries, and boarding houses, for instance. For low-income people they are crucial as a place of survival (Silas et al. 2012: 13).

Often, *kampungs* are wrongly associated with poverty or considered as slums. This association has a historic reason, since original *kampungs* developed without formal planning and had only basic infrastructure and poor housing quality (Silas et al. 2012: 9). Indeed, many inner-city *kampungs* still show these characteristics, but conditions cannot be generalised and the word '*kampung*' does not automatically signify 'slum' (Obermayr 2017: 95). Rather, a wide variety of *kampungs* exists, differing in their social and economic conditions, their degree of informality, and their residents' socio-economic strata. Densely populated *inner-city kampungs* with improved infrastructure exist next to *kampungs* with inadequate housing conditions or *squatter kampungs* with high degrees of informality as well as newer *kampungs* at the edges of the cities with richer inhabitants (Tunas & Peresthu 2010; Samyahardja et al. 2006).

For most Indonesians, *kampungs* are more than a settlement type. They represent a place inscribed with meaning, symbols, and belonging. Many have grown up in the *kampung*, where they have lived and worked, where the streets are filled with life and interaction, where residents have learned to form a larger community. Identities and a sense of community are created here, as captured by Lea Jellinek (1991) or Robbie Peters (2013) in their comprehensive work on *kampungs* in Jakarta and Surabaya. In a way, the *kampung* reflects the cultural and social fabric of the Indonesian '*urban society*' (Rolnik 2013b: 6–7).

18.2.1 The urban divide: formality vs. informality

The urban fabric in Indonesian cities is divided into formal and informal areas. Officially planned areas contrast sharply with the more irregular pattern of *kampungs*. Urban *kampungs* are an integral part of Indonesian cities, scattered as patches within the more formal urban landscape. Considering dimensions, *kampungs* cover only small areas of the city, but harbour most of the population. In Surabaya, for instance, *kampungs* covered only approximately 7 % of the city's space in 1988, but accommodated 60 to 70 % of the city's residents (Silas et al. 2012: 15). These numbers have not much changed and can be more or less transferred to all other Indonesian cities (Ford 1993; Silas 1992).

The divide between formal and informal areas developed historically (Tunas & Peresthu 2010; Samyahardja et al. 2006). During colonial times, vacant land between existing indigenous villages was used to produce European and Chinese quarters. Development was oriented at European models, including a well-planned layout with tightly packed townhouses constructed from solid materials. Rural *kampungs* surrounded these quarters, characterised by detached houses with much open space built from non-permanent building materials (bamboo and timber) (Röll 1981: 68–79; Obermayr 2017: 94). With urban growth, the formal city grew around these indigenous villages, encroaching on them and slowly incorporating them (McCarthy 2003).

The foundation of this dichotomous city was laid already in colonial times, but the divide became stronger in the second part of the 20th century. Under the rule of Sukarno, active government interventions produced monumental and symbolic buildings in Jakarta, while simultaneously rural-urban migration became stronger. The existing *kampungs* densified, land was subdivided, and gradually ever more people lived in this settlement type (Obermayr 2017: 98). After the takeover of Suharto, economic growth accelerated in the 1970s, pulling even more migrants to the cities (Samyahardja et al. 2006; Zahnd 2005). The former villages transformed into inner-city *kampungs* characterised by cramped one- or two-storey houses, separated only by narrow alleys, and informal building and management processes. Soon they became overcrowded and new squatter *kampungs* begun to emerge in various locations (Firman 1999: 72).

This dual structure of Indonesian cities can be easily observed in satellite images. In figure 31, an area of Surabaya is illustrated. In that satellite image, the formally planned

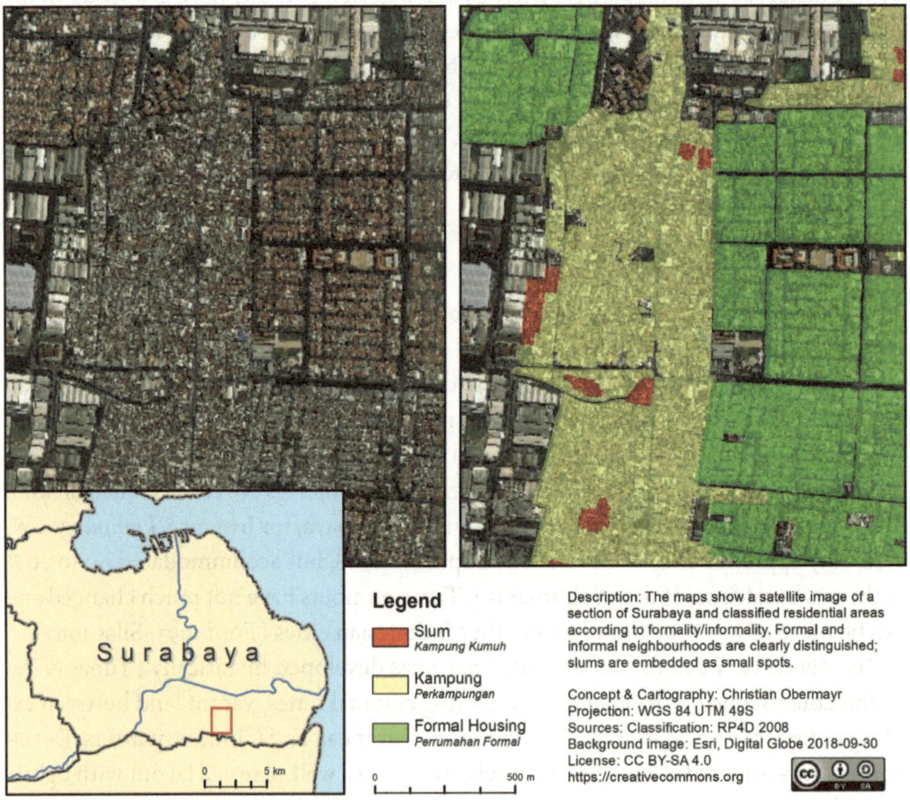

Fig. 31 *Kampungs*, formal housing, and slums – a typical urban divide in Indonesian cities
Source: Illustration by author

housing areas are clearly distinguishable from areas built informally. Formal areas show a planned layout, structures are larger and more homogeneous, and streets are wide and in a rectangular shape. Informal areas, by contrast, show diverse and smaller structures, wide streets are rare, and the small alleys in these *kampungs* are barely visible. Nevertheless, only some small patches in these informal areas are characterised as slums (*kampung kumuh*) according to Surabaya's city government (Pemerintah Kota Surabaya 2008).

18.2.2 Slum- and squatter settlements – *kampung kumuh dan kampung liar*

Indonesian authorities generally recognise inner city *kampungs* and include them – though not as a priority – in their urban development planning. Some areas within *kampungs* are considered as substandard with inadequate housing conditions, lacking infrastructure, and with bad access to services. These patches are called *kampung kumuh*, meaning 'dirty *kampung*', a term used for areas with inadequate housing and bad living qualities. Most of these 'slum patches' within existing *kampungs* are nevertheless recognised by the government – even without ownership rights (*hak milik*) – and in most cases they are eligible to receive government support and participate in upgrading or social programmes.

Other residential areas are not recognised since they are considered illegal. These settlements are called *kampung liar*, meaning 'illegal *kampung*', or squatter settlements. They mostly developed in the second half of the 20th century by processes of infiltration, when inner-city *kampungs* had become overcrowded due to accelerated urbanisation. New residents – often migrants from rural areas – settled on unused land on riverbanks and railway lines, in parks, or in graveyards and created squatter settlements (Samyahardja et al. 2006; Bawole 2007: 106). Often the land is government-owned and not designated for housing since it is prone to natural hazards (eg flooding) (Rindarjono 2014). Unmapped and contradicting spatial plans, these settlements are 'invisible' in urban development plans and the residents are threatened by evictions. The government refrains from investments and the implementation of upgrading or social assistance programmes. Thus, these settlements are the poorest neighbourhoods with the worst living conditions (Rolnik 2013b: 7).

Both settlement types, *kampung kumuh* and *kampung liar*, are characterised by high population densities, marginality, deteriorated housing conditions, and bad access to basic services. Processes of infiltration have created them gradually. Residents are often rural migrants and work in the urban informal sector as rickshaw (*becak*) drivers, street hawkers, scavengers, tailors, casual construction workers, and others. This type of works gives them only unsecure income and they are stigmatised and marginalised due to their origin (Silas 1989; Tunas & Peresthu 2010; Rindarjono 2014).

18.2.3 The legal status of *kampungs*

Tenure rights in *kampungs* are complex, consisting of a combination of western, individual, customary, and collective rights (Das 2017). The Indonesian system of land ownership is a mixture of formalised, registered land and informal land regulated by customary law. This dual land system has historical reasons, since the Dutch did not extend their land administration system to all areas and the situation became even more complex during the Japanese occupation and the chaotic times of the struggle for independence (Tunas & Peresthu 2010: 319–320; Monkkonen 2013: 258; Asnawi 2005: 31). The basic agrarian law of 1960 was established to overcome this dual system, but has not succeeded up to now.

The traditional system of land ownership (*hak adat*) prevailed and remains in place today. Most of the residents in *kampungs* have not officially registered their property or land to obtain the right of ownership (*hak milik*), since the official registration at the National Land Agency (Badan Pertanahan Nasional, BPN) is considered too cost-intensive and time-consuming. In addition, the necessity is not seen, since their residency is well legitimised through their duration of stay, social recognition within the community, and land-related documents issued by lower tiers of government. The local authorities (*lurah, camat*, and respective RTs/RWs) in fact legitimise the residency of residents by issuing identity cards, collecting land and building taxes, and providing letters confirming their residency. These factors generate a *de facto* security of tenure in such a way that informal property or use rights can even be sold on the large informal housing market (Supriatna 2016; Monkkonen 2013).

Issuing formal titles, one of the favoured measures of formalisation in international titling programmes, seems to have only a marginal impact on perceived tenure security and housing consolidation in Indonesia (Reerink & Gelder 2010). Rather, the informal system in place already provides enough *de facto* tenure security for residents, encouraging incremental upgrading activities and consolidation (Warren & Lucas 2013; Guinness 2016). From this perspective it can be stated that Indonesia's housing market remains affordable for the urban poor because of, not despite, the large informal part of it (Monkkonen 2013).

18.3 Recent urban developments: implosion – explosion

Continuing urbanisation has produced two major trends for the shape and structure of Indonesian cities. The first one is the massive expansion of urban areas into the peripheries, transforming the landscape and absorbing smaller towns and villages. The second one is the transformation of inner-city areas and *kampungs*. In the centres, increased densification and skyscraper development has put massive pressure on still existing inner-city *kampungs* and their residents. Lefebvre has termed these processes as 'implosion-explosion', the breaking up of the traditional city and its dissolution into fragments distributed over large areas (Lefebvre 1970 [2003]: 10).

Disintegrating urban patterns – *desakota*

The first trend is the formation of an increasingly disintegrated and deconcentrated urban landscape. Cities expand rapidly into their hinterland, forming polycentric metropolitan regions and urban corridors along major transport links. New towns have developed in the urban peripheries, land prices are increasing rapidly and the old core regions lose their centrality (Fahmi et al. 2014; Dieleman 2011; Sudarmo 1997). Between 1996 and 2007 more than 70 % of urban population growth took place in suburban areas, having outpaced the growth rates of urban cores (World Bank 2013b: 102). This suburbanisation trend has accelerated in the last decades, cutting through administrative boundaries and causing rapid changing land use patterns (Zahnd 2005: 51–52; Firman 2009).

The transformation of the urban-rural landscape is rarely properly planned and steered by regulations. Outside the administrative boundaries of the city, real estate companies are developing large-scale residential areas for the middle class, gated communities, industrial complexes, recreational facilities, and huge shopping malls, sometimes forming new satellite towns and superblocks. The *tissue urbain* is spreading from a core ribbon-like in all directions along arterial roads. Formal development is happening at the street edges, buildings are tightly packed, in many cases blocking access to the areas behind, where mixed areas with less density, new *kampungs*, and informal settlements have evolved (Firman 2009; 2014b; Fahmi et al. 2014; Spreitzhofer 2007; Herlambang et al. 2019). Despite a tight *de jure* regulatory system, only market laws rule these developments (Monkkonen 2013).

The described transformation processes mainly concern Jakarta, but also other cities and towns. In Surabaya and Solo, for instance, adjacent districts outside the formal city boundaries are growing rapidly. There, suburbanisation tendencies have created new centres (*Solo Baru* south of Solo and *Sidoarjo* south of Surabaya). Metropolitan regions are emerging, which need new coordination mechanisms and governance systems (World Bank 2013b: 102). Terry McGee (1991) has theorised these processes as the formation of *desakota* regions. Similar to the western concept of 'urban sprawl' *desakota* describes areas where the difference between village (*desa*) and city (*kota*) are increasingly blurred, areas consisting of a mesh of light urban structures covering increasingly more territory (Miller 2013). Characteristics are a mix of urban and rural structures with residential, agricultural, commercial, and industrial functions in close proximity (Ford 1993; Obermayr 2017: 100). Facing these developments and due to decentralisation policies introduced starting in 1998, metropolitan governance has become a major challenge for Indonesian cities and their surrounding districts not yet addressed by proper institutional arrangements (Firman 2014a; Hudalah et al. 2013a; Hudalah et al. 2013b).

Under the influence of globalisation, tendencies of polarisation and fragmentation are increasing. Similar to other world regions (Coy & Kraas 2003), processes of economic globalisation shapes the structure of Indonesian cities, integrating some areas and excluding others (Firman 1999: 72). The existing urban divide is furthered and new disparities and fragmented areas within the country and within cities are beginning to emerge (Kraas 2003; UN-Habitat 2008c). Up to now, social segregation is less pronounced in Indonesian cities and many *kampungs* are still diverse, with residents from all social strata. Inequality is on the rise, though, visible in the spatial expression of segregated residential areas with homogeneous inhabitants. A mosaic of heterogeneous city fragments is increasingly emerging (Kraas 2003, 2005; Simone 2010).

Transformation of the city core and inner-city *kampungs*

The second trend is the transformation of the city core and inner-city *kampungs*. New business districts, shopping malls, offices, and hotels need space that can only be provided by vertical growth or by grabbing land from informal or semi-formal areas. Inner-city *kampungs* have increasingly come under pressure as the competition for land in central areas has intensified. Urban land for development has become scarce and housing prices have skyrocketed. *Kampungs* in prime locations have thus become the target for redevelopment (Shirleyana & Sunindijo 2018: 558). Powerful economic forces try to expand their business activities into these areas and lobby with the government to evict or revitalise *kampungs*. The results are evictions of squatter settlements and market-based expulsions of former (legal) *kampung* residents (Rolnik 2013b: 8–9). Thousands of *kampungs* have been demolished in Jakarta, and in many areas of the capital *kampung* life has become a story from the past (Jellinek 2012).

Though under pressure, many inner-city *kampungs* still exist today. It is less regulations and building codes that save many *kampungs* from redevelopment, but more a combination of formal and informal processes within the *kampungs* itself. New constructions require a building permit by the city government and depend on the approbation of district and sub-district heads as well as RW and RT leaders. This collective approval has prevented large-scale redevelopments of inner-city *kampungs* up to now. Only at their edges, facing larger roads, have office buildings and commercial estates been allowed (Das 2017).

Nevertheless, the settlement type of the *kampung* needs protection. *Kampungs* are a place of survival for low-income communities and it can be argued that they are a good alternative in terms of sustainability and resilience compared to other residential areas (Dianingrum et al. 2017; Shirleyana & Sunindijo 2018). They have high densities, allowing many people to live near the centre, avoiding long commutes and thus generating less traffic. The ecological impact of *kampung* dwellers is certainly less compared to middle-class apartment towers or single-family homes on the outskirts. Most importantly, in terms of social sustainability, the *kampung* offers a vibrant community life with mutual assistance (*Gotong Royong* cf. box 12). Therefore, remaining inner-city *kampungs* are to be seen as a rare achievement that needs special treatment and protection (Das 2017).

Box 12: *Gotong Royong*

The Javanese term *Gotong Royong* refers to the idea and practices of mutual support, solidarity, and local cooperation within the community. In absence of state support, communities rely on *Gotong Royong* to realise collective projects in self-help (Kamil 2014; King & Idawati 2010). These practices are a common characteristic of Indonesia's *kampungs*.

18.4 Indonesia's housing situation, housing demand, and provision

Indonesia's urban population lives in various types of housing. A striking observation is that few tenement blocks exist in Indonesian cities (with the exception of Jakarta) and the industrial production of high-rise residential buildings has only just begun in recent years. On the contrary, the majority of Indonesia's urban population lives in one- or two-storey houses, which are located in urban *kampungs* of various densities. There are no reliable data and estimates are dependent on definitions and regionalisation. However, it can be said that approximately 60 to 80% of urban residents live in *kampungs* (Silas 1992; Shirleyana & Sunindijo 2018) – an estimate that includes all types of *kampungs*, not only the poor or informal ones (on the characteristics of *kampungs* cf. chapter 18.2). This perspective is reflected in relevant laws (eg fixed-term contracts in social housing), implemented housing programmes (eg focusing on improved access to mortgage loans), and the non-existence of policies for rental housing. Most efforts of the Indonesian government since the 2000s, for instance, have focussed on making the poor bankable, increasing their access to credit, enabling them to buy their own homes.

Home ownership is the preferred housing option, more so in rural than in urban areas and in smaller towns than in larger cities. Approximately 80% (2018) of all Indonesians live in properties they or their relatives own, including formal or informal ownership (BPS 2019c; Rolnik 2013b: 6). The remaining 20% are in the rental sector (cf. figure 32). Most of the rental arrangements are through informal and flexible lease arrangements that provide less security of tenure than ownership, but are preferred by various groups in certain stages of life. Home-ownership is clearly favoured over rental housing among residents and can be considered as a hegemonic discourse in the country's housing policies.

Based on population growth, an annual housing demand of 800,000 to 1 million new homes is estimated (Sudarmo 1997; Asnawi 2005: 37). Since these numbers have never been met by supply in the last decades a large housing backlog has accumulated and continues to increase. Estimates of this backlog vary widely, amounting to anywhere between 6 and 12 million units (World Bank 2017: 2). In addition, 8 to 15 million units (or around 20 % of all housing units) are considered substandard (Stalker 2007: 31; World Bank 2015b).

A housing crisis has unfolded, exaggerated by globalisation tendencies. Since the 2000s, investments in housing as a safe asset have increased, as has the influx of global capital (Herlambang et al. 2019). In addition, the large increase of urban population, combined with a shortage of land for development has led to soaring land and housing prices, making it more difficult for low- and medium-income groups to acquire homes in formal housing markets. Only 20 % of the Indonesian population can afford to purchase a house in the formal market. Another 40 % might be enabled to acquire formal housing solutions with assistance, but the bottom 40 % of Indonesia's society cannot afford to buy a house, even at subsidised rates (UN-Habitat 2008b; Utomo 2014; Perumnas 2016: 164). The production crisis has become an affordability crisis and has led to overcrowding and the growth of slums (Rolnik 2013b; World Bank 2015b).

Much of the large annual housing demand is satisfied by informal construction activities. According to a World Bank report (2015b), the private sector produces approximately 400,000 units annually, while the public sector accounts for an overall number of 200,000 housing solutions, leaving a gap of 200,000 to 400,000 units that must be supplied by the informal sector. Other estimates assume that even more, namely 60 to 80 % of all new houses built are provided by the informal sector (Asnawi 2005: 37–41; Bredenoord & Lindert 2010; Monkkonen 2013; Septanti 2014: 45). In these estimates the formal modes of housing provision (private sector, public housing, and cooperatives) account together for only for 20 to 40 % (cf. figure 32). Despite all efforts to increase public and private housing production, these numbers have barely changed over the years. The formal sector was unable to meet the demand and the gap is largely filled by the people's own efforts (Permanent Mission of the Republic of Indonesia 2012: 7–8). Only in recent years do some of the latest reports and data suggest that this pattern might be about to change.

Fig. 32 Share of rental housing and home ownership (A) and estimated share of formal and informal housing production per year (B)
Sources: Illustration by author. Data compiled from BPS (2019c) for graph A; from Asnawi (2005), Bredenoord & Lindert (2010), Monkkonen (2013) and Septanti (2014) for graph B

19 Indonesia's Housing Policies

The content and organiation of Indonesia's housing policies are explored from a historic perspective in this section. Important milestones structure three successive phases of housing policies. From the identification and analysis of these phases, two dimensions of the organisation of Indonesia's housing domain are derived and analysed: actors and rules of the game.

19.1 Phases of housing policies in Indonesia

Indonesian housing policies have a long history and follow broadly the international discourse. Intervention strategies have been introduced to promote all areas of housing provision, both formal and the informal. Three successive phases of housing policies are apparent (cf. figure 33). In a first period after independence, housing policies were not a priority and public housing dominated the discussion, though never reaching scale. Later, under the New Order regime of Suharto, self-help housing strategies became pronounced, introducing large-scale slum upgrading measures. Since the 2000s, the enabling approach emerged, concentrating on community empowerment, capacity building, and housing finance systems. The three phases correspond broadly with major political shifts in the country.

19.1.1 Phase I: public housing and absence of the state – 1945 to 1967

The first phase of housing policies was characterised by the absence of the state and some limited public housing measures. Shortly after Indonesia's independence, the country faced a period of political unrest. In those years, housing policies had no priority and if any, the established models from the colonial government were continued. It was written into the constitution of 1945 that 'every person shall have the right to live in physical and spiritual prosperity, to have a home and enjoy a good and healthy environment' (art. 28H, para. 1), which was interpreted as an acknowledgement of the

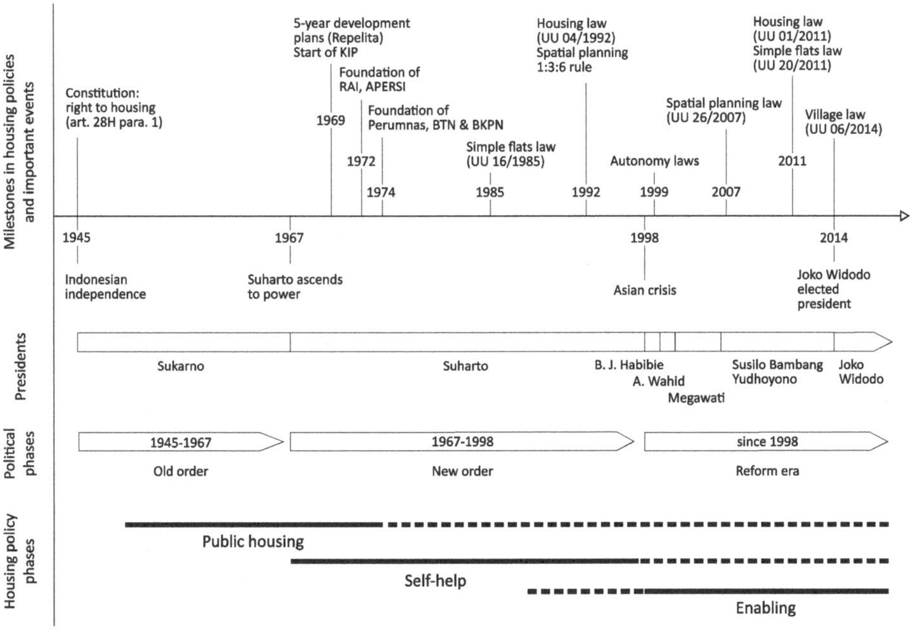

Fig. 33 Milestones in housing policies and housing policy phases in Indonesia
Source: Illustration by author

right to housing for everyone. The responsibility to realise this goal was seen to lie with the state, a young nation lacking resources and capacities to realise this task immediately.

Public housing models from Europe were regarded as the right means to address the housing question. It was presumed that mass housing could be provided by a capital-intensive housing industry. Thus, a public housing scheme was initiated in the 1950s initially intended to accommodate civil servants. Soon these measures ran into difficulties, since the necessary capital and housing technologies were not available. They never reached scale and the policy can be considered as a general failure (Asnawi 2005: 32–33).

Against intensifying urbanisation and the evolving housing shortage of those years, the state appeared helpless. Urban intervention strategies remained punctual, focusing on limited development projects or the establishment of satellite towns in and around Jakarta. These measures soon proved insufficient to cope with rapid urban growth. The state failed to develop comprehensive strategies or proper urban development plans due to a lack of capacities and resources (Tunas & Darmoyono 2014: 167–172).

19.1.2 Phase II: self-help – 1966 to 1998

The establishment of major housing organisations, the introduction of development plans and the necessary legal framework for housing issues as well as the implementation of large slum upgrading programmes characterises the second phase of housing policies in Indonesia. After Suharto took over the government, five-year development plans (Rencana Pembangunan Lima Tahun, or REPELITA) were introduced in 1969, aiming to develop the country in economic and social terms. In the second REPELITA (1974–1979), housing policies became more pronounced. Since 1969 Indonesia had already initiated the first round of slum upgrading programmes and in 1974 the National Board for Housing Policies (Badan Kebijakan Perumahan Nasional, or BKPN) was established, chaired by the ministry of housing and public works but also including members from various other ministries and organisations related to housing.

The same year saw also the foundation of a national savings bank (Bank Tabungan Negara, or BTN), tasked with the development of a national mortgage credit scheme (KPR), and the establishment of the state-owned public housing company (Perusahaan Umum Pembangunan Perumahan Nasional, or Perumnas), to promote public housing production. Beside these state-owned organisations, associations of private housing developers also formed as lobbying organisations in 1972: the simple and very simple house developers association, (the Asosiasi Pengembang Rumah Sederhana, or APERSI) and Real Estate Indonesia (REI) (Asnawi 2005: 34; Tunas & Darmoyono 2014: 167–172).

Since the second REPELITA, the view gained ground that the public housing approach introduced in the 1950s with the state as a housing provider had failed. The government thus begun to withdraw from public housing, focusing instead on slum upgrading programmes, ie the famous Kampung Improvement Programme (KIP). Since the late 1970s, comprehensive slum upgrading programmes focusing on community infrastructure became the main vehicle of Indonesia's housing policies (cf. chapter 20.1). Perumnas continued its operations, but together with the private sector it could not reach more than one third of the annual housing need of one million units in the 1980s and 1990s (Asnawi 2005: 34; Sudarmo 1997: 240).

In 1992, the first Housing and Settlements Law was enacted (UU 04/1992), intended to better manage urban sprawl by an improved land management system. Spatial planning was developed further by introducing 20-year master plans for all urban areas. In addition, a regulation for 'balanced' development (the 1:3:6 rule) was adopted, intended to mix social classes in housing developments and to force private developers to provide low-income housing (Spreitzhofer 2007; Sudarmo 1997: 235–239). This new rule required that luxury, medium-income, and low-income housing be constructed in the ratio 1:3:6 (cf. chapter 19.3.1).

The 1990s saw the rise of new initiatives and approaches, signaling the ascendancy of the period of enabling policies. Influenced by global discussions around Habitat II, the rhetoric changed towards participative and community-based approaches. This was reflected in the new initiatives developed and the changes made to the existing programmes. The community-based housing development (CBHD) approach was developed to enhance cooperative housing (cf. chapter 20.3); and the KIP approach moved to its second phase, now pronouncing also economic and social aspects, and highlighting community-based planning and resident participation. The enabling approach slowly emerged and various housing finance schemes were implemented to serve different income groups (Sudarmo 1997).

19.1.3 Phase III: enabling approach – since 1998

Poverty alleviation programmes, an increased involvement of the state in direct housing production, an agenda to shift responsibility to regional and local levels, and a massive turn towards housing finance policies characterise the latest phase of housing policies in Indonesia. Former top-down initiatives are increasingly balanced with bottom-up approaches. Slum upgrading schemes transformed into broader poverty alleviation programmes with strong emphasis on community empowerment. A housing finance system was developed, establishing new institutions and extending subsidised mortgage loans. All these developments took place under the paradigm of the enabling approach, aiming to enable the community, the government, and the private sector to contribute to the overall housing production. The private sector was thought to be enabled to provide more housing also for low-income groups; the government was to be enabled by devolving power and transferring responsibilities and the community was to be enabled by empowering them to handle their own affairs and increase self-help housing production. The result is a mix of measures and programmes driven by local, provincial, and national governments that contribute to the overall goal of reducing the housing backlog and solving the housing crisis over the long term.

The new phase of housing policies was triggered by the Asian financial crisis in 1998, the monetary crisis (*Krismon*) that followed, and the political shift towards democracy. In the *Krismon* years Indonesia's property market collapsed, developers went bankrupt, and housing projects were discontinued. Banks had provided huge loans to the property sector, despite unreliable market information and mortgage lending capacities (Permanent Mission of the Republic of Indonesia 2012). Poverty alleviation became a priority to address escalating poverty degrees. The KIP was transformed into broader poverty alleviation strategies, introducing social assistance programmes and community empowerment programmes such as the Urban Poverty Alleviation Project (Proyek Penanggulangan Kemiskinan di Perkotaan, or P2KP) or the National Programme for Community Empowerment (Program Nasional Pemberdayaan Masyarakat, or PNPM) (cf. chapter 20.4).

Simultaneously, decentralisation policies were introduced starting in 1998, devolving power to local governments. With the Spatial Planning Law of 2007 (UU 26/2007), provinces and municipal governments were obliged to create their own master plans and zoning regulations (Herlambang et al. 2019). The revised Housing and Settlements Law (UU 01/2011) further reinforced and extended these new obligations: responsibility for respective low-income communities was transferred as well as as the authority to monitor, plan, and implement housing programmes and projects on their own accord. (Booth 2003; Kersting et al. 2009: 171–175; Jones 2017: 2). In addition, local governments were now required to create detailed settlement and housing development plans (cf. chapter 19.3.2). Consequently, numerous local initiatives emerged to improve the living conditions of the poor and housing production at the local level. Governments at all levels were now required to work as an enabler, focusing to improve regulatory frameworks, planning, infrastructure, and the financial environment to create a good working climate for all stakeholders in the housing sector (Sudarmo 1997; Permanent Mission of the Republic of Indonesia 2012).

From 2001 onwards the challenge of insufficient housing finance systems was increasingly addressed, shifting much of the government's efforts towards the development of housing markets (Permanent Mission of the Republic of Indonesia 2012; Rolnik 2013b). The goal was market empowerment: to make housing credit more affordable for low-income people in order to enable them to buy their own homes (Dahiya 2012: 51). Adopted in the long-term development plan (2004–2025), this goal was to be achieved by measures of institutional development, synergising of funding from different levels, and the establishment of new mortgage finance mechanisms (Permanent Mission of the Republic of Indonesia 2012). In 2001, interest rate subsidies (SSB) and down payment subsidies (SBUM) were introduced as well as micro-loans in 2006 and a housing finance liquidity scheme (Fasilitas Likuiditas Pembiayaan Perumahan, or FLPP) in 2010. All these initiatives targeted the demand side to increase access to mortgage loans for lower-income people. Simultaneously, measures on the supply side were taken, such as the ease of regulations and building permits in an effort to increase housing production by the private sector.

By 2007, the real estate sector had overcome the *Krismon* and began to prepare land for large development projects. So-called superblocks – large-scale integrated projects of residential, commercial, and recreational facilities – began to emerge, first in Jakarta's outskirts, and from 2010 onwards also in other cities. The private sector became more influential, cooperating with the authorities in public-private partnerships, providing assistance in developing master plans and zoning regulations, and even influencing the housing law of 2011 by lobbying for a relaxation of the 1:3:6 rule (Herlambang et al. 2019). Indonesia's housing policies are more and more adapted to the needs of the private sector, as is visible in the increased focus on housing finance. This development can be considered as 'neoliberalising urbanism' (ibid.), increasingly penetrating Indonesia's housing policies, where the government has to work as an enabler to adapt policies to the needs of the private sector in the desperate belief that the housing crisis could be addressed in that way.

In line with this shift towards housing finance, ambitious national initiatives were announced. In 2003, a million housing programme and in 2006 the initiative to develop 1,000 towers were put forward. These programmes worked strongly with housing subsidies and public-private partnerships to improve housing finances, but were initially not very successful (cf. chapter 20.6). They did manage, however, to bring in housing subsidies as a means for adequate housing policies and better financial housing markets. In a way, they prepared another massive housing initiative introduced under the succeeding government.

With the inauguration of Joko Widodo as Indonesian president in 2014, a new era of housing policies began to take shape. The Indonesian government showed increasing political will to address the housing challenge by more comprehensive and determined measures and strategies. Housing became a priority and the authorities committed themselves to ambitious targets in the next five-year development plan (RPJMN 2014–2019). Commitments were made to reach universal access to safe drinking water and sanitation and the eradication of slums until 2019 (known as the 100-0-100 target[6]) (World Bank 2016b: 3). To achieve this, a number of sectoral programmes were initiated with international support (World Bank, ADB, etc). Programmes in the housing domain comprised slum upgrading, community empowerment, and assistance for incremental housing improvements. Existing programmes were continued and enlarged (eg NSUP, KOTAKU, NAHP). As an umbrella initiative the One Million Houses Programme (PSR) was established in 2015, aiming to synergise all efforts and stakeholders. By expanding access to housing finance through different incentives (SSB, SBUM, and FLPP), by activating the private sector, but relying also on all other programmes and furthering direct provision by national and local governments (rusunawa), the goal was to provide one million houses per year. Indeed, the initiative has reached this target for the first time in 2018 (Jones 2017: 11–12; The Jakarta Post 2019).

19.2 Actors in Indonesia's housing policies

Four main groups of actors are involved in Indonesian housing policies. These are governmental organisations, civil society, the private sector, and international organisations.[7]

6 The Indonesian target 100-0-100 refers to 100 % of households with access to clean water, 0 % slums, and 100 % with access to proper sanitation.

7 These four groups were developed following roughly the classification of Sonia Roitman (2016: 193–194). During the social network analyses carried out in the two case study cities of Surabaya and Surakarta, the groups were extended by several other sub-groups. An overview about my classification of actor-groups in Indonesia's housing sector is provided in chapter 12.4.

Government actors: Governmental organisations have the greatest role to play, since they are the main actors designing and implementing housing policies. Government agencies and companies can be distinguished. Government agencies at all levels are involved, but the most important ones are the national and the city level for creating and realising policies. The provincial and the *kelurahan* level are less important, since they rarely have the responsibility for introducing their own housing policies. At the national level, two ministries must be mentioned: the Ministry of Development Planning with its agency, the National Development Planning Agency (Badan Perencanaan Pembangunan Nasional, or BAPPENAS), and the Ministry of Public Works and Housing (Kementerian Pekerjaan Umum dan Perumahan Rakjat, or KPUPR)[8]. The former creates the national long-term development plans, sets general strategic goals and aligns and balances the policies between the different ministries. The latter implements and regulates all initiatives and programmes related to housing and infrastructure development. KPUPR usually has branches in every city and district, known locally as the Department of Public Works (Dinas Pekerjaan Umum, or DPU). These branches are formally integrated into local or provincial governments, but also follow national directives. Similarly, the National Land Administration Agency (Badan Pertanahan Nasional, or BPN), works nearly independently through branches in every region and city, and is responsible for registering existing land and aiming to formalise all areas. At the city and province level, the Regional Development Planning Agency (Badan Perencanaan dan Pembangunan Daerah, or BAPPEDA) is the most important coordinating agency. Among all governmental agencies, it is primarily the latter, which has become more powerful in the last years of decentralisation policies.

Government-owned companies are involved in housing production and infrastructure development. In 1974, the state-owned public housing company Perumnas and the national savings bank, BTN, were established to promote public housing production and develop a system of housing loans. Other organisations have a more indirect or supporting role. The National Electricity Company (Perusahaan Listrik Negara, or PLN) and the Water Supply Corporation (Perusahaan Daerah Air Minum, or PDAM), for instance, are state-owned companies involved in all housing projects due to their near monopoly in their respective fields.

Private sector: This group includes private developers, construction companies, conventional banks, and their lobby organisations. These actors produce mostly housing for middle and upper classes and are rarely involved in the design and implementation of housing policies (some exceptions are their corporate social responsibility activities). In the last decades, however, they have been increasingly targeted by governmental policies, aiming to increase private sector housing production. In 1972, the

8 The Ministry of Public Works (*Kemen PU*) and the Ministry of Housing (*Kemenpera*) were merged in 2014, following the inauguration of the new president, Joko Widodo.

lobbying organisations of the real estate sector, REI and APERSI, were founded, aiming to influence policies in favour of their clientele.

Civil society: This group consists of research institutions, the informal governance system of RTs and RWs (cf. chapter 17.5), international and national NGOs as well as CBOs. Universities have become important advisors for local housing policies, as for instance in Surabaya in the case of ITS. With their research, they evaluate existing programmes and develop new ideas for housing interventions. Since Indonesia's turn to democracy, increasingly more NGOs have been founded (eg the Solo-based NGO Solo Kota Kita, or the Jakarta-based Urban Poor Consortium, or UPC). Their activities range from advocacy for local residents threatened by eviction to monitoring housing policies towards the proposal and realisation of their own projects. At the international level, these NGOs are increasingly networking and supporting each other, for example through joint projects and mutual learning under the umbrella of the Asian Coalition for Housing Rights (ACHR).

At the neighbourhood level, the RT and RW organisation is of particular relevance for the implementation of housing programmes. This informal administrative structure offers an easy way to reach the community and has been used for decades to implement and realise housing policies. In the last years, the government has begun explicitly strengthening the neighbourhood level by its community empowerment programmes. One example is the PNPM programme, where self-organised working groups (BKM, LKM) were established (cf. chapter 20.4.1).

International organisations: Many multilateral organisations, bilateral organisations from the realm of development cooperation, and foundations are involved in Indonesia's housing policies. Private foundations (the Rockefeller Foundation and the Bill Gates Foundation) have supported several housing programmes and international development cooperation is also involved in different projects every once in a while. The UN organisations UN-Habitat and UNEP have supported several programmes, mainly through their expertise and advice. The largest support, and with this also the largest influence, is exerted by the World Bank and the Asian Development Bank (ADB). Since the 1970s, they have issued loans for housing programmes (in the case of the World Bank) and have in that way significantly influenced Indonesia's housing policies.

19.3 Rules of the game: housing legislation

Several formal rules have been established at the national level to regulate all aspects in the housing sector. The most important laws are mentioned in figure 33, but it would go too far to analyse all of these rules here. Therefore, only two are selected and briefly explored: 'the 1:3:6 policy' to demonstrate the difference between a well-intended regulation and reality and the Housing and Settlements Law (UU 01/2011) as the latest milestone in Indonesia's housing legislation.

19.3.1 The 1:3:6 policy

In 1992, the Indonesian ministers of Internal Affairs, Housing, and Public Works adopted a joint decree aiming to promote socially integrated housing (*Lingkungan Hunian Berimbang*) and to avoid segregation tendencies in private housing production (SKB 648–384/1992). Commonly, private developers tend to create housing complexes that are directed to one social income group, endemically high- or middle-income groups, resulting in homogeneous neighbourhoods. Private developers avoid social mixing, since they perceive it as less attractive for customers, more complicated to realise, and less profitable. Therefore, a national regulation was established, ruling that new developments should have a mix of luxury (*Rumah Mewah*), medium (*Rumah Menengah*) and basic houses (*Rumah Sederhana*) in the ratio of 1:3:6. This meant that each housing project had to consist of three medium and six low-cost housing units for each luxury housing unit built (Rukmana 2015; Tunas & Darmoyono 2014). In such a way, it was intended to force the private sector to increase their housing production down the income levels and create harmonious, socially mixed neighbourhoods instead of segregated enclaves (KPUPR 2016: 79; Sudarmo 1997: 235–239).

In the Housing and Settlements Law of 2011 (UU 01/2011) and specified in a regulation of the housing ministry (Permenpera 10/2012) this rule of integrated housing was confirmed, albeit in a more relaxed version. Lobbying associations of developers succeeded to ease the rule, relaxing it from a 1-3-6 restriction to a ratio of 1-2-3 (Herlambang et al. 2019: 641). All new residential projects are obliged to follow this rule. It is compulsory for larger projects (> 1,000 houses) *on the same site*, and for smaller projects within the same city or district (UU 01/2011 Art. 34–36).

Although the 1-3-6 rule was adopted with good intentions, implementation was inadequate in the 1990s and also today remains unsatisfying (Rukmana 2018: 84–85). This has two reasons. The first is that the poorest segment of society was not reached, since even the simplest houses were still not affordable for this group. The other is that the private sector did not realise the necessary numbers, avoiding the rule wherever possible. The construction of homogeneous neighbourhoods with luxury property is preferred since profit margins are much higher (Asnawi 2005: 40).

Enforcement of the law remained weak. During the turmoil in the aftermath of the Asian financial crisis and the following years of institutional reorganisation, effective enforcement was impossible. Penalties for non-compliance with the rule were different in every region. In West Java, for instance, it was allowed to substitute low-income housing units with cash subsidies in the 1990s. (Sudarmo 1997: 239–240; Yuniati 2013). Later reports from Jakarta show that developers not complying with the rule are still not penalised (Yap 2015: 3).

In Solo, developers use many creative ways to avoid or circumvent the building restrictions. As pointed out during several talks and interviews with private developers, the common way would be to create luxury housing in sought-after locations, sell these units with high profit margins, and then, often years later, create the low-income dwellings on cheap land in urban peripheries or – in absence of controls – not at all. Among these developers, the view prevailed that low-income housing production would not yield enough profits (Interview 24). In such ways, the well-intended rule established in 1992 had little effect in increasing the housing stock for low-income people.

19.3.2 The Housing and Settlements Law (UU 1/2011)

The Indonesian Housing and Settlements Law (UU 01/2011) regulates various things in the housing and settlement system. Besides general principles, obligations for governments at different administrative levels, and an explicit section on slum settlements, a wide variety of articles regulates the arrangements of houses and settlements, spatial planning, facilities and public services, house and infrastructure design and construction, issues of maintenance, supply of land, the housing financial system, and rights and obligations for all involved parties.

The housing law acknowledges four principles:

a. It reaffirms article 28H paragraph 1 of the 1945 Constitution of the Republic of Indonesia stating that 'every person shall have the right to live in physical and spiritual prosperity, to have a home and to enjoy a good and healthy environment'.
b. It recognises the obligation of the state to create appropriate conditions allowing everyone to live in affordable, safe, and adequate housing throughout Indonesia.
c. It calls for greater state involvement in providing and facilitating housing developments
d. It calls for the need of "balanced development" (*Hunian berimbang*) which recognises the needs of low-income people (MBR).

The document includes a whole section on low-income people (*Masyarakat Berpenghasilan Rendah*, or MBR) and slum houses (*Perumahan Kumuh*) and slum settlements (*Permukiman Kumuh*). The document also defines the responsibilities and tasks of the three tiers of governments (national, province, and city/district) required to carry out all duties in the arrangement of housing and settlements in Indonesia. Among the many tasks and obligations for cities and districts, two points stand out: First, municipalities are now required to prepare development plans for settlement and housing development and implement them accordingly. Second, municipalities are explicitly mentioned as responsible for the realisation of housing for low-income people. This is to be supported and facilitated by the allocation of substantial funding. It falls in the authority of the city government to provide land for the construction of housing and settlements for low-income groups and to facilitate the slum upgrading and slum prevention in their area of jurisdiction (UU 01/2011 art. 15–16).

The housing and settlement law also explains and recommends adequate measures to intervene in the housing domain: Housing programmes are to be developed containing components such as subsidies, self-help stimuli, tax incentives, relaxing licensing rules, bank insurances, land supply, land certification, or the construction of infrastructure and public facilities (UU 01/2011 art. 54). The government has to take on a supporting role, guaranteeing legal frameworks, facilitating housing finance, and providing public infrastructure. It is the obligation of the government to provide financial incentives for new housing constructions and also for improving the existing housing stock.

In addition, strategies are recommended to deal with slums: Regional governments are obliged to determine slum locations and monitor them closely as a precondition for implementing upgrading or relocation measures (UU 01/2011 § 97–100). All measures have to be implemented in a just, humane, and economic way (§ 96). For slums that are located in areas not in accordance with the spatial plan or in hazardous areas, relocations must be carried out. All others are to be upgraded (houses and community infrastructure). Relocations are implemented by local authorities aiming to realise better housing conditions and to guarantee the communities' safety. These relocations must involve all tiers of government and have to take place in a participative way, involving also the affected communities (§ 101). Community participation in all measures is considered as essential. However, this is also accompanied by obligations: The community has to take on a supporting role for housing and settlement developments initiated by the state. The community is expected to help with the preparation of plans, to implement housing construction in self-help, to repair and maintain infrastructure, and control all of the government's activities (§ 131–132).

With this housing and settlement law, for the first time a comprehensive legal framework is available to address the housing challenge for low-income people and the authority to do so was explicitly transferred to local and provincial governments. Obligations of all actors, including the community, are clearly outlined. The starting signal was given for lower tiers of government to identify slum areas and housing problems within their jurisdiction, prepare development plans, and implement projects and programmes to prevent slum expansion and upgrade the existing housing stock (Jones 2017: 12).

When reading between the lines it becomes obvious that general opinions are transported in the document: (1) that self-help housing can solve the housing challenge; (2) that these self-help abilities of the community need to be enabled by a bundle of measures, especially financial enablement, and (3) that home-ownership is the preferable mode of housing for everyone. These opinions have developed from the context; they are reflected in the applied housing policies from the last 30 years. The next section categorises and analyses past and current policies, exploring their impact and consequences.

20 Indonesia's Housing Programmes

This section illustrates the content of Indonesia's housing programmes, and explains and assesses some of the implemented initiatives in more detail. The goal is to give an overview on Indonesia's housing interventions and to derive latest developments and policy changes. Since programmes and policies change rapidly and are difficult to categorise (cf. box 13), only the most important housing programmes, their evolution and procedures, mechanisms and outcomes are explored.

Programmes applied over the last 30 years are analysed and categorised in seven groups: i) slum upgrading, ii) public housing, iii) cooperative housing, iv) community empowerment, v) housing financial policies, vi) subsidies for incremental housing, and vii) larger national initiatives (cf. table 23). These programmes span different periods, apply different approaches, and show varying results (cf. table 24). There is no clear trend, various programmes are applied simultaneously and if terminated they often reappear years later under different names and with slightly changed content. Nevertheless, an expansion in the number of programme types is visible from 2000 onwards. Well-introduced measures such as slum upgrading and public housing are now accompanied by newer approaches of community empowerment and housing financial policies. The latter has become the main leverage for the Indonesian state to encourage the private sector to increase production and the people to access credit for house purchases.

Box 13: Difficulties in giving an overview on Indonesia's housing programmes

The objective of providing a good overview of the Indonesian housing programmes was a difficult one. The analysis is based on my experience from the fieldwork, informal discussions with Indonesian experts, the collection and review of literature at local universities, and a comprehensive review of international sources. Since there is – to my knowledge – no comprehensive over all presentation of Indonesia's housing policies, it was difficult to gain a deep insight. Some programmes, especially those with international participation, are well documented, while mechanisms and results of other activities in the housing sector were more difficult to grasp.

Generally, many programmes and housing initiatives coexist in Indonesia, frequently overlapping each other in their objectives and sometimes using similar mechanisms and target groups. Some of them were only short-lived programmes, soon terminated and marked as failure. Others were applied for longer periods, but continued under different names with slightly changed mechanisms and foci. Moreover, over time, components from past programmes were merged and presented as new housing initiatives, even though they were merely a continuation of previous measures. For these reasons, a categorisation and clear temporal presentation of Indonesia's housing policies was difficult. The analysis presented here can therefore certainly not claim to be exhaustive, although every effort has been made to provide as much detail as possible.

Table 23 Selected Indonesian housing programmes and initiatives 1989–2019

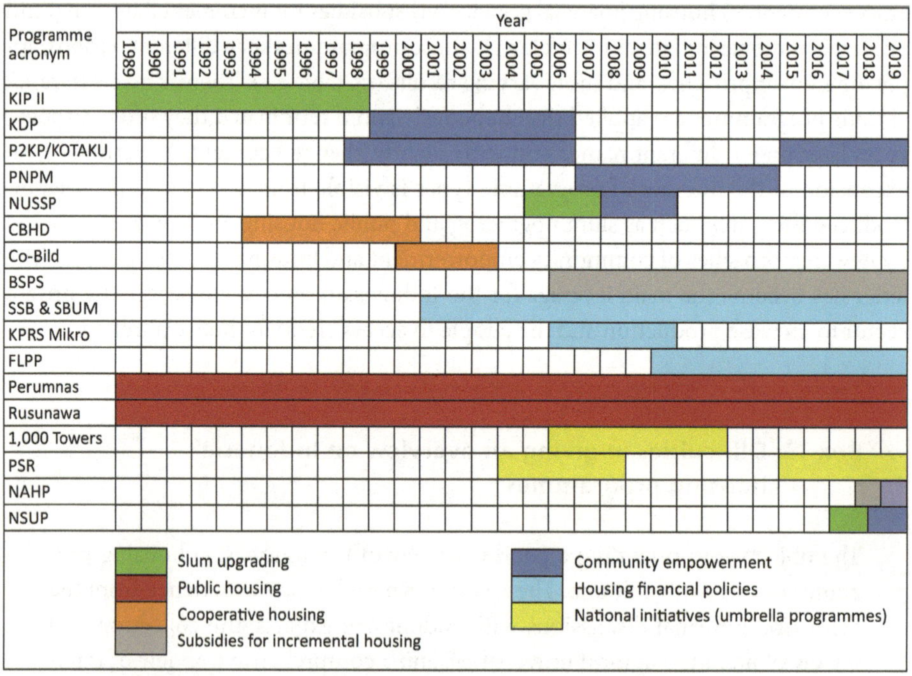

Source: Table by author

Note: Illustrated time ranges are approximate estimates for each housing programme and initiative. For acronyms, see the glossary

Table 24 Selected Indonesian housing programmes: years of implementation, components, and performance

Programme acronym	Years	Programme components	Reported performance
KIP I	1969–1980s	– Slum upgrading – Physical infrastructure – Top down	36 million people reached [c] 85,000 ha slums improved [c]
KIP II	1980s – 1998	– Slum upgrading – Physical infrastructure – Social and economic aspects – Community planning & participation	
KDP	1998–2006	rural – Poverty alleviation – Community empowerment	Implemented in all rural and urban villages
P2KP	1999–2006	urban – CDD approach – Infrastructure improvements	
KOTAKU	Since 2015	urban – Refocus on slum upgrading – CDD approach	11,067 *Kelurahan* [h] 23,656 ha slums [h]
PNPM	2006–2014	– Poverty alleviation – Community empowerment – CDD approach – Infrastructure improvements	21 million people reached [l]
NUSSP	2005–2010	– Slum upgrading – CDD approach – Infrastructure improvements – Micro loans	1.2 million households reached [d]
CBHD	1994–2000	– Cooperative housing – Community empowerment – Demand-driven approach – Subsidised loans	1,887 houses realised (1994–2000) [j]
Co-Bild	2000–2003		10,000 households [d]
BSPS	Since 2006	– Subsidy for incremental self-build housing	544,000 beneficiaries (2010–2013) [b]
KPRS-Mikro KPRS-Bersubsidi	2006–2010	– Micro loans for home improvements – Mortgage subsidies – Mortgage interest rate buy down	50,000 households [a]
FLPP	Since 2010	– Conditional funds for lenders – Down payment assistance – Subsidised interest rates	650,000 units (2011–2019) [c]
Perumnas	Since 1974	– State-owned public housing company – Provision of different housing solutions	approx. 16,000 new housing units per year [i]

Programme acronym	Years	Programme components	Reported performance
Rusunawa Development	Since 1985	– Low-cost rental housing in social housing multi-storey blocks	approx. 13,720 units in 2012 [d] approx. 21,000 units in 2018 [g]
1,000 towers	2006–2012	– National initiative to build 1,000 high-rise residential towers – Public-private partnerships – Land provision, tax exemptions, subsidised loans	120 towers realised by 2010 [e]
PSR	Since 2015	– National initiative to build one million homes annually – Umbrella initiative combining several programmes	3.5 million houses realised (2015–2018) [g]
NAHP	Since 2018	– Mortgage-linked down payment assistance – Subsidy for incremental self-build housing (expansion of BSPS) – Support programme for PSR	120,000 houses improved (2017–2018) [f]
NSUP	Since 2016	– Slum upgrading – Urban infrastructure and services	2.5 million beneficiaries (2016–2019) [k]

Sources: Table by author. Data compiled from **[a]** Permanent Mission of the Republic of Indonesia (2012), **[b]** World Bank (2017: 6), **[c]** Tunas & Peresthu (2010: 318), **[d]** National Development Planning Agency – BAPPENAS (2012: 102), **[e]** Kusno (2013: 159), **[f]** Harrison (2019), **[g]** Ministry of Public Works and Housing – KPUPR (2019), **[h]** Ministry of Public Works and Housing – KPUPR (n.d.), **[i]** Perumnas (2018: 11), **[j]** Asnawi (2005: 77), **[k]** Soraya (2019), **[l]** Republic of Indonesia (2016: 92)
Note: For acronyms, see the glossary

20.1 Slum upgrading: Indonesia's experience

Slum upgrading is one of the oldest intervention strategies in Indonesia's housing sector. Already under colonial rule the low housing quality and bad living conditions in Indonesia's *kampungs* were seen as problematic, since unhealthy conditions were regarded as the origin of diseases spreading to the European quarters (Cobban 1974: 403–404; Dianingrum et al. 2017: 44). In 1905 the Dutch thus introduced first upgrading and clearance measures (*Kampoeng Verbetering*) for the *kampungs* in worst condition (Obermayr 2017: 101). The dual land system of land rights (customary and western property rights) within the *kampungs* (cf. chapter 18.2.3), however, proved a difficult factor for realising measures on a larger scale. The interventions remained punctual. After Indonesian independence, the problems grew worse caused by rising rural-urban migration flows targeting the inner-city *kampungs*. Political conditions, however, were unstable, leaving little space to address urban development problems and the inadequate housing conditions in the *kampungs*. At the beginning of Suharto's New Order, not much had been achieved. At that time, 80 % of Jakarta's *kampungs* lacked sanitation facilities and even the supply of electricity (Spreitzhofer 2007: 267–279; Obermayr 2017: 101).

This changed from 1969 onwards. Based on the colonial experiences, Suharto's government introduced an extensive slum upgrading programme, soon to be known as Kampung Improvement Programme (KIP). The programme was seen as a breakthrough since it recognises *kampungs* as an essential housing option for low-income people and acknowledges measures of *in situ* upgrading instead of evictions as a proper policy (World Bank 2003). Nevertheless, evictions were also a welcome means of the authoritarian government to clear land for large-scale development projects (Reerink 2006).

20.1.1 Three phases of slum upgrading

Initially, KIP focused solely on the improvements of physical infrastructure, but soon evolved into an internationally respected and integrated upgrading scheme. Three generations can be identified (cf. figure 34): an initial phase focusing on infrastructure (KIP I, 1970s), a more comprehensive phase, trying to incorporate social and economic aspects (KIP II, 1980s and 1990s) and the latest phase of community-driven development (CDD) emphasising community empowerment and poverty alleviation (CDD, 2000s and ongoing).

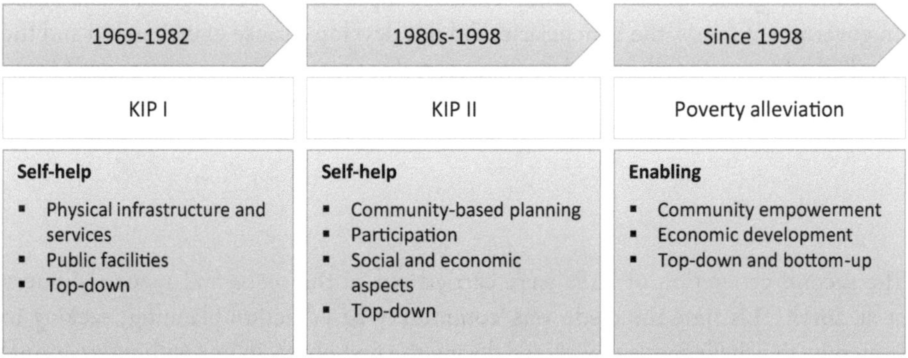

Fig. 34 Three generations of Kampung Improvement Programmes (KIPs) in Indonesia
Source: Illustration by author

Phase I

In the first generation of Kampung Improvement Programmes (1969–1982), the provision of basic infrastructure and public facilities were the main concerns. Efforts comprised the pavement of roads and alleys, the installation of sanitation systems, drainage channels, and water infrastructure (pipes, public toilets, and water taps) as well as the establishment of schools and health facilities (Tunas & Peresthu 2010). The idea was that improved infrastructure and services would also stimulate the renovation of individual houses (Andavarapu & Edelman 2013: 187). The programmes were implemented in a top-down manner, the kinds of improvements were determined by the state and the affected communities contributed their work power. The communities hardly had a say in this early stage of KIP (Zahnd 2005: 67–69; Jones 2017). After successful pilot phases (1969–1975) in Surabaya and Jakarta, where 89 *kampungs* or 2,400 ha with over 1.2 million inhabitants were reached (Bawole 2007: 38–41; Tunas & Peresthu 2010; Darrundono 2005), the programme was endorsed as national policy in 1979 and became an essential part of Indonesia's national five-year development plans (REPELITA). Thanks to UN funding and using World Bank and ADB loans the measures were scaled up, reaching now more than 190 cities and engaging whole neighbourhoods in the upgrading processes.

In retrospect these first generations of KIPs are widely seen as successful, showing impressing figures: by 1977 more than 5,000 ha of 'slum areas' had been improved and by 1982 more than 16 million residents benefited from the programmes (Tunas & Peresthu 2010: 318; Darrundono 2005). Nevertheless, there were also some drawbacks. Since the programme design was implemented top-down by state agencies and based on government funds, the beneficiaries did not develop a sense of ownership and the installed infrastructure degraded over the years due to insufficient maintenance (Asnawi 2005: 69–72).

Phase II

The second generation of KIPs were carried out in the 1980s and 1990s (Minnery et al. 2013). This time the credo was 'community-based action planning', seeking to overcome the challenges encountered during the first phase. In line with international recommendations, programmes were now designed to be more participative and comprehensive, still focusing on physical upgrading, but aiming to integrate also economic and social aspects. Training and other measures were realised to improve community organisation and capacities (technical knowledge and skills) and raise awareness of the community about the need and benefits of improved urban environments. Those affected were now involved in planning and had a voice in prioritising improvements made in their *kampung*. The goal was to better meet the needs of affected communities and to develop the community's capacity of self-help and a sense of ownership for the realised improvements (Yap 2015). The traditional habits in Indonesian *kampungs* of mutual assistance and volunteering for community activities (*Gotong Royong* cf. box 12) were incorporated in this approach (Andavarapu & Edelman 2013: 187).

In this second generation of KIPs, the goals had broadened, but funding had not. Less means were now available for many more tasks. The programme remained top-down in nature, demanding community participation and indeed creating social cohesion, but real bottom-up initiative could hardly be initiated top-down. The expectations that communities would develop more ownership and gradually learn to become more proactive to manage their livelihoods and to take care of the environment was only partly achieved (Tunas & Darmoyono 2014: 170; Minnery et al. 2013).

Phase III

After the Asian financial crisis, a new round of programmes was initiated, now obliged to deal with escalating poverty degrees. Officially, the KIP as a slum upgrading programme was discontinued; improvement programmes were moreover broadened, including now several sub-programmes with the overall goal of poverty alleviation (eg the Kecamatan Development Programme (KDP), Jaring Pengaman Sosial (JPS), a programme to establish a social safety net, and P2KP). These efforts followed an integrated approach, trying to reach livelihood improvements by addressing physical, economic, and social aspects equally. The slum upgrading programmes (KIPs) had evolved into community empowerment programmes (Darrundono 2005).

Under the medium-term development plan for 2004–2009 (RPJMN) three pillars of poverty alleviation strategies were announced: (1) direct support for the poor, (2) community empowerment, and (3) lending to small and medium enterprises (JICA 2018: 308). In a first pillar, social assistance programmes were initiated focusing on reducing the economic burden of the poor. Examples are the *Raskin* programme (subsidised rice), *Jemkesmas* (health insurance) or PKH (conditional cash transfers for poor families) (TNP2K 2014). The second pillar focused on community empowerment and the respective programmes are P2KP, KDP, and PNPM. The third pillar had a focus on the development of micro-enterprises by establishing proper credit systems (Suryahadi et al. 2010: 11).

In line with the discussions at the international level on enabling policies, the objective moved gradually towards community empowerment focusing on participation of the community in planning and design (Dianingrum et al. 2017). Beside the development of autonomous and self-reliant communities, the empowerment approach aims to improve the economic situation in the *kampungs* by providing assistance in the form of micro-credit with low interest rates and marketing training. These efforts were more broadly based poverty reduction strategies with many stakeholders involved trying to mobilise and synchronise the support of affected communities, public agencies, and international donors for community empowerment (Spreitzhofer 2007; Darrundono 2005).

20.1.2 Kampung Improvement Programmes – results and criticism

Indonesia's Kampung Improvement Programme (KIP) is recognised as one of the best examples of slum upgrading and poverty alleviation in the world. Over 30 years of implementation (1969–1998) the programmes reached more than 36 million people, improving approximately 85,000 ha of slum area throughout Indonesia. (Tunas & Peresthu 2010: 318). The main positive outcomes were upgraded living conditions, poverty reduction, and better access to infrastructure and services (Pugh 2001). The programme has gradually evolved from a project-based slum upgrading programme focusing on infrastructure towards a fully-fledged poverty alleviation programme that is community based and integrates social, economic, and physical aspects (Keivani & Werna 2001a: 88). The goal moved from provision of services to the empowerment of the community, in order to enable their self-help capacity.

The secret of the programme was the focus on community infrastructure, not on the improvements of individual housing. By developing a mechanism for community empowerment, community engagement in improving and maintaining their living environment were unleashed. This prevented gentrification tendencies in most cases, the programmes were low-cost, urban livelihoods were improved, and residents simultaneously enjoyed higher land values in their upgraded *kampungs*. (World Bank 2003: 68–70).

The programmes encountered also a bulk of criticism. Early KIP measures focused only on the establishment of physical infrastructure, leaving the question of operation and maintenance unsolved. Poor training of facilitators and project coordinators, lacking synchronisation and integration of neighbourhood and city development, as well as the unsolved land question were the main points of criticism (Tunas & Peresthu 2010: 318; World Bank 2003: 68–70). Not formalising tenure in the *kampungs* had benefits, since gentrification effects were eased and the displacement of low-income dwellers was only reported for some cases (Kusno 2011: 316), but also had negative consequences since some upgraded *kampungs* were later demolished to make way for larger development projects (Yap 2015).

All KIP measures remained national initiatives and were introduced in a top-down manner. Local governments were required to react and implement the national targets (Minnery et al. 2013). Even though this changed gradually over the years – most of all during the transition in the *Reformasi* era since 1998 – real bottom-up initiative could hardly be brought about in a top-down manner. Consequences were that *kampung* dwellers did not develop a sense of ownership of the resulting improvements and did not feel responsible for maintenance, resulting in a neglect of follow-up for the established improvements. Increasing awareness among community members is regarded as the largest challenge (Asnawi 2005: 72). Although discontinued after 1998, the programmes had a long-lasting legacy for all follow-up measures (Minnery et al. 2013). Basic infrastructure had been established as well as cooperatives to maintain it. Social assets and cohesion has been enhanced by the foundation of community based organisations (CBOs). These CBOs can be quickly activated should they be needed. All follow-up programmes can build on these experiences and can use the mechanism of community organisation to realise further upgrading goals.

20.1.3 The National Slum Upgrading Project – NSUP

The opinion is widespread that today Indonesia's *kampung*s are in moderate shape and mostly equipped with proper infrastructure (Interview 26). However, with the adoption of the 100-0-100 goal in Indonesia's national medium-term development plan (RPJMN 2015–2019), the need of another round of infrastructure upgrading was considered as necessary to reach the goal of 0 % slums, 100 % access to water, and 100 % of households with proper sanitation. Therefore, along with other programmes focusing on water supply and sanitation, the National Slum Upgrading Project (NSUP) was launched in 2016, once again focusing on the improvement of urban infrastructure and services, but also promoting capacity building for local governments, supporting their efforts of slum prevention, and monitoring (World Bank 2016: 3).

The programme is jointly funded by the central, provincial, and local governments and is supported by the World Bank and the Asian Infrastructure and Investment Bank. It builds on experiences of the community empowerment programmes (cf. chapter 20.4), but has a more city-wide upgrading agenda focusing also on connecting infrastructure. In the 154 target cities, five programme components are carried out: institutional development, capacity building for local governments and communities, investments in infrastructure and services, technical assistance, and disaster response. The capacity-building measures include training through experts and community facilitators to create Slum Improvement Action Plans at the city level to be developed by municipal authorities and Community Settlement Plans at the community level to be developed by the community prior to the upgrading activities. These plans include area-level improvements of roads, sanitation, water, and drainage systems, but also smaller-scale community infrastructures such as footpaths, sanitation, and drainage improved by the community using the mechanism established through the community empowerment programmes (World Bank 2016b). From its implementation in 2016 until 2019, the programme has already improved the livelihoods of 2.5 million people (Soraya 2019).

The legacy of preceding slum upgrading and community empowerment programmes is clearly visible in the project design of the latest of Indonesia's slum upgrading programmes. The improvement of physical infrastructure is still necessary in many of Indonesia's slums and wherever possible, the upgrading activities are carried out with maximal participation of the community leveraging their self-help resources.

20.2 Public housing

Public housing has never been strong in Indonesia. In the first decades after independence, the government realised only few projects due to limited financial means. In the 1970s, direct provision of housing by the state was considered a failure and the approach was abandoned. As a substitute, the state-owned public housing company Perumnas and other institutions were established. Nevertheless, housing production remained low. It was only in the 2000s that the governemnts once again became involved in direct housing provision. Since those years, the construction of low-cost rental flats (*rusunawa*) for low-income dwellers is increasingly promoted throughout the country.

20.2.1 The state-owned public housing company Perumnas

The state-owned public housing company Perumnas was founded in 1974 with the objective of developing housing and settlement solutions for all Indonesians, focusing particularly on low-income groups (Bawole 2007: 92–98). The national savings bank BTN supports Perumnas by offering business loans and long-term mortgage loans (20 years) for customers. Those with low or medium incomes benefit from subsidised interest rates and low down payments (Tunas & Peresthu 2010; Tunas & Darmoyono 2014).

Residential projects realised by Perumnas include housing, facilities, and infrastructure. The company constructs different types of 'landed' houses[9], classified as basic houses and very basic houses (*rumah sederhana* and *rumah sangat sederhana*) with surface areas of 18 to 36 m^2. Two other options are the healthy modest house (*rumah sederhana sehat)* and the growing core house (*rumah inti tumbuh*). The latter is a core house that can be gradually expanded by the new owner. Perumnas also offers empty land parcels for those who want to build their houses on their own (Tunas & Peresthu 2010: 318).

Since 1983, the company has pioneered vertical housing. Vertical apartment blocks were developed, several stories tall and hosting hundreds of flats. These towers were divided in two categories according to the types of flats they host. There are complexes

9 'Landed housing' is used as a term for all housing units with less than two storeys. It also represents the counterpart to the term vertical housing.

offering simple owner-occupied flats (*rumah susun sederhana milik*, or *rusunami*) or simple rental flats (*rumah susun sederhana sewa*, or *rusunawa*). Both categories are seldom mixed and tenements are managed either by Perumnas itself or by local authorities. As a company, Perumnas is required to make profit, which cannot be achieved by focusing solely on low-income housing. Therefore, the company is also involved in the construction of luxury housing, the hotel and retail sector, and estate management (Perumnas 2013: 64).

Perumnas is an important housing corporation, but output measured in realised housing units has always remained low. Between 1974 and 2004 Perumnas provided 450,000 units, which is not much more than 15,000 units per year (Rolnik 2013b: 6; Bawole 2007: 92–98). Despite moderate growth – 24,231 units were produced in 2018 – these numbers have hardly changed, with approximately 16,000 units produced annually between 2010 and 2018 (Perumnas 2018: 11). Considering the estimated demand, this production is far from sufficient. The main reasons for this are the lacking financial abilities of the government and the difficulties in finding appropriate land (Tunas & Peresthu 2010: 318; Perumnas 2013: 51). In addition, the housing units constructed were often not suitable to residents' needs. They were constructed outside the city centres in the form of unpopular simple flats (*rusunami* and *rusunawa*) in high-rise apartment blocks (Spreitzhofer 2007: 264). Often, these blocks suit neither informal workers nor *kampung* dwellers or migrants and have a bad reputation (cf. box 14). They are too far away (high transport costs), do not offer space for a home-based business, and are in most cases not affordable, even with subsidised loans (Evers & Korff 2000: 168; Spreitzhofer 2007: 264).

Box 14: High-rise apartment blocks – alien to Indonesians?

Most Indonesians reject tenement blocks as a proper way to live. During many discussions and throughout the interviews this topic was always present. As housing costs are on the rise, increasingly more experts propose high-rise vertical apartment blocks (more than five floors) as a solution. However, most Indonesians have grown up in the *kampung*, in one- to two-storey houses; they feel an aversion towards this type of housing, seeing it as alien to their culture. In addition, the first tenement blocks in many Indonesian cities were *rusun* (simple flats), five stories tall and assigned to low-income people, which goes along with a certain stigmatisation: '[...] if it is called rusun, no one imagines rich persons' (Interview 22).

At first, I was sceptical of their claims. Wasn't life better in modern apartment blocks with all its amenities and services (water, sanitation, electricity,

AC)? During my stays in Surabaya and Solo, I had the opportunity to experience the differences myself. Indeed, living in the two types of housing is very dissimilar. Living in the *kampung* might mean inadequate housing conditions and limited or faulty water connections, but also means living in a community. Everybody knows everybody, with all its positive and negative aspects. Social networks are strong, but also social control and denunciation. Life is happening on the streets and meeting and chatting with neighbours at the local street stalls and shops is a daily routine. Even in larger cities, these special conditions are maintained, giving the Indonesian urban *kampung* its famous vibe and its fame of being a village in the city.

Quite the contrary is the experience in a modern high-rise apartment block designed for the middle class. Living in a 40 m² flat on the 17th floor of a high-rise apartment twin block was the other experience I had during my stay. In this anonymous environment, interactions with neighbours are minimal, limited to short greetings in the elevator. It felt familiar to me, being similar to Europe. The common space at the ground floor and the surrounding area was highly formalised, with no street stalls, and the area was mainly used as a parking lot.

Comparing these two experiences, I suddenly understood the unpleasant feeling which seemed to beset most Indonesians when talking about tenement blocks. Too strong is the contrast between lively *kampungs* and bare high-rise blocks. Living and housing conditions are often inadequate in *kampungs*, but they offer an unbeatable atmosphere of encounter and interaction, resulting in strong social networks and high social capital. Nevertheless, high-rise blocks begin to dominate the skylines in the larger Indonesian cities symbolizing progress and prosperity for the affluent middle class. They are seen as a profitable investment and represent good business opportunities for developers and the building industry. *Kampungs* are increasingly under pressure to 'revitalise', a term understood as a complete demolition and reconstruction of whole areas (Zahnd 2005: 55). Since the vertical *kampung* exists only as an idea not (yet) realised, Indonesia has to cultivate and maintain its existing *kampungs* carefully or has to accept that this type of settlement will become a tale from the past.

20.2.2 Social housing: the *rusunawa* programme

From the 1980s onwards, social housing was revived in the form of simple rental flats in multi-storey houses (*rusunawa*). In those years, building land in cities had become increasingly scarce, so land prices exploded. Walkable low-cost rental flats in low rise towers were seen as the solution to high urban density and poverty (Kisnarini 2015: 53). Initial concerns that living in such flats would not be suitable for low-income residents were gradually swept aside. Rather, the upward growth of tenements was seen as the only solution in the face of ever-increasing land prices. In addition, the variability of housing consumption patterns in the course of household life cycles[10] was increasingly recognised by the authorities and experts alike. This fact not only justified the existence of social housing, but also made it seem urgently necessary. *Rusunawa* slowly became an acknowledged housing option for low-income groups (Widiyani 2017: 9–10).

Based on these considerations, a first law on social housing, the Simple Flats Law (UU 16/1985), was adopted in 1985. Direct provision of housing through the state was reintroduced with the official goal of reducing the proportions of people living in slum and squatter settlements and providing adequate housing for low-income groups in urban areas. In the beginning, the production of social rental housing blocks faced great difficulties since no experiences with the planning, managing, and design of such rental flats was available. The design question dominated the debate. How many floors should social housing blocks have and how much space was needed for each unit? Initially each flat was designed with only 18 m^2 for each household, a number that has meanwhile (2011) changed to 30 m^2 (Kisnarini 2015: 53). Such fundamental questions had to be answered first before other management and distribution problems could be addressed.

In the 2000s, the production of social housing blocks accelerated. Vertical housing was increasingly considered as the solution to the housing problems in bigger cities. The 1,000 towers programme was initiated in an attempt to activate the private sector to build low-income housing units (cf. chapter 20.6), but the state also increased the direct provision of *rusunawa* blocks. With the revision of the Housing and Settlements Law (UU 01/2011) and the Simple Flats Law (UU 20/2011), the legal basis and more expensive and detailed regulations were laid to promote *rusunawa* development (Siagian 2015). The responsibility to create new social housing stock and to handle slum areas was now in the hands of local and provincial governments and the ministry of housing urged local authorities to make more efforts to address the problem of affordable housing and slums. Funding for the construction of new multi-storey rental towers was now completely provided by the central government, while local governments had to provide the necessary land and were obliged to take over management and maintenance after completion. Local governments selected tenants based on their income, giving priority to those households targeted by relocations and evictions (World Bank 2017: 6).

---

10 During the life cycle of a household, residents choose their housing according to their economic and social abilities and needs corresponding to the stages of their lives.

Throughout the country 110 twin blocks, consisting of two blocks, three to five storeys tall with 50 to 100 units each (unit size of 20 to 30 m^2), were developed in 2010 until 2012 (Kisnarini 2015: 53). Most of the new rental housing blocks were constructed in Jakarta and only few blocks were realised in other cities in the 2000s. Bandung, for instance, had only three 'towers' in 2016 with 849 units available (Jones 2017: 18). Surabaya in contrast had already finalised some blocks in the 1990s and in 2015 all together 18 projects had been finished, providing 4,469 units (cf. chapter 24.3). In Solo, *rusunawa* construction only began in 2004 with six blocks (560 units) finalised by 2011 (cf. chapter 28.3). However, with a more comprehensive legislative framework in place since 2011 and the continued political will of the national government, local governments seem to be more committed to increase the production of *rusunawa*. In 2018 the Ministry of Public Works and Housing reported the provision of approximately 21,000 flats in new *rusunawa* blocks (KPUPR 2019).

Still, the development of social housing is hindered by the prevailing aversion against vertical housing, a certain stigmatisation of residents living in *rusunawa*, and the general rejection of rental housing (cf. box 14). Vertical housing is considered as alien to Indonesian culture and requires a changed lifestyle, as pointed out during several interviews: '[...] the government also does not prepare the people to live in such houses. For example, the livelihood must be changed. But can you imagine, if the fisherman living in that place? They will bring all their equipment to their flats ... some of them are also rubbish pickers and the house will become very slum' (Interview 23). People relocated from *kampungs* to *rusunawa* are forced to adapt to a new lifestyle that is very different and cannot replicate culture and social capital from *kampung* life (Jones 2017; Das 2017). In addition, the realised units of the 1990s and 2000s are in very bad shape due to insufficent maintenance and bad management (Sari et al. 2015). They are known as places of the poor and *rusunawa* residents thus are associated with poverty. Furthermore, rental housing is not seen as a permanent condition in Indonesian society. Even housing experts consider rental accommodation as a needed property type for each city, but only as a temporary solution during household lifecycles of residents who cannot afford their own property yet.

Other problems with *rusunawa* blocks are related to their location, associated costs, and their building design. Since land is increasingly scarce in urban areas, *rusunawa* housing is often realised in peripheral locations. This makes them unattractive for the urban poor who cannot bear increased transport costs to their places of work, often located close to the city centre (Kusno 2013: 165). Increased living costs are also mentioned in other respects. Residents of social housing have to pay rent as well as the costs for electricity and water, which are –though subsidised – often higher than in informal settlements. These increased costs are an additional burden for household expenditures that have to be paid from fluctuating incomes. Another aspect is the design of social housing that is often not suitable to the needs of low-income groups. Since many of them work in the informal sector, many of their jobs require space for small home-based business, which is not offered in *rusunawa* (Evers & Korff 2000: 168). For these reasons, *rusunawa* is a housing option not necessarily preferred by the poor.

20.3 Cooperative housing: CBHD and Co.BILD

Cooperative housing is another housing option that has been supported since the 1990s. The Community Based Housing Development (CBHD) and the Community Based Initiatives for Housing and Local Development (Co.BILD) concepts have been established since 1994 and since 2000, respectively. They promote cooperative housing, ie housing projects realised by organised groups of residents for owner occupation (Winayanti & Lang 2004: 46–48; Asnawi 2005). The programmes were established with the aim of supporting these cooperatives and promoting this demand-driven approach of housing production as an alternative to the regular provider-driven approach. By doing this, it is possible to overcome the problems of the provider approach (ie only for middle and upper income groups, speculation tendencies). In addition, it is possible to utilise the people's management skills and self-help abilities in housing production.

Initially, NGOs organise people in need of housing as CBOs to initiate the planning and construction process. The community is fully in charge pf collectively designing and deciding about their housing project. The actual housing construction then is realised using the community's workforce, contract work, or a mixture of both (Sudarmo 1997). The concept followed the ideas of Turner (1972) to unleash the productive skill of the community (freedom to build) as demonstrated in informal modes of housing production.

In CBHD, the community is enabled to create their own housing and the government acts only as an enabler, not as a provider of housing (Agustina 2006: 79). Authorities have the task of regulating and facilitating the whole process by counselling activities, the simplification and acceleration of building regulations and permits, and the provision of tailor-made credit arrangements (Asnawi 2005). As one of the actions, the Triguna Credit Scheme was introduced, a mortgage loan programme subsidised by the national government and provided by conventional banks with low interest rates (Sudarmo 1997: 241). Not individuals, but the established CBOs receive the loan if a number of preconditions are met (approval of city government and BPN, existence of construction plans, availability of land, etc). In that way, credit defaults of individual members could be mitigated by the CBO, creating higher reliability for the banks (Asnawi 2005: 78–80).

The approach did not reach scale but was seen as an advancement in housing production. Units realised were more suitable to the communities' needs, but in the period 1994–2000, only 1,887 houses were realised under the CBHD approach. A major drawback were the difficulties in persuading conventional banks to provide construction loans to CBOs. The banks insisted on compliance with many rules and treated the applicants equal to regular housing projects, where target groups must be bankable (Asnawi 2005: 76). This problem was overcome in the follow-up programme Co.BILD starting in 2000. Now, the bank BTN became the main provider of loans and a revolving funds system was introduced, where communities could obtain small loans without collateral (Asnawi 2005: 82–83; Winayanti & Lang 2004: 46–48). This second generation of cooperative housing was more successful, with roughly 10,000 units constructed (BAPPENAS 2012:102).

The experience with housing cooperatives in Indonesia were mainly positive. They showed that this mode of housing provision makes it possible both to build homes and to create community. The collective planning and building process produced social capital and enhanced social cohesion, creating and forming a community. Shortcomings of private housing production can be circumvented by such an approach. Nevertheless, cooperative housing does not reach the poorest since knowledge, skills, willingness, and a certain amount of capital is required. The main drawback is the availability of cheap land not located in peripheries and and lacking well-established infrastructure. Only with strong state support, political commitment, and an integration into wider residential development planning could this mode of housing production be scaled up (Asnawi 2005; Sudarmo 1997).

20.4 Community empowerment

Community empowerment programmes have been introduced in Indonesia since 1998 as part of a wider poverty alleviation strategy. They build strongly on experiences made in the Kampung Improvement Programmes and can be seen as their continuation and evolution. The objective of programmes in this category is still slum upgrading, but the focus has moved towards community empowerment to reach the goal of healthy and liveable settlements. Several programmes fall in this category: the Kecamatan Development Programme (KDP, 1998–2006) working in rural areas and the Urban Poverty Project (Proyek Penanggulangan Kemiskinan di Perkotaan, P2KP, 1999–2006). Both programmes pioneered the so called community driven development (CDD) approach and were later merged into the National Programme for Community Empowerment to be Autonomous (Program Nasional Pemberdayaan Masyarakat Mandiri, or PNPM-Mandiri, henceforth PNPM), which ran from 2007 to 2014. The CDD approach was rated to be so effective that this mechanism was also used for another programme, the Neighbourhood Upgrading and Shelter Sector Project (NUSSP). Using loans from the Asian Development Bank, this project was a mixture of community empowerment and slum upgrading.

This section explores NUSSP and the PNPM programme in more detail to illustrate the Indonesian understanding of community empowerment and community driven development.

20.4.1 The PNPM programme

In 2007, President Susilo Bambang Yudhoyono (2004–2014) introduced a national programme (PNPM) to combine all poverty alleviation programmes of Indonesia under one operational umbrella with the goal of developing autonomous communities. Co-founded by the World Bank and the Government of Indonesia, the programme had an annual budget of Rp 13.6 trillion in 2012 (approx. EUR 1,200 million)[11], with 75 % of the projects carried out in rural areas (BAPPENAS 2012: 20; PSF 2015).

The main purpose of the PNPM was to empower communities and to improve their living conditions by enhancing their capacity of self-help and self-management (Interview 05, 20). The goal was to develop communities that were independent and autonomous, aware of poverty alleviation strategies, and ready to take initiative for improving the quality of life in their neighbourhoods (Roitman 2016: 195). The programme focused on establishing and institutionalizing CBOs, which were seen as the central driving force for neighbourhood development. The communities were required to set up these CBOs and to formulate community development plans to receive direct cash transfers from the national level as incentives for local infrastructure projects. Private consultants and NGOs facilitated the process, giving advice and technical assistance (PSF 2015). 'The community is empowered to do planning, effective financing, then its implementation using the stimulant funds' (PNPM-Facilitator, Interview 20).

The PNPM programme was a continuation of the KDP and the P2KP programmes that had been launched to mitigate escalating poverty levels in the years after the Asian Crisis. These poverty alleviation programmes had the objective of supporting communities in economic and social aspects and organising them in order to make them more resilient against external shocks (Roitman 2016: 195; Minnery et al. 2013). Especially P2KP focused on informal and community-based housing delivery in urban areas (Jones 2017: 11–12). Since both programmes had proven very successful, they were merged and massively extended within the PNPM framework (they became known as PNPM-Rural and PNPM-Urban). Beside these two core programmes, the PNPM framework is also a collection point for several sub-programmes related to poverty alleviation and social assistance (Suryahadi et al. 2010).

The mechanism: community-driven development

PNPM uses a mechanism known as the community-driven development approach (CDD-approach) developed and applied in the preceding KDP and P2KP programmes. Under KDP, this approach was introduced, channelling funding for infra-

11 Exchange rate of 1€ = Rp 11,500 (2012, received from https://fxtop.com).

structure improvements from the central government directly to beneficiaries via block grants (Ensminger 2017: 33). All authority to use these funds for planning, designing, and implementing development activities was given to the communities putting them in the centre of the development process (ADB 2012).

The KDP projects were small in scale and comprised mostly establishment or improvement of infrastructure. The details and budget for each project had to be posted on public information boards to promote transparency. The idea was that by skipping official government channels and transferring funds directly to the communities, residents themselves became engaged in planning, managing, and implementing activities for enhancing their neighbourhood. It turned out that the realised infrastructure projects were of better quality and cost less than measures implemented in the traditional way (World Bank 2013a). Delays and corruption within local governments could be circumvented and projects involved voluntary work of the community, which made it cheap. Beside better infrastructure, more importantly, the community became better organised. By working together in planning and implementing small projects, social capital, awareness of poverty issues, and organisational skills were developed. This mechanism was transferred to the P2KP programme and is the central approach of the PNPM programme.

The PNPM actor-network structure in Solo

The actor-network structure of the PNPM programme is exemplified for the city Solo in Figure 35. Numerous actors at different spatial scales are involved. At the international level, the World Bank and other development cooperation organisations significantly supported the PNPM programme by providing loans. In the beginning, 50 % of the funds originated from the World Bank and the other half from the government of Indonesia (namely the Ministry of Public Works and Housing, or PUPR). This amount diminished over the years; in 2014, the government of Indonesia financed more than 70 % (PSF 2015).

All funding for the PNPM was channelled through the PNPM support facility (PSF), a board or working group consisting of representatives from the World Bank and the major national ministries involved in planning and housing issues (BAPPENAS, Ministry of Finance, Ministry of Social Welfare, Ministry of Economy, PUPR, etc). The tasks were to distribute and harmonise all PNPM activities and to transfer funding directly to the community organisations (BKM, LKM) at the neighbourhood level (Friedman 2014). Other actors involved at the national level are Patiro, a national NGO supporting and disseminating the programme, PDAM, and PLN, the national water and electiricity companies, which are important for all projects related to infrastructure.

At the city level, three actors are the most important: a team of consultants, the Regional Poverty Eradication Coordination Team (Tim Koordinasi Penangulangan

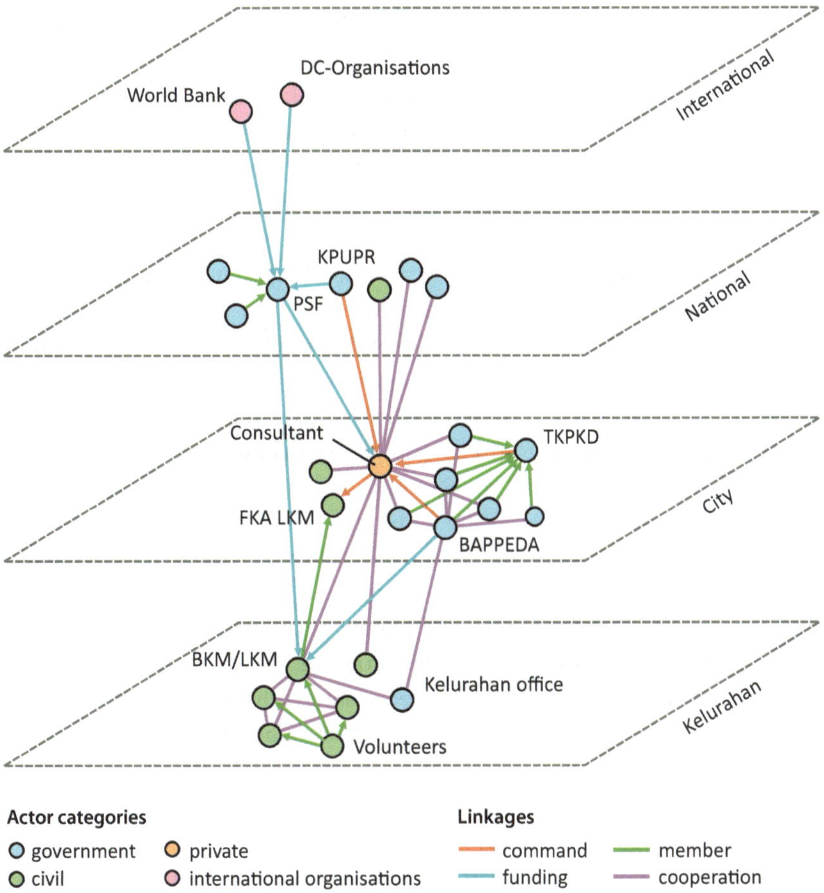

Fig. 35 Network of actors and linkages in the PNPM-Urban Programme in Solo
Source: Illustration by author. Data compiled from three expert interviews in Solo (Interview 12,19,20), Jakimow (2017, 2018), Roitman (2016), PSF (2015), and Friedman (2014)
Note: For acronyms, see the glossary

Kemiskinan Daerah, or TKPKD), and the central board of all community organisations (FKA LKM). In every city, private consultants were appointed and trained to work as PNPM facilitators. They had the task of disseminating the programme, promoting community participation by establishing community organisations (BKM, LKM), mediating between community and all tiers of government, advising the community, and organising trainings for technical and financial management (Interview 20). These facilitators were supposed to enhance the communities' capacities to propose, plan, and implement projects (Friedman 2014). In Solo, around 40 people worked as PNPM facilitators in 2014, with one person as city coordinator (Interview 20).

The local government agencies (DPU, BAPERMAS, DKK, BAPPEDA, DTRK, etc) have a supporting role within the PNPM programme. They form a citywide working group (the TKPKD) under the leadership of BAPPEDA and the mayor, giving advice to the consultants and FKA LKM. It is important to align proposed development projects of the community with urban development planning and spatial plans. Therefore, consultants have frequent meetings with TKPKD to discuss the community proposals (Interview 20). FKA LKM is the central board of all community organisations (BKM, LKM) within the city. These committees hold regular meetings to discuss proposed projects and exchange experiences from different neighbourhoods. At this committee, representatives of all established BKM and LKM units meet regularly to discuss proposed projects and to exchange experiences.

At each neighbourhood level, local committees of volunteering community members were formed, called Badan Keswadayaan Masyarakat (BKM) or Lembaga Keswadayaan Masyarakat (LKM). These CBOs are the main actors central for all activities, receiving funding directly from PSF and additional budget allocated by BAPPEDA. They were tasked to carry out all activities, to develop, plan, implement, and monitor the measures together with the community. Consisting of around ten individuals per quarter (*Kelurahan*), BKMs and LKMs were divided into three units obliged with financial issues (eg financial management, micro-credit), social affairs (eg trainings, services for groups with special needs) and implementation of infrastructure improvements (eg construction or renovation of houses, drainage channels, roads). They carried out a broad variety of projects, among them infrastructure-related measures and the establishment of micro-loan systems. Their tasks were to coordinate with the government (*Kelurahan* office and citywide agencies), to raise additional funding, to organise the community, to create proposals and a community development plan as well as to implement all kinds of poverty alleviation measures for improving their neighbourhood. For these tasks, they are supported and counselled by the consultant and other experts (cf. interview 20)

Programme sequence and implementation in Solo

In Solo, the PNPM programme started in 2008. It has a regular programme component and several supporting programmes (eg PLPBK, USRI, PNPM Pariwisata). All of the city's *Kelurahans* received the basic component, consisting of three-year cycles and aiming at community empowerment (see below). After one *kelurahan* has completed such a three-year cycle, the community there is considered 'empowered' and other supporting programmes can be carried out using the established structure of BKM or LKM. In Solo, however, these programmes (ie PLPBK as a community-based environmental management programme) had reached only pilot stage in 2014.

The main component of the PNPM programme has two phases including several steps:

Part I: Preparation
1) Socialisation of the programme
2) Commitment
3) Formation of CBO

Part II: 3-year cycle of implementation
4) Self-assessment on poverty in the neighbourhood
5) Development of a three-year development plan
6) Project prioritisation (depending on funds)
7) Implementation
8) Monitoring success

In the preparation phase, the programme is made known and disseminated by the consultants and the local government. Communities need to commit formally to the programme (it can be declined). If accepted, they must volunteer and form a CBO (BKM, LKM). In Solo, every *kelurahan* has one BKM or LKM.

In the actual implementation phase, the established CBO surveys the neighbourhood, identifies poverty-related problems (food, drainage, access to water supply and sanitation, housing structure, etc) and discusses solutions together with all residents. From these activities project proposals are developed (including schedule and budget needs) to be included in a three-year development plan. If approved by the consultant and the city government a block grant is transferred by the PSF to the CBO, amounting to Rp. 75 to 350 million depending on the respective neighbourhood's poverty level. Funds received rarely meet the proposed budget, which is why projects need to be prioritised. When the incentive funds have arrived, projects are implemented and after the three-year cycle, its success is monitored. In the second and third year of one project cycle only steps 6 and 7 are repeated (Interview 20).

One of the interviewed RTs in Kelurahan Pucang Sawit of Solo describes his experiences with the PNPM as follows: 'In this area PNPM has been only working on the issue of woman empowerment. They distributed a loan, a soft loan, to the female groups, so that those groups can develop their economic activity. They can produce something and sell those goods to the market. It is a programme, which is fully participatory in its approach. It all depends on the peoples' initiative; people can propose something than government tries to facilitate it. That one is PNPM' (RT in Pucang Sawit, Interview 05).

Results of the PNPM programme

The PNPM programme is reported as a general success. In its implementation period, it became massive, spending more than one billion Euros every year and employing more than 9,000 facilitators throughout the country. It is regarded as the largest and most successful CDD programme in the world, completing 50,000 sub-projects and benefiting more than 60 million people (Republic of Indonesia 2016: 92; KPUPR 2016: 78; OECD 2013: 66). These are only the tangible results. More important are the positive effects on social capital and community organisation reflected indirectly in decreasing poverty levels and enhanced community self-help abilities (World Bank 2013a).

Side effects of the PNPM were improvements of local governance. Even though the programme was designed to bypass lower tiers of government by transferring funds directly to the communities, local government agencies became increasingly involved in all projects since their approval and advice on spatial planning and urban development was necessary. In that way a process of interaction between communities and local governments was initiated, that – over time – encouraged local governments to become more responsive to community needs and to adopt 'pro-poor' policies. Slowly, the central notions of CDD (ie self-management of funds and participatory planning) became integrated in local development planning procedures (ADB 2016; World Bank 2016b).

Critical voices argue that the results of the programme are more questionable. Huge debts are accumulated at the international level for improvements of community infrastructure that is in many cases not properly aligned with regional development planning (Rolnik 2013b; Jakimow 2018). Despite all control mechanisms, corruption remained a problem within the programmes and sometimes projects were realised only for reporting success not because they were needed by the community (Sari 2017). As in many other programmes for the poor in Indonesia, one large drawback is that PNPM measures are only intended for 'legal' and official citizens in an area. All 'illegal' residents, ie those without official registration as for instance the residents of squatter settlements, are excluded from this programme, even though they have the greatest need (Roitman 2016).

Follow-up: the village law and KOTAKU

Under the new president Joko Widodo, the PNPM programme was discontinued in 2014. Instead, the Village Law (UU 06/2014) was issued, granting greater autonomy and additional funds to the village level (Jakimow 2018; TNP2K 2014: 121–123). This law was seen as the next step of decentralisation policies, bringing more development to the regions and serving as an effort to reduce the pull factor of cities (KPUPR 2016: 78). In many respects, the law builds on the PNPM programme, institutionalising the CDD approach for development projects at the village level (ie participatory project design, planning, and implementation). The PNPM programme had not been based on official legislation, but was an executive-run programme, which could be terminated anytime. With the new law, this has changed. The CDD approach has been furthered at the village level, transforming the mechanism into a regular governance process (Howes & Davies 2014: 171; ADB 2016).

The PNPM programme was largely dismissed, but in many villages and urban quarters the created governance procedures and structures remained in place. Local authorities have learned to work with the community, and the residents have been taught to introduce their own projects, to organise themselves, and to solve their problems by means of self-help. Capacities of communities and local governments are growing with such projects and further development programmes and measures can build on established procedures of implementation.

Also in urban areas the CDD approach was continued. There, the PNPM was transformed into the KOTAKU programme (Kota Tanpah Kumuh, or city without slums) from 2015 onwards. Basically, KOTAKU is a continuation of the P2KP programme, refocussing on slum upgrading to achieve the 100-0-100 target of the Jokowi administration. KOTAKU is established as a national collaborative platform for slum upgrading, uses the established mechanisms (the CDD approach) and is financed by multiple sources, including the Indonesian government, communities, and the private sector, but also international funding provided by the ADB, the World Bank, and the Asian Infrastructure and Investment Bank (KPUPR n. d.).

20.4.2 The Neighbourhood Upgrading and Shelter Sector Project

In 2005 the Indonesian ministry of housing introduced another slum upgrading programme, known as the Neighbourhood Upgrading and Shelter Sector Project, or NUSSP. The aim was to improve slum neighbourhoods and to provide better access to appropriate housing for low-income people. The project ran from 2005 until 2010 and was funded by loans from the ADB in collaboration with national and local (districts and cities) budgets. The project had several components: improving planning and upgrading initiatives for low-income neighbourhoods, capacity building for local authorities, and provision of better access to housing finance (micro-credit). In the five-year period of implementation, the project reached 1,353 *kampungs* and villages in 32 cities or districts with more than one million households (Hartono 2009; BAPPENAS 2012: 102; Chomistriana 2011: 51–52).

Mechanism of NUSSP

As in other upgrading programmes (eg KIP), the project focused on the establishment and improvement of community infrastructures, ie public sanitation facilities, neighbourhood roads, drainage channels, garbage collection facilities, to name a few. The distinguishing element is the project design. A CDD approach similar to other Indonesian community empowerment initiatives is employed (eg KDP, P2KP, and PNPM). Assisted and trained by project facilitators, community self-help organisations, BKMs, were formed. These BKMs were tasked with surveying the neighbourhood, developing neighbourhood upgrading plans, and realising infrastructure constructions either through community self-construction or by contracting the work to third parties. The goal was to establish independent and responsive institutions at the community level to improve community self-reliance (Chomistriana 2011: 50–51; ADB 2012).

The activities followed this procedure (Hartono 2009):

1) Socialisation of the programme (spread the information)
2) Small-scale community meetings where the facilitators identify persons to form a cadre
3) Community meetings at larger scale, formation of a community self-help organisation (BKM)
4) Self-survey conducted by BKMs about their neighbourhood
5) Participatory planning process to develop a neighbourhood upgrading plan
6) Implementation and monitoring
7) Consultation with the government

Results of NUSSP

The quality of infrastructure provided was found to be better compared to improvements made without a CDD approach, which was attributed to high degrees of participation and the establishment of BKMs that created a sense of ownership for the established measures. An ADB study (ADB 2012) found that the existence of BKMs are tied either to the NUSSP project – they were created for the upgrading process – or already existed when the respective area had participated in other community empowerment programmes preceding NUSSP. In the latter case or in areas with long lasting traditions of mutual assistance (*Gotong Royong* cf. box 12), the degree of participation in beneficiary communities was higher and upgrading and maintenance results were better than in areas without such traditions or established BKMs. Generally, BKMs proved not to be lasting institutions. When the process of construction ended, maintenance practices also diminished and BKMs dissolved in many cases (ADB 2012). Considering the goal of lasting community self-help organisations, this is a major drawback.

20.5 Housing financial policies: mortgage loans, micro-credit, and FLPP

Housing finance is usually out of reach for Indonesia's urban poor. Over 60 % of Indonesians work in the informal sector, lacking a regular income and thus access to the financial system (World Bank 2015b). Consequently, they are considered as 'unbankable' by commercial banks, thereby deny them mortgage loans. Financial institutions also avoid smaller loan arrangements due to perceived high risks and operational costs (Dahiya 2012: 51). As a result, mortgage lending is underdeveloped in Indonesia and accounted for only 2.8 % of GDP in 2012, compared to 7 % in India and 19 % in Thailand (World Bank 2017: 3). Low-income residents do not use loans for housing construction and improvements at all, or obtain them from informal moneylenders at poor conditions.

To address these challenges, the Indonesian government has developed financial organisations and several intervention strategies from the 1970s onwards. The goal is financial enablement to increase access to housing finances. The first step was the foundation of BTN in 1973, tasked with the creation of a subsidised mortgage loan scheme. In close cooperation with Perumnas and REI, first loans were issued for housing construction. Perumnas produced primarily simple housing units for low-income people, while the private developer cooperation REI and the building industry preferred the production of more expensive housing for the upper class. These first steps to increase access to mortgage credit were well intended, but mainly benefited members of middle- and high-income groups who were able to fulfil the requirements. For this reason the subsidised credit system neither reached scale nor the urban poor (Asnawi 2005: 45).

Since formal financial markets largely failed, additional measures were taken to expand access to loans down the income ladder. Since 2001 'interest rates subsidies' have been given (SSB) and since 2002 down payment subsidies are also available (SBUM). Since 2006, the Ministry of Finance allowed local cooperatives to become active in this segment of housing finance to work as intermediaries between banks and loan recipients. In that way, risks and operational costs could be externalised and the conventional banks became more willing to give loans. By 2010 this subsidised micro-credit for home improvements, known as KPRS-Mikro, reached more than 50,000 households for self-help housing development (Permanent Mission of the Republic of Indonesia 2012).

In 2010, a centre for housing finance (since 2015 PPDPP)[12] was established with the central task to channel and administer funds for housing development for low-income people. The institution supervises and manages the FLPP mechanism, a housing loan liquidity scheme for people with low- to moderate incomes. The goal is to enhance mortgage affordability for more people and to promote in that way investments in the housing industry and further economic growth and employment in that sector (World Bank 2015b; Perumnas 2013: 90).

---

12 The Centre for Housing Finance (*Pusat Pembiayaan Perumahan*, or PPP) was transformed to the Centre for Housing Finance Fund Management (PPDPP) in 2015, following the fusion of the ministry of public works and the ministry of housing (*Kemenpera* and *KemenPU into KemenPUPR*). The centre reports directly to this ministry.

Under this programme, subsidised home mortgage loans and down payment assistance is provided through financial institutions for low-income first homebuyers. Beside the Ministry of Housing and the Ministry of Finance, a number of national and local banks are involved. The loans are heavily subsidised. Of each mortgage loan, 70 % is covered by the government and only 30 % by banks. These shares later increased to 90 % as compared to 10 % (World Bank 2017: 6). Compared to market interest rates of 12 % the FLPP scheme offers a 20-year loan at a fixed rate of 8,5 % (2010). These rates decreased to 7.25 % in 2012 and to 5 % since 2015. All people with monthly incomes no higher than Rp. 4 million are eligible for the programme (Permanent Mission of the Republic of Indonesia 2012).

In the period from 2011 to 2019 approximately 650,000 units (72,000 units per year) were constructed using the subsidised mortgage loan provided by the FLPP scheme (PPDPP 2019). Major drawbacks were high costs for the state, the exclusion of Indonesians with non-fixed incomes, and the exclusive support of projects pursued by private developers. In 2016, nearly 60 % of the government's budget for housing was spent on the FLPP programme and the majority of Indonesians with informal incomes were excluded (World Bank 2017: 8–9; Utomo 2014). Since banks require fixed incomes to pay the monthly installments, FLPP is not suitable for the poor who have informal occupations and cannot meet this requirement. As a result the FLPP mechanism works only for medium-income people (Agustina 2006: 79). The FLPP programme thus can be regarded as a massive housing programme for the middle class and as a subsidy for the private housing industry. As is too often the case, the trickle-down effects of such policies is not about to happen.

20.6 Ambitious national initiatives

In the 2000s, housing policies were increasingly prioritised and successive governments announced an increasing number of new initiatives to address the housing backlog. The Million Houses Programme (2003) of President Susilo Bambang Yudhoyono (2004–2014) and the 1,000 tower programme (2006) of vice president Jusuf Kalla were ambitious examples. Both were short-lived initiatives that largely failed, but paved the way for successive strategies such as the FLPP scheme and the ambitious PSR programme of the Jokowi government.

The 1,000 tower programme

Jusuf Kalla, vice president of Indonesia (2004–2009 and 2014–2019), announced the 1,000 tower programme in 2006. He stipulated that the Indonesian government would construct 1,000 high-rise residential towers throughout Indonesia using public-private partnerships (Herlambang et al. 2019: 637). In only five years, by 2011, all towers were to be finished, half of them in Jakarta (Kusno 2013: 61). Two forms of housing units were intended: (1) simple rental flats (*rusunawa*) in walkable towers targeting informal workers, students, and temporary migrants and (2) simple owner-occupied flats (*rusunami*) in high-rise apartments constructed at low cost (Permanent Mission of the Republic of Indonesia 2012: 10; Herlambang et al. 2019). Expectations were that these residential low-cost towers within the city boundaries would be a real option for the urban poor to become homeowners. Purchase prices were capped at Rp. 144 million, and subsidised housing loans as well as tax exemptions were prepared for low-income dwellers (below Rp. 4.5 million income per month) (Pathoni 2012). The towers were constructed in collaboration with the private sector under public-private partnerships and with Perumnas. Private developers rushed to the programme, attracted by the promise of free land for the projects in the highly competitive Jakarta land market and to ease building permits.

After only four years, in 2010, the subsidies for the programme were halted, since the programme completely failed to reach the target group (Kusno 2013: 163). The private sector argued that poor planning and lacking incentives from the government were responsible. They complained that land was too expensive to construct units at the capped rate. In fact, demand from low-income people was low due to persisting difficulties in obtaining loans. For these reasons the market for *Rusunami* already constructed were broadened to the middle- and upper-income groups (Pathoni 2012). When the programme was terminated in 2012, only 120 of the 1,000 towers had been realised, nearly all of them occupied by residents of the middle and upper class. Even though failing its objectives, the 1,000 tower programme proved that subsidised housing combined with political will can achieve some results. It paved the way for the FLPP programme, in which now less the supply side (the developers), but more the demand side (the customers) were considered for subsidies (Kusno 2013: 159).

Jokowi's initiative for one million houses – PSR and NAHP

In 2015, the newly elected president Jokowi made the provision of affordable housing and the reduction of the housing backlog an explicit priority of his policy (Widiyani 2017: 8). He introduced the One Million Houses Programme (*Program Satu Juta Rumah*, or PSR), to be a broad umbrella initiative for addressing housing demand and the existing housing deficit. As the name suggests the goal is to produce one million new houses annually, 70 % to be designated for low-income residents. This goal is to be achieved by continuing and expanding all existing strategies, by synergising the efforts of all stakeholders and by encouraging the private sector in particular to produce housing for low-income groups.

One component of PSR is a number of incentives targeting supply and demand sides to improve the housing finance system. On the supply side, these incentives entail efforts to simplify bureaucratic processes (eg making it easier, faster, and less costly to obtain building permits) and the preparation of land for construction purposes. On the demand side, the financial abilities of customers are to be increased by subsidised mortgage loans and low down payments using revised versions of FLPP, SSB, and SBUM schemes (Perumnas 2016: 165).

Soon it was recognised that improved housing finance would not be enough to reach the poorest part of society, those considered as 'unbankable'. Therefore, a PSR supporting programme was introduced in 2018 with significant support from the World Bank: The National Affordable Housing Programme (NAHP). This programme has two components: (1) another mechanism to improve access to housing finance in the form of mortgage-linked down payment assistance and (2) an expansion of the home improvement assistance programme for incremental upgrading activities (the BSPS programme cf. box 15). Bantuan Stimulan Perumahan (BSPS) is a programme that provides direct subsidies for incremental home improvement and construction and had already been implemented successfully in rural and periurban areas and was now to be scaled up and expanded to urban areas (World Bank 2017). Due to various reasons (eg better attractiveness of other subsidies) the first component has not been very successful up to now, while the second programme component resulted in the renovation of 120,000 houses in the years 2018 and 2019 (Harrison 2019).

Box 15: BSPS: Direct subsidies for incremental self-build housing

Since 2006, the Indonesian government provides home improvement assistance (Bantuan Stimulan Perumahan, or BSPS), a subsidy for incremental home improvements (Rolnik 2013b: 7). The programme targets mainly rural and periurban areas, aiming at the lowest income households (monthly income below Rp. 1.5 million or approx. 100€[13]; under NAHP below 3.1 million) (World Bank 2017: 18). If eligible, a household can receive an amount of Rp. 10 to 30 million (approx. 650 to 2,000€[13]) for renovation, repairs, sanitation, expansion, or even new construction (World Bank 2017: 6). This subsidy is intended to enable residents to buy construction materials and to undertake renovations in the form of self-help (World Bank 2015b). Over the course of only three years (2010–2013) the programme reached 544,000 beneficiaries (World Bank 2017).

13 Exchange rate: 1€ = Rp. 15,000 (09/2019, received from https://fxtop.com).

Combining and synergising the different approaches and programmes, the overall results of the PSR initiative are reported as remarkable. Approximately 3.5 million houses have been 'realised' from 2015 until 2018 and the target of 1.1 million houses was allegedly reached for the first time in 2018 (KPUPR 2019; The Jakarta Post 2019; Perumnas 2018: 153). These results are presented in more detail in chapter 21.1.

21 The Impact of Indonesia's Housing Policies – an Assessment

Having explored Indonesia's cities and settlements, recent urban developments, the housing situation, housing policies, and applied programmes over the last decades, the question remains of what governmental interventions in the housing sector can really achieve, especially with regard to the poorest population groups. This section explores this question and provides an analysis and assessment of the claim of most Indonesian housing programmes to target the poor. For this goal, the target groups of the housing programmes implemented are analysed as well as allocated budgets. The section closes with the finding that only three approaches reach Indonesia's low-income groups.

21.1 Recent achievements: spending, housing provision, and improvements

In recent years, the Indonesian government reports significant progress in housing provision and improvement. The country shows a remarkable decline in poverty levels and proportions of the urban population living in slums since the 2000s (cf. chapter 17.2 and 17.3). This success is not only the result of continued economic growth, but can also be attributed to the combined efforts of poverty reduction strategies, housing interventions, decentralisation policies, and the long-term commitment to slum alleviation. Since the inauguration of the Jokowi government in 2014 housing policies have been prioritised even more. Government spending on housing has increased as well as the housing provision measured in units produced per year. This allegedly has resulted in a reduction in the housing backlog of the country. In addition, housing standards have improved, as measured by various indicators.

Government spending on housing has long been criticised for being too low. Only 1.8 % of the national budget was allocated for housing and infrastructure in 2013, housing alone accounted for 0.4 % (Rolnik 2013b: 5; World Bank 2017: 7). Even though Indonesia had increased its budget allocation in the preceding years, in 2013 expenditures for housing were much lower compared to other countries in the region – Thailand spent 35 times as much and the Philippines five times more (World Bank 2017: 7). Under the Jokowi administration and with the introduction of PSR spending in the housing sector doubled (mainly used for the FLPP and BSPS schemes), but is still seen as insufficient (ibid.).

The results reported recently for the PSR programme are nevertheless remarkable. Since its introduction in 2015, approximately 3.5 million houses have been 'realised' by 2018 and the target of 1.1 million houses was allegedly reached for the first time in 2018 (KPUPR 2019; The Jakarta Post 2019; Perumnas 2018: 153). Data provided by the Ministry of Public Works and Housing for the year 2018 suggest that of these 1.1 million houses 70 % are designated for low-income people (cf. table 25). Combined efforts of the national and regional governments have provided 328,885 units for low-income groups while the private sector accounts for 447,364 units. This sudden explosion of annual housing production after decades of undersupply is surprising. This can be partly explained by the fact that these figures include not only newly built houses, but also those households that received subsidies for housing improvements (eg BSPS). Nevertheless, especially the high numbers supplied by the private sector are surprising. It is reasonable to assume that also many houses for the middle class appear in this data. Further studies are needed to verify these positive claims of Indonesia's Ministry of Public Works and Housing.

Table 25 Housing provision in Indonesia 2018

Indicator	Realised units	
Housing for low-income groups	785 641	11 655
National government through the Ministry of Public Works and Housing	217 064	4 525
Low-cost rental flats (*rusunawa*)	111 821	200 884
Special houses	447 364	9 430
Self-help housing	458	102 391
Regional governments	8 934	
Low-cost rental flats (*rusunawa*)		
Subsidies for incremental self-build housing (BSPS)		
Private sector		
Corporate Social Responsibility		
Community		
Housing for high-income groups	346 980	
Private sector	290 656	
Individuals	56 324	
Total	1 132 621	

Source: Table by author. Data from the Ministry of Public Works and Housing – KPUPR (2019)

Not only housing production has increased massively, also housing standards have improved throughout the country. Considering the housing indicators published by BPS (2019a) the percentage of households with access to improved drinking water and improved sanitation has increased significantly over the last decades (cf. figure 36). In 2018, 73.7 % of Indonesian households had access to improved drinking water

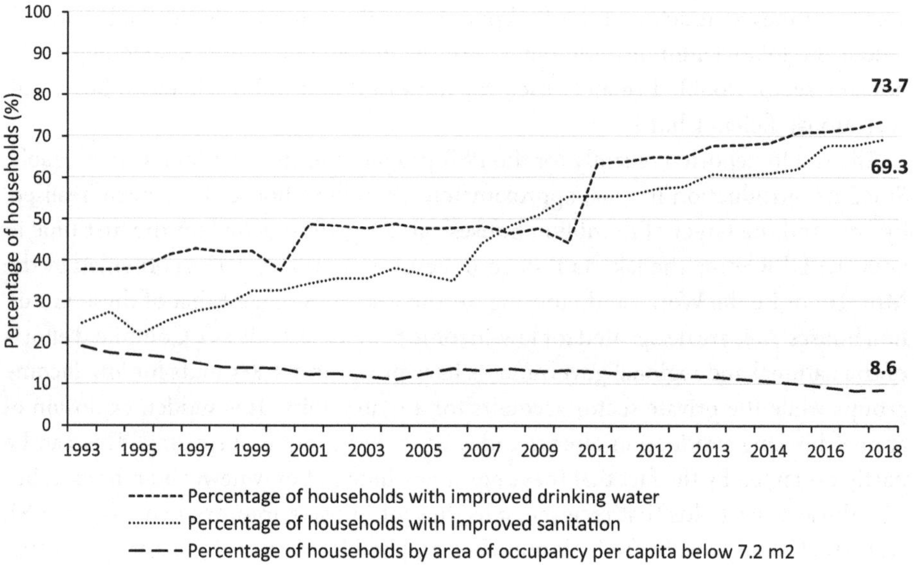

Fig. 36 Housing indicators in Indonesia 1993–2018
Source: Illustration by author. Data from Badan Pusat Statistik Indonesia – BPS (2019a)

and 69.3 % to improved sanitation. Per capita living space – one indicator for housing quality – has also significantly improved. While in 1993 nearly 20 % of all Indonesian households had less than 7.2 m^2 living space per resident, this number decreased to only 8.6 % of households in 2018. These positive developments must be noted and can be attributed to increased government efforts. Nevertheless, the target of the Jokowi administration to reach full access to improved sanitation and slums and zero percent slums by 2019 (the 100-0-100 target) has not been reached.

This positive development in terms of housing provision and improvements in housing quality is remarkable, and the intervention strategies applied seem to have a significant impact. However, it is not clear which programmes and which modes of housing provision had the greatest effect and which population groups benefited most. Therefore, in the following section, the programmes are examined according to their effect on different modes of housing provision and income groups.

21.2 Impact of housing programmes depending on household income

Applied housing intervention strategies always have more benefits for specific income groups over others (cf. chapter 15.2.1). To capture the impact of different programmes for specific income groups an integrated infographic was developed (cf. figure 37). It integrates the three aspects of (I) household income distribution, (II) modes of housing provision and (III) housing programmes. Part I of the illustration shows a rough estimation of Indonesia's population structure depending on household income, as created by Markus Zahnd (2005: 63). Part II represents – in a modified version – the dominating modes of housing provision, as developed by Ramin Keivani and Edmundo Werna (2001a). Finally, part III shows and assesses some of Indonesia's housing programmes and measures, as described in chapter 20. Each of the programmes has an impact on one of the modes of housing provision, which in turn are beneficial for some income groups and not for others.

Household income levels are usually categorised in low-income, middle-income and high-income levels. For this graph, low and medium income categories are further subdivided in order to relate these categories to the different modes of housing provision in the country. The estimation of the household income distribution shows that roughly 60 % of Indonesian households are low-income households with 10 % having income levels insufficient for sustaining their livelihoods. The middle class with lower-middle and upper-middle income levels amounts to roughly 30 %, while households with high income are less than 10 %. The income levels are related to modes of housing provision, illustrated in part II of figure 37. The formal modes of housing provision comprise activities of the private sector (ie individual housing production and that of the real estate sector), direct interventions of the public sector (ie social housing, slum upgrading, and sites and services) and cooperative housing. The informal housing production consists of squatting, informal subdivisions, and informal rental housing.

For upper-middle- and high-income households, formal housing delivery by the private sector is the dominant mode of housing provision. Direct public housing interventions target low-income people, but – in the case of social housing – have difficulty reachinig the poorest and serve more the upper segment of low-income people and the lower-middle class. Slum upgrading in contrast has benefits for all low-income groups, even though interventions usually do not focus on housing provision, but on community infrastructure and facilities. Also housing cooperatives do not reach the poor, since they require a substantial amount of organisation and capital to be realised. As illustrated in chapter 18.4, most houses in Indonesia are provided by informal modes of housing provision. Informal subdivision and informal rental arrangements are the dominating options for low-income people and also for large parts of the middle class. In many cases, the poorest have to rely on squatting.

Indonesian housing programmes and their impact on various modes of housing provision are illustrated in part III of figure 37. A single programme always addresses at least one of these modes of housing provision and therefore beneficiaries are predominantly households of a specific income group. The establishment of better financial institutions and the promotion of accessibility of mortgage loans in the FLPP programme or other housing financial subsidies (SSB, SBUM), for instance, does help individuals, private developers, and also the social housing production. It reaches, thus, mostly only the middle- and higher-income groups and has less impact on households with poor income levels, despite dissonant rhetoric of the programmes. Also some regulations, such as the 1:3:6 rule target the real estate sector, trying to expand private sector activities down the income ladder, but largely fail due to ignorance and insufficient control (cf. chapter 19.3.1). Direct provision from Perumnas, the national Indonesian housing company, is of greater benefit for groups with lower-middle and low household income. Besides its market orientation, the corporation also produces affordable housing for low-income residents, though never reaching scale.

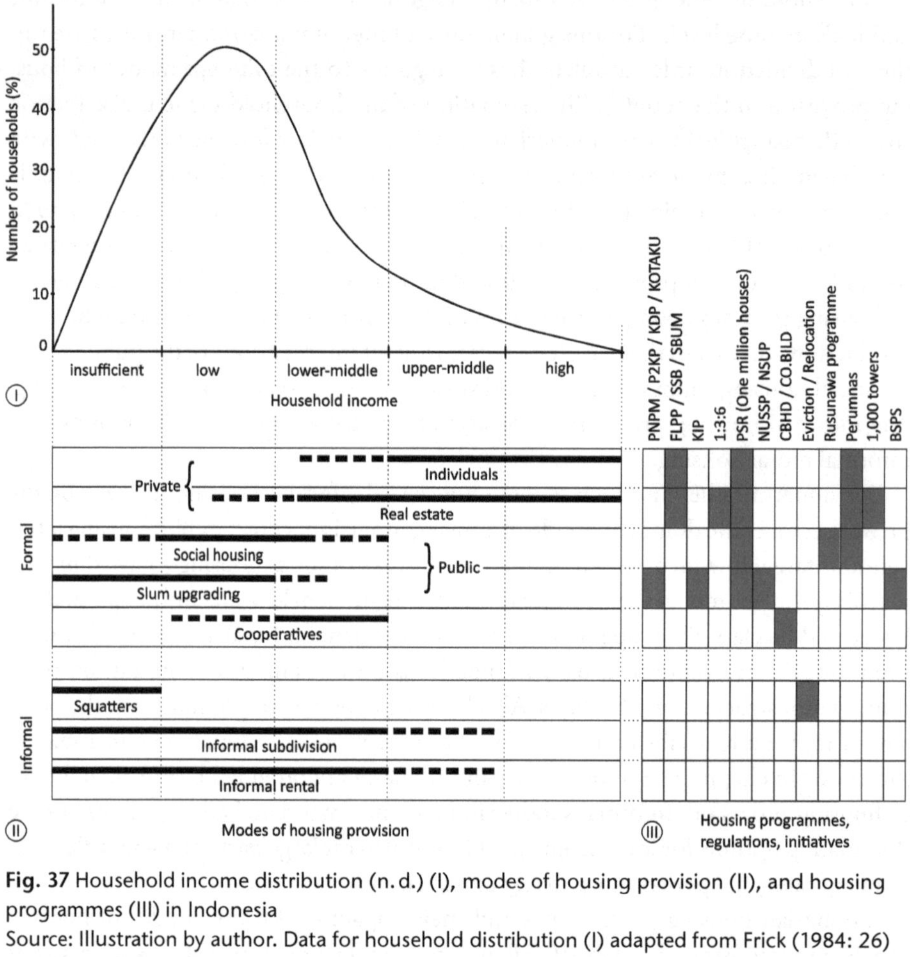

Fig. 37 Household income distribution (n. d.) (I), modes of housing provision (II), and housing programmes (III) in Indonesia
Source: Illustration by author. Data for household distribution (I) adapted from Frick (1984: 26)

Slum upgrading programmes, such as KIPs, NUSSP, and NSUP, as well as the community empowerment programmes, such as P2KB, PNPM, and KOTAKU, are better suited to reach the poorest and low-income households. Even though they only rarely provide direct housing improvements, they improve living conditions in poor neighbourhoods and enhance community self-organisation and self-help abilities. More direct support for homeowners is provided through the BSPS programme. Using incentives in the form of direct cash transfers for home improvements, the programme reaches many poor households in a direct way. Cooperative housing is a mode of housing delivery in Indonesia which is hardly developed, but would have high potential (cf. chapter 20.3). It has been supported in the CBHD and Co.Bild schemes with moderate success. The drawback here is that it also did not reach the poorest and concepts need improvement if this is to change. The Initiative to build one million houses anually (PSR) has reached scale in recent years, combining and enlarging several programmes under one umbrella (FLPP, BSPS, etc). The initiative combines approaches targeting most formal modes of housing provision and thus all income groups. The latest numbers are promising, but further studies are needed to evaluate the impact of this initiative.

In the informal housing sector – 60 to 80 % of housing is produced informally (cf. chapter 18.4) – only few measures and programmes exist. For squatters the only pursued option is eviction and relocation to social housing units. What has become obvious is that all housing programmes target the formal modes of housing provision. There are no measures in place to support informal markets, even though informal processes provide the substance of Indonesia's housing production. As in many other countries, there are also no policies in place to support or expand formal or informal rental housing.

The analysis shows that most of Indonesia's housing programmes favour middle- and upper-income groups. They target the private mode of housing provision and it is this mode which has seen most growth in recent years. This mode of provision, however, does not reach the poor. Only the public modes of provision do this, but since realised quantities are too small, for most, the only option remains the informal sector. Slum upgrading and community empowerment programmes are more promising than social housing. Though not providing new housing stock, these programmes improve living conditions and increase the communities' capacities of self-help. Empowerment and upgrading must be seen as the key mechanism that has contributed to the achievements in housing quality improvement over the last years.

Budget allocation for housing reflects this inequitable distribution. Housing programmes that favour middle- and higher-income groups and the building industry are clearly preferred considering the annual budget for housing interventions (World Bank 2015b, 2017). In 2016, nearly 60 % of the government's budget allocation was spent on the FLPP programme, a programme that excludes all residents with informal incomes and reaches only the upper part – the bankable part – of low-income households. Only the rest was shared by programmes tailored more to the needs of low-income people: among others mainly the public rental housing programme (*rusunawa*), neighbourhood upgrading programmes, and the incremental home subsidy programme (BSPS) (Utomo 2014; World Bank 2015b). These findings throw a different light on the success story told by official reports. The housing deficit seems to be diminishing, but for the poorest of the poor only few approaches exist that would really lead to an improved housing situation for all.

21.3 Housing for the poor? Financial enablement, self-help, and eviction/resettlement

Only few of the strategies and programmes presented here have benefits for the poor. Three approaches, depending on household income, are applied (cf. table 26): Financial enablement, self-help strategies, and resettlement. The upper part of low-income households is considered as 'bankable', meaning that families of this group can afford to buy a house provided on the formal markets when supported by better access to housing finances or the provision of cheap housing options or land (= financial enablement). The second group is the middle part of all households with low income, people with informal occupations, who mostly live in informal or semi-formal settlements (*kampungs*). These households are considered as 'unbankable', as unreachable by financial housing incentives, due to their irregularities of income and/or because they do not have legalised ownership rights to their properties. For this group the self-help housing is the only option. The government provides direct support for incremental housing development and improvement as well as indirect assistance through a range of slum upgrading and community empowerment programmes. The third group consists of the very poor, the lowest segment of low-income households, those without even informal tenure rights and/or local citizenship. For residents belonging to this

Table 26 Three types of government support for low-income households in Indonesia depending on income

	Household income →		
Household categorisation	insufficient	very low	low
	'Non-bankable'		'Bankable'
Government support	*Resettlement* – Social housing in multi-storey low-income rental houses (*rusunawa*)	*Self-help housing* – Support for housing development and housing improvement (BSPS) – Slum upgrading programmes (KIP, NUSSP, etc) – Community empowerment programmes (PNPM, KOTAKU, etc)	*Financial enablement* – Increased access to housing finances: subsidised mortgage loans and interest rates (FLPP, SSB, SBUM, etc) – Provision of simple houses or ready to build land parcels (Perumnas)

Source: Illustration by author. Adapted from Utomo (2014)

group, government support is limited to one approach: resettlement to social housing (*rusunawa*).

In most of Indonesia's *kampungs* the approaches of resettlement or self-help housing are applied, since residents are not bankable, even when assisted. *Kampungs* are managed according to their legal status. In settlements considered as squatters (*kampung liar*) the resettlement approach is followed, while households with *de facto* ownership rights and legal citizenship can benefit from various government support programmes (community empowerment, slum upgrading, and social assistance).

Resettlement to low-cost rental flats in social housing blocks is considered the only option for the poorest and this approach has become national strategy (BAPPENAS 2012: 101; Jones 2017). In practice there is some tolerance and ambiguity. Local governments have only limited options and struggle to provide social housing in adequate numbers. Due to that, squatters are often temporarily tolerated. However, the prospect of eviction looms like the sword of Damocles above such settlements and when larger development projects are on the way local governments tend to facilitate evictions (Rolnik 2013b: 7). Even though the idea is to compensate residents by relocating them to *rusunawa*, in reality this option reaches only some of the original dwellers. In fact, evictions are still carried out in the country using military and police forces. The problem is that relocations are not suitable for everyone and not practical in all areas. The two cases of Surabaya and Solo exemplify the differences in applied measures, even though they follow the same national strategy.

22 Summary: A Story of Success and Failure

In this chapter, the current state of Indonesia's housing situation, the organisation and content of the country's housing policies, and the impact of programmes for low-income people has been examined and illustrated. The following questions guided the analysis:

Which intervention strategies are implemented on the Indonesian scale to address the housing challenge?
- What is the housing situation in Indonesia?
- What are rules of the game and central actors in Indonesia's housing domain?
- Which measures, strategies, and programmes were applied to what effect?

The Indonesian housing situation can be described as a continuing housing crisis. The country's cities are growing rapidly, and the demand for urban services and housing is constantly increasing. Vast urban-rural landscapes are emerging (*desakota*) and the distinctive element of Indonesian settlements, the *kampung*, is threatened by modernisation and redevelopment. Developers and the state, as the main actors of formal housing provision, have shown themselves incapable of providing adequate quantities to meet the annual demand. Therefore, self-build solutions are the only option for most Indonesians, resulting in 60 to 80 % of all new units produced informally. Due to these trends, a large housing backlog of approximately twelve million units has accumulated and an existing 15 million houses are considered substandard (cf. chapter 18). In recent years however, housing indicators show some positive trends: poverty levels have come down and the number of people living in slums is remaining constant despite rapid urban growth (cf. chapter 17). This testifies not only to the positive economic development and achievements of the reform policies of the last decades, but also to the success of Indonesian housing policies.

Indonesia's housing policies have evolved since the 1970s, involving increasingly more actors and gradually establishing the legal framework as the formal rules of the game. Since then, more and more organisations and housing associations have been founded; the programmes and strategies have become increasingly sophisticated, as have the corresponding laws and regulations. Three successive phases, in which housing policies orient at overreaching paradigms, can be identified: public housing, self-help, and enablement (cf. chapter 19). Within these paradigms a broad set of intervention strategies have been developed, tested, and rolled out, so that today a confusing number of different approaches and projects are applied simultaneously (cf. chapter 20). For decades, slum upgrading programmes and later community empowerment programmes have been applied with great success. The mechanism of CDD used to provide community infrastructure and develop the communities' self-help abilities can be considered as the best practice of international reputation. These very successful initiatives have been accompanied by the traditional public housing approach, support for housing cooperatives, and, in more recent years, by the massive extension of housing financial policies and direct housing subsidies (cf. chapter 20). The three Indonesian phases of housing policies correspond with international phases, though with some delay. While the World Bank moved to a neoliberal agenda in the 1990s and the enabling approach became dominant on the global scale, this change did not happens until the 2000s in Indonesia. Only then did financial housing policies focusing the private sector and public-private partnerships grow in importance.

Under the Jokowi government, housing policies have become priority, with a focus on leveraging large resources for housing development and initiating massive umbrella initiatives. These efforts are reported as very successful with more than one million units realised in 2018. However, an analysis of the impact of various programmes on different target groups according to income shows that most initiatives do not benefit low-income groups, but more so middle- and upper-income groups (cf. chapter 21). Also spending on housing shows this unequitable distribution. Most programmes and allocated funds aim at private modes of housing provision that have only limited benefits for the poor. For low-income groups only three approaches are applied depending on household income: (1) Financial enablement for those creditworthy; (2) assistance for self-help housing (slum upgrading and empowerment) for those who are not creditworthy, but acknowledged as legal citizens; and (3) resettlement to social housing blocks for all others (the poorest). Most people in slum and squatter settlements fall under the last category. Often, they are not legally recognised and therefore are not eligible to participate in most assistance programmes. Strategies are needed that go beyond resettlement policies to prevent the development of areas of exclusion and poverty.

V. CASE STUDY: SURABAYA

This chapter presents the results of the empirical fieldwork in Surabaya, arriving at deep insights into the content and organisation of Surabaya's housing policy arrangement. The first section introduces the city by presenting the latest socio-economic and demographic data, illustrating historic phases of urban development and exploring the current housing situation. The second section examines the city's applied housing policies, identifying municipal policies for the poor, and analysing two housing measures in more detail – social housing and resettlement programmes. By telling the story of slum clearances taking place along Surabaya's rivers, the policy arrangement towards squatters unfolds. The third section presents and analyses the actor influence network, dominant discourse strands, and rules of the game shaping housing policies in the city. The final section summarises the results and reveals the main characteristics of Surabaya's housing policy arrangement. The following questions guide this chapter:

<u>What are the characteristics of Surabaya's policy arrangement in the housing domain?</u>

- What intervention strategies and programmes are realised for the poor and what do they achieve?
- Which actors are relevant in the housing domain and what influence do they hold?
- What strands shape the local discourse on housing the poor?
- What are the formal and informal rules of the game?

23 Introduction to Surabaya

With about three million inhabitants, Surabaya is the second largest city in Indonesia. Located on the northern coast of Java Island, approximately 800 km east of Jakarta, the city was founded close to the river mouth of the Kali Mas[1], one of the tributaries forming the lowlands of the Brantas River delta. The city is the capital of East Java Province and borders two districts, Gresik to the west and Sidoarjo to the south, while the Java Sea limits the urban area to the north and east (cf. figure 38). Administratively, Surabaya is divided into 31 sub-districts (*kecamantan*) that are composed of 154 quarters (*kelurahan*), 1,368 community units (RW), and 9,120 neighbourhood units (RT) (Pemerintah Kota Surabaya 2017: 34). After two city extensions (1931 and 1965), the current administrative area covers 326.8 km² (Soemarno 2011: 91–96). Selected data are provided in table 27.

As a delta city, most of the urban area is located only a few meters above sea level (3–8 m) and only the south-western part is characterised by a hilly landscape, reaching heights of 25 to 50 m (Bawole 2007: 298–301). Due to these conditions, the city is prone to flooding in some areas, mostly caused by heavy rain events and less by inundation of seawater. Compared to Jakarta, however, the problem of flooding is less dramatic. A functioning drainage system and good water management is nevertheless essential for the city. The climate is tropical with an annual average temperature of 27.1 °C and a precipitation total of 1,679 mm (Pemerintah Kota Surabaya 2019). Temperatures hardly fluctuate and it is rather the precipitation that divides the year into a wet season (November to April) and a dry season (May to October). Indonesians have adapted to these conditions by having all activities take place mainly in the morning. Compared to Solo and Yogyakarta, however, the temperature felt in Surabaya is much hotter, a result of lower altitude and the magnitude of soil sealed by built-up areas.

Surabaya is the most important centre of industry, finances, and trade in East Java and serves as the central transport hub for a region with approximately 40 million inhabitants (Das 2017; Gervasi 2011). Looking back at a long industrial history – already

1 '*Kali*' is the Javanese term for river.

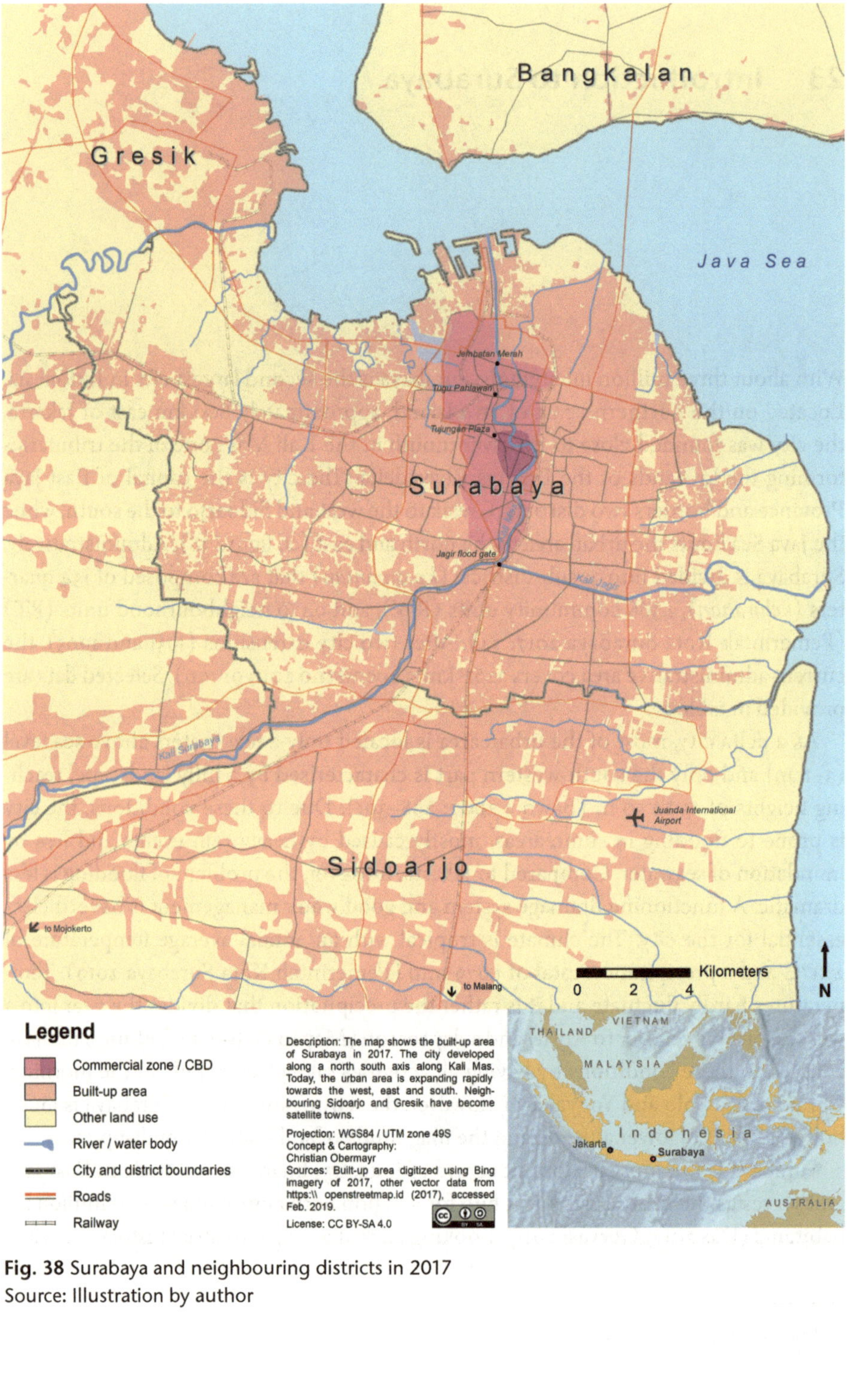

Fig. 38 Surabaya and neighbouring districts in 2017
Source: Illustration by author

Table 27 Administrative and population data, Surabaya

Indicator	Source	Value
Administrative divisions 2017	[a]	31 *Kecamatan*, 154 *Kelurahan* 1 368 RW, 9 120 RT
City area since 1965 (km^2)	[b]	326.8
Population 2018*	[c]	2 885 555
Population of the urban region** 2010	[d]	6 100 000
Population of the metropolitan region 2010	[e]	9 000 000

Source: Table by author. Data compiled from: **[a]** Pemerintah Kota Surabaya (2017), **[b, c]** BPS Surabaya (2020), **[d]** World Bank (2015a: 150–151), **[e]** Das (2017: 4)
Note: * Population data projected from the 2010 census; ** Urban region defined as continuous built-up area derived from satellite imagery

in colonial times the city had a significant base of heavy industry supporting sugar milling, railways, and shipping (Dick 2002: 253) – the region has meanwhile developed a large industrial base producing a wide variety of consumer goods and products of manufacturing (textiles, furniture, chemicals, metals, etc) and is home to large shipyards and extractive industries (oil, gas) (Dick 2002: 314–330). After the industrial boom of the 1970s, which lasted well into the 1990s, most heavy industries have decentralised outside the city boundaries to the neighbouring districts due to the need for cheap land. Surabaya itself is becoming increasingly a service centre with many job opportunities in large-scale trade, retail, restaurants, financial services, and a strong construction sector as is visible in the rapidly developing skyline of office towers that are hosting banks and insurances (Dick 2002: 321–324; Pemerintah Kota Surabaya 2017: 106–107).

Three million people officially inhabit the city, but considering the large number of temporary and informal workers, the numbers are probably much higher. After decades of suburbanisation, the borders towards the two neighbouring districts have blurred, and estimates suggest a number of six million people living in the urban agglomeration with continuous built-up area. Summing up all residents of the official metropolitan region composed from six surrounding districts (called *Gerbangkertosusila*[2]), more than nine million people are recorded, making the area the second largest urban agglomeration in Indonesia (Das 2017: 4).

2 *Gerbangkertosusila* is an acronym of the districts Gresik, Bangkalan, Mojokerto, Surabaya, Sidoarjo and Lamongan.

23.1 Latest data on population, poverty, and human development for Surabaya

Some recent data on population, poverty, and human development are provided in table 28 and table 29. These data are obtained from various official sources and thus show some inconsistencies due to dissimilarities in data collection (see box 16 for details). However, it can be concluded that Surabaya's population is continuously increasing mostly due to in-migration and the data suggest improvements in human development and poverty. Although the figures for natural population change (cf. [F] in table 28) and for the migration balance [I] have come down in recent years, the total population [B] is growing, though with a decreasing tendency. For the period from 2013 to 2018, the annual increase was approximately 13,000 on average considering the projected data from BPS (cf. [A[1]] in table 29), or as much as approximately 63,000 considering

Box 16: Population data: census data and civil registration data

Indonesian population data are obtained from different sources resulting in differing datasets. The first one are census data collected every ten years during a population census. At the time of writing, the last census happened in 2010 and the years in between are projected. The enumeration uses two approaches: a *de jure* approach, ie recording all people in their permanent residence, and a *de facto* approach, ie enumerating anyone found during 'census day' in a specific area. This is necessary since the *de jure* approach excludes many groups (eg homeless people, remote communities, people living in squatter settlements, ie all people not formally registered).

The second source is the civil registration register holding data obtained from lower administrative units. In every small neighbourhood unit, respective RT leaders collect data on births, deaths, marriage, and migration. These data are reported to the next higher administrative level. People moving into a neighbourhood are obliged to register, even though it depends on the neighbourhood and the RT how strictly this regulation is carried out. In that way *d -facto* population data are aggregated for larger administrative areas.

Both methods have their drawbacks and are not 100 % accurate. As is the case for Surabaya and Solo, projected population data are lower than the civil registration data obtained from the quarters and villages (*kelurahan/desa*) and the inaccuracy has consequences for all calculated data. This issue must be kept in mind when interpreting any data related to population (BPS Surakarta 2020b: 29–30).

Table 28 Demographic data from the civil registration register, Surabaya

Indicator	Year						
	2012	2013	2014	2015	2016	2017	2018
Registered population [A]	3 125 576	3 200 454	2 853 661	2 943 528	3 016 653	3 074 883	3 094 732
Population change on prev. year [B]		74 878	-346 793	89 867	73 125	58 230	19 849
Population change per year (%) [C = (B/A)*100]		2.34	-12.15	3.05	2.42	1.89	0.64
Registered births [D]	40 190	46 405	45 437	31 225	31 572	30 814	32 585
Registered deaths [E]	20 322	15 394	24 351	17 803	20 304	21 762	20 532
Natural population change [F = D-E]	19 868	31 011	21 086	13 422	11 268	9052	12 053
Registered immigrants [G]	111 594	65 048	67 416	46 654	43 495	38 404	39 005
Registered emigration [H]	30 210	21 181	31 287	22 015	26 925	25 361	27 951
Migration balance [I = G-H]	81 384	43 867	36 129	24 639	16 570	13 043	11 054

Source: Table by author. Data compiled/calculated from Pemerintah Kota Surabaya (2019)
Note: [A, D, E, G, H] Data from the civil registration register. Data inconsistencies: figures for natural population change [F] and migration balance [I] do not add up to population change per year [C]

Table 29 Data on population (projected), poverty and human development, Surabaya

Indicator	Year						
	2012	2013	2014	2015	2016	2017	2018
Projected population [A']	2 805 718	2 821 929	2 833 924	2 848 583	2 862 406	2 874 699	2 885 555
Population change on prev. year [B']		16 211	11 995	14 659	13 823	12 293	10 856
Population change per year (%) [C' = (B'/A')*100]		0.57	0.42	0.51	0.48	0.43	0.38
Poor people	175 357	169 316	164 084	165 788	161 153	154 946	140 815
Poverty line in Rp. per person per month (in €)*	339 208 (28)	372 511 (27)	393 151 (25)	418 930 (28)	438 283 (30)	474 365 (31)	530 178 (32)
Percentage poor (%)	6.25	6.00	5.79	5.82	5.63	5.39	4.88
Human Development Index (HDI)	78.05	78.51	78.89	79.47	80.38	81.07	81.74

Source: Table by author. Data compiled/calculated from BPS Surabaya (2020)
Note: Projected population data [A'] based on the 2010 census. *Currency converted using historical annual average conversion rates from fxtop.com

data from the civil registration register (excluding the year 2014). The cause of this population increase is primarily in-migration, less so natural population change (cf. [F] and [I] in table 28). The share of migration in population growth is probably even under-represented, considering that most migrant workers and students, to name a few examples, will not report a changed place of residence.

In the period from 2012 to 2018, the Human Development Index has increased, reaching 81.74 in 2018, and the number of poor people has decreased from approximately 175,000 (2012) to approximately 140,000 (2018). This means that only 5 % of Surabaya's residents officially live below the national poverty line (2018). Compared to the national average – HDI 0.71 (2018) and poverty 9.42 % (2019) – these data are promising, telling a story of a successful urban economy and effective upgrading and social programmes. The poverty line, calculated as minimum monthly consumption expenditures per capita, has continuously been raised over the last years, but remains on a very low level (28 to 32€ per month) considering the rising cost of living in the city (on the calculation of the poverty line cf. box 11).

23.2 Phases of urban development

Surabaya's city development can be categorised in several phases that are strongly entangled with the political and socio-economic history of the city. During these phases, informal and formal processes characterise the production of space, struggling for dominance. Under colonial rule, the dual city emerged, where the walled European settlement coexisted with the Javanese town. Later under the colonial regime, the city became increasingly formalised and tight control was executed. After World War II, in a situation of political turmoil and economic stagnation informality resurged and dominated all urban development processes, while after the take-over of Suharto a regime of law and order was executed and formal processes began to resurge as the predominant mode of production of space. This duality, the conflict between the formal and informal city or in other words the conflict between colonial city and *kampung* continues until today and has become deeply inscribed in Surabaya's urban structure (Dick 2002: 325–326).

23.2.1 Pre-colonial urban development

The oldest reports of a settlement at the mouth of the Brantas River date back to the 13th century and the official date of foundation was set to 1293, when Radan Wijaya, the ruler of the Majapahit Kingdom, won a significant victory here (Soemarno 2011: 85–88). Protected by the offshore island of Madura and equipped with a natural harbour, the location was favourable for the foundation of a city. Soon the settlement became an important port city due to its prime position at the trade route between the Spice Islands (Maluku islands) and Malacca (Malay Peninsula). As such, it attracted Malay and Arab traders who settled near the harbour, a quarter today known as *Ampel*. Further to the south, the pre-colonial centre was located. Similar to the seats of Javanese kingdoms (Solo and Yogyakarta), this centre showed the characteristics of a typical Javanese palace city: the palace (*kraton*) as home for the local ruler in the centre, a large open square (*alun-alun*) close by and a general city structure oriented at the compass rose. Today, this arrangement has been completely overhauled by urban restructuring during colonial times and by modernisation processes. Only street and block names south of today's Hero's Monument (*Tugu Pahlawan*) refer to this Javanese origin (Silas et al. 2012: 57–65).

When the Dutch arrived during the 17th century, they occupied the northern coast of Java in 1679 and set up a trade post in Surabaya to control the sea trade. On the western side of the Kali Mas, just north of the Javanese centre, the walled European quarter was established and on the eastern side the Chinese, Malay, and Arab quarters were located (Soemarno 2011: 91–92). While Malay and Arab quarters had already existed before the Dutch arrived, the Chinese quarter grew after the Dutch occupation since the Europeans actively promoted the immigration of Chinese, who were considered as more loyal workers (Dick 2002: 325–334). During colonial times, the European quarter developed into the central business district and still today it is one of the busiest areas, characterised by bustling activity at one of its traditional markets.

In the 18th an 19th centuries, Surabaya developed into the most important centre in the Dutch East Indies, even outpacing Batavia (Jakarta) in population and economic significance (Soemarno 2011: 88; Dick 2002). At the beginning of the 20th century, roads and railways connected the vast agricultural interior of East Java with the port of Surabaya, which functioned as the main export route for cash crops, such as rubber, tea, coffee, tobacco, and, most importantly, sugar cane (Peters 2013: 4). At that time, 75 % of the colony's sugar cane was produced on Dutch plantations located in Surabaya's surroundings, and the city ranked as one of the great port cities of modern Asia, alongside Calcutta, Rangoon, Singapore, Bangkok, Hong Kong, and Shanghai (Dick 2002).

23.2.2 City development under Dutch occupation

During colonial rule, urban development happened along a north-south axis following major transport links (roads and rivers). At the end of the 18th century, suburbanisation tendencies set in, causing a city expansion towards the south. Similar to Jakarta, the better-off European population moved away from the crowded city centre of the European quarter to garden towns established further south (Dick 2002: 340). The starting signal for this development was given by the construction of a large mansion for the governor in Simpang, which remains the seat of the governor of East Java today (Gedung Grahadi). In the following period more and more country houses were built in this area, so that a garden city emerged, soon to be known as Surabaya's upper town (*bovenstad*), contrasting the already existing lower town (*benedenstad*). From 1900 onwards, the significance of this upper town increased and the foundation was laid for today's city centre in the Tujungan area (Dick 2002: 361). This city expansion to the south accelerated from the 1860s onwards, fuelled by the construction of a large boulevard (Darmo Boulevard) including a steam tramline (since 1890) connecting *Wonokromo* and the red bridge (*Jembatan Merah*) (Peters 2013: 25). Along this north-south axis more and more garden cities developed. In the beginning of the 20th century railway lines were constructed at both sides of the Kali Mas, opening urban development to the east and west and allowing the decentralisation of industries and workshops in greater distance to the old town. Only with the recession after World War I did this development come to an end (Dick 2002: 340–358).

All expansions of the formal city came at the expense of indigenous settlements located everywhere in between the formal urban structures. These *kampungs* had to give way to roads and garden suburbs (Dick 2002: 125). The residents were evicted and had to resettle in one of the prevailing *kampungs* or move to fringe areas. Under the colonial regime these measures were accompanied by the prohibition of street vending, begging and squatting (Soemarno 2011). Howard W. Dick (2002: 357) estimates that 15,000 to 23,000 people were evicted in this first urban expansion to the south by the 1920s, mostly without compensation. The results were housing shortages and increasing overcrowding in the remaining *kampungs*. On the eve of World War II, Surabaya is portrayed as an orderly western city, a 'tropical Holland' (Buitenweg 1980), a '[…] prosperous middle class world of white washed offices and garden suburbs […]' (Dick 2002: 360). This viewpoint contrasted sharply with that of expelled *kampung* dwellers suffering from colonial control.

After World War I the city entered a phase of economic stagnation and decay which lasted well into the 1960s. Due to the crisis of the sugar export industry in the 1930s, Surabaya lost its stake in the international economy and Jakarta emerged as the more important city in the Dutch colony. During World War II, Japanese troops occupied Surabaya (1942–45) and the city had to endure intense fighting, with many casualties during Indonesia's struggle for independence (1945–49). Sukarno and Hatta proclaimed independence in Jakarta, but it was in Surabaya where resistance against reoccupation by Western powers was fiercest. Intense fighting erupted when British troops arrived in 1945 to take back control from the Japanese. Indonesian military forces and civilians from the *kampungs* resisted fiercely, trying to prevent the re-establishment of the colonial system at all costs. The events are known as the 'Battle of Surabaya' and brought a reputation for the city as being a 'City of Heroes' (*Kota Pahlawan*). Despite this strong resistance, the battle was lost, causing many casualties and severe destructions. Particularly those *kampungs* where resistance had been fiercest were severely damaged during the fighting. Residents fled the city and population numbers dropped to 200,000 from 400,000 inhabitants at the eve of World War II (Peters 2013: 6–7). In the following years, the struggle raged on in Java's rural areas and it was only in 1949 that the Dutch finally accepted the independence of their former colony.

23.2.3 Post-colonial urban development: 'city of *kampungs*'

When peace was restored and independence achieved in 1949, Surabaya's population began to increase rapidly. The city's residents returned and land-urban migration rose sharply. Since the plantation sector in East Java had collapsed due to war and revolution, many peasants were deprived of their livelihoods. Left without choice, people flocked to the city seeking work and a place for survival (Peters 2013: 7–8). In 1952, the city recorded already 920,000 inhabitants and by 1965, more than 1.5 million people were living in Surabaya (Soemarno 2011: 90–91). *Kampungs* were rebuilt, but could not accommodate the massive influx of new residents. Soon existing *kampungs* became even more overcrowded than in colonial times and the river channels, railway lines, and all available space became occupied by quickly built squatter settlements. Overwhelmed by this development and in uncertain political and economic times, the municipal government did not react. The bureaucracy consisted of former colonial civil servants and among them the opinion prevailed that harsh measures against squatters and the informal sector may not be applied. The new government was to be different compared to the colonial regime. As a result, informality became the dominant force shaping the production of space and the presence of the poor in the streets became an ordinary sight (Peters 2013: 10). From these days, Surabaya gained another reputation, that of a 'city of *kampungs*', a city with many overcrowded and informal areas that were beyond state control (Dick 2002: 364–368).

During this first phase of post-colonial development (1949–1969), urban development happened predominantly towards the south, since no transport network existed towards the east and west. A ribbon development appeared along major roads (cf. figure 39) and this southward urban extension was supported by the relocation of the

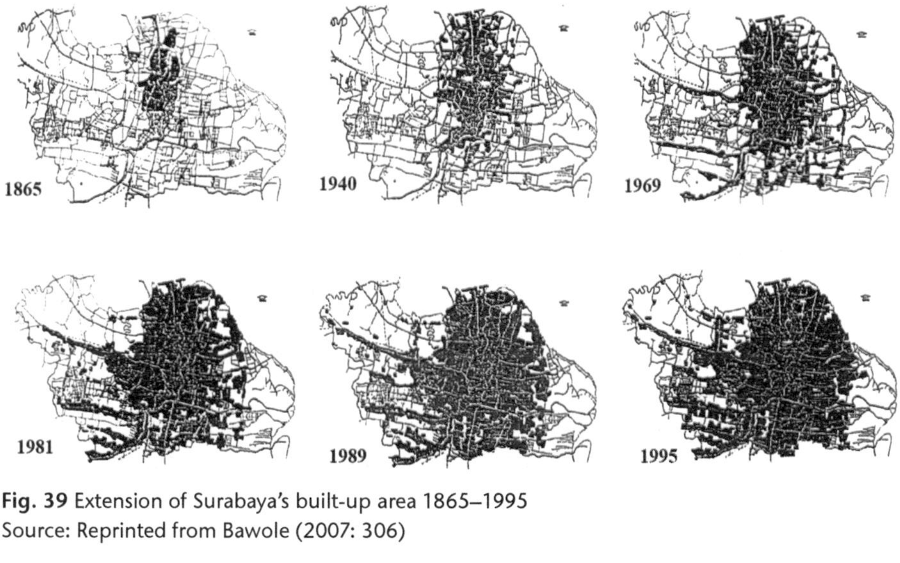

Fig. 39 Extension of Surabaya's built-up area 1865–1995
Source: Reprinted from Bawole (2007: 306)

provincial government offices and the airport (1956) to the neighbouring district of *Sidoarjo* (Soemarno 2011: 94; Dick 2002: 373–374).

When General Suharto became president in 1965, this development ended. Suharto had justified his claim to power by his duty to defend the state from the activities of the Indonesian Communist Party (Partai Komunis Indonesia, or PKI). After his seizure of power, he initiated massive anti-communist persecutions with actions against the PKI and mass killings of suspected communists. The results were devastating for Indonesia, with an estimated nationwide death toll of between 200,000 and 1,000,000 people. Surabaya and its informal settlements suffered particularly from these actions. The city was regarded as a centre of communism, especially its *kampungs*, where the PKI indeed enjoyed substantive support (Peters 2013: 54–56). In absence of the state, the party had established an alternative organisational structure in the *kampungs*, providing social support for those in need. For this reason, massive raids against informal settlements happened and many inhabitants fled the city or lost their lives. The city administration began to execute a stricter regulatory regime in the following years, evicting squatters and street stalls and performing crackdowns on suspected communists (Peters 2013: 10–11). These events and the continuing actions against informal areas are still today seen in the historic relationship between municipality and *kampung* dwellers. From a city where the production of space was dominated by informal processes, the city became again a highly regulated city, where law and order were tightly enforced. *Kampung* dwellers were on the one hand regarded as heroes in the struggle of independence, and on the other were now portrayed as communists, and enemies of the state.

23.2.4 Masterplan, *kampung* improvement, evictions, and real estate boom

From the late 1960s onwards, the stricter regime of law and order soon translated into urban development projects. The first citywide master plan was developed (finished in 1970), triggered by the need for urban planning that resulted from slum clearances and the extension of the city boundaries (1965) (Dick 2002: 375–376). The goal was to push back informal processes perceived as causing chaotic land use patterns, to create an orderly city, and to achieve better state control of informal areas (Soemarno 2011: 96).

The introduction of KIP in 1969 (cf. chapter 20.1) was another means to achieve this goal. Many informal *kampungs* were now formalised by handing out land certificates – ironically an old PKI demand, now fulfilled under the New Order government. This encouraged many to invest into their homes and neighbourhoods and was one of the reasons for the success of the programmes. Both, the master plan and the KIP programmes were developed in close cooperation with ITS and Professor Johan Silas, well-known names in the city associated with successful urban planning and regeneration (King & Idawati 2010: 215; Peters 2013: 69–74). They advocated on the one hand for the preservation and improvement of *kampungs* instead of demolition and evictions, but on the other for the exertion of tight state control to prevent unauthorised squatting. These are still the general guidelines for the municipality today. According to Peters (2013: 4–15), informality was tolerated in the *kampungs* as a necessity to absorb surplus labour, but not on the streets and in the formal city, where it was seen as the tangible expression of disorder, as '[…] threatening safety and causing political conflict and radicalism' (Peters 2013: 12). Various phases of the KIPs transformed large parts of the city and brought improved neighbourhoods and housing conditions.

For Surabaya's riverbank settlements the master plan of 1970 did not bring any good since it allowed a regularisation of all areas not in accordance with the plan. The municipality withdrew temporary permits from the 1960s onward and declared riverbank occupation as illegal. The 'lower Brantas Project' was initiated in 1975 and aimed to clear the riverbanks of the Kali Mas, where an estimated 20,000 households, or 100,000 people, had built their homes between Wonokromo and Jembatan Merah. Over the next years, the evictions were carried out and people had to move to new land further south (Karang Pilang) offered as compensation. At that time, resistance was no option, since this would have been interpreted as communist agitation and would have provoked a violent response (Dick 2002: 399–405).

In economic terms, Surabaya entered a phase of rapid economic development most visible in a real estate boom (Peters 2013: 98–104). Luxury projects with upper-class housing, shopping malls, and even golf courses began to develop in greater distance to the centre as satellite towns. These large-scale real estate projects emerged at first towards the east and south, and later, with the establishment of the western toll road, also towards the west (Silas 2002). In the 1980s the central north-south development axis became increasingly replaced by a west-east urban development axis (Soemarno 2011: 85–106). In the 1990s, large new town projects with more than 1,000 ha were planned and most of the land in the western part of the city was sold to private developers. In the east, urban expansion was more scattered in smaller projects and the conservation zone limited further urban growth (Dick 2002: 393–397). These developments were only temporarily halted by the Asian financial crisis of 1998 and the real estate boom continued in the 2000s.

23.2.5 Today's urban structure and latest urban developments since the 2000s

From these historic urban development phases, today's urban structure emerges. Most of the city's area is used for housing (appoximately. 40 %) while industrial and commercial zones cover around 6 % and 4 %, respectively (Pemerintah Kota Surakarta 2012: 3–7 and 3–8). The commercial zone stretches approximately from the 'Old Town' in the north around *Tugu Pahlawan* towards the district of Wonokromo in the south, roughly towards the Jagir floodgate. It is surrounded by residential and mixed-use areas. The two main industrial areas are located in the southeast (*Rungkut*) and northwest of the city, but many industries have decentralised to the neighbouring district of Gresik. North of the commercial zone, the harbour and the military zone are located. To the east, a large mangrove conservation zone protects the coastline against subsidence and flooding. A distinctive feature of the city are large areas (16.8 %) used for aquaculture (mostly fishponds) east and northwest of the centre. These areas are under pressure from urban development and are generally decreasing in size. Just the same is happening to agricultural land within the city boundaries. While in 2001 approximately 16 % of the urban territory was used for rice cultivation (Bawole 2007: 298), this proportion has decreased dramatically in the following years. Nearly all of this land has been transformed in recent years and in 2018 only around 2,500 ha (approx. 0.8 %) of the city area is used for agricultural purposes. As a result, land is getting increasingly expensive, with consequences for the availability of housing and housing costs.

The centre has shifted from the Javanese town in pre-colonial times towards the colonial town further north and later to the present central business district. Approximately situated in the triangle between Hotel Majapahit[3], Plaza Surabaya, and Tujungan Plaza, the latter two both large shopping malls constructed in the 1990s, the new economic and political centre has formed. In addition, the city parliament, the seat of the mayor, and other authorities are located in this area. Upon my visit in 2015, this new centre distinguished itself by its very orderly appearance with wide streets and clean intact pavements, flanked by greenery. Shopping malls and administrative buildings were lined up along streets that were congested by motorbikes and cars. Particularly striking were the pretty sidewalks, where street stalls and other informal activities are banned, leaving a modern and glossy but somehow deserted impression. It seems that law and order enforcement are very efficient in these parts of the city.

Since the 2000s, Surabaya's urban policies were dominated by the dogma of city revitalisation and beautification. After the economic crisis in the late 1990s, the real estate boom set in again, with the proliferation of large-scale shopping malls and high-rise apartment blocks as air-conditioned citadels for the upper class throughout the city. A skyline is beginning to emerge and Surabaya is increasingly establishing itself as a centre of commerce and services (cf. figure 40). Urban disorder and informality, which had surged again during the Asian crisis, were pushed back and the city government promoted clearance operations against street vendors and informal settlements. Oriented at the vision laid out in the long-term development plan (RTRW 2005–2025), Surabaya is envisioned as a 'City of international trade and services of local character [...] smart, clean and ecologically friendly'. A business-friendly, orderly, and beautiful city attracting tourists and investments alike was to be developed (Bunnell et al. 2013). Since 2005, the city is branded as *'Sparkling Surabaya'* and for this goal the city govern-

3 Hotel Majapahit is a colonial hotel that was founded in 1911 as the Hotel Oranje. It became famous when Indonesian revolutionaries tore down the Dutch flag and exchanged it with the Indonesian flag in September 1945, marking the symbolic beginning of the struggle for independence (Dick 2002: 361).

Fig. 40 Emerging skyline of Surabaya
Photo: Christian Obermayr, 2015

ment strives to create a city of order with many clean parks, footpaths shaded by trees, and no poverty visible on the streets (Peters 2013: 157–217).

Latest urban developments are taking place to the west, to the east, and to the south in the neighbouring district of Sidoarjo. To the east, the remaining areas are developed with large-scale housing estates, putting increasing pressure on remaining marshlands and mangrove areas. This trend, however, will be limited by the sea and probably by the protected mangrove conservation zone. Most of the latest urban development is happening to the west and south, still in the form of ribbon development along major transport links, but slowly also filling up available space in between. Besides the realisation of more large-scale real estate projects, informal building activities have also increased, transforming the landscape with small-scale housing projects, realised often without permits, public facilities, or infrastructure (Soemarno & Sudarma 2014). To the south, urban expansion has spilled over to the district of Sidoarjo, a development supported by the decentralisation of industries, governmental offices, and the growing international airport in this area.

A new mayor, Tri Rismaharini (referred to as 'Ibu Risma'), was elected in 2010, marking simultaneously a turning point and a continuation of existing urban policies. Risma has a background in urban planning and is considered as one of the progressive figures among Indonesia's new leaders with no ties to the old political regime. Influenced by her long work at the city's Department for Cleaning and Gardening (Dinas

Kebersihan dan Pertamanan, or DKP), she continued the general dogma of city beautification, giving special attention to public space and environmental issues (parks, waste collection, and environmental improvements) (Bunnell et al. 2013). Connected to this thematic priority are some initiatives aiming to increase the city's *kampungs* (eg the Green and Clean Programme), but no extra attention is given to the prevailing housing question.

23.3 Surabaya's housing situation

From the city's history, the duality of formal and informal housing areas has been inscribed in urban structure (cf. figure 42). In planning documents, residential areas are characterised as (1) formal areas, ie areas developed by the private sector following building codes and zoning regulations and (2) *kampungs*, ie all other areas that developed informally. Commonly, the word '*kampung*' describes diverse settlement types with different housing conditions and in various stages of consolidation, but they are distinguished from slums (*kampung kumuh*) and squatter settlements (*kampung liar*). This distinction is made according to housing and infrastructural conditions and legal status (cf. chapter 18.2.2 for a more detailed discussion).

In figure 41, Surabaya's housing areas are illustrated, classified as formal housing, *kampungs*, and slums. *Kampung* housing can be found throughout the city, often surrounding other built-up areas and mostly located in the older parts of the city. Towards the west, two major ribbons are visible, indicating informal housing activities along arterial roads. Areas with inadequate housing conditions (*kampung kumuh*) are nested within better-off *kampungs*. These patches of slum housing are the more frequent the closer an area is located to the city centre. Formal housing areas, in contrast, are generally located in greater distance to the central business district (CBD), towards the south, east, and west. Since these parts of the city are more recent city extensions, it can be concluded that formal housing developments have been the dominating form of areal city development over the last decades. The map does not indicate squatter *kampungs* (*kampung liar*), as they are only rarely mapped and not acknowledged in urban planning. Squatter settlements are located near the harbour, in the old town, the Chinese, Arab, and Malay quarter (*Ampel*), and generally on government-owned land along the railway lines and the river courses (Interview 36).

Data on housing, informality, and access to infrastructure are not available or published only for specific occasions and periods. Therefore, the number of people living in formal or informal areas, as well as those living in slum or squatter settlements can only be estimated. The same is valid for data concerning specific housing conditions (eg permanent, non-permanent, adequate, or inadequate). For these reasons, no clear statement can be made on the number of slum or squatter dwellers in Surabaya. What can be estimated is a proportion of 60 % of all residents living in *kampungs* (Shirleyana

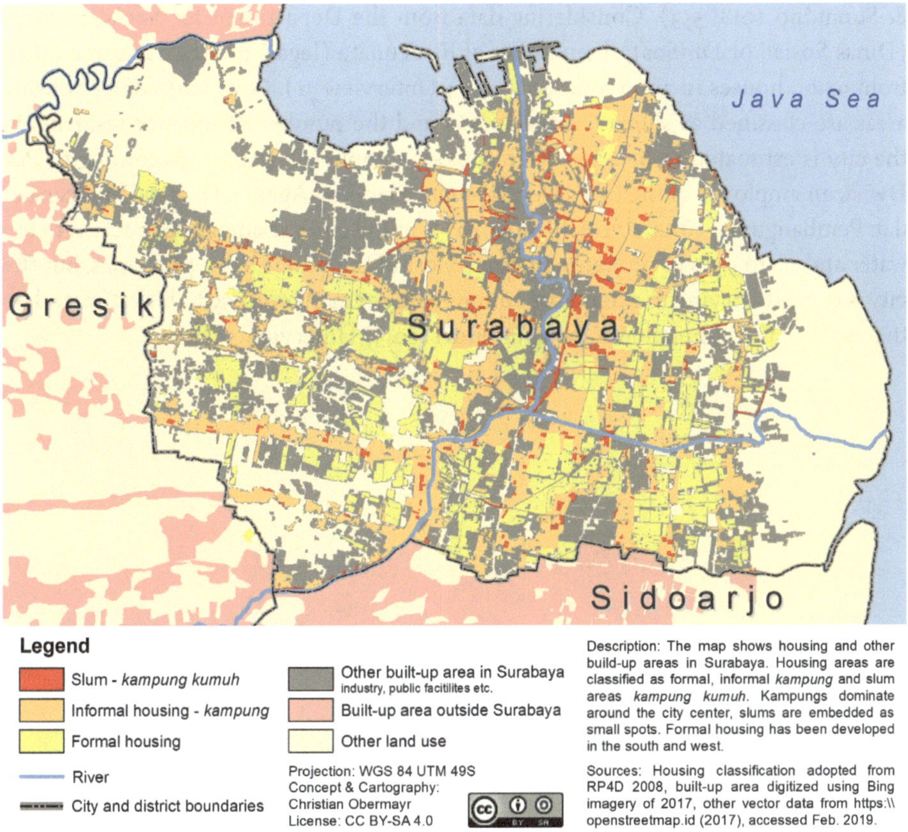

Fig. 41 Housing and other built-up areas in Surabaya 2008
Source: Illustration by author

Fig. 42 Housing types in Surabaya: slum areas (left), formal *kampungs* (middle), luxury housing (right)
Photos: Christian Obermayr, 2015

& Sunindijo 2018: 553). Considering data from the Department for Social Services (Dinas Sosial, or DinSos), the number of inadequate (legal) houses has come down from 9,000 houses in 2009 to 1,600 in 2014 (Interview 31). Only 0.6 % of all housing areas are classified as slums (Interview 36) and the number of squatter residents in the city is estimated to be 200,000 to 300,000 people (Das 2017). According to Pak Dwija, an employee of the city's Development Planning Agency (Badan Perencanaan dan Pembangunan Kota, or BAPPEKO), 93 % of the city's residents have access to tap water and 40 to 50 % to proper sanitation. Most of the others use septic tanks, but the city is currently trying to extend the communal system. According to his estimate, less than 20 % of the population is living in slums (2015) (Interview 39).

24 Content: Housing Policies in Surabaya

This section analyses the *content* of Surabaya's policy arrangement in the housing domain, meaning the principles, the objectives and measures, the target, and the outcome of governance processes. Based on information and findings from expert interviews, several field visits, and enriched with secondary literature the design and implementation of housing policies is explored. To start with, an overview of various housing and urban development programmes in Surabaya is provided, focusing thereinafter on measures for the poorest parts of society: evictions and resettlement to low-cost social housing units.

24.1 Housing and urban development programmes in Surabaya

Applied housing programmes in Surabaya can be classified according to the settlement type they are primarily targeting (cf. figure 43): (1) formal areas (2) *kampungs* (3) *kampung kumuh* (slum) and (4) *kampung liar* (squatter). For these four settlement types, different housing policies have been applied, which are either the local shaping of national housing programmes or initiatives developed by the municipal government on its own accord. In general, the national housing programmes and initiatives explored in chapter 20 have also been initiated and carried out in Surabaya, ie slum upgrading, public housing, cooperative housing, community empowerment, financial housing policies, and umbrella initiatives (for a periodic overview cf. table 23, table 24, and Dianingrum et al. (2017)). These programmes target mostly the *kampungs*, with the exception of financial policies that are primarily used as incentives for formal housing development by the private sector. For squatter settlements, no explicit national housing programme exists, and resettlements by local authorities is recommended.

The municipal government has pioneered several additional measures, testifying to the potential for innovative urban policies originating from Surabaya. Examples are a community empowerment programme (C-KIP), a social assistance programme with cash transfers for poor families (Rehabilitasi Sosial Daerah Kumuh, or RSDK), a programme for economic empowerment of the *kampungs* (Kampung Unggulan), and a city beautification initiative (Green & Clean). These initiatives target the city's *kampungs*

	Settlement type			
	Formal settlements (not *kampung)*	*kampung*	*kampung kumuh* (slum)	*kampung liar* (squatter settlement)
National Policies	**Financial policies** FLPP, KPRS-Mikro, SSB & SBUM	**Community Empowerment:** P2KP/KOTAKU, PNPM, NUSSP **Subsidies for incremental housing:** BSPS		
		Cooperative housing: P2KP/KOTAKU CBHD, Co-Bild	**Slum upgrading:** KIP, NUSSP, NSUP NAHP	
		Social housing: *rusunawa* programme		
Additional Municipal Policies		**Community empowerment:** C-KIP **City beautification:** Green and Clean **Economic empowerment:** Kampung Unggulan		**Resettlement:** Relocation to *rusunawa*
		Social assistance: RSDK		

Fig. 43 Applied housing and urban development programmes in Surabaya according to targeted settlement type
Note: Programmes highlighted are analysed in more detail
Source: Illustration by author

and, in the case of RSDK, are open for residents of squatter settlements. For the latter, the municipality pursues a policy of resettlement in combination with the national public housing programme of *rusunawa* development.

These measures of the municipality are not fully-fledged housing programmes; they are much more indirect support programmes for the communities focusing on awareness raising, economic empowerment, and environmental issues. The reason is that there is a common understanding among the city's experts (Interview 36, 39) that there would be no need for further upgrading programmes. The opinion dominates that most *kampungs* have been well improved over the last decades and the issue of 'basic shelter' provision is seen as accomplished. Therefore, other topics related to *kampung* improvement are prioritised, now focusing on wider topics of sustainability, environmental issues, community participation, and economic empowerment.

In order to grasp the dimension 'content' – the principles, measures, and objectives – of Surabaya's policy arrangement, it is expedient to briefly examine the municipality's programmes before analysing the two policies of public housing and resettlement in more detail.

24.2 *Kampung*-centred urban policy

Since the 1960s, Surabaya's city government has chosen to preserve existing *kampungs* in contrast to other Indonesian cities, where *kampungs* often had to give way for urban development projects. This *kampung*-centred urban development policy is closely related to the advocacy of Professor Johan Silas and fellow experts at the ITS and alumni who propagated a policy that acknowledges *kampungs* as '[...] inseparable from the city' (Silas et al. 2012: 5). The long-lasting collaboration between the housing lab at ITS (Lab Perumahan dan Permukiman) and the local authorities has produced an understanding of *kampungs* as an integral part of the city, as residential areas that need special assistance (Das 2017). Most of Surabaya's *kampungs* thus have been continuously improved and 'regularised' over the years using the consecutive cycles of the KIP (Silas 1989, 1992). After 30 years of KIP activities, basic infrastructure and public facilities exist in almost all of the city's *kampungs*. As a result, this settlement type prevails even close to the CBD and covers large parts of the urban area, providing housing for an estimated 60 % of the population (Shirleyana & Sunindijo 2018: 553; Das 2017).

After 1998, when the famous KIP programme was terminated at the national level (cf. chapter 20.1.1), Surabaya city authorities decided to continue a local variant: the Comprehensive Kampung Improvement Programme (C-KIP). Compared to overall urban development, however, which became more rapid during the 1990s, the *kampungs* were considered as falling behind. For that reason, C-KIP was initiated in order to speed up *kampung* improvement and further support community organisation (Interview 26). The actions were not limited to the poorest *kampungs*, but aimed to strengthen and assist overall *kampung* development in the city.

C-KIP was a top-down initiated community empowerment programme aiming to promote the communities' self-management capacities through community participation and foster in that way their resilience (UN-Habitat 2002b; Das 2009, 2015a). The approach was to establish lasting CBOs enabling the communities to develop, plan, initiate, and realise development on their own accord with minimal state support (cf. the enabling approach, chapter 15.1.3). To achieve this, community development consultants were deployed to assist and train the community (empowerment and capacity building) and to synchronise efforts at the neighbourhood level with local government planning and wider urban development (Bawole 2007: 40–41). Compared to the previous national KIP programmes, C-KIP funding was much more limited, and only based on local funds (municipality and community) (Interview 39). The focus was not on physical improvements – only one-fifth of the budget was used for that – but on the establishment of a mechanism of community-managed revolving credit schemes (micro-credit) for upgrading projects, support for small enterprises and community development (Das 2015b: 21–26, 2017). The main purpose was to improve access to finance for the community and local enterprises and strengthen in that way their capacities to improve their local environment, business, and infrastructure in self-help. C-KIP ran from 1998 until 2007 and was than replaced by the national community empowerment programme (the PNPM programme, cf. chapter 20.4.1). The programme brought significant improvements for community participation and organisation, increasing the self-management capacities in Surabaya's *kampungs* (Das 2015b).

Some years after the start of the C-KIP programme, Surabaya's authorities also launched RSDK in 2003. This programme is a social assistance measure focusing not on the infrastructure of whole settlements, as larger slum upgrading programmes do, but on individual assistance for the poorest households. Overseen by DinSos, the programme involves the renovation of individual houses considered in bad condition, as well as social assistance for people in need (eg food expenses of elderly people) (Interview 31). According to the head of this department, Pak Narko (Interview 34), funding is very limited and if there were to be too much applicants, it would not be sufficient. Therefore, '[...] the programme is not too much promoted' (Interview 34).

Eligible households receive a support of approximately Rp. 10 million (appox. 700€[4]), an amount almost completely used for building materials. The selection process is top-down; households are proposed by working groups (Unit Pembinaan Keluarga Miskin, or UPKM) set up in each *kelurahan*. These working groups consist of local leaders (RT, RW, *lurah*) and members from the community (eg members from the women's association). Besides these actors, other departments of the municipality (eg BAPERMAS, DinKes) and experts from the local universities might also be involved in some cases, giving recommendations on single households or areas that need assistance through the programme (Interview 31, 34). In order to be selected, families must be citizens of Surabaya (with a valid identity card, or KTP[5]) and considered as poor families or to be living in inadequate conditions as assessed by the working groups. A waiting list with proposed households exists in each quarter and usually it takes up to one year until an eligible household receives funds from the programme. In such a way, every year on average 500 households are supported (Interview 34). According to data received from DinSos this programme has helped to bring down the numbers of uninhabitable homes in Surabaya from 8,941 in 2009 to 1,595 in 2014 (Interview 31).

In line with the city's efforts to improve its *kampungs*, another initiative has gained momentum over the last years: the Green and Clean Programme. Since 2004, the city government has increased its efforts to create a better waste management system in the city, focusing on activities to reduce waste at its source (UN-Habitat 2008a; Gervasi 2011; Prasetiyo et al. 2019). In 2005, a local newspaper (Java Pos) begun supporting these activities by initiating a competition among communities to clean up their environment. Prize money was announced to be received by the best participating kampungs. The initiators were surprised by the enormous response: by 2009, already 30 % of *kampungs* participated (Bunnell et al. 2013) – and the authorities decided to continue and promote this competition on a regular basis twice a year.

---

4 Exchange rate: 1€ = Rp. 14,400 (Avg. 2015, received from https://fxtop.com).

5 The national identity card (*Kartu Tanda Penduduk*, or KTP) states personal details including place of residence, religious affiliation, and marital status. It is required to be eligible for social and governmental services in respective administrative areas.

Today, the initiative is facilitated and supported by the city's Department for Cleaning and Gardening (DKP) with the goal of creating a cleaner and greener environment. In each round of the competition, a jury assesses the efforts of participating *kampungs*. The best-performing *kampungs* are to receive an award and prize money that can be used for improvements in their settlement or for other measures benefiting the community. To ensure a fair competition, several leagues of *kampungs* are established depending on socio-economic structure and development status. In that way 'less advanced' *kampungs* do not compete with 'more developed' *kampungs*, but only with their equals. Every year the categorisation is addressed anew and it is possible for the leading *kampungs* of one ranking to ascend to the next league in the following year.

The activities for the programme are organised at the community level and tied to efforts of improving the self-management capacities within the *kampungs*. There are facilitators contracted by the city government to promote the process of self-organisation and self-help. The community is organised in several working groups that perform different activities at the household or neighbourhood level: tree planting, waste separation, waste collection, urban gardening, new economic products, production of goods from recycled materials, and so on (Silas et al. 2012: 105). Every year a jury consisting of several experts visits the participating *kampungs* and assesses their performance. Members of this jury originate from different governmental agencies, local universities, representatives of NGOs, and contracted facilitators. The composition of the jury changes every year. Each representative assesses indicators related to his or her field of expertise. These indicators change every year and local people do not know them in advance. One representative of the municipal Department of Health (Dinas Kesehatan, or DinKes) for instance, used as criteria in 2015 the amount of mosquito larvae found in standing water and knowledge about mosquitos as well as indicators connected to a 'healthy house' (*rumah sehat*), such as ventilation and building material. Data on these indicators are directly collected during the field trips, mainly through methods of observation and interviewing the residents.

The day when the jury arrives to assess progress is celebrated as a festive day, where the whole neighbourhood gathers. The jury is invited to walk through the area and the improvements made during the year are proudly presented (eg the creation of a vertical herbal garden on a previously empty house wall). Also new products they have created in their home-based industries (eg products from recycled materials, food, drinks produced from their small-scale urban gardening projects) are presented to the jury (cf. figure 44). According to jury members, the motivation to participate in the 'green and clean competition' is less about the prize money or the award and more about pride.

Initially the programme focused only on cleaning and greening, as the name suggests, but meanwhile other aspects and ideas for improving life in the *kampungs* have been included (Prasetiyo et al. 2019). Among them are infrastructure improvements, issues of a healthier environment, a better sanitation system, and the existence of

Fig. 44 Results of the Green and Clean Programme (top) and the Kampung Unggulan Programme (bottom)
Note: The communities proudly present their awards won in the 'green and clean competition' (top-left); plants are grown everywhere in the *kampungs (*top-middle); the jury-team on an evaluation trip (top-right); one *kampung* has specialised in *tempe* production (bottom-left); new products developed in the *kampungs* (bottom-right)
Photos: Christian Obermayr, 2015

home-based industries (Interview 38). Urban experts and practitioners judge the Green and Clean Programme as very successful and it has received several international awards due to its success and its community-based design (Interview 26, 47). The initiative has shown its potential and since its first implementation Surabaya has become in many ways a greener city and the amount of waste produced has significantly dropped (Bunnell et al. 2013; UN-Habitat 2014b; Prasetiyo et al. 2019).

The impact of the Green and Clean initiative is not limited to these hard factors, but it enhances community collaboration and has fuelled creativity and innovation. As one of the interviewed experts puts it: 'There are incredible numbers of ideas that have sprung up in the different kampungs' (Interview 26). Residents have developed innovative ideas to improve their environment (eg composters, which are small tons to produce soil from recycled organic waste). The programme has greatly increased public awareness of environment issues (Silas et al. 2012: 5) and has also brought economic gains (eg by the establishment of a waste bank system or the production of goods from recycled materials). Pak Mustakim, an employee of BAPPEKO, even states that from all programmes aiming to improve living conditions in *kampungs*, the Green and Clean initiative had the greatest impact (Interview 47).

Another aspect of the *kampung*-centred policy in Surabaya is the improvement of economic opportunities for *kampung* residents. For this goal, the municipality has introduced an economic empowerment programme since 2010, called Kampung Unggulan Programme. Having received upgrading programmes and empowerment programmes over the last decades, the *kampungs* were considered to be ready to receive what is seen as the next stage of development: a better economic base. It was decided to create a programme focusing on economic development within the *kampungs*, more precisely to support the development of small and medium enterprises (Dianingrum et al. 2017: 44–46). Different initiatives were started. They range from the support of marketing activities for the *kampung* products, to basic training for residents (eg how to set up a small enterprise), to initiatives that promote whole neighbourhoods around one product (eg *kampungs* specialised in producing typical dishes: the *kampung tempe, kampung lontong*). The goal is to make local products serving for subsistence ready for a larger market (Interview 26). Administrative buildings and shopping malls are used to present *kampung* products to a wider public, enabling communities to sell them at city scale. According to interviewed experts (Interview 32, 36), these incentives have been successful. *Kampung* products are in high demand by the growing middle class and production can hardly satisfy this demand.

Over the last decades, Surabaya's *kampungs* have received three generations of supporting programmes. The first generation targeted infrastructure (KIP), the second improved community organisation (C-KIP, Green and Clean), and the third is now aiming to improve local economies (Green and Clean, Kampung Unggulan). All these initiatives are designed and initiated in close cooperation between universities and the authorities. They all aim in one way or another to preserve existing *kampungs* by creating better housing conditions and livelihoods within these neighbourhoods. The view dominates that only in such a way can *kampungs* be preserved as a distinct and fascinating settlement type, mitigating the threats posed by market forces and globalisation processes. Surabaya, in this regard, has pioneered several approaches to improve life in its *kampungs*. The *pro-kampung* programmes illustrated here, however, target only acknowledged settlements and citizens, but not squatter settlements (*kampung liar*) or residents without valid citizenship. These groups, estimated to be 200,000 to 400,000 people, are excluded from supporting programmes (Das 2017). The only policy pursued for them is public housing for citizens or resettlement and eviction for non-citizens.

24.3 Social housing: Surabaya's social housing blocks (*rusunawa*)

The national public housing programme (*rusunawa* programme) is one option for poor citizens of Surabaya to satisfy their housing needs. Through this programme, the housing backlog is to be eased by the provision of low-cost rental apartments in high-rise social housing blocks. The flats are explicitly designated for low-income people and the programme is implemented throughout Indonesia (cf. chapter 20.2.2). As on the national scale, also in Surabaya, public housing did not have much significance in the past. Due to limited funds, only few public housing projects were realised starting in the 1950s. The houses built were mainly occupied by civil servants and military personnel, as these groups were the only ones with a stable, albeit low, income. The first vertical 'towers' in the city were built in 1983 (Urip Sumoharjo). It was only in the 2000s that construction significantly accelerated. In the 30-year period from 1975 to 2005 only seven *rusunawa* with 2,184 flats were finished, but in the ten-year period from 2005 to 2015 ten additional *rusunawa* were realised with another 2,285 units (cf. table 30). In 2015, low-cost rental flats exist in 18 spots, providing all together 4,469 housing units.

The city's *rusunawa* differ in size and shape. There are either compact blocks or twin-blocks separated by empty space in between. Each block has a height of three to five floors and accommodates approximately 50 flats. The standard twin-block has approximately 100 flats, but in some spots (eg Sombo) several blocks have been realised in close proximity with more than 600 flats. Usually these tenements stand out from the normal city structure, where building heights are no more than one or two floors. Each of the flats has a size of 18 to 24 m^2 with an attached bathroom and kitchen accommodating families with up to four individuals[6] (Interview 30).

The latest *rusunawa* developments are located increasingly in the urban periphery. This pattern becomes obvious considering figure 45 showing existing *rusunawa* of the city for the year 2015. Due to land scarcity, brought about by rapid urban growth, the authorities have difficulties in finding space for new developments and must fall back on existing land resources in less favourable areas (Interview 28). Therefore, new *rusunawa* are located at a greater distance to the work opportunities of the centre, often close to the rivers or the city boundaries.

Several governmental bodies are involved in the construction and management of *rusunawa* in Surabaya. Since both the city and the provincial government are obliged to provide units in *rusunawa* for their low-income population (MBR), both authorities strive to realise new projects (Interview 30, 37). Usually they propose projects and provide the land, while funding for the construction is obtained from the national budget. For this reason, there is a dual structure with 16 of the 18 *rusunawa* managed by

6 There might be exceptions from this rule, eg if a family has more than two children.

Table 30 Social housing blocks (*rusunawa*) in Surabaya 2015

Name	Year completed	Management	Blocks	Floors	Size per unit (m²)	Units
Urip Sumoharjo	1983	City	4	4	21	120
Dupak Bangunrejo	1989	City	6	3	18	150
Sombo	1990	City	10	4	18	618
Penjaringan Sari I	1991	City	3	4	18	240
Waru Gunung	1996	City	10	5	21	480
Penjaringan Sari II	2004	City	6	4	21	288
Wonorejo	2004	City	6	4	21	288
Randu	2007	City	6	5	21	288
Tanah Merah	2009	City	8	5	21	388
Gunung Sari	2010	Province	3	5	34	268
Penjaringan Sari III	2010	City	2	5	24	96
Grudo	2011	City	2	5	24	99
Pesapen	2012	City	2	5	24	100
Jambangan	2012	City	1	5	24	50
Siwalankerto	2013	City	2	5	24	99
Sumur Welut	2014	Province	4		24	396
Bandarejo	2014	City	2		24	99
Remokalisari	2015	City	5		24	396
						Total 4469

Source: Table by author. Data compiled from Kisnarini (2015: 61–62), from the provincial (DPU) and municipal government (DPBT)
Note: The data from the three sources are inconsistent, particularly the indicator 'year completed'. The most reasonable value is used

the municipality (3,805 units), while two *rusunawa* – Gunung Sari and Sumur Welut, with 664 units – are managed by the province (cf. table 30). This structure has consequences for the occupancy, which is done according to citizenship, meaning that only citizens of Surabaya holding an identity card (Kartu Tanda Penduduk, or KTP) with an appropriate place of residence are eligible to apply for a flat in one of the municipality's *rusunawa*. The same applies for the *rusunawa* managed by the province.

Besides these two categories of *rusunawa* (provincial and municipal) meant for low-income people, there are also other *rusun* towers (owner-occupied or rental) with similar designs but intended for other target groups. According to data provided by the provincial government (DPU East Java, Interview 37), there are at least 14 other *rusun* blocks in Surabaya, providing another 2,356 units that are composed of owner-occupied flats, company flats, student flats, and apartments for police or military personnel. These other low-cost flats are managed by the respective organisations, ie the military, the police, companies, universities, schools, or Perumnas. The construction of these

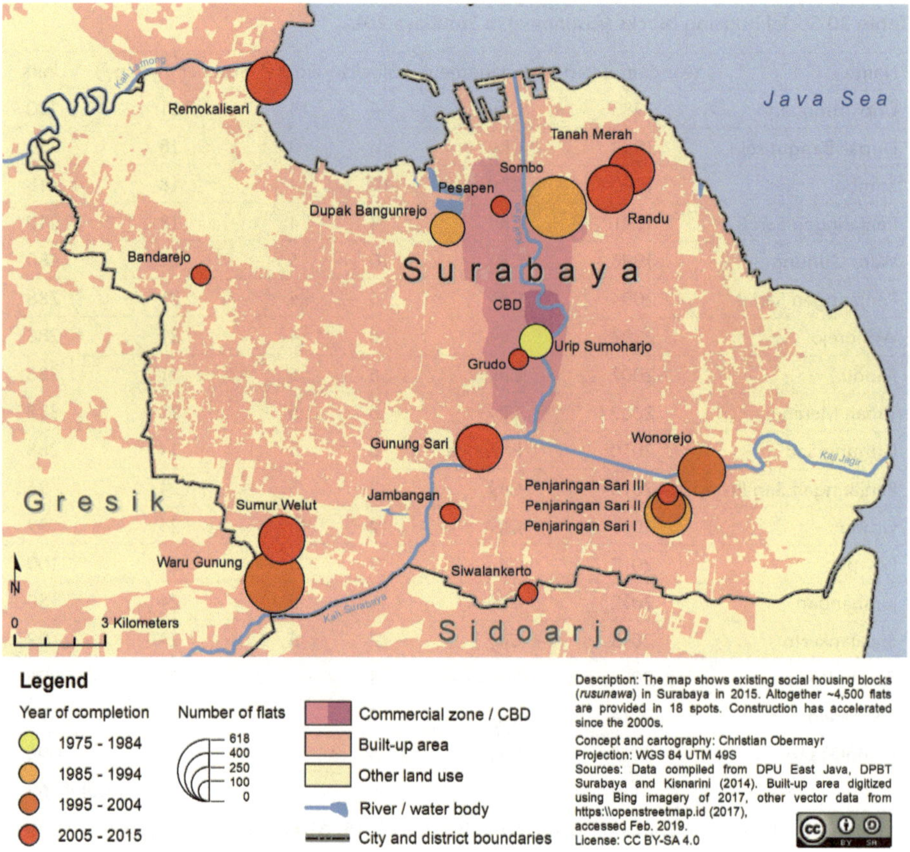

Fig. 45 Social housing blocks (*rusunawa*) in Surabaya 2015
Source: Illustration by author

rusun towers is also funded from the national budget and has equally accelerated in recent years (cf. figure 46). Overall, roughly 35 % of all *rusun* constructed in Surabaya are designated not for low-income people, but allocated to the mentioned target groups. These data raise the question of whether funding is used reasonably and whether these other groups are really in such a desperate need of accommodation compared to the poor. Since these other *rusun* towers do not target the poor, they are excluded from a closer analysis in this work.

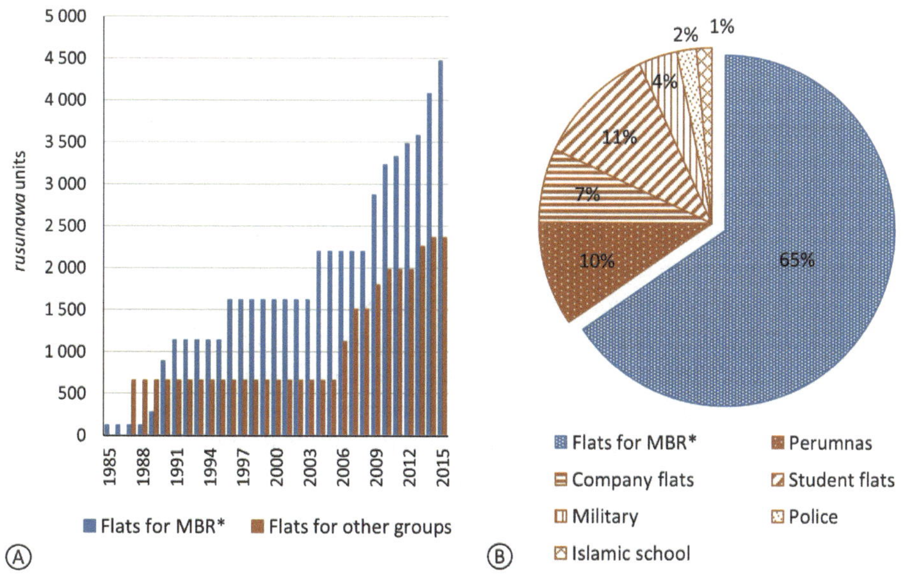

Note: * MBR is the Indonesian acronym for *Masyarakat Berpenghasilan Rendah,* translatable as 'low-income people'.

Fig. 46 Flats in social housing blocks (*rusunawa*) for the poor (flats for MBR) and for other groups 1985–2015 (A); Proportional number of *rusunawa* units according to target groups in 2015 (B)
Source: Illustration by author. Compiled/calculated using data provided by the provincial (DPU) and municipal government (DPBT) (= Interviews 30 and 37)

24.3.1 Rents and application process in Surabaya's *rusunawa*

Rents in *rusunawa* are low and depend on the storey in which a specific flat is located. Since none of the social housing blocks has an elevator or air-conditioning, it is more exhausting and inconvenient to live on the upper floors. For these reasons, occupants prefer the lower floors. This is also reflected in monthly rents set by the city government through local regulations (*Perwali*). With Rp. 22,000 to 39,000 (appox. 1.5–2.7€[7]) the cheapest flats are those on the upper floors, while flats in the ground floor are considerably more expensive with Rp. 48,000 to 87,000 (appox. 3–6€[7]) (Perwali 13/2015). These rents cover the accommodation only and are used for maintenance purposes (repair costs, cleaning, etc). Additional costs for electricity and water consumption must be paid separately. Considering an estimated monthly income of approximately

7 Exchange rate: 1€ = Rp. 14,400 (Avg. 2015) and 1€= Rp. 15,300 (Avg. 2013, received from https://fxtop.com).

Rp. 700,000 (appox. 46€*) on average for *rusunawa* residents in 2013, the expenses for rent amounts to only 3 to 13 % of average incomes depending on the floor, an amount regarded as affordable by the authorities (Interview 47). An office responsible for the management and rent collection is located in each of the blocks. The Department for Construction and Land Management (Dinas Pengelolaan Bangunan dan Tanah, or DPBT) oversees the municipality's *rusunawa* and the Department of Public Works at the provincial level manages the provincial's *rusunawa*. These departments also handle the allocation of flats to the people in need.

The application process for a rusunawa flat has several conditions. Only citizens of Surabaya can apply for one of the units in the municipality's *rusunawa* and the same applies for one of the units in the provincial's *rusunawa*. The applicants must provide extensive records, proving their citizenship, marriage status, and salary to apply for a flat (Interview 29, 42). Conditions are the possession of a KTP Surabaya or KTP East Java, no other property is allowed and household income must be below one million Rupiah per month (2015) (Interview 30,47). Single households are not allowed and families with children and those affected by relocation measures have priority for the allocation of flats. According to an interviewed resident: '[...] the application process is not easy and time consuming. You need the permission of your RT, the RT of the kampung you are staying at the moment. You have to visit DPBK several times' (Interview 48). Others confirmed this procedure and stated that the application process would be easier if there is already a relation to government officials in place. Asked if it was possible to select the unit within the *rusunawa*, the residents denied, but one of them admitted the existence of this possibility '[...] if you pay one million rupiahs' (Interview 51).

All existing *rusunawa* in Surabaya were fully occupied in 2015 and for the municipality's blocks, 2,800 families were registered on a waiting list in 2014 (Interview 29,30). Considering these data, it can be said that another half of the existing flats in *rusunawa* are needed to meet the demand. To address this challenge experts and authorities discuss the construction of 15-floor *rusunawa* towers (Interview 29, 36).

24.3.2 Example for *rusunawa* housing: Penjaringan Sari I–III

The development of low-cost rental apartment blocks can be illustrated using the examples of the *rusunawa* Penjaringan Sari I–III. During the fieldwork phase in 2015, three complexes were encountered that were developed through three consecutive construction phases in the southeast of the city. In a first phase, three blocks with four floors each and 250 flats was constructed in 1991 (Penja I), while in a second phase six additional blocks were finished in 2004 with 288 flats (Penja II). In 2010, the third construction phase resulted in a twin-block with a new design, five floors, and another 96 flats (Penja III). The development continues and in 2019, another twin-block was finished nearby (*Penja IV*).

Each flat in one of these towers consists of only one room with an adjacent kitchen and bathroom. The size of the flats has increased over the years from 18 m^2 (Penja I) to over 21 m^2 (Penja II) to 25 m^2 (Penja III) – a trend visible also for all other *rusunawa* in Surabaya. In the oldest complex, Penja I, not all flats have a private bathroom and the kitchen is shared on every floor. In the second complex (Penja II) this has changed and now every single flat has a private kitchen and bathroom. In addition, on the ground floor more public space was provided and a wide parking lot, facilities that Penja I is lacking. The third complex, Penja III, is even more spacious and modern. Flats are larger and the new design allows for better air circulation. Outside the building a park was created, including a sports ground. From these observations, it can be concluded that *rusunawa* housing has improved over the years in terms of design, unit size, and provided facilities. Impressions of rusunawa housing are provided in figure 47.

Fig. 47 Impressions from Surabaya's social housing blocks (*rusunawa*)
Note: *Rusunawa* Gunung Sari viewed from outside (top-left), and inside (bottom); new *rusunawa* Penja III (top-right) won several prizes due to its innovative design
Photos: Christian Obermayr, 2015

The municipality manages all three *rusunawa* and in each of the blocks, an RT is responsible for all administrative tasks. The allocation of flats is done by the city government (DPBT) according to applications and urgency of housing needs in their records. Penja I and II were constructed explicitly as an alternative housing option for those affected by the municipality's relocation programmes, even though the resident structure has meanwhile changed, so that today not all occupants are people relocated from other areas in Surabaya. In Penja III, in contrast, people are chosen according to the official list and this new *rusunawa* has won several prizes due to its innovative design (Interview 48). According to one of the RTs in Penja II (Interview 42), one third of the flats is still occupied by the original residents. They originate from a riverbank settlement cleared in 2004. In the other flats the occupation has changed; there would appear to be quite a fluctuation. He describes Penja II as 'very good, a nice place and very quiet' and estimates an average occupation in each flat of three people, but mentions that sometimes up to seven share a flat of 21 m^2. As in all other *rusunawa*, rents in Penja II depend on the floor, ranging from Rp. 38,000 to Rp. 53,000. The costs for services even surpass this monthly rent with monthly costs of Rp. 15,000 for water and Rp. 60,000 for electricity per household (Interview 42).

While people in Penja I and Penja II may stay in their flats as long as they desire, residents of Penja III fall into a new regulation issued in 2010 that allows a maximum stay of nine years only. Some of the interviewees in Penja II even consider their flat as their property. They claim that they would have bought the flat from a previous tenant or in one case from a government employee. These claims indicated that residents are not necessarily only appointed by the responsible department, but that rights to stay are traded informally – at least in the older *rusunawa*. The view that *rusunawa* flats belong to the occupant might be due to the fact that many of these residents were resettled from the riverbanks and offered a flat as compensation. An experience of living in social housing is provided in box 17.

Box 17: Living in social housing (Penja II) – an experience

One of the residents in Penja II gave insights into his life in the *rusunawa* (Interview 50). He was one of the people affected by the clearance of riverbank squatters in the year 2002. As compensation, the government promised to relocate him and his family (wife and one child) to a *rusunawa* to be built in the near future. His home was demolished and since the new *rusunawa* was not ready, he had to move to a rented accommodation payed as compensation by the government. After one year, however, the compensation was running out and they moved into the *rusunawa* block. At that time, the building was not finished and in the beginning, they had to live without water and electricity. He and his wife work in the informal sector as a construction worker and an informal street vendor. The main problems with this work is the irregular income, but they never had problems paying the rent or expenses for water and electricity in the *rusunawa*. From the original residents relocated only few remain in Penja II. The municipal government carries out surveys, but usually they do not come personally. This, he suggests, is the reason why there are many people without a proper Surabaya ID-card (KTP) living in the house.

Today, after more than ten years of occupation, he admits to be mostly satisfied with the housing situation. He states the facilities are good, especially the existence of a private bathroom, kitchen, and water tap. Some problems occur since the pipes in the house are too small, which is why they are easily blocked. Management and rents are considered generally good, but when the roof was damaged, the government reacted very slowly to repair it. He has already considered moving to another place, since he wants to live in his own house. He has already bought a small house in Bratang Tangkis knowing that this riverbank *kampung* is considered illegal. The cheap price and the long existence of this settlement, however, were reasons for him to buy. In the near future, he plans to move there.

24.3.3 Challenges of *rusunawa* housing in Surabaya

The challenges of the city's *rusunawa* housing are similar to those on the national scale. Also in Surabaya, a general aversion to vertical housing and a rejection of rental housing is present, combined with a certain stigmatisation of *rusunawa* resident and challenges of management and maintenance (cf. chapter 20.2.2). Specific problems in Surabaya are of an organisational nature, related to available land for new developments and the length of the rental contracts.

The diversified competences between the government bodies at different scales is not optimal. Since the national, city, and provincial governments are involved with different agencies, the process to construct new *rusunawa* requires a close coordination and cooperation between these government agencies. This structure is time-intensive and prolongs the construction process significantly. In addition, responsibilities are shared for certain groups of the population (according to citizenship), but with many exceptions. This procedure requires additional time-consuming coordination.

Another, more urgent problem is the availability of land for future projects. Land prices are increasing rapidly, making it more difficult to find suitable land within the city boundaries (Interview 29, 36). Therefore, new projects are realised in already densely populated areas or at increasing distances to the city centre. Both solutions have unfavourable consequences. In the case of new *rusunawa* projects in densely populated neighbourhoods, the projects have high conflict potentials with existing communities, requiring mediation. Existing residents seldom welcome new *rusunawa* blocks in their neighbourhood, due to fears of increasing crime. If the new *rusunawa* are located at a greater distance to the commercial centre, other problems occur. On the one hand, infrastructure and access to urban services has to be extended to these areas, causing higher project costs, and on the other, future residents suffer higher transport costs in more remote areas. Mostly employed in the informal sector, *rusunawa* residents require central locations to sustain their livelihoods, the locations must be easily accessible through public transport, and should be close to work and school (Kisnarini 2015: 56–58).

Another issue present in Surabaya is related to the length of stay in *rusunawa* housing. Initially, the *rusunawa* managed by the city government were meant for permanent occupation, allowing the occupants to stay as long as desired. This has changed with a local regulation issued in 2010 (Perda 02/2010). Now the rental contract is limited to three years with possible extensions to nine years if the preconditions (income) are met. This new rule applies only for new contracts and exempts families already staying in *rusunawa* flats. The new regulation was created to address on the one hand the still existing backlog of units and on the other because the view dominates that after a certain period of time occupants would be able to purchase their own property (Interview 29). According to Professor Silas, studies confirm that most residents are able to purchase their own property after approximately seven years (Interview 36). In such a way, the regulation is a measure to guarantee that existing social housing really benefits those who need it most. Considering the increasing land scarcity and rising prices in Surabaya, however, it is highly questionable whether future residents will be able to purchase their own property.

24.4 Eviction and relocation of squatter settlements

Surabaya's policy to deal with its squatter settlements (*kampung liar*) is eviction for non-citizens and resettlement to social housing for citizens. Since independence, the city has struggled to cope with rapid urban growth and the sprawl of settlements in areas not designated for housing. Among municipal agencies and experts, the favoured policy option is relocation. The strategy is to provide rental accommodation in social housing blocks (*rusunawa*) for citizens of Surabaya and compensation payments for (informal) house owners. All others (non-citizens) are to be evicted.

Squatter settlements at the riverbanks have received particular attention, since they are the most visible and resistant hurdle to the broad agenda of progressive revitalisation. They are seen as one of the obstacles for achieving better flood control and a more beautiful city. In the 1990s, cleaning the rivers was a central concern and the Kali Mas, the central south-north branch of the Brantas River, was the focus. Among others, actions taken were the greening of riverbanks, the prosecution of uncontrolled waste disposal into the river, the improvement of sanitation facilities along the rivers' *kampungs*, and the relocation of industries and squatter settlements (Santosa 2000). The goal was and still is to model other famous waterfront cities (ie Singapore), envisioning green corridors through the city with pleasant walkways and beautiful riverfronts without the embarrassing sight of untidy and semi-permanent shacks associated with poverty (King & Idawati 2010).

24.4.1 Informal settlements on Surabaya's riverbanks

Informal settlements exist particularly at the riverbanks of the Kali Surabaya, the Kali Mas and the Kali Jagir. The Kali Surabaya enters the city from the south and separates into two branches in the Wonokromo district: the Kali Mas and the Kali Jagir (cf. figure 48). As the main distributary, the Kali Mas flows north, passing the city centre and reaching the sea at Surabaya's port district. The city originally developed at its estuary. The second branch, running east towards the sea, is the Kali Jagir, an artificial channel constructed during the 19th century to regulate the water levels of the Kali Surabaya. The historic Jagir floodgate (Pintu Air Jagir) controls the water flow in this 50-metre-wide channel and the riverbanks are fortified and embanked. The tidal range of the Java sea reaches until the floodgate and the difference between low and high tide is one to one-and-a-half metres (Bawole 2007: 344).

Fig. 48 Kali Surabaya separates into Kali Mas and Kali Jagir within the city boundaries. Both photos show Kali Jagir east of Jagir Floodgate
Source: Illustration by author. Photos: Christian Obermayr, 2015

In many spots along these channels, informal settlements have developed since the 1960s, mostly from squatting on government-owned land. Estimations speak of 15 riverside communities (*kampungs*) in the city, with 3,000 households or roughly 9,000 inhabitants (ACHR 2009). Their development cannot be generalised; it must rather be contextualised for each specific area. The settlements developed during different periods, for various reasons, and with diverse types of legitimisation. Usually, free land is occupied by a pioneer group of settlers, who might have obtained permission from local authorities or local companies to construct temporary shacks close to their work or for other reasons. Over time, these temporary shelters consolidated into houses that were more permanent and if not evicted, new residents were drawn in, and the settlements expanded.

Settlements along Kali Jagir

One example of such riverside settlements is the area east of the Jagir Floodgate along Kali Jagir. In 2006, both sides of the river were occupied by houses, forming several *kampungs*. The residents of the houses at the southern riverbank, between the floodgate and the Panjang Jiwo Bridge, were simply referred to as the Jagir Settlement (derived from the name of the *kelurahan* most of this area belongs to). At the northern side, three communities occupy the levee: Kampung Baru, Bratang Tangkis (henceforth 'Bratang'), and Baratajaya (cf. figure 49).

Bratang is the only one of the four settlements that has two lines of houses, separated by a small alley at the top of the embankment (cf. figure 50). In 2006, all of the houses in Bratang faced the street behind the second row or the alley in the middle. The rear of the houses was directed towards the river. The three other *kampungs* consisted only of one row of houses, their front side also facing the street or alley. Usually, kitchen and sanitary facilities are located closest to the river and sometimes this back part is built on silts above the channel. In the eyes of some, these run-down and 'messy' riverbanks leave a shabby expression. As they are clearly visible from the Jagir Bridge, the main southern entrance towards Surabaya, this view would be embarrassing for the city.

Due to the proximity of Wonokromo market to the west and a larger access road running parallel to the river, the Jagir Settlement at the southern river side consisted of a mixture of residential houses and small shops (particularly to the west). In the *kampungs* at the northern side, the residential function dominated and still dominates today (Bawole 2007: 333). Most people worked in the informal sector, as street vendors, pedicab drivers, or garbage gatherers, for instance, an observation that has not changed over the years. All four *kampungs* existed for several decades, although occupants have partially changed when houses were sold (Setiawan 2010). According to a survey conducted in 2003, only 2 % of the residents were migrants from other areas; all

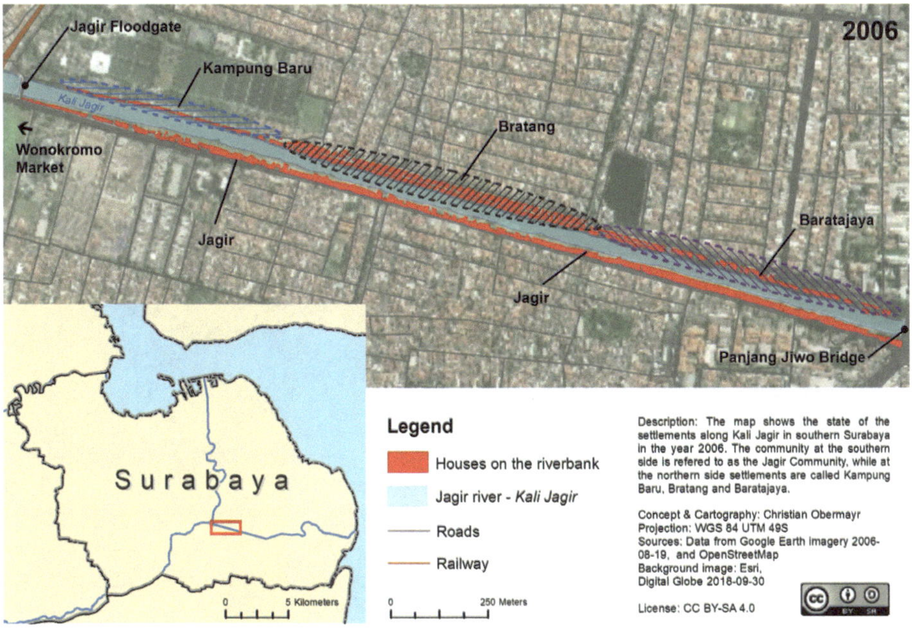

Fig. 49 Settlements along Kali Jagir in 2006
Source: Illustration by author

Fig. 50 Kampung Bratang at the northern riverbank of Kali Jagir (left); an alley separates the two rows of houses in Bratang (right)
Photos: Christian Obermayr, 2015

others have lived there for several decades (Bawole 2007: 313). Bratang is considered the oldest and most respected settlement, while Kampung Baru is certainly the youngest and poorest with the worst reputation.

Kampung Baru is located between Kampung Bratang and the Jagir Floodgate. It is the newest and poorest of the four *kampungs* (*baru* means 'new') consisting of one row

Fig. 51 The houses of Kampung Baru formed at the northern levee of Kali Jagir
Photo: Christian Obermayr, 2015

of one-storey houses, directly built on the levee (cf. figure 51). There is a small path, one or two metres wide, behind the houses and the wall of a water-processing factory (PDAM). From the four *kampungs* considered here, it is the most run-down settlement, generally associated with crime, prostitution, and disorder. Some shacks had probably been built already in the 1960s, but a more intensive development happened during the 1990s (King & Idawati 2010; Das 2017). The residents claim to have lived in this *kampung* for more than 20 years and approximately 75 % of them hold Surabaya citizen status, even though there is no RT-structure. In their struggle for survival, they work in the informal sector, mostly as street vendors, garbage collectors, and sex workers (Interview 41, Interview 40). The scavenging activity seems to have expanded from a squatter community nearby (Lumumba), located close to the railway line. The informal activities are clearly visible in the western part of Kampung Baru, while the eastern part is more respectable, and used for residential purposes. There, also a mosque was built and residents try to seek connection to Bratang, since this area is considered as more secure from eviction (King & Idawati 2010: 222–224).

Kampung Bratang is the oldest and most secure of the four informal settlements, home to roughly 450 households (Das 2017). It consists of two lines of small (less than 50 m^2), one- or two-storey houses on both sides of an alley running along the levee. Most of the houses are built today from semi-permanent or permanent materials and have expanded over time upwards or towards the river. The development started in the

1950s, with informal workers (pedicap drivers) obtaining permission from government officials to build houses on this state-owned land against the payment of small compensations (King & Idawati 2010). Initially, raw huts were built between banana trees, coconut trees, and bamboo near the river. The settlement consolidated and drew migrants from East Java, who gradually receiving citizen status, a status seen as achieved when 'Surabaya' is officially stated as their place of residence on their national identity card (KTP) (Subroto 2013; Das 2017). In 1966, the *kampung* was included in the RT-system of the adjacent *kelurahan* and efforts of the municipality to demolish the houses in 1974 turned out with no consequence (Interview 44). The settlement expanded in the 1980s and 1990s, consisting increasingly of formal workers (mainly construction workers) and former members of the Indonesian armed forces (King & Idawati 2010: 222).

The third settlement, Kampung Baratajaya, has formed east of Kampung Bratang, stretching until the Panjang Jiwo Bridge. This settlement consists of only one line of houses, and looks less permanent than neighbouring Bratang. This squatter community developed in the 1990s as a community of recyclers, cleaners, and waste collectors. Indonesia's transmigration programme had brought them temporarily to Surabaya, but during the political turmoil in the 1990s, the relocation plan was halted, leaving them stranded in Surabaya. Lacking an RT structure and any kind of permission, the eviction threat looms high over this settlement (Das 2017). Figure 52 presents the respective alley in each of the three *kampungs*.

Fig. 52 The respective alley through the three informal settlements Kampung Baru (A), Bratang (B), and Baratajaya (C)
Note: Bratang is the most consolidated settlement. The alley provides public space for all kind of day-to-day activities. It is the place where children play and where residents encounter each other
Photos: Christian Obermayr, 2015

The Jagir community at the southern riverbank of Kali Jagir started to develop in 1964, when traders from the Wonokromo market (west of the Jagir floodgate) were evicted due to the development of a public transport terminal (Bemo Terminal). Searching for space to continue their business, roughly 50 ironmongers moved their shops to the western part of the Jagir region (Lay 2017: 42). This was the starting signal for further development of the riverbank and slowly the entire southern waterfront became occupied by pedicap drivers and others, who built their housing and shops there. In 1968, the village administration tried to prohibit the eastward development of the settlement, but after negotiations and against a small payment, people were allowed to stay and became recognised as citizens, allowing them to obtain an official identity card (KTP) stating Surabaya as their place of residence. The status of the settlement became further strengthened in 1975, when the residents began to pay land taxes and in 1983 when the state-owned electricity company, PLN, started to service the area. Meanwhile, the resident structure began to change, since use rights were traded and new inhabitants moved in (Setiawan 2010).

24.4.2 Central arguments for evicting riverside communities

Besides being illegal and squatting land that does not belong to them, advocates of relocation policies argue that informal settlements at the riverbanks would destroy the functions of the river and cause flooding, pollute the environment, particularly the water in the rivers, and cause a bad image of the city due to the poor and shabby houses.

The first argument goes that the residents of riverside communities would cause flooding in other areas due to their habit of putting all their garbage into the rivers. This waste would cause not only bad water quality, but would also settle in the riverbeds as sediment, affecting the water flow and proper functioning of the river. This would result in a reduced carrying capacity and in higher flood levels in other areas (Some et al. 2009: 464–466). The government thus argues that it is of utmost importance to dredge the riverbeds regularly and to fortify the riverbanks against higher water levels and erosion. For this task, it must be possible to access the rivers with heavy equipment and to maintain the channels on a regularly basis. Therefore, access roads to the rivers are needed and houses close to the larger river beds cannot be allowed (Bawole 2007: 339). Indeed, many areas of Surabaya are prone to flooding and sedimentation is one of the problems. Flooding occurs mostly from heavy rainfalls during the rainy season, when the drainage system cannot handle the water volume, but are not caused from rivers overflowing their banks. Just the same as Jakarta, Surabaya is built on an estuary where land subsidence is a common problem reinforced by human activities. Large parts of the city are situated below sea level. The uncoordinated urban development has sealed ever greater areas of open space, causing increased run-off and flooding. Problems identified are drainpipes that are too small or clogged, floodgates and pumps not working properly, and sedimentation, reducing the capacity of reservoirs and riverbeds. Certainly, riverside communities are contributing to this sedimentation process by their habit of discarding waste into the river. Nevertheless, the deposition of industrial plants located upriver and the amount dumped by residents in formal settlements is probably much greater. Finally, the sedimentation is only one of the reasons for flooding (King & Idawati 2010; Bawole 2007). Still, it has been common to blame someone for floods, why not the riverbank communities?

The second argument is that riverbank communities would pollute their environment and the rivers. In a survey conducted in 2003, Bawole (2007: 340) reports that none of the houses in the Jagir region had a septic tank and untreated sewage was running directly to the river. This has meanwhile changed, and today most of the houses still at the riverbanks have a septic tank, where wastewater is treated. Tellingly, this upgrading measure was not supported by government funds but was built by the communities through self-help. Considering pollution of the river, it can still be observed (in 2015) that people from riverside communities put some of their garbage and sewage into the river. It is, however, difficult to tell if this habit is the only cause of the bad water quality in Surabaya's rivers. Dumping waste into the rivers seems to be not only a habit of people in riverside communities, but also a habit of most people living in Surabaya – observable in many other spots.

The third and last argument is more an underlying rationale behind riverbank revitalisation and not often articulated openly: the riverside communities would cause a bad image of the city (Bawole 2007: 349–350). Certainly, the non-permanent houses are not a pleasant sight due to bad housing structures and the bare association and confrontation with poverty. Unlike inner-city *kampungs*, which are usually hidden from direct street-view, located in back-alleys behind a facade of more permanent houses facing the streets, the riverside communities are openly visible for all visitors. In that way, they have received more attention, and seeking solutions for these areas has become one of the pressing issues to be addressed by the municipal authorities.

24.4.3 The 2002 evictions

In 2002, it was decided to clear all of Surabaya's riverbanks of informal settlements to reduce pollution and flood risks and revitalise the riverbanks (King & Idawati 2010: 215). All *kampungs* in question received an eviction notification, including the Jagir *kampungs*. A first stage of evictions took place, with roughly 1,150 houses demolished in three *kampungs* along Kali Surabaya and Kali Jagir, east of the Panjang Jiwo Bridge (Nginden, Wonrejo, and Semampir). The initiators were the Irrigation Department of the East Java provincial government supported by the municipality. The affected residents were offered public housing flats, but at this point, they were not ready yet. In the case of settlements along Kali Jagir (further downstream, east of Nginden Bridge) Paulus Bawole (2007: 311–313) reports the eviction of 864 families, only 165 of whom were relocated to temporary barracks. Compensations of 3.5 million Rp. were paid per demolished house, an amount far too low to cover the property value lost. Other sources

Fig. 53 Kali Jagir towards the east
Note: East of the Nginden Bridge (A) and the Panjang Jiwo Bridge (B): squatters were cleared here in 2002. A pier was established, the riverbanks are tidy and orderly (A) but sometimes used as a dumping place for all kinds of garbage (B). Middle-class-residential towers are under construction
Photos: Christian Obermayr, 2015

(Das 2017) speak of 1,150 households demolished using police forces and violence. Many of the residents had no choice but to rent elsewhere or to improvise shelters in empty spots close by. In 2004, some 700 residents were eventually resettled to public housing units. The measures were accompanied by a media campaign, describing riverside *kampungs* as illegal areas of criminality and prostitution. In that way the forceful evictions were justified and it was also made sure that the remaining *kampungs* would understand the need for their relocation (King & Idawati 2010: 216–217).

The government successfully cleared large areas along the two river channels. East of Nginden Bridge the riverbanks are today clear from any settlements. Instead, new residential apartment blocks for the middle class have sprung up or are under development close to the channel (cf. figure 53). There is reason to follow Bawole's assessment and to presume that the interest of private investors to develop these projects have contributed their part to the eviction decision (Bawole 2007: 311–313). The challenge of informality, however, is not solved. Evicted residents have to find other housing options, intensifying housing problems in other areas of the city.

24.4.4 Resistance: foundation of NGOs and settlement upgrading

The 2002 evictions triggered reactions from university activists, who formed an NGO named Jerit, which aimed to organise all vulnerable groups in Surabaya. Since local leaders (RTs) did not take the lead, they persuaded the remaining riverbank communities to organise themselves outside the traditional RT system to resist the eviction attempts of the government. They formed a federation of *kampungs*, an organisation called the Riverside Community Rights Defenders (Paguyuban[8] Pembela Tanah Strenkali, or PPTS) or. In 2005 it became known as the Strenkali People's Movement (Paguyuban Warga Strenkali, or PWS), a civil society organisation uniting resident associations from several riverside communities under the common goal of continuing their life along the riverbanks (Some et al. 2009: 464; Taylor 2015).

Besides resisting eviction, PWS aims at developing the communities in cultural, economic, and social terms, to establish social cohesion and environmental awareness. Activities range from the introduction of community saving groups, joint upgrading activities, and waste management to the reintroduction of traditional medicine, children's education, and so on. The organisation's structure is based on participatory principles – every three years the leadership and *kampung* coordinators are elected. In 2007, 5 out of 15 riverside communities, representing 887 of 2,107 households were members of PWS (ACHR 2009: 46): Bratang, Gunung Sari, Kebraon, Kareng Pilang, and Semampir. In

---

8 '*Paguyuban*' derives from the Javanese word *guyub*, which means the gathering of people with a common emotional link (King & Idawati 2010).

2010, the communities of Baratajaya and Kampung Baru also joined. Of these, Bratang has always been the vanguard of resistance and the backbone of the organisation. In order to achieve the ultimate goal of being granted a permanent right to stay, PWS tried to negotiate alternative solutions with the government and took efforts to change the public perception of the riverside communities (King & Idawati 2010; Subroto 2013).

From the beginning, PWS was supported by UPLINK, a broad-based national NGO with branches all over Indonesia[9]. UPLINK provided advice on community organisation, technical help for house design and settlement planning, and, most importantly, national and international contacts, as for instance to the Asian Coalition of Housing Rights (ACHR) (Some et al. 2009: 464). With the help of this support, they approached the national minister of public works in 2002, who was persuaded to ask the provincial and municipal government to halt all evictions and to form a joint team of community and government members for discussing alternative solutions (ibid.).

They also initiated a technical study (2002) supported by Gadjah Mada University (from Yogyakarta), to determine the water quality of Surabaya's rivers. The study found that the riverside communities cause only 15 % of the river's pollution while 60 % comes from factories. In that way one of the government's central arguments for evictions was invalidated. The study also proposed an alternative solution: Instead of widening and deepening the rivers, which would involve the clearance of a 10 to 15-metre-wide corridor along all riverbanks – this was the municipal government's proposal based on national legislation – the study proposed a compromise of opening only a three to five-metre-wide path along the banks. This alternative would allow an access path for dredging and maintenance activities, but would simultaneously avoid the eviction of an estimated 8,000 dwellers. With both options on the table, the provincial parliament, which has jurisdiction over the riverbanks, had to make a decision (Some et al. 2009; Taylor 2015; Das 2017).

Though the decision was still pending, PWS began to develop its organisation in the following years, forging alliances and introducing various measures to improve the communities. They set up a waste management system, founded community savings groups, and undertook some upgrading initiatives. By street construction (paving), housing improvements, and greening they tried to demonstrate the communities' willingness to take initiative. These actions were disseminated through the local media, telling stories about life in riverside *kampungs* and improvements made. The goal was to destroy the stigma of riverside communities being dirty places damaging the environment and harbouring criminals. By showing the government and the wider public the community's

---

9 UPLINK was established in 2002 as a national network in order to show the people's strength by helping to establish community organisations and support them in their development. This is done by developing relations with other organisations, such as universities, other NGOs, and advocacy and law groups. The network also provides advice and technical assistance with the goal of facilitating community organisations that are not dependent on external organisations or funding (Some et al. 2009).

capacity to improve their environment and their houses through self-help, it was hoped to influence the upcoming decision (Bawole 2007: 339; Some et al. 2009: 466).

After years of negotiations, the provincial House of Representatives (DPRD) decided that the social costs of evicting 8,000 people would be too high and vowed in favour for the riverside communities. A new regulation was adopted in 2007 (Perda 09/2007), banning new housing constructions along the river, but allowing existing communities to stay, under the condition that settlements be upgraded in the next five years. The existing houses were to be realigned in such a way that their front sides faced the river, a path along the channel was to be opened as an access road and a community waste management system had to be installed (Interview 44). Among the residents, this decision was celebrated as a success and many initiatives were started to realise the required measures. Using revolving loans acquired from the ACHR and funds from community saving groups, the residents of Bratang tried hard to upgrade their houses with the help of Arkom, a group of community architects (Das 2017). The upgrading activities started in 2008, during which they rearranged and resized their houses in a joint community action, moving them back from the riverbank to establish riverside walkways (Subroto 2013). For wastewater treatment shared septic tanks were installed, lanes were paved, and a solid waste composting system was set up (ACHR 2009, 2010, 2014).

The results of the upgrading process looked quite impressive in 2015 (cf. figure 54). Even though the riverside walkway was not paved yet, the efforts of the community in Bratang were clearly visible. Houses were largely renovated, improved in their quality and structure. The regulation had, however, also unintended consequences. When Bratang was secured by the new regulation and residents started upgrading their houses, some residents used the chance to build new houses in Kampung Baru and Baratajaya and simultaneously the further construction of new houses along the rivers was pr-e

Fig. 54 Bratang: the alley along the river Kali Jagir
Note: Houses close to the river were moved back and realigned. Their front side now faces the river. This measure was a requirement of the city government to clear space for an access road
Photos: Christian Obermayr, 2015

vented on a legal basis. PWS succeeded in turning the government-favoured approach of relocation to public housing units into an approach of community-driven on-site settlement upgrading (Some et al. 2009: 466; Bawole 2009).

24.4.5 The looming threat: the evictions of 2009 and 2016

Despite the decision of the provincial parliament in favour of the riverside communities in 2007, many authorities still saw relocation of squatter settlements as the only viable solution to revitalise Surabaya's riverbanks. Among municipal and provincial authorities, the view dominates that squatters need to be evicted. Only the good relationship between PWS and the provincial parliament provided some institutional support and fortunately for the residents of Bratang, the areas along Surabaya's rivers fall under the province's jurisdiction (Some et al. 2009: 473–474).

Such a positive relation is not necessarily enough, as the following events showed: In 2009, another phase of demolitions and clearances of riverside houses took place. Beside some other communities, the Jagir settlement, just across from Bratang, was demolished. The municipal government initiated this eviction even though the jurisdiction about the land close to the rivers is in the hands of the provincial government. Using police forces, the houses were demolished and the eviction resulted in 380 families being made homeless. Only 236 of them held citizenship and were thus eligible to move into one of the public housing flats (*rusunawa*) prepared by the city government in Randu (Kecamatan Kenjeran) and Wonorejo (Kecamatan Rungkut). Of these, only 130 families took the opportunity; for the others it remains unclear where they moved or where they are today (Setiawan 2010; Sur 2009).

This eviction took place in violation of the regional regulation of 2007, which allowed limited settlements along Surabaya's rivers, particularly in the Jagir region, under the condition that houses are more than five metres away from the channel. Ignoring provincial legislation and the plea of the communities, the eviction was carried out by the municipal authorities. These events show that no remaining riverside community can be secure, since the threat of eviction still looms above them. This proved true again some years later in 2016, when the latest eviction events happened in the surveyed Jagir region. This time the western part of Kampung Baru and the eastern part of Baratajaya were demolished. The same reasons were put forward again: the houses are illegal, they disturb the function of the river and Kampung Baru is home to sex workers. No option of relocation was offered to the residents of the 48 houses demolished (Lintartika 2016).

In figure 55, three stages of housing development in the Jagir region are mapped for the years 2006, 2015, and 2018. The evictions can be clearly recorded. The southern riverbank of the Jagir river was cleared in 2009 (Jagir) and in 2016 the eastern and western parts of the northern riverbank were cleared (Kampung Baru and Baratajaya). The

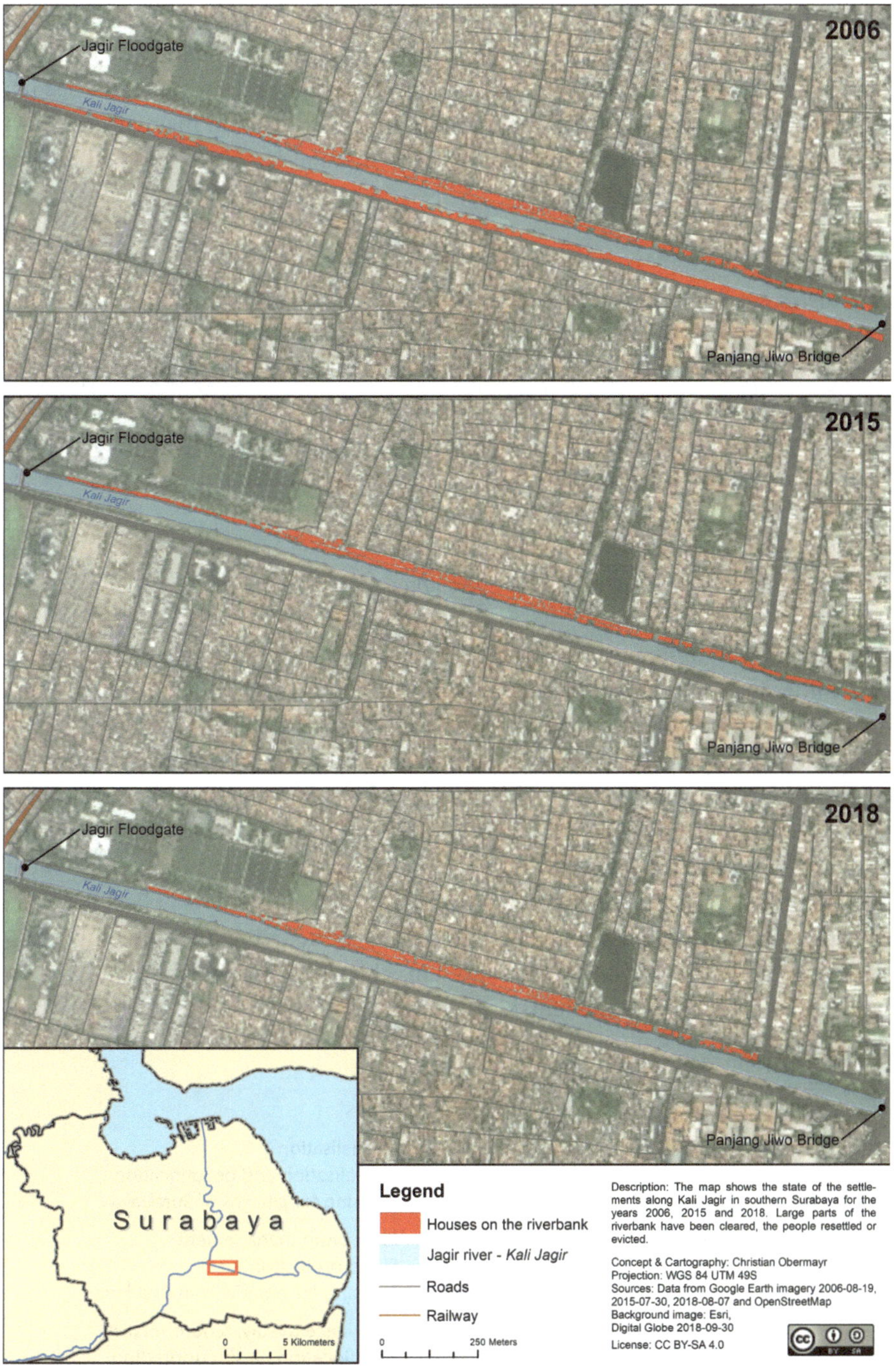

Fig. 55 Informal settlements along Kali Jagir 2006, 2015, and 2018
Source: Illustration by author

eviction threat slowly moves towards the remaining houses in Bratang. Even though the community there has struggled hard to improve their settlements, when considering the strong pro-eviction stance among authorities, they cannot be totally secure. Ever more, it is important for this community to strengthen and maintain their organisation and links to other institutions to be continuously able to resist all further eviction attempts of the government.

24.4.6 Discussion: the policy arrangement towards squatters

Powerful actors, institutions, and discourses have formed a stable policy arrangement for dealing with riverside communities in Surabaya. Opposing perspectives among actors, overlapping and inconsistent regulations, and prevailing assumptions and misinterpretations about the residents have hindered a lasting solution up to now.

Actors: different interests and opposing perspectives

Several actors with different interests are involved in the long struggle with riverside communities in Surabaya (cf. table 31). Supported by ITS, the city government has a strong interest in formalising all areas within the city boundaries with the goal of revitalising and beautifying the city. The provision of housing is also a central concern, although only for citizens of Surabaya. The provincial government is another main actor with a say in the management of riverside communities, since the riverbanks formally fall under the province's jurisdiction. The main interests are river basin management and flood protection as well as the provision of housing for all people in East Java. The riverbank communities themselves know that they are squatting illegally on government-owned land. They have a strong interest in achieving a lasting right to stay, tenure security, to upgrade their settlements.

Table 31 Actors and their central interests

Actors	Interests
City government and ITS	– Formalisation – Revitalisation and beautification – Housing for citizens of Surabaya
Provincial government	– River basin management – Flood protection – Housing for people from East Java
Riverside communities (PWS)	– Allowance to stay, tenure security – No relocation, in situ upgrading

The municipal government and academic experts from ITS have long positioned themselves as proponents of an eviction and relocation policy. All informal settlements are seen as an unsolved problem that can only be addressed by relocation (Interview 27). The municipal authorities never accepted the provincial regulation of 2007. As one of the employees at the Department of Spatial Planning (Dinas Cipta Karya dan Tata Ruang, or DCKTR) puts it: 'The NGOs are just protesting about eviction. In Surabaya, there is also the Jagir community. Why should we give permit for them? All people have the same rights. So that is no solution' (Interview 29).

The resistance of the communities and the supporting NGOs have even reinforced this perspective. They did not back down and accept a well-meant proposal elaborated by ITS and the municipal and provincial authorities in 2002 that would have included relocations to social housing flats, provision of land and infrastructure, and loans on favourable conditions. Instead, they refused; a behaviour uncommon towards the demands of authorities in Indonesia. 'NGOs intervened and told the people to resist', Johan Silas, a renowned housing expert at ITS, explained. Later, in 2004, they were ready to accept the offer, but the option was no longer on the table since the land necessary for the development of social housing was assigned to other purposes and the government had changed after an election (Interview 46).

Academic experts have also expressed their concern about the further growth of informal settlements on empty riverbanks. This happened, for instance, after the adoption of the 2007 regulation in the case of Kampung Baru (Interview 36 and 46). They propose therefore that empty riverbanks be put to another use, fostering for instance recreational activities of adjacent *kampung* residents, in order to implement more control and to prevent further squatting (Interview 46).

Responsibility for the riverside communities is subject to debate. The municipal authorities claim that 'people on the riverbanks are the obligation of the province' (Interview 29), and in the eyes of housing experts of ITS, riverbank residents, NGOs, and the provincial authorities are to be held responsible for not having achieved a solution. The riverbanks fall under the jurisdiction of the province and the city cannot be held accountable. 'The city government wants to solve the problem, but until now nothing has happened. So the government can only write letters to the provincial government. The answer: silence' (Interview 36). The municipal government, however, is not as powerless and innocent as suggested here. The municipal authorities had initiated the 2009 eviction of the Jagir community and at least in this case the city government is not innocent in the development of the settlement in the first place. The community had started to develop due to relocations of traders in 1964, KTP documents were granted in 1968, and the community had payed land taxes for decades. These facts rendered them an official part of the city, tolerated over the years and recognised as citizens (Setiawan 2010). The municipality therefore cannot deny its responsibility and must question their stance of caring only for citizens and not for all people living in the city.

With the election of Ms Tri Rismaharini (Ibu Risma) as the first female mayor in 2010, new players emerged in the policy arrangement of Surabaya, but did not bring about a radical change with regard to the city's policy on squatters. Considered as progressive and open-minded, bringing about a more inclusive form of governance, the new mayor opened up communication with the riverside communities, assuring them tenure security and citizenship (KTP). The general policy, however, did not change. Little was done to assist *in situ* upgrading activities in informal settlements. Instead, the construction of more social housing blocks was proclaimed, retaining the dominating policy against squatters: relocation (Taylor 2015; Das 2017).

The provincial authorities take a more ambivalent stance with regard to the riverside communities. It is recognised that the problem of informal settlements needs to be solved and just the same as the municipal employees, the province seeks to relocate the residents to social housing blocks. The provincial parliament's decision of 2007 to grant a right to stay is respected, but in the long run relocation is seen as inevitable. It is acknowledged that social housing should not be located in the outskirts of Surabaya, but close to the old settlements. Otherwise, social ties and income possibilities would be lost and the residents would be burdened by long travel distances (Interview 35, 37). To achieve this, cooperation with the municipality is seen as crucial. It is argued that the municipal government should take initiative and come up with a proposal (Interview 37).

Both provincial and municipal authorities seek relocation as the goal for all riverside communities. Dependent on citizenship (East Java or Surabaya), one of the two authorities is responsible for providing adequate housing alternatives in social housing blocks. Since the construction and management of social housing blocks are clearly separated among these two government bodies, this perspective raises the question of whether any further relocations can be realised in a just way and with adequate alternatives, considering the availability of social housing units. In the case of future relocations, space in both municipal and provincial housing blocks needs to be available simultaneously *and* close to the old riverside community. Such an undertaking seems to be difficult enough, but needs concrete cooperation between all actors involved.

Institutions: unclear jurisdiction and overlapping and inconsistent regulations

A number of inconsistent and overlapping regulations impede a proper management of Surabaya's riverbanks. Officially, the jurisdiction over these areas lies in the hands of the provincial water department, although the municipal government manages the settlements. This ambiguity must be attributed to the short history of decentralisation policies in Indonesia, failing to distribute competencies clearly and causing follow-up problems.

Even though there is no *de jure* responsibility of the provincial government for the squatters, *de facto* the city government has an important say in this matter, since the settlements are located within the city boundaries. There is a strong interest that the riverfronts be formalised and cleared from settlements. Therefore, the municipality tries to foster and support the process of relocation. As far as Surabaya's citizens are concerned, the city is responsible for ensuring their well-being, but considering migrants from outside Surabaya, employees of BAPPEKO state: 'Illegal people are not our priority' (Interview 27), meaning that the municipality is not responsible for migrants from outer areas.

The 2002 evictions were based on an East Java governor's decree (134/1997) about the boundaries of Surabaya's rivers. After the riverside communities protested against evictions and the long negation processes, the exceptional provincial regulation of 2007 was adopted, stating that existing settlements were allowed to stay at the riverbanks under certain conditions. Some years later, a clarification letter of the national ministry challenged this regulation, stating that the agreed boundary against the river's edge would be not wide enough according to national law. The provincial government was consequently asked not to apply the regulation of 2007 (Setiawan 2010). Up to now, the validity of the 2007 regulation is under debate and the different administrative bodies have not yet come up with a more consistent regulation.

Discourses: presuming residents are migrants and not poor

The non-achievement of a possible solution is further hampered by prevailing assumptions about residents in informal settlements. Among Surabaya's authorities, the perspective dominates that residents are migrants from outside Surabaya who are not really poor. They claim and they use their shelters in the informal settlements only as temporary places to work in the city, but have another property somewhere else. From this view, they would be using any grant or compensation from the government not for improving their lives and their houses *in situ*, but for their original home in other areas. 'Since the status in the informal settlement is insecure, they will not invest there, but use their earnings for their property in their hometown. For these people any direct government intervention in the informal settlement is useless' (Interview 29).

This fear of supporting people who were not in need led to a specific perspective on these settlements: those people are not poor; they are migrants from other areas; and they steal land belonging to the government. A policy of eviction is thus justified. 'Illegal people are not our priority. They should go home' (Interview 27). This perception was supported by actual fraud cases that took place and led to the rule that only citizens of Surabaya were eligible to benefit from municipal programmes (ie settlement upgrading, social assistance, empowerment, health care, etc). In that way residence status can be controlled more easily. These assumptions also provide a good excuse for the municipality not to implement assistance programmes to support and improve informal settlements.

In fact, these assumptions are exaggerated in the case of the riverside communities. While it is true that informal settlements generally hold a higher degree of migrants from other areas, since they provide cheap housing options and are therefore the focal point for first-time migrants, in the case of the riverbank communities, evidence from several studies suggests otherwise. A study conducted by ITS in 2002 found that over two thirds of riverside residents in the Wonokromo region were registered citizens of Surabaya, a status not easily given to migrants (Soemarno 2010). Considering the Jagir region between the Jagir Floodgate and the Panjang Jiwo bridge, Paulus Bawole found in 2006 that roughly 80 % had been living in the same area for more than 15 years (Bawole 2007: 313). In addition, the eviction of 2009 showed that most of the residents in the Jagir region were holding a KTP of Surabaya.

24.4.7 Eviction, relocation or in situ upgrading?

In general, policies for informal settlements should consider several options, ranging from *in situ* upgrading to relocation to evictions. Evictions might beautify and revitalise one area, but do not solve the challenge of poverty. Evicted residents are likely to move to another informal settlement or become squatters elsewhere. Other options must be considered first. Relocations to social housing units might be a solution, but this policy must be designed with care. *In situ* upgrading has some advantages over other options: communities are not broken and isolated in remote flats, but the existing social ties are maintained and strengthened. Relocations usually shatter this structure, making affected residents even more vulnerable.

For all these policy options, it is necessary to design the implementation with the community from the beginning. Evictions should always be only the last resort and if performed, the process must follow guidelines outlined by the United Nations (UN 2014), involving the communities and providing adequate compensation (Setiawan 2010; Kothari & Vasquez 2015). What is crucial for all policy options is to develop a good relationship between authorities and affected residents. Such a relationship needs time and a changed perception about dwellers in informal settlements. Understanding the dwellers' potentials and capabilities, recognising them as part of the city and their homes as settlements that need special attention is the foundation needed to design an adequate pro-poor policy.

In the case of evictions in Surabaya, the residents are promised an alternative accommodation in one of the *rusunawa*. Residents affected by evictions are thus prioritised as occupants of social housing blocks over the 'normal' applicants on the list. This applies only for residents of Surabaya with a valid identity card (KTP), however, and excludes all others from this alternative housing solution. All residents of East Java, but not Surabaya, are considered to be under the responsibility of the provincial government. In such cases, they might be eligible for social housing of the provincial government. The two existing *rusunawa* of the provincial government are indeed explicitly designated for squatters that are affected by relocations (Interview 28, 29, 37). To be eligible, an identity card (KTP) stating an area within East Java as the place of residence is necessary. Since there are only two provincial *rusunawa* within the city boundaries, evictions of squatter settlements might happen in the city, but alternative housing for the relocation might be located further away. The interviewed government officials are well aware that relocations to remoter areas might cause follow-up problems and are not optimal for the needs of the affected residents (Interview 35, 37).

This procedure is not optimal. The socio-economic structure in squatter settlements is usually very diverse, with many migrants from other areas and informal residents calling it their home. In the case of a planned relocation, therefore, different solutions apply for the residents depending on their citizenship, and for some there might be no compensation at all. The procedure is also complicated, requiring close cooperation between the government bodies and free space in both types of *rusunawa*. Due to these reasons, not all of the relocated people are treated equally.

The riverside communities favour *in situ* upgrading. They have proven their willingness and capacity to improve the living environment and their houses. With the support of NGOs, such as ACHR, they have achieved a lot. Meeting the requirements of the authorities, they have realigned their houses in a creative and efficient way, using limited space and materials suited to their needs. They have also shown their readiness to take care of the environment by implementing a waste management system and septic tanks. Nevertheless, Surabaya's authorities have not moved away from their chosen policy option of relocation. For riverside communities this means continued uncertainty. The resettlement option remains on the table and increasingly more social housing is developed in the city. Even the provincial authorities seem to be in favour of relocations in the long run. For Bratang, a provincial employee of DPU stated that there would be 'a plan to relocate the other residents at the northern side of Kali Jagir, this is ongoing' (Interview 35). The negotiations are continuing and the general dogma to regulate all informal areas is not questioned. The authorities are more concerned with the challenge of how to realise it and overcome the difficulty of finding adequate land, than to question the overall policy (Interview 37). A first step for achieving a solution in Surabaya would be to restart from scratch, leaving behind the poisoned relations between government bodies and the communities. All options must be brought back to the table, including all actors, discussing and negotiating possible solutions and implementing them by means of collective action.

25 Surabaya's Housing Policy Arrangement

This chapter analyses three dimensions of Surabaya's policy arrangement in the housing domain, namely actors, power, and discourses. The fourth dimension, rules of the game, is presented in chapter 31.4. The interplay of these three dimensions shape, together with the fourth dimension 'rules of the game'[10], applied housing policies in the city. Based on data collected by expert interviews and the network surveys, the first part of this chapter explores the actor network structure of Surabaya's policy arrangement including its power relations. Dominant discourses related to housing policies are presented thereinafter, arriving at the impression of a centralistic and top-down housing policy arrangement in Surabaya.

25.1 Actors and power: the influence network

Actors and power are relevant for the organisation of Surabaya's housing policy arrangement. The collected network data and the social network analysis applied makes it possible to draw a network influence map (for details on the methods see chapter 12). Altogether, the influence network consists of 65 nodes (ie actors, such as institutions, organisations and individuals) and 152 edges (ie relations among actors). Actors were categorised in four groups: government, civil sector, private sector, and international organisations. They share values of 60.0 %, 26.2 %, 9.2 %, and 4.6 % respectively (cf. figure 56). Clearly, government actors were named most frequently as relevant stakeholders shaping housing policies, but also the private sector and the civil society play a role. International organisations are less relevant in the network; if at all, they appear mostly as lenders for specific programmes. Of all actors, most are place-based, executing their main activities at the city (46 %) or neighbourhood level (15.3 %). Since Surabaya is the capital of East Java, the different agencies of the provincial government are also located in the city. Many of them were also mentioned as having a stake in Surabaya's housing

10 The 'rules of the game' dimension is explored in chapter 31.4 for both cities.

policy (9.2 %). Of course, actors from the national level also exert significant influence as they create national guidelines or national housing programmes to be implemented at the local level (21.5 %). Furthermore, despite all decentralisation efforts, most of the funds used in housing policies are more or less directly derived from the national level.

Surabaya's actor network in the housing domain is visualised in figure 57. Actors perceived as most influential by interviewed experts become clearly visible. Most of them are government organisations. These hubs are embedded in the centre of the network and are characterised by many and strong relations with each other. Actors from civil society (research institutions, NGOs, CBOs, residents) are located more at the network periphery, having larger distances to pass to reach most influential actors.

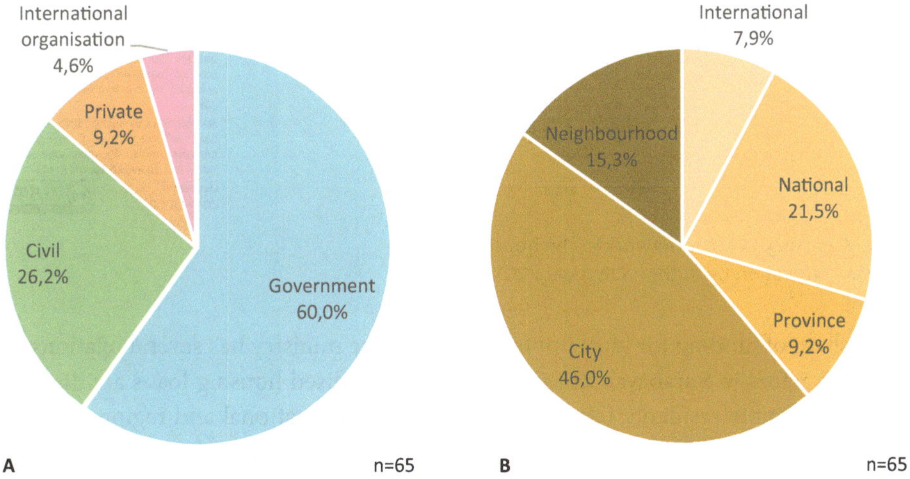

Fig. 56 Categorisation (A) and spatial levels (B) of 65 actors in Surabaya's housing policy network
Source: Illustration by author. Own data (2015)
Note: For details on the actor categorisation, see figure 15

Surabaya's Development Planning Agency (BAPPEKO) stands out as the most influential actor shaping the direction of housing policies. This result is not surprising, since it is this governmental agency that defines the development strategy of the city, creates new programmes, and supervises all other municipal agencies. BAPPEKO has the authority to issue directives for subordinate agencies and the power to prioritise the funds received from the national level (Interview 27). In the words of an employee of DPU: 'Everything we do is by the instruction through BAPPEKO. BAPPEKO is the policy maker' (Interview 29). Coordination within the network does rarely happen horizontally, but the network is organised hierarchically (Interview 33).

The national Ministry of Public Works and Housing (KPUPR) is the second most influential actor (half the value of BAPPEKO). This ministry creates the technical guidelines, rules, national housing programmes, and, most importantly, provides the

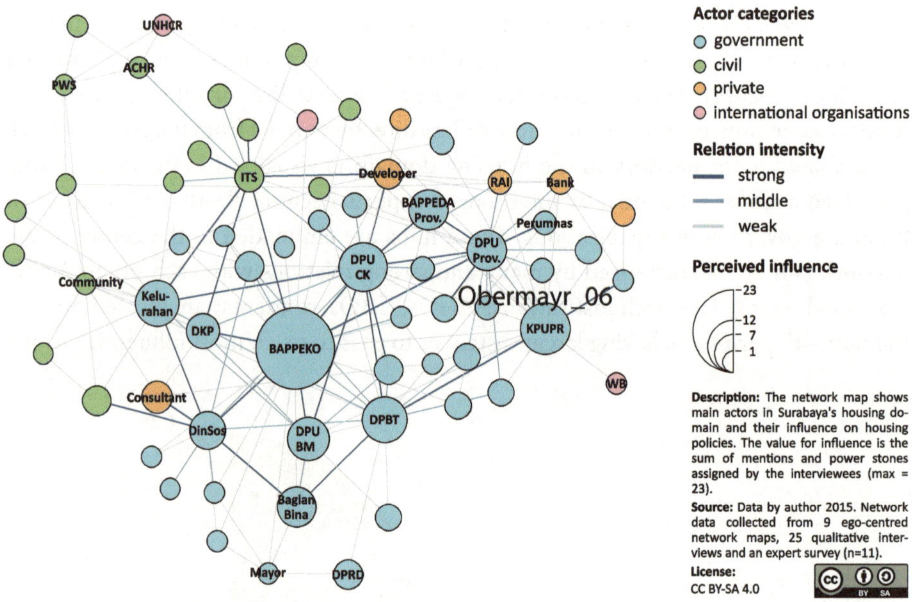

Fig. 57 Surabaya's actor network in the housing domain
Source: Illustration by author. Own data 2015

lion's share of funding for local implementation. The ministry has several relations to different actors in Surabaya's housing domain. Subsidised housing loans are disseminated to eligible residents (cf. chapter 20.5), involving national and regional banks, private developers, and their lobbying groups. Relations do also exist with DPBT and DPU Prov., with funds provided for the development of social housing (*rusunawa*), and to the two departments of DPU (Dinas Pekerjaan Umum Cipta Karya, or DPU-CK, and Dinas Pekerjaan Umum Bina Marga, or DPU-BM), guiding them in all technical questions. The national ministry also has the task of evaluating the work of BAPPEKO on a regular basis (Interview 27).

A number of municipal agencies share the next ranks of important actors. Two subdivisions of DPU are perceived as important players in Surabaya's housing domain. All activities related to development and maintenance of infrastructure (ie roads, bridges, drainage system, public facilities, etc) are handled by the Bina Marga section (DPU-BM) and all issues related to urban planning (ie spatial planning, zoning, regional spatial plan, building permits) and the general layout and design of residential areas are managed by the Cipta Karya section (DPU-CK) (Interview 28). The two sections are required to work closely together, since both are important for the development and management of the urban system. In the case of challenges concerning this cooperation, BAPPEKO works as a mediator. Ties to the sister agency at the province level (DPU Prov.) do exist, but are not very strong. Often BAPPEKO has to coordinate the two DPU sections (Interview 29).

Interestingly, three other municipal agencies stand out in the network: the Department for Construction and Land Management (DPBT), the Department for Social Services (DinSos) and the Department for Cleaning and Gardening (DKP). This is because important housing or upgrading programmes fall under their responsibility – DinSos manages the RSDK programme, DPBT the *rusunawa* programme, and DKP the Green and Clean Programme (cf. chapter 24.2). Often, private consultants (ie contracted professionals) are hired for these programmes to facilitate the implementation process. In this regard, the local administration at the neighbourhood level (*kelurahan*) plays a decisive role, since it is important for programme implementation and as an intermediary towards the communities. The RT/RW system is used for data collection and dissemination of information (Interview 33).

Another surprising result is the importance assigned to two of the province's administrative agencies (DPU Prov. and BAPPEDA). These two agencies are the mirrors of corresponding agencies at the city level. They have certainly indirect influence via their responsibilities to create overreaching development planning strategies and spatial plans at the provincial level, but because of decentralisation policies over the last years, the provincial level has lost much of its power in contrast to the city or district level (*kota/kabupaten*). The importance assigned here by the interviewees might be explained by the role of the provincial government in the relocation policies carried out along Surabaya's riverbanks. Equipped with the responsibility of supervising all rivers and their banks in East Java, the relocation of squatters to social housing units is the central task of the province's public works agency.

Political leaders (mayor) and representatives – the local House of Representatives (DPRD) – are located only at the periphery of the housing policy network. This suggests that housing policy in the city is not prioritised by politicians, but rather left to other actors and their expertise. Nevertheless, the role of the mayor was regarded as central by the interviewees. 'If there is a good housing policy, it depends on the leader' (Interview 46). 'If you want to achieve something, you have to discuss with Ibu Risma' (Interview 30). Furthermore, the importance of the mayor is credited indirectly. All referrals to subordinated institutions, such as Bagian Bina, Bagian Hukum, and Bagian Kesra, are indirect significations for the importance of local leadership. These institutions are part of the city government, directly subordinated to the mayor and have an instructing role for all other agencies including BAPPEKO. They do not instruct details on programme implementation, but supervise and coordinate the implementation of the medium and long-term development plans. In other words, they convey that outlined measures and programmes should be implemented, but leave the design and implementation to BAPPEKO as the city's central planning and coordinating agency (Interview 33). It can be concluded, however, that the priority of Surabaya's mayor is not housing, but other aspects of urban development (ie economic development and urban revitalisation).

International organisations, such as the World Bank or UN-Habitat, seem not to influence local housing policies in Surabaya, or at least not directly. They are probably more indirectly involved, by funding housing and upgrading programmes via KPUPR. The same is valid for most organisations of civil society (NGOs or CBOs). They are only located at the network's periphery; their influence on housing policies is considered as marginal by experts.

Beside the indicator of perceived influence presented in figure 57, additional centrality indicators (betweenness, degree, and closeness centrality) were calculated using social network analysis. These are commonly regarded as power indicators (cf. chapter 12.4). Together with the two indicators for perceived influence (PI1 derived from the ego-centred network maps and PI2 derived from the expert survey), they were included in a table showing the 15 most important actors in Surabaya's housing domain (cf. table 32). For each indicator the actors' rank within the network is presented

Table 32 The 15 most important actors in Surabaya's housing domain in terms of influence and centrality

#	Actor name	Category	Level	Perceived influence		Centralities			Average
				(PI1)	(PI2)	Betweenness (BC)	Closeness (CC)	Degree (DC)	
				Rank					
1	BAPPEKO	government	city	1	1	1	1	1	1
2	DPU CK	government	city	3	3	4	2	2	2.8
3	DPBT	government	city	4		2	5	4	3.8
4	DPU Prov.	government	province	7	4	4	4	3	4.4
5	Kelurahan	government	neighbourhood	5		6	6	6	5.8
6	ITS	civil	city	13	10	3	3	5	6.8
7	KPUPR	government	national	2	2	13	12	9	7.6
8	DPU BM	government	city	6	5	15	8	10	8.8
9	DinSos	government	city	10	13	8	7	7	8
10	Bapemas	government	city	14	14	14	9	8	11.3
11	DKP	government	city	11		17	11	10	12.3
12	Developer	private	city	14	25	13	10	9	11.5
13	Community	civil	city	36		7	14	8	20
14	Bagian Bina	government	city	9	28	21	18	17	16.3
15	BAPPEDA	government	province	8		22	22	31	23.8

Source: Table by author. Each indicator is calculated/derived from survey data (2015). Data for PI1 derived from ego-centred network maps (n = 9) and for PI2 from an expert survey (n = 11). BC, CC, and DC are calculated from the network graph of Surabaya's housing domain
Note: The top 10 actors for each indicator were included in the table featuring their rank (some were excluded for PI2 due to irrelevance). Influence indicators were directly assessed by experts (PI1 by Net-Map Method, PI2 by expert survey), while centrality indicators were calculated from the network graph using social network analysis (cf. chapter 12.4). The table is sorted by average rank

separately. By connecting perceived influence with centrality indicators, some interesting results become visible. Not surprisingly, most of the actors perceived as influential show also high centrality degrees (eg BAPPEKO rank one for all indicators). Some actors, however, are perceived as influential, but show only low centralities and vice versa. This is the case for KPUPR, which is perceived as very influential, but not as very important considering centrality indicators. While the ministry is certainly one of the most important actors in Indonesia's housing domain, this is not reflected in centrality, since there are not many relations to other actors within the city.

The most striking aspect, however, is the position that a local university, ITS, suddenly gained. While not regarded in the top ten considering the influence indicators, it looks different regarding centrality indicators. ITS seems to have a large stake in Surabaya's housing policy, but is not perceived as influential. Looking at the network, it can be guessed that ITS is an important gatekeeper that links the civil sector (especially residents and communities) with governmental organisations. It appears that the activities of this university over the last decades – *in situ* research in the *kampungs* and involvement in programmes related to urban upgrading, revitalisation, and urban design – have brought trust among the communities and a reputation of being an appreciated partner for government agencies. Furthermore, many alumni of ITS currently work in high positions in the city government, as for instance the incumbent mayor, Ibu Risma. For that reason the view on 'good' urban planning, *kampung* upgrading, and sound housing policies taught at ITS is also the dominant perspective among many government employees. Professor Johan Silas, former head of the housing lab at ITS and co-founder of the famous KIP programme, is a well-known and respected person in expert circles. During many interviews, these connections were emphasised, more frequently as ties to other universities or research institutions within the city or beyond. Summarising, it can be concluded that ITS is significantly shaping applied housing policies in Surabaya.

Another interesting finding from the comparison of indicators was once again the position of DPBT. This government agency is confirmed as an important stakeholder considering the centrality indicators. This was surprising, since the agency does not have many competencies and is only responsible for the *rusunawa* programme. It might be interpreted as a clue on the importance of this programme. Indeed, the social housing programme is increasingly prioritised on the national level and flats in social housing are generally perceived as the only solution for low-income people. Since the programme gained momentum in Surabaya over the last years as well, this might explain the prominent position of DPBT in the network. The communities, residents, and private developers are neglected considering the influence indicators assessed by experts. However, they gain importance when considering centrality indicators. These findings might also suggest that their influence is underrepresented by relying only on indicators of perceived influence. Certainly, the communities have an important role, since for many programmes their work and participation is required; nevertheless, this participation is more or less prescribed from above and arises less from the communities themselves as grass-root initiatives. Therefore, the findings might be interpreted more as non-participation of these actors in shaping local housing policies despite their importance in the network and for implementation processes. It seems that of the civil actors only ITS can significantly influence local housing policies.

These findings suggests that Surabaya's housing policies are mostly produced in a negotiation process between important governmental agencies, or are imposed from above (from Jakarta). Provincial agencies are involved in some aspects, especially in issues connected to the river channels. ITS seems to be involved in the negotiation process, but hardly the communities and residents at the local level or the private sector. The latter might influence housing policies at the national scale through lobbying organisations, but further research would be necessary to determine this assumption.

25.2 Discourse strands on how to house the poor in Surabaya

The discourses on how to deal with the city's poor population is entangled with the other policy arrangement dimensions and with applied housing policies. Several discourse strands could be depicted from expert interviews (cf. figure 58). Some are programme-specific or circle around one specific policy (eg resettlement of squatters). Others are more general, related to urban policies in the city. The most obvious strands are illustrated here, revealing hegemonic perceptions on slum dwellers, squatters, and proper strategies to address the housing challenge in Surabaya.

25.2.1 Becoming green, clean, and smart

In general, terms, the urban policies of Surabaya do not prioritise housing as the main challenge, but focus on other urban development issues. The problem of existing slums and squatters is seen as minor by housing experts: 'Housing is not the problem anymore in Surabaya [...] the problems are more connected to sustainability and the environment, not to providing basic shelter [...] the land is very regulated and every piece of land has an owner' (Interview 10). After decades of KIPs and other social assistance programmes, housing for the poor is considered as accomplished, and the housing challenge as largely addressed. With this dominant perception, it is not surprising that mayor Tri Rismaharini (Ibu Risma) has put a focus on other issues of rapid urban development, namely to achieve a green and orderly city. This is in line with Surabaya's quiet endeavour to imitate Singapore as a smart waterfront city (Mahizhnan 1999; King & Idawati 2010). In this regard, her urban policy is seen as good practice among the interviewed experts. It can be exemplified in the perceived importance of DKP, which seems to get priority among the city's numerous departments. This agency

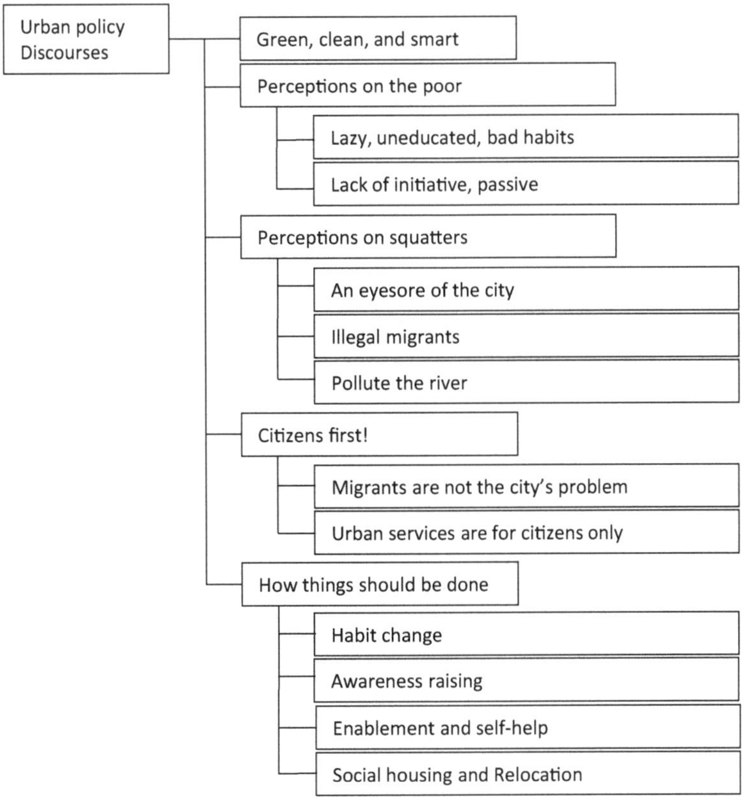

Fig. 58 Category tree for the thematic analysis of expert interviews in Surabaya
Source: Illustration by author

manages the Green and Clean Programme (cf. chapter 24.2) and was mentioned frequently during expert interviews. In addition, opinions about Ibu Risma's policy in Surabaya reflect this agenda:

> The policy, she always talks about the policy of the municipality, look at this, we have so many gardens, along the rivers, many places are upgraded, very green, this is true, it is good. But, unfortunately I found some places she didn't touch yet, and what did she say, oh yes, this is the next programme. [...] actually, if you see the housing area, it is very cool, because from the gardens along the street. But behind the surface, there is a small river, and it is very smelly and full of garbage there. [...] So she never touched it. It means that some places, which people can see directly, are properly maintained. Even for the upgrading of some part of the area, Risma's strategy is very good, not only the physical things, but the people. They touch also the community (Interview 46).

This clean, green, and smart agenda propagated by the city government is generally accepted and supported by all government officials. The policies are seen as 'touching the community' meaning that lasting changes are achieved in some fields and many initiatives are considered as successful. There are, however, also some critical thoughts on the city beautification agenda of the municipal government. Focusing this agenda means also to prioritise areas and population segments important for the city's image, but possibly neglecting other areas and marginalised population groups. Such policies are not sustainable, as some warning voices argue:

> If they only think about how to make the city beautiful, it cannot be sustainable. [...] three or four years later it will deteriorate again. But if the leader is concerned about how to improve the capability of the people, in order to develop and maintain the facilities, than it will be sustainable. So that's why, the KIP programme actually is also the programme of people empowerment (Interview 46).

It is argued that a strategy is needed that focuses on enhancing the capabilities of the people. If strategies centre only on city beautification and on the creation of a good business climate, the city might become more beautiful and proper in the short term, but will deteriorate again in the long run. Thus, it is seen as important to address the people, to increase their capabilities, to empower them to make their own living and improve their neighbourhood (Interview 46).

25.2.2 Perceptions on slum and squatter dwellers: bad habits, passive, lack of initiative

Slum dwellers are considered as poor, uneducated, and having bad habits by most of Surabaya's city authorities. Not structural reasons are seen as the causes of their bad behaviour, but their habits – something learned and internalised from childhood. The people's limited capabilities and these internalised practices are held responsible for causing inadequate environmental conditions in their settlements – 'they just do not know better than to pollute their environment' (Interview 39). From this perspective, to improve their livelihood, a proper strategy should focus on the next generation:

> [...]so we have to find a strategy how to cut this link [to their parents], this connection to the previous generation, it means this young children, we have to give them and teach them how to live in a good environment, so when they grow up and become parents, they change their habits (Interview 46).

Government officials also complain about a lack of initiative and willingness from the people to do their part in improving their livelihoods. It is explained that dwellers in inadequate units are waiting for the government to take action, but that when the authorities offer support for urban upgrading or training, the affected residents are '[...] not really committed to the programme and [would] not show up for trainings' (Interview 32). They are described as remaining passive without any self-initiative. One of the interviewees puts it as follows: '[...] people who live there, they do not know how to maintain the area. They just wait for the government programme. If there is no government programme to develop this area, they just take it easy about the situation' (Interview 46).

All these perceptions of slum dwellers are generally also assigned to squatters living in informal settlements along the city's river channels. These squatters are considered to be illegal migrants; their settlement to be an eyesore and posing an obstacle for a proper management of rivers and drainage channels. Two lines of argumentation can be found: First, it is argued that informal settlements would disturb a proper water flow in the riverbeds and generally alter the river's course (Interview 37, 10). This would cause more frequent flood events in other areas. Indeed, informal settlements located at riverbanks tend to gradually size parts of the riverbed due to the residents' activities – they build houses on stilts at the riverbed's edge and perform small-scale land reclamation by putting material and garbage into the channels. In some cases, this might have altered the channel width. Narrower river channels then might cause a higher frequency of flood events up- or downstream. This argumentation is often heard among officials, but could not be verified when visiting corresponding areas and consulting local residents or academic experts (Interview 40, 44, 46). The second argumentation is that informal settlements along the rivers would pollute the channels, since garbage and wastewater is put into them. 'They have reclaimed large parts of the river, they put all their waste into the river and only when there is a study, they clean up the kampung' (Interview 36). These activities could also be observed during field visits, but were made out of necessity and in absence of other options. Nevertheless, the visible contamination of the river channels and the surroundings of informal settlements is frequently reinterpreted as caused by the dwellers' bad habits (Interview 37, 43).

These two lines of argumentation are the underlying rationale and justification for all actions taken against informal settlements. It is thus not surprising that under this perception the only valid option is removal of existing squatters and close supervision of vacant areas along the channels to prevent reoccupation (Interview 37, 10). Relocating squatter dwellers to social housing is the strategy favoured (Interview 43, 30). Such a measure would not only benefit the affected dwellers, but would also represent an absolute necessity for the greater public good. People fighting such evictions must be aware of this reasoning to give no cause for any actions. In the case of the Strenkali community (PWS), which is still resisting any relocation attempts by the government (cf. chapter 24.4.4), the residents have understood these dominant perceptions. They try to adapt their activities in order to avoid any causes for relocation. 'They know they have to be clean' (Interview 36), otherwise they will be removed. Other reasoning for the removal of squatters, such as the interest of developers to commodify nearby land and the desire to tell the story of a beautiful and orderly world city without the eyesore of informal settlements sprawling in viewable places, are prudently kept secret.

This stance against riverbank dwellers in Surabaya and the only policy option of removal is supported by assuming them as migrants from outside Surabaya. 'If you have a deeper observation about them, you will see that they are coming from another area [...]' (Interview 29). Although these assumptions were refuted in several studies – results show very different origins of the inhabitants for specific settlements (cf. chapter 24.4.6) – the perception of 'illegal migrants' settling along the city's rivers prevails. Picturing them as the 'others', as strangers compared to Surabaya citizens makes it certainly easier to enforce clearing measures.

25.2.3 Citizens of Surabaya first!

> 'Pulang saja!' ['They should go home!'] (Interview 27)

Connected closely to the perceptions about slum and squatter dwellers is another recurring discourse strand related to citizenship. According to the institutions in place, only citizens of the respective administrative units are eligible to receive assistance from governmental programmes. This means that only residents of Surabaya holding a valid residence permit for the city (KTP) are eligible for assistance programmes (RSDK, public housing, or relocation). This has consequences for all housing or supporting programmes of the city government, in particular for the social housing programme (*rusunawa* programme) and the relocation programme.

Consequently, Surabaya's city authorities see themselves as not responsible for residents without a residence permit in the city. In the case of the relocation programme, for instance, an alternative housing option cannot be provided in the municipalities' social housing blocks (*rusunwa*). Government employees at BAPPEKO state openly that 'Illegal people are not the priority for Surabaya. Citizens of Surabaya come first' and, when asked what policy exists for them, the answer is '[...] they should go home (pulang saja)' (Interview 27). In these statements, the perception on squatters is reflected as being migrants from outside Surabaya. The view dominates that their home district is responsible for them, or the provincial government, but not the city government of Surabaya. Practical policy consequences are that in the case of relocation policies alternative housing options must be provided in social housing blocks managed by both the provincial and municipal government. This, of course, causes follow-up problems connected to coordination and spatiality (relocation options should be close to the old place, social cohesion should not be disturbed, etc).

25.2.4 How things should be done: habit change, awareness, enablement

From the perceptions of Surabaya's low-income dwellers and from the experiences with past upgrading programmes, a common understanding about necessary components of adequate housing policies and implementation procedures has emerged. There is consensus among interviewed experts about the nature of housing policies for the poor. Physical upgrading and enabling policies are seen as good strategies for existing formal *kampungs*. For informal areas, relocation to *rusunawa* is commonly seen as the only option. A general recurring perspective on a good approach to achieving lasting effects are measures that aim to initiate a 'habit change' among residents. Raising awareness, that the environment in informal settlements should not be dirty and housing structure should not be shabby, is seen as crucial. Strategies implemented, therefore, involve often so-called 'facilitators' – private professionals – who ensure the sound implementation of programmes and teach the community for instance how to recycle garbage and how to stop polluting their environment, especially the rivers and drainage channels (Interview 27). Nevertheless, it is also recognised that the poorest need support for physical improvements in housing and infrastructure:

> The most important thing is to raise the awareness of the community, that they do not produce slum areas; if they are poor, they should be helped with infrastructure; for those who are not poor, raising awareness might be enough. The Municipal Government is unlikely to provide jobs for all of them, so they have to create their own jobs, city counsellors provide tools to empower them. We help with physical and socio-economic issues (Interview 27).

This statement, made by employees at Surabaya's influential development planning agency, BAPPEKO, points to the dominant perspective about the role of the city government in housing policies. Tasks are to raise awareness among the community, to support self-help activities using training, and to raise the community's capacity to help themselves. Support for physical upgrading of housing and infrastructure is given, but considered as not expedient when not accompanied by other measures. 'Task of the city government is not to create jobs for all, but to provide social and economic assistance' (Interview 39). The perspective is perfectly in line with recommended strategies under the 'enabling approach' propagated on the global level, where the authorities' role is not to implement direct measures, but to work as an enabler, encouraging the communities' self-help abilities.

Experiences with past slum upgrading programmes support the view of how things should be done. Decades after the implementation of the first KIPs, it has become clear that physical upgrading alone is not sufficient: 'If you see my kampung now, before it had also a KIP programme, but now it's also bad again. [...] It means that people who live there, they do not know how to maintain the area. They just wait for another government programme' (Interview 46). From these observations, it is concluded that people have developed high expectations for government programmes, depleting their efforts to help themselves. Accordingly, a shift towards more comprehensive measures within an enabling environment are seen as the solution, where the upgrading of physical conditions is only one aspect that cannot be maintained without simultaneous improvements in social, economic, and organisational terms.

25.3 Characteristics of Surabaya's policy arrangement

From the analysis, the characteristics of Surabaya's housing policy arrangement unfold. Each of the dimensions has specific attributes that characterise the overall arrangement and result in city-specific housing policies. Table 33 illustrates the characteristics for each dimension. Considering actors and power, Surabaya's arrangement is quite hierarchically organised and clearly dominated by BAPPEKO. This municipal authority is by far the most important actor when it comes to shaping housing policies in the city. It is only with some distance that other actors in the network are mentioned. These are mainly other municipal authorities, which have a leading role in various programmes. All government organisations derive their influence largely from authoritative resources (ie laws and regulations). The mayor and the city's House of Representatives are positioned at the edge of the network and are not considered important for housing policies. This does not mean that they do not have any influence, but it seems that this influence is not primarily used in housing and that other policy areas are focused instead. Some of the important actors in Surabaya are also not place-based. National ministries, particularly KPUPR, are important for funding and for providing the general strategic direction. In some cases, also the provincial authorities have a say in Surabaya's housing policies, especially when the riverbanks of Surabaya are concerned. In this case, conflicting interests and unclear jurisdictions and responsibilities have led to contradictory outcomes of relocation policies.

Non-governmental actors, ie residents, NGOs, the private sector, and universities, have little influence on the general strategic direction of housing policies and hardly have a say in decision-making. ITS is the big exception here. After decades of collaboration with the municipal government and the communities, ITS has gained a good reputation for providing sound solutions and has influenced the municipal government to pursue a *kampung*-centred policy for many decades. Based on its dispositional power within the network, ITS has become an important gatekeeper and intermediary between government and communities. The university has formed an actor coalition with the municipal authorities, collaborating on many issues and sharing the same understanding about proper housing policies for the poor (*kampung*-centred, law and order, formalisation, enablement). Other non-governmental actors are less influential. The residents' participation is limited to programme implementation – where it is strong and much promoted – but does not influence strategic directions. Equally low is the influence of NGOs and CBOs on housing policies at the city level. Their impact

Table 33 Characteristics of Surabaya's housing policy arrangement

Actors – Hierarchical network – Mostly government actors (60%) – Several municipal agencies have programme lead: DPU, DinSos, DPBT, and DKP – Provincial agencies are present – Non-governmental actors (ITS, consultants) works as intermediaries – Communities and their working groups (*Pokjas*) participate in project implementation – KPUPR provides funding and strategic directions – International actors are absent	**Power** – BAPPEKO is by far the most influential actor – Government actors are most powerful – Power is largely derived from rules and is based on authoritative resources – Exception: Dispositional power of ITS – Communities and residents hardly have a say in decision-making – Mayor and House of Representatives are not relevant
Rules of the game – Local authorities are responsible for their low-income population (UU 01/2011) – Requirement to draw spatial plans for settlement development – Only citizens are eligible for social housing – Riverbanks are in the formal responsibility of the province – Social housing is only temporary (9 years) – Social housing is managed by municipal authorities (DPBT) and provincial authorities (DPU)	**Discourses** – Green, clean, and smart city is the goal – Slum/Squatter dwellers are poor, uneducated, lazy, have bad habits, and are passive; they do not know better – Squatters are migrants, they are an eyesore, they pollute the river and disturb the water flow – Awareness building and enabling is the right approach to improve housing conditions – Social housing, relocations, evictions – Citizens first!
Applied policies *Type of programme* – Community and economic empowerment (C-KIP and Kampung Unggulan programme) – City beautification (Green and Clean) – Social housing (*rusunawa* programme) – Resettlement: relocation to *rusunawa* – Social assistance (RSDK)	 *Implementation procedure* – Top-down by the local government – Mediated by non-governmental actors – Resident participation in programme implementation not in decision-making

Source: Table by author
Note: Rules of the game are presented in chapter 31.4, where they are examined in more detail

is mostly limited to neighbourhoods or quarters (*kelurahan*) where they strongly contribute to self-help initiatives and programme implementation. Only rarely do they gain citywide attention by organising the communities (as in the case of PWS protesting against evictions). The private sector, developers, and their advocacy organisations also did not appear as important for housing policies for low-income people during this study. The reason is probably their disinterest in housing provision for the poor since it is not profitable. Nevertheless, a large influence on the rules of the game in Indonesia's housing sector at the national level can be presumed, along with an aim to shape laws in their favour.

Several rules of the game influence Surabaya's housing policy arrangement (cf. chapter 31.4). There are national rules and regulations derived from housing laws that determine the resources and capacity of each actor in the network (eg the dominance of BAPPEKO) as well as their tasks and responsibilities. Large parts of new responsibilities have only been established recently with the enactment of the housing and settlement law, (UU01/2011) – eg the requirement of establishing a more detailed planning and monitoring system for residential areas. Other rules influence applied housing policies more directly: only citizens of Surabaya can benefit from housing programmes, social housing flats are for temporary accommodation only, and the riverbanks (and squatter settlements located there) fall under the jurisdiction of the provincial government. In Surabaya, these rules cause manifold follow-up problems of coordination and conflicting interests. A dual structure of agencies at the provincial and municipal levels is the result, with overlapping responsibilities lacking coordination and transparency. For residents who are affected by relocations and demand compensation, for instance, this uncertainty and lack of transparency creates a flawed image of authorities and does not exactly contribute to more trust in the city government.

Several discourse fields characterise Surabaya's housing discourse. These are the general orientation of urban policies, dominant views on slum and squatter residents, and opinions on sound housing policies. The interviewees no longer regarded the provision of housing as the central topic of urban development. After many years of Kampung Improvement Programmes, the housing issue and the problem of informality is considered as largely solved. Therefore, the aim of the city administration is now to create a clean, green, and smart urban environment. Considering slum and squatter residents, the respondents were relatively united in their opinion. In general, slum dwellers were considered as poor, uneducated, and passive. The reason for poor environmental conditions and insufficient housing structures in their settlements would be their bad behaviour and their laziness. Even worse were the opinions about squatter residents. For the most part, they are not seen as citizens of Surabaya and the image prevails that they pollute the river channels and disturb a proper water flow. These views were found in one form or another among all the experts interviewed. This narrative therefore serves as a justification and breeding ground for the realisation of forced evictions. In general, however, resettlement to social housing is preferred, at least for citizens of Surabaya. All others are not eligible for municipal assistance. There is a consensus that social housing is the only solution for informal settlements. For formalised settlements, however, physical upgrading, social and economic support through empowerment programmes, and, in general, the enabling approach is considered to be appropriate.

The aspects of these four dimensions culminate in Surabaya's policy arrangement, from which the city's housing policy emerges. The city government implements a variety of programmes that are related to livelihood improvements and go beyond pure housing provision. In addition to the national social housing programme, which is strongly promoted, the city has implemented local initiatives for city beautification, community and economic empowerment, and a social assistance programme for families in need. Resettlement to *rusunawa* is being supported for the remaining informal settlements. Surabaya implements all these measures top-down, often in strong cooperation or with the advice of a local university (ITS). In the cases of measures for the *kampungs,* residents are involved in programme implementation, but not in decision-making.

26 Summary: Kampung-centred and Excluding

This chapter has examined and analysed Surabaya's housing policies and the content and organisation of Surabaya's housing policy arrangement. The following questions guided the analysis:

What are the characteristics of Surabaya's policy arrangement in the housing domain?
- What intervention strategies and programmes are realised for the poor and what do they achieve?
- Which actors are relevant in the housing domain and what influence do they hold?
- What strands shape the local discourse on housing the poor?
- What are the formal and informal rules of the game?

Tropical Holland, City of Heroes, City of Kampungs, Sparkling Surabaya – Surabaya has already received many names that stand for past eras, for certain characteristics of its inhabitants, for the urban structure, or for a visionary future. In all these terms there is a true core and all these terms can be associated with the housing question. Historically, Surabaya has always been a dual city, where the European city ('tropical Holland') stood in stark contrast to the indigenous villages, the Indonesian *kampungs*. This duality between formal and informal space production has continued throughout the 20th century and is responsible for recurring conflicts over land and housing. The inhabitants of the *kampungs* were celebrated as heroes after independence, so that the informal production of space dominated until the 1960s. During this period the city grew rapidly, the *kampungs* became more and more crowded and informal settlements spread to all open spaces. Informality dominated the street scene and soon the city was known nationwide as the 'City of Kampungs'. In the 1970s, the city administration began to react. With the advice of architects and civil engineers from ITS, the city government began to pursue a *kampung*-oriented policy. This policy aimed at maintaining, formalising, and gradually improving existing *kampungs* on the one hand, and took a firm stance against illegal settlements, not shying away from forced evictions, on the other. This policy of preservation on the one hand and rigid action against informality on the other has, with some exceptions, not changed until today. After decades of slum upgrading programmes (KIPs), the city has become known among experts for its successful approach towards slums. Since the 2000s, the trend of city revitalisation and beautification has intensified. Branded as 'Sparkling Surabaya', every part of the city is made to 'shine', to be attractive for investors and tourists. Informal settlements do not fit into this picture of a city that is being presented as a second Singapore, as a green, clean, and smart city. Similar to colonial times, a new tropical world-class city is imagined, a city that once again is named together with the other great metropolises of Asia.

In order to realise this vision, the city administration has developed various strategies that go beyond the housing sector. National and an increasing number of local programmes are implemented. One of the most important housing programmes in the city is the national *rusunawa* programme. Besides Jakarta, Surabaya was one of the country's pioneers in implementing social housing and since the 1990s, the programme has been pursued with great determination. Over the years, the design of social housing blocks was considerably optimised and more flats are being completed every year. Nevertheless, the demand is by far greater than the supply. After the termination of the national KIPs, the city decided to continue efforts for improving living conditions in the *kampungs*. Several locally funded initiatives were started that were now less concerned with physical upgrading, but rather follow the enabling approach, aiming to improve the residents' self-help capacities. Among these programmes are C-KIP, Green and Clean, Kampung Unggulan, and the RSDK programme. What all these programmes have in common is an approach of providing incentives to initiate economic or social development. Ideally, the communities maintain this development later on. The Green and Clean Programme for example, offers prize money for the best idea and the cleanest neighbourhood. Through the competitive mechanism, innovative ideas are furthered and simultaneously the winning neighbourhoods improve their *kampung* using the prize money, which is earmarked for this purpose. In this way a gradual improvement of living conditions in the neighbourhoods is achieved at low cost. This policy of dealing with the formal *kampungs* contrasts sharply with the way the city's informal settlements are addressed. The prevailing view is that only relocation to social housing is a viable option for squatter settlements. The goal is to gradually clear all 'illegally' occupied areas in the city. The example of the riverbank communities shows that this is by no means an easy task. The inhabitants have organised themselves and do not give up their homes easily, especially since the offered alternative in social housing is only for registered citizens of Surabaya, excluding all others. Different responsibilities between provincial and city government further complicate the situation. So far, there is no solution in sight.

The implemented programmes are based on a specific policy arrangement in the housing domain with its four dimensions: actors, power, rules of the game, and discourse. Considering actors and power, the development planning agency BAPPEKO is by far the most important actor in Surabaya's housing policy network. The network itself is organised hierarchically and consists largely of government actors. Apart from BAPPEKO, several other municipal actors are important, depending on their role in the implementation of individual programmes. Hardly any other actors from civil society or the private sector are relevant in the network; only the local university, ITS, is an exception. As an intermediary between communities and government and an advisor of the city government, ITS has significantly influenced housing policies over the last decades. The constellation of actors in the network is largely based on authoritative resources that are derived from national law. These laws are interpreted quite strictly in Surabaya, which causes problems in some cases. The rule that only registered citizens of Surabaya are eligible to benefit from assistance programmes, for instance, excludes a large part of the population. Another example is the unclear jurisdiction over the riverbanks, which creates problems for riverbank communities, which must prepare for further forced evictions. This is also reflected in the housing discourse that serves to justify further evictions. Slum and squatter residents are portrayed as poor, uneducated, lazy, passive, and having bad habits. The city's goal for urban development is to achieve a green, clean, and smart city. In such a city, there is no place for poor neighbourhoods that are seen as an eyesore to be eradicated. Therefore, the city's experts consider it the best strategy to relocate squatters to social housing and to demolish their homes.

The analysis reveals a stable policy arrangement in Surabaya's housing domain that is hierarchically organised and shaped most of all by agencies from the city administration. These governmental agencies create the city's housing policy and implement it top-down. Participation of non-governmental actors is virtually non-existent at the strategic and decision-making level. Regarding resulting housing policies, a clear separation in dealing with formal and informal housing has become perpetuated. Backed by an ideology of formalisation, formal settlements can benefit from many supportive measures. Informal settlements, in contrast, are only intended to be demolished, their residents to be moved elsewhere or relocated to social housing. Even with the election of Tri Rismaharini as mayor in 2010, not much has changed. However, Surabaya does indeed take a leading role in the preservation and further development of traditional *kampungs*. A variety of ideas and innovative processes have evolved, as for instance through the Green and Clean Programme. However, the poorest parts of society are excluded from the city's support. Surabaya's housing policy can therefore only partly be described as progressive and certainly not as inclusive. Whether this finding can clearly be linked to the described policy arrangement must be analysed from a comparative perspective.

VI. CASE STUDY: SURAKARTA (SOLO)

This chapter presents the results of the empirical fieldwork in Surakarta (Solo), arriving at deep insights in the content and organisation of Solo's housing policy arrangement. The first section introduces the city by presenting the latest socio-economic data, examining Solo's urban structure and urban development trends, and exploring the current housing situation in the city. The second section analyses the city's applied housing policies. After briefly identifying urban policies for the poor, three intervention strategies are examined in more detail – social housing and resettlement programmes and the row-housing concept. Through this analysis, the progressive character of the implemented policies becomes apparent. The third section presents and analyses the actor influence network and dominant discourse strands shaping applied housing policies in the city. The final section summarises the results and reveals the main characteristics of Solo's housing policy arrangement. The following questions guide this chapter:

<u>What are the characteristics of Solo's policy arrangement in the housing domain?</u>
- What intervention strategies and programmes are realised for the poor and what do they achieve?
- Which actors are relevant in the housing domain and what influence do they hold?
- What strands shape the local discourse on housing the poor?
- What are the formal and informal rules of the game?

27 Introduction to Solo

Surakarta, more commonly known as 'Solo'[1], is a medium-sized Indonesian city of about 520,000 inhabitants (2019) in the centre of Java Island, roughly 500km east of Jakarta. The city is located in a flatland corridor between high volcanoes that limit the view to the east and west (East: Mt. Lawu 3,265m; West: Mt. Merapi 2,914m and Mt. Merabu 3,142m), where important transport links are running from north to south. Administratively, the city belongs to Central Java Province (Java Tengah) with the provincial capital of Semarang located approximately 100 km to the north-west. Three districts (*kabupaten*) surround the city (Sukoharjo, Boyolali, and Karanganyar) and the longest river of Java, the Bengawan Solo River, marks the city boundary to the east. The city extends over an area of 44 km^2 and is divided in five sub-districts (Laweyan, Serengan, Pasar Kliwon, Jebres, and Banjarsari), composed of 54 quarters (*kelurahan*), 626 community units (RW), and 2,786 neighbourhood (RT) units (BPS Surakarta 2019: 15). Selected data are provided in table 34.

Table 34 Administrative and population data, Solo

Indicator	Source	Value
Administrative divisions 2019	[a]	5 *Kecamatan*, 54 *Kelurahan* 626 RW, 2 786 RT
City area (km^2)	[b]	44.04
Population 2019*	[c]	519 587
Population of the urban region** 2010	[d]	2 125 000
Population of the metropolitan region 2019*	[e]	5 788 234

Source: Table by author. Data compiled from: **[a]** BPS Surakarta (2019), **[b, c]** BPS Surakarta (2020b), **[d]** World Bank (2015a: 152–153), **[e]** BPS Boyolali (2020)
Note: *Population data projected from the 2010 census; ** Urban region defined as continuous built-up area derived from satellite imagery

1 The city's official name is Surakarta and this name is found often in government documents and maps. However, since the residents call their city 'Solo' this denomination is also preferred in this study.

The topography of Solo's urban area is mostly flat, with an altitude of approximately 85m above sea level. Only in the northern part, north of Kali Anyar, does the landscape becomes more hilly with altitudes reaching 135m at maximum (Fabrianti 2010: 11). The climate is tropical with hardly any temperature fluctuations during the year, an annual temperature average of 27.3 °C and annual precipitation sums of 1.800mm (BPS Surakarta 2020b). Depending on diverging monsoon conditions, the year is separated into a rainy season ranging approximately from November until May and a dry season from June until October. During the dry season, the conditions are slightly hotter but feel more convenient due to less humidity. Since all of the rain is concentrated in a few months of the year, with peaks in December and January, riverine flooding occurs frequently during these months. Especially the eastern parts of the city, close to the Bengawan Solo River, are affected by recurring flood events.

Solo is a cultural, economic, and political centre of regional and national significance. Together with Yogyakarta, a city of similar size roughly 60 km to the southwest, the city is regarded as the home of Javanese culture. Both cities trace their origin to the Mataram kingdom and Solo became a palace city in 1745, when the ruler of Mataram kingdom, Pakubuwono II, moved his court during the Javanese succession wars to this strategic place close to the Bengawan Solo River. Unlike the port cities at the northern coast of Java island (Semarang, Surabaya, Jakarta), Solo and Yogyakarta were less influenced by the Dutch during colonial times since they remained autonomous vassal states. Both cities were important seats of rivalling parts of the ruler family, forming separate Javanese kingdoms, which gave up their authority to the Indonesian republic after independence (Vorlaufer 2009: 88). Traces of this history can still be found in both cities, eg the *kraton*, the palace and home of the sultan, and the surrounding areas, where the cultural and historic heart of both cities is located. Although Solo's sultan is deprived from any political power today, he remains an important figure in cultural and traditional terms. In many respects, both cities have been rivals in the past. While Yogyakarta developed as a centre of services, tourism, and science, Solo's economy is more based on trade, manufacturing (chemical and textile products), construction as well as restaurant and hotel services (BPS Surakarta 2020b). Solo is not only an important industrial centre and trade hub in the region, known for its textile products (Batik) and traditional handicrafts, but also an important centre of education, with two universities. In recent years, the city has been promoting its cultural heritage, establishing itself increasingly as major tourist destination, attracting mostly domestic tourists.

Officially, Solo has a population of around 520,000 inhabitants (2019) excluding informal and temporary residents. This number suggests a medium-sized city, but considering the continuous built-up area in the surroundings, an urban agglomeration emerges (cf. figure 59) – home to an estimated 2.1 million people (World Bank 2015a: 153). The official metropolitan region, including six surrounding districts reaches far into rural areas (known as *Subosukawonosraten*[2]) and is, with approximately 5.8 million inhabitants, even larger.

27.1 Latest data on population, poverty and human development, Solo

Some of the latest data on population, human development, and poverty are provided in table 35. The population data are obtained from the statistical department of the city (BPS Surakarta), reflecting a projection from the 2010 nationwide population census. According to these data, 518,000 people were living in Solo in 2018, a number that has grown by 12,474 people or 0.41 % annually from 2012 to 2018. These numbers, of course, reflect only the *de facto* population – everyone with official place of residence in Solo, and excludes all informal residents (temporary workers, residents of informal settlements, etc). Drawing on the civil registration register[3], this population number shows, with 575,230 people, considerably higher records (BPS Surakarta 2020b: 35). Whatever the real numbers of Solo's inhabitants, the available data suggest

Table 35 Data on population (projected), poverty and human development, Solo

Indicator	Year						
	2012	2013	2014	2015	2016	2017	2018
Projected population [A]	505 413	507 825	510 077	512 226	514 171	516 102	517 887
Population change on prev. year [B]		2412	2252	2149	1945	1931	1785
Population change per year (%) [C = B/A)*100]		0.47	0.44	0.42	0.38	0.37	0.34
Poor people	60 475	59 679	55 920	55 710	55 910	54 900	46 990
Poverty line in Rp. per person per month (in €)*	361 517 (30)	403 121 (29)	385 467 (24)	406 840 (27)	430 293 (29)	448 062 (30)	464 063 (28)
Percentage poor (%)	12.02	11.75	10.96	10.88	10.87	10.64	9.07
Human Development Index (HDI)	78.44	78.89	79.34	80.14	80.76	80.85	

Source: Table by author. Data compiled/calculated from BPS Surakarta (2020a)
Note: [A] Projected population data are based on the 2010 census; *Currency converted using historical annual average conversion rates from fxtop.com

2 *Subosukawonosraten* is an acronym of the districts *Sukoharjo, Boyolali, Surakarta, Karanganyar, Wonogiri, Sragen and Klaten*. The area of this metropolitan region stretches far into rural areas, and the southern part of Wonogiri even touches the Indian Ocean. The designation as metropolitan region thus is a bit misleading; it is moreover an artificial construct for administrative purposes.

3 The civil registration register holds data obtained from lower administrative levels. It uses a *de facto* approach, compared to the *de jure* approach used in census data.

a slowly growing population, but population growth is happening most of all in the suburban areas in the surrounding districts. Increasingly more commuters are recorded from outside Solo, raising the city's day population to more than 1.5 million (Yayasan Kota Kita 2015: 8).

The city shows promising improvements in the last years considering poverty levels and human development. In the period from 2012 to 2018, the the Human Development Index has continuously increased, reaching 80.85 in 2017, and the number of poor people has decreased from approximately 60,000 (2012) to 47,000 (2018). The official poverty degree was 9.07 % in 2018. This calculation is based on the official poverty line[4], which was set to a monthly per capita income of Rp. 464,000 (appox. 28€) for the year 2018. With these data Solo clearly beats the national average considering the HDI (0.71 in 2018) and poverty degree (9.42 % in 2019). Spatial analysis using geographical information technologies suggest that poverty is not concentrated in segregated neighbourhoods, but rather a certain amount of poverty is evident in all areas of the city (Obermayr 2017: 121). Most poor people live in the more densely populated areas, in the southeastern part of the city, those areas that are prone to riverine floods. Other concentrations of poverty are on the riverbanks, along railroad lines and generally on government-owned land where informal settlements have spread. Even though living costs can be considered as cheap compared to the largest Indonesian cities of Jakarta and Surabaya, the opposite is true compared to other cities in Central Java. Monthly minimum consumption expenditures (ie the poverty line) are highest in Solo, even outpacing this indicator for the provincial capital Semarang (RKPD 2018: II – 17). Other data on poverty are provided by the Department for Social Services (DinSos) based on their social assistance programmes. These data describe poverty with a degree of 16.8 % (2018) for the city, meaning that 86,000 people can be considered as poor (BPS Surakarta 2019: 158). All available statistical data, however, tell a story of successful development, improvements in living conditions, and reduction of poverty over the last decade.

27.2 Historical roots and urban development

In the area where today the city of Surakarta (Solo) is located, only few small villages could be encountered at the beginning of the 18th century. The area belonged to the Sultanate of Mataram, an empire controlling large parts of Central Java from its seat in Plered near Kotageda, today a neighbourhood of Yogyakarta (Qomarun & Pray-

4 Every year, the central statistics agency sets an annual poverty line at the national, provincial and district levels. The calculation is based on a bundle of food and non-food items and specifies the monthly minimum consumption expenditures per capita (cf. box 11 for details). People who have an income below this line are considered as being poor.

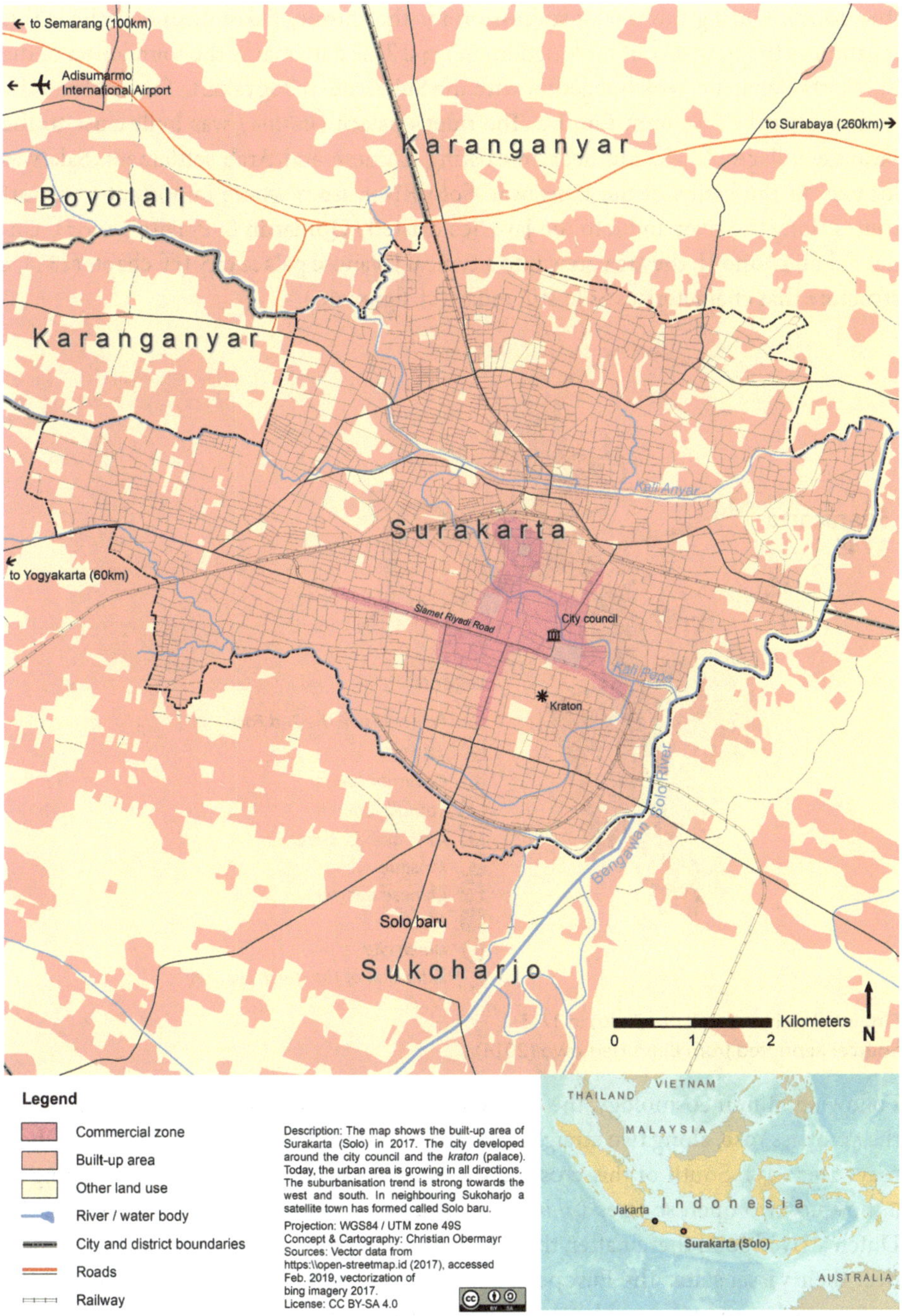

Fig. 59 Surakarta (Solo) and surrounding districts 2017
Source: Illustration by author

itno 2007). During the war of succession for the throne, Pakubuwono II chose this location as the new seat of his kingdom in 1745. This date marks the foundation of the Surakarta Sunanate, which together with the Sultanate of Yogyakarta formed from the remnants of the Mataram Empire. The ruler's palace (*kraton*) was built close to the Javanese village of Sala and near an existing Chinese and Arab settlement. Sala was located on the banks of the Bengawan Solo River, from where important transport routes along the river and into the Java Sea existed (Qomarun & Prayitno 2007). Under Pakubuwono II, the area grew into a typical Javanese palace city (cf. chapter 18.1), a structure that characterises Solo still today (cf. figure 60).

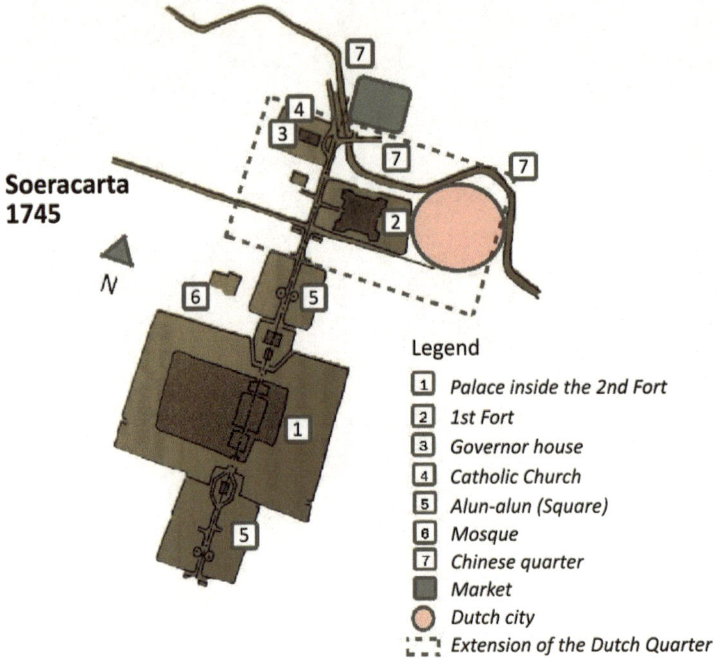

Fig. 60 Sketch of Surakarta (Solo) in 1745
Source: Reprinted from Bimo Hernowo (2016)

Following Hindu cosmology, the different elements of the city core were oriented at the compass rose, along two straight lines from west to east and north to south (Obermayr 2017: 93). South of this crossing the palace complex was located, consisting of a mosque, two open squares (*alun-alun*), and the actual palace buildings. When the Dutch arrived soon thereinafter, they established a fort nearby in order to exert power over their vassal state. The European quarter grew around this fort, consisting of the governor's house and a residential area towards the east. Towards the northeast the central market is located (Pasar Gede), surrounded by the former Chinese settlement that was incorporated into the city and remains until today an important commercial zone. The governor's house and buildings nearby are the seat of the city administration today and Pasar Gede is still the most important traditional market of Solo. All areas surrounding this historical heart of the city were slowly filled by residential areas (*kampungs*) characterised by their irregular structure. Although continuously reshaped over the years, this historical area remains today the cultural and political heart of the city. From this city core, urban development took place in all directions during different urban development phases. In the 19th century, more and more migrants came to the city and the individual quarters increasingly segregated (into Javanese, European, Chinese, and Arab quarters). Near the city centre, and especially in the European quarter, urban planning was based on European guidelines and architecture. In between and further away from the centre, however, a rather unregulated urban development began. To the east, the Arab settlement and the Javanese village became part of the city, but Bengawan Solo River limited further urban extensions. In the second half of the 19th century, river trade lost more and more of its importance. The river increasingly silted up, making it more difficult to navigate. This was due to the introduction of the plantation system by the Dutch, which caused deforestation in many areas, leading to increasing erosion and consequently to the silting up of the rivers (Qomarun & Prayitno 2007). In addition, from 1873 onwards the railroad connected Solo with Semarang, so that the transport of goods completely shifted to the railways. This also changed the orientation of urban development. Initially, the city had developed eastwards towards the river, but now the railroad stations in the north (Balapan and Solo Jebres) and the central road towards the west (connection to Semarang and Yogyakarta) were the focal points of urban expansions. By 1945 the city had extended north towards the railway line and to the west along the central development axis of Slamet Riyadi road roughly until the stadium Sriwedari.

When Indonesia gained independence, the Sunanate of Surakarta lost much of its previous influence. Subsequently, the mayor and the city administration became actors that are more important and the following years were characterised by unregulated urban development. This changed under the New Order, when the city government began to exert a tighter grip. It was only in the 1970s when a construction boom set in that urban development became increasingly dominated by market forces, and especially on the central western axis, higher and more modern buildings were developed. The old centre slowly lost its importance, showing signs of deterioration, and a new business centre emerged further west (Zaida & Arifin 2010). In the 1980s, the real estate boom accelerated similar to other Indonesian cities. More and more banks and hotels opened branches in the city and the first shopping centres were built. This boom continued until the end of the 1990s, when a financial and political crisis set in, sweeping away the Suharto regime (Qomarun & Prayitno 2007).

27.3 Today's urban structure and latest developments since the 2000s

From this historic urban development, today's urban structure emerges (cf. figure 59). Solo's urban landscape is characterised by built-up structures mostly one or two storeys tall. Only few higher buildings, latest hotel developments, shopping malls or tenements, stand out of this structure (cf. figure 61). According to BPS, 66 % of Solo's area is dedicated for residential purposes and roughly 100,000 houses are located in the city (DPU Surakarta 2011). Most of these residential houses are located in urban *kampungs* and accommodate a household of five persons on average, ie the (greater) family. Frequently, the ground floor is used for commercial activities: small shops, home-based industries, or food stalls are located there (Obermayr 2017:123).

The political and economic heart of the city is located in the southeast around the Kraton and the historic European quarter. Around these areas, many *kampungs* are located and population densities are highest, with up to 15,000 people per km^2 in the sub-districts of Pasar Kliwon and Serengan. Nevertheless, residential houses rarely reach more than three floors. Further east, towards the river, poverty and informality increases and the area is frequently threatened by riverine floods. The other three sub-districts in the northern and western part of the city show lesser population densities, which is also reflected in land use patterns. Altogether, in 2016, 66 % or 29.07 km^2 of the city area is used for housing purposes and roughly 17 % is needed for commercial and industrial activities (BPS Surakarta 2019: 13). Fallow land (2.5 %) and agricultural land (4.4 %) can still be found in the two northern sub-districts of Jebres and Banjarsari located north of Kali Anyar (ibid.). These northern areas are the city's least developed regions, still characterised by a village atmosphere and existing agricultural activities. Rice and other crops are still cultivated in some areas and chickens running on the smaller roads are a frequent sight. This is likely to change. Developers realising housing and real estate projects increasingly target the area and also the authorities aim to develop the area by the extension of infrastructure and services. Soon there will be nothing left of the agriculture and the village character.

Most residents consider Slamet Riyadi Road as the centre of the city. This central road leads west from the historic centre, cuts through the whole city and from there to Yogyakarta and Semarang. Most commercial activities are concentrated along this road: modern shopping malls, hotels, banks, and other high-rise office buildings. This trend continues to the west, where new hotels and shopping malls have been built in more recent times, spilling over the city limits, as is visible in the emergence of large suburbs. In the eastern district, Jebres, Solo's state university, UNS, is located and the surrounding district is clearly directed to the needs of 20,000 students, characterised by dormitories and food-stalls. Small-scale Industries are scattered all over the city, but concentrate in the eastern and western edges. Larger industrial estates are located outside the city boundaries, most importantly towards the west in Sukoharjo.

Fig. 61 Solo's 'skyline' and latest hotel and office developments
Photos: Christian Obermayr, 2014–2017

In 2001, Solo's authorities announced a new vision for the city's future development: Solo was to become a cultural city, based on trading, services, education, tourism, and sports. The slogan 'Solo, the Spirit of Java' was born (Zaida & Arifin 2010). This vision is to be achieved by integrated policies and comprehensive revitalisation measures. After the economic crisis in the late 1990s, informality had been on the rise in Solo. The government tried to address this development by formalisation policies. New market houses were built throughout the city to accommodate informal street vendors and resettlement policies were initiated for the many informal settlements in the city.

The revitalisation measures also included the traditional batik industry, which is being promoted as a distinctive element of the city. Various projects have also been initiated in an attempt to make the city more attractive for tourists. One of these projects is the revitalisation of the historical centre, which is to become a tourist magnet. In addition, the creation of new large hotels has been allowed, aiming to increase comfort for external visitors. The northern ring road and the expansion of the airport to the north of the city, finally, should provide a development boost for the neglected northern region.

Latest urban developments, however, are increasingly taking place outside the city boundaries. Due to rising land prices within the city and increasing motorisation, industrial and residential suburbanisation has become a strong urban development trend over the last decades (Buchori et al. 2020). Industries are increasingly developed towards the east and west, along arterial roads towards Surabaya and Yogyakarta/Semarang respectively. These new centres of manufacturing are accompanied by new residential developments, resulting in an urban landscape that consumes more and more land. Towards the south, another massive urban expansion has taken shape, not driven by the development along major transportation links, but by the activities of real estate investors and developers. There, a new urban centre has been established in Grogol called 'new Solo' (Solo Baru). Located around a shopping mall (Hartono Mall) the most exclusive villas and large estates for high-income groups can be found. Increasingly more trade activities, retail stores, and shopping malls are concentrated in this area and this agglomeration has already reached the status of a satellite town with an estimated 100,000 inhabitants. Around this area increasingly more residential projects are developed in former green paddy fields, characterised as so-called 'clusters' – gated housing areas of 20 to 50 rowhouses constructed by developers for high- to middle-income groups (cf. figure 62 and figure 63). These suburbanisation tendencies have happened mostly unplanned. Spatial planning efforts are still based on district boundaries and up to now no effective planning regime is in place for the greater Solo region. Follow-up problems are increasing traffic congestion in and around Solo as well as the continuing transformation of fertile agricultural land.

27.4 Solo's housing situation

As in other Indonesian cities, the common settlement type in Solo is the *kampung*. In planning documents (eg RKPD 2018) residential areas are categorised into four types: traditional residential, flood-prone residential areas, slum and squatter settlements, and suburban residential areas. This categorisation differs from the one in Surabaya, where formal and informal settlements are more clearly distinguished. Traditional residential areas in Solo are mostly located in the historical regions of the city close to the centre and comprise all areas of cultural and architectural value (eg *kraton* and surrounding area, *kampung* areas). Historically, the formal city and colonial buildings

Fig. 62 Middle-class housing developments at Solo's southern urban fringe
Photos: Christian Obermayr 2016

Fig. 63 Gates, walls, and security guards ensure privacy in these so-called 'clusters' – middle-class housing developments in Solo's suburbs
Photos: Christian Obermayr, 2016

have enclosed these cultural sites and inner-city *kampungs*. Over the years, *kampungs* have been continuously subdivided and are thus characterised by high population densities (Obermayr 2017: 123–124).

Thanks to upgrading efforts in the past (eg KIP programmes; cf. chapter 20.1) most of the areas were improved and regularised over the years (owner-occupation), but many of them also show signs of deterioration (DPU Surakarta 2011: 22). Since city authorities consider these historical quarters, including inner-city *kampungs*, as unique and worth protecting, they receive special attention, and revitalisation efforts are ongoing (RKPD 2018: IV, 18–22). Towards Bengawan Solo River, east of the centre, some of the most densely populated *kampungs* are located, characterised by a more deteriorated condition. These areas are frequently affected by riverine floods or flooding caused by heavy rainfall events. Infrastructure (drainage channels, flood protection), and housing and environmental conditions are inadequate and need attention by governmental programmes.

Slum (*kampung kumuh*) and squatter areas (*kampung liar*) are distinguished from 'ordinary' *kampungs*. They can be differentiated according to legal status as well as housing and infrastructure conditions (cf. chapter 18.2.2). Slum areas (here used as a catch-all term for substandard housing areas) cover 360 ha or 12.9 % of Solo's residential area and are seen as a serious challenge for the city administration (SK Walikota 413.21/38.3/1/2016). They are scattered throughout the city (cf. figure 64), but are mostly in the more densely populated southern part of the city (south of Kali Anyar). Smaller

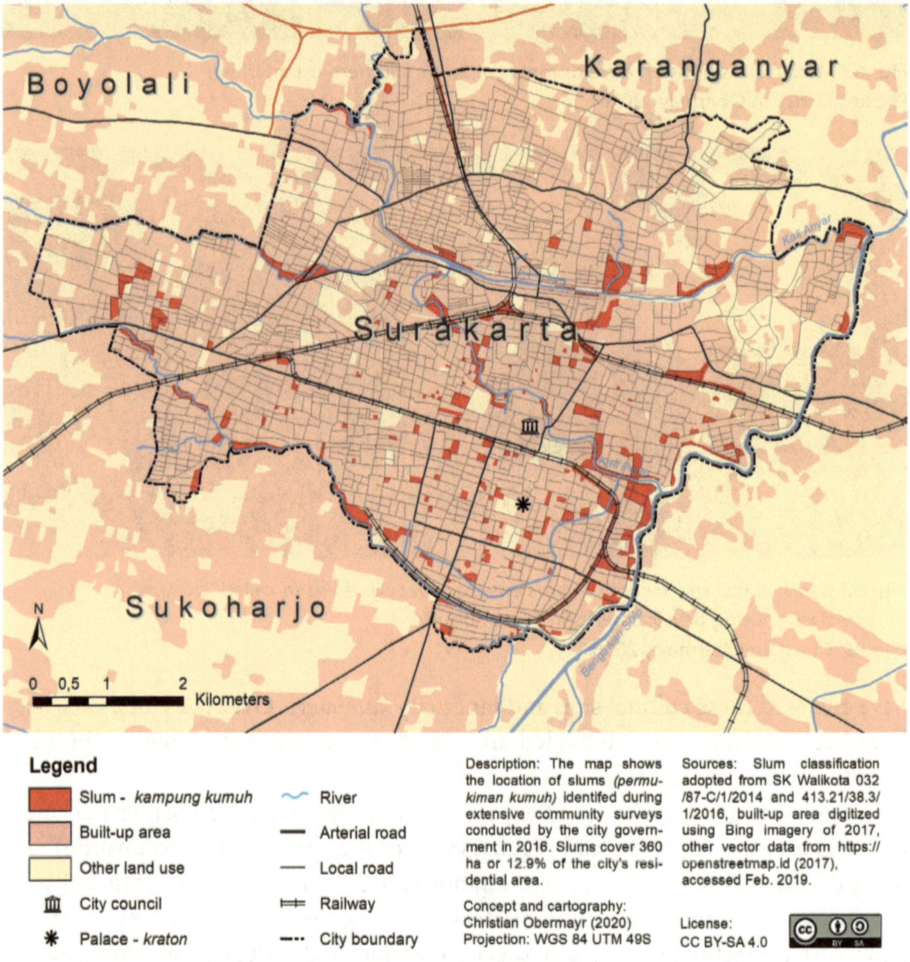

Fig. 64 Location of slum areas in Solo 2016
Source: Illustration by author. Data from SK Walikota 032/97-C/1/2014 and SK Walikota 413.21/38.3/1/2016

patches of substandard housing considered as slums can be found within almost every better-off *kampung*, but inadequate conditions are most severe at the riverbanks, along railway tracks, near the centres of economic activities, at some graveyards, and on other patches of government-owned land. There, the settlements are considered squatter settlements (*kampung liar*), or unauthorised and illegal settlements (Obermayr & Astuti 2016; SK Walikota 032/97-C/1/2014; SK Walikota 413.21/38.3/1/2016). Altogether, Solo is considered as having a large amount of sub-standard houses and a serious housing backlog, which has worsened over the years. Estimates suggest that 18,000 houses are sub-standard in the city and 20,000 to 33,000 further units would be needed to meet the housing demand (DPU Surakarta 2011: 12–13).

28 Content: Housing Policies in Solo

This chapter analyses the *content* of Solo's policy arrangement in the housing domain, meaning the principles, objectives and measures, the target, and the outcome of governance processes. Based on information and findings from expert interviews, several field visits and enriched with secondary literature the design and implementation of housing policies is explored. To start with, an overview of various housing and urban development programmes is given, focusing thereinafter on measures for the poorest parts of society: relocations of residents of squatter settlements to low-cost social housing units.

28.1 Housing and urban development programmes in Solo

Applied housing programmes in Solo can be classified according to the settlement type they are primarily targeting (cf. figure 65): (1) formal areas (2) *kampungs* (3) *kampung kumuh* (slum) (4) *kampung liar* (squatter). For these four settlement types, different housing policies have been applied, which are either the local shaping of national housing programmes or initiatives developed by the municipal government on its own accord. In general, the national housing programmes and initiatives explored in chapter 20 have also been initiated and carried out in Solo – ie slum upgrading, public housing, cooperative housing, community empowerment, financial housing policies, and umbrella initiatives (for a periodic overview table 23 and table 24). A city-specific account of the community empowerment programme PNPM-Mandiri in Solo is given in chapter 20.4.1. All of these national programmes target mostly *kampungs*, with the exception of financial policies that target the private sector as incentives for formal housing developments. For squatter settlements, no explicit national housing programme exists, and resettlements by local authorities is recommended.

Since the decentralisation policies were introduced in the beginning of the 2000s, bringing more autonomy for the city, Solo's government has introduced a number of additional innovative urban policies and housing programmes. Examples are the introduction of a city-wide participatory planning process (*musrenbang*), the formalisation

	Settlement type			
	Formal settlements (not *kampung*)	*kampung*	*kampung kumuh* (slum)	*kampung liar* (squatter settlement)
National Policies	**Financial policies** FLPP, KPRS-Mikro, SSB & SBUM	**Community Empowerment:** P2KP/KOTAKU, PNPM, NUSSP **Subsidies for incremental housing:** BSPS		
		Cooperative housing: P2KP/KOTAKU CBHD, Co-Bild	**Slum upgrading:** KIP, NUSSP, NSUP NAHP	
		Social housing: *rusunawa* programme		
Additional Municipal Policies		**Slum upgrading:** RTLH programme RTLH-cluster		**Resettlement:** *program relokasi*
		Row-housing: *rumah deret* programme		

Fig. 65 Applied housing and urban development programmes in Solo according to targeted settlement type
Note: Programmes highlighted are analysed in more detail
Source: Illustration by author

and relocation of the numerous street vendors in the city, a local slum upgrading programme (Rumah Tidak Layak Huni, or RTLH programme) and an upgrading programme for whole neighbourhoods involving international actors (RTLH cluster). Initiatives to realise better participatory planning or the relocation of the street vendors are not housing programmes; they illustrate the commitment to allow citizens and marginalised groups to participate in urban development. The city's initiative of slum upgrading targets the city's traditional settlements, its *kampungs*. For the city's squatter settlements (*kampung liar*), the city government pursues a policy of relocation to other parts of the city (*program relokasi*) or to social housing (*rusunawa* or *rumah deret*). Solo's housing policy is difficult to look at out of context, as the implementation process builds on a sequence of other urban policies applied. Therefore, this sequence is briefly presented in the following section before taking a closer look at the policies of social housing and resettlement.

28.2 Inclusive and balanced urban policies

Since 2001, national decentralisation policies opened the opportunity for Solo's city government to have more autonomy in designing and implementing urban policies. A number of new policies emerged that build on each other and significantly changed political style and policy trajectories of the city. Urban authorities began to experiment with a new approach of participatory planning. The old system of top-down-implemented policies with only few participatory elements at the implementation stage, which was inherited from the Suharto era, was increasingly considered as inadequate to deliver sound results. A senior municipal employee who participated in a study tour on participatory governance and decentralisation policies to the Philippines (funded by the Ford Foundation), brought the idea of participatory planning back to Solo (Phelps et al. 2014; Widianingsih 2006). He founded an NGO aiming to promote this approach and after broad discussions with the Regional Development Planning Agency (Badan Perencanaan dan Pembangunan Daerah, or BAPPEDA), local universities and the mayor, Solo introduced a new planning mechanism to be known as participatory development planning, or *Perencanaan Pembangunan Partisipatif* (Widianingsih & Morrell 2007).

After some difficulties in the first years of implementation, the approach of participatory planning and budgeting was successfully implemented and has been applied ever since. The mechanism introduces annual citizens' meetings at different administrative levels (neighbourhoods, quarters, and citywide) to discuss, prioritise, and decide about development issues in respective areas. Development plans for the following years are created and implemented drawing on local budget (the Anggaran Pendapatan dan Belanja Daerah, or APBD). The change towards this new planning paradigm was a slow process, since old norms, values and traditions inherent to Javanese culture prevailed (cf. box 18) and the existing top-down planning mechanisms were persistent and difficult to overcome. Since 2004, however, the approach has been rolled out nationwide and its name changed to *musrenbang*, short for *Musyawarah Perencanaan Pembangunan* (Cabannes 2018; USAID 2009). Today, *musrenbang* is applied throughout Indonesia and is regarded as an effective way to create awareness on development issues, raise citizen participation, create ownership for introduced measures, reduce potential conflicts, and promote democracy (Obermayr 2017: 136–137).

Box 18: Javanese culture – an obstacle for participatory processes?

Solo is regarded as home to Javanese culture and it is precisely this culture which is seen as an obstacle for participatory processes. Javanese culture is patrimonial and hierarchical (Widianingsih & Morrell 2007: 8); respect has to be paid to the elderly and to all persons with a high social status. This is reflected in the Javanese language: there are differing versions of salutation and words, depending on the social status of the partner in a conversation. This means that differing words must be used when addressing elderly persons, someone with a high status (eg the mayor or sultan), a friend, or a child. In Solo, this tendency is strong, reinforced through history. At the royal court of a Javanese kingdom, ordinary citizens were not regarded as equals. For present policies, this means that relations between leaders and community are often characterised as patron-client systems, where open discussions and critcism are only rarely expressed. As a European researcher with presumed high status, I encountered these cultural norms frequently, with conversation partners neither addressing my potential misconduct nor criticizing other presumed high-ranked persons, such as government officials.

With the election of Joko Widodo (Jokowi) as mayor of Solo in 2005, a new political style emerged. He introduced a balanced policy aiming at the economic and social development of the city between tradition and modernity. Jokowi succeeded in balancing the interests of the different associations (civil and economic) in the city (Luebke et al. 2009). Under his leadership, comprehensive measures were introduced to improve the living conditions in the city for all – acknowledging marginalised groups as equal partners as well. With his background as a businessperson, he was well connected to local business elites, having an open ear for their demands. His deputy mayor, Fransiskus Xaverius Hadi Rudyatmo, on the other hand was well connected to CBOs in the city (Ortiz 2014: 252). During his time as mayor of Solo, Jokowi was known for his unannounced visits in many government offices and for penalising any misbehaviour of government officials. In addition, Jokowi repeatedly made unannounced visits in various parts of the city, listening to the complaints and needs of local residents. These visits, to be known as *blusukan*, earned him the reputation of being a mayor who values the opinions of citizens and is concerned about their problems.

Under Jokowi, several measures were introduced targeting the informal sector and informal settlements. Well-known is the successful relocation of street vendors to revitalised traditional markets (Obermayr 2017: 138–139; Taylor & Song 2016). Since the Asian financial crisis, the number of street vendors had increased in the city. They were soon regarded as a problem, since their street stalls blocked pedestrian areas, sidewalks, and public parks, caused traffic congestion, and increased waste around their locations. Jokowi succeeded in addressing the problem through informal encounters with the street vendor associations. In over 50 meetings, he convinced them to agree to be relocated to newly constructed market houses. The city promised several years of free use of the kiosks in these new market houses, legal status of the traders' business, tax exemptions, assistance with marketing efforts, and free management trainings. A symbolic event was organised in 2006, a procession where the street vendors moved to their new market places. Overall, 13 such new traditional market houses were newly constructed or revitalised, expressing the commitment of the city government to support small-scale traders and traditional markets. Some other rules were enacted, such as a ban to transform traditional markets into modern shopping malls or the ban to establish new shopping malls within close proximity. The peaceful relocation soon drew international attention and is regarded as best practice (UN-Habitat 2008d; Gervasi 2010). In addition, the economic elites of the city approved Jokowi's policy for small and medium traders, since a more regularised urban landscape was also in their interest. After the successful relocation and revitalisation of the traditional marketplaces, Jokowi gave permission for the establishment of large real estate developments in the city. The best example is the construction of Solo Paragon Mall, a large shopping centre with a connected multi-storey luxury hotel. In such a way his policy in these first years can be described as between tradition and modernity, recognizing the need of modernising Solo's economy, but simultaneously preserving and promoting traditional trade and cultural heritage (Luebke et al. 2009). The latter can be exemplified by other revitalisation initiatives in the city. In an endeavour to promote tourism, Solo is marketed as a 'City of Culture' or as 'The Spirit of Java'. The traditional Batik district is revitalised and promoted, as well as other cultural heritage sites and the palace of the Sultan as important points of interest for tourists. Simultaneously, hotel development is massively promoted, as has become visible in an emerging city skyline, with skyscrapers standing out of the established urban structure.

In terms of housing policies, the city had participated in many of the national Kampung Improvement Programmes of the past, but in 2007 the municipality introduced its own slum upgrading programme, called Program Pemberian Bantuan Pembangunan / Perbaikan Rumah tidak Layak Huni (Programme RTLH). Fully funded by the local government, the programme aims to assist residents of houses considered as uninhabitable in their efforts at renovating their homes using a community-driven approach as in other Indonesian programmes (cf. chapter 20.4). For every eligible household[5] a grant of two million Rupiah was provided as an incentive for upgrading. Community-based working groups (*Klempok Kerja*, or *Pokja*) facilitated the projects, which soon became a crucial element of the programme. Consisting of respected community members, these *Pokjas* worked as the interface between community and government, managed government funds, and encouraged residents to jointly upgrade their houses in self-help (Obermayr 2017: 141–145). The programme demonstrates the political will of Solo's government to address the challenge of inadequate housing in the city without waiting for national support. Even though it is top-down initiated with participatory elements only at the implementation level, the programme can be regarded as very successful with a total of 6,280 houses renovated between 2006 and 2014 (Bapermas Surakarta 2014).

Similar to the street vendor management, this programme also drew international attention. UN-Habitat decided to choose Solo as one of the international pilot cities for the organisation's idea to establish slum upgrading facilities (SUF), technical advisory facilities that focus on the financial enablement of low-income people and promotes local housing projects by mobilising local financial means (UN-Habitat

---

5 Only residents of Solo with valid residency in the city (KTP) are eligible.

2006a, 2006b). A facility with some employees was established as an independent agency based in Solo's government: Badan Layanan Umum Daerah Griya Layak Huni (BLUD). Directly subordinated to the mayor, but closely cooperating with other agencies, such as BAPERMAS, architects, and banks, the agency's mission is to develop and facilitate comprehensive upgrading measures by making loans available for slum dwellers and attracting additional funding from new national or international actors. The agency supports interested citizens of Solo (a Solo ID-card is needed) in technical, legal, and economic issues (business plan), provides information on possible support from other programmes (eg the RTLH programme) and connects them to banks, providing guarantees for the repayment of loans. The goal is to bundle all available resources to achieve the best result for all applicants and to prove the possibility of mobilising commercial bank funding for housing improvements (Obermayr 2017: 145–148; UN-Habitat 2011). Several comprehensive neighbourhood projects were realised, to be known as the RTLH cluster, in Ketelan, Setabeland, and Kratonan. In all cases, households received the grant from the RTLH programme and could obtain additional loans on favourable conditions from different banks. Corporate social responsibility activities could be mobilised and the upgrading activities were organised once again by the established working groups (*Pokjas*) and carried out by the communities in self-help. In the pilot areas, the results were impressive: whole neighbourhoods were substantially renovated, including the improvement of public infrastructure and services. Nevertheless, the approach remained complicated. On the one hand, it was difficult to convince banks to provide risky loans and on the other slum dwellers were reluctant to get into debts as they had no experiences with such formal loans. Despite a proof of concept in the pilot areas, the activities were not scaled up and SUF has not succeeded in attracting significantly new funding from other international or national donors (UN-Habitat 2011). In 2013, UN-Habitat decided to end the support and closed down its facilities (Interview 16). The concept did have, however, an impact on wider Indonesian housing policies, as reflected in the Housing and Settlements Law adopted in 2011 (for details cf. chapter 19.3.2). In this law, it is recognised that there is a need to establish national or local finance facilities to provide housing guarantees or insurance for enabling low-income dwellers to obtain loans.

The sequence of these three programmes focusing on marginalised groups testified to the commitment of the municipality to address the city's problems. The city gained a reputation as a model of urban governance, introducing progressive and innovative urban policies (Yuwono 2014; Taylor 2015; Phelps et al. 2014; Taylor & Song 2016). The effect was international attention, and international actors such as UN-Habitat appeared at the scene. This involvement, in turn, established Solo also as a venue for international conferences. In 2010, the third Asia Pacific Ministerial Conference on Housing and Urban Development (APMCHUD) was held in Solo with over 700 international participants discussing proper policies to address the housing challenge in their respective countries (APMCHUD 2010; Lourenço & Astuti 2011).

The introduction of these balanced and inclusive policies in Solo had already started before Jokowi became mayor of the city, but were significantly promoted during his seven years in office (2005–2012). The successes of this new political style in Solo paved the way for Jokowi's political career, which led him first to become Governor of Jakarta (2012–2014) and later President of Indonesia (since 2014). When he left the city, however, the new style of governance by no means disappeared with him. Rather, a reformed bureaucracy was left behind with established routines that were sustained. This can certainly be attributed to Jokowi's former deputy mayor, who is now the acting mayor of Solo. This continuity can be best understood by illustrating policies for marginalised groups in more detail, focusing on their crucial element: community-based working groups implementing the programmes. The policies described so far target mostly acknowledged citizens of Solo, but not residents of squatter settlements (*kampung liar*) or residents without citizenship (KTP). These groups represent a large part of Solo's population but are excluded from most government aid programmes. Nevertheless, in an ongoing effort to regularise urban space, Solo's authorities are also trying to reach them with appropriate measures. Similar to Surabaya, the options are public housing for citizens and resettlement for non-citizens.

28.3 Social housing in Solo

Within the national social housing programme, Solo is increasingly realising new social housing blocks (*rusunawa*). All constructed tenements are property of the city government. As in other Indonesian cities and districts, a local DPU branch largely plans and implements the buildings. City and national government share the costs. While the latter provides funding for the construction, the required land as well as all planning and management obligations have to be funded from the local budget (Interview 22). Compared to larger Indonesian agglomerations, this trend is relatively new to the city. In Jakarta and Surabaya, *rusunawa* were constructed much earlier, probably mainly due to the higher cost of building land in these larger cities. In Solo, the first block was realised only in 2004 with 96 units designated for low-income people (Bagalon I). Since that time, however, construction activities accelerated and by 2019, thirteen *rusunawa* have been finished, providing altogether 1,020 flats (cf. figure 66). National policies have fueled this development and there is a growing recognition that a certain amount of social housing is needed to help solving the housing crisis in Indonesia. This recognition became increasingly evident in the 2000s and is visible in several initiatives and laws – ie in the 1,000 tower programme, with the enactment of the housing law (UU 01/2011), and with the large PSR initiative of the Jokowi government (cf. chapter 20.2.2 for more details).

The social housing blocks developed in Solo have a similar shape and design to other *rusunawa* throughout Indonesia (for Surabaya cf. chapter 24.3). The favoured design has developed from a compact block towards a twin block five storeys tall and with up

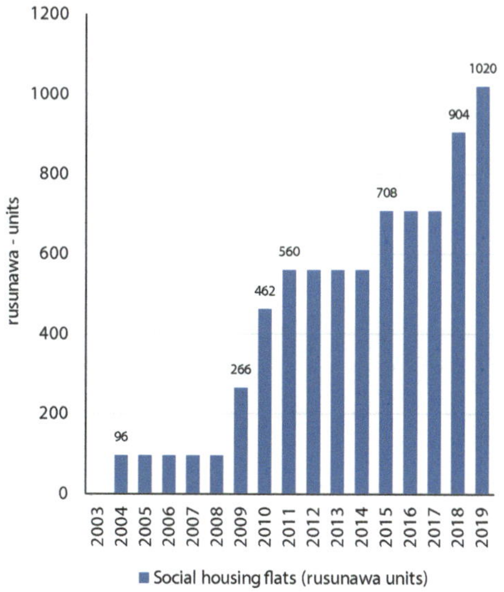

Name	Year completed	Size per unit (m^2)	Units
BAGALON I	2004	21	96
BEGALON II	2009	21	96
JURUG I	2009	27	74
JURUG II	2009	24	98
SEMANGGI I	2010	24	98
SEMANGGI II	2010	24	98
KERKOV	2011	24	98
MOJOSONGO A	2015	24	74
MOJOSONGO B	2015	24	74
PUTRI CEMPO A	2018	24	98
PUTRI CEMPO B	2018	24	98
PUTRI CEMPO C	2019	36	58
PUTRI CEMPO D	2019	36	58
TOTAL			1 020

Fig. 66 Social housing blocks (*rusunawa*) and available flats in Solo 2003–2019
Source: Illustration by author. Data obtained from DPU Surakarta (= Interview 22)

to 98 units in one block (cf. figure 67). The latter has advantages, since it allows better air circulation compared to the compact block. Over the years, the size of single flats has increased from 21 to 36 m^2 recognising the necessity of more space for a single family. While rental flats are located in the upper floors, the ground floor of most *rusunawa* is used as public space for the residents – often it is reserved as a parking lot. Rents decrease as the floor rises, all of which are approximately Rp. 100,000 per month plus electricity and water, which must be paid individually for each unit (Interview 19). Every Solo citizen can apply for a flat, provided he or she can prove to be a registered resident of the city. For a successful application process, several documents are needed proving citizen and marriage status as well as monthly salary. Unmarried couples are not allowed and in 2015 applicants had to prove a salary that was below the limit of Rp. 2.5 million (appox. 166€) per month. It is not allowed to possess other property and applications have to be submitted to DPU, where an extra section has been formed to manage all issues related to social housing in Solo. Families and households to be relocated are prioritised in the allocation of rental flats. Government employees see the development of *rusunawa* in Solo as a solution for both low-income citizens in the need for housing as well as families that are targeted by the relocation policies of the city (Interview 15). In this regard, the municipal government sometimes also assigns flats to households that are non-citizens of Solo (Interview 29).

According to employees of the Department of Public Works (Interview 22) the demand for flats in *rusunawa* is increasing. They state there is a waiting list of 500 families (2015) which is getting larger every year. A local regulation was passed in 2016 (Perwali

Fig. 67 Social housing in Solo: *Rusunawa* Jurug and *Rusunawa* Semanggi
Photos: Christian Obermayr, 2014

15/2016) stipulating that only one-year contracts would be made to be extended up to a maximum of five years. This limit was introduced on the one hand to allow as many families as possible benefiting from social housing; on the other hand, beneficiaries are expected to be able to buy their own property after some years due to the subsidised rents.

Despite the acceleration in construction of *rusunawa,* the new developments face difficulties concerning land and budget limitations. As in Surabaya, also in Solo the latest *rusunawa* developments are increasingly located in the urban peripheries due to the limited availability of suitable land. Peripheral locations, however, cause some well-known follow-up problems, such as isolation of communities and difficulties reaching public facilities and jobs. In order to prevent this, the municipal government is permanently looking for alternative solutions. More and more, squatter areas come into focus, and concepts are being developed to realise social housing directly on site. However, according to the technical regulations for social housing, a land plot of 5,000 m^2 is needed at minimum to develop social housing blocks using national funding. This is the only way the standard *rusunawa* twin block, which is currently being realised all over Indonesia, can be built on such a property. Since there are hardly any such areas left in Solo, the city government has come up with the idea of developing social housing blocks with different design and smaller size on state land that is occupied by squatters (Interview 19, 22). In these areas, some smaller projects have been realised that are known as rowhouses (*rumah deret*). The approach is considered quite successful, but as lacking the financial means to be replicated on a large scale (cf. chapter 28.5 for more details).

28.4 Resettling squatter settlements – 'Program Relokasi'

Solo's policy for dealing with its squatter settlements (*kampung liar*) is resettlement to social housing or to other areas within the city boundaries. As in other Indonesian cities, these settlements are mostly located on government-owned land along the city's rivers and railway lines (cf. chapter 27.4). They developed historically but are considered illegal according to Indonesian law. In the case of the riverbank communities, a certain amount of space near the river courses has to be free from any buildings according to law (cf. box 19). Solo's city government thus is obliged to clear its riverbanks and formalise the land in question. A large-scale resettlement programme has been initiated in 2007, called 'Program Relokasi', in order to regularise the riverbanks of Bengawan Solo River, which marks the eastern border of Solo.

Box 19: Management of Indonesian rivers

The management of Indonesian rivers and their extent is regulated in the government regulation of 2011 (PP 38/2011). According to this regulation, the authorities are obliged to delineate the river boarders under their authority considering a certain amount of space outside the riverbed, usually the riverbank, as part of the river. Depending on several factors, eg the river's physical and geomorphological condition (size and depth), catchment area, the river status as embanked (*bertangul*) or not, and whether it is passing through areas defined as a city (*perkotaan*) or not, the authorities are obliged to define the space between riverbed and river boundary. The distance between riverbed and river border – the riverbank – can range from three meters (embanked small river channels within cities) up to 100 meters (in the cases of undisturbed rivers in rural areas). These riverbank areas are to be managed by local, provincial, or national authorities for inner-urban, cross-district, or cross-provincial river courses respectively. According to the government regulation of 2011 (PP 38/2011) certain activities are restricted in the riverbank area, among them the construction of any buildings.

This regulation has many implications for existing settlements along rivers and channels. Frequently, houses are located within the prohibited zone, their residents not possessing legal claims to the land. Sometimes, however, the dwellers have inhabited their houses in these zones for many decades. In some cases, also households with legal rights (certificates of ownership or usage) can be found due to historic reasons. Managing this complicated situation is not an easy task for the government of Solo and requires intensive negotiations with existing dwellers.

With a length of 600 km and a catchment area of 16.000 km^2, Bengawan Solo River is the largest river system on Java Island (Lasminto et al. 2016). The river's waters are an important source for the irrigation of rice fields and recurring floods provide necessary nutrients from volcanic origin, which is one of the reasons for the region's fertile soils and high harvest yields. Flood events are frequent and affect all settlements and cities along the river course. The eastern part of Solo was flooded several times, the worst flood event happened in 1966, when large parts of the city were flooded one to two meters high (Zein 2010). Since the 18th century, the Dutch government had implemented several measures of flood protection, such as the construction of floodgates and canals, but only few measures were realised. After the 1966 event, the Indonesian government made a second, more ambitious attempt to control the riverine floods. With the help of Japanese development assistance, a master plan for the whole river system was developed, which includes various measures such as the construction of large retention areas, canals, dams, dikes, and the fortification of the riverbanks (Lasminto et al. 2016).

At the riverbanks of this river in Solo, settlements and individual houses existed long before independence. After the 1966 flooding a levee was constructed and the tributaries emptying into Bengawan Solo River were fortified by floodgates. The levee construction faced the problem of existing houses at the riverbanks, which had received land certificates issued by the Sultan of Surakarta (Interview 15). These certificates were not in accordance with the modern Indonesian land system[6], but the authorities nevertheless recognise them. At the time the levee was constructed, however, it was decided to realise it closer to the river, to avoid problems associated with expropriation and demolition of houses (Interview 02). The result was that a levee several meters high separated existing settlements consisting of scattered houses on the riverbanks. Some were now located behind the levee, supposedly protected from riverine floods, others were located in front of it, still endangered by flooding. The levee was realised at approximately a 50–100 m distance to the riverbed and all land between the river and the levee was announced as being government-owned. In the following decades, the levee was continuously improved and heightened.

Over the years, the settlements at the riverbanks in front of the levee grew continuously in size. Consisting only of few houses with certificates issued by the Sultan prior to 1966, a slow infiltration process set in starting in the 1980s (Interview 11). More and more families established their houses without legal permission, but often with the approval of their neighbours. Since the authorities did not react, temporary shelters grew into houses that were more permanent and the settlement consolidated. Residents were a mixture of migrants from outside Solo, but also Solo citizens seeking a cheap place to stay (Interview 11). These newcomers had no option to obtain land

6 The modern Indonesian land system started to develop with the enactment of the basic agrarian law of 1960.

titles and remained semi-legal owners with a *de facto* claim to the land they lived on (Obermayr 2017: 125). The results were more or less densely populated riverbanks in Solo, with residents having various and complicated claims of ownership or use rights for the land they were occupying. Some have legal certificates; others claim to possess customary rights, as they have been living there for decades. This constellation is also present today and complicates any intervention attempt.

28.4.1 The flood event of 2007 – disaster relief – a window of opportunity

In December 2007 another severe flooding hit Solo. The levee broke and the waters inundated the city, flooding large parts of it up to 4 meters high (Zein 2010: 12–13). A local resident in Pucang Sawit explained: 'In 2007, there was a huge flood. It was the most serious flood the community experienced ever' (Interview 02). The flooding affected mostly the densely populated neighbourhoods in the southeast. The authorities counted 6,368 houses damaged by the flood, 3,761 of them badly (Interview 06). Destruction was most severe at the riverbanks. The event was tragic, but it opened also a window of opportunity for the city government to implement a long-cherished plan to formalise and redevelop the riverbanks, clear them from slum and squatter settlements, and establish a green belt at Solo's eastern border.

The city government pursued several goals with its relocation policy. The primary reason, according to officials, would be to help residents to mitigate the effects of the flood (Interview 06, 10, 19). 'The main reason behind relocation programme was the city government was concerned about the destiny of the condition of the people who are flooded that year' (Interview 06). However, this was not the only reason. The opportunity should also be taken to solve the problem of the 'illegal' houses at the riverbanks, to restore the function of the river, and to establish a green belt (Interview 06, 11, 18). Squatters were commonly perceived as disturbing the function of the river with their activities. Once people have been resettled, according to this view, it would be easier to implement flood control measures and protect the riverbanks against erosion (Interview 18).

The national government, through the Coordinating Ministry for Human Development and Cultural Affairs (Kementerian Koordinator Pembangunan Manusia dan Kebudayaan, or Kemenko PMK) and the Ministry of Social Affairs (Kementerian Sosial, or Kemsos), agreed to provide assistance for all victims of the flood. The disaster relief for the 6,368 affected households was divided according to several criteria (cf. figure 68). The damaged houses were categorised into heavily (3,761) and lightly (2,607) damaged units. The inhabitants of the 2,607 less damaged houses received help from Kemsos in the form of building materials to renovate their houses in self-help (Interview 14). For each of the 3,761 heavily damaged units a Rp. 8.5 million (appox. 680€) grant was provided by Kemenko PMK earmarked to repair or rebuild the houses in another place.

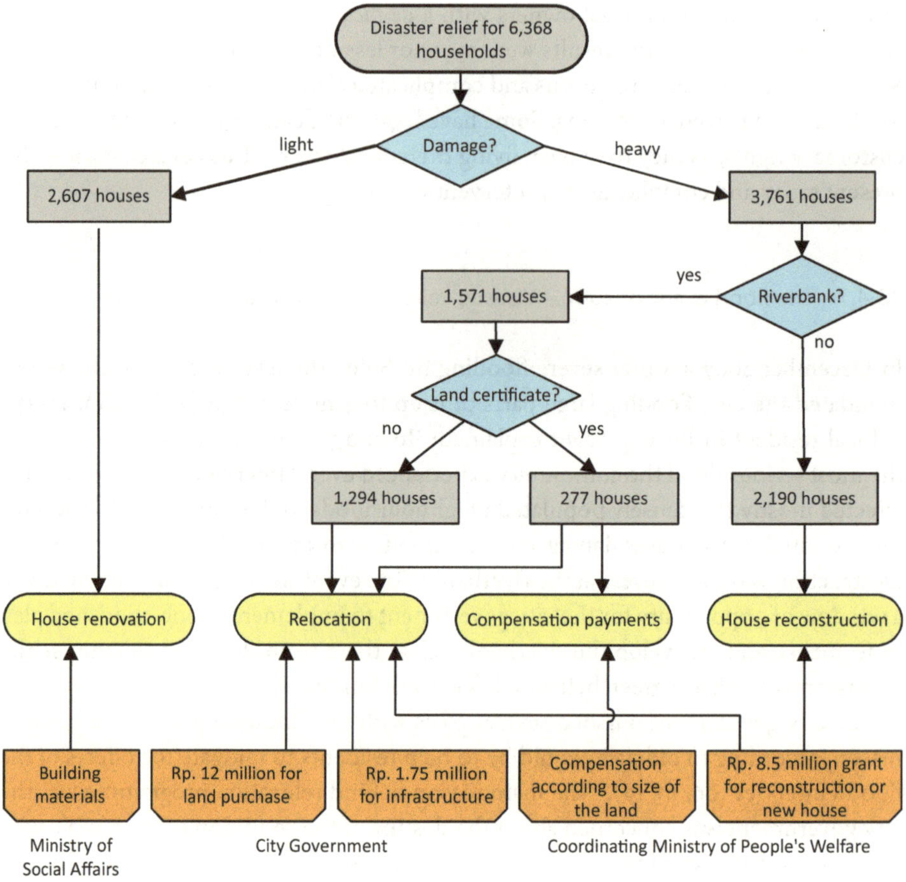

Fig. 68 Disaster relief for 6,368 households affected by the 2007 flood in Solo
Source: Illustration by author. Data obtained from Bapermas Surakarta

Since 1,571 houses were located at the riverbanks, considered as a too dangerous place to live, the city government proposed an additional plan to relocate the residents to safer areas. To reach this goal, additional funds were raised from the local budget (ABPD). Adding to the national help of Rp. 8.5 million (appox. 680€[7]) for reconstruction, for each of the 1,571 households at the riverbank without legal land status Rp. 12 million (appox. 960€) were allocated for the purchase of new land (50–60 m^2) and Rp. 1.75 million (appox. 140€) for the construction of infrastructure in the new locations (Interview 06). For each household the assistance agreed upon sums up to an amount of Rp. 22.25 million (appox. 1,800€).

7 Currency converted using historical annual average conversion rates (2007) from fxtop.com.

All households on government-owned land at the riverbank were eligible for these compensation payments. The only conditions were to be recognised as official victims of the flood and to agree to the resettlement programme. Both citizens of Solo and also those without official residence status (stated in the identity card KTP) were considered, provided the respective district head (*lurah*) confirmed that they had lived in the neighbourhood for many years (Obermayr 2017: 149). A member of the city government pointed out that in this case all riverbank dwellers were treated equally: '[...] Illegal or legal, the government's obligation when there is a disaster is that they remain citizens' (Interview 14). Households at the riverbank with legal land status (277 households), however, were to receive higher compensation payments drawing on funds from Kemenko PMK. For them the amount of compensation is calculated individually during an independent appraisal, valuing the land according to market prices. Depending on the size of their land, they received usually more than the Rp. 12 million offered residents occupying state land. However, the size of the house was not taken into account. Here the same value was used as for all others (Interview 15). In total, national transfers covered approximately 70 % of the cost for the disaster relief measures including the relocation (Interview 06).

28.4.2 The approach: participatory resettlements

For the actual process of relocating the informal riverbank communities, Solo's city government initiated a participatory resettlement approach (Phelps et al. 2014; Taylor 2015; Obermayr 2017). The experience from preceding programmes (street vendor management, RTLH programme) were used to design a people-centred approach of relocation (Obermayr & Sandholz 2017; Obermayr & Astuti 2016). The process involved many stakeholders and required great efforts of coordination. On the government side, the Agency for Community Empowerment (Badan Pemberdayaan Masyarakat, or BAPERMAS) was the leading agency, but also DPU, the Department for Spatial Planning (Dinas Tata Ruang Kota, or DTRK) and the mayor himself were significantly involved. The agencies of the city formed a team under the coordination of BAPERMAS overseen by the regional development planning agency BAPPEDA. Other governmental organisations at the supra-regional level were also involved, such as BPN – responsible for land certification – and the River Basin Management Agency (Balai Besar Wilayah Sungai Bengawan Solo, or BBWS/BS), which is responsible for inter-communal river management. Beside these government actors, the resettlement approach also involved experts in the fields of architecture, geography, and spatial planning from local universities as well as CBOs that were formed during the implementation process. An overview of involved actors and their tasks is provided in table 36.

The process of relocating the communities consisted of several steps. In a first step, the city government announced the resettlement plan as one part of the support for

Table 36 Actors involved in the relocation programme in Solo and their role

Actor	Role
National	
Coordinating Ministry of People's Welfare (Kemenko PMK)	– Grant for land purchase
Ministry of Social Affairs (Kemsos)	– Grant for building materials – Compensation payments for land owners
BBWS/BS	– Authority over the riverbank areas, maintaining the river, dam fortification, floodgates, riverbank fortification, water pumps, etc
BPN	– Land certification
Province	
DPU (Central Java)	– Provision of the drainage system
City	
Mayor	– Issues regulation to formalise the riverbanks – Important for discussions
BAPPEDA	– Coordination between government agencies – Budget planning
Bapermas	– Lead agency of the relocation programme – Community empowerment and education – Coordination between government agencies and communities
DPU	– Construction work, infrastructure: roads, lightning, sanitation, advice for house construction for the people
DTRK	– Spatial planning, design arrangement of houses, site plan, coordinates with community and *Pokja*
DKP and BLH	– Post-relocation development: park and greening, planting of trees in the old area (urban forest)
kelurahan	– Coordination at the local level – Programme facilitation – Provision of identity cards (KTP)
Pokja	– Community working group: Search of land, community organisation, realisation of house construction
PDAM	– Water supply
PLN	– Electricity supply
BLUD	– Provision of bank warranties
UNS	– Partner in discussions

Source: Table by author. Information based on Interviews conducted in Solo 2011 and 2014 flood victims. More than 24 community meetings were organised to disseminate the information and discuss the resettlement plan with the affected population. These meetings were attended by representatives of the city administration, in particular by former mayor Jokowi (2005–2012) and employees of BAPERMAS. During these meetings, the planned project was explained in detail to the people concerned, including the planned process and compensation payments. Eligible residents had to provide details on their situation: condition and size of their property (house and land) as well as proof of ownership. These data were verified and an independent surveyor determined the value of the land (Interview 06). After this process, a regulation (SK Walikota) was passed by the city to put the agreement on resettlement on a legal basis. The individual households were required to sign a statement letter in which they declared their consent. This was a prerequisite for the compensation payments. Finally yet importantly, a Memorandum of Understanding (MoU) was signed with BBWS/BS. In this document, the future use of the riverbanks as a recreational area is regulated (Interview 06).

The city administration succeeded in convincing most of the inhabitants of the riverbank by promising legal land certificates, general acknowledgement as citizens (KTP, meaning access to social programmes), and compensation payments considered as sufficient. Finally, yet importantly, the fact that the mayor, as a person of high reputation and status asked for something from ordinary citizens, also played a decisive role (cf. box 18). Only those dwellers with legal land tenure – roughly a quarter of all residents at the riverbanks – refused to be relocated, claiming that the land price or the value of the house had been underestimated and demanding higher compensations payments (Taylor 2015; Obermayr & Sandholz 2017). One of them explained: 'It is not fair because for example all buildings are valuated the same, also those with two stories. The government can only give 8.5 million, which is in fact not fair for people who have quite good houses' (Interview 03). For some of the larger families a new house with only 40 m² was also not an option (Interview 10). The authorities acknowledge their right to stay – 'It is their own risk. We must not force' (Interview 14) – but discuss other solutions with them.

In a second step, community-based steering groups (*Pokjas*), were founded at quarter level (*kelurahan*) to guide and implement the entire resettlement process (*Pokja Relokasi*). The members of these working groups consisted of the district head (*lurah*) and respected members from the local council, the LPMK. Their task was to organise the community, to mediate between community and government agencies, and to manage and allocate the financial resources (Astuti & Prasetyo 2014; Obermayr & Astuti 2016). In the first wave of resettlements, it was agreed that the affected families would pool their compensation claims in the hands of the respective working group at *kelurahan* level (Obermayr 2017: 151). Below these working groups, so-called '*Subpokjas*' were established at neighbourhood level – working groups consisting of several respectable persons from each neighbourhood. Usually respective RTs and RWs volunteered for this job, taking on the tasks of looking for suitable land, and organiing the community members and later on the construction activities.

In a third step, the established working groups and the residents themselves searched for affordable land to create the new settlement. This was a crucial point of joint decision-making and community participation. In a normal relocation case, the city government alone would determine the location of the new settlement based on their own assessment. This location might be considered as ideal by the government, but not necessarily by the community. 'They search for their own land and move as they wish. If they move based on the direction of the government, it may not be according to their needs. They are looking for BAPERMAS because this programme is empowering, not a river cleaning project' (Interview 15). People chose the land based on three considerations: first, they wanted to move together to one new spot, in order to sustain relations and their social network, which had sometimes formed over decades. The two other considerations were land availability and price. Most spots were too small for all families and they had to decide who was going to live in which location (Interview 06).

People were allowed to choose the right location for a new settlement that has easy access to their places of work and other public facilities (Interview 14). After land was found that could be purchased at a reasonable price, the location was proposed to the lead agency, BAPERMAS, which together with DTRK checked the possibility to create a new settlement there (accordance to the master plan, environmental conditions, access to urban services, etc). If the area was considered suitable and after consultations with *Pokja* and the community, DTRK created a site plan of the new village and the land was purchased by the city government. After this moment, which is marked by a formal agreement between *Pokja* and the government about the relocation, people receive the financial aid (Rp. 8.5 million per household) and are required to leave their old place. Residents are obliged to move to the new area and to demolish their old houses within a period of two months (Interview 06).

The fourth step was the construction of the houses. Together with the families to be relocated, the respective working groups decided if the houses were to be constructed in self-help or by private contractors. Depending on the purchase price of the land, the residents had to contribute their own labour to build the houses. The construction was entirely organised by the people themselves, only public infrastructure (water, sanitation, and electricity) was provided by the respective department (DPU). Depending on the land price achieved, more or less money was left to be invested into the building structure of the settlement. Therefore, the realised houses differ in their quality depending on location. Each house must remain in the possession of the new owner for at least five years before it can be sold (Interview 06). When the new settlement was finished, the future residents drew lots to determine the plot of land to be owned by each household (Interview 15). After that the community moved as a whole or in small groups to the new area and the land certification process began, carried out by BPN. Within the relocation programme, this was free of charge for all participating households and the agency promised a quick processing.

28.4.3 The case of Ngemplak Sutan

The relocation of riverbank dwellers from Kelurahan Pucang Sawit to Kelurahan Mojosongo illustrates the resettlement process (cf. figure 69). Organised by the *Pokja* relocation at *kelurahan* level and guided by 13 *subpokjas* altogether 268 households (HH) were resettled in groups of different size (Interview 08). Nearly all of them chose the northeast of Solo, Mojosongo, as their new home (Interview 12). This area is characterised by a hilly landscape, and population densities and land prices were low back in 2007. Therefore, most of the families to be resettled could find land for their new homes. Over the last years, however, private investors have bought most of the remaining open space to develop new projects. Urban development has accelerated and is furthered by the finalisation the northern ring road (Pihan 2018: 38). A number of new settlements were created for people relocated from Kelurahan Pucang Sawit (cf. figure 69): Ngemplak Sutan (112 HH), Solo Elok (89 HH), Donohudan (36 HH), Mipitan (8 HH), Kedung Tungkul (18 HH), and Sabrang Lor (5 HH) (Interview 12).

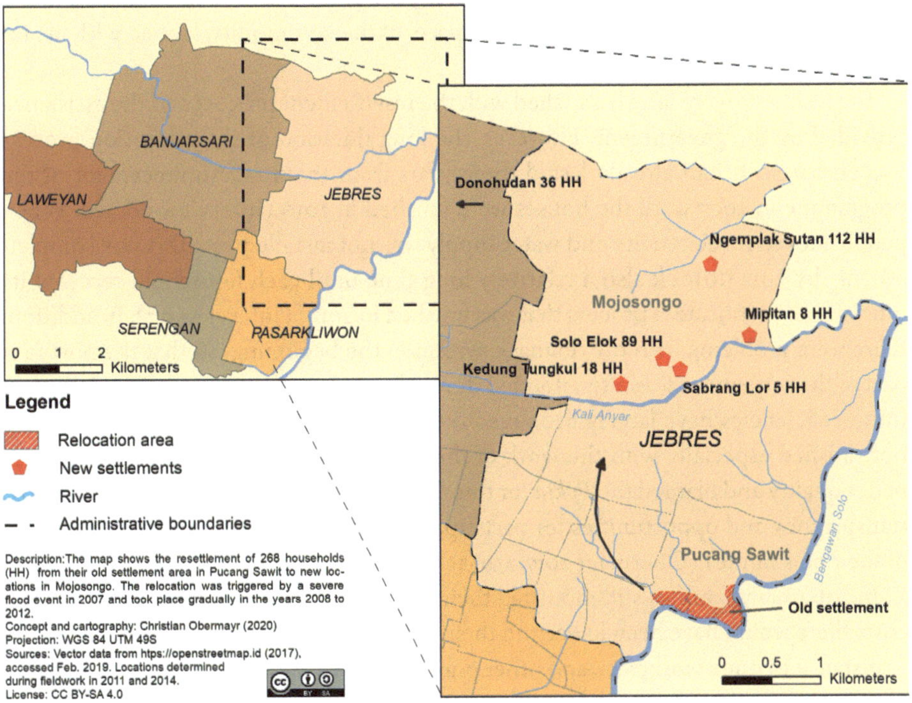

Fig. 69 Resettlement of 268 households in Solo in the years 2008–2012
Source: Illustration by author

The largest settlement – Ngemplak Sutan – was subject to several studies (Astuti 2012; Obermayr 2017; Höferl & Sandholz 2017; Pihan 2018). The results can be summarised as follows: Ngemplak Sutan was completed in 2009, consisting of 112 houses built by a private contractor. The houses all had the same size of 40 m^2 and consisted of one room without separations and an attached bathroom. The walls were made of brick, the roof made of corrugated sheet and the floor left as pure soil. Between 2009 and 2010, the families from Pucang Sawit gradually moved in. After initial difficulties people settled in relatively quickly. Many of them had already expanded and improved their houses in 2011 (enlargement with a second floor, separating walls within the house, floors concreted or laid out with tiles, new roof, plastering, building a veranda). This process continued and by 2014 the individual houses appeared further improved (cf. figure 70 and figure 71). Some of the residents also use their houses or the nearby surroundings as a workplace, and small businesses and stores were established. In the meantime, the residents also began to improve the settlement as a whole and appropriated space through the creation of symbolic physical-material objects. These are, for instance, a small mosque established in 2013 or the entrance gate to the settlement, symbolising a joint identity. Both objects are the material aspect of collective social practices marking a 'representational space' – the 'lived space' of the community, loaded with meaning and a collective history.

The residents were largely satisfied with the resettlement process and the assistance provided by the government. However, the long duration of the relocation process was criticised. It had already lasted three years from the first announcement of the programme in 2007 until the houses were finished in 2010 (Interview 06, 10). When people moved in, electricity and water supply was not installed yet. This was completed only by 2012. It took also a relatively long time until each household received its official land certificate, a process that was finished in 2014[8] (Interview 07). In addition, there were problems with the drainage system in the beginning, so that the northern part of the settlement was often flooded during heavy rain. In the meantime, however, these deficiencies have largely been resolved by construction measures. People were not satisfied especially with the work of the *Pokja*. They had expected a house with better quality and blamed the *Pokja* for this. There was also criticism of the lack of cost transparency and opportunities for participation (eg in the appearance and structure of their new home) (Obermayr 2017: 159–161).

In 2011, many families still mourned their old settlement, explaining that the living costs there would have been lower and their house larger (Obermayr 2017). The greater distance to one's workplace and other public facilities was felt to be a disadvantage

---

8 The process of certification takes only 60 days according to an employee of BPN (Interview 07). In the case of Ngemplak Sutan, however, the completion lasted more than four years. According to the interviewee, this was due to several revisions of the site plan and to missing documents that need to be submitted by the residents.

Fig. 70 Ngemplak Sutan in 2011 (A), 2014 (B) and 2017 (C)
Photos: Christian Obermayr

Fig. 71 A new mosque and self-help improvements in Ngemplak Sutan 2014
Photos: Christian Obermayr, 2014

in the new settlement. However, better public services (fresh water connection and sanitation facilities), more safety from natural hazards, and the legal land title are considered as strong advantages. Especially the land certificate, a thing they had never possessed before, enabled them to feel more secure and allows taking on mortgage loans. In the meantime, residents have adapted their social practices to local conditions and pointed out they would look to the future with confidence (Interview 02, 04, 06).

In the original area, the houses of the former residents were demolished and a park was created by the city's environmental agency (Badan Lingkungan Hidup, or BLH) and DKP (cf. figure 72). They also introduced the concept of a so-called 'urban forest' and planted the now empty riverbank areas partly with mango trees. The remaining neighbourhood benefited from this development (Obermayr & Sandholz 2017). Al-

Fig. 72 Revitalised riverbank area in front of the levee after the relocation
Photo: Christian Obermayr, 2017

though there is some criticism about poor management and insufficient maintenance of the park area (Interview 05), the resettlement has solved some of the sanitation problems in the area and the impression is that there are also fewer infectious diseases. This is attributed to the better health situation resulting from the fact that the area is less densely populated (Interview 02, 03). The residents from neighbouring *kampungs* have also won a park, which is mainly used by children and young people as a playground and meeting point. In addition, residents grow other things besides the harvest from the planted mango trees.

28.4.4 Status of the relocations in 2014 – constraints and evaluation

While the aid for the renovation of the destroyed houses became available relatively quickly, the resettlement project proved to be more protracted. Of the 1,571 households that lived on Solo's riverbanks in 2007 and were eligible for the programme, 277 had a legal land title (cf. table 37). For these, extra negotiations had to be conducted on the amount of compensation payments, which slowed down the process. The largest resettlement actions took place between 2008 and 2010. During this period, 993 of the households were resettled and by 2012, the relocation of 1,024 squatter households was accomplished. With rising land prices throughout the city, it became more and more difficult to find suitable land and to raise the necessary funds. Nevertheless, by 2014, 1,184 of the squatter households were relocated to other places in the city. For all residents with legal land tenure, negotiations dragged on. Of these, 84 households remained to be relocated in 2014.

In 2014, seven years after the beginning of the programme, 1,377 of the 1,571 families at the riverbank had been relocated. Asked for the reason why not all households have been relocated, an employee of BAPERMAS pointed out that the resettlement is always voluntary no matter whether there is a legal land certificate or not. 'They are allowed to move as they wish. We discuss with them continuously to make them aware and understand about the danger of flooding. But if they have a house in good condition, they often don't want to move' (Interview 15). In addition, he mentioned budget constraints and complications due to entangled regulatory issues. The people with land certificate proved to be the most difficult cases. It is not only more expensive to relocate them, as they are entitled to higher compensation payments that need to be negotiated individually, it is also very complicated, since their land rights have to be transferred to the formal land system first (Interview 12). Usually they have inherited the land from their parents or grandparents, and the traditional rights must be properly registered, before the land can be released (to become government-owned land). Only after that are people allowed to receive the compensation payments and resettle to another area (Interview 15).

Over the years, the process of resettlement began to change. While during the window of opportunity provided by the flood event of 2007, the people-centred approach described above using community-based working groups was favoured, later more and more individual solutions were sought. The approach changed from large-scale relocations of whole communities into a concept of gradually relocating individual households. On the one hand, this was due to the increasing difficulties in finding affordable land, and on the other hand there were also problems with the community-based working groups. After suspected fraud cases (Interview 04, 08), the scheme where the working groups managed the funds was abandoned in 2014 and the compensation is now paid out directly to eligible households using individual bank accounts. These measures have increased transparency and acceptance. In addition, the new locations can now be located outside the city limits – eg in Karanganyar or Sukoharjo (Interview 08).

The city government of Solo has managed to revitalise and regularise large parts of its riverbanks and resettle residents of squatter settlements to new areas using an inclusive and people-centred approach. In contrast to other Indonesian cities, Solo decided to consider the inhabitants of the riverbank settlements as human beings and to refrain from using forced evictions. On the contrary, through negotiations and the provision of various incentives, the government was able to convince the inhabitants of the squatter settlements to agree to the government's plan to rebuild their settlement elsewhere. By leaving the relocation process to the affected residents themselves and providing financial support to them, no matter their legal status of residency, the city government proved its confidence in the abilities of the residents and its willingness to acknowledge them as equal partners.

Table 37 Households at Solo's riverbanks in 2007 and realised relocations by 2014

Households at the riverbank 2007		Realised relocations		Not yet realised
		Until 2012	Until 2014	
Squatters	1,294	1,024	1,184	110
Residents with legal status (*hak milik*)	277	76	193	84
Total	1,571		1,377	194

Source: Table by author. Data Source: Bapermas Surakarta (2015)
Note: 'hak milik' is the official certificate for freehold property

The key to success was a project structure in which government actors only had an enabling role and the actual project implementation was left to community-based working groups. This approach not only saved funds of the city administration, but also created ownership among residents, another crucial element of this approach. Nevertheless, such a large-scale intervention project was only feasible during the window of opportunity provided by the flood event of 2007. Triggered by this event, large disaster relief funds of the national government became suddenly available, allowing the relocation project to be initiated. For a sustained resettlement policy aiming to gradually regulate all of the city's informal settlements, however, continued efforts are needed and a flexible approach is required. In view of rising land prices, new solutions are necessary, such as resettlement to social housing blocks (*rusunawa*), *in situ* row houses (*rumah deret*), or new land outside the city limits.

28.5 A new approach: *in situ* row-housing: the *rumah deret* programme

Since 2014, the municipal government has initiated a new approach for formalising squatter settlements located at the city's riverbanks: the *rumah deret* programme. As in similar experiments in Jakarta (Guinness 2016: 217), the idea is to gradually relocate people from their sub-standard houses to newly constructed 'rowhouses' (*rumah deret*) nearby, avoiding the disadvantages of larger resettlements to more peripheral areas and simultaneously formalizing and revitalising the riverbank (improved environmental conditions and enhanced flood protection). Most of all, residents of the smaller rivers in Solo are now the centre of focus, with attempts to find solutions on the same spot (Interview 06). In the past, the approach was to relocate residents of riverbank squatters to other areas within the city boundaries (cf. chapter 28.4) or to newly established social housing blocks (cf. chapter 28.3). These approaches are increasingly difficult to implement due to increased land prices and the limited availability of land for *rusunawa* construction. Therefore, an alternative approach had to be developed.

The *rumah deret* approach was first used in the revitalisation project of Kali PePe, a central river channel running through the city. The river is known for its bad environmental quality and is used as a dumping place of all kinds of waste, which can be observed at its river mouth (cf. figure 73). The goals of the revitalisation project were to regularise the river, create a better environment, and protect nearby quarters from riverine floods. Measures introduced are an annual dredging of the riverbed, the fortification of the riverbanks, technical improvements of the floodgates, the greening of the riverbanks, and a rearrangement of the area for pedestrian use. For these measures, a three-metre-wide corridor along the channel was to be cleared from all buildings. To achieve this, existing houses had to be demolished, their inhabitants moved. The rowhouse idea was a welcome and communicable housing alternative to be presented to the affected residents (Interview 19).

Fig. 73 The river mouth of stream Kali Pepe. Wastewater from the city is mixing with the waters of Bengawan Solo River. Despite this pollution, locals use the spot for fishing
Photo: Christian Obermayr 2018

Several rowhouses were developed on state land in close proximity to Kali PePe. These houses are government-owned tenements or owner-occupied apartment buildings three to four storeys tall. The ground floor was designed as public space, which can be used for meetings, festivals, and economic activities. The two or three upper floors are for residential purposes, where in the case of tenements a monthly rent of Rp. 100,000 is to be paid to the government (2014). This amount of rent is comparable to other social housing units in Indonesia and can be considered as affordable for the urban poor (comparable rent-level at market prices would be roughly Rp. 1,000,000 for a flat with equivalent amenities (Interview 19)). In some cases, (eg land owned by the sultan, but occupied for decades by royal servants) units in rowhouses were also sold to future residents offering a favourable financial model. In the case of the rowhouses built in Keprabon residents had previously lived in the same spot in a riverside *kampung*. During the project, people dismantled their homes carefully preserving reusable materials for temporary shelters built at the edges of the same land plot. After they had moved to these temporary shelters the residents also participated with the design and the construction of the new three-storey building (ACHR 2014).

The project is carried out and coordinated by DPU, which has a leading role. Other place-based agencies involved are similar to the relocation programme BAPPEDA, BAPERMAS, and DTRK, realising different tasks of the project (spatial planning, dissemination, etc). Since the riverbank is under the responsibility of BBWS/BS and land certification is under the responsibility of BPN, much coordination work needs to be done with these non-place based actors (Interview 19). Between 2014 until 2018, altogether five such house projects were realised, accommodating 126 families.

In contrast to common public housing (*rusunawa*), where large twin-blocks are constructed requiring a minimum land area of 5,000 m², Solo's row houses can be realised on much smaller plots, which are more easily available. The residents for these houses are selected from the squatter areas nearby, sometimes even from the same plots where the rowhouses are to be built. In the latter case, the former residents get an emergency place to stay during the construction. As in the relocation programme, people must neither own land nor hold citizenship of Solo (KTP) to be eligible to apply for a flat in such a house. The condition is that dwellers near the channel need to prove that they have lived on the spot for the last decades (Interview 19). Later, when flats are still available or become available, they will be treated like the other city flats (*rusunawa* units) and the corresponding eligibility conditions apply (Solo-KTP, income limit).

The *rumah deret* approach demonstrated some advantages over other strategies: First, the houses are nearly completely financed from the city government's budget, ensuring less bureaucracy, better involvement of the dwellers in the process, and smoother and faster development. Second, the houses can more easily be realised compared to common public housing blocks (*rusunawa*), since they require less space due to their smaller size. Third, and most importantly, the houses are built on the same plots or in close proximity to the former living areas of future inhabitants and offer space for small shops or home-based industries in the ground floor. In such a way, social ties to neighbours as well as the customer base of the economic activities of the future inhabitants can be maintained (Interview 15). Affected residents are also less likely to resist the project, since they receive improved housing conditions in the same spot. As a result, former squatter areas near Kali PePe were transformed into revitalised areas with improved livelihoods and the area became a government-owned asset, generating rents and economic activities (Interview 15).

Due to these advantages, the approach of *rumah deret* has proven feasible for revitalising riverbanks without interrupting communities too much. It is a means to overcome the difficulties to find adequate land either for *rusunawa* development or for the relocation programme. The approach also has its constraints, however. Unlike the *rusunawa* programme and the programme relocation, no funding from the central government is available. Thus, this approach poses a much higher burden for the city budget. Furthermore, it does not target low-income people only, since the new rowhouses are designated to people already occupying a specific area regardless of whether they are rich or poor (Interview 22). Nevertheless, Solo's city government has proven its willingness to overcome the challenge of squatter settlements within the city by pioneering another new approach without falling back on simple evictions or slum clearances.

29 Solo's Housing Policy Arrangement

This section analyses three dimensions of Solo's policy arrangement in the housing domain (actors, power, and discourses). Together with the fourth dimension of 'rules of the game'[9], the interplay of these three dimensions shape applied housing policies in the city. Based on data collected by expert interviews and the network survey, the first part explores the actor network structure, including power relations. Dominant discourses related to housing policies are presented after this, arriving at deep insights into the characteristics of Solo's housing policy arrangement.

29.1 Actors and power: the influence network

Actors and their relations with each other form a housing policy network that significantly shapes the organisation of Solo's housing policy arrangement. The collected network data were used as an input for a social network analysis that makes it possible to illustrate the results in a network influence map (for details on the methods used cf. chapter 12). Solo's network is constituted of 72 nodes (ie actors, such as institutions, organisations, and individuals) and 193 edges (ie relations among actors). Actors were categorised in four groups: government, the civil sector, the private sector, and international organisations. They share values of 48.6 %, 30.6 %, 12.5 % and 8.6 % respectively (cf. figure 74). Not surprisingly, government actors clearly dominate the network, but also stakeholders from the civil sector (ie NGOs, CBOs, research institutions) hold a significant share. In addition, international organisations were mentioned quite often, testifying to the activities of development cooperation organisations (US-AID, GIZ, UN-Habitat, World Bank, or JICA) providing funding and advice. Most of the actors are place-based, carrying out their main activities at city level (47.2 %), or neighbourhood level (15.3 %). A significant number of actors, however, is not place-based. Actors from the national level (19.4 %), the international level (12.5 %), and the provincial

9 The dimension of 'rules of the game' is explored in chapter 31.4 for both cities.

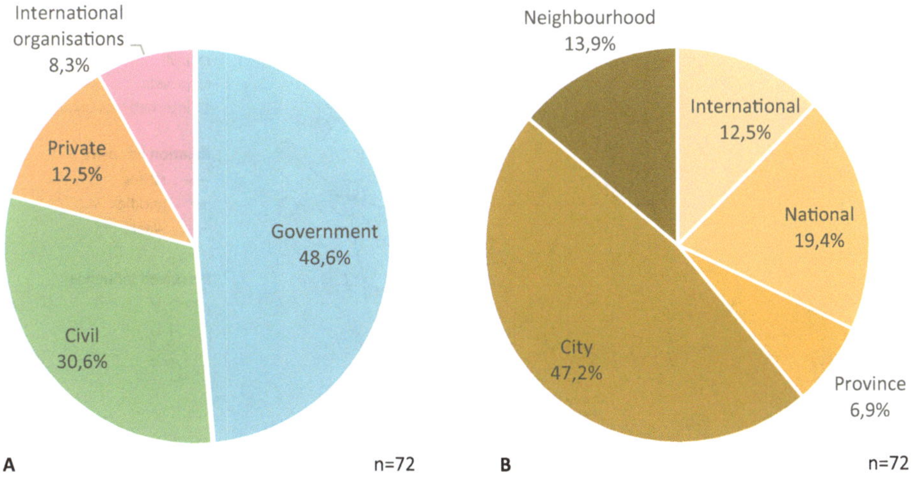

Fig. 74 Categorisation (A) and spatial levels (B) of 72 actors in Solo's housing policy network
Source: Illustration by author. Own data (2015)
Note: For details on the actor categorisation, cf. figure 15

level (6.9 %) have a stake in Solo's housing policy network. Especially the national level is important, since actors at this level provide much of the funding for local programmes, as well as strategic directives of applied housing policies.

Solo's actor network in the housing domain is visualised in figure 75. Actors with a high number of relations appear in the centre of the graph, and nodes of the most influential networks are illustrated larger. The most important actors are exclusively government actors at different administrative levels that are well linked to each other. Actors from society (research institutions, NGOs, CBOs and residents, etc) and the private sector (developers, banks, etc) are less influential and located more on the fringes of the network. However, some of these actors are located in the centre and are quite well connected to other stakeholders, showing a high centrality rating. In addition, several international organisations are active in the city, but with little perceived influence.

The local DPU branch and BAPPEDA are the most influential actors in Solo's housing domain. In the case of BAPPEDA, this result was expected, since this governmental agency creates the general development strategy for the city, oversees the budget and has the task of coordinating all other departments of the city administration. 'All agencies are centred on BAPPEDA[…]' (Interview 14) and tasks are '[…] planning, monitoring and coordination. To integrate programmes and to formulate strategies' (Interview 17). More surprising was the result for DPU. This department is even considered as more influential than BAPPEDA in housing policies (considering indictors for perceived influence), even though it has lower values considering the centrality indicators (cf. table 32). DPU has the task of developing and managing all kinds of public

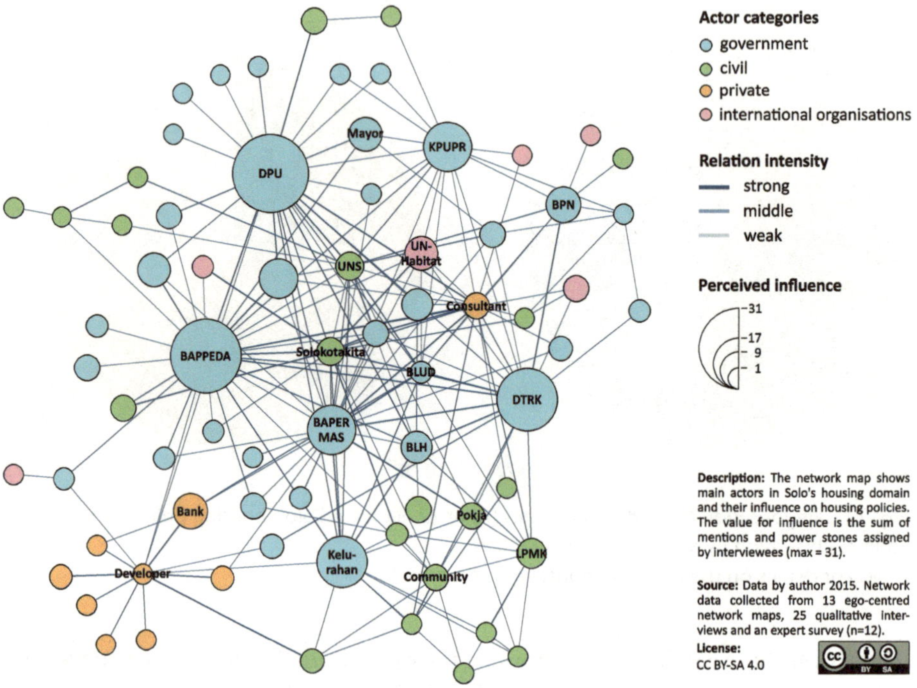

Fig. 75 Solo's actor network in the housing domain
Source: Illustration by author. Own data 2015

infrastructure (eg roads, public facilities, street lightning) and is the central player in Solo when it comes to social housing. It has a leading role in the *rusunawa* and in the *rumah deret* programme. The tenements are mainly built by this organisation, and DPU is responsible for contracting and management. DPU is involved in one way or another in all other housing programmes (RTLH, Relocation). In the case of the relocation programme, for example, in addition to the construction of infrastructure and the connection to public services, technical assistance for the construction of houses is provided in the form of consultancy (Interview 19).

Two departments of the city administration stand out next in the ranking and are considered as very important for local housing policies: BAPERMAS and DTRK. DTRK is naturally involved in many of the housing programmes, since all issues related to spatial planning – ie the spatial plan, zoning, site plans, building permits, and the general layout and design of residential areas are managed by this department. A speciality of Solo, however, is the importance assigned to BAPERMAS. This agency, which has the broadly formulated task of community empowerment, was chosen as the leading agency for the local slum upgrading programme (Programme RTLH) and the relocation programme (Program Relokasi). Its role is to oversee these projects, verify data and proposals, assist the community, and facilitate the implementation process (Interview 15). Based on strong ties to other municipal agencies, to authorities on the ground (the *kelurahan* offices) as well as to the communities and their working groups (*Pokja*), BAPERMAS oversees and coordinates the implementation of the programmes. In the case of the relocation programme, for instance, DTRK and DPU are involved as equal partners, forming a team for realising all issues related to spatial planning, infrastructure, and public facilities while the community based working groups (*Pokja*) organise the community and realise the relocation. Together with the *kelurahan* offices as the lowest formal administrative bodies of the city government these working groups at neighbourhood level are the actors responsible for implementing the programmes supervised by BAPERMAS.

The Ministry of Public Works and Housing (KPUPR is, of course, also among the most important actors for Solo's housing policies albeit only ranking in sixth place considering perceived influence. The ministry provides much of the funding and creates the technical guidelines, rules, and national housing programmes and initiatives. It is well connected to most of the place-based authorities, particularly to DPU, guiding this agency in all technical questions and providing the funds for the development of social housing blocks (*rusunawa*). There are also relations with various international organisations that are needed to finance loans for national housing initiatives. These funds are channelled to local authorities via KPUPR.

The mayor of Solo and the city's House of Representatives (DPRD) are only located at the periphery of the network and their role is not explicitly mentioned as very important for housing policies. Nevertheless, the mayor has strong ties to BAPPEDA and DPU and the role of the mayor is considered as important: 'The mayor gives instructions to BAPPEDA and the house of representatives controls the budget of each agency' (Interview 14). As has been pointed out in the content section (cf. chapter 28), Solo's mayor had a central role for initiating policies. During Jokowi's term of office in 2007, for example, he was a decisive factor in the resettlement programme. By directly addressing the people he succeeded in convincing affected residents to be relocated thanks to the authority he gained by his office. However, the mayor seems to only give the general direction, and is not unconditionally involved in the process and the technical details of implementing programmes. This assumption is also supported by the fact that both the way programmes were implemented and the general political direction were maintained, even when Jokowi was no longer mayor. This suggests that the mayor's position is not the only decisive factor for the implementation of a political direction. International organisations are present in Solo's housing network. Interviewees mentioned the World Bank, GIZ, US-AID, and JICA. They do not directly influence housing policies in the city, but are involved in a project-based manner or by funding housing and upgrading programmes via KPUPR at the national level. An exception is UN-Habitat. This organisation is perceived as having comparably more influence on Solo's housing policies. This is mainly due to past activities, ie the temporary establishment of Solo as a pilot city for UN-Habitat's slum upgrading facility (BLUD) (cf. chapter 28.2).

Beside the indicator of perceived influence, which was derived from ego-centred network maps, additional centrality indicators were calculated for each actor in the network using social network analysis. Three indicators were calculated: betweenness, degree, and closeness centrality). These three indicators are commonly regarded as 'power indicators' and are therefore predestined to complement the indicators of perceived influence. The results are several tables with values for each indicator that can be ranked. These rankings were combined and included into a table showing the 15 most important actors in Solo's housing domain (cf. table 32). For each indicator the actor's rank within the network is presented separately and an average is calculated.

The comparison between the different methods for calculating power produces some interesting results. Many of the actors regarded as most influential by the interviewees show also high centrality degrees, confirming the assumption about their influence. Others, however, are perceived as influential by interviewees, but show only low centralities and vice versa. An actor with a value for perceived influence and lower centrality values is BPN. Since this agency is mostly needed for land certification, the importance assigned by the interviewees can be interpreted to mean that formalisation of squatter settlements is still an important issue in the city. BPN's low centrality indicators, however, suggest that this organisation is perceived as powerful in all matters of land acquisition, but has only limited influence on applied housing policies.

The most interesting aspects revealed by the calculation of centrality indicators, however, is the appearance of actors in high rankings that are not considered as very influential by local experts. The comparison with centrality indicators catapults some non-governmental actors into the centre of attention. As already illustrated in figure 75, the actors UNS, Solo Kota Kita, UN-Habitat and 'consultant' appear with central positions in the housing policy network. Local experts do not perceive UNS and Solo Kota Kita as very influential, but both actors have an important mediating role. Both show high centrality values reflecting their large networks to government agencies, actors from the civil society (other NGOs, universities, and the communities) as well as relations to international organisations. Mostly, they are not directly involved in creating or implementing housing policies, but through their activities, they are important stakeholders influencing indirectly urban policies. Solo Kota Kita, for instance, has completed several projects and reports on Solo's *kampungs* and has, for instance, in collaboration with volunteers and students from UNS, created a database on the different *kampungs*, revealing problems and deficits. In such a way, the framework for new ideas and problem-solving policies was laid. For many of the upgrading programmes, private professionals are hired (eg the PNPM programme) as facilitators for programme implementation. These consultants are also not considered as influential, but they show high centrality values. Since they work with many actors from all sectors, they have a bridging function between the authorities on the one hand and the communities and *Pokjas* on the other.

Table 38 The 15 most important actors in Solo's housing domain in terms of influence and centrality

#	Actor name	Category	Level	Perceived influence (PI1)	Perceived influence (PI2)	Centralities: Betweenness (BC)	Centralities: Closeness (CC)	Centralities: Degree (DC)	Average
				Rank					
1	BAPPEDA	government	city	2	2	1	1	1	1.4
2	DPU	government	city	1	1	2	2	2	1.6
3	BAPERMAS	government	city	5	5	4	3	3	4
4	DTRK	government	city	3	4	7	5	5	4.8
5	KPUPR	government	national	6	3	8	10	8	7
6	Kelurahan	government	neighbour-hood	4	19	5	7	11	9.2
7	UNS	civil	city	15	13	9	6	6	9.8
8	Solo Kota Kita	civil	city	16	11	11	9	7	10.8
9	BLH	government	city	12	10	12	11	12	11.4
10	BPN	government	national	8	7	10	20	13	11.6
11	Consultant	private	city	17	40	6	4	4	14.2
12	BLUD	government	city	35	6	15	8	10	14.8
13	LPMK	civil	neighbour-hood	14	8	16	22	14	14.8
14	Bank	private	national	9	15	18	26	21	17.8
15	PDAM	government	city	7	12	42	14	18	18.6

Source: Table by author. Each indicator is calculated/derived from survey data (2015). Data for PI1 derived from ego-centred network maps (n = 13) and for PI2 from an expert survey (n = 12). BC, CC and DC are calculated from the network graph of Solo's housing domain
Note: The top 10 actors for each indicator were included in the table featuring their rank (some were excluded for PI2 due to irrelevance). Influence indicators were directly assessed by experts (PI1 by Net-Map Method, PI2 by expert survey), while centrality indicators were calculated from the network graph using social network analysis (cf. chapter 12.4). The table is sorted by average rank

It can be concluded that Solo's housing policy network is shaped mainly by governmental agencies, which are also the most influential actors. However, a high number of actors from civil society also characterises the network. Some of them hold central positions in the network, mediating between residents and government organisations. Many of them are also involved in programme implementation. Therefore, Solo's housing policy network can be described as an arrangement where government agencies are the crucial players designing policies top-down, but allow and promote the presence and participation of actors from civil society needed to communicate and implement many of the governmental programmes.

29.2 Discourse strands on how to house the poor in Solo

The discourses on how to deal with the city's poor population is entangled with the other policy arrangement dimensions and with applied housing policies. The conducted expert interviews make it possible to derive several discourse strands (cf. figure 76). Some are programme specific (eg the goals of resettlement policies), whereas others are more general, related to urban policies in the city. The most obvious strands are illustrated here, revealing hegemonic perceptions on squatters and on proper strategies to address the housing challenge in Solo.

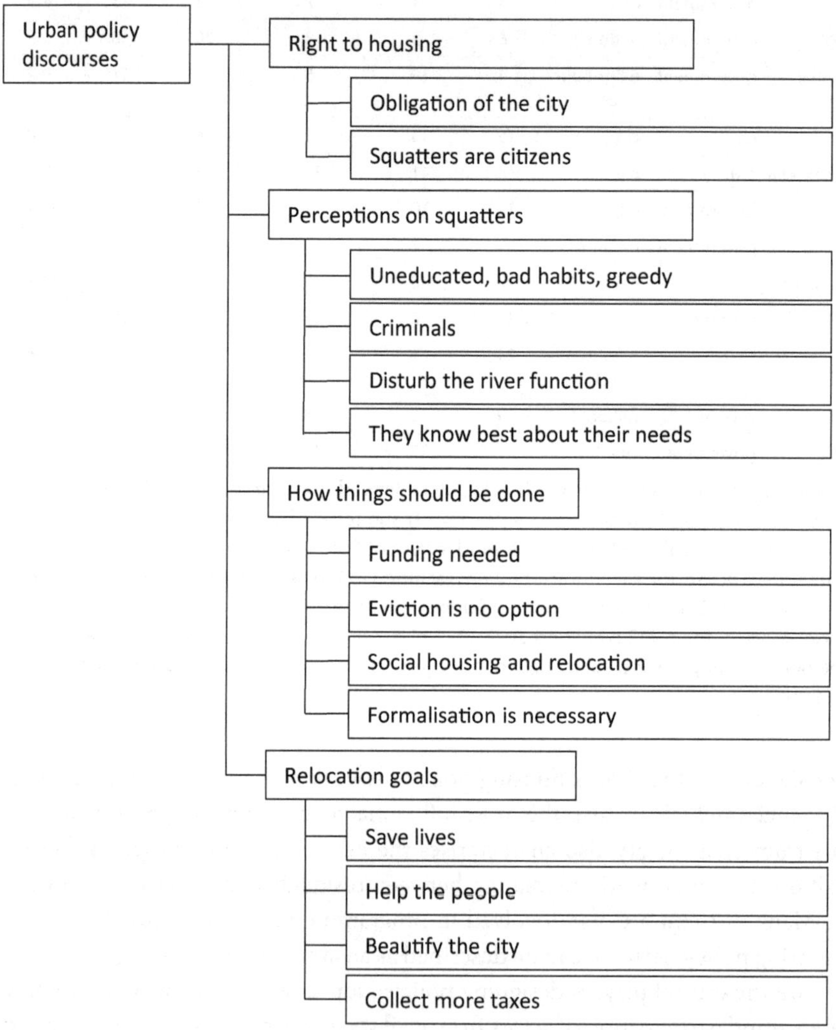

Fig. 76 Category tree for the thematic analysis of expert interviews in Solo
Source: Illustration by author

29.2.1 Housing provision – a central task for the authorities

Solo's government officials accept and acknowledge the obligation of the city to provide housing for its citizens. During several expert interviews, a pragmatic understanding of how to deal with squatter and slum settlements became apparent. Most housing experts in the city believe that this challenge is one of the central tasks of the city administration. Mostly, responsibilities are not denied or shifted to the national authorities, and it is recognised that it is the municipality's obligation to provide adequate and affordable housing for the poor. This opinion was found in interviews with employees of several departments, among them BAPPEDA, DPU, and DTRK and also in the interviews with academic experts. They widely agree that '[...] the provision of housing is mandatory for government affairs [...]' (Interview 22).

Most frequently, this opinion was encountered when asking about the goals of the city's resettlement policy: '[...] the land is very dangerous for residents; they have to be moved to another location that is more suitable. This is part of the right to housing. So the government is compulsory to give the right to land and the right to housing' (Interview 12). The relocation programme was in fact carried out without making a difference between citizens and non-citizens living on the riverbanks (with or without official residency in Solo). Both groups were equally eligible to receive support from this government policy, provided they agreed to the relocation and to the registration procedure in their new location. This approach is remarkable, since differences are usually made in terms of eligibility between citizens (with KTP) and migrants (without KTP). It could be argued that this rule was simply suspended given the magnitude of the 2007 disaster as one of the interviewees suggested: 'Homes that are on government-owned lands are automatically declared illegal. But illegal or legal, the government's obligation, when there is a disaster, is that they remain citizens' (Interview 14). In fact, however, this view is not programme-specific or only due to the flood disaster of 2007. It is also evident in other housing programmes, especially those set up by the city administration. This is the case, for example, with the rowhouse programme (*rumah deret*), where citizenship plays a role, but the rule is not strictly applied. In many cases, the duration of living in the city is seen as a more decisive point for eligibility rather than any formal papers.

29.2.2 Perceptions on squatters: uneducated and bad habits, but with amazing skills

Perceptions on slum and squatter dwellers (or the poor in general) differ widely among Solo's authorities and housing experts. On the one hand, these groups are afflicted with many prejudices, casting them as uneducated people with bad habits; on the other hand, they are recognised as an important part of the city, as people that live under difficult circumstances but have amazing abilities of self-help.

Many interviewees transported their perception on squatter dwellers of being uneducated and having generally bad habits. For example, the authorities of Mojosongo expressed their fears about the new arrivals (people resettled from the riverbanks) in their area: 'We hope that people in the new relocation have a commitment to help each other, become wealthier and will have a better behaviour; that they will improve their behaviour, maybe more care with the environment something like this. Because when they were at the riverbank, they did not care how to put the garbage in the right place' (Interview 09). This statement indirectly presents the opinion that the reason for the bad living conditions at the riverbanks must lie in the bad behaviour of the residents and it is assumed that this behaviour is caused by a lack of education. Other government officials confirm these perceptions and cast riverbank dwellers as uneducated, and as not thinking about their own future: It would be difficult to '[…] attract their participation [in government programmes] and attract their concern about how to make their future life' (Interview 19, BAPPEDA). Riverbank dwellers are also considered as uneducated because they occupy land that does not belong to them. Some interviewees even regarded them as criminals since they have stolen land. It is assumed that they do not occupy state land out of a necessity to survive, but out of pure calculation in order to make profit from it (Interview 11). Winny Astuti, a renowned lecturer at UNS and involved in many of the city's housing programmes, however, puts this assumption into perspective and explains that people are sometimes simply not aware that they occupy government-owned land. She also explains that they have the wrong perceptions about the relocation policy letting them appear as greedy:

> So, I mean some people don't know that they stay in [state land that is restricted.] Some people do not understand. They live at the dam […] and when they get land, actually it should be communicated that this is the benefit for them. Because they do not have land at all and now they received land and got houses, but still because they are not involved, no education. So, people feel that they could get more and more. I mean it should be explained to them. The measures are for the benefit of the city […] (Interview 12).

In her statement she criticises a lack of communication about the programme ('it should be communicated') which results in these wrong perceptions and causes an attitude among relocated residents of being greedy ('[they] feel they could get more and more'). The perception about the poor than is that they are greedy, but she claims that it is not their fault, but more caused by lacking communication and missing explanations.

In addition, other government officials agree that in particular squatters need to be educated. They have to learn that they are illegally occupying land and that their life along the rivers is dangerous due to flood events. The informal settlements on the riverbanks are perceived as disturbing the function of the river and preventing proper management. Therefore, the goal of the relocation is 'to bring the function of the riverbank back. It means that the water can flow without any obstacles' (Interview 06).

By removing these 'obstacles' – the houses along the riverbanks – the opinion is expressed that floods could be prevented. 'Our role is to educate the public that if the land is not normalised the impact will be another flood' (Interview 18).

Some city government officials articulated contrary perceptions on marginalised groups as well. They ascribe – entirely in the spirit of Turner (1968a) – astonishing abilities to the inhabitants of the riverbanks (Interview 14). This assessment is based on past programmes implemented in the city together with local residents. In all these programmes, it was always the communities that organised themselves and that were ready to create working groups to implement the projects. Since this approach was used for the relocation of street vendors, for slum upgrading, and for the resettlement of riverbank residents, Solo's authorities have understood that marginalised groups have the ability to help themselves if they are properly supported.

29.2.3 How things should be done: formalisation and participatory approaches

> *'Kita tidak boleh memaksa!'* ['We must not force!'] (Interview 14).

From these perceptions on slum and squatter dwellers and from the experiences with past participatory programmes, a common understanding on implementation procedures and about the necessity to provide adequate housing can be derived. There is a consensus among Solo's authorities on the nature of housing policies for the poor. Approaches to be pursued are social housing, *in situ* slum upgrading and relocation policies to formalise all land in question. Regarding procedures it is agreed to continue the participatory approach developed in the city, where the initiatives are implemented top-down by the authorities, but during the implementation stage authorities only assist, letting communities and their working groups realise the projects through self-help. This procedure has the advantage of creating more ownership for the projects among communities and mitigating the funding constraints faced by the city government. A lack of financial means was frequently mentioned as the largest constraint for scaling housing policies (Interview 14, 15, 17). Although the city budget has increased since the introduction of decentralisation policies, much of the annual funds are still received from the national government.

A recurring perspective among interviewed experts was a general agreement on the necessity of formalisation. Informality is seen as a phenomenon that needs to be addressed and it would be in the interest of the city administration to enforce the formal plans and rules. The relocation programme of 2007 is widely regarded as very successful in this respect. It is seen as a first step to overcome the challenge of squatter settlements in the city. Authorities frame the relocation programme as an assistance for the people: 'We offer them to relocate, this programme is open and not by force. We are not structuring or evicting, but we want to save lives. Because people who live on the banks live in dangerous conditions to themselves and outside the flood area because their homes are a water park if flooded' (Interview 15). The story told is that the city government's primary interest is in helping the people, but this is not the only goal. Certainly, in view of the 2007 disaster, the initial focus was on direct aid, but from a long-term perspective the objectives are different, namely the formalisation of the entire urban area and the beautification of the city. Even without the flood event, the resettlement measures would continue, as recent years have shown. It is in the interest of the city government to formalise all areas of the city for various reasons. One of them is increased revenues: '[...] because when the government gives legal status to the people they will pay tax and everything' (Interview 12). This was already the main reason when relocating the street vendors to formal marketplaces in 2006. It can be concluded that the flood event of 2007 offered an opportunity and reasoning to introduce far-reaching resettlement measures for the goal of formalising all areas in the city. An employee of BPN pointed out: '[...] when the land is not normalised, the impact for Solo city will be flood again such as in 1966 and 2007' (Interview 18). This reasoning seems pretentious, and suggests that the squatters would be to blame for the floods in the city. This is very unlikely; the causes for the unusual flood event are to be seen in the high precipitation sums at the end of 2007 (Satrio 2010).

The doctrine of formalisation is mainly carried out by ongoing relocation policies. It is widely acknowledged that resettlement can only be conducted by encouragement and participation of the dwellers, not by using forced evictions. It is necessary to convince the people to move to another place or to accept government programmes: 'The programme is not eviction, because this causes social problems. [...] we must not force (Kita tidak boleh memaksa!)' (Interview 14). Indeed, the relocation policies are voluntary and many households still resisted and stayed at the riverbanks. They were allowed to do so provided they have some legal land certificate. Nevertheless, these residents report from indirect pressure. The city government, for example, would no longer look after access to water and electricity, nor would it maintain the paths on the riverbank, so that supply bottlenecks would increasingly occur. The goals are, the residents assume, to convince them in the end to agree to the resettlement (Interview 05).

In Solo, the interviewed experts agree that a multiplicity of approaches is necessary to overcome the challenge of slum and squatter settlements in the city. The authorities consider social housing (*rusunawa*) and the slum upgrading programme (RTLH) as the best options for low-income people. The focus, however, has been on formalisation strategies over the last years. Since two decades, the city government pursues a formalisation approach aiming to regulate all areas and aspects of urban life. For all informal settlements, this means relocation to new formal settlements or social housing in the variants of *rusunawa* towers or *rumah deret* (Interview 14, 19).

29.3 Characteristics of Solo's housing policy arrangement

From the analysis, the characteristics of Solo's housing policy arrangement unfold. Each of the dimensions has specific attributes that fit into an overall picture and result in specific housing policies. Table 6 provides an overview of these attributes. With regard to the dimensions of actors and power, Solo's policy arrangement is organised through a hierarchical actor network with multiple power hubs. Authorities of the municipality are most influential, significantly shaping the implementation of national housing policies, and have created local programmes. Most influential among these hubs are BAPPEDA and DPU, but power is also shared with subordinated municipal agencies that appear quite influential in the network and have important roles in the implementation of programmes. These agencies derive their power largely from authoritative resources (ie laws and regulations). The mayor and the House of Representatives, in contrast, are less relevant in the network. The House of Representatives is hardly mentioned and only the mayor is considered to have some influence in terms of general policy directions. On the national level, KPUPR and BPN are considered as important. The former is relevant for funding purposes and for providing the general strategic direction, the latter is necessary to regulate informal settlements.

Non-governmental actors, ie NGOs, the private sector, or academic institutions hardly influence the general strategic direction of housing policies. Nevertheless Solo's actor network shows a great diversity of actors from different sectors involved. Some of them occupy central positions in the network (UNS, Solo Kota Kita, Consultants). Based on their dispositional power, they are important for programme implementation and work as intermediaries between authorities and communities. In addition, international actors are present in Solo's policy network. They hold no direct influence, but often have a stake in specific projects or are involved as funding organisations. Communities and residents are located only peripherally in the actor-influence network and hardly have a say in shaping housing policies. Their participation, however, is needed for project implementation, where it is strong and much promoted by the authorities. The private sector, developers, and their advocacy organisations are equally not considered as important. The obvious reason is that the profit margin in housing development for low-income people is not high enough.

Several rules of the game (presented for both cities in chapter 31.4) shape Solo's housing policy arrangement. There are national rules and regulations derived from housing laws that determine the resources and capacity of each actor in the network (eg the dominance of BAPPEDA) as well as their tasks and responsibilities. Only with the enactment of the housing and settlement law, (UU01/2011) have new responsibilities and obligations been established. Some other rules were found that influence more directly applied housing policies: only official citizens of Solo are eligible to receive support from government programmes, rental contracts in social housing are of a temporary nature, and the riverbanks within the city are under the official responsibility of the provincial government. However, these rules are not strictly implemented in Solo; there is room to manoeuvre. The decision about support for non-citizens, for instance, is made in a case-specific manner, *de facto* residency outdoing the condition of formal citizenship. In the case of the riverbanks, a non-place-based agency may be officially responsible, but the city administration recognises the riverbanks and their inhabitants as the task of the municipality and implements appropriate measures. By bending rigid rules, manifold problems and conflicting interests can be avoided, focusing instead on finding pragmatic solutions that are people-oriented.

Several dominant discourse fields characterise Solo's housing discourse. These are the general orientation of urban policies, dominant views on slum and squatter residents, and opinions on sound housing policies. Interviewed experts often articulated the goal of a green, cultural, and inclusive city that recognises the provision of housing for all as mandatory for government affairs. This opinion was hegemonic. The views about slum and squatter residents were more diverse and not dominated by one opinion. Many described these population groups as poor, uneducated, and with bad habits. Others emphasised their amazing abilities of self-help and self-organisation. Considering proper means to address the housing challenge for the poor, there is a consensus that a multiplicity of approaches (social housing, slum upgrading, empowerment, and relocations) and formalisation policies are needed. A regulated urban environment is seen as a necessity. Programme implementation is to be done using a participatory approach wherever possible and forced evictions are not at all seen as an option.

The aspects of these four dimensions culminate in a policy arrangement, from which the city's housing policy emerges (cf. table 39). The city administration implements a multiplicity of approaches, including national empowerment and social housing programmes, a local slum upgrading initiative, and the resettlement programme. Solo implements these measures top-down with non-governmental actors having a mediating and facilitating role. In many cases, the residents and their working groups are involved in programme implementation, but not in decision-making.

Table 39 Characteristics of Solo's housing policy arrangement

Actors	Power
– Network with multiple hubs – Mostly government actors (48.6 %) – High diversity of actors (administrative level/sector) – Several municipal agencies have programme lead: DPU, BAPERMAS – Non-governmental actors (Solo Kota Kita, UNS, consultants) work as intermediaries – Communities and their working groups (*Pokjas*) participate in project implementation – KPUPR provides funding and strategic directions – International actors are present	– BAPPEDA and DPU are most influential – Government actors are most powerful – Power is shared among hubs – Power is largely derived from rules and is based on authoritative resources – Exception: Dispositional power of UNS, Solo Kota Kita, Consultants and Kelurahan – Communities and residents have hardly a say in decision-making – Mayor and House of Representatives are not relevant

Rules of the game	Discourses
– Local authorities are responsible for their low-income population (UU 01/2011) – Requirement to draw spatial plans for settlement development – Only citizens are eligible for social housing – Non-citizens are sometimes also eligible – Riverbanks are in the formal responsibility of the province, but the municipality feels responsible for squatters on the riverbank – Social housing is only temporary (5 years) – Social housing managed by municipal authorities (DPU)	– Inclusive, green, and cultural city is the goal – Housing provision is an obligation of the city – Slum/squatter dwellers are poor, uneducated and have bad habits, but have astonishing capacities of self-organisation and self-help – Squatters are citizens but disturb the function of the river – Social housing, relocations, and slum upgrading – Participatory approach for implementation – Formalisation is a necessity, but evictions are no option
Applied policies	
Type of programmes	*Implementation procedure*
– Slum upgrading (RTLH programme) – Social housing (*rusunawa* programme) – Resettlement of informal settlements – Row Housing (*rumah deret*)	– Top-down by the local government – Mediated by non-governmental actors – Resident participation in programme implementation (Pokjas) not in decision-making – Community empowerment

Source: Table by author

Note: Rules of the game are presented in chapter 31.4, where they are examined in more detail

30 Summary: Progressive and Inclusive

This chapter has examined and analysed Solo's housing policies and the content and organisation of Solo's housing policy arrangement. The following questions guided the analysis:

What are the characteristics of Solo's policy arrangement in the housing domain?

- What intervention strategies and programmes are realised for the poor and what do they achieve?
- Which actors are relevant in the housing domain and what influence do they hold?
- What strands shape the local discourse on housing the poor?
- What are the formal and informal rules of the game?

Since the beginning of the 2000s, policies in Solo show a progressive character. The introduction of a participatory budget, the peaceful resettlement of street vendors, and slum upgrading and resettlement programmes with strong citizen participation rightly earned the city the reputation of pursuing innovative urban policies. However, the search for the reasons for these innovations has proven difficult. In many cases, Solo's success is attributed to one person: Joko Widodo (Jokowi). He was mayor in Solo from 2005 to 2012, later governor of Jakarta, and is now acting president of Indonesia. However, the analysis shows that progressive initiatives already existed in the city before Jokowi took office and continued after he left for Jakarta. This suggests the existence of a stable policy arrangement in place prior to Jokowi that provided a breeding ground for innovative urban policies. Certainly, the person Jokowi reinforced this trend. By introducing balancing urban policies aiming to reconcile the interests of different actors in the city while at the same time recognising marginalised groups as partners, he laid the foundation for the vision of a city between tradition and modernity and above all, for a city that makes policies for its citizens.

The municipality's intervention strategy in the housing sector consists of various programmes. In some cases, national programmes are simply implemented locally, in others the city uses its new freedoms gained through decentralisation policies and has started to set up its own initiatives. The confusing multitude of programmes and supporting measures makes it difficult to assess their effect on the city as a whole. For this reason, the analysis was limited to a few programmes, which were deemed sufficient to paint an overall picture. One of the most visible programmes has become the national social housing programme (*rusunawa* programme). Since the 2000s, social housing blocks have increasingly become part of the urban landscape and the number of social housing units has been increasing year by year. In this respect, the municipality has also implemented a number of pilot projects that break up the rigid design and concept of *rusunawa*: smaller apartment blocks (*rumah deret*), better adapted to local conditions, have been developed, financed with local funds. To upgrade existing *kampungs,* the city administration has set up its own slum upgrading programme, which has been running relatively successfully for several years now. In the RTLH programme, households in need of refurbishment have been able to apply for assistance from the city since 2007. The support consists of an incentive directed to whole communities, which form working groups (Pokja) and contribute their labour to carry out improvements of individual houses or community infrastructure. Since its creation, the programme has been running continuously and helping to upgrade and improve existing *kampungs*. Dealing with informal settlements is a particular challenge in Solo. A policy of formalisation is applied for squatter settlements located in many parts of the city. This means the attempt to resettle squatter dwellers either to social housing or to newly built settlements elsewhere in the city. In this process, the self-organisation of the communities into different working groups was utilised again. They carried out the resettlement largely on their own initiative, supported by the city administration in technical and legal questions. This resulted in broad participation by affected residents to implement the resettlement. Over the years, numerous resettlement projects have been carried out which can be regarded as quite successful. Large parts of the urban areas formerly occupied by informal settlements are now public space and the resettled people have largely been able to improve their housing situation. Even though the housing programmes analysed are only one part of all measures implemented, they testify to the stakeholders' commitment for finding solutions to address the challenge of housing.

The implemented measures are based on a specific policy arrangement with its four dimensions of actors, power, rules of the game, and discourses. In Solo, housing policy is largely created by various government actors and implemented top-down. The central actor in the housing-policy network is the Regional Development Planning Agency (BAPPEDA), but several other municipal departments are of similar importance, resulting in a network structure characterised by several power hubs. Although the main actors in the arrangement clearly come from the government, Solo's network is also characterised by a variety of actors from different sectors and administrative levels. Non-governmental actors such as CBOs, NGOs, and consultants play a decisive mediating role and affected communities and their working groups are strongly involved in project implementation. The background for this constellation are rules that are largely determined by national laws. In particular, the housing and settlement law of 2011 set standards in the housing sector and underlines the responsibility of local governments to provide adequate housing. Local government actors have also recognised this as their central task, as is evident from the significance of this issue in analysed housing discourses. Although slum and squatter residents are still labelled with the usual judgements (uneducated, criminal, and bad habits) by some government actors, there is also an understanding that these population groups are quite capable of organising themselves and helping themselves if they are given appropriate support. The discourse is shaped by the vision of a regulated city, which is why attempts are being made to relocate all informal settlements in the city and to fully regulate the urban landscape. However, an approach is predominant that contains a mixture of persuasion and participation and does not consider forced evictions as an option. The residents of informal settlements, often migrants from outside the city, are mostly recognised as equal partners and attempts are made to find solutions collaboratively.

The analysis reveals the existence of a policy arrangement that results in top-down initiated housing policies, characterised by a variety of participative processes and elements in programme implementation. Housing policies follow multiple approaches with the aim of providing adequate and affordable housing for all. The progressive character of policies in Solo seems to have continued since the 2000s, suggesting a relatively stable policy arrangement. The city has succeeded in initiating a process of continuous improvements that take into account the needs of marginalised groups. Solo's housing policy and its policy arrangement can therefore largely be described as inclusive and pro-poor. However, whether the characteristics of the described policy arrangement can be so clearly linked to the implemented programmes and to what extent Solo is en route to becoming a city that recognises the right to the city for all, must be analysed from a comparative perspective. This requires comparing the characteristics found with other cities and testing them against the normative goal of Lefebvre's possible-impossible utopia of an 'urban society'.

VII. COMPARISON AND DISCUSSION

This chapter juxtaposes and compares policy arrangements and their outcome in the housing domain of the two case study cities of Surabaya and Solo and tests the conditions found against the normative foundation of governance derived from Lefebvre's theories. In a first step, applied housing policies in both cities are compared as well as each of the four dimensions of policy arrangements – actors, power, rules of the game and discourses – and similarities and differences between the cities are derived. This analysis reveals the characteristics and nature of unique policy arrangements and housing policies in the two cities. In a second step, these characteristics are tested against a conceived policy arrangement that would be present in Lefebvre's possible-impossible world of an 'urban society'. This analysis concludes that in both cities only few elements are present within the respective policy arrangement that would promote a societal transformation towards an 'urban society'. While both cities have introduced housing policies to achieve adequate housing policies for all, the policies of Solo are more people-centred, participative, and respectful of marginalised groups. Thus, clearly, Solo's policy content respects the right to the city far more than Surabaya's policies do.

The following research questions guide this chapter:

- What are similarities and differences of the identified policy arrangements in Surabaya and Solo (content and organisation)?
- What are formal and informal rules of the game in the two cities?
- To what extent are global and national recommendations implemented at the local level?
- Do identified policy arrangements respect the right to the city and adequate housing?

31 Comparison of Surabaya and Solo

In this section, the two case study cities of Surabaya and Surakarta (Solo) are compared regarding their housing policies and their policy arrangements in place. Of course, in many respects, both cities are unique and a comparison is not feasible. Solo is a medium-sized city of 500,000 inhabitants with moderate centrality, while Surabaya is a metropolis of more than three million inhabitants, the capital of East Java, and the second largest Indonesian agglomeration. Naturally, the challenges and problems in these two cities vary or are of different dimension. Therefore, necessary reductions are made and the analysis is limited to the housing policies and the characteristics of the two existing policy arrangements. To start with, however, some basic socio-economic data are provided, comparing poverty and human development in the two cities.

Table 40 shows the poverty line, the percentage of poor population, and the HDI for Indonesia, Surabaya, and Solo. The indicators suggest higher human development and less poverty for the two cities compared to the national average. These findings underline the advantages of cities compared to rural areas in terms of socio-economic opportunities, urban infrastructures, and service provision. However, living costs are also higher in cities. To capture this, the Indonesian statistical agency calculates poverty lines for each territorial unit[1]. If a person's income falls below this threshold, he or she is classified as poor. When interpreting the data, it must be borne in mind that the indicators for Indonesia always include a rural-urban bias, since rural areas are generally characterised by lower values for human development and higher poverty levels.

In the years 2012 to 2018, poverty lines were raised in both cities and at national average. This is due to economic development, which is accompanied by rising wages and considerable inflation. The Human Development Index reflects this, too. It continuously rose over the years, reaching values of more than approximately 0.8 in both cities, which is considerably higher than the national average (appox. 0.7). In both cities, the number of people living in poverty decreased in the years 2012 to 2018. In Solo, there was a decrease from 12 % to 9 %, which is higher than the national average. In

1 The poverty line is calculated as monthly per capita income. For details on the calculation, see Box 11.

Table 40 Comparison of poverty line, percentage of poor population and human development, Indonesia, Surabaya and Solo

Indicator	Year						
	2012	2013	2014	2015	2016	2017	2018
Indonesia							
Poverty line in Rp. per person	248 317	271 158	302 306	330 306	354 087	373 559	399 761
per month (in €)*	(21)	(20)	(19)	(22)	(24)	(25)	(24)
Percentage poor (%)	11.96	11.37	11.25	11.22	10.89	10.64	9.79
Human Development Index (HDI)**	67.7	68.1	68.9	69.55	70.18	70.81	71.39
Surabaya							
Poverty line in Rp. per person	339 208	372 511	393 151	418 930	438 283	474 365	530 178
per month (in €)*	(28)	(27)	(25)	(28)	(30)	(31)	(32)
Percentage poor (%)	6.25	6.00	5.79	5.82	5.63	5.39	4.88
Human Development Index (HDI)**	78.05	78.51	78.89	79.47	80.38	81.07	81.74
Solo							
Poverty line in Rp. per person	361 517	403 121	385 467	406 840	430 293	448 062	464 063
per month (in €)*	(30)	(29)	(24)	(27)	(29)	(30)	(28)
Percentage poor (%)	12.02	11.75	10.96	10.88	10.87	10.64	9.07
Human Development Index (HDI)**	78.44	78.89	79.34	80.14	80.76	80.85	

Source: Table by author. Data for Indonesia compiled/calculated from BPS (2019b: 51, 2020); data for Solo compiled/calculated from BPS Surakarta (2020a); data for Surabaya compiled/calculated from BPS Surabaya (2020)
Note: * Currency converted using historical annual average conversion rates from fxtop.com
** HDI is multiplied by 100 in this dataset

Surabaya, the decrease was smaller, but the city already reached very low levels with only 5 % of residents living in poverty in 2018. While the values of human development are similar in both cities, this difference in poverty levels is remarkable. Of course, the larger economic base of the city suggests better and more income-earning possibilities which could explain lower values for poverty in Surabaya. From my personal impression, however, poverty levels and living costs appeared much higher in the city compared to Solo. It could also be explained by questioning the value for the poverty line in Surabaya. This value could be set too low, so that many people are not defined as poor. Living costs are much higher in Surabaya compared to Solo and even when considering better income opportunities, it is barely imaginable to live from Rp. 530 0000 (appox. 32€) per month in that city. In Solo, however, this seems rather conceivable considering lower living costs. Taking this into account, the percentage of the poor in Surabaya to be below 5 percent appears to be underestimated.

Overall, it can be said that the two indicators of poverty and human development have improved in both cities during the period covered here and are thus in line with the national average. Neither city stands out due to a particularly advantageous development. The low poverty rate for Surabaya is striking, which either is an underestimate or could be the result of successful housing policies prior to the period under study.

The often-heard statement that the problem of basic shelter has already been solved in Surabaya supports the latter.

31.1 Applied housing policies

The city governments of Surabaya and Solo implement the national housing strategy and associated programmes. Only in recent years did the municipalities added their own programmes funded from the local budget. Due to the large number of different strategies and policies, only resettlement programmes and social housing policies have been examined in more detail in addition to the local initiatives. While the two cities have very different programmes of local origin, the national programmes show fewer differences in terms of content and more in terms of implementation.

General urban policies and programmes

Since the end of the Suharto Era in 1998, Indonesian municipalities have been emancipating themselves more and more from Jakarta and are now able to start their own housing programmes and initiatives, which no longer necessarily need to be approved by Jakarta or depend on national funds. In both cities, new programmes and initiatives were therefore started in the 2000s. In Surabaya, due to the long tradition of slum upgrading and the dominance of a *kampung*-centred policy, the focus of interest remained on improving *kampungs* (cf. chapter 24.2 for details). After the national KIP programme expired in 1998, Surabaya's city administration developed its own programmes to further develop the *kampung* improvement approach and build on past successes. First, C-KIP was initiated, which aimed less at physical upgrading than at promoting the self-management capacities of the communities. The idea was that, through a combination of training measures and micro-credit, CBOs should be enabled to implement improvements in the neighbourhood on their own initiative. This community empowerment approach was strongly based on the internationally propagated enabling approach, which has been recommended on a global level since the 1990s. In a certain respect, this approach can be seen as a further development of the older national improvement programmes. The Green and Clean Programme also went in this direction, following the principle of enablement, aiming to strengthen community self-management. Through the element of competition between different *kampungs* and the prize money to be awarded to the winner, incentives were set for the communities to improve their neighbourhood on their own and thus contribute to a desired city beautification. As the latest programme cycle, the Kampung Unggulan Programme was developed, which is designed to promote the local economies in the *kampungs* (economic empowerment). All these programmes aim in one way or another to preserve existing *kampungs* by creating better housing conditions and livelihoods within these neighbourhoods. Surabaya clearly takes a pioneering role in Indonesia in developing new approaches to improve life in *kampungs*.

At the beginning of the reform era after 1998, Solo initially focused on other topics (cf. chapter 28.2 for details). In contrast to Surabaya, the previous top-down planning system was increasingly questioned and the city administration tried to introduce the idea of participatory planning and budgeting in the city. Community meetings at different levels should decide on parts of the city budget and priorities for future development. This approach became known as *musrenbang* and is now implemented in many cities in Indonesia. Since 2005, with Jokowi as mayor, an inclusive and balanced urban policy began to emerge in the city, trying to balance tradition and modernity. Marginalised groups became more and more focused. This was reflected in the resettlement of the street vendors. After lengthy negotiations with their representatives, they were persuaded to move to newly built market halls, regulating their formerly informal businesses. Since 2007, a locally financed slum upgrading programme (RTLH) has also been set up. This programme aimed to improve individual houses using the CDD approach. In keeping with the spirit of the times, the improvements were carried out by community working groups, which had extensive powers and received limited state funding. Due to the success of these measures, international actors (UN-Habitat) became increasingly aware of the city's policy and began to join the programme in order to test new ideas of slum upgrading. Based on the idea of financial enablement, the focus of these activities were to make informal residents 'bankable'. As many people as possible should be able to receive loans to enable them to invest in their houses. The implementation of these programmes and measures has shown Solo's commitment to its poor population and to the provision of adequate housing. In many respects, Solo has tested diverse and innovative ideas (participation, community-driven, financial enablement), which are clearly based on international discussions and have now partly found their way into national strategies and initiatives.

Resettlement policies

In both cities, a policy of resettlement is being pursued with regard to informal settlements. However, there are clear differences in the implementation of these measures. The aim of resettlement is to formalise as many regions of the city as possible and to transfer them to the intended land use. This is the declared aim in both cities. Informal settlements had developed mainly along rivers, railway lines and, in some cases, cemeteries. In Surabaya, this development was particularly noticeable shortly after independence, when the city grew very fast and the administration did not take action against these settlements. This only changed in Suharto's New Order from the 1970s onwards. Since then, the city has implemented a rigid policy against any form of informality, which continues to this day. However, Surabaya's urban structure is still characterised by a duality between formal and informal areas, which changes in one direction or another depending on the economic and political situation.

Just as in Solo, a flare-up of informality was observed after the Asian crisis in 1998, when the number of street vendors and the size of informal settlements increased rapidly. Prior to these collective experiences, both cities had come to realise that a regulated and formalised urban landscape is an absolute necessity. In Solo, however, the emergence of informal settlements began later, was less massive in scale, and was characterised by a different legal situation. Before the introduction of a modern land system in the 1960s, Solo's Sunan had in many cases distributed land use rights to people who now live on government land. Since the 1980s, however, processes of infiltration have led to an increasing expansion and densification of informal settlements, especially along the city's river courses, which has led to the inhabitants of squatter settlements being increasingly perceived as a problem.

Nevertheless, a different perception of the informal settlements in both cities can be observed, which is also reflected in the measures taken and the way they are implemented. In Solo, the informal settlements seem to be perceived as less alien and threatening, their inhabitants are accepted as residents of the city, the settlements as part of the city. Only the poor housing, living, and environmental conditions are perceived as a problem. In Surabaya, too, the settlements on the riverbanks are perceived as inadequate in terms of living and housing conditions, but other backgrounds also play a role. For historical reasons, informality is generally quickly perceived as a threat to existing power structures and thus also to the formal city. This is also the case with informal settlements, which must be prevented from expanding, as they represent a breeding ground for resistance against the ruling order.

This different perspective on informal settlements is reflected in the measures taken. While Solo pursues an approach that tries to convince the inhabitants of the informal settlements to move to alternative housing options through incentives and broad participation possibilities, the approach in Surabaya is much more authoritarian and strict. Although there are similar negotiations on the modalities of resettlement, the means of forced evictions are applied very quickly if the negotiations fail. Solo's government, in contrast, does not consider forced eviction as a viable option at all. Differences are also made with regard to the inhabitants. In Surabaya, only residents with an official residence in the city are offered some form of compensation or an alternative place to live, while all others, migrants and long-time but unregistered residents, are rarely offered this option. In Solo, on the other hand, most resettlement actions made no or hardly any distinction between these groups.

Both cities have set up resettlement programmes to deal with their informal settlements. In Surabaya, actions began in the 1980s to clear squatter settlements in the city centre and along the central river channel running through it. Later, since the 1990s and 2000s, these measures were extended to more and more areas further away from the city centre. The measures are very restrictive and the municipality only offers social housing as an alternative for squatter dwellers. However, this option is only available to a fraction of the affected population, namely those who have been able to obtain an official residence permit. All others are usually evicted and the administration does not see it as its duty to take care of these residents. In Solo, on the other hand, massive resettlements took place especially at the end of the 2000s. A major resettlement programme was initiated following a severe flood event, which mainly affected the squatter settlements along the rivers. In doing so, the city relied on the tried and tested community-driven approaches that had already been used for the resettlement of street vendors and the RTLH programme. Many negotiations convinced the communities to resettle and they were granted extensive possibilities to codetermine the programme. Community-based working groups were entrusted with finding new locations and managing the process. Through this participatory approach, the city government succeeded in resettling a large part of the residents without using force. No coercive measures are planned for the residents remaining along the rivers either; instead, an attempt is made to find solutions together.

Social housing policies

Both cities have been promoting the national social housing programme (*rusunawa* programme) since the 2000s and increasingly more social housing blocks with tenements for low-income residents are realised (cf. chapters 24.3 for Surabaya and 28.3 for Solo). This trend towards a provider approach is driven by national housing policies and initiatives (eg the 1,000 towers programme, the housing law UU 01/2011 and PSR) and a sustained political commitment (cf. chapter 20.6). In Surabaya, this development set in significantly earlier compared to Solo. In both cities *rusunawa* development accelerated since the 2000s. By 2015 Surabaya had realised 4,469 flats in *rusunawa* and Solo 708. In relative numbers these are 138 flats per 100,000 inhabitants in Solo and 157 flats per 100,000 inhabitants for Surabaya. In both cities, employees of the city administration report annually increasing numbers of applications for flats in *rusunawa*, even though many Indonesians consider this type of living still as alien to their culture (cf. box 14). Design and size of realised blocks and flats are similar and follow the same national designs and trends (from single blocks to twin blocks and increasing size of single flats). Differences are present most of all in the management structure. In Surabaya, there is a dual management structure for *rusunawa* towers meant for low-income people. Some *rusunawa* are managed by the provincial government and others by the municipal government, both realised in locations within the city boundaries. This has consequences for the occupancy[2] and results sometimes in overlapping

2 For eligibility an official residence (KTP) in Surabaya or East Java is required depending on *rusunawa*.

responsibilities for the same target groups. In the case of relocation policies against squatter settlements, for instance, the city government and the provincial government partly shift the responsibility to each other, so that a lot of coordination work is necessary to offer an alternative housing solution for affected residents. In the eyes of the inhabitants, this leads to incomprehensible delays and to the feeling that they are left alone. In addition to social housing for low-income groups, also other *rusun* towers (owner-occupation or rental) are realised in Surabaya for other target groups. These are student flats, company flats, and apartments for police or military personnel. These developments are not (yet) present in Solo. In this city, *rusunawa* developments are relatively new, starting only in 2004, and no dual management structures are present. All issues related to social housing are concentrated in one department (DPU) and additional *rusun* towers for other target groups are not present, even though there are plans in this regard for the near future.

Both cities face the challenge of increasing land prices and the decrease of areas available for further development of *rusunawa*. This problem is addressed by several measures. One option pursued is to develop increasingly peripheral locations, though the problems related to this trend (stigmatisation, increased distance to public facilities and jobs) are well recognised in both cities. An additional possibility to deal with the rising demand for social housing flats is the enactment of temporal limits for rental contracts, in order to give more households the possibility to benefit from a flat in a *rusunawa*. Both cities have therefore adopted respective regulations. In Surabaya, the rental contracts are limited to nine years, while in Solo rental contracts are signed on an annual basis with a maximum period of five years. These regulations are based on the widespread assumption that the inhabitants will be able to buy their own property after a few years. Whether this is true, however, may be questioned. Solo has come up with another innovative solution to this challenge. Instead of developing full-scale *rusunawa* towers, the city government has realised some pilot projects, ie rowhouses (*rumah deret*), which are smaller in scale and can thus be realised on smaller land plots directly on the site of existing squatter settlements. Even though this new idea demands complicated discussions with existing communities and a lot more planning and design work (due to individual design of the houses for each project), the successful realisation of some smaller projects can be regarded as proof of concept and might be a solution for other cities as well.

Different policies in Surabaya and Solo

Local housing policies can indeed be considered innovative in both cities. Surabaya is clearly a pioneer and thought leader in the development of the Indonesian *kampung*. Solo, on the other hand, pursues holistic approaches towards marginal groups, who are acknowledged as citizens and, through community-based working groups, the implementation of improvements is placed in the hands of the communities. In both cities, the aim is to regulate urban space completely. There are differences particularly with regard to the inhabitants of squatter settlements (*kampung liar*) or inhabitants without registered residence. The approach in Surabaya seems to be much stricter and fiercer than in Solo. In general, informal residents are usually excluded from aid programmes but in Solo, they are nevertheless often considered, as the example of resettlement has shown (on the resettlement, cf. chapter 28.4). Social housing is being promoted in both cities and is increasingly perceived as the solution for the poor population. There are also many links to international discourses. Since the end of the 1990s, for example, the ideas of the enabling approach have been implemented in a wide variety of programmes in both cities. Efforts have been made to strengthen community organisations to enable them to carry out their own projects. This can be seen on the one hand as a neoliberal outsourcing of central tasks of the city administration, on the other hand as a favourable extension of participation possibilities for the inhabitants. Also in line with international recommendations is the attempt of financial enablement of the inhabitants. In both cities, various measures are being taken to make the inhabitants 'bankable', ie to enable them to take out a loan or mortgage and use this money to improve their housing. This measure can also be interpreted as a further attempt of neoliberal urban development, as an attempt to include as many aspects as possible in the circulation of capital. The trend towards more social housing, on the other hand, can be derived less from the international discussion, but is due to national trends. Initiatives from Jakarta are pushing social housing construction, while it is rejected internationally as being too cost-intensive. The different design of individual programmes can be traced back to the different policy arrangements in the two cities. These are therefore examined comparatively in the following sections.

31.2 Actors and power

The actor influence networks in the housing domain of the two cities show similarities and differences. In both networks, government actors are the dominant policy-makers and actors from other sectors (civil and private) are less important for housing policies. The characteristics of the housing policy networks in Surabaya and Solo are presented in table 41. The metrics are similar considering nodes, edges, density, and average degree centrality. Solo's network consists of more nodes (72) compared to Surabaya (65) and actors have more relations (193) to each other than in Surabaya (152). This can be interpreted as a first indication that a greater number of actors is involved in policy-making processes in Solo compared to Surabaya. Considering actor categories and the actors' spatial scales more differences become visible. Government actors mostly shape both networks. In Surabaya, they hold a share of 60 %, while Solo's network consists of slightly less than 50 % government actors. Solo's network is clearly characterised by a higher

Table 41 Network characteristics of the housing policy networks in Surabaya and Solo

		Surabaya	Solo
Metrics*	Nodes	65	72
	Edges	152	193
	Density	0.073	0.074
	Average degree centrality	4.677	4.836
	Average path length	2.58	2.55
Actor category** [%]	Government	60	48.61
	Civil	26.15	30.56
	Private	9.23	12.5
	International organisations	4.62	8.33
Spatial level*** [%]	International	7.69	12.5
	National	21.54	19.44
	Province	9.23	6.94
	City	46.15	47.22
	Neighbourhood	15.38	13.89

Source: Table by author. Own data 2015
Note: * Network metrics were calculated performing a social network analysis (cf. chapter 12.4) ** Actors are categorised in four classes 'government', 'civil', 'private' and 'international organisations'. Each of these classes consists of several sub-classes. The category 'private', for instance, consists of private companies, banks, developers, associations, and professionals. Under 'civil', research institutions, NGOs, CBOs, the community, and individuals are subsumed. For more details, see figure 15 *** Depending on the main activities, a spatial level was assigned to each actor

diversity of actors from different sectors. This is a second indication that Solo's network involves more non-governmental actors in the policy-making process. Considering the spatial scales of involved actors, shares are similar in the housing policy networks of the two cities. Most important for both city's housing policies is the city level, followed by the national level. This result is not surprising, since housing programmes are exclusively conceptualised at these two levels. In Surabaya, some agencies at the provincial level are influential, insisting on their responsibility over the riverbanks and interfering with their own policies of resettlement and social housing in the affairs of the municipal authorities. In Solo's housing policy network, actors from the provincial level are not influential. Instead, more international actors are considered as relevant compared to Surabaya. These are the results of recent development cooperation activities in the city and are mainly due to the activities of UN-Habitat, which temporarily classified Solo as a pilot city for one of its slum upgrading facilities.

Actor categorisation by type proved more difficult than expected, but since required for the network analysis, it was decided to develop a generalised categorisation in four classes: 'government', 'civil', 'private', and 'international organisation'. Each of these classes consists of several sub-classes (cf. figure 15). Government agencies (eg Kementerian, Dinas, Kelurahan), state-owned companies (eg Perumnas, PLN) and government institutions (ie all representative bodies of the people: LPMK, Mayor, DPRD, APEKSI, etc) as well as mentioned government programmes[3] were subsumed in the category of 'government'. Multilateral organisations (eg World Bank, UN, ADB) and development cooperation organisations (GIZ, USAID, etc) were subsumed in the category of 'international organisations'. The category of 'private sector' consists of private companies, including construction companies, banks, developers (investors), associations (eg advocacy groups: REI, APERSI), and professionals (eg consultants, notaries, programme facilitators). In the fourth category, 'civil society', research institutions (universities and other research institutions), non-governmental organisations (eg UPC, ACHR), CBOs (eg BKM, *Pokja*), individuals, and the community[4] were included.

When comparing the two calculated network graphs (cf. figure 77), further similarities and differences become clear. In both networks, government actors are not only in the majority, they are also the most influential actors in the network. Among them, the respective development planning agencies (BAPPEDA/BAPPEKO) stand out as the most influential actors. These are the central policy makers, giving directives, steering, and coordinating all other agencies. Of particular importance is also KPUPR influencing local housing agendas by higher-level programmes, through housing legislation

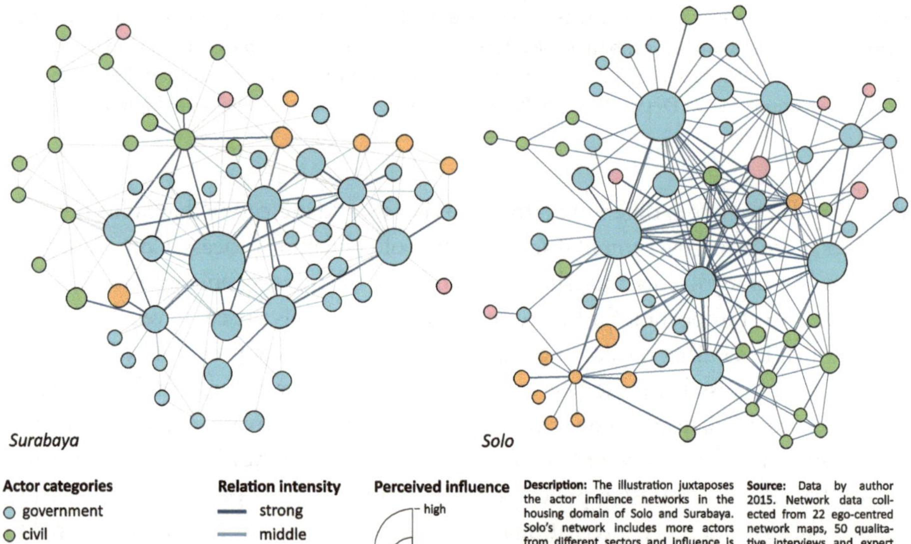

Fig. 77 Actor influence networks in the housing domain of Surabaya and Solo
Source: Illustration by author. Own data (2015)

---

3 Sometimes government programmes were mentioned as actors. Usually the interviewees meant the working group established around a specific programme.

4 The 'community' was frequently mentioned as an actor by the interviewees.

and by the transfer of national funds. Actors from other sectors (civil and private) are in the minority and not perceived as influential in both networks. Surprisingly, the mayor and the House of Representatives are not considered of much relevance for housing policies in both networks, even more so in Surabaya.

While Surabaya's housing policy network is organised very hierarchically with one dominant actor, multiple power centres structure Solo's network, sharing influence on housing policies. In Surabaya, BAPPEKO is by far perceived as the most important actor steering housing policies and giving strategic directions. The respective agency in Solo, BAPPEDA, holds also the rank as the most important actor, but with less distance to other stakeholders. In Solo's network, especially DPU is considered as equally important in influencing housing policies. Considering the overall network structure, Solo's network shows multiple hubs and government actors holding similar values for influence. The ability to influence housing policies seems to be more shared among Solo's governmental agencies compared to Surabaya, where a clear hierarchical structure is present under the leadership of BAPPEKO.

Both networks are characterised by a number of governmental agencies with central positions and high influence in housing policies. These are agencies needed for specific tasks related to settlement development, spatial planning, or provision of urban services and infrastructure (eg sections of DPU, DTRK), or agencies that have a leading role for the implementation of specific programmes. In Solo these are the empowerment agency BAPERMAS, which handles the slum upgrading and relocation programmes, and DPU as the agency managing the social housing provision. In Surabaya, in contrast, the empowerment agency BAPERMAS is much less important, with no role in housing programmes, but is responsible for empowering small and medium enterprises throughout the city. Other agencies emerge as more important in Surabaya's housing domain. These are DinSos, DPBT, and DKP, which is responsible for the social assistance programme (RSDK), social housing provision (*rusunwa*), and the Green and Clean Programme respectively.

The emergence of different government agencies as influential players in the housing domain in the two cities reflects differing priorities of housing policies for the poor. In Solo, the management of the national *rusunawa* programme is assigned to a sub-section of DPU, while in Surabaya a stand-alone agency (DPBT) is responsible for social housing. Even though the growing importance of social housing is increasingly recognised in the two cities, established structures suggest that *rusunawa* housing is even more prioritised in Surabaya. In that city, *rusunawa* housing is considered as the overall solution for low-income people and as the main option for relocating squatter settlements. Considering the programmes and initiatives developed locally, another difference becomes obvious: In Solo, all locally developed housing programmes, ie slum upgrading and relocation programmes, are concentrated under the leadership of BAPERMAS, an agency that considers community empowerment as its central task. In Surabaya, in contrast, housing provision is not seen as the city's greatest challenge anymore; the strategy has shifted to a focus on more comprehensive urban development issues. This finding is reflected in the emergence of other agencies considered as important players. These are DinSos as lead agency of a social assistance programme and DKP as lead agency for the Green and Clean Programme. In other words, while Solo is favouring community empowerment using approaches of participatory relocations and *in situ* slum upgrading, Surabaya focuses on *kampung* revitalisation to achieve an orderly city and *rusunawa* housing provision as well as social aid programmes for its low-income dwellers.

Table 42 Similarities and differences of the actor influence networks of Surabaya and Solo

Similarities of both networks	
– Government actors are in the majority and also the most influential actors – Development planning agencies (BAPPEDA or BAPPEKO) are the most important policy-makers – Several municipal agencies have important roles – KPUPR influences local housing policies – Actors from other sectors (civil and private) are less important – The mayor and the House of Representatives (DPRD) are not relevant in both networks – Some non-governmental actors have high centralities and are needed as intermediaries – Communities and their working groups are needed for programme implementation – Private sector is irrelevant for housing policies for the poor	
Differences of both networks	
Surabaya	*Solo*
– Hierarchical network dominated by BAPPEKO – Lower diversity of actors from different sectors – Importance of gov. agencies reflects priorities: DPBT (social housing), DinSos (social aid) and DKP (revitalisation) – The local university ITS has an outstanding role as gatekeeper and intermediary – Municipal agencies and ITS form a coalition – Rivalry between municipal and provincial authorities	– Multiple hubs of influential government agencies – Higher diversity of actors from different sectors – Importance of gov. agencies reflects priorities: DPU (social housing), BAPERMAS (empowerment) and BPN (formalisation) – Some non-governmental actors have important roles as intermediaries (UNS, Solo Kota Kita, consultants) – International organisations are present

Source: Table by author

In addition, non-governmental actors have important roles in both housing policy networks, even if not perceived as influential. Communities and their working groups are needed for programme implementation and this process is steered by non-governmental organisations that have high centralities based on their position in the network. These organisations work as intermediaries between authorities and residents, facilitating the realisation of projects. In Solo, these are the local university, UNS, a place-based NGO (Solo Kota Kita), and various consultants that are hired for programme implementation. In Surabaya, this task is filled mostly by the local university, ITS. This university has an outstanding role in the city, shaping local housing policies, since it is not only a gatekeeper and intermediary between communities and authorities, but also forms a development coalition with municipal agencies (shared understandings, alumni).

In summary, it can be said that government actors significantly influence housing policies in both cities. The residents play a role only in implementation, not in decision-making. The policy network in Surabaya appears much more hierarchical and is characterised by fewer and less diverse actors compared to Solo. While both cities implement their policies top-down, the network structure suggests that in Solo more actors from civil society have a say in applied housing policies than is the case in Surabaya. Similarities and differences of the actor influence networks in Surabaya and Solo are presented in table 42.

31.3 Discourse strands and fields

The discourse on how to deal with the poor population in the two cities shows interesting differences. They can be assigned to three discourse fields: First, the general orientation of urban policy; second, views on slum and squatter dwellers; and third, components of sound housing policies (cf. table 43). These differences are entangled with other dimensions of policy arrangements in the two cities and influence significantly the case-specific content of housing policies. The main differences between the existing discourse strands are presented below[5].

Strong differences exist in the orientation of urban policies between the two cities. In Surabaya, housing issues are no longer perceived as the central problem of the city. After years of slum-upgrading and resettlement programmes, the challenge of basic shelter is largely seen as addressed. Rather, the city propagates revitalisation and beautification policies oriented at the model of Singapore, including its disputed law and order policies. In contrast to that, the discourse about the general direction of urban policies in Solo is more dominated by the housing issue. Although there are discourse strands that include urban beautification and revitalisation policies – very visible in the endeavour to establish Solo as a cultural city and a major tourist destination – there is a strong awareness about the need to address the challenge of inadequate housing. The provision of housing is seen as obligation of the city, a central task that needs to be addressed.

The views on slum and squatter dwellers show similarities and differences among experts and government employees in both cities. Rather negative opinions were encountered among government officials. Especially in Surabaya, slum dwellers are perceived as lazy and uneducated; they are seen as not wanting to improve their living conditions on their own initiative, but rather waiting for help from the city govern-

5 For more details on the individual cases, see chapters 25.2 for Surabaya and 29.2 for Solo.

ment. The bad living conditions in the settlements are regarded as a result of bad habits – something they have learned and internalised from childhood. These characteristics are also assigned to residents of squatter settlements at the riverbanks. They are considered as illegal migrants, their settlements as an eyesore of the city, posing an obstacle for a proper management of the river channels. According to this view, since they pollute their environment and disturb a proper water flow in the rivers, the best policy would be relocation or eviction. Most of these judgements about slum and squatter settlements can also be found in interviews with Solo's authorities. However, the opinions differ more widely compared to Surabaya. Many of the interviewees agreed that especially the inhabitants of squatter settlements are uneducated and greedy; sometimes they were also called criminals. In this perspective, they occupied land illegally and were now trying to profit from this situation by demanding compensation payments for their resettlement. These opinions, however, were less predominant in Solo. Among government officials, there was also the view that the inhabitants of informal settlements formed an important part of society. With appropriate government support, they were very capable and interested in improving their livelihoods.

Table 43 Three discourse fields and related discourse strands in Surabaya and Solo

Surabaya	Solo
Urban policy orientation	
– Green, clean, and smart	– Inclusive, green, and cultural
	– Housing is an obligation of the city
Views on slum- and squatter dwellers	
– Lacy, uneducated, bad habits	– Uneducated, bad habits, greedy
– Lack of initiative, passive	– Criminals
– An eyesore of the city	– Disturb the river function
– Illegal migrants	– Skilful and capable of self-help
– Pollute their environment	– Squatters are citizens ['*Kita tidak boleh memaksa!*']
– Citizens first! ['*Pulang saja!*']	
Components of sound housing policies	
– Habit change	– More funding is needed
– Awareness raising	– Eviction is no option
– Enablement and self-help	– Formalisation
– Social housing and relocation	– Multiplicity of approaches

Source: Table by author
Note: Discourse fields and strands derived from 50 expert interviews using thematic analysis (cf. chapter 12.2 for details)

The third discourse field appearing in both cities were differing views on components of sound housing policies for the poor. Local experts of both cities consider resettlement policies and social housing as the option for squatter settlements. For deteriorated but 'legal' urban areas (*kampung kumuh*), Solo's authorities favour slum upgrading programmes while the municipality of Surabaya promote enabling policies. In Surabaya, the view dominates that incentives for self-help provided by the state are key to the success of all housing policies. This view is in congruence with the enabling approach dominating the global discussions, where the state does not provide housing, but works as a facilitator to enable residents to improve their situation in self-help. Since poor residents are widely considered as uneducated and as having bad habits, it would be key to change their behaviour, in order to reach the best results. Therefore, policies of enablement that include awareness raising are propagated. This view dominated in nearly all of the interviews conducted in Surabaya. Empowerment of legal residents (economic and community enablement) and eviction or relocation of illegal residents is the pursued housing policy. In Solo, the enabling approach was less present in the interviews. Even though Solo's government relies strongly on the skill of the communities for implementing housing programmes in self-help, this issue was less pronounced as a component of sound housing policies. This could indicate that Solo's authorities do not consider enabling policies to be important or that the process of empowerment has already become a recognised practice in Solo's housing policies. The programmes already successfully implemented using a participatory approach suggest the latter. In the city, there is a consensus that social housing, *in situ* slum upgrading, and relocation activities are the proper means to overcome the challenge of housing for the poor. A strong imperative of formalisation is present and interviewed authorities widely agree that a regularised urban landscape is a precondition for proper urban management. Resettlement in particular is highlighted as a necessary means. This is to be achieved through relocation to social housing in the form of new settlements, *rusunawa* towers, or *rumah deret*, but only by convincing the residents, not by use of force. Forced evictions are not considered as an option, since squatters are acknowledged as part of the city.

The largest difference encountered in both cities is the attitude of government employees against squatter dwellers: It can be summarised by two apt quotations that are representative for the opinion of the respective city government: When asked about the city's policy for squatter settlements, a government employee in Surabaya made the statement 'Pulang saja!', which means 'They should go home'. Since squatters are considered illegal migrants, the general opinion of the city administration is that they should go back to their hometowns, or be properly registered and placed in formal housing. In contrast to this, when asked about the resettlement of the squatter settlements in Solo, the statement 'Kita tidak boleh memaksa!' was made by a government employee, which means 'we must not force them! [to be relocated]'. Squatters are considered equally as people illegally occupying government-owned land, but a proper strategy would be to convince them to be relocated instead of using forced evictions. In these two statements, the difference between both cities in dealing with their poor population becomes clear. In Surabaya, interviewees made clear differences between citizens and non-citizens, the latter not being of priority. In Solo, this distinction is less clear and it is acknowledged that forced evictions are not an option at all. Discussing these different positions on squatters in Surabaya and Solo with a colleague from UNS, who knows both cities well, the response spoke for itself: 'In Solo, I don't know, they are part of the city somehow. It is different in Surabaya. In Solo they have lived on the banks for years, they belong to the city' (Interview 12).

31.4 Rules of the game: regulative institutions

Different regulative institutions shape the organisation of housing policy arrangements in both cities. National law is the main source for these rules. They are reflected in the division of competences and allocation of resources between agencies of the municipal government. As in all other Indonesian cities, the governance system of Surabaya and Solo is organised hierarchically, with the respective mayor supervising all activities of municipal agencies. During Suharto's New Order, the central government appointed mayors, but in the reform era beginning in the late 1990s this changed. Since 2005, citizens directly elect their mayors, increasing greatly their accountability. From the social network analyses, the respective development planning agencies (BAPPEKO/BAPPEDA) have clearly emerged as the most powerful actors in respective housing policy arrangements. A number of national laws has determined the existence of such agencies in all Indonesian territorial units since the 1960s. Over the decades the competences, responsibilities, and resources of these government bodies have increased, making them the central actor for regional development planning. Subordinated to these leading agencies, several other departments are established according to respective thematic fields (environmental, economic, social, construction etc). Usually, these departments exist in all Indonesian cities, having more or less the same tasks and responsibilities. This pattern, however, might also vary more significantly in some cases, since the mayor and/or BAPPEDA/BAPPEKO might prioritise certain issues or sectors. In both cities, social network analysis showed that some departments (and related thematic issues) are considered more influential than others, indicating priorities in housing policies. For Solo, this is the case for DPU, BAPERMAS, and DTRK while for Surabaya DKP, DinSos, and DPBT reach particular significance in the network analysis.

Considering the housing domain, relevant regulations for regional governments are derived from the national housing and settlement law (UU 01/2011). This document sets the obligations and authority for regional governments (ie the city government and the provincial government) to address housing challenges within their jurisdiction. It states the obligation to identify and monitor residential areas, prepare development plans, and implement measures to improve existing housing stock and provide new housing for their respective population (cf. chapter 19.3.2). While the law and other national documents give general directives and recommendations to address the housing challenge, no clear guidelines on specific procedures or the stakeholders to be involved are provided. Municipal governments have the freedom to decide which of the recommended measures suits local circumstances best and what agencies are assigned with this task. The adoption of the housing and settlement law, however, was the starting signal for more intensive planning in the housing sector. The cities now have the task of drawing up long-term plans (20 years) for the development of settlements (Strategi Pengembangan Permukiman dan Infrastruktur Perkotaan, or SPPIP) in addition to their existing master and development plans. For this reason, the city administrations were forced to classify their residential areas for the first time and to map slum areas precisely. The existence of maps, in turn, means a certain acknowledgement of slum areas, which previously simply did not appear in planning documents. Now these areas are designated as priority regions for development (Interview 17).

Beside the general rules of the game shaping the organisation of governance, several context-specific rules were encountered during the fieldwork in Surabaya and Solo. Their more precise manifestation in the respective city can be understood best from a context-specific perspective (cf. chapters 24 and 28). Three different rules were encountered that pose considerable challenges for the implementation of adequate housing policies:

- Only citizens with official place of residence (KTP) can benefit from government programmes
- Social housing blocks can be rented only temporarily
- The cities' riverbanks are managed by separate intercommunal authorities

The first rule states that only official citizens (with legal residence) can receive support from government programmes. This fact excludes large parts of the *de facto* population from any governmental support (eg migrants, temporary or informal residents). Consequences are problems for programme implementation and results, since far-reaching targets of improving whole neighbourhoods can hardly be achieved. However, there are differences between the two cities in the implementation of this rule. In Surabaya, authorities seem to follow it more strictly than in Solo. It can be illustrated when considering the resettlement activities: while in Surabaya relocation of riverbank dwellers into social housing was exclusively reserved for citizens, the participation in resettlement programmes of Solo was also possible for non-citizens (without official residents). Nevertheless, also in Solo all other governmental support is bound to an officially documented place of residence (KTP) within the city boundaries.

The second rule states that rental contracts in social housing must always be limited in time. This rule also has negative consequences. On the one hand, fixed-term contracts mean higher fluctuation and more fairness, as it ensures that that the limited amount of social housing units reaches those who need it most. On the other hand, it is illusory to think that after nine (Surabaya) or five (Solo) years of living in such a flat residents are ready to purchase their own property considering soaring land prices. In Surabaya, the rule also creates unequal treatment, since residents of older social housing units are exempted from this regulation.

The third rule concerns the riverbanks in both cities that are officially under the jurisdiction of another government agency at a higher level. The management of Indonesian rivers and their extent is regulated in the government regulation of 2011 (PP38/2011) where management responsibilities are defined. Any construction activities are prohibited according to this regulation. In Solo there seems to be a good relationship between the city authorities and BBWS/BS. A memorandum of understanding has been signed clarifying responsibilities and land use issues. Solo's authorities are free to relocate existing riverbank dwellers and then use the area as park or conservation zone. In turn, BBWS/BS is responsible for all issues related to flood control. In contrast to this harmonious relationship, relations between Surabaya's authorities and the respective provincial agencies responsible for river management are tense. Jurisdiction over the riverbanks is disputed between both sides, complicating any supportive measures for (and repressive measures against) informal riverbank communities. *De jure,* the provincial government is responsible for all issues related to Surabaya's rivers, including the banks, but the municipal government has a strong interest in relocating squatters on the riverbanks to clear this perceived eyesore of slum settlements within the city boundaries. Due to this constellation and against resisting communities the implementation of relocation policies to social housing blocks is very complicated and demands strong coordination between all involved actors (for more details cf. chapter 24.4).

31.5 Juxtaposing housing policy arrangements

The two cities show different characteristics in their policy arrangements, which is also reflected directly and indirectly in the policies implemented (cf. table 44). Both cities have a network of actors in the housing sector, which is strongly dominated by government actors. This is much more pronounced in Surabaya, where the network is organised much more hierarchically and power is concentrated in the hands of one governmental actor. Looking at the diversity of actors, this becomes particularly evident. The number of non-governmental actors in Solo is higher and more diverse, while in Surabaya only one non-governmental is important in the network. Equally insignificant, however, are the residents in both cities. They are only needed to implement programmes and measures, which is what both cities are trying to promote (community empowerment), but they have little influence on decision-making or the design of the programmes.

There is little difference between the two arrangements in terms of formal rules, since most of them are based on national laws. The only difference is the actual implementation of these rules. In Solo, rules are interpreted somewhat more broadly than in Surabaya, so that, for example, also unregistered residents can receive support from the government. In addition, informal rules that have to do with the history as a palace

Table 44 Similar and different characteristics of policy arrangements in the housing domain of Surabaya and Solo

	Similarities	Speciality in Surabaya	Speciality in Solo
Actors	– The actor network consists mostly of government actors from different administrative levels – Several municipal agencies have important roles in implementing policies – Actors from other sectors (civil or private) are part of the network – Non-governmental actors are needed as intermediaries or for implementing measures – Mayor and local House of Representatives are located peripheral	– Network is hierarchical – Several agencies from the provincial government are present in the network – The local university ITS is an important player and works as intermediary	– Network has multiple hubs – More actors from other sectors (civil and private) area present than in Surabaya – Several non-governmental actors work as intermediaries – Community-based working groups (POKJA) for programme implementation – International organisations are present
Power	– The respective development planning agency (BAPPEDA or BAPPEKO) is the most important policy-maker – KPUPR has an important superior role – Government actors are the most important policy makers – Power is largely derived from rules and is based on authoritative resources	– BAPPEKO is most powerful and dominates the network – ITS has an important role as intermediary based on dispositional power	– BAPPEDA and DPU are most influential – Power is shared among several gov't agencies – Some non-governmental actors have an important role as intermediaries based on dispositional power
Discourses	*Urban policy orientation* – Housing is an obligation of the city	– Green, clean, and smart	– Inclusive, green, and cultural
	Views on slum and squatter dwellers – Lazy, uneducated, bad habits – Lack of initiative, passive – Disturb the river function	– An eyesore of the city – Pollute the environment	– Skillful and capable of self-help – Squatters are citizens
	Components of sound housing policies – Enablement and self-help – Awareness raising – Formalisation	– Habit change – Eviction – Social housing and relocation	– More funding is needed – Eviction is no option – Multiplicity of approaches

	Similarities	Speciality in Surabaya	Speciality in Solo
Rules	– Organisation of the administration is hierarchical – Only citizens are eligible for support – Social housing is temporary – The riverbanks are managed by intercommunal authorities	– Non-citizens are excluded – Unclear and contradictory management of riverbanks	– Sometimes non-citizens benefit from programmes – Riverbanks are managed by the city
Housing Policies	– Social housing and resettlement – Other national programmes: community empowerment, subsidies, cooperative housing, slum upgrading	– *Kampung*-centred policies – Community, financial, and economic empowerment – City beautification	– Inclusive and balanced policies – Slum upgrading – Rowhouses

Source: Table by author

city are also important and the consensus-oriented Javanese culture is much stronger in Solo. This means that conflicts tend to be avoided, as is the case with the search for harmony inherent to Javanese culture. Furthermore, the size of the city probably plays a role. It is quite conceivable, for example, that the lax interpretation of rules in Solo is related to the fact that access to decision-makers is easier and more open in a smaller city than would be the case in a larger city as in Surabaya.

In terms of discourses, there are clear differences between the two cities, particularly when considering the perception of slum and squatter dwellers. While this part of the population is perceived as negative in both cities, this is much more evident in Surabaya. In Solo there are not only negative voices; some officials admit that slum and squatter dwellers do have skills and potential and can therefore be partners in implementing upgrading programmes. In Surabaya, on the other hand, a thoroughly negative image of these groups prevails. The authorities in both cities believe that sound housing policies should follow a policy of formalisation and adopt the recommendations of the enabling approach. Community empowerment, CDD, and awareness raising are the corresponding catchwords. In Surabaya, social housing, relocation and eviction are seen as measures against informal settlements. In Solo, in contrast, eviction is not considered as a viable option.

What conclusions can be drawn from this comparison? It has become clear that the urban policies of both cities rightly have a reputation for being progressive and innovative. However, these innovations are of dissimilar nature and happen in different areas within the housing sector. In Surabaya, the progressive character of housing policies is content-related and refers to the policies of dealing with existing *kampungs*. The city government has committed itself to the task of protecting this settlement type with supportive measures and furthering its development with new ideas. In addition, innovations are also happening in the field of social housing. The social-housing blocks are constantly being improved, especially in technical respects and design questions. This progress in terms of content takes place within a hierarchical policy arrangement, in which policy is prescribed top-down and one actor, the development planning agency, has a decisive influence on the strategies in the housing domain. The success of the project is also due to the cooperation with the local university, ITS, which acts as a mediator to the communities and contributes technical expertise. However, this coalition between authorities and ITS leaves no place for informality, which is reflected in the policy towards marginalised groups and the associated discourses. It can therefore be concluded that in a hierarchically organised policy arrangement consisting almost exclusively of government actors, progress in the housing sector can be achieved on a content-related level.

In Solo, on the other hand, innovation is mainly to be seen in the progressive political style that has gradually emerged since the 2000s. Starting with attempts to make politics more efficient and closer to the citizens through participatory budgeting and planning, the relation between authorities and citizens as well as the way they interact has gradually changed. This is evident in the programmes implemented: the relocation of street vendors, the local slum-upgrading initiative, the resettlement programme, and the row-housing idea. All these programmes are characterised by cooperation between the city government and communities, with the communities being responsible for programme implementation mediated and guided by NGOs and consultants. This does not mean that these activities are developments initiated by the community or grass-root initiatives, they remain nevertheless top-down initiated measures. However, it does mean that the authorities are willing to recognise the communities as valuable project partners and not only as aid recipients. This progressive policy style developed in a diverse policy arrangement, whose network structure is characterised by a multitude of actors from different sectors and levels. Not one actor alone dominates the network, but rather influence is distributed among several governmental and non-governmental actors. Within this diverse network, an approach of collaboration is adopted vis-à-vis residents of informal settlements,whereby they are acknowledged them as citizens of the city. It can be concluded that a diversely organised policy arrangement in which power is shared between different actors can result in a progressive political style that enables inclusive processes. Such a style, which recognises citizens as partners, allows participation, and aims at broad cooperation is to be seen as the decisive factor for the success and wide acceptance of Solo's housing policies.

32 Surabaya and Solo and Lefebvre's 'Urban Society'

32.1 The production of space in Indonesia: Surabaya and Solo

The production of space in the two cities manifests itself in conceived, perceived, and experienced moments of space production. These moments or processes are simultaneously collective and individual, and an analysis can be carried out at different scales. In this section, the collective production of space and its three dimensions is described for the national scale and for the two case studies. The starting point for this is 'spatial practice' and 'perceived space'. Spatial practice projects social practice to the terrain and 'representations of space' as well as 'representational spaces' are already inscribed. From a city perspective, spatial practice manifests itself in all physical-material objects of the built environment, in the morphology of the city.

With regard to the topic of housing, both cities are characterised by historically grown formal and informal quarters, which are based on different kinds of space production. Even though most of the *kampungs* are now formalised and, strictly speaking, no longer informal settlements, they have nevertheless developed informally. Of the three moments producing space, the representations of space were – and still are – not the dominating force in this settlement type, but rather the other two moments of space production. *Kampungs* have developed in an environment where planning and formal rules did not apply or were irrelevant. Similar to other informal settlements around the world space is produced collectively in the resident's everyday practices (Rothfuß 2012: 153–157). Space is less conceptualised; it is more lived and experienced. This origin is reflected in *kampungs*, in narrow alleys, in individual houses stacked one upon another, in a constantly changing appearance. However, one can also recognise elements Henri Lefebvre missed in the functional cities of Europe during the 1960s. In *kampungs*, life on the streets pulsates, there is no separation between living, working, and idling; there is a diversity of social groups; and the streets are central places where everything comes together, encounters each other, concentrates. Representational space, symbols, and experiences have a great significance for the production of space. Since an estimated 60 % of Indonesians still live and grow up in *kampungs*, this type of settlement forms the horizon of experience for many Indonesians and it is home to the community idea that characterises Indonesian society.

In addition to these informal settlements, however, more and more formal quarters have been built since the arrival of the Europeans. Initially, these were only the European neighbourhoods in the larger cities, but with the introduction of western standards in urban planning, the formal and planned city expanded and encroached into the *kampung*. These informal settlements were gradually surrounded by the formal city, so that today's mosaic of formality and informality emerged. With the real estate boom since the 1980s at the latest, the formal city – and with it the logic of exchange value – expanded massively and has now reached almost all areas. Formal planning is considered gold standard and is constantly shaping the ideas of planners and architects to a greater degree. Conceived space, the representations of space of planners and architects, dominates, creating alleged knowledge that is shaped by an ideology of formalisation and capitalist commodification. This is the background of urban planning, clearly aiming at formalisation. In Solo, as well as in Surabaya the objective is to create a proper, highly regulated city, a city where informality has been eradicated. This notion underlies all policies carried out and is made explicit in the resettlement of street vendors and residents of informal settlements and in the implementation of titling programmes to formalise all parts of the city. As a result, the still existing *kampungs* are coming under increasing pressure of redevelopment. Formalised through titling programmes, it is usually only their small-scale structure and informal community control that prevents these diverse neighbourhoods from being revitalised by powerful real estate companies. This probably would result in the expulsion of present residents.

Urban development in Indonesia today is similar to what Lefebvre termed 'implosion-explosion' when he described developments in France of the 1960s. The built environment is exploding, resulting in a fragmented landscape. Everywhere, new residential areas, and business or industrial districts are created, separated according to their function. The old city centre is imploding, slowly losing importance and giving way to the *'desakota'*, an amalgam of built environment, neither city nor countryside. Private investors are developing large residential areas for the middle and upper classes, consisting of homogenised rowhouses or high apartment blocks. However, the promise of a higher living standard comes at a price. Contact with neighbours is limited to essentials; urban life is not happening here. These new and luxurious apartments are nothing more than 'machines for living' and thus stand in stark contrast to the vibrant and lively *kampungs*. Increasing inequality and fragmentation, coupled with processes of inclusion and exclusion, are becoming more and more apparent. This is the background of today's urban development in Indonesia, which can clearly be described as neoliberal urbanisation with tendencies towards a functional and homogenising production of space.

These trends are also reflected in Surabaya and Solo. The described policy arrangements and the associated housing policies result in a certain type of conceived space.

In both cities, there are strong tendencies towards homogenisation and formalisation, a repression of informality, which suggests a dominance of one moment of space production (*representations of space*) and an underlying ideology of capitalist commodification. A strong planning culture prevails and although many of the increasingly specific rules are not (yet) strictly exercised, the trend is clearly in this direction. More and more formal laws and rules are being enacted with the aim of subjecting all areas of life under formal rules. This puts pressure on still existing informal settlements. In both cities, resettlement programmes are in place that aim to clear the city from informality. The dominant position of formalisation is also reflected in housing discourses. Squatter settlements and their inhabitants are generally perceived as a problem since these settlements illegally occupy land, withholding it from any commodification. Even if, as Solo's government propagates, resettlement is actually carried out for the protection and benefit of the inhabitants, the underlying logic is clearly to be assigned to the societal formation of the 'industrial society'.

These tendencies are also evident in public space. In Surabaya, for instance, areas of highly regulated public space can be observed all over the city. This observation is only conspicuous since it does not match the common appearance of other Indonesian cities where streets are filled with the bustling activities of street vendors, where the city bursts with life. The city government refers to this development with pride. They claim having pushed back the chaos of informality and that the city is be on track to become a 'modern' city. The exclusion of marginalised parts of the population is accepted as necessary to reach an orderly city. In Surabaya's centre, there are sidewalks of good quality, but they are not used as such, they are mostly deserted. Since street vending is prohibited, they are empty or used as parking lots for motorbikes, if at all. The new places of urban life are more and more the well-designed and air-conditioned shopping malls, which are mushrooming in all parts of the city. They have become the preferred weekend getaway destination for the middle class, as they invite consumption in an air-conditioned environment. However, this logic leads to the exclusion of large parts of the population, for whom a visit to these temples of consumption is simply out of reach due to the costs.

The production of space in Surabaya and Solo aims at formalisation and the homogenisation tendencies of neo-liberal urbanisation have hardly been addressed so far. However, local government does not only welcome these general trends. In both cities, attempts are being made to protect the traditional production of space by introducing various regulations. In Solo, for example, the city government promotes traditional markets and grants building permits for new shopping malls only hesitantly. Of course, these measures are also based on a conception of space that does not call into question a general formalisation and the eradication of informality. This is evident in the case of the street vendor relocation, where the municipality succeeded in moving them to newly built market halls. In such a way, the representation of space conceived by planners is inscribed in space as *spatial practice*.

In summary, it can be said that the production of space in Indonesia and the two cities is similar to what Lefebvre described and criticised as the societal formation of the 'industrial society'. Of the three moments of space production, representations of space – the concepts devised by planners and architects, dominate and outdo the other two moments. Although there are still numerous informal developments, these are slowly pushed back. The logic of formalisation and commodification is hegemonic and gradually all areas of the city are subjected under this ideology.

32.2 Societal transformation towards an 'urban society'?

As we have seen in the previous chapter, the production of space in the two cities generally follows the logics of space production in an 'industrial society'. However, Henri Lefebvre has also predicted the emergence of a new societal formation, an 'urban society', where the right to the city is realised. In chapter 8, criteria and characteristics for sound housing policies that respect the right to the city, for policy arrangements in the 'urban society' and for this formation itself were developed. The question now arises whether and to what extent these theoretically conceived criteria are present in the two cities studied.

Policy arrangements in an 'urban society'?

The characteristics of policy arrangements in an 'urban society' – in the following often referred to as 'ideal' policy arrangements – can be conceived for each of the four dimensions of actors, power, rules, and discourses. The dimension of actors in an 'ideal' arrangement would be characterised by a network of actors from different sectors. Actors in such a network would create policies together and jointly decide on strategies and programmes. Such networks exist in the policy arrangements of Surabaya and Solo. However, they consist mostly of government actors and are less a network of actors determining policies, but the most powerful players. Decisions are rarely made in collaboration and policies are largely created and implemented top-down. A diverse network consisting of actors from different backgrounds and sectors, which was deduced as 'ideal' from theory, is not present. This is most of all the case in Surabaya, while Solo's network is more diverse, consisting of more actors from civil society. In both arrangements, however, the latter are only involved as advisors or mediators and have hardly any influence on decision-making. In terms of content, government actors in an 'ideal' arrangement would be open to new ideas, would allow alternative space production and would show patience and willingness to deal with such alternatives. This aspect is present in Solo, at least to a certain degree. For example, there is openness among central actors towards new approaches of governance and the implementation of alternative housing options. There is also willingness to accept different views and to enter into discussion with actors from civil society. In doing so, the authorities appear open and patient, but without relinquishing decision-making power. This is particularly evident in the implementation of programmes, in which the communities' working groups are strongly involved. This openness towards new ideas is also evident in Surabaya, though not necessarily with regard to the poorest parts of the city, but in the search for ways to improve and support existing (formalised) *kampungs*.

With regard to the question of power distribution in such a network, in an 'ideal' policy arrangement power would be evenly distributed, all inhabitants of a city would have a say in the creation and implementation of housing policies, and there would be broad opportunities for participation. This is only partially realised in the cities' arrangements. In both networks, government actors clearly dominate, conceiving representations of space to be implemented. In addition, Surabaya's network is much more hierarchically organised, dominated by one governmental actor. In Solo, on the other hand, there are several power hubs, which implies a better distribution of power. However, since all these actors come from the government, it cannot be regarded as a genuine joint decision-making process or power sharing. Residents only have the opportunity to participate in the implementation process. This is even encouraged in both cities by promoting the self-management capacities of the communities. However, this is probably done not out of the willingness to include more citizens in decision-making processes, but more out of the consideration of achieving cost reductions and better ownership in project implementation.

The 'ideal' policy arrangement of an 'urban society' would have not static but flexible rules limiting or allowing actors' conduct. Planning would not predesign any aspect of physical space, but rather promote a flexible space design that is allowed to change. This aspect cannot be found in Surabaya or Solo. Rules are clearly dictated by the ideology of formalisation, there is no room for a different kind of space production. Land use plans have to be followed and functionalism is the dominant doctrine in urban planning. In Solo, however, these rules are not applied in all circumstances; there is sometimes a deviation. Rules that exclude non-citizens from government assistance, for instance, were simply not applied in several programmes. Instead, there is a certain flexibility. Such a flexibility was also encountered when studying the city's resettlement programme. In the newly built settlements for relocated people, the general guidelines and land use plans had to be followed, but except for these framework conditions, the city government did not enforce any other rules. To a certain extent, the residents were allowed to handle and develop their new settlement on their own and to their desire. In Surabaya, on the other hand, official rules are enacted much more rigorously and there is no acceptance of alternative approaches or a different production of space that does not respect the prevailing regulations.

The discourses within the 'ideal' arrangement of an 'urban society' would be characterised by openness towards different lifestyles and social practices. Diversity would be understood as a central resource of the city, a resource that is actively promoted. However, the low acceptance of informal settlements and their inhabitants shows that tolerance and the recognition of diversity is not far advanced in either city. There are strong prejudices against informality, casting informal settlements not only as illegal, poor, and dirty but their inhabitants also as uneducated, lazy, and as criminals. Only in Solo can some positive voices be heard, recognising the skills and potentials of slum and squatter dwellers. Nevertheless, informal lifestyles and practices are not seen as desirable, rather as something that should be pushed back.

From this comparison of policy arrangements empirically analysed with characteristics of 'ideal' policy arrangements conceived theoretically, it can be concluded that both cities show only few elements considered as 'ideal'. This is not surprising, since the conceived criteria represent the normative goal to be achieved. Citizen participation is limited in both cities, housing policies are initiated top-down and government actors in particular determine these policies. However, there is also a tendency of more actors to become involved, even if only in the implementation of measures. The comparative analysis reveals also that in Solo many more elements of an 'ideal' policy arrangement can be encountered, than in Surabaya. Solo's arrangement is less hierarchical, power is more evenly distributed, actors are more open to new ideas, and the arrangement allows for more participation than would be the case in Surabaya. These general characteristics are reflected in applied housing policies.

Sound housing policies in an 'urban society'?

From a Lefebvrian perspective, sound housing policies would be those that respect the minimum standards of adequate housing as defined by the United Nations but extend them by including elements of the right to the city (cf. chapter 6.5). This includes the right to all resources that a city offers, the right to participate, the right of appropriation, and the right to a renewed urban life. This extended understanding of adequate housing in certain ways is only partially realised in Surabaya and Solo. Although both cities have committed themselves to housing provision for their poor population, this does not apply to all societal groups and usually only takes into account the minimum standards of adequate housing. In Surabaya, large efforts are being made to preserve existing *kampungs*. They have been recognised as a central resource of the city that needs protection. To achieve this, it is envisaged to support and improve the self-management capacities of residents, seeking to enable them to carry out their own projects to improve their livelihoods in self-help. Allowing *kampung* dwellers to have a say in the development of their neighbourhood is certainly in line with the right to the city. However, for other parts of society, especially for marginalised groups, the same efforts are not being made. For them, the right to the city is given little consideration in Surabaya. Although there is a general commitment to housing provision for the poor, this is only applied to officially registered residents of the city. For all others, the right to the city is completely denied. Even for those who are eligible to receive support programmes, allocated flats in social housing blocks do not necessarily correspond to the right to participation and to a renewed urban life. Often located in the urban periphery, not socially mixed, without places of encounter, designed as pure housing machines, many of these social housing blocks do not offer what is understood here as an extended concept of adequate housing. Social housing in its current form is not more than a temporary permission to live in the city in minimum housing standards. This is not enough to be termed as adequate housing. Nevertheless, promoting social housing means an essential support for people with very low income and enables many to live in the city. Therefore, the social housing blocks realised so far are a first and necessary step, but with great potential for qualitative and quantitative improvement. Solo's initiative of row houses seems to go into this direction trying to better balance the needs articulated by residents with the idea of social housing.

The failure to realise adequate housing, however, is particularly evident in the way the challenge of informal settlements is addressed in both cities. This settlement type and informality in general have no place in either city and the authorities do not question the logics of formalisation and functionalism. Therefore, both cities carry out resettlements though using different approaches. While Surabaya's authorities consider resettlements to social housing as the only option and are quick to apply forced evictions, Solo's government chooses an approach that respects elements of the right to the city to a far greater degree. Such elements are the right to participate in the resettlement process and the permission to appropriate the chosen location for the new settlement autonomously. The general attitude against informal settlements, thus, denies adequate housing for them, even though programme implementation in Solo shows some progressive aspects.

From this analysis, it can be concluded that sound housing policies – here understood as housing policies that aim to realise adequate housing including the right to the city – are only to some degree present in both cities. In Surabaya, sound housing policies can be found with respect to the traditional *kampungs* where participative processes and the appropriation of space is strongly promoted by the authorities. At the same time, however, the city denies large parts of its population the right to the city and adequate housing. This is different in Solo. In Solo's housing policies various elements of the right to the city can be found. Participation, inclusion and commitment to marginalised groups characterise many of the projects implemented. From a comparative perspective, therefore, Solo's housing policy can be described as more 'sound' than the housing policies of Surabaya.

Promoting an 'urban society'?

The policy arrangements and housing policies in Surabaya and Solo show only few elements of an 'urban society'. The question arises of how the existing elements can be furthered and promoted. The Indonesian *kampung* with its informal processes of space production can provide some insights. The *kampung* has meanwhile been recognised as being worthy of protection, but it is unclear how this could be achieved. How can structures resulting from informal space production be protected and furthered in a system that propagates formalisation and commodification? Is it conceivable for planners and architects to set only framework conditions and allow an informal production of space? Of course, building regulations, zoning laws, and land use plans have not been enacted without reason and often already serve the purpose of limiting further commodification processes. Nevertheless, it should be considered how the other moments of the production of space could be supported. In the *kampungs* of Surabaya, this is attempted by community empowerment programmes. These programmes are intended to strengthen self-organisation and self-management in the *kampungs*, in order to achieve improvements from within the community. However, this goes hand-in-hand with formalisation, as ownership is seen as a basic prerequisite for residents to invest in their homes. Although various studies show that no official land titles are necessary to reach *de facto* security of tenure and deem informal rights as sufficient, the ongoing formalisation trend is not questioned (Guinness 2016; Jellinek 1991; Warren & Lucas 2013; Monkkonen 2013). However, the fact that the formalisation of *kampungs* can even result in expulsion by market forces and further marginalisation is ignored.

Would it not be worth considering breaking the dominance of an ideology of formalisation that tries to impose an exchange value on every piece of land? In the words of Henri Lefebvre: is it possible to imagine a city where the production of space is not dominated by representations of space, but in which the other two moments of space production are more pronounced? This is by no means an argument to abolish spatial planning. On the contrary, conceived space is an inseparable part of the three-dimensional production of space. In another societal formation, however, the weighting of the three dimensions would be different. It is obvious that the dominance of conceived space must be pushed back and its content altered. At present, representations of space are characterised by formalisation, exchange value, and commodification. Connected to this is always the ideology of capitalist exploitation that tries to penetrate as many areas of life as possible. Spatial planners and experts of the city administrations reproduce this logic in their daily work without questioning the basic principles. How could alternatives look like?

An example from Solo shows that it is quite possible to combine formal and informal space production. This is the process of relocation resulting in the new settlement of Ngemplak Sutan, which was finished in 2009. In this case, the city government abandoned the primacy of planning – the dominance of conceptualised space – to a certain degree and allowed the other two dimensions of space production to flourish. The authorities – remarkably – recognised the abilities of the people to choose the location of their new settlement and that the result is better than if experts, architects, and urban planners had done this for them. In this way, it is recognised that the production of space is not the sole result of a conception of space by experts, but also consists of the other two dimensions of space production. Only the residents themselves know about their demands on the new space, which depend on their previous spatial practices and the previous representational space. They will therefore examine their choice of a location of the new settlement to see if their previous way of life is possible there. If, for example, their place of work is located in the city centre or their children have to commute to distant schools, residents will have to change their spatial practices (find another place of work or another school) or make demands on the representations of space to take this into account in the conception (for example, by planning a connection with public transportation). The authorities also allowed informal processes of space production. Although the city government planned the layout of this settlement and a private company constructed basic houses in uniformity, only after the residents moved in, did the actual production of space begin. Residents started to improve their new settlement in a joint effort; they redesigned their houses, added another floor, or collectively changed certain public places. An entrance monument was built to demarcate the newly created *kampung* from the rest of the city, a collective symbol of identity. A place for the neighbourhood watch was built, parts of the public space are used for economic activities, a place for urban gardening, and some houses had to make way for a mosque. A new piece of city has been created; the people have appropriated space, and it is now charged with symbols and meaning; representational space has been produced. These spatial practices were achieved primarily through informal negotiations and discussions among the residents under the mediation of local leaders. Official representations of space created by the city government are only important as a framework allowing the community's processes of space production to evolve. The non-dominance of conceptualised space can be regarded as one of the reasons for the relocation's success.

The discussion here has raised some important questions and the examples from Surabaya and Solo have shown that housing policies and policy arrangements that are based on a different, alternative production of space do seem possible. In such a constellation, it is not representations of space that dominate, but rather other production processes have become of equal importance. Identifying and finding ways to promote such emerging elements of an 'urban society' is the task of scholars.

33 Summary: Policy Arrangements for Adequate Housing

This chapter has compared and discussed policy arrangements and housing policies in Surabaya and Solo. The conditions found were tested against the normative foundation of governance derived from theory. The following questions guided this chapter:

- What are similarities and differences of the identified policy arrangements in Surabaya and Solo (content and organisation)?
- What are formal and informal rules of the game in the two cities?
- To what extent are global and national recommendations implemented at the local level?
- Do identified policy arrangements respect the right to the city and adequate housing?

The comparison of housing policies between the two cities reveals that urban policies in both cities rightly have a reputation of being progressive and innovative. These innovations, however, happen in different areas of the housing sector. While in Surabaya this progressive character refers to the policies of dealing with existing traditional settlements, the Indonesian *kampungs,* in Solo, the innovative character is to be seen in the progressive political style and the holistic approach for dealing with marginalised groups with many participatory elements. In both cities, corresponding initiatives are carried out as well as social housing and resettlement policies. The goal is to regulate urban space completely. There are differences, particularly with regard to the inhabitants of squatter settlements or residents without registered residence. The approach in Surabaya against these groups is much fiercer and stricter than in Solo. Social housing has become a national trend and is increasingly seen as the solution to house low-income groups.

Links to the international discussion on adequate housing are present in both cities. Many measures and strategies implemented increasingly follow the enabling approach. Community enablement and financial enablement is visible in a number of projects. It is attempted to increase community organisation and management capacities to handle their own affairs and improve their neighbourhoods and houses in self-help. To achieve this there are also increased efforts to make residents 'bankable', ie to enable them to take on loans for home improvements. This trend can be interpreted as a characteristic of neoliberal urbanisation, as an attempt to assign exchange value to every piece of urban space. On the other hand, it can also be interpreted as favourable extension of participation possibilities for the residents to have a say in the production of space.

The policy arrangements in the housing domain of the two cities show similarities and differences. Both arrangements are organised mainly through government actors in which decision-making is concentrated in few hands and policies are prescribed and implemented in a top-down manner. Participation of residents is widely limited to programme implementation. Surabaya's arrangement is organised more hierarchically than Solo's arrangement where power is more widely shared between larger numbers of actors. More actors from civil society are involved in the policy network in Solo, working as mediators between government and communities. Little difference in terms of official rules were encountered, since most of them are derived from national law. However, while in Surabaya rules are strictly applied, in Solo they are interpreted somewhat more loosely. As a result, unregistered residents might be able to profit from government programmes more likely in Solo than is the case in Surabaya. These circumstances are reflected in the discourses present in each city, most of all in strands considering informality or squatters. In both cities, they are mostly regarded very negatively, but in Solo, there are some voices acknowledging their skills and potentials as well. Overall, Surabaya's policy arrangement is more hierarchically organised, stricter, and has less possibilities of participation, while Solo's arrangement appears more open, has several power hubs, and involves more actors from civil society. This is reflected in applied policies and the way the government deals with its poor population. While both arrangements produce somewhat progressive policies, considering marginalised groups, Solo's arrangement results in more participative and inclusive policies.

When testing the empirically found arrangements and housing policies against criteria derived from theory, it becomes obvious that both cities show only few aspects of 'ideal' arrangements or *sound* housing policies. Sound housing policies – here understood as housing policies that aim to realise adequate housing including the right to the city – are only to some degrees present in the cities investigated. In both cities, the production of space is dominated by the representations of space conceptualised by city authorities and following an ideology of formalisation and commodification. Citizen participation is limited and policies are implemented in a top-down manner. In Surabaya sound housing policies can be found with respect to the traditional *kampungs*; at the same time, however, for large parts of the population the right to the city and adequate housing is denied. In Solo, on the other hand, participation, inclusion, and commitment to improve the livelihoods of marginalised groups is present in many projects implemented. Considering housing policies for the poor, therefore, Solo's housing policy can be described as more 'sound' than the housing policy of Surabaya.

The comparative analysis revealed important findings: First, housing policies and policy arrangements that are based on a different alternative production of space do seem possible. Second, policy arrangements and housing policies studied empirically show only few elements of 'ideal' aspects conceived from theory. Third, more of these 'ideal' aspects are present in Solo as compared to Surabaya. Fourth, Solo's housing policy is more inclusive and sound compared to Surabaya. These findings indicate an important conclusion: A policy arrangement that meets the conceived criteria of 'ideal' arrangements seems to be more likely to produce *sound* housing policies that benefit the poor. To verify this conclusion, however, further research and more case studies in other cities are needed.

VIII. CONCLUSION

The question why more than one billion people must live in inadequate housing marked the beginning of this book. From this supposedly simple question, a comprehensive analysis developed, which no longer asked only for the reasons for the present situation, but increasingly looked for solutions to achieve the goal of adequate housing for all. This goal was set out in the SDGs (target 1 of SDG 17) adopted by the international community in 2015. In order to find answers, the first approach of this work looked into applied housing policies to explore the most promising and successful measures. This analysis of individual programmes, however, whether slum upgrading, core housing, or social housing, repeatedly came to the conclusion that the success of each measure depends on an enormous and opaque number of factors on different scales. Programmes of the same kind seemed to have different impacts even in neighbouring cities of the same country. The realisation matured that there is no such thing as a 'best practice' that can be applied everywhere and due to the unique nature of cities – their '*Eigenlogik*' – this also cannot be expected. Instead, many different paths must be taken to achieve the goal of adequate housing for all. From this insight, it became apparent that it is not the question of the best housing policy that is decisive, but rather the question of under what circumstances successful strategies can arise in the first place. More and more the focus shifted to local governance as a decisive factor for the development of 'sound' housing policies. Therefore, the aim of this book was to gain a better understanding of the relationship between forms of urban governance and resulting housing policies. Despite the increased research on governance since the 1990s, this relationship has not yet been explored to a great extent. This may be due to the practicability of such research, the lack of analytical concepts, but perhaps also to the necessary normative colouring of such an endeavour. The latter is also deliberately reflected in the main research question of this work:

Main research question

Which modes of local governance produce 'sound' housing policies that realise adequate housing for the poor?

This question was approached from four different angles. The first one searched for 'sound' modes of governance and housing policies at the global and the Indonesian level. A second approach was theoretical, developing a normative compass for governance and housing policy based on theories of Henri Lefebvre and operationalising the concept of policy arrangements to study urban governance. A third approach was empirical, applying detailed analyses of the Indonesian cities Surabaya and Surakarta (Solo). A fourth approach, finally, compares the two cities, their housing policies, and related forms of governance.

Results from context

The search for 'ideal' forms of governance and 'sound' housing policies out of context was the subject of the first approach. To this end, the debate on appropriate housing strategies, applied housing programmes, and measures and projects at the international and Indonesian level were traced from a historical perspective and subjected to a critical analysis. The aim was to classify these intervention strategies, identify advantages and disadvantages, and evaluate the respective programmes according to their success.

The analysis showed that the issue of housing has become increasingly important at the international level over the years. Facing a worsening housing crisis, the international community committed itself at three international conferences on human settlements (Habitat I–III) to address the challenge. Since Habitat I in 1976, the recommended strategies for the housing sector have changed significantly. Three phases are identified and the Human Settlements Programme of the United Nations (UN-Habitat) and the World Bank have gradually emerged as opinion leaders. In a first phase, social housing was seen as the appropriate strategy, while in a second phase more project-based self-help programmes such as slum upgrading and core housing were recommended. In the current third phase, the enabling approach and comprehensive sectoral policies are considered the key to success. On the one hand, this development can be seen as a gradual learning process, overcoming deficits of past approaches. On the other hand, it can also be understood as a proliferation of neoliberal practices, since the new enabling strategy is designed to achieve the greatest possible effect with as few resources and as little government as possible against the background of an ideology of formalisation and commodification.

The enabling approach has become the dominating strategy in the housing sector

Meanwhile, the enabling approach has become the dominating strategy in the housing sector. It is not so much an applied housing measure or programme, but rather an approach under which various programmes with different objectives can be subsumed. The approach seeks to enable government actors, the private sector, and the communities to realise more quantities and quality in the housing sector. The aim is to strengthen the self-management and self-help capacities of the communities by enabling them to carry out projects independently (community enablement) and to gain access to mortgage loans (financial enablement). Simultaneously, it is attempted to use incentives to enable the private sector to expand housing production down the income ladder (private sector enablement). In this model, the state refrains from direct interventions and merely has the task of providing appropriate framework conditions. Although this approach is currently the most recommended strategy, individual nations also pursue their own approaches that differ considerably from international recommendations. The housing policy of Indonesia is one of the examples. The three phases of internationally recommended strategies are reflected – though with some delay – in applied programmes, but the country also pursues its own path. For several decades, Indonesia has successfully implemented slum upgrading and later community empowerment programmes, which have rightly become known as 'best practice'. In the last years an increasing number of programmes that follow the enabling approach were implemented. At the same time, however, social housing has been massively expanded so that more and more council flats are available for the poorest parts of the population.

Informal modes provide more than 50 % of the produced housing stock

In a second step of the analysis, the approaches recommended during the three phases were linked to the modes of housing provision present in the Global South. Formal and informal modes of housing provision with several sub-categories are distinguished. Informal modes provide more than 50 % of the produced housing stock (eg squatter or informal subdivisions), but almost all approaches target the formal modes of housing provision (by private sector or the state). In addition, housing policies generally refocused from state to private provision over the last decades. Since all modes of provision favour one part over other parts of society, this shift is also associated with changing target groups. Low-income people tend to secure their housing needs informally or through state provision which is why the observable shift is more beneficial for middle- and upper income groups. This result indicates that the changing housing policies of recent years brought about by the enabling approach must be reviewed critically. They may have produced more housing in quantitative respects, but do not reach the poor and cause negative effects in many cases. Despite the successful extension of housing markets the argument of 'filtering-down' cannot be sustained against empirical evidence. Therefore, this market-based strategy must be reconsidered. It remains incomprehensible why alternative modes of housing production such as cooperatives, rental housing, and the entirely informal modes of provision are hardly considered as options.

Informal housing is the only option for the majority of Indonesia's population

This is also evident in Indonesia. More and more of the country's housing programmes are being set up in an attempt to increase the market's production of housing through a massive extension of housing finance policies and direct housing subsidies. These measures, however, primarily benefit middle and higher income groups and are not suitable for providing housing for the poor. For the country's low-income groups only three approaches remain: 1) financial enablement for those creditworthy, 2) assistance for self-help housing and 3) resettlement to social housing. Only the third option – resettlement – targets all residents of informal settlements and most slum and squatter dwellers. Therefore, informal housing production is likely to continue to be the only option for the majority of Indonesia's population. However, as at the international level, this fact is still ignored and hardly any approaches have been developed to better consider or promote informal housing production.

There is no one-size-fits-all approach for *'sound'* housing policies

It can be concluded that there is no one-size-fits-all approach for 'sound' housing policies. Individual projects or programmes may well be considered successful, but might only benefit specific population groups, are often not transferable to other cities and are too small in scale facing the ongoing urbanisation trend. The outcome document, the New Urban Agenda, from the latest conference on human settlements in 2016, recognises this fact by recommending diverse housing delivery options. Applied housing policies must be tailored to the context and deploy an interplay of approaches that addresses different modes of housing provision.

The contextual approach has brought us closer to finding 'ideal' forms of governance and 'sound' housing policies. Suitable modes of governance are flexible and able to employ various housing approaches considering differing modes of housing provision. For housing policies that seek to prioritise the poor, public housing, alternative approaches, and support for informal modes of provision are of particular relevance. However, the analysis also revealed the fundamental need for a normative goal that goes beyond 'adequate' housing. This requirement of a normative direction for governance and housing policies can only be found through a theoretical approach.

Results from theory

The theoretical approach to the main research question aimed at developing a normative direction for 'adequate housing' and 'sound' housing policies on the one hand and at operationalising a useful analytical concept for the empirical analysis of governance on the other. In the search for a normative direction, the theories of Henri Lefebvre were examined in detail. From his theory of the production of space, an alternative approach towards urbanisation emerges, opening up a new perspective into a possible future that is to be achieved with the right to the city.

Lefebvre comprehends space not as a physical-material thing, but as a social product, as the result of three intertwined production processes. Space is conceived, perceived, and lived. Following these thoughts, space does not exist naturally, but is continuously produced and reproduced by social actors. Space becomes a historically specific reflection of societal relations, something always in motion and always changing. This understanding of space shifts the object of analysis away from physical things in space towards collective production processes of space and it moves the focus to an exploration of possibilities for far-reaching changes towards a societal transformation. Based on this understanding of the production of space, Lefebvre observes the phenomenon of urbanisation. He conceptualised it as processes of 'implosion' – dissolving the traditional city – and 'explosion' – expanding a *tissue urbain* over the country – and he developed a strategic hypothesis: that of a completely urbanised society. With this hypothesis, it becomes possible to comprehend urbanisation as a macro-societal historical phenomenon, a development towards a new societal formation: the 'urban society'. He conceptualised this new formation as a possibility, a possible future space-time configuration of society, which follows the 'industrial society' as a new episode in history. By conceptualising it, its characteristics and emergence become analysable. He describes the 'urban society' as an upcoming societal formation where economic rationality and the dominance of exchange value is replaced by another world where productivism has become meaningless and use value is prioritised. As in today's debates on post-growth, Lefebvre conceived a new world in which economic logics no longer stand above everything and in which use value has triumphed over exchange value.

The *'urban society'* is an upcoming societal formation in which use value has triumphed

Based on this understanding of urbanisation, however, the classical understanding of the city as a clearly definable socio-spatial unit becomes obsolete. In the search for a new definition of the city, Lefebvre conceived three levels of societal reality, giving the city a mediating role between a private and a global level. Through this mediating function he redefines the city as a social and mental form characterised by centrality, difference, encounter, and simultaneity. In the city, he argues, exchange, assembly, and encounter are made possible, creating a milieu in which innovation and new ideas can flourish. By definition, the city becomes a crucial societal resource for 'the possible' to emerge, a breeding ground of the 'urban society'. To advance the emergence of this new formation Lefebvre formulates the right to the city, meaning the right to a changed urban world, a reformed and renewed urban life shaped by difference, encounters, and simultaneity. It includes also the right to the place that is to bring about this change: places of exchange, assembly, and encounter: the city. The right to the city, thus, is a 'cry and demand' for such places from which the transformation towards an 'urban society' might suc-

The city is a crucial resource for societal transformations

The right to the city demands a reformed and renewed *urban* life

ceed. These insights from Lefebvre's theories makes it possible to imagine a new formation of society, its three levels of societal reality and respective dimensions of the production of space. The mediating level of the city is of particular interest since at this level politicians, planners, and architects conceive *representations of space* and create applied housing policies. Both are the result of a process of policy-making within a specific mode of governance.

For the empirical analysis of these modes of governance the policy arrangement approach developed by Arts et al. (2006) was adapted and operationalised. A policy arrangement consists of four interlinked dimensions – actors, power, rules, and discourses. These four dimensions form a temporarily stable arrangement in a specific policy domain, in the case of this work the housing domain. Based on Giddens' structuration theory and informed by a neo-institutional perspective, actors' practices are assumed to be structured by institutions and power relations. Both structure and agency are considered important for the policy-making process. For the empirical application, the four dimensions of this approach were defined as actor networks, regulatory institutions, resources and influence as well as policy discourse strands. Together they form specific arrangements that shape the design and outcome of housing policies. Operationalised through appropriate empirical methods these criteria can be applied in case studies and thus make it possible to compare individual aspects as well as entire arrangements. In addition, this analysis grid also allows testing the existing arrangements against a desirable arrangement conceived as a possible policy arrangement in an 'urban society'.

Adequate housing means access to all resources of the city

From these theoretical insights some important conclusions considering the main research question can be drawn. Modes of governance are analysable employing the policy arrangements approach and Lefebvre's theories provide a normative compass to assess them empirically. The characteristics of policy arrangements, related housing policies, and the meaning of adequate housing in a future societal formation of an 'urban society' can be imagined. Doing this, adequate housing means more than the minimum standards defined by the United Nations; it also means access to all resources of the city, access to a renewed urban life, and the possibility of participating in the production of space. Adequate housing must include the right to the city. A 'sound' housing policy tries to achieve adequate housing defined in this way, giving citizens far-reaching opportunities for participation and the appropriation of space. Policy arrangements that produce such housing policies are not organised hierarchically and are not composed solely of government actors, but include a multitude of actors from different fields who are actually involved in the decision-making processes. Rules would be flexible and local governments would actively engage and promote ideas from civil society, not negating alternative concepts and lifestyles from the onset. On the contrary, actors in such an arrangement would see diversity as a crucial resource of the city, a resource that generates innovation and is therefore promoted. In this way, the conditions are created to help an 'urban society' to break through and to achieve the goal of inclusive cities respecting adequate housing for all.

Empirical results and results from the comparison

A third approach to the main research question was made from an empirical perspective. This involved a detailed analysis of the housing policy and policy arrangements of the two cities Surabaya and Surakarta (Solo) chosen as case studies. The subsequent comparison and the normative compass developed made it possible to identify characteristics of 'ideal' forms of governance that would allow the appearance of better housing policies.

In the city of Surabaya, with its 3 million inhabitants the second largest city in Indonesia, the housing question was one of the most important issues of urban development throughout the 20th century. In nowhere else in Indonesia, apart from Jakarta, does the duality of formal and informal production of space become so apparent. Today, the city's housing policy can be described as *kampung*-oriented but also as excluding. On the one hand, the city's urban *kampungs*, crowded inner-city settlements, have been formalised and improved since the 1970s through several cycles of the famous Kampung Improvement Programme. On the other hand, the city follows a strict and rigid course against all informal settlements, excludes residents not registered and does not refrain from forced evictions. Conditions in former slum areas have improved over the years and the city administration shifted its attention to other support programmes. In line with the enabling approach, community empowerment projects are increasingly carried out using incentives to enhance community organisation and local economies. Since the political turnaround in the late 1990s, more and more programmes of local origin have been set up for this purpose. Against informal settlements the municipality pursues a policy of resettlement and eviction. This approach led to many conflicts, especially since the offered alternative of council flats is limited to registered residents and excludes all others. Social housing is seen as the only solution for the poor. The social housing tenements have been technically optimised and production has accelerated in recent years, but quantities will not meet the constantly increasing demand any time soon. Altogether, Surabaya's housing policies can rightly be described as innovative in several fields pioneering the design of social housing and the future development of the traditional *kampungs*. However, for the poor no policy alternative has been developed except social housing. For these reasons Surabaya's housing policies can only partly be assessed as progressive and certainly not as inclusive.

Surabaya's housing policy is *kampung*-oriented but excluding

This all takes place in a policy arrangement in the housing domain that is organised hierarchically and mainly consists of government actors. The Development Planning Agency (BAPPEKO) plays a key role in determining local housing policies and is by far the most important actor. One of Surabaya's universities, the Sepuluh Nopember Institute of Technology (ITS), has a special role to play. It is a source of ideas for new policies; it mediates between government and communities and has an important advisory function for the implementation of new policies. Other actors from civil society have hardly a say in Surabaya's housing policies. The distribution of power in this arrangement is based on authoritative resources determined by national rules and laws and the city administration implements formal rules quite strictly with only few exceptions. The discourse among housing experts in the city is characterised by a negative view on slum and squatter residents. They are described as being lazy, uneducated, poor, and passive. In this view, due to their bad habits, they are themselves responsible for the inadequate conditions of their neighbourhoods. This view serves as a justification for further resettlements and slum clearances aiming to achieve a green, clean, and smart city without the eyesore of informal settlements. The analysis revealed the existence of a policy arrangement in Surabaya's housing sector that has been stable over the last decades. The rise of Tri Rismaharini to become mayor of Surabaya in 2010 did not change this arrangement and brought hardly any new impetus for the housing sector. The city's housing policy remains top-down organised, offers little opportunity for civil society participation, is characterised by an ideology of formalisation and results in progressive concepts towards traditional *kampungs*, but also in the exclusion of the poor.

In the city of Surakarta (Solo), a medium-sized city in Central Java with a population of about 520,000, the challenge of housing has a different dimension, simply because of the size of the city. However, there are also many densely populated slum and squatter settlements especially along the rivers and railway lines. Since the 2000s, the city pursued a balanced urban policy manoeuvring between tradition and modernity that tries to address informality by including marginalised groups as development partners. This was reflected in a number of measures such as the introduction of a participatory planning system, the peaceful resettlement of informal street vendors as well as slum upgrading and resettlement projects carried out by the communities. All these programmes use incentives and persuasion to encourage the affected population to organise themselves into working groups and then implement the planned programmes. Through this CDD, astonishing results have been achieved at low cost. In the spirit of the enabling approach, state actors take on a supporting and advisory function in these measures. In addition to these programmes of local origin, the national social housing programme has been advanced in recent years, even if the demand is still far from being satisfied. In some pilot projects, the strict design and concept of tenements was refined by developing smaller rowhouses (rumah deret). Considering informal settlements, the city administration pursues the long-term goal of resettlement and formalisation. However, evictions are not considered as opportune. Instead, attempts are made to cooperate with the communities to find solutions for resettlements to other areas. People who are not officially registered as residents are frequently included in the projects, even though they are not entitled by law to receive aid from the city. Despite the continuing problem of providing housing for all, Solo's housing policy can therefore be described as progressive and inclusive.

Solo's housing policy is progressive and inclusive

This housing policy is based on a policy arrangement organised through an actor network that is composed mostly of government actors. In Solo, too, the Regional Development Planning Agency (BAPPEDA) is the most important actor, but other municipal agencies are largely responsible for various housing programmes. The network structure is not hierarchical, but rather characterised by various power hubs and a number of civil society actors play an important mediating and advisory role. The rules of conduct are based on national laws, but exceptions are made in application, for example when migrants are taken into account in the resettlement programmes. The discourses among the city's experts show that they consider the goal of achieving adequate housing as their central task and that they do indeed focus strongly on marginalised groups. Although slum and squatter residents are associated with the usual negative prejudices (uneducated, lacy, bad habits), there are also voices that acknowledge their ability for self-organisation and self-help. The city administration aims to formalise all areas of the city in the long-term. However, this is not to be done by force, but through an approach based on cooperation, participation, and persuasion. The analysis shows that a stable policy arrangement has been in place since the beginning of the 2000s from which progressive policies have emerged. This is often credited to Joko Widodo (Jokowi) who was mayor of the city from 2005 to 2012. However, even before he took office innovative policies had emerged in Solo. Jokowi seems to have significantly promoted and consolidated this arrangement so that it still exists after his further career as governor of Jakarta and acting president of Indonesia.

Comparison of housing policies and policy arrangements

The analysis of the housing policies in the two cities revealed a differentiated picture. In both cities, a bundle of increasingly sophisticated housing policies can be observed extending national efforts of social housing and incentives for the private sector. Furthermore, there is a growing consensus that traditional *kampungs* need to be protected against urban renewal, although it is not yet clear how this is to be achieved. Since the political turnaround in 1998, both cities are increasingly taking the initiative in launching their own local programmes. Many of these initiatives follow the internationally recommended enabling approach. One of the most important components is community enablement, which attempts to promote organisational and management capacities of communities in order to enable them to carry out projects independently. These efforts were reflected in a number of successful projects that enabled many to have say in the production of space. The long-term goal in both cities is the complete regulation of urban space, to be achieved by suppressing informality and by performing resettlements. However, there are clear differences in implementation. The approach in Surabaya is much more authoritative and strict compared to Solo, where the emphasis is more on cooperation and participation. This can be traced back to historical experiences with informality. In Solo, informal settlements are seen as an integrated part of the city which is in need of support, whereas in Surabaya, against the background of strong squatting activities and migration tendencies during the 20th century, informal settlements are perceived very negatively. Overall, Solo's housing policy is more clearly focused on aiding the poor to meet their housing needs than is the case in Surabaya. There, only few support measures exist for marginalised people. The city government prefers to focus on the expansion of formal housing production and on promoting and preserving already formalised *kampungs*.

Surabaya's policy arrangement is more hierarchically organized, stricter and has less possibilities of participation, while Solo's arrangement appears more open, has several power hubs and involves more actors from the civil society

These housing policies are reflected in policy arrangements that also show similarities and striking differences. Both are organsed mainly through an actor network comprised predominantly of government actors. Decision-making is concentrated in a few hands and policies are prescribed and implemented in a top-down manner. Participation of residents is widely limited to programme implementation and not to decision-making. However, Surabaya's arrangement is much more hierarchically organised than Solo's arrangement, where power is more shared in an actor network that is larger and more diverse. Actors from civil society have a say in Solo's network and there are significantly more possibilities of participation. Official rules derived from national law set the general rules of conduct, strictly applied in Surabaya, while interpreted somewhat more broadly in Solo. As a result, unregistered residents are more likely to benefit from government measures in Solo than in Surabaya. These circumstances are also apparent in discourses on marginalised groups. They are mostly regarded very negatively in Surabaya, while in Solo also their skills and potentials are acknowledged. Overall, Surabaya's policy arrangement is more hierarchical, stricter, and has less possibilities of participation, while Solo's arrangement appears more open, has several power hubs, and involves more actors from the civil society. Applied policies and the way the government deals with its poor population reflect these characteristics. Both arrangements produce somewhat progressive policies, but considering marginalised groups, Solo's arrangement results in more participative and inclusive housing policies.

The comparison of the two cities makes it possible to derive some indications for the main research question. The city government of Solo seems to be more interested in achieving access to adequate housing for all. This suggests that Solo's policy arrangement is more likely to produce 'sound' housing policies for the poor. An interplay of factors characterises Solo's arrangement: a less hierarchical organisation of the actor network, a better distribution of power, the inclusion of actors from the civil sector, but also openness to alternative approaches, the willingness to cooperate and discuss with actors from civil society, and finally a discourse that acknowledges marginalised groups as citizens and partners for development. Together, these aspects have created a fertile ground from which innovative and progressive approaches and an overall inclusive and pro-poor policy has emerged. However, it should be investigated further whether these characteristics also apply to policy arrangements in other cities that are believed to produce 'sound' housing policies for the poor.

***'Ideal'* policy arrangements and *'sound'* housing policies?**

By comparing these empirical findings with criteria for 'ideal' policy arrangements and 'sound' housing policies derived from theory, it becomes clear that both cities so far show only few of the conceived criteria. This was not surprising since they are the normative goal to be achieved. The production of space in both cities still functions according to the logics inherent to the 'industrial society' with its strong tendency towards homogenisation and formalisation, a repression of informality, and an underlying ideology of capitalist commodification. These logics are not questioned; informality has no place in either of the cities. Elements of 'sound' housing policies, understood as housing policies that aim to realise adequate housing and the right to the city, hardly exist. Neither social housing policies in their present form, granting only temporary permission to live in the city at minimum housing standards, nor the resettlement approaches towards informal settlements can be assessed as *'sound'*. For marginalised groups the right to the city and adequate housing remains largely denied.

For marginalised groups the right to the city and adequate housing remains largely denied

Nevertheless, primarily in Solo some elements of such 'sound' housing policies and 'ideal' policy arrangement are present. These are the commitment to improve housing conditions for the poor, the implementation procedure of projects, and the manner in which marginalised groups are addressed in a participative and inclusive way. Also Solo's policy arrangement

Solo's policy arrangement is more likely to produce *'sound'* housing policies for the poor shows elements that are congruent with an 'ideal' arrangement conceived for an 'urban society': among them are a less hierarchical actor-network, a more equal power distribution, open-minded actors, and opportunities for participation. Though not reaching the characteristics of an 'ideal' arrangement, Solo's mode of governance seems to be on the right track.

This normative compass contributes to achieve adequate housing for all

The results of such a comparison with theory provides further indications for the main research question. In fact, an alternative production of space does seem possible, although few elements of a corresponding housing policy and governance constellation were encountered so far. However, it has been shown that especially Solo's housing policies and mode of governance do meet some of the conceived criteria. Since the results of these policies are beneficial for the poor, it is reasonable to conclude that the theoretically developed criteria are indeed a viable consideration to be pursued. The implementation of this normative compass contributes to achieving adequate housing for all. It is therefore crucial to further develop this normative foundation of governance and housing policies and to continue looking for empirical examples. In such a way, not only adequate housing for all might become reality, but also a societal transformation towards an 'urban society' is advanced.

Modes of governance for achieving adequate housing for all?

The results of this study do not allow formulating a definitive answer to the question raised at the beginning of this work. However, they have brought us closer to the search for 'ideal' conditions of governance and housing policies that realise adequate housing for all. Findings from the contextual analysis suggest that there are no 'best practices' in housing policies but rather a need for a variety of measures that take into account the different modes of housing provision. Such a variety evolves only in modes of governance that are flexible and allow different approaches to coexist. From a theoretical perspective, it became clear that the definition of adequate housing should be expanded to include elements of the right to the city. Such a definition means more than just the minimum standards of adequate housing defined by the United Nations but also access to all resources of the city, access to a renewed urban life, and the possibility to participate in the production of space. From these considerations, a normative compass was developed which provides a basis for defining 'ideal' policy arrangements. A large network of actors from different levels and background equally participating in decision-making processes would organise such arrangements. Actors would be flexible and open-minded, would regard diversity as a crucial resource of the city, and would allow and promote other dimensions of the production of space. The empirical analysis showed that such properties are not completely unreasonable. On the contrary, some elements of 'ideal' policy arrangements and sound housing policies were present in both case studies, especially in Solo. These elements are in line with the theoretically conceived criteria for an 'ideal' governance configuration. From these results, it can be concluded that the criteria conceived theoretically represent indeed a significant contribution for a normative foundation of governance needed to achieve the goal of adequate housing for all. These findings, however, still need further backing from other case studies. Further research is also needed to identify factors that prevent or encourage such modes of governance, before intervention strategies might be developed in order to help such governance to emerge. This could be a crucial cornerstone in achieving the goal of adequate housing for all and a means to promote a societal transformation towards an 'urban society'.

References

Aalbers, M. (2008): The Financialization of Home and the Mortgage Market Crisis. *Competition & Change*, 12 (2), pp. 148–166.

Aalbers, M. (2016): The financialization of housing. A political economy approach. London, New York: Routledge (Routledge studies in the modern world economy, 158).

Abrahamson, M. (2014): Urban sociology. A global introduction. New York: Cambridge University Press.

Abrams, C. (1964): Housing in the Modern World. London: Faber & Faber.

ACHR – Asian Coalition for Housing Rights (2009): Asian Coalition for Community Action (ACCA), first year report, Indonesia. <http://www.achr.net/upload/files/Indonesia%20First%20Year%20Report%20Dec%202009%20PART%202.pdf> (accessed 2023/03/04).

ACHR – Asian Coalition for Housing Rights (2010): Asian Coalition for Community Action (ACCA), second year report, Indonesia. <http://www.achr.net/upload/files/Indonesia%20yr%202%20Extract30.pdf> (accessed 2019/04/02).

ACHR – Asian Coalition for Housing Rights (2014): Asian Coalition for Community Action (ACCA), fifth year report, Indonesia. <http://www.achr.net/upload/files/Indonesia%205-6.pdf> (accessed 2016/04/01).

ADB – Asian Development Bank (2006): From Poverty to Prosperity: A Country Poverty Analysis for Indonesia. <http://www.adb.org/sites/default/files/institutional-document/33087/files/poverty-assessment-ino.pdf> (accessed 2016/08/03).

ADB – Asian Development Bank (2012): The Neighborhood Upgrading and Shelter Sector Project in Indonesia. Sharing Knowledge on Community-Driven Development. Manila.

ADB – Asian Development Bank (2016): Toward Mainstreaming and Sustaining Community-Driven Development in Indonesia. Understanding Local Initiatives and the Transition from the National Rural Community Empowerment Program to the Village Law. Manila.

ADB – Asian Development Bank (2019): Basic Statistics 2019. <https://www.adb.org/publications/basic-statistics-2019> (accessed 2019/10/21).

Affolderbach, J. & Mössner, S. (2014): Der Institutionenbegriff in den Wirtschafts- und Sozialwissenschaften. In: Oßenbrügge, J. & Vogelpohl, A. (eds.): Theorien in der Raum- und Stadtforschung. Einführungen. Münster: Westfälisches Dampfboot, pp. 176–194.

Aguilera, T. & Smart, A. (2016): "Squatting North, South and Turnabout: A Dialogue Comparing Illegal Housing Research". In: Anders, F. & Sedlmaier, A. (eds.): Public Goods vs Economic Interests: Global Perspectives on the History of Squatting: Routledge, pp. 29–55.

Agustina, S. I. (2006): Manual for Facilitator Organized Self-Help Rental Flat Housing in Indonesia. In: Ministry of Public Works (ed.): Public Works International 2006. Jakarta, pp. 79–88.

Alexandri, G. & Janoschka, M. (2017): Who Loses and Who Wins in a Housing Crisis? Lessons From Spain and Greece for a Nuanced Understanding of Dispossession. *Housing Policy Debate,* 146 (3), pp. 1–18. doi:10.1080/10511482.2017.1324891

Allen, J. (2003): Lost Geographies of Power. Malden, Oxford, Melbourne, Berlin: Blackwell.

Amin, A. (1999): An Institutionalist Perspective on Regional Economic Development. *International Journal of Urban and Regional Research,* 23 (2), pp. 365–378. doi:10.1111/1468–2427.00201

Andavarapu, D. & Edelman, D. J. (2013): Evolution of Slum Redevelopment Policy. *Current Urban Studies,* 1 (4), pp. 185–192. doi:10.4236/cus.2013.14021

APMCHUD (2010): The Solo Declaration. Asia Pacific Ministerial Conference on Housing and Urban Development. Surakarta.

Arnouts, R. (2010): Regional nature governance in the Netherlands. Four decades of governance modes and shifts in the Utrechtse Heuvelrug and Midden-Brabant. Dissertation. Wageningen University: Wageningen.

Arnouts, R., van der Zouwen, Mariëlle and Arts, B. (2012): Analysing governance modes and shifts – Governance arrangements in Dutch nature policy. *Forest Policy and Economics,* 16, pp. 43–50. doi:10.1016/j.forpol.2011.04.001

Arts, B. & Leroy, P. (eds.) (2006): Institutional Dynamics in Environment Governance. Dordrecht: Springer (Environment & Policy, 47).

Arts, B., Leroy, P. and Tatenhove, J. van (2006): Political Modernisation and Policy Arrangements. A Framework for Understanding Environmental Policy Change. *Public Organization Review,* 6 (2), pp. 93–106.

Arts, B. & Tatenhove, J. van (2000): Environmental policy arrangements: a new concept. In: Goverde, H. (ed.): Global and European polity? Organisations, policies, contexts. Aldershot: Ashgate, pp. 223–238.

Arts, B. & Tatenhove, J. van (2004): Policy and Power. A conceptual Framework between the 'old' and 'new' Paradigm. *Policy Sciences,* 37 (3–4), pp. 339–356.

Arts, B. & Tatenhove, J. van (2006): Political Modernisation. In: Arts, B. & Leroy, P. (eds.): Institutional Dynamics in Environment Governance. Dordrecht: Springer (Environment & Policy, 47), pp. 21–43.

Arts, B., Tatenhove, J. van and Leroy, P. (2000): Policy Arrangements. In: Tatenhove, J. van, Arts, B. & Leroy, P. (eds.): Political Modernistation and the Environment. The Renewal of Environmental Policy Arrangements. Dordrecht: Kluwer Academic Publishers (Environment & Policy, 24), pp. 53–70.

Asnawi, S. T. (2005): Ansätze zur Entwicklung von neuen Wohnvierteln mit Bewohnerbeteiligung für niedrige Einkommensgruppen in Indonesien. Modellprojekte in Semarang im Vergleich. Dissertation. Universität Kassel: Kassel.

Aspinall, E. & Mietzner, M. (2014): Indonesian Politics in 2014: Democracy's Close Call. *Bulletin of Indonesian Economic Studies,* 50 (3), pp. 347–369. doi:10.1080/00074918.2014.980375

Astuti, W. (2012): Laporan Penelitian: Karakteristik "Community-Based Housing Development" dan Kontribusinya Terhadap Pengentasan Kemiskinan. Studi Kasus Kota Surakarta Indonesia. Universitas Sebelas Maret.

Astuti, W. & Prasetyo, D. A. (2014): Model of Community-based Housing Development (CBHD) of Bedah Kampung Program in Surakarta Indonesia. *Procedia Environmental Sciences,* 20, pp. 593–601. doi:10.1016/j.proenv.2014.03.072

Atkinson, A. (2004): Promoting Environmentalism, Participation and Sustainable Human Development in Cities of Southeast Asia. In: Westendorff, D. (ed.): From Unsustainable to Inclusive Cities. Geneva: UNRISD, pp. 15–57.

Attoh, K. A. (2011): What kind of right is the right to the city? *Progress in Human Geography,* 35 (5), pp. 669–685. doi:10.1177/0309132510394706

Auclair, C. (2005): The Millennium Declaration and the Habitat Agenda. *Habitat Debate,* 11 (3), p. 9.

Bähr, J. (2005): Stadtgeographie II. Regionale Stadtgeographie. Braunschweig: Westermann.

Bähr, J. & Mertins, G. (2000): Marginalviertel in Großstädten der Dritten Welt. *Geographische Rundschau,* 52 (7/8), pp. 19–26.

Bapermas Surakarta – Badan Pemberdayaan Masyarakat Surakarta (2014): Rekapitulasi Pemberian Bantuan Pembangunan Perbaikan Rumah Tidak Layak Huni Bagi Masyarakat Miskin Kota Surakarta Tahun 2006–2014. Surakarta.

Bapermas Surakarta – Badan Pemberdayaan Masyarakat Surakarta (2015): Rekapitulasi Relokasi Rumah Bengawan Solo 2014. Dataset received from BAPERMAS. Surakarta.

BAPPENAS – Badan Perencanaan Pembangunan Nasional (2012): Report on the achievement of the millennium development goals in Indonesia 2011. <https://planipolis.iiep.unesco.org/sites/default/files/ressources/indonesia_mdg_2011.pdf> (accessed 2023/03/04).

Baross, P. & Linden, J. van der (eds.) (1990): The transformation of land supply systems in Third World Cities. Aldershot: Avebury.

Bawole, P. (2007): Informelle Siedlungen an Flussufern in gefährdeten Stadtgebieten Indonesiens. Fallstudien in den Städten Medan, Yogyakarta, Malang und Surabaya. Dissertation. Universität Stuttgart: Beuren, Stuttgart.

Bawole, P. (2009): The Settlement of Stren-Kali-Wonokromo-Surabaya: "The City Image Based on the Development of Marginal Society". *DIMENSI,* 37 (1), pp. 1–8.

Bazoglu, N. (2005): The need for a more ambitious target. *Habitat Debate,* 11 (8), p. 8.

Belina, B. (2011): Kapitalistische Raumproduktionen und ökonomische Krise. Zum Begriff des spatial fix bei David Harvey. *Zeitschrift für Wirtschaftsgeographie,* 55 (4), pp. 239–252. doi:10.1515/zfw.2011.0018

Belina, B., Heeg, S., Pütz, R. and Vogelpohl, A. (2013): Neuordnung des Städtischen im neoliberalen Zeitalter – Zur Einleitung. *Geographische Zeitschrift,* 101 (3–4), pp. 125–131.

Belina, B. & Michel, B. (2007): Raumproduktionen. Zu diesem Band. In: Belina, B. (ed.): Raumproduktionen. Beiträge der radical geography; eine Zwischenbilanz. Münster: Westfälisches Dampfboot (Raumproduktionen: Theorie und gesellschaftliche Praxis, 1), pp. 7–34.

Benwell, M. C., Haselip, J. and Borello, J. A. (2013): Housing, Security, and Employment in Post-Neoliberal Buenos Aires. *Latin American Perspectives,* 40 (2), pp. 146–167. doi:10.1177/0094582X12467759

Benz, A., Lütz, S., Schimank, U. and Simonis, G. (eds.) (2007): Handbuch Governance. Theoretische Grundlagen und empirische Anwendungsfelder. Wiesbaden: VS Verlag.

Berking, H. & Löw, M. (2008): Die Eigenlogik der Städte. Neue Wege für die Stadtforschung. Frankfurt: Campus (Interdisziplinäre Stadtforschung, 1).

Bertuzzo, E. T. & Nest, G. (2016): From the Ruins of 21st Century's Urban Development: the Paradigm of Self-organization. In: *TRIALOG,* 124/125 (1–2), pp. 39–50.

Bimo Hernowo (2016): Urban History of Surakarta 1745–1945. Architecture Amalgamation and Its Urban Structure. Utrecht University. Utrecht, June 2016.

Blum, S. & Schubert, K. (2011): Politikfeldanalyse. Wiesbaden: VS Verlag.

Bogumil, J. & Seuberlich, M. (2014): Lokale Politikforschung – Eine politikwissenschaftliche Sicht auf Stadt und Raum. In: Oßenbrügge, J. & Vogelpohl, A. (eds.): Theorien in der Raum- und Stadtforschung. Einführungen. Münster: Westfälisches Dampfboot, pp. 45–56.

Booth, A. (2003): Decentralisation and poverty alleviation in Indonesia. *Environment and Planning C: Government and Policy,* 21 (2), pp. 181–202. doi:10.1068/c0127

Bork, T., Kraas, F. and Yuan, Y. (2011): Governance challenges in China's urban health care system – the role of stakeholders. *Erdkunde,* 65 (2), pp. 121–135. doi:10.3112/erdkunde.2011.02.02

Bourdieu, P. & Wacquant, L. J. D. (2013): Reflexive Anthropologie. Frankfurt am Main: Suhrkamp.

Bower, R. (2016): Who Decides and Who Provides? The Anarchistic Housing Practices of John Turner as Realizations of Henri Lefebvre's Autogestive Space. *Alternatives: Global, Local, Political,* 41 (2), pp. 83–97. doi:10.1177/0304375416684856

BPS Boyolali – Badan Pusat Statistik Boyolali (2020): Population by Regency/Municipality in Jawa Tengah Province (thousand), 2015–2019. <https://boyolalikab.bps.go.id/statictable/2020/08/06/1131/jumlah-penduduk-menurut-kabupaten-kota-di-provinsi-jawa-tengah-ribu-2015–2019.html> (accessed 2020/08/07).

BPS Surabaya – Badan Pusat Statistik Kota Surabaya (2020). <https://surabayakota.bps.go.id/> (accessed 2020/04/24).

BPS Surakarta – Badan Pusat Statistik Kota Surakarta (2019): Kota Surakarta Dalam Angka 2019. <https://surakartakota.bps.go.id/publication/2019/08/16/18c08be6770cc96c4497cbec/kota-surakarta-dalam-angka-2019.html> (accessed 2019/07/21).

BPS Surakarta – Badan Pusat Statistik Kota Surakarta (2020a). <https://surakartakota.bps.go.id/> (accessed 2020/04/20).

BPS Surakarta – Badan Pusat Statistik Kota Surakarta (2020b): Kota Surakarta Dalam Angka 2020. Surakarta.

BPS – Badan Pusat Statistik Indonesia (2019a): Indicators of Housing 1993–2018. <https://www.bps.go.id/statictable/2009/03/12/1537/indikator-perumahan-1993–2018.html> (accessed 2020/01/15).

BPS – Badan Pusat Statistik Indonesia (2019b): Perkembangan Beberapa Indikator Utama Sosial Ekonomi Indonesia. Jakarta.

BPS – Badan Pusat Statistik Indonesia (2019c): Statistics Indonesia. <https://www.bps.go.id/> (accessed 2019/10/21).

BPS – Badan Pusat Statistik Indonesia (2019d): Statistik Indonesia Dalam Infografis 2019. <https://www.bps.go.id/publication/2019/09/26/c90ef44501d430ddb065bec5/statistik-indonesia-dalam-infografis-2019.html> (accessed 2023/03/04).

BPS – Badan Pusat Statistik Indonesia (2020): Human Development Index by Province [New Method], 2010–2019. <https://www.bps.go.id/> (accessed 2020/04/27).

Braun, V. & Clarke, V. (2006): Using thematic analysis in psychology. *Qualitative Research in Psychology,* 3 (2), pp. 77–101. doi:10.1191/1478088706qp063oa

Bredenoord, J. & Lindert, P. van (2010): Pro-poor housing policies: Rethinking the potential of assisted self-help housing. *Habitat International,* 34 (3), pp. 278–287. doi:10.1016/j.habitatint.2009.12.001

Bredenoord, J., Lindert, P. van and Smets, P. (2010): Equal access to shelter: Coping with the urban crisis by supporting self-help housing. *Habitat International,* 34 (3), pp. 274–277. doi:10.1016/j.habitatint.2009.11.017

Bredenoord, J., Lindert, P. van and Smets, P. (eds.) (2014): Affordable Housing in the Urban Global South. Seeking sustainable solutions. London: Routledge.

Brenner, N. (1999): Globalisation as Reterritorialisation: The Re-scaling of Urban Governance in the European Union. *Urban Studies,* 36 (3), pp. 431–451.

Brenner, N. (2012): What is critical urban theory? In: Brenner, N., Marcuse, P. & Mayer, M. (eds.): Cities for people, not for profit. Critical urban theory and the right to the city. London, New York: Routledge, pp. 11–23.

Brenner, N. (2013): Theses on Urbanization. *Public Culture,* 25 (1(69)), pp. 85–114. doi:10.1215/08992363-1890477
Brenner, N. (ed.) (2014a): Implosions/Explosions. Towards a study of planetary urbanization. Berlin: Jovis.
Brenner, N. (2014b): Introduction: Urban Theory without an Outside. In: Brenner, N. (ed.): Implosions/Explosions. Towards a study of planetary urbanization. Berlin: Jovis, pp. 14–30.
Brenner, N. & Schmid, C. (2015): Towards a new epistemology of the urban? *City,* 19 (2–3), pp. 151–182. doi:10.1080/13604813.2015.1014712
Brenner, N. & Theodore, N. (2002): Spaces of neoliberalism. Urban restructuring in North America and Western Europe. Malden, Mass, Oxford: Blackwell.
Brenner, N. & Theodore, N. (2003): Cities and the Geographies of "Actually Existing Neoliberalism". *Antipode,* 34 (3), pp. 349–397.
Bromley, R. (2003): Peru 1957–1977: How time and place influenced John Turner's ideas on housing policy. *Habitat International,* 27 (2), pp. 271–292. doi:10.1016/S0197-3975(02)00049-8
Bronger, D. (ed.) (2007): Marginalsiedlungen in Megastädten Asiens. Berlin, Münster: LIT.
Brown, A. & Kristiansen, A. (2009): Urban Policies and the Right to the City: Rights responsibilities and citizenship (MOST-2 Policy Papers). <http://unesdoc.unesco.org/images/0017/001780/178090e.pdf> (accessed 2016/04/26).
Buchori, I., Pangi, P., Pramitasari, A., Basuki, Y. and Wahyu Sejati, A. (2020): Urban Expansion and Welfare Change in a Medium-sized Suburban City: Surakarta, Indonesia. *Environment and Urbanization Asia,* 11 (1), pp. 78–101. doi:10.1177/0975425320909922
Buckley, R. & Simet, L. (2015): An agenda for Habitat III. Urban perestroika. *Environment and Urbanization,* 28 (1), pp. 64–76. doi:10.1177/0956247815622131
Buitenweg, H. (1980): Krokodillenstad. Katwijk aan Zee: Servire.
Bunnell, T., Miller, M. A., Phelps, N. A. and Taylor, J. (2013): Urban development in a decentralized Indonesia: Two Success Stories? *Pacific Affairs,* 86 (4), pp. 857–876. doi:10.5509/2013864857
Bunting, J. (2005): Global goals for local change. *Habitat Debate,* 11 (3), p. 11.
Burgess, R. (1978): Petty Commodity Housing or Dweller Control? A Critique of John Turner's Views on Housing Policy. *World Development,* 9/10 (6), pp. 1105–1133.
Burgess, R. (1982): Self-Help Housing Advocacy: A Curious Form of Radicalism. A Critique of the Work of John F. C. Turner. In: Ward, P. M. (ed.): Self-help housing. A critique. London: Mansell, pp. 56–98.
Burgess, R. (1996): An adjustable Agenda? *TRIALOG,* 50 (3), pp. 8–9.
Burgess, R., Carmona, M. and Kolstee, T. (eds.) (1997): The challenge of sustainable cities. Neoliberalism and urban strategies in developing countries. London: Zed Books.
Cabannes, Y. (2018): Highlights on some Asian and Russian Participatory Budgeting Pioneers. <https://www.ucl.ac.uk/bartlett/development/sites/bartlett/files/pub_asiarussia_2.pdf> (accessed 2019/08/11).
Caldeira, T. & Holston, J. (2015): Participatory urban planning in Brazil. *Urban Studies,* 52 (11), pp. 2001–2017. doi:10.1177/0042098014524461
Campbell, P. (2013): Collateral Damage? Transforming Subprime Slum Dwellers into Homeowners. *Housing Studies,* 28 (3), pp. 453–472. doi:10.1080/02673037.2013.759543
Caprotti, F., Cowley, R., Datta, A., Broto, V. C., Gao, E., Georgeson, L., Herrick, C., Odendaal, N. and Joss, S. (2017): The New Urban Agenda. Key opportunities and challenges for policy and practice. *Urban Research & Practice,* 11 (3), pp. 1–12. doi:10.1080/17535069.2016.1275618
Castree, N., Kitchen, R. and Rogers, A. (2013): Dictionary of Human Geography. Oxford: Oxford University Press.

Chaudhry, S. (2014): Forced to the fringes. Disasters of 'Resettlement' in India. Housing and Land Rights Network, Habitat International Coalition – South Asia. New Delhi.

Chen, J., Stephens, M. and Man, Y. (eds.) (2013): The future of public housing. Ongoing trends in the East and the West. Heidelberg: Springer.

Chiodelli, F. (2016): International Housing Policy for the Urban Poor and the Informal City in the Global South. A Non-diachronic Review. *Journal of International Development,* 28 (5), pp. 788–807. doi:10.1002/jid.3204

Choguill, C.L. (2007): The search for policies to support sustainable housing. *Habitat International,* 31 (1), pp. 143–149. doi:10.1016/j.habitatint.2006.12.001

Chomistriana, D. (2011): Indonesia: Neighbourhood Upgrading and Shelter Sector Project – Toward Cities without Slums. In: Steinberg, F. & Lindfield, M. (eds.): Inclusive cities. Manila: Asian Development Bank (Urban Development Series), pp. 47–62.

Christaller, W. (1933 [2006]): Die zentralen Orte in Süddeutschland: eine ökonomisch-geographische Untersuchung über die Gesetzmäßigkeit der Verbreitung und Entwicklung der Siedlungen mit städtischen Funktionen. Darmstadt: Wissenschaftliche Buchgesellschaft.

Citiscope (2016): Question of the Day: What key issue is missing from the New Urban Agenda? 25 experts weigh in on the Habitat III outcome strategy being adopted this week in Quito. Citiscope, 2016-10-17.

Clegg, S. (1989): Frameworks of Power. London: Sage. doi:10.4135/9781446279267

Cobban, J. (1974): Uncontrolled urban settlement: The kampung question in Semarang (1905–1940). *Bijdragen tot de Taal-, Land- en Volkenkunde,* 130 (4), pp. 403–427.

Cohen, B. (2006): Urbanization in developing countries: Current trends, future projections, and key challenges for sustainability. *Technology in Society,* 28 (1–2), pp. 63–80. doi:10.1016/j.techsoc.2005.10.005

Cohen, M.A. (2015): From Habitat II to Pachamama. A growing agenda and diminishing expectations for Habitat III. *Environment and Urbanization,* 28 (1), pp. 35–48. doi:10.1177/0956247815620978

Contesse, M., Vliet, B.J. van and Lenhart, J. (2018): Is urban agriculture urban green space? A comparison of policy arrangements for urban green space and urban agriculture in Santiago de Chile. *Land Use Policy,* 71, pp. 566–577. doi:10.1016/j.landusepol.2017.11.006

Cope, M. & Kurtz, H. (2016): Organizing, Coding, and Alayzing Qualitative Data. In: Clifford, N. et al. (eds.): Key Methods in Geography. London: Sage, pp. 647–665.

Coy, M. (2001): Institutionelle Regelungen im Konflikt um Land. *Geographica Helvetica,* 56 (1), pp. 28–33.

Coy, M. (2004): The fragmentation of the Brazilian city. Recent tendencies and challenges for urban policy. *Ágora,* 10 (1/2), pp. 9–22.

Coy, M. & Kraas, F. (2003): Probleme der Urbanisierung in den Entwicklungsländern. *Petermanns Geographische Mitteilungen,* 147 (1), pp. 32–41.

Croese, S., Cirolia, L.R. and Graham, N. (2016): Towards Habitat III. Confronting the disjuncture between global policy and local practice on Africa's 'challenge of slums'. *Habitat International,* 53, pp. 237–242. doi:10.1016/j.habitatint.2015.11.037

Crump, J., Newman, K., Belsky, E.S., Ashton, P., Kaplan, D.H., Hammel, D.J. and Wyly, E. (2008): Cities Destroyed (Again) For Cash: Forum on the U.S. Foreclosure Crisis. *Urban Geography,* 29 (8), pp. 745–784. doi:10.2747/0272–3638.29.8.745

Dahiya, B. (2012): Cities in Asia, 2012: Demographics, economics, poverty, environment and governance. *Cities,* 29 (2), pp. 44–61.

Dahm, B. & Ptak, R. (1999): Südostasien-Handbuch. Geschichte, Gesellschaft, Politik, Wirtschaft, Kultur. München: Beck.

Dang, T.K.P., Zouwen, M. van der and Arts, B. (2019): Challenges of Forest Governance: the Case of Forest Rehabilitation in Vietnam. *Public Organization Review*, 19 (4), pp. 425–452. doi:10.1007/s11115-018-0414-x
Daniel, M.M. & Hunt, R.J. (2014): Changing housing policies and housing provision in Jos, Nigeria. *Habitat International*, 42, pp. 203–213. doi:10.1016/j.habitatint.2013.11.004
Darrundono (2005): The first large-scale upgrading programme: an Indonesian success story. *Habitat Debate*, 11 (3), pp. 15–17.
Das, A. (2009): The Contribution of Participation to Slum Upgrading: Comparing Indian and Indonesian Cases. In: Santosa, H., Astuti, W. & Astuti, D.W. (eds.): Sustainable slum upgrading in urban area. Surakarta: Universitas Sebelas Maret (CIB Working Commission W110), pp. 27–50.
Das, A. (2015a): Autonomous but constrained: CBOs and urban upgrading in Indonesia. *Cities*, 48, pp. 8–20. doi:10.1016/j.cities.2015.05.009
Das, A. (2015b): Participatory slum upgrading: lessons from post-decentralization India and Indonesia. *Journal of Indonesian Regional Development and Environment*, 1, pp. 15–34.
Das, A. (2017): A City of Two Tales. Shelter and Migrants in Surabaya. *Environment and Urbanization Asia*, 8 (1), pp. 1–21. doi:10.1177/0975425316686501
David, B. (2012): Machtverschiebungen zwischen Indonesiens Zentrum und Peripherie. *Aus Politik und Zeitgeschichte*, 62 (11–12), pp. 23–30.
Davis, M. (2006): Planet of Slums. New York: Verso.
Death, C. & Gabay, C. (2015): Doing Biopolitics Differently? Radical Potential in the Post-2015 MDG and SDG Debates. *Globalizations*, 12 (4), pp. 597–612. doi:10.1080/14747731.2015.1033172
Deffner, V. (2006): Lebenswelt eines innerstädtischen Marginalviertels in Salvador da Bahia (Brasilien) : Umgang mit sozialer und räumlicher Exklusion aus Sicht der armen Bevölkerungsgruppen. *Geographica Helvetica*, 61 (1), pp. 21–31.
Desai, V. & Loftus, A. (2013): Speculating on Slums: Infrastructural Fixes in Informal Housing in the Global South. *Antipode*, 45 (4), pp. 789–808. doi:10.1111/j.1467–8330.2012.01044.x
Devas, N. (ed.) (2004): Urban governance, voice, and poverty in the developing world. London: Earthscan.
Dianingrum, A., Faqih, M. and Septanti, D. (2017): Development of Kampung Improvement Program in Surabaya, Indonesia. *The International Journal of Engineering and Science*, 6 (7), pp. 41–47. doi:10.9790/1813–0607014147
Dick, H. (2002): Surabaya, city of work. A socioeconomic history, 1900–2000. Athens, Ohio, London: Ohio University Press.
Dieleman, M. (2011): New town development in Indonesia. Renegotiating, shaping and replacing institutions. *Bijdragen tot de taal-, land- en volkenkunde / Journal of the Humanities and Social Sciences of Southeast Asia*, 167 (1), pp. 60–85. doi:10.1163/22134379–90003602
DiGaetano, A. (2009): The Birth of Modern Urban Governance: A Comparison of Political Modernization in Boston, Massachusetts, and Bristol, England, 1800–1870. *Journal of Urban History*, 35 (2), pp. 259–287. doi:10.1177/0096144208327914
DiGaetano, A. & Strom, E. (2003): Comparative Urban Governance: An Integrated Approach. *Urban Affairs Review*, 38 (3), pp. 356–395.
Doornbos, M. (2001): 'Good Governance'. The Rise and Decline of a Policy Metaphor? *Journal of Development Studies*, 37 (6), pp. 93–108. doi:10.1080/713601084
Dowall, D.E. (1989): Bangkok: A Profile of an Efficiently Performing Housing Market. *Urban Studies*, 26 (3), pp. 327–339.
DPU Surakarta – Dinas Pekerjaan Umum (2011): Executive Summary: Penyusunan Data Dasar RP4D Kota Surakarta. Surakarta.

Duff, C. (2017): The affective right to the city. *Transactions of the Institute of British Geographers*, 42 (4), pp. 516–529. doi:10.1111/tran.12190

Dyos, H.J. (1967): The Slums of Victorian London. *Victorian Studies*, 11 (1), pp. 5–40.

Edelman, M., Oya, C. and Borras, S.M. (2013): Global Land Grabs: historical processes, theoretical and methodological implications and current trajectories. *Third World Quarterly*, 34 (9), pp. 1517–1531. doi:10.1080/01436597.2013.850190

Engels, F. (1845 [1969]): Condition of the Working Class in England. Panther Edition. Moscow: Institute of Marxism-Leninism. doi:10.14714/CP65.121

Engels, F. (1892 [1970]): Über die Umwelt der arbeitenden Klasse: aus den Schriften von Friedrich Engels: ausgewählt von Günter Hillmann. Gütersloh: Bertelsmann (Bauwelt Fundamente, 27).

Ensminger, J. (2017): Corruption in community-driven development. A Kenyan case study with insights from Indonesia. CMI – Chr. Michelsen Institute (U4, 9). <https://www.cmi.no/publications/6291-corruption-in-community-driven-development> (accessed 2020/03/12).

Etzold, B. (2011): Die umkämpfte Stadt. Die alltägliche Aneignung öffentlicher Räume durch Straßenhändler in Dhaka (Bangladesch). In: Holm, A. & Gebhardt, D. (eds.): Initiativen für ein Recht auf Stadt. Theorie und Praxis städtischer Aneignungen. Hamburg: VSA, pp. 187–220.

Etzold, B. (2013): The Politics of Street Food. Contested Governance and Vulnerabilities in Dhaka's Field of Street Vending. Stuttgart: Franz Steiner Verlag (Megacities and Global Change, 13).

Etzold, B., Jülich, S., Keck, M., Sakdapolrak, P., Schmitt, T. and Zimmer, A. (2012): Doing institutions. A dialectic reading of institutions and social practices and its relevance for development geography. *Erdkunde*, 66 (3), pp. 185–195. doi:10.3112/erdkunde.2012.03.01

Evans, B., Elisei, P., Rosenfeld, O., Roll, G., Figueiredo, A. and Keiner, M. (2016): HABITAT III – Toward a New Urban Agenda. *disP – The Planning Review*, 52 (1), pp. 86–91. doi:10.1080/02513625.2016.1171053

Evers, H.-D. (2007): The End of Urban Involution and the Cultural Construction of Urbanism in Indonesia. *Internationales Asienforum*, 38 (1–2), pp. 51–65.

Evers, H.-D. & Korff, R. (2000): Southeast Asian Urbanism. The Meaning and Power of Social Space. Münster: Lit Verlag.

Fabrianti, F. (2010): Flood Risk Perception and Coping Mechanism of Local Community. A Case Study in Part of Surakarta City, Central Java Province, Indonesia. Master Thesis. Gadjah Mada University: Yogyakarta.

Fahmi, F.Z., Hudalah, D., Rahayu, P. and Woltjer, J. (2014): Extended urbanization in small and medium-sized cities: The case of Cirebon, Indonesia. *Habitat International*, 42, pp. 1–10. doi:10.1016/j.habitatint.2013.10.003

Fassmann, H. (2004): Stadtgeographie I. Braunschweig: Westermann.

Ferguson, B. & Smets, P. (2010): Finance for incremental housing; current status and prospects for expansion. *Habitat International*, 34 (3), pp. 288–298. doi:10.1016/j.habitatint.2009.11.008

Fernandes, E. (2007): Constructing the `Right To the City' in Brazil. *Social & Legal Studies*, 16 (2), pp. 201–219. doi:10.1177/0964663907076529

Firman, T. (1999): Indonesian cities under the "Krismon": A great "urban crisis" in Southeast Asia. *Cities*, 16 (2), pp. 69–82.

Firman, T. (2009): The continuity and change in mega-urbanization in Indonesia: A survey of Jakarta–Bandung Region (JBR) development. *Habitat International*, 33 (4), pp. 327–339. doi:10.1016/j.habitatint.2008.08.005

Firman, T. (2010): Multi local-government under Indonesia's decentralization reform: The case of Kartamantul (The Greater Yogyakarta). *Habitat International,* 34 (4), pp. 400–405. doi:10.1016/j.habitatint.2009.11.005

Firman, T. (2014a): Inter-local-government partnership for urban management in decentralizing Indonesia: from below or above? Kartamantul (Greater Yogyakarta) and Jabodetabek (Greater Jakarta) compared. *Space and Polity,* 18 (3), pp. 215–232. doi:10.1080/13562576.2014.959252

Firman, T. (2014b): The need for a national urban development policy in Indonesia. *Jakarta Post,* 2014-09-20.

Flagge, I. (ed.) (1999): Geschichte des Wohnens. 1945 bis heute: Aufbau, Neubau, Umbau. Band 5. Wüstenrot Stiftung. Stuttgart: DVA.

Flick, U. (2011): Triangulation. Wiesbaden: Springer Fachmedien (Qualitative Sozialforschung).

Flick, U. (2016): Qualitative Sozialforschung. Eine Einführung (7th ed.). Reinbek bei Hamburg: Rowohlt.

Flick, U. (2019): An Introduction to qualitative research (6th ed.). Los Angeles [i. a.]: Sage Publications.

Follmann, A. & Trumpp, T. (2013): Armutsbekämpfung oder Bekämpfung der Armen? Weltstadtvisionen und Slum-Räumungen in Delhi. *Geographische Rundschau,* 65 (10), pp. 4–11.

Ford, L. R. (1993): A Model of Indonesian City Structure. *Geographical Review,* 83 (4), pp. 374–396.

Freeman, L. C. (1978): Centrality in Social Networks. Conceptual Clarification. *Social Networks,* 1 (3), pp. 215–239.

Freytag, T. (2014): Raum und Gesellschaft. In: Lossau, J., Freytag, T. & Lippuner, R. (eds.): Schlüsselbegriffe der Kultur- und Sozialgeographie. Stuttgart: Ulmer (UTB), pp. 12–24.

Freytag, T., Gebhardt, D., Gerhard, U. and Wastl-Walter, D. (eds.) (2016): Humangeographie Kompakt. Berlin, Heidelberg: Springer.

Frick, H. (1984): Rumah sederhana. Kebijaksanaan Perencanaan dan Konstruksi. Yogyakarta: Kanisius.

Friedman, J. (2014): Expanding and Diversifying Indonesia's Program for Community Empowerment, 2007–2012. Innovations for Successful Societies. Princeton University. <https://successfulsocieties.princeton.edu/sites/successfulsocieties/files/Expanding%20and%20Diversifying%20_Indonesia_ToU_1.pdf> (accessed 2023/03/07).

Friendly, A. (2013): The right to the city: theory and practice in Brazil. *Planning Theory & Practice,* 14 (2), pp. 158–179. doi:10.1080/14649357.2013.783098

Frings, M. (2012): Zivilgesellschaft in Indonesien. *Aus Politik und Zeitgeschichte,* 62 (11–12), pp. 43–49.

Fromhold-Eisebith, M. & Eisebith, G. (2019): What can Smart City policies in emerging economies actually achieve? Conceptual considerations and empirical insights from India. *World Development,* 123. doi:10.1016/j.worlddev.2019.104614

Fuhse, J. (2018): Soziale Netzwerke. Konzepte und Forschungsmethoden (2nd ed.). Konstanz, München: UVK Verlagsgesellschaft mbH (UTB Sozialwissenschaften, 4563).

Fukuyama, F. (2013): What Is Governance? *Governance: An International Journal of Policy, Administration, and Institutions,* 26 (3), pp. 347–368. doi:10.1111/gove.12035

Furman, J., Stiglitz, J. E., Bosworth, P. and Radelet, S. (1998): Economic Crises: Evidence and Insights from East Asia. *Brookings Papers on Economic Activity,* 29(2), pp. 1–135.

Galiani, S. & Schargrodsky, E. (2010): Property rights for the poor: Effects of land titling. *Journal of Public Economics,* 94 (9–10), pp. 700–729.

Gamino, D. K. (2012): Annäherung an ein unbekanntes Land. *Aus Politik und Zeitgeschichte,* 62 (11–12), pp. 3–8.

Ganapati, S. (2010): Enabling Housing Cooperatives: Policy Lessons from Sweden, India and the United States. *International Journal of Urban and Regional Research,* 34 (2), pp. 365–380. doi:10.1111/j.1468–2427.2010.00906.x

Ganapati, S. (2014): Housing cooperatives in the developing world. In: Bredenoord, J., Lindert, P. van & Smets, P. (eds.): Affordable Housing in the Urban Global South. Seeking sustainable solutions. London: Routledge, pp. 102–116.

Garreau, J. (1992): Edge city: life on the new frontier. New York: Anchor Books.

Garschagen, M. & Porter, L. (2018): The New Urban Agenda: From Vision to Policy and Action. *Planning Theory & Practice,* 19 (1), pp. 117–121. doi:10.1080/14649357.2018.1412678

Geoffrey, P., Durand-Lasserve, A. and Rakodi, C. (2009): The limits of land titling and home ownership. *Environment and Urbanization,* 21 (2), pp. 443–462.

Gervasi, M. (2010): Surakarta, Indonesia: Empowering the Informal Sector: Street Vendor Management. UCLG – Committee on Social Inclusion, Participatory Democracy and Human Rights of United Cities and Local Governments. <https://www.uclg-cisdp.org/sites/default/files/Surakarta_2010_en_final.pdf> (accessed 2012/08/09).

Gervasi, M. (2011): Surabaya, Indonesia: Green and clean initiative. Centre for Social Studies, University of Coimbra. <http://www.uclg-cisdp.org/sites/default/files/Surabaya_2010_en_final.pdf> (accessed 2014/11/28).

Ghosh, A. & Kamath, L. (2012): Decentralisation and Local Government Innovation in Providing Urban Services for the Poor in South and South-east Asia. *Space and Polity,* 16 (1), pp. 49–71.

Giddens, A. (1984): The constitution of society. Outline of the theory of structuration. Cambridge: Polity Press.

Gilbert, A. (2002): On the mystery of capital and the myths of Hernando de Soto. What difference does legal title make? *International Development Planning Review,* 24 (1), pp. 1–19. doi:10.3828/idpr.24.1.1

Gilbert, A. (2004a): Helping the poor through housing subsidies. Lessons from Chile, Colombia and South Africa. *Habitat International,* 28 (1), pp. 13–40. doi:10.1016/S0197–3975(02)00070-X

Gilbert, A. (2004b): Learning from others. The spread of capital housing subsidies. *International Planning Studies,* 9 (2–3), pp. 197–216. doi:10.1080/1356347042000311776

Gilbert, A. (2007): The Return of the Slum: Does Language Matter? *International Journal of Urban and Regional Research,* 31 (4), pp. 697–713. doi:10.1111/j.1468–2427.2007.00754.x

Gilbert, A. (2009): Extreme Thinking About Slums and Slum Dwellers. A Critique. *SAIS Review,* 29 (1), pp. 35–48. doi:10.1353/sais.0.0031

Gilbert, A. (2011): Ten Myths Undermining Latin American Housing Policy. *Revista de Ingenieria,* 35, pp. 79–87.

Gilbert, A. (2015): Rental housing. The international experience. *Habitat International,* 54, pp. 173–181. doi:10.1016/j.habitatint.2015.11.025

Gomes da Silva, K. (2018): The new urban agenda and human rights cities: Interconnections between the global and the local. *Netherlands Quarterly of Human Rights,* 36 (4), pp. 290–310. doi:10.1177/0924051918806721

Gottdiener, M., Budd, L. and Lehtovuori, P. (2016): Key concepts in urban studies (2nd ed.). Los Angeles: Sage (Sage key concepts).

Gould, E. R. L. (1900): The Housing Problem in Great Cities. *The Quarterly Journal of Economics,* 14 (3), pp. 378–393.

Grell, B. (2014): Recht auf Stadt. In: Belina, B., Naumann, M. & Strüver, A. (eds.): Handbuch kritische Stadtgeographie. Münster: Westfälisches Dampfboot, pp. 366–371.

Grindle, M.S. (2007): Good Enough Governance Revisited. *Development Policy Review*, 25 (5), pp. 533–574. doi:10.1111/j.1467–7679.2007.00385.x
Guelf, F.M. (2010): "La révolution urbaine". Henri Lefebvres Philosophie der globalen Verstädterung. Dissertation. Technische Universität Berlin: Berlin.
Guillot, C. (2005): Urban Patterns and Polities in Malay Trading Cities, Fifteenth through Seventeenth Centuries. *Indonesia*, 80, pp. 39–51.
Guinness, P. (2016): Land and housing security for the urban poor. In: Robinson, K.M. & McCarthy, J.F. (eds.): Land & development in Indonesia. Searching for the people's sovereignty. Singapore: ISEAS Publishing (Indonesia update series), pp. 206–224.
Handzic, K. (2010): Is legalized land tenure necessary in slum upgrading? Learning from Rio's land tenure policies in the Favela Bairro Program. *Habitat International*, 34 (1), pp. 11–17. doi:10.1016/j.habitatint.2009.04.001
Harding, A. & Blokland-Potters, T. (2014): Urban theory. A critical introduction to power, cities and urbanism in the 21st century. Los Angeles: Sage.
Hardoy, J.E. & Satterthwaite, D. (1989): Squatter citizen. Life in the urban third world. London: Earthscan.
Harris, R. (2015): International Policy for Urban Housing Markets in the Global South since 1945. In: Miraftab, F. & Kudva, N. (eds.): Cities of the global South Reader. London, New York: Routledge (Routledge urban reader series), pp. 122–131.
Harrison, D.H. (2019): Disclosable Version of the ISR – National Affordable Housing Program – P154948 – Sequence No: 05 (English). World Bank Group. Washington D.C. <http://documents.worldbank.org/curated/en/267061559778207400/Disclosable-Version-of-the-ISR-National-Affordable-Housing-Program-P154948-Sequence-No-05> (accessed 2020/01/15).
Hartono, I.G. (2009): Sustainability of Neighborhood Upgrading and Shelter Sector Project (NUSSP). In: Santosa, H., Astuti, W. & Astuti, D.W. (eds.): Sustainable slum upgrading in urban area. Surakarta: Universitas Sebelas Maret (CIB Working Commission W110), pp. 3–13.
Harvey, D. (1978): The urban process under capitalism. A framework for analysis. *International Journal of Urban and Regional Research*, 2 (1–4), pp. 101–131. doi:10.1111/j.1468–2427.1978.tb00738.x
Harvey, D. (1979): Social justice and the city. London: Arnold.
Harvey, D. (2006): The limits to capital. London, New York: Verso books.
Harvey, D. (2007): Kleine Geschichte des Neoliberalismus. Zürich: Rotpunktverlag.
Harvey, D. (2008): The Right to the City. *New Left Review*, 53, pp. 23–40.
Harvey, D. (2012): Rebel Cities. London, New York: Verso books.
Hay, C. & Wincott, D. (1998): Structure, Agency and Historical Institutionalism. *Political Studies*, 46 (5), pp. 951–957.
Heeg, S. (2014): Rugulationstheorie: Akkumulationsregime und Regulationsweise. In: Oßenbrügge, J. & Vogelpohl, A. (eds.): Theorien in der Raum- und Stadtforschung. Einführungen. Münster: Westfälisches Dampfboot, pp. 156–175.
Heineberg, H. (2017): Stadtgeographie (5th ed.). Paderborn: Schöningh (UTB).
Helmsing, A.H.J. (2002): Decentralisation, enablement, and local governance in low-income countries. *Environment and Planning C: Government and Policy*, 20 (3), pp. 317–340. doi:10.1068/c0040
Herlambang, S., Leitner, H., Tjung, L.J., Sheppard, E. and Anguelov, D. (2019): Jakarta's great land transformation: Hybrid neoliberalisation and informality. *Urban Studies*, 56 (4), pp. 627–648. doi:10.1177/0042098018756556
Hernández, F., Kellett, P. and Allen, L.K. (eds.) (2010): Rethinking the informal city. Critical perspectives from Latin America. New York: Berghahn Books (Remapping cultural history, 11).

Herz, A., Peters, L. and Truschkat, I. (2015): How to do qualitative strukturale Analyse? Die qualitative Interpretation von Netzwerkkarten und erzählungsgenerierenden Interviews. *Forum: Qualitative Sozialforschung*, 16 (1).

Hilpert, T. (2000): Le Corbusiers "Charta von Athen" (2nd ed.). Basel: Birkhäuser.

Höferl, K.-M. & Sandholz, S. (eds.) (2017): Urban Resilience in Indonesia. Assessing and Evaluating Development Strategies in Yogyakarta and Surakarta. Innsbruck: Innsbrucker Studienkreis für Geographie (inngeo – Innsbrucker Materialien zur Geographie, 17).

Hollstein, B. (2006): Qualitative Methoden und Netzwerkanalyse – ein Wiederspruch? In: Hollstein, B. & Straus, F. (eds.): Qualitative Netzwerkanalyse. Konzepte, Methoden, Anwendungen. Wiesbaden: VS Verlag für Sozialwissenschaften, pp. 11–36.

Holm, A. (2013): Recht auf Stadt – Soziale Bewegungen in umkämpften Räumen. *p|art|icipate – Kultur aktiv gestalten*, 2. <http://www.p-art-icipate.net/cms/recht-auf-die-stadt-soziale-bewegungen-in-umkampften-raumen/> (accessed 2016/06/28).

Holm, A. (2015): Das Recht auf die Stadt. In: Stadtpolitisches Bündnis "Wem gehört die Stadt?" (ed.): Wem gehört die Stadt? Ein Reader zum Thema "Recht auf Stadt". Mannheim, pp. 4–9.

Holm, A. & Gebhardt, D. (eds.) (2011): Initiativen für ein Recht auf Stadt. Theorie und Praxis städtischer Aneignungen. Hamburg: VSA.

Holtkamp, L. (2007): Local Governance. In: Benz, A. et al. (eds.): Handbuch Governance. Theoretische Grundlagen und empirische Anwendungsfelder. Wiesbaden: VS Verlag, pp. 366–377.

Howes, S. & Davies, R. (2014): Survey of Recent Developments. *Bulletin of Indonesian Economic Studies*, 50 (2), pp. 157–183. doi:10.1080/00074918.2014.938403

Hudalah, D., Firman, T. and Woltjer, J. (2013a): Cultural Cooperation, Institution Building and Metropolitan Governance in Decentralizing Indonesia. *International Journal of Urban and Regional Research*, 38 (6), 2217–2234. doi:10.1111/1468–2427.12096

Hudalah, D., Zulfahmi, F. and Firman, T. (2013b): Regional Governance in Decentralizing Indonesia: Learning from the Success of Urban-Rural Cooperation in Metropolitan Yogyakarta. In: Bunnell, T., Parthasarathy, D. & Thompson, E. C. (eds.): Cleavage, Connection and Conflict in Rural, Urban and Contemporary Asia. Dordrecht: Springer, pp. 83–98.

Huff, A. S. (2008): Designing Research for Publication. Los Angeles: Sage.

Jäger, S. (1993): Kritische Diskursanalyse. Eine Einführung. Duisburg: Duisburger Institut für Sprach- und Sozialforschung.

Jahn, T. & Lux, A. (2009): Problemorientierte Diskursfeldanalyse – neue Methode und Anwendungsmöglichkeiten. Institut für sozial-ökologische Forschung (ISOE-Studientexte, 15).

Jakimow, T. (2017): Becoming a Developer: Processes of Personhood in Urban Community-driven Development, Indonesia. *Anthropological Forum*, 27 (3), pp. 256–276. doi:10.1080/00664677.2017.1379005

Jakimow, T. (2018): Negotiating Impossibilities in Community-driven Development in Indonesia. *Journal of Developing Societies*, 34 (1), pp. 35–55. doi:10.1177/0169796X17753001

Jansen, D. (2006): Einführung in die Netzwerkanalyse. Grundlagen, Methoden, Forschungsbeispiele. Wiesbaden: VS Verlag.

Jehle, V. M. (2017): "Housing" und "Slum-Upgrading" im Rahmen des United Nations Human Settlements Programme. Diplomarbeit. Universität Innsbruck: Innsbruck.

Jellinek, L. (1991): The wheel of fortune. The history of a poor community in Jakarta. Honolulu: University of Hawaii Press.

Jellinek, L. (2012): Ways of Knowing Indonesia. The Personal Journey of an Academic and Activist. In: Purdey, J. (ed.): Knowing Indonesia. Intersections of self, discipline and nation. Clayton, Victoria, Australia: Monash University Publishing (Monash Asia series).

Jessop, B. (2001): Institutional Re(turns) and the Strategic – Relational Approach. *Environment and Planning A*, 33 (7), pp. 1213–1235.

JICA – Japan International Cooperation Agency (2018): Review of Indonesia's Development and Capan's Cooperation. Its Past, Present and Future in the Republic of Indonesia. <http://open_jicareport.jica.go.jp/pdf/12307831.pdf> (accessed 2019/09/24).

Jones, B. G. (2012): 'Bankable Slums': the global politics of slum upgrading. *Third World Quarterly*, 33 (5), pp. 769–789.

Jones, G. A. & Ward, P. M. (1994): The World Bank's 'New' Urban Management Programme: Paradigm Shift or Policy Continuity? *Habitat International*, 18 (3), pp. 33–51.

Jones, P. (2017): Formalizing the Informal: Understanding the Position of Informal Settlements and Slums in Sustainable Urbanization Policies and Strategies in Bandung, Indonesia. *Sustainability*, 9 (8), p. 1436. doi:10.3390/su9081436

Joshi, S. & Sohail Khan, M. (2010): Aided self-help: The Million Houses Programme – Revisiting the issues. *Habitat International*, 34 (3), pp. 306–314. doi:10.1016/j.habitatint.2009.11.010

Kaika, M. (2017): 'Don't call me resilient again!': the New Urban Agenda as immunology … or … what happens when communities refuse to be vaccinated with 'smart cities' and indicators. *Environment & Urbanization*, 29 (1), pp. 89–102. doi:10.1177/0956247816684763

Kamil, M. (2014): Participatory Design. The social role of architecture in kampung upgrading. *Inside Indonesia*, 118, 2014-11-25. <https://www.insideindonesia.org/participatory-design> (accessed 2019/11/21).

Kearns, A. & Paddison, R. (2000): New Challenges for Urban Governance. *Urban Studies*, 37 (5–6), pp. 845–850. doi:10.1080/00420980050011118

Keivani, R. & Werna, E. (2001a): Modes of housing provision in developing countries. *Progress in Planning*, 55 (2), pp. 65–118. doi:10.1016/S0305-9006(00)00022-2

Keivani, R. & Werna, E. (2001b): Refocusing the housing debate in developing countries from a pluralist perspective. *Habitat International*, 25 (2), pp. 191–208. doi:10.1016/S0197-3975(00)00024-2

Kelle, U. (2014): Mixed Methods. In: Baur, N. & Blasius, J. (eds.): Handbuch Methoden der empirischen Sozialforschung. Wiesbaden: Springer, pp. 153–166.

Keller, R. (2011): Diskursforschung. Eine Einführung für SozialwissenschaftlerInnen (4. Aufl. Wiesbaden: VS Verlag für Sozialwissenschaften / Springer Fachmedien Wiesbaden GmbH Wiesbaden (Qualitative Sozialforschung, 14). doi:10.1007/978-3-531-92085-6

Kern, A. (2016): Produktion von (Un-)Sicherheit – Urbane Sicherheitsregime im Neoliberalismus. Münster, Westf: Westfälisches Dampfboot (Raumproduktionen: Theorie und gesellschaftliche Praxis, 22).

Kersting, N., Caulfield, J., Nickson, R. A., Olowu, D. and Wollmann, H. (2009): Local Governance Reform in Global perspective. Wiesbaden: VS Verlag für Sozialwissenschaften (Urban and Regional Research International, 12).

King, R. & Idawati, D. E. (2010): Surabaya Kampung and Distorted Communication. *Sojourn: Journal of Social Issues in Southeast Asia*, 25 (2), pp. 213–233. doi:10.1355/sj25-2c

Kipfer, S., Saberi, P. and Wieditz, T. (2013): Henri Lefebvre. Debates and controversies. *Progress in Human Geography*, 37 (1), pp. 115–134. doi:10.1177/0309132512446718

Kisnarini, R. (2015): Functionality and adaptability of low cost apartment space design: a case of Surabaya Indonesia. Dissertation. Technische Universiteit Eindhoven: Eindhoven.

Kooiman, J. (2003): Governing as governance. London: Sage.

Kooiman, J. & Jentoft, S. (2009): Meta-Governance: Values, Norms and Principles, and the Making of Hard Choices. *Public Administration,* 87 (4), pp. 818–836. doi:10.1111/j.1467–9299.2009.01780.x

Kothari, M. (2007): Basic Principles and Guidelines on Development-based Evictions and Displacement. In: United Nations Human Rights Council (UNHRC): Report of the Special Rapporteur on adequate housing as a component of the right to an adequate standard of living, Miloon Kothari. UN Doc. A/HRC/4/18, 5. February. <http://www.ohchr.org/Documents/Issues/Housing/Guidelines_en.pdf> (accessed 2017/01/16).

Kothari, M. & Vasquez, P. (2015): Policy Debate | The UN Guidelines on Forced Evictions: A Useful Soft-Law Instrument? *International Development Policy | Revue internationale de politique de développement,* 6.2. doi:10.4000/poldev.2188

KPUPR – Kementerian Pekerjaan Umum dan Perumahan Rakjat (2016): Indonesia National Report for Habitat III. <http://habitat3.org/wp-content/uploads/National-Report_INDONESIA.pdf> (accessed 2019/10/04).

KPUPR – Kementerian Pekerjaan Umum dan Perumahan Rakyat (n. d.): Tentang Program Kota Tanpa Kumuh (Kotaku). <http://kotaku.pu.go.id/page/6880/tentang-program-kota-tanpa-kumuh-kotaku)> (accessed 2020/03/18).

KPUPR – Kementerian Pekerjaan Umum dan Perumahan Rakyat (2019): Capaian Program Satu Juta Rumah Per 31 Desember 2018 Tembus 1.132.621 Unit. <https://pu.go.id/berita/capaian-program-satu-juta-rumah-per-31-desember-2018-tembus-1-132-621-unit> (accessed 2023/03/07).

Kraas, F. (2003): Verstädterungs- und innerurbane Entwicklungsprozesse in Südostasien. In: Feldbauer, P., Husa, K. & Korff, R. (eds.): Südostasien. Gesellschaften, Räume und Entwicklung im 20. Jahrhundert. Wien: Promedia, pp. 196–211.

Kraas, F. (2005): Stadtentwicklung und Stadtvisionen in Südostasien. *Geographische Rundschau,* 57 (10), pp. 68–72.

Kraas, F. & Mertins, G. (2014): Megacities and Global Change. In: Kraas, F. et al. (eds.): Megacities. Our global urban future. Dordrecht: Springer (International year of planet Earth), pp. 1–6.

Krätke, S. (2014): Cities in Contemporary Capitalism. *International Journal of Urban and Regional Research,* 38 (5), pp. 1660–1677. doi:10.1111/1468–2427.12165

Kratzer, A. & Ammering, U. (2019): Rural innovations in biosphere reserves – A social network approach. *Journal of Rural Studies,* 71, pp. 144–155. doi:10.1016/j.jrurstud.2019.01.001

Kumar, S. (2008): Urban Housing Policy and Practice in the Developing World. In: Colby, I. C., Sowers, K. M. & Dulmus, C. N. (eds.): Comprehensive Handbook of Social Work and Social Welfare: Social Policy and Policy Practice. New York: Wiley

Kusno, A. (2011): The green governmentality in an Indonesian metropolis. *Singapore Journal of Tropical Geography,* 32 (3), pp. 314–331. doi:10.1111/j.1467–9493.2011.00440.x

Kusno, A. (2013): After the new order. Space, politics and Jakarta. Honolulu: University of Hawaii Press (Writing past colonialism).

Kuymulu, M. B. (2013): The Vortex of Rights: 'Right to the City' at a Crossroads. *International Journal of Urban and Regional Research,* 37 (3), pp. 923–940. doi:10.1111/1468–2427.12008

Lasminto, U., Lumantara, E., Widyastuti, H. and Zharin, F. (2016): Flood Assessment of Bengawan Solo River. *ARPN Journal of Engineering and Applied Sciences,* 11 (24), pp. 14443–14450.

Lay, C. (2017): Volunteers from the Periphery (Case Studies of Survivors of the Lapindo Mudflow and Stren Kali, Surabaya, Forced Eviction). *Southeast Asian Studies,* 6 (1), pp. 31–61.

Lefebvre, H. (1940 [2009]): Dialectical Materialism. Translated by John Sturrock. Minneapolis: University of Minnesota Press.

Lefebvre, H. (1968 [2016]): Das Recht auf Stadt. Nautilus Flugschrift. Hamburg: Edition Nautilus.
Lefebvre, H. (1968 [1996]): Writings on Cities. Selected, translated and introduced by Eleonore Kofman and Elizabeth Lebas. Cambridge, Mass.: Blackwell.
Lefebvre, H. (1970 [2003]): The Urban Revolution. Translated by Bonnonno, R. Minneapolis: University of Minnesota Press.
Lefebvre, H. (1973[1976]): The Survival of Capitalism. Reproduction of the Relations of Production. New York: St. Martin's Press.
Lefebvre, H. (1974 [1991]): The Production of Space. Translated by Nicholson-Smith, D. Maiden, Oxford, Victoria: Blackwell Publishing.
Leggewie, C. (2015): Wie tot ist die "Charta von Athen"? Zur Unöffentlichkeit unserer Städte. *Informationen zur Raumentwicklung* (4), pp. 361–368.
Leitner, H., Peck, J. and Sheppard, E. S. (eds.) (2007a): Contesting neoliberalism. Urban frontiers. New York, London: The Guilford Press.
Leitner, H., Sheppard, E. S., Kristin, S. and Anant, M. (2007b): Contesting Urban Futures: Decentering Neoliberalism. In: Leitner, H., Peck, J. & Sheppard, E. S. (eds.): Contesting neoliberalism. Urban frontiers. New York, London: The Guilford Press, pp. 1–25.
Leon, J. K. (2015): The role of global cities in land grabs. *Third World Quarterly,* 36 (2), pp. 257–273. doi:10.1080/01436597.2015.1015787
Leroy, P. & Arts, B. (2006): Institutional Dynamics in Environmental Governance. In: Arts, B. & Leroy, P. (eds.): Institutional Dynamics in Environment Governance. Dordrecht: Springer (Environment & Policy, 47), pp. 1–19.
Leroy, P. & Tatenhove, J. van (2000): Political modernization theory and environmental politics. In: Spaargaren, G., Mol, A. P. J & Buttel, F. H. (eds.): Environment and global modernity. London: Sage, pp. 187–209.
Lifferink, D. (2006): The Dynamics of Policy Arrangements: Turning Round the Tetrahedron. In: Arts, B. & Leroy, P. (eds.): Institutional Dynamics in Environment Governance. Dordrecht: Springer (Environment & Policy, 47), pp. 45–68.
Lin, Y., Hao, P. and Geertman, S. (2015): A conceptual framework on modes of governance for the regeneration of Chinese 'villages in the city'. *Urban Studies,* 52 (10), pp. 1774–1790. doi:10.1177/0042098014540345
Link, J. & Link-Heer, U. (1990): Diskurs, Interdiskurs und Literaturanalyse. *Zeitschrift für Literaturwissenscahft und Linguistik,* 20 (77), pp. 88–99.
Logan, J. R. & Molotch, H. L. (1987): Urban Fortunes: The Political Economy of Place (20th ed.). Barkley, Los Angeles, London: University of California Press.
Longhurst, R. (2016): Semi-structured Interviews and Focus Groups. In: Clifford, N. et al. (eds.): Key Methods in Geography. London: Sage, pp. 143–156.
Lourenço, J. M. & Astuti, Z. B. (2011): Intertwining Big Events and Urban Strategy within Life Cycle Analysis: the case of Solo, Central Java, Indonesia. In: Schrenk, M., Popovich, V. & Zeile, P. (eds.): Real CORP 2011. Change for Stability. Lifecycles of Cities and Regions. The Role and Possibilities of Foresighted Planning in Transformation Processes. Proceedings of the 16th International Conference on Urban Planning, Regional Development and Information Society. Schwechat-Rannersdorf: CORP, pp. 493–504.
Löw, M. (2008): Soziologie der Städte. Frankfurt am Main: Suhrkamp Verlag.
Luebke, C. v., McCulloch, N. and Patunru, A. A. (2009): Heterodox Reform Symbioses. The Political Economy of Investment Climate Reforms in Solo, Indonesia. *Asian Economic Journal,* 23 (3), pp. 269–296. doi:10.1111/j.1467–8381.2009.02012.x

Mader, P. (2018): Contesting Financial Inclusion. *Development and Change,* 49 (2), pp. 461–483. doi:10.1111/dech.12368

Mahizhnan, A. (1999): Smart cities: The Singapore case. *Cities,* 16 (1), pp. 13–18. doi:10.1016/S0264-2751(98)00050-X

Mangin, W. (1967): Latin American squatter settlements: a problem and a solution. *Latin American research review,* 2 (3), pp. 65–98.

Marcuse, P. (2010): From critical urban theory to the right to the city. *City,* 13 (2–3), pp. 185–197. doi:10.1080/13604810902982177

Martínez-Alier, J., Pascual, U., Vivien, F.-D. and Zaccai, E. (2010): Sustainable de-growth: Mapping the context, criticisms and future prospects of an emergent paradigm. *Ecological Economics,* 69 (9), pp. 1741–1747. doi:10.1016/j.ecolecon.2010.04.017

Marx, B., Stoker, T. and Suri, T. (2013): The Economics of Slums in the Developing World. *Journal of Economic Perspectives,* 27 (4), pp. 187–210.

Marx, K. (1844 [1968]): Karl Marx, Friedrich Engels. Schriften, Manuskripte, Briefe bis 1844. Berlin: Dietz Verlag (Werke, 40).

Marx, K. (1858 [1983]): Grundrisse der Kritik der politischen Ökonomie. Berlin: Dietz Verlag (Werke, 42).

Marx, K. (1867 [1965]): Das Kapital: Kritik der politischen Ökonomie. Stuttgart: Kröner.

Marx, K. & Engels, F. (1844 [1988]): Economic & Philosophic Manuscripts of 1844 and the Communist Manifesto. New York: Prometheus Books.

Massiah, G. (2016): Proposals for a "Good Use" of Habitat III. AITEC Address to Movements, Local Authorities, Researchers. *TRIALOG,* 124/125 (1–2), pp. 24–30.

Matthews, F. (2012): Governance and State Capacity. In: Levi-Faur, D. (ed.): Oxford handbook of governance. Oxford: Oxford University Press (Oxford handbooks), pp. 281–293.

Mattissek, A. & Glasze, G. (2015): Discourse analysis in German-language human geography. Integrating theory and method. *Social & Cultural Geography,* 17 (1), pp. 39–51. doi:10.1080/14649365.2014.961532

Mattissek, A., Pfaffenbach, C. and Reuber, P. (2013): Methoden der empirischen Humangeographie. Braunschweig: Westermann (Das Geographische Seminar).

Mattissek, A. & Prossek, A. (2014): Regieren und Planen. In: Lossau, J., Freytag, T. & Lippuner, R. (eds.): Schlüsselbegriffe der Kultur- und Sozialgeographie. Stuttgart: Ulmer (UTB), pp. 198–211.

May, B. (2015): Dezentralisierung – Eine wechselvolle Geschichte. In: Stange, G., Jordan, W. & Großmann, K. (eds.): Handbuch Indonesien. Berlin: Horlemann, pp. 230–246.

Mayer, M. (2011): Recht auf die Stadt-Bewegungen in historisch und räumlich vergleichender Perspektive. In: Holm, A. & Gebhardt, D. (eds.): Initiativen für ein Recht auf Stadt. Theorie und Praxis städtischer Aneignungen. Hamburg: VSA, pp. 53–78.

Mayntz, R. & Scharpf, F. W. (1995): Der Ansatz des akteurszentrierten Institutionalismus. In: Mayntz, R. & Scharpf, F. W. (eds.): Gesellschaftliche Selbstregelung und Steuerung. Frankfurt am Main: Campus, pp. 39–72.

Mayring, P. (2000): Qualitative Inhaltsanalyse. *Forum Qualitative Sozialforschung,* 1 (2). doi:10.17169/fqs-1.2.1089

Mayring, P. (2015): Qualitative Inhaltsanalyse. Grundlagen und Techniken. Weinheim, Basel: Beltz.

McCarthy, P. (2003): Urban Slum Reports: The case of Jakarta, Indonesia. UN-Habitat. <http://www.ucl.ac.uk/dpu-projects/Global_Report/pdfs/Jakarta.pdf> (accessed 2012/06/18).

McGee, T. G. (1991): The emergence of Desakota Regions in Asia: Expanding a Hypothesis. In: Ginsburg, N. S., Koppel, B. & McGee, T. G. (eds.): The Extended Metropolis. Settlement Transition in Asia. Honolulu: University of Hawaii Press, pp. 3–26.

Mengay, A. & Pricelius, M. (2011): Das umkämpfte Recht auf Stadt in Brasilien. Die insitutionalisierte Form der "Stadt Statute" und die Praxis der urbanen Wohnungslosenbewegung MTST. In: Holm, A. & Gebhardt, D. (eds.): Initiativen für ein Recht auf Stadt. Theorie und Praxis städtischer Aneignungen. Hamburg: VSA, pp. 245–270.

Mertins, G. (1984): Marginalsiedlungen in Großstädten der Dritten Welt. *Geographische Rundschau,* 36 (9), pp. 434–442.

Milbert, I. (2006): Slums, Slum Dwellers and Multilevel Governance. *The European Journal of Development Research,* 18 (2), pp. 299–318. doi:10.1080/09578810600717222

Miller, M. A. (2013): Decentralizing Indonesian City Spaces as New 'Centers'. *International Journal of Urban and Regional Research,* 37 (3), pp. 834–848. doi:10.1111/j.1468–2427.2013.01209.x

Minnery, J., Argo, T., Winarso, H., Hau, D., Veneracion, C. C., Forbes, D. and Childs, I. (2013): Slum upgrading and urban governance: Case studies in three South East Asian cities. *Habitat International,* 39, pp. 162–169. doi:10.1016/j.habitatint.2012.12.002

Misselwitz, P. (2018): Koproduktive Ansätze zur Lösung der globalen Wohnraumkrise. Zwischen informellen Selbstversorgungspraktiken, Staat und Markt. *Geographische Rundschau,* 70 (6), pp. 10–15.

Mitchell, D. (2012): Right to the City. Social Justice and the Fight for Public Space. New York: Guilford Publications.

Mitchell, D. & Heynen, N. (2009): The Geography of Survival and the Right to the City: Speculations on Surveillance, Legal Innovation, and the Criminalization of Intervention. *Urban Geography,* 30 (6), pp. 611–632. doi:10.2747/0272–3638.30.6.611

Monkkonen, P. (2013): Urban land-use regulations and housing markets in developing countries: Evidence from Indonesia on the importance of enforcement. *Land Use Policy,* 34, pp. 255–264. doi:10.1016/j.landusepol.2013.03.015

Moosenberger, K. & Stocker, G. (2001): The Evolution of Urban Regime Theory. The Challenge of Conceptualization. *Urban Affairs Review,* 36 (6), pp. 810–835.

Moreno, E. L. (2005): How far is the world from the slum target? *Habitat Debate,* 11 (3), pp. 4–5.

Mukhija, V. (2001): Enabling Slum Redevelopment in Mumbai. Policy Paradox in Practice. *Housing Studies,* 16 (6), pp. 791–806. doi:10.1080/02673030120090548

Müller, W. & Sträter, D. (2011): Wer lenkt die Stadt? Wie die Neoliberalisierung der Stadt die kommunale Selbstverwaltung aushebelt. In: Belina, B. (ed.): Urbane Differenzen. Disparitäten innerhalb und zwischen Städten. Münster: Westfälisches Dampfboot (Raumproduktionen, 9), pp. 132–162.

Mumford, E. (2002): The CIAM Discourse on Urbanism, 1928–1960. Cambridge, Mass.: The MIT Press.

Nakamura, S. (2016): Does slum formalisation without title provision stimulate housing improvement? A case of slum declaration in Pune, India. *Urban Studies,* 54 (7), pp. 1715–1735. doi:10.1177/0042098016632433

Neudert, E. (2001): Armut und Marginalität in Städten der "Dritten Welt". Sozioökonomische Analyse eines Railwayslums in Bombay unter besonderen Berücksichtigung von Gender-Aspekten. Diplomarbeit. Eberhard-Karls-Universität: Tübingen. Geographisches Institut.

Newman, M. E. J. (2010): Networks. An introduction. Oxford: Oxford University Press.

North, D. C. (1990): Institutions, institutional change and economic performance. Cambridge: Cambridge University Press.

Novira, N. (2017): The Illegal Conversion of Rice Field to Oil Palm Smallholder Estate. Between Government's Target and Landowners' Decision. Dissertation. University of Innsbruck: Innsbruck.

Nuissl, H. & Heinrichs, D. (2013): Slums: perspectives on the definition, the appraisal and the management of an urban phenomenon. *Die Erde,* 144 (2), pp. 105–116.

Obermayr, C. (2013): Anzeichen für eine nachhaltige Stadtentwicklung in Indonesien? Der Umgang mit dem informellen Sektor und Slumsiedlungen in Surakarta. *Südostasien,* 29 (1), pp. 35–37. doi:10.11588/soa.2013.1.4128

Obermayr, C. (2017): Sustainable City Management. Informal Settlements in Surakarta, Indonesia. Cham: Springer. doi:10.1007/978-3-319-49418-0

Obermayr, C. & Astuti, W. (2016): Paradigm shifts in the international housing debate and its local implications for Surakarta's approaches on housing the poor. In: Rachmawati, R., Pomeroy, G. & Mookherjee, D. (eds.): Rapid Urbanization and Sustainable Development in Asia. The 13th International Asian Urbanization Conference Proceedings. Yogyakarta: Badan Penerbit Fakultas Geografi, Universitas Gadjah Mada, pp. 571–580.

Obermayr, C. & Sandholz, S. (2017): Participatory Resettlements in Surakarta, Indonesia. Changing Livelihoods for the Better or the Worse? *TRIALOG,* 126/127 (3–4/2016), pp. 43–50.

OECD (2010): OECD Economic Surveys: Indonesia. OECD Publishing. doi:10.1787/97892640 00000-en

OECD (2013): Development Co-operation Report 2013: Ending Poverty. OECD Publishing. doi:10.1787/dcr-2013-en

OECD (2015): The Metropolitan Century. Understanding Urbanisation and its Consequences. Paris: OECD Publishing. doi:10.1787/9789264228733-en

Oestereich, J. (1996): From Habitat I to Habitat II. The way from Vancouver to Istanbul. *TRIALOG,* 49 (2), pp. 56–62.

Ortiz, B.J. (2014): The Promise of Prosperity through Urban Revitalization in the Philippines and Indonesia under a Devolved and Neoliberal Regime. In: South-South Tricontinental Collaborative Programme (ed.): Inequality, Democracy and Development under Neoliberalism and Beyond. Bangkok, pp. 232–258.

Park, R. E., Burgess, E. W. and McKenzie, R. D. (1925): The City. Chicago: The University of Chicago Press.

Parnell, S. (2016): Defining a Global Urban Development Agenda. *World Development,* 78, pp. 529–540. doi:10.1016/j.worlddev.2015.10.028

Pathoni, A. (2012): Indonesia's 1000-Tower Plan Falls Flat. *The Wall Street Journal,* 2012-10-11. <https://www.wsj.com/articles/BL-SEAB-1206> (accessed 2023/03/07).

Pemerintah Kota Surabaya (2008): Rencana Pembangunan dan Pengembangan Perumahan dan Permukiman (RP4D) Kota Surabaya Tahun 2008–2018. Surabaya.

Pemerintah Kota Surabaya (2017): Statistik Sektoral Kota Surabaya tahun 2017. <https://www.surabaya.go.id/id/berita/49832/statistik-sektoral-kota-surabay> (accessed 2019/01/25).

Pemerintah Kota Surabaya (2019): Statistik Sektoral Kota Surabaya Tahun 2019. <https://surabaya.go.id/id/berita/52759/statsekt2019> (accessed 2020/04/15).

Pemerintah Kota Surakarta (2012): Penyusunan Strategi Pembangunan Permukiman dan Infrastruktur Perkotaan (SPPIP) Kota Surakarta Tahun Anggaran 2012. Surakarta.

Perda – Peraturan Daerah Kota Surabaya (Perda 09/2007): Penataan Sempadan Kali Surabaya dan Kali Wonokromo.

Perda – Peraturan Daerah Kota Surabaya (Perda 02/2010): Pemakaian Rumah Susun.

Perera, G. (2007): Claiming the Right to the City: A Question of Power. *Race, Poverty and Environment,* 15 (1), pp. 12–13. <http://www.reimaginerpe.org/files/15.Perera.pdf> (accessed 2018/09/05).

Perlman, J. E. (1976): The Myth of Marginality: Urban Poverty and Politics in Rio de Janeiro. Berkeley, Los Angeles, London: University of California Press.
Perlman, J. E. (2010): Favela. Four decades of living on the edge in Rio de Janeiro. Oxford, New York: Oxford University Press.
Perlman, J. E. (2017): Cities without Slums are Cities without Soul. Re-thinking Concepts and Consequences of Marginality in the Favelas of Rio de Janeiro. In: *TRIALOG*, 123 (4), pp. 4–12.
Permanent Mission of the Republic of Indonesia (2012): Responses submitted by the Government of Indonesia. Questionnaire on Housing Financing Policies and Programs. <http://www.ohchr.org/Documents/Issues/Housing/Housingfinancing/Indonesia.pdf> (accessed 2015/05/19).
Permenpera – Peraturan Menteri Perumahan Rakyat (Permenpera 10/2012): Penyelenggaraan Perumahan dan Kawasan Permukiman dengan Hunian Berimbang.
Perumnas (2013): Products Transformation for Business Growth Enhancement (Annual Report). <https://perumnas.co.id/assets/img/laporan-tahunan/pdf/Annual_Report_2013.pdf> (accessed 2023/03/07).
Perumnas (2016): The best Legacy for Excellent Performance (Annual Report). <https://perumnas.co.id/assets/img/laporan-tahunan/pdf/Annual_Report_2016.pdf> (accessed 2023/03/07).
Perumnas (2018): Giving Added Value through Continuous Transformation (Annual Report). <https://perumnas.co.id/assets/img/laporan-tahunan/pdf/Annual_Report_2018.pdf> (accessed 2023/03/07).
Perwali – Peraturan Walikota Surabaya (Perwali 13/2015): Tarif Sewa Rumah Susun Sederhana Sewa Wonorejo, Penjaringansari II, Randu, Tanah Merah Tahap I, Tanah Merah Tahap II, Penjaringansari III, Grudo, Pesapen, Jambangan, Siwalankerto, Romokalisari Tahap I dan Romokalisari Tahap II di Kota Surabaya.
Perwali – Peraturan Walikota Surakarta (Perwali 15/2016): Pengelolaan Rumah Susun Sederhana Sewa Pemerintah Kota Surakarta.
Peters, R. (2013): Surabaya, 1945–2010. Neighbourhood, State and Economy in Indonesia's City of Struggle. Copenhagen: NIAS Press (Southeast Asia publications series).
Phelps, N. A., Bunnell, T., Miller, M. A. and Taylor, J. (2014): Urban inter-referencing within and beyond a decentralized Indonesia. *Cities*, 39, pp. 37–49. doi:10.1016/j.cities.2014.02.004
Pierre, J. (2005): Comparative Urban Governance. Uncovering Complex Causalities. *Urban Affairs Review*, 40 (4), pp. 446–462.
Pierre, J. (2006): Debating governance. Authority, steering, and democracy (2nd ed.). Oxford: Oxford University Press.
Pihan, S. A. (2018): Leben im Kampung. Master thesis. University of Innsbruck: Innsbruck. <http://diglib.uibk.ac.at/ulbtirolhs/content/titleinfo/2873787> (accessed 2019/09/11).
Plessis, J. (2005): The growing problem of forced evictions and the crucial importance of community-based, locally appropriate alternatives. *Environment and Urbanization*, 17 (1), pp. 123–134.
Porter, L. (2011): Interface: Informality, the Commons and the Paradoxes for Planning: Concepts and Debates for Informality and Planning. *Planning Theory & Practice*, 12 (1), pp. 115–153.
PPDPP – Pusat Pengelolaan Dana Pembiayaan Perumahan (2019): Realisasi Penyaluran Dana FLPP Tahun 2010–2020 (Bulan Berjalan). <https://ppdpp.id/kinerja-penyaluran-dana-flpp-2/> (accessed 2019/12/05).
PP – Peraturan Pemerintah Republik Indonesia (PP 38/2011): Sungai.
Prasetiyo, W. H., Kamarudin, K. R. and Dewantara, J. A. (2019): Surabaya green and clean: Protecting urban environment through civic engagement community. *Journal of Human Behavior in the Social Environment*, 29 (8), pp. 997–1014. doi:10.1080/10911359.2019.1642821

Priebe, J. (2014): Official Poverty Measurement in Indonesia since 1984. A Methodological Review. *Bulletin of Indonesian Economic Studies,* 50 (2), pp. 185–205. doi:10.1080/00074918.2014.938406

PSF – PNPM Support Facility (2015): 2014 PSF Progress Report. <https://www.dfat.gov.au/sites/default/files/indonesia-pnpm-support-facility-progress-report-2014.pdf> (accessed 2023/03/07).

Pugh, C. (1994): Housing policy development in developing countries. *Cities,* 11 (3), pp. 159–180. doi:10.1016/0264-2751(94)90057-4

Pugh, C. (1997): Poverty and Progress? Reflections on Housing and Urban Policies in Developing Countries, 1976–96. *Urban Studies,* 34 (10), pp. 1547–1595. doi:10.1080/0042098975358

Pugh, C. (2001): The Theory and Practice of Housing Sector Development for Developing Countries, 1950–99. *Housing Studies,* 16 (4), pp. 399–423. doi:10.1080/02673030120066527

Purcell, M. (2002): Excavating Lefebvre: The right to the city and its urban politics of the inhabitant. *GeoJournal,* 58 (2–3), pp. 99–108.

Purcell, M. (2003): Citizenship and the right to the global city: reimagining the capitalist world order. *International Journal of Urban and Regional Research,* 27 (3), pp. 564–590.

Purcell, M. (2006): Urban Democracy and the Local Trap. *Urban Studies,* 43 (11), pp. 1921–1941.

Purcell, M. (2013a): Possible Worlds. Henri Lefebvre and the Right to the City. *Journal of Urban Affairs,* 36 (1), pp. 141–154. doi:10.1111/juaf.12034

Purcell, M. (2013b): The right to the city: the struggle for democracy in the urban public realm. *Policy & Politics,* 43 (3), pp. 311–327. doi:10.1332/030557312X655639

Qomarun & Prayitno, B. (2007): Morfologi Kota Solo (Tahun 1500–2000). *Dimensi Teknik Arsitektur,* 35 (1), pp. 80–87.

Rakodi, C. (2003): Politics and performance: the implications of emerging governance arrangements for urban management approaches and information systems. *Habitat International,* 27 (4), pp. 523–547. doi:10.1016/S0197-3975(03)00004-3

Redclift, M. (2005): Sustainable development (1987–2005): an oxymoron comes of age. *Sustainable Development,* 13 (4), pp. 212–227. doi:10.1002/sd.281

Reerink, G. (2006): The Price of Uncertainty: Kampung Land Issues in Post-Suharto Bandung. *IIAS Newsletter* (40), p. 14.

Reerink, G. & Gelder, J.-L. van (2010): Land titling, perceived tenure security, and housing consolidation in the kampongs of Bandung, Indonesia. *Habitat International,* 34 (1), pp. 78–85. doi:10.1016/j.habitatint.2009.07.002

Republic of Indonesia (2016): Indonesia National Report for Habitat III. <http://habitat3.org/wp-content/uploads/National-Report_INDONESIA.pdf> (accessed 2017/07/18).

Republic of Indonesia (2019): Voluntary National Reviews (VNR). Empowering People and Ensuring Inclusiveness and Equality. <https://sustainabledevelopment.un.org/content/documents/2380320190708_Final_VNR_2019_Indonesia_Rev3.pdf> (accessed 2020/02/03).

Right to the City Alliance (n. d.): Who we are. <https://www.righttothecity.org/who-we-are> (accessed 2023/03/07).

Rindarjono, M. G. (2014): "Slum" Urban Inequality: Reclamation, Inundation and Social Impact in Central Java, Indonesia. Yogyakarta: Media Perkasa.

RKPD (2018): Rencana Kerja Pemerintah Daerah Kota Surakarta (RKPD). Kota Surakarta. Surakarta.

Roberts, B. (2014): Managing Systems of Secondary Cities. Policy Responses in International Development. Brussels: Cities Alliance.

Roitman, S. (2016): Top-Down and Bottom-Up Strategies for Housing and Poverty Alleviation in Indonesia: The PNPM Programme in Yogyakarta. In: Attia, S. et al. (eds.): Dynamics and

resilience of informal areas. International perspectives. Cham: Springer International Publishing, pp. 187–210.
Rojas, E. (2018): "No time to waste" in applying the lessons from Latin America's 50 years of housing policies. *Environment and Urbanization*, 3 (1), 1–16. doi:10.1177/0956247818781499
Röll, W. (1981): Indonesien. Entwicklungsprobleme einer tropischen Inselwelt. Stuttgart: Klett.
Rolnik, R. (2013a): Late Neoliberalism: The Financialization of Homeownership and Housing Rights. *International Journal of Urban and Regional Research*, 37 (3), pp. 1058–1066. doi:10.1111/1468-2427.12062
Rolnik, R. (2013b): Report of the Special Rapporteur on adequate housing as a component of the right to an adequate standard of living, and on the right to non-discrimination in this context on her mission to Indonesia. Report to the Human Rights Council (UN Doc. A/HRC/25/54/Add.1).
Rolnik, R. (2013c): Ten years of the City Statute in Brazil: from the struggle for urban reform to the World Cup cities. *International Journal of Urban Sustainable Development*, 5 (1), pp. 54–64. doi:10.1080/19463138.2013.782706
Ronneberger, K. & Vogelpohl, A. (2014): Henri Lefebvre: Die Produktion des Raumes und die Urbanisierung der Gesellschaft. In: Oßenbrügge, J. & Vogelpohl, A. (eds.): Theorien in der Raum- und Stadtforschung. Einführungen. Münster: Westfälisches Dampfboot, pp. 251–270.
Rossi, U. (2017): Cities in global capitalism. Cambridge, UK, Malden, MA: Polity Press (Urban futures).
Rothfuß, E. (2012): Exklusion im Zentrum. Die brasilianische Favela zwischen Stigmatisierung und Wiederständigkeit. Bielefeld: Transcript.
Rothfuß, E. (2014): Stigmatisierung und Alltag in brasilianischen Favelas. Das Beispiel Calabar in Salvador da Bahia. *Geographische Rundschau*, 66 (5), pp. 12–17.
Roy, A. (2005): Urban Informality. Towards an Epistemology of Planning. *Journal of the American Planning Association*, 71 (2), pp. 147–158.
Roy, A. (2014): Slum-free cities of the Asian century: Postcolonial government and the project of inclusive growth. *Singapore Journal of Tropical Geography*, 35 (1), pp. 136–150. doi:10.1111/sjtg.12047
Roy, A. & AlSayyad, N. (eds.) (2004): Urban Informality – Transnational Perspectives from the Middle East, Latin America, and South Asia. Lenham: Lexington Books.
Rukmana, D. (2015): The Transformation of Indonesian Housing Policies. Indonesia's Urban Studies. <http://indonesiaurbanstudies.blogspot.co.at/2015/09/the-transformation-of-indonesian.html> (accessed 2016/08/11).
Rukmana, D. (2018): Upgrading Housing Settlement for the Urban Poor in Indonesia: An Analysis of the Kampung Deret Program. In: Grant, B., Liu, C.Y. & Ye, L. (eds.): Metropolitan Governance in Asia and the Pacific Rim. Singapore: Springer Singapore, pp. 75–94.
Rusliandy & Megawati, E. (2016): Civil Servants Rationalization in Indonesia. In: Wekke, I.S. et al. (eds.): Proceedings of the International Conference on Ethics in Governance (ICONEG 2016), No. 84. Makassar: Atlantis Press (Advances in Social Science Education and Humanities Research, 84), pp. 490–494.
Rutz, W. (1985): Die Städte Indonesiens. Städte und andere nicht-landwirtschaftliche Siedlungen, ihre Entwicklung und gegenwärtige Stellung in Verwaltung und Wirtschaft. Berlin, Stuttgart (Urbanisierung der Erde, 4).
Saharan, T., Pfeffer, K. and Baud, I. (2018): Shifting approaches to slums in Chennai. Political coalitions, policy discourses and practices. *Singapore Journal of Tropical Geography*, 35 (2), pp. 1–18. doi:10.1111/sjtg.12244

Samyahardja, P., Subiantoro, I. and Saraswati (2006): The Understanding of Physical Development Forces for Estimation of Administrative Definition of Urban Areas. In: Ministry of Public Works (ed.): Public Works International 2006. Jakarta, pp. 95–104.
Santosa, H. (2000): Environmental management in Surabaya with reference to National Agenda 21 and the social safety net programme. *Environment and Urbanization,* 12 (2), pp. 175–184. doi:10.1177/095624780001200214
Sari, A. A., Shirleyana and Feliciani, F. A. (2015): Optimizing visual Quality of Facade in Social Housing. Paper presented at International Seminar on Partnership for Sustainable Housing and Urban Development. Surabaya, 2015-10-15.
Sari, Y. I. (2017): When village development fails. *Inside Indonesia,* 128, 2017-05-09.
Sassen, S. (2009): When Local Housing Becomes an Electronic Instrument: The Global Circulation of Mortgages – A Research Note. *International Journal of Urban and Regional Research,* 33 (2), pp. 411–426. doi:10.1111/j.1468–2427.2009.00868.x
Satrio, R. P. (2010): Flood Characteristics of Upper Solo River Sub-basin. <http://www.icharm.pwri.go.jp/training/master/pubilication/pdf/2010/panji.pdf> (accessed 2012/02/05).
Satterthwaite, D. (2016): A new urban agenda? *Environment and Urbanization,* 28 (1), pp. 3–12. doi:10.1177/0956247816637501
Satterthwaite, D. (2018): Will the New Urban Agenda Have Any Positive Influence on Governments and International Agencies? *Planning Theory & Practice,* 19 (1), pp. 121–123. doi:10.1080/14649357.2018.1412678
Schechla, J. (2016): Habitat III's Seven Deadly Sins of Omission. In: *TRIALOG,* 124/125 (1–2), pp. 31–38.
Schiel, T. (2015): Reformasi. In: Stange, G., Jordan, W. & Großmann, K. (eds.): Handbuch Indonesien. Berlin: Horlemann, pp. 97–107.
Schiffer, E. (2007): Net-Map toolbox. Influence Mapping of Social Networks. <https://netmap.files.wordpress.com/2008/06/net-map-manual-long1.pdf> (accessed 2014/02/14).
Schiffer, E. & Hauck, J. (2010): Net-Map: Collecting Social Network Data and Facilitating Network Learning through Participatory Influence Network Mapping. *Field Methods,* 22 (3), pp. 231–249. doi:10.1177/1525822X10374798
Schmid, C. (2005): Stadt, Raum und Gesellschaft. Henri Lefebvre und die Theorie der Produktion des Raumes. Stuttgart: Steiner (Sozialgeographische Bibliothek, Bd. 1).
Schmid, C. (2011): Henri Lefebvre und das Recht auf die Stadt. In: Holm, A. & Gebhardt, D. (eds.): Initiativen für ein Recht auf Stadt. Theorie und Praxis städtischer Aneignungen. Hamburg: VSA, pp. 25–52.
Schmid, C. (2014): Networks, Borders, Differences: Towards a Theory of the Urban. In: Brenner, N. (ed.): Implosions/Explosions. Towards a study of planetary urbanization. Berlin: Jovis, pp. 67–80.
Schmid, C. (2018): Journeys through planetary urbanization. Decentering perspectives on the urban. *Environmental Planning D: Society and Space,* 1–20. doi:10.1177/0263775818765476
Scholz, F. (2002): Die Theorie der fragmentierenden Entwicklung. *Geographische Rundschau,* 54 (10), pp. 6–11.
Scholz, F. (2003): Globalisierung und "neue Armut". *Geographische Rundschau,* 55 (10), pp. 11–13.
Scholz, F. (2006): Entwicklungsländer. Entwicklungspolitische Grundlagen und regionale Beispiele. Braunschweig: Westermann.
Scholz, U. (1992): Transmigrasi – ein Desaster? Probleme und Chancen des indonesischen Umsiedlungsprogramms. *Geographische Rundschau,* 44 (1), pp. 33–39.
Schott, C. (2015): Indonesien. Ein Länderporträt. Berlin: Ch. Links Verlag.

Schulze, H. (1997): Neo-Institutionalismus. Ein analytisches Instrument zur Erklärung gesellschaftlicher Transformationsprozesse. Osteuropa-Institut der Freien Universität Berlin (Arbeitspapiere es Bereichs Politik und Gesellschaft, 4).

Scott, W. R. (2014): Institutions and organizations. Ideas, interests and identities. Los Angeles, London, New Delhi, Singapore, Washington DC: Sage.

Scruggs, G. (2016): Historic consensus reached on 'right to the city' in New Urban Agenda. Citiscope, 2016-09-09.

Senge, K. (2011): Das neue am Neoinstitutionalismus. Der Neo-Institutionalismus im Kontext der Organisationswissenschaft: VS Verlag.

Sengupta, U., Murtagh, B., D'Ottaviano, C. and Pasternak, S. (2018): Between enabling and provider approach: Key shifts in the national housing policy in India and Brazil. *Environment and Planning C: Politics and Space,* 36 (5), pp. 856–876. doi:10.1177/2399654417725754

Septanti, D. (2014): Functionality and Adaptability of Coastal Low Income Houses in Java Indonesia. Dissertation. Eindhoven University of Technology.

Serdült, U. (2002): Soziale Netzwerkanalyse: eine Methode zur Untersuchung von Beziehungen zwischen sozialen Akteuren. *Österreichische Zeitschrift für Politikwissenschaft,* 31 (2), pp. 127–141.

Setiawan, R. P. (2010): Penggusuran Permukiman Liar di Stren Kali Jagir: Sebuah Tinjauan dari Sisi Hukum dan Humanisme. Conference Paper: Seminar Nasional Perumahan Permukiman dalam Pembangunan Kota 2010. doi:10.13140/RG.2.1.1044.5283

Sheng, Y. K. & Kirinpanu, S. (2000): Once Only the Sky was the Limit: Bangkok's Housing Boom and the Financial Crisis in Thailand. *Housing Studies,* 15 (1), pp. 11–27. doi:10.1080/02673030082441

Shirleyana, S. H. & Sunindijo, R. Y. (2018): City of Kampung: risk and resilience in the urban communities of Surabaya, Indonesia. *International Journal of Building Pathology and Adaptation,* 36 (5), pp. 543–568. doi:10.1108/IJBPA-02-2018-0025

Siagian, R. (2015): The Analysis of vertical Housing Policy in Jabodetabek Area. Paper presented at International Seminar on Partnership for Sustainable Housing and Urban Development. Surabaya, 2015-10-16.

Sieverts, T. (1997): Zwischenstadt. Zwischen Ort und Welt, Raum und Zeit, Stadt und Land. Wiesbaden: Springer (Bauwelt Fundamente, 118).

Silas, J. (1989): Marginal settlements in Surabaya, Indonesia: problem or potential? *Environment and Urbanization,* 1 (2), pp. 60–70. doi:10.1177/095624788900100207

Silas, J. (1992): Government-community partnerships in kampung improvement programmes in Surabaya. *Environment and Urbanization,* 4 (2), pp. 33–41. doi:10.1177/095624789200400204

Silas, J. (2002): Toll roads and the development of new settlements: The case of Surabaya compared to Jakarta. *Bijdragen tot de Taal-, Land- en Volkenkunde,* 158 (4), pp. 677–689.

Silas, J., Setyawan, W., Ernawati, R. and Okitasari, M. (2012): The Kampungs of Surabaya entering the 21st Century. Planning and Revitalization of Surabaya Kampungs. Surabaya: City Government of Surabaya.

Simone, A. (2010): City Life from Jakarta to Dakar. Movements at the Crossroads. New York: Routledge.

SKB – Surat Keputusan Bersama Menteri dalam Negeri, Menteri Pekerjaan Umum dan Menteri Perumahan Rakyat (SKB 648–384/1992): Pedoman Pembangunan Perumahan dan Permukiman dengan Lingkungan Hunian Yang Berimbang.

Smets, P., Bredenoord, J. and Lindert, P. van (2014): Introduction. Governance, sustainability and affordability of low-income housing. In: Bredenoord, J., Lindert, P. van & Smets, P. (eds.):

Affordable Housing in the Urban Global South. Seeking sustainable solutions. London: Routledge, pp. 1–14.
Soederberg, S. (2014): Subprime Housing Goes South: Constructing Securitized Mortgages for the Poor in Mexico. *Antipode,* 47 (2), pp. 1–19. doi:10.1111/anti.12110
Soederberg, S. (2017): Universal access to affordable housing? Interrogating an elusive development goal. *Globalizations,* 14 (3), pp. 343–359. doi:10.1080/14747731.2016.1253937
Soemarno, I. (2010): A 'Simple' Solution Proposal for Riverbank Settlement Problems in Surabaya. *Environment and Urbanization Asia,* 1 (2), pp. 209–222. doi:10.1177/097542531000100207
Soemarno, I. (2011): Urban land policy and housing development in Indonesia. Surabaya as a case study. Saarbrücken: Lambert Academic Publishing.
Soemarno, I. & Sudarma, E. (2014): Small Scale Real Estates Development and Spatial Planning 'Adjustment' in Surabaya, Indonesia. In: CIB Working Commission W110: Informal Settlements and Affordable Housing. Durban 2014 Conference Proceedings, pp. 1115–1123.
Soja, E.W. (1989): Postmodern geographies. The reassertion of space in critical social theory. London, New York: Verso.
Some, W., Hafidz, W. and Sauter, G. (2009): Renovation not relocation. The work of Paguyuban Warga Strenkali (PWS) in Indonesia. *Environment and Urbanization,* 21 (2), pp. 463–475. doi:10.1177/0956247809343766
Soraya, G. (2019): Disclosable Version of the ISR – Indonesia National Slum Upgrading Project – P154782 – Sequence No: 07 (English). World Bank Group. Washington D. C. <http://documents.worldbank.org/curated/en/748821572515682725/Disclosable-Version-of-the-ISR-Indonesia-National-Slum-Upgrading-Project-P154782-Sequence-No-07> (accessed 2020/03/19).
Soto, H. d. (2002): Freiheit für das Kapital! Warum der Kapitalismus nicht weltweit funktioniert. Berlin: Rowohlt.
Spreitzhofer, G. (2007): Marginalisierte Kampungs, zentralisierte Superblocks? Aspekte der Regionalentwicklung in Metro-Jakarta. In: Bronger, D. (ed.): Marginalsiedlungen in Megastädten Asiens. Berlin, Münster: LIT, pp. 251–296.
Stake, R. (1995): The art of case study research. Thousand Oaks, California: Sage.
Stalker, P. (2007): Let's Speak Out for MDGs. Achieving the Millennium Development Goals in Indonesia. <https://www.undp.org/indonesia/publications/lets-speak-out-mdgsachieving-mdgs-indonesia-2008-edition> (accessed 2023/03/07).
Steinbrink, M. (2013): Soziale Netzwerkanalyse für HumangeographInnen. Einführung in UCINET und NetDraw in fünf Schritten. Potsdam: Universitätsverlag Potsdam (Potsdamer Geographische Praxis, 5).
Stone, C.N. (1989): Regime politics. Governing Atlanta, 1946–1988. Lawrence: University Press of Kansas.
Stone, C.N. (1993): Urban Regimes and the Capacity to Govern – A Political-Economy Approach. *Journal of Urban Affairs,* 15 (1), pp. 1–28. doi:10.1111/j.1467–9906.1993.tb00300.x
Subroto, G. (2013): Pesona Kampung Pinggir Kali. Blogpost. <http://ayorek.org/2013/05/pesona-kampung-pinggir-kali/> (accessed 2019/03/02).
Sudarmo, S.P. (1997): Recent Developments in Indonesian Urban Development Strategy. In: Burgess, R., Carmona, M. & Kolstee, T. (eds.): The challenge of sustainable cities. Neoliberalism and urban strategies in developing countries. London: Zed Books, pp. 230–244.
Suhartini, N. & Jones, P.R. (2019): Urban Governance and Informal Settlements: Lessons from Jayapura, Papua, Indonesia. Cham: Springer International Publishing.
Sullivan, J. (1992): Local Government and Community in Java: An urban Case Study. Singapore: Oxford University Press.

Supriatna, A. (2016): Land Tenure Security: De Facto or de Jure Tenure. The case of urban kampung in Jakarta, Indonesia. In: Rachmawati, R., Pomeroy, G. & Mookherjee, D. (eds.): Rapid Urbanization and Sustainable Development in Asia. The 13th International Asian Urbanization Conference Proceedings. Yogyakarta: Badan Penerbit Fakultas Geografi, Universitas Gadjah Mada, pp. 544–556.

Sur, C. (2009): Penghuni Rusun Di-deadline. *TRIBUNnews.com*, 2009-12-12. <https://surabaya.tribunnews.com/2009/12/06/penghuni-rusun-di-deadline> (accessed 2019/12/12).

Surat Keputusan Walikota Surakarta (SK Walikota 032/97-C/1/2014): Penetapan Lokasi Perumahan dan Permukiman Kumuh di Kota Surakarta. <http://ciptakarya.pu.go.id/bangkim/perdakumuh/upload/skbupwal/SK%20Walikota%20Surakarta.pdf> (accessed 2019/10/03).

Surat Keputusan Walikota Surakarta (SK Walikota 413.21/38.3/1/2016): Penetapan Lokasi Kawasan Lingkungan Perumahan dan Permukiman Kumuh di Surakarta.

Suri, S. N. & Taube, G. (2014): Governance in Megacities: Experiences, Challenges and Implications for International Cooperation. In: Kraas, F. et al. (eds.): Megacities. Our global urban future. Dordrecht: Springer (International year of planet Earth), pp. 195–200.

Suryahadi, A., Yumna, A., Reku Raya, U. and Marbun, D. (2010): Review of Government´s Poverty Reduction Strategies, Policies, and Programs in Indonesia. SMERU Research Institute. Jakarta.

Tatenhove, J. van, Arts, B. and Leroy, P. (2000a): Political Modernisation. In: Tatenhove, J. van, Arts, B. & Leroy, P. (eds.): Political Modernistation and the Environment. The Renewal of Environmental Policy Arrangements. Dordrecht: Kluwer Academic Publishers (Environment & Policy, 24), pp. 35–52.

Tatenhove, J. van, Arts, B. and Leroy, P. (eds.) (2000b): Political Modernistation and the Environment. The Renewal of Environmental Policy Arrangements. Dordrecht: Kluwer Academic Publishers (Environment & Policy, 24).

Tatenhove, J. van & Leroy, P. (2000): The Institutionalisation of Environmental Politics. In: Tatenhove, J. van, Arts, B. & Leroy, P. (eds.): Political Modernistation and the Environment. The Renewal of Environmental Policy Arrangements. Dordrecht: Kluwer Academic Publishers (Environment & Policy, 24), pp. 17–33.

Taylor, J. (2015): A tale of two cities: comparing alternative approaches to reducing the vulnerability of riverbank communities in two Indonesian cities. *Environment and Urbanization*, 27 (2), pp. 621–636. doi:10.1177/0956247815594532

Taylor, J. & Song, L. (2016): Return to the Streets. *Cityscape*, 18 (1), pp. 71–88.

Taylor, L. (2016): Case Study Methodology. In: Clifford, N. et al. (eds.): Key Methods in Geography. London: Sage, pp. 581–595.

Taylor, M. (2007): Community Participation in the Real World: Opportunities and Pitfalls in New Governance Spaces. *Urban Studies*, 44 (2), pp. 297–317.

The Australian National University (2013): Indonesia provinces and capital cities, including maritime boundaries – 2013: CartoGIS, College of Asia and the Pacific. <https://asiapacific-archive.anu.edu.au/mapsonline/base-maps/indonesian-provinces> (accessed 2023/03/08).

The Jakarta Post (2019): Housing program exceeds 1 million target in 2018. *The Jakarta Post*, 2019-01-09. <https://www.thejakartapost.com/news/2019/01/09/housing-program-exceeds-1-million-target-in-2018.html> (accessed 2020/01/10).

Tibaijuka, A. K. (2009): Building Prosperity. The Centrality of Housing in Economic Development. London: Earthscan.

TNP2K – National Team for the Acceleration of Poverty Reduction (2014): Reaching Indonesia's Poor and Vulnerable and Reducing Inequality: Improving Programme Targeting Design and Processes. <http://www.tnp2k.go.id/images/uploads/downloads/Report_REACHING_Mar30_LR.pdf> (accessed 2018/11/21).

Tunas, D. & Darmoyono, L. T. (2014): Self-Help Housing in Indonesia. In: Bredenoord, J., Lindert, P. van & Smets, P. (eds.): Affordable Housing in the Urban Global South. Seeking sustainable solutions. London: Routledge, pp. 166–180.

Tunas, D. & Peresthu, A. (2010): The self-help housing in Indonesia: The only option for the poor? *Habitat International,* 34 (3), pp. 315–322. doi:10.1016/j.habitatint.2009.11.007

Turner, J. (1968a): Housing priorities, settlement patterns and urban development in modernizing countries. *Journal of the American Institute of Planners,* 34 (6), pp. 354–363.

Turner, J. (1968b): Uncontrolled Urban Settlement: Problems and Policies. *International social development review,* 1, pp. 107–130.

Turner, J. (1977): Housing by people: towards autonomy in building environments. New York: Pantheon Books.

Turner, J. & Fichter, R. (eds.) (1972): Freedom to build. Dweller control of the housing process. New York: Macmillan.

Tyrrell, N. (2016): Making Use of Secondary Data. In: Clifford, N. et al. (eds.): Key Methods in Geography. London: Sage, pp. 519–536.

UNCHR – United Nations Commission on Human Rights (1993): Forced Evictions. Resolution 1993/77. UN doc. E/CN.4/RES/1993/77, 10 March.

UNCHS – United Nations Centre for Human Settlements (1988): Global Strategy for Shelter to the Year 2000. <https://www.ircwash.org/sites/default/files/UN-HABITAT-1990-Global.pdf> (accessed 2019/05/08).

UN-DESA – United Nations Department of Economic and Social Affairs (2013): World economic and social survey 2013. Sustainable development challenges. New York: United Nations.

UN-DESA – United Nations Department of Economic and Social Affairs (2014): World Urbanization Prospects: The 2014 Revision, CD-Rom Edition.

UN-DESA – United Nations Department of Economic and Social Affairs (2018a): World Urbanization Prospects: The 2018 Revision. [key facts]. <https://esa.un.org/unpd/wup/Publications/Files/WUP2018-KeyFacts.pdf> (accessed 2018/06/20).

UN-DESA – United Nations Department of Economic and Social Affairs, Population Division (2018b): World Urbanization Prospects: The 2018 Revision, Online Edition.

UN-DESA – United Nations Department of Economic and Social Affairs, Population Division (2019): World Population Prospects 2019. Custom data acquired via website. <https://population.un.org/wpp/DataQuery/> (accessed 2019/12/20).

UNDP – United Nations Development Programme (2005): A home in the city. Achieving the Millennium Development Goals. London: Earthscan.

UNGA – United Nations General Assembly (2002): Strengthening the mandate and status of the Commission on Human Settlements and the status, role and functions of the United Nations Centre for Human Settlements (Habitat). UN doc. A/RES/56/206, 26 February.

UNGA – United Nations General Assembly (2015): Transforming our world: the 2030 Agenda for Sustainable Development. UN doc. A/RES/70/01, 21 October.

Unger, K. (2016): Habitat for People – Not for Profit. The need for social regulation of real estate markets. *TRIALOG,* 124/125 (1–2), pp. 71–80.

UN-Habitat – United Nations Human Settlements Programme (1976): The Vancouver Declaration on Human Settlements. UN doc. A/CONF.70/15, 11 June.

UN-Habitat – United Nations Human Settlements Programme (1996): The Habitat Agenda. Istanbul Declaration on Human Settlements. UN doc. A/CONF.165/14, 14. June.

UN-Habitat – United Nations Human Settlements Programme (2002a): Housing rights legislation. Review of international and national legal instruments (Series of publications in support of the Global Campaign for Secure Tenure, 5).
UN-Habitat – United Nations Human Settlements Programme (2002b): Kampung Improvement Program Comprehensive (Best Practice Database). <http://mirror.unhabitat.org/bp/bp.list.details.aspx?bp_id=2986> (accessed 2017/08/09).
UN-Habitat – United Nations Human Settlements Programme (2003a): The Challenge of Slums: Global Report on Human Settlements 2003. London: Earthscan.
UN-Habitat – United Nations Human Settlements Programme (2003b): The Global Campaign on Urban Governance. Concept Paper, 2nd Edition March 2002. Nairobi.
UN-Habitat – United Nations Human Settlements Programme (2007): Forced Evictions – Towards Solutions? Second Report of the Advisory Group on Forced Evictions to the Executive Director of UN-HABITAT. Nairobi.
UN-Habitat – United Nations Human Settlements Programme (2008a): Green and Clean Initiative. <http://mirror.unhabitat.org/bp/bp.list.details.aspx?bp_id=1217> (accessed 2017/08/09).
UN-Habitat – United Nations Human Settlements Programme (2008b): Housing Finance Mechanisms in Indonesia. Nairobi.
UN-Habitat – United Nations Human Settlements Programme (2008c): State of the world's cities 2010/2011. Bridging the urban divide. London: Earthscan.
UN-Habitat – United Nations Human Settlements Programme (2008d): Surakarta: Empowering the Informal Sector: Street Vendor Management (Best Practice Database). <http://mirror.unhabitat.org/bp/bp.list.details.aspx?bp_id=1216> (accessed 2017/08/09).
UN-Habitat – United Nations Human Settlements Programme (2009a): Good Urban Governance: Towards an Effective Private Sector Engagement. Nairobi.
UN-Habitat – United Nations Human Settlements Programme (2009b): The Right to adequate housing. Factsheet 21. Geneva.
UN-Habitat – United Nations Human Settlements Programme (2010): The State of the Asian Cities 2010/11. Fukuoka.
UN-Habitat – United Nations Human Settlements Programme (2013): State of the World Cities 2012/2013. New York: Routledge.
UN-Habitat – United Nations Human Settlements Programme (2014a): Sustainable Cities and Human Settlements in the Post-2015 UN Development Agenda. <http://sustainabledevelopment.un.org/content/documents/1653SustainableCities.pdf> (accessed 2014/11/17).
UN-Habitat – United Nations Human Settlements Programme (2014b): The Green and Clean Program of Kampung Gundih, Surabaya, Indonesia (Best Practice Database). <http://mirror.unhabitat.org/bp/bp.list.details.aspx?bp_id=4741> (accessed 2017/08/09).
UN-Habitat – United Nations Human Settlements Programme (2015a): The State of Asian and Pacific Cities 2015. Urban transformations Shifting from quantity to quality. London.
UN-Habitat – United Nations Human Settlements Programme (2015b): United Nation's Millennium Development Goals database. <http://mdgs.un.org/unsd/mdg/> (accessed 2019/12/12).
UN-Habitat – United Nations Human Settlements Programme (2016): Urbanization and Development: Emerging Futures. World Cities Report 2016. Nairobi.
UN-Habitat – United Nations Human Settlements Programme, Slum Upgrading Facility (2006a): SUF Action Planning Methodology and Development Guidelines. Nairobi.
UN-Habitat – United Nations Human Settlements Programme, Slum Upgrading Facility (2006b): The SUF Handbook. An Approach to Financial Action Planning for Slum upgrading and New Low-income Residential Neighbourhoods. Nairobi.

UN-Habitat – United Nations Human Settlements Programme, Slum Upgrading Facility (2011): Slum Upgrading Facility Pilot Programme End of Programme Evaluation. Nairobi (Evaluation report, 4/2011).
UNHRC – United Nations Human Rights Council (2007): Adequate housing as a component of the right to an adequate standard of living. UN doc. A/HRC/RES/6/27, 14 December.
UNHRC – United Nations Human Rights Council (2014): Adequate housing as a component of the right to an adequate standard of living. UN doc. A/HRC/RES/25/17, 14 April.
UN – United Nations (1948): Universal Declaration of Human Rights. UDHR. General Assembly resolution 217A.
UN – United Nations (2001): Millennium Development Goals. <http://www.un.org/millennium goals/environ.shtml> (accessed 2012/07/07).
UN – United Nations (2010): The Millennium Development Goals Report 2010. New York.
UN – United Nations (2014): Forced Evictions. New York (Fact Sheet, 25).
UN – United Nations (2015a): Sustainable Development Goals. <http://www.un.org/sustainable development/> (accessed 2016/01/29).
UN – United Nations (2015b): The Millennium Development Goals Report 2015. New York.
UN – United Nations (2017): New Urban Agenda. <http://habitat3.org/wp-content/uploads/NUA-English.pdf> (accessed 2017/11/14).
UN – United Nations (2018): Tracking Progress Towards Inclusive, Safe, Resilient and Sustainable Cities and Human Settlements. SDG 11 Synthesis Report – High Level Political Forum 2018. <https://www.un-ilibrary.org/content/books/9789210472401> (accessed 2023/03/08).
USAID (2009): Musrenbang as a Key Driver In Effective Participatory Budgeting. Key Issues and Perspectives for Improvements. <http://pdf.usaid.gov/pdf_docs/PNADQ129.pdf> (accessed 2012/02/05).
Usman, S., Mawardi, M. S., Poesoro, A., Suryahadi, A. and Sampford, C. (2008): The Specific Allocation Fund (DAK): Mechanisms and Uses. Jakarta: SMERU Research Institute.
Utomo, N. T. (2014): Affordable Housing Finance Policies on Indonesia. Director of Housing and Settlement Ministry of National Development Planning Republic of Indonesia. 2014-05-28, Washington DC.
UU – Undang Undang Republik Indonesia (UU 16/1985): Rumah Susun.
UU – Undang Undang Republik Indonesia (UU 04/1992): Perumahan dan Permukiman.
UU – Undang Undang Republik Indonesia (UU 26/2007): Penataan Ruang.
UU – Undang Undang Republik Indonesia (UU 01/2011): Perumahan dan Kawasan Permukiman.
UU – Undang Undang Republik Indonesia (UU 06/2014): Desa.
Veronika Deffner & Christoph Haferburg (2012): The Bourdieusian Perspective on Space, Cities and Power Relations in German-speaking Human Geography. *Geographische Zeitschrift*, 100 (3), pp. 164–180.
Vickers, A. (2005): A History of Modern Indonesia. Cambridge: Cambridge University Press.
Vogelpohl, A. (2011): Städte und die beginnende Urbanisierung. Henri Lefebvre in der aktuellen Stadtforschung. *Raumforschung und Raumordnung*, 69 (4), pp. 233–243. doi:10.1007/s13147-011-0105-3
Vorlaufer, K. (2009): Südostasien. Brunei, Indonesien, Kambodscha, Laos, Malaysia, Myanmar, Osttimor, Philippinen, Singapur, Thailand, Vietnam. Darmstadt: Wissenschaftliche Buchgesellschaft.
Wachsmuth, D. (2018): Researching the Global Right to the City. In: Harrison, J. & Hoyler, M. (eds.): Doing global urban research. London: Sage, pp. 153–168.

Waeyenberge, E. van (2017): Crisis? What crisis? A critical appraisal of World Bank housing policy in the wake of the global financial crisis. *Environment and Planning A,* 13 (1), 1–22. doi:10.1177/0308518X17745873

Wardenga, U. (2002): Räume der Geographie – zu Raumbegriffen im Geographieunterricht. <https://homepage.univie.ac.at/christian.sitte/FD/artikel/ute_wardenga_raeume.htm> (accessed 2018/08/16).

Warren, C. & Lucas, A. (2013): Indonesia's Land Titling Program (LAP) – The Market Solution? In: Lucas, A. E. & Warren, C. (eds.): Land for the people. The state and agrarian conflict in Indonesia. Athens: Ohio University Press (Southeast Asia series, 126), pp. 93–113.

WBGU – Wissenschaftlicher Beirat der Bundesregierung Globale Umweltveränderungen (2016a): Der Umzug der Menschheit: Die transformative Kraft der Städte. Berlin: WBGU.

WBGU – Wissenschaftlicher Beirat der Bundesregierung Globale Umweltveränderungen (2016b): Stellungnahme. Empfehlungen zur "UN-Konferenz über Wohnraum und nachhaltige urbane Entwicklung – Habitat III". Berlin: WBGU.

Wehrhahn, R. (2014): Ghettos und Slums: Begriffe, Konzepte, Diskurse. *Geographische Rundschau,* 66 (5), pp. 4–11.

Weichhart, P. (2018): Entwicklungslinien der Sozialgeographie. Von Hans Bobek bis Benno Werlen (2nd ed.). Stuttgart: Steiner.

Wekesa, B.W., Steyn, G.S. and Otieno, F. (2011): A review of physical and socio-economic characteristics and intervention approaches of informal settlements. *Habitat International,* 35 (2), pp. 238–245. doi:10.1016/j.habitatint.2010.09.006

Werlen, B. (1999): Zur Ontologie von Gesellschaft und Raum (2nd ed.). Stuttgart: Steiner.

Werlen, B. (2008): Sozialgeographie. Eine Einführung. Bern: UTB.

Werlin, H. (1999): The Slum Upgrading Myth. *Urban Studies,* 36 (9), pp. 1523–1534.

Westendorff, D. (2004): Sustainable Development for Urban Poor: Applying a Human Rights Approach to the Problem. In: Westendorff, D. (ed.): From Unsustainable to Inclusive Cities. Geneva: UNRISD, pp. 191–245.

Wetzstein, S. (2017): The global urban housing affordability crisis. *Urban Studies,* 54 (14), pp. 3159–3177. doi:10.1177/0042098017711649

Wicakasono, S. (2006): Indonesia. In: Roberts, B. & Kanaley, T. (eds.): Urbanization and Sustainability in Asia. Case Studies of Good Practice. Manila: ADB, pp. 155–187.

Widianingsih, I. (2006): Local Governance, Decentralization, and Participatory Planning in Indonesia: Seeking a New Path to a Harmonious Society. In: Ahmad, R. (ed.): The role of public administration in building a harmonious society. Selected proceedings from the Annual Conference of the Network of Asia-Pacific Schools and Institutes of Public Administration and Governance (NAPSIPAG). Manila: ADB

Widianingsih, I. & Morrell, E. (2007): Participatory Planning in Indonesia. Seeking a new path to democracy. *Policy Studies,* 28 (1), pp. 1–15. doi:10.1080/01442870601121320

Widiyani, W.N.M. (2017): Rusunawa Sustainability Assessment and the Impact to Residents' Capabilities. Rusunawa Jatinegara Barat, Indonesia. Master thesis. Université Grenoble Alpes: Grenoble.

Wiering, M. & Immink, I. (2006): When water management meets spatial planning: a policy-arrangements perspective. *Environment and Planning C: Government and Policy,* 24 (3), pp. 423–438. doi:10.1068/c0417j

Willer, D., Lovaglia, M.J. and Markovsky, B. (1997): Power and Influence: A Theoretical Bridge. *Social Forces,* 765 (2), pp. 571–603.

Winayanti, L. & Lang, H. C. (2004): Provision of urban services in an informal settlement: a case study of Kampung Penas Tanggul, Jakarta. *Habitat International,* 28 (1), pp. 41–65. doi:10.1016/S0197-3975(02)00072-3
Wirth, L. (1938): Urbanism as a Way of Life. *Journal of Sociology,* 44 (1), pp. 1–24.
World Bank (1992): Governance and Development. Washington, DC.
World Bank (1993): Housing: Enabling Markets to Work. Washington, DC.
World Bank (2003): Cities in Transition: Urban Sector Review in an Era of Decentralization in Indonesia (East Asia Urban Working Paper Series, 7).
World Bank (2013a): Indonesia: Evaluation of the Urban Community Driven Development Program Program Nasional Pemberdayaan Masyarakat Mandiri Perkotaan (PNPM-Urban). Policy Note. <https://openknowledge.worldbank.org/handle/10986/17870> (accessed 2020/01/17).
World Bank (2013b): Planning, connecting, and financing cities – now: priorities for city leaders. Washington, DC.
World Bank (2015a): East Asia's Changing Urban Landscape. Measuring a Decade of Urban Growth. Washington, DC.
World Bank (2015b): Program-For-Results Information Document (PID). Concept Stage. <http://documents.worldbank.org/curated/en/852761468269376515/pdf/P154948-PID-June-6-Final.pdf> (accessed 2020/01/09).
World Bank (2016a): Global Monitoring Report, 2015/2016. Development Goals in an Era of Demographic Change. Washington, DC.
World Bank (2016b): Indonesia – National Slum Upgrading Project. <http://documents.worldbank.org/curated/en/226091468417040569/Indonesia-National-Slum-Upgrading-Project> (accessed 2020/03/16).
World Bank (2017): Indonesia – National Affordable Housing Program Project (English). <http://documents.worldbank.org/curated/en/121201489975262694/Indonesia-National-Affordable-Housing-Program-Project> (accessed 2020/01/15).
World Bank (2019): GDP per Capita (constant 2010 US$) – Indonesia. <https://data.worldbank.org/indicator/NY.GDP.PCAP.KD?end=2018&locations=ID&start=1961&view=chart> (accessed 2019/12/12).
World Charter for the Right to the City (2005). <https://www.right2city.org/document/world-charter-for-the-right-to-the-city/> (accessed 2023/03/09).
Yap, K. S. (2015): The enabling strategy and its discontent: Low-income housing policies and practices in Asia. *Habitat International* (54), pp. 166–172. doi:10.1016/j.habitatint.2015.11.026
Yayasan Kota Kita (2015): The Angkots of Solo. Solo. <http://workworkworkwork.work/kotakita/publications-docs/The%20Angkots%20of%20Solo_150528.pdf> (accessed 2023/03/09).
Yuniati, V. (2013): Inclusionary housing in Indonesia: The role of balanced residential ratio 1:3:6 in Makassar. Master thesis. Erasmus University Rotterdam: Rotterdam.
Yuwono, T. (2014): Jokowi's local Government in Surakarta – Lessons Learned from Good Governance Best Practice. *Global Journal of Politics and Law Research,* 2 (4), pp. 26–41.
Zahnd, M. (2005): Traditionelle Stadtquartiere in Semarang und Yogyakarta, Indonesien. Möglichkeiten der Revitalisierung und innovativen Nutzung des historischen Städtebaus. Dissertation. Universität Stuttgart: Stuttgart.
Zaida, S. N. A. & Arifin, N. H. S. (2010): Surakarta: Perkembangan Kota sebagai Akibat Penguruh Perubahan sosial pada bekas Ibukota Kerajaan di Jawa. *Journal Lanskap Indonesia,* 2 (2), pp. 83–92.

Zein, M. (2010): A community-based approach to flood hazard and vulnerability assessment in flood prone areas. A Case Study in Kelurahan Sewu, Surakarta City – Indonesia. Master thesis. Gadjah Mada University: Yogyakarta.

Zhu, J. (2007): Commons and Anticommons: Role of the State in the Housing Market. In: World Bank & IPEA (eds.): Land and Urban Policies for Poverty Reduction. Brasilia: The World Bank (Proceedings of the Third International Urban Research Symposium held in Brasilia 2005), pp. 295–310.

Zimmer, A. & Sakdapolrak, P. (2013): The Social Practices of Governing: Analysing Waste Water Governance in a Delhi Slum. *Environment and Urbanization Asia*, 3 (2), pp. 325–341. doi:10.1177/0975425312473228

Glossary

This glossary provides English translations and explanations of Indonesian acronyms and terms. It was compiled with great care. Most of the translations are official, but some are also my own and might not reflect the exact meaning. The descriptions include additional information that may not be exhaustive.

ACHR	Asian Coalition for Housing Rights. A network of Asian professionals, NGOs and CBOs committed to address poverty and housing problems by joint actions and projects.
ADB	Asian Development Bank. A multilateral development bank founded in 1965.
alun-alun	Town square, a distinctive element of the Indonesian city. Usually in front of the ruler's palace.
APBD	*Anggaran Pendapatan dan Belanja Daerah.* The regional budget and annual financial plan approved by the regional house of representatives.
APBN	*Anggaran Pendapatan dan Belanja Negara.* The national budget and annual financial plan approved by the house of representatives.
APERSI	*Asosiasi Pengembang Rumah Sederhana / Sangat Sederhana Indonesia.* Indonesian housing development association committed to the construction of simple and very simple houses.
BBWS/BS	*Balai Besar Wilayah Sungai Bengawan Solo.* River Basin Management Agency of *Bengawan Solo River.*
BAPE(R)MAS	*Badan Pemberdayaan Masyarakat.* Agency for Community Empowerment. Part of the city administration in Surabaya and Solo.
BAPPEDA	*Badan Perencanaan dan Pembangunan Daerah.* Regional Development Planning Agency.
BAPPEKO	*Badan Perencanaan dan Pembangunan Kota Surabaya.* Development Planning Agency of the city Surabaya.
BAPPENAS	*Badan Perencanaan Pembangunan Nasional.* National Development Planning Agency.

becak	Three-wheeled pedicab.
bemo	Minibus for public transport.
benedenstad	Lower town. Name for the old parts of colonial Surabaya (including port and central business district).
BKM	*Badan Keswadayaan Masyarakat.* Community self-help organisation. Working group established at the neighbourhood level tasked to develop, plan, and implement housing and neighbourhood improvements.
BKPN	*Badan Kebijakan Perumahan Nasional.* National Board for Housing Policies. Founded in 1974 as an effort to harmonise the activities of stakeholders in the housing sector.
BLH	*Badan Lingkungan Hidup.* Environmental Agency. Part of the city administration in Surabaya and Solo.
BLUD	*Badan Layanan Umum Daerah.* Regional Agency for General Services. Part of the city administration in Solo.
BPS	*Badan Pusat Statistik.* The Central Statistics Agency, a government agency with regional branches tasked to created statistical databases.
BPN	*Badan Pertanahan Nasional.* The National Land Administration Agency, a government agency with regional branches responsible for land registration.
BSPS	*Bantuan Stimulan Perumahan.* Subsidy for incremental home improvements.
bupati	Head of a district (*kabupaten*).
camat	Head of a sub-district (*kecamatan*).
CBO	Community based organisation.
CDD	Community-driven development. A community empowerment approach used in several Indonesian housing programmes since the 1990s.
DC-Organisation	Organisation working in development cooperation (eg GIZ, US-AID)
DCKTR	*Dinas Cipta Karya dan Tata Ruang.* Department of Spatial Planning. Part of the city administration in Surabaya.
desa	Village. Administrative division in rural areas, equivalent to the adm. level *kelurahan* (quarter).
DinKes	*Dinas Kesehatan.* Department of Health.
DinSos	*Dinas Sosial.* Department for Social Services. Part of the city administration in Surabaya and Solo.
DinKop	*Dinas Koperasi dan Usaha Mikro, Kecil dan Menengah.* Department for Cooperatives and Small and Medium Enterprises. Main

	task is to promote local economic development. Part of the city administration in Surabaya and Solo.
DISPERINDAG	*Dinas Perindustrian dan Perdagangan.* Department for industry and trade. Manages and promotes local industries and trade (eg traditional markets). Part of the city administration in Surabaya and Solo.
DKP	*Dinas Kebersihan dan Pertamanan.* Department for Cleaning and Gardening. Manages public spaces (especially urban parks) and organizes waste collection. Part of the city administration in Surabaya.
DPBT	*Dinas Pengelolaan Bangunan dan Tanah.* Department for Construction and Land Management. Manages most social housing units (*rusunawa*) in Surabaya. Part of the city administration in Surabaya.
DPR *DPR-RI* *DPRD*	*Dewan Perwakilan Rakyat.* House of Representatives. At the national level (DPR-RI) this is one of the two elected national legislative assemblies. Similar representative councils (DPRD) exist at regional levels of provinces (*provinsi*), districts (*kabupaten*) and cities (*kota*).
DPU *DPU-BM,* *DPU-CK*	*Dinas Pekerjaan Umum.* Department of Public Works. Develops and manages infrastructure (roads, bridges etc) through local branches in each Indonesian city. Is part of the city administration in Surabaya and Solo. The department has local variations and subdivisions – eg in Surabaya: *Dinas Pekerjaan Umum Bina Marga* (DPU-BM) for road management and *Dinas Pekerjaan Umum Cipta Karya* (DPU-CK) for the management of settlements.
DTRK	*Dinas Tata Ruang Kota.* Department for Spatial Planning. Part of the city administration in Solo.
FKA LKM	Central board of all community organisations (BKM/LKM) in Solo during the PNPM-programme.
FLPP	*Fasilitas Likuiditas Pembiayaan Perumahan.* A housing finance liquidity scheme established in 2010 for people with low- to moderate incomes providing subsidised interest rates for obtaining loans.
GIZ	Deutsche Gesellschaft für Internationale Zusammenarbeit. German development agency.
hak milik	Official certificate of freehold property. Foreigners are not allowed to obtain this certificate.
HDI	Human Development Index. The HDI combines measures of life expectancy, educational attainment and income in a single value

	between 0 and 1. It was developed as an alternative to other indicators, such as GDP/per capita, for measuring development. The nearer the value is to 1, the better is the human development in a region.
ITS	*Institut Teknologi Sepuluh Nopember.* The Sepuluh Nopember Institut of Technology, a public university in Surabaya.
Jabodetabek	Acronym for the metropolitan region Jakarta composed from Jakarta, Bogor, Depok, Tangerang and Bekasi.
JICA	Japan International Development Cooperation Agency.
kabupaten	District. Administrative division in rural areas, equivalent to the adm. level *kota* (city).
kali	Javanese term for 'river'.
kampung	An urban village – a distinctive Indonesian settlement type.
KDP	*Kecamatan Development Programme.* Sub-district development programme for poverty alleviation and community empowerment using the CDD approach (1998–2006).
kecamatan	Sub-district. An administrative division in urban and rural areas.
kelurahan	Quarter. An administrative division in urban areas, equivalent to the rural division 'village' (*desa*).
Kemenpera	*Kementerian Perumahan Rakyat.* Ministry of Housing. Since 2014 merged with the Ministry of Public Works to KPUPR.
Kemen PU	Kementerian Pekerjaan Umum. Ministry of Public Works. Since 2014 merged with the Ministry of Housing to KPUPR.
Kemenko PMK	*Kementerian Koordinator Pembangunan Manusia dan Kebudayaan.* Coordinating Ministry for Human Development and Cultural Affairs (formerly Coordinating Ministry of People's Welfare). Coordinates and synchronises governance in human development and culture.
Kemsos	*Kementerian Sosial.* Ministry of Social Affairs.
KIP	*Kampung Improvement Programme.* An Indonesian slum upgrading programme introduced in 1969 and running well into the 1990s. Internationally recognised for its success.
kota	City – an administrative division in urban areas, equivalent to the district level (*kabupaten*).
KOTAKU	*Kota Tanpa Kumuh. City without Slum.* An Indonesian slum upgrading programme established in 2015 using the CDD approach.
KPUPR	*Kementerian Pekerjaan Umum dan Perumahan Rakjat.* Ministry of Public Works and Housing. The central ministry formulating and implementing national policies for all issues related to infrastruc-

	ture (roads, bridges, drainage channels, facilities, etc), settlement, and public housing development.
KTP	*Kartu Tanda Penduduk.* National Identity Card. The compulsory Indonesian identity card states personal details including place of residence, religious affiliation, and marital status. It is issued by local governments and required to be eligible for social and governmental services in respective administrative areas.
LKM	*Lembaga Keswadayaan Masyarakat.* Community self-help organisation. Working group established at the neighbourhood level tasked to develop, plan and implement housing and neighbourhood improvements.
lurah	Head of a quarter (*kelurahan*)
MBR	*Masyarakat Berpenghasilan Rendah.* Low-income people.
MDGs	Millennium Development Goals. Eight international development goals established in 2000 to be reached in 2015. They were established at the United Nations Millennium Summit.
NAHP	National Affordable Housing Programme. Housing programme for improving access to housing finance established in 2018. Supporting programme of the One Million Houses Programme (PSR) of the Jokowi government supported by the World Bank.
NSSUP	Neighbourhood Upgrading and Shelter Sector Project. An Indonesian slum upgrading programme using the community driven development approach.
NSUP	National Slum Upgrading Project. Comprehensive initiative established in 2016 focusing on slum upgrading (urban infrastructure and services), community empowerment, capacity building and institutional development. Supported by the World Bank and AIIB.
NGO	Non-governmental organisation.
PDAM	*Perusahaan Daerah Air Minum.* The State Water Supply Company.
Perumnas (*Perum Perumnas*)	*Perusahaan Umum Pembangunan Perumahan Nasional.* The national housing cooperation. Founded in in 1974 this state-owned public housing company has the goal to provide housing for all Indonesians, focussing particularly on low-income groups.
PKI	*Partai Komunis Indonesia.* The Indonesian Communist Party.
PLN	*Perusahaan Listrik Negara.* The State Electricity Company.
PLPBK	*Penataan Lingkungan Permukiman Berbasis Komunitas.* Community-based Environmental Management (supporting programme of PNPM).
PNPM (Mandiri)	*Program Nasional Pemberdayaan Masyarakat – Mandiri.* National Programme for Community Empowerment – to be autonomous.

	Follow-up programme of KDP and P2KP; main targets were poverty alleviation and community empowerment by using the CDD mechanism. The programme run from 2006 to 2014.
Pokja	*Kelompok Kerja.* Working Group. Established for most programmes among governmental agencies to promote cross-sectoral cooperation and among community members to implement and realise governmental programmes at neighbourhood level.
P2KP	*Proyek Penanggulangan Kemiskinan di Perkotaan.* Urban Poverty Alleviation Project. The urban expression of the KDP programme focusing on community empowerment for poverty reduction. The programme run from 1999 to 2006.
PPDPP	*Pusat Pengelolaan Dana Pembiayaan Perumahan.* Centre for Housing Finance Fund Management, formerly known as the Centre for Housing Finance (Pusat Pembiayaan Perumahan, or PPP). Manages the Funds for the FLPP programme.
PSF	PNPM Support Facility. Manages the funds of the PNPM programme. A working group consisting of representatives from the World Bank and major national ministries.
PSR	*Program Satu Juta Rumah.* The One Million Houses Programme. An umbrella initiative of the Jokowi administration of 2015 to produce one million houses annually.
PWS	*Paguyuban Warga Stren Kali.* Strenkali People's Movement. A civil society organisation uniting resident associations from several riverside communities in Surabaya.
REI	*Real Estate Indonesia.* Real Estate Indonesia. An association and lobby organisations of private developers founded in 1972.
Repelita	*Rencana Pembangunan Lima Tahun.* Five-year Development Plan.
Rp.	Indonesian Rupiah 1€ = approx. 15,000 Rp. (09/2019)
RPJM	*Rencana Pembangunan Jangka Menengah.* Medium-term Development Plan (5 years).
RPJP	*Rencana Pembangunan Jangka Panjang.* Long-term Development Plan (25 years).
RP4D	*Rencana Pembangunan Pengembangan Perumahan dan Pemukiman di Daerah.* Regional Development Plan for Housing and Settlements.
RSDK	*Rehabilitasi Sosial Daerah Kumuh.* Slum Area Social Rehabilitation. Social assistance programme for poor families in Surabaya.
RT	*Rukun Tetangga.* Ward. Smallest Indonesian administrative unit, consisting of 20 to 100 households, headed by the *Ketua RT* (RT-leader).
RTRW	*Rencana Tata Ruang Wilaya.* Regional Spatial Plan.

RTLH	*Rumah Tidak Layak Huni.* Sub-standard house.
rusun	*Rumah Susun Sederhana.* Simple flats – often used as synonym for social housing
rusunami	*Rumah Susun Sederhana Milik.* Simple owner occupied flats / owner occupied apartments.
rusunawa	*Rumah Susun Sederhana Sewa.* Simple rental flats / low-cost rental apartments.
RW	*Rukun Warga.* Neighbourhood. Indonesian administrative unit consisting of several RT, headed by the Ketua RW (RW-leader).
SDGs	Sustainable Development Goals. As a follow-up of the MDGs, the United Nations established these 17 global goals in 2015 to be reached until 2030.
SK Walikota	*Surat Keputusan Walikota.* A regulation decreed by the mayor.
SKK or YKK	*Solo Kota Kita or Yayasan Kota Kita.* Our City Solo or Our City Foundation, an Indonesian NGO based in Solo.
Solo	Informal name for the city Surakarta.
SPPIP	*Strategi Pengembangan Permukiman dan Infrastruktur Perkotaan.* Housing and Urban Infrastructure Development Strategy. Strategy developed for 20 years in all urban areas.
SUF	Slum Upgrading Facility. UN-Habitat sponsored local facilities designated to raise local funding for slum upgrading and financial enablement of low-income residents.
tempe	Local food made from soybeans.
TKPKD	*Tim Koordinasi Penangulangan Kemiskinan Daerah.* Regional Poverty Eradication Coordination Team. A citywide working group of government agencies in the PNPM programme.
UGM	*Universitas Gadjah Mada.* Gadjah Mada University. A university in Yogyakarta.
UNCHS	United Nations Centre for Human Settlements. Founded in 1978 as an outcome of Habitat I, UNCHS transformed into the United Nations Human Settlement Programme in 2002.
UNESA	*Universitas Negeri Surabaya.* State University Surabaya.
UN-Habitat	United Nations Human Settlement Programme. A fully-fledged UN-Programme established in 2002 to promote sustainable human settlements development and adequate shelter for all.
UNS	*Universitas Sebelas Maret.* Sebelas Maret University. A university in Surakarta.
UNDP	United Nations Development Programme.
UNESCO	United Nations Educational, Scientific and Cultural Organisation.
UPC	Urban Poor Consortium. Jakarta based NGO fighting nationwide for the rights of the urban poor to land, water and housing.

UPKM	*Unit Pembinaan Keluarga Miskin.* Supporting unit for poor families. A working group set up in the quarters *(kelurahan)* of Surabaya to carry out supporting activities for poor households, mainly within the RSDK programme.
USAID	United States Agency for International Development. The official agency of the United States for development cooperation.
USRI	Urban Sanitation and Rural Infrastructure Programme. A support programme for the PNPM programme.
UU	*Undang Undang.* Indonesian law.
YKK	*Yayasan Kota Kita Surakarta.* Surakarta-based NGO concerned with urban planning, citizen participation, and urban design.

Index

Index of persons and organisations

Index of places

Subject index